IFAC HANDBOOK

Scope of the Handbook

This Handbook brings together for continuing reference background information about the International Federation of Accountants (IFAC) and the currently effective pronouncements issued by IFAC as of July 1, 19

How this Handbook is Arranged

The contents of the Handbook are arranged by Section as follows:

International Federation of Accountants (General Information) 1

Statements of Policy of Council:

- Recognition of Professional Accountancy Qualifications 6

International Professional Practice Statements:

- Assuring the Quality of Professional Services 20

Auditing 33

Ethics 537

Education 591

Financial and Management Accounting 695

Information Technology 927

Membership 969

Public Sector 971

International Federation of Accountants
535 Fifth Avenue, 26th Floor
New York, New York 10017

Telephone: +1 (212) 286-9344
Telefax: +1 (212) 286-9570
Internet: http://www.ifac.org

Changes of Substance from the 1998 Handbook

INTERNATIONAL PROFESSIONAL PRACTICE STATEMENT

- Included revised Statement of Policy of Council "Assuring the Quality of Audit and Related Services" now referred to as International Professional Practice Statement 1 "Assuring the Quality of Professional Services."

AUDITING

- Included revised IAPS 1005 "The Special Considerations in the Audit of Small Entities."

The following Standards have been approved for release by the International Auditing Practices Committee (IAPC). They can be found at the end of the Auditing Pronouncements. They are effective for financial periods ended after 31/December 2000 and, are included for informational purposes only.

- Revised ISA on "Going Concern."
- New ISA on "Communications of Audit Matters with Those Charged with Governance."

EDUCATION

- IEG 7 "Education and Training Requirements for Accounting Technicians" has been withdrawn and has been issued as Study 2 "An Advisory on Education and Training of Technical Accounting Staff."
- Included summaries of Discussion Paper "Practical Experience" and Study 2 "An Advisory on Education and Training of Technical Accounting Staff."

FINANCIAL & MANAGEMENT ACCOUNTING

- Changed Terms of Reference for the Financial and Management Accounting Committee.
- Included summaries of International Management Accounting Studies - IMAS 7 "The Measurement and Management of Intellectual Capital: An Introduction, IMAS 8 "Codifying Power and Control: Ethical Codes in Action, IMAS 9 "Enhancing Shareholder Wealth by Better Managing Business Risk, and IMAS 10 "Target Costing for Effective Cost Management: Product Cost Planning at Toyota Australia."
- Included summaries of Annual Theme Booklets - (1998) "Into the Twenty-first Century with Information Management and, (1999) "The Role of Management Accounting in Creating Value."

INFORMATION TECHNOLOGY

- Included new Information Technology Guideline 2 "Managing Information Technology Planning for Business Impact."

INTERNATIONAL FEDERATION OF ACCOUNTANTS

Organization

The International Federation of Accountants (IFAC) came into being as a result of initiatives put forward in 1973 and formally approved at the International Congress of Accountants in Munich in 1977. The mission of IFAC is the worldwide development and enhancement of an accountancy profession with harmonized standards, able to provide services of consistently high quality in the public interest. It is a non-profit, non-governmental, non-political international organization of accountancy bodies.

Through cooperation with member bodies, regional organizations of accountancy bodies and other world organizations, IFAC initiates, coordinates and guides efforts to achieve international technical, ethics and education pronouncements for the accountancy profession.

Membership

Membership in IFAC is open to accountancy bodies recognized by law or general consensus within their countries as substantial national organizations of good standing within the accountancy profession. Membership in IFAC automatically includes membership in the International Accounting Standards Committee (IASC). The membership of IFAC member bodies comprises more than 2,000,000 accountants in public and private practice, education and government service.

Assembly

The Assembly, which consists of one representative from each member accountancy body, elects the members of Council, establishes the basis of financial contributions by members and adopts changes to the IFAC Constitution.

Council

The Council, which consists of representatives from 18 countries elected by the Assembly for 2½ year terms, supervises the general IFAC work program, the budget and as appropriate, oversees specific committee projects. The Council appoints an Executive Committee from among its membership to carry out its policy and decisions.

The work program of Council is implemented primarily by smaller working groups or the following standing technical committees:

- Education
- Ethics
- Financial and Management Accounting
- Information Technology
- International Auditing Practices
- Membership
- Public Sector

EDUCATION COMMITTEE

Terms of Reference

To develop standards, guidelines and other pronouncements on prequalification education for members of the profession and on matters relating thereto, and on continuing professional education for members of the profession and on matters relating thereto, and to promote understanding and acceptance of such standards and guidelines.

Recognizing the importance of education and training in enabling the profession to be able to provide services of consistently high quality in the public interest, the Committee is expected to act as catalyst for bringing together the developed and the developing nations and to assist in advancing accounting education programs worldwide, particularly in areas where this will assist economic development.

ETHICS COMMITTEE

Terms of Reference

The IFAC Ethics Committee reports to Council. It will consult with and advise Council on all aspects of ethical issues and develop appropriate guidance on these issues for Council's ultimate approval. It will also actively promote good ethical practices to IFAC's member bodies and to the public at large.

The committee will achieve its objectives by:

- scheduling working sessions at appropriate locations and including seminars/consultation with the host bodies on appropriate topics

- organizing, at its discretion, Ethics Fora to broaden discussion, attempting to coordinate such activities with other IFAC-wide activities

- ensuring that all proposed guidance is subject to an appropriate exposure period, as with other IFAC pronouncements; the committee may issue such Exposure Drafts on its own authority, but it may, as appropriate, seek selected viewpoints prior to exposure, and

- regularly contributing to the *IFAC Quarterly,* member body journals and other media on ethics issues.

In presenting its recommendations to the Council, the Committee will explain the results of the exposure process and any other information to assist the Council in making its decisions. No exposure draft will be released or proposal on the revision or issuance of guidance on ethics and related issues presented to Council unless it is approved by at least three-fourths of the committee members.

FINANCIAL AND MANAGEMENT ACCOUNTING COMMITTEE

Terms of Reference

The Financial and Management Accounting Committee (FMAC) is a standing committee of the Council of IFAC.

Its mission is:

- To support IFAC member bodies in the global development and promotion of the financial and management accounting aspect of the profession.

The vision of the Committee is:

- To lead the profession to recognize that the scope of management accounting has expanded to the extent that it has become an essential component of contemporary management processes for the achievement of strategic intent.

The general objectives of the Committee are:

- To achieve increased recognition of the professional capabilities of management accountants.

- To provide a source of comment and suggestions from a management accounting point of view on issues that fall within the terms of reference of other committees of IFAC.

- To encourage management accounting research, by member bodies and others, into matters of importance and assist in disseminating the results internationally.

- To select and disseminate information on best practices in management accounting.

- To identify the future directions of management accounting practice and communicate the implications of this to the profession at large.

- To influence and assist IFAC member bodies in developing and promoting the financial and managerial aspects of the profession.

The Committee has also been given the specific responsibility to issue, on behalf of the Council of IFAC, pronouncements on management accounting in the form of "practice statements," and "studies," and other publications.

INFORMATION TECHNOLOGY COMMITTEE

Terms of Reference

To monitor research and promote information technology advancements and its impact on the accountancy profession as a whole.

3

INTERNATIONAL AUDITING PRACTICES COMMITTEE

Terms of Reference

The objective of the International Auditing Practices Committee, on behalf of the IFAC Council, is to improve the quality and uniformity of practice throughout the world by:

- Issuing International Standards on Auditing.

- Issuing guidance on the application of International Standards on Auditing.

- Promoting the adoption of the Committee's pronouncements as the primary authority for the setting of National Standards and Guidance and for use internationally for cross border offerings.

- Promoting the endorsement of International Standards on Auditing by legislators and securities exchanges.

- Promoting debate with practitioners, users and regulators throughout the world to identify user needs for new standards and guidance.

"International Standards on Auditing" is a generic term for standards to be applied in the audit of financial statements and standards to be applied in providing related services and reporting on the credibility of information.

Each country which has a member on the Committee shall have one vote. The affirmative vote of at least three-quarters of the countries but not less than ten (10), represented at a meeting, shall be required to approve a proposed pronouncement for exposure or a definitive pronouncement for issuance.

Dissentient opinions will not be included in the exposure drafts or pronouncements issued by the Committee.

MEMBERSHIP COMMITTEE

Terms of Reference

The purpose of the IFAC Membership Committee is to recommend policies and procedures and implement programs designed to maintain and increase membership in IFAC as the world body for the accountancy profession.

The Membership Committee may:

- Commission research within its approved budget.

- Design and implement programs consistent with the activities and responsibilities approved by Council.

- Recommend to Council policies and procedures for adoption by IFAC.

- Communicate directly with present and potential member bodies and Regional Organizations.

- Recommend to Council the admissions of bodies applying for IFAC membership.

- Recommend to Council the suspension of a member body.

PUBLIC SECTOR COMMITTEE

Terms of Reference

To develop programs aimed at improving public sector financial management and accountability including:

- developing accounting and auditing standards and promoting their voluntary acceptance;
- developing and coordinating programs to promote education and research; and
- encouraging and facilitating the exchange of information among member bodies and other interested parties.

The Committee has been given the authority to issue, on behalf of the Council of IFAC, pronouncements on accounting, auditing and reporting in the public sector. The affirmative vote of at least three-quarters of the members of the Committee present at a meeting shall be required to approve a definitive standard for issuance.

A quorum of nine Committee members is required for a vote to be held.

From time to time small working groups, ad hoc committees or task forces will be appointed to work on special projects and their terms of reference will be determined by Council as deemed necessary.

Recognition of
Professional Accountancy Qualifications
Statement of Policy of Council

INTRODUCTION

1. The mission of the International Federation of Accountants (IFAC) is the worldwide development and enhancement of an accountancy profession with harmonized standards, able to provide services of consistently high quality in the public interest. Inherent in this mission statement is the understanding that services of consistently high quality implies that professional standards governing those services are also of consistently high quality. Consistently high standards will facilitate the international practice of the accountancy profession.

2. Accountants have traditionally practiced internationally, both as individuals and as firms. The main impetus behind this movement has been the globalization of business, which has accelerated especially in recent years. As enterprises became multi-national, they asked that their financial advisors be equally multi-national. As a result, professional accountants have organized themselves into global organizations, providing a wide range of services throughout the world.

3. Notwithstanding these developments, national professional institutes and national regulatory authorities have been reluctant to accept the professional qualifications of foreign accountants for regulated services. Conditions of residence, citizenship, special educational criteria and examinations have been set, conditions which are, in many cases, impossible to meet. Moreover, some of these criteria do not pertain to the professional qualifications. Given the international scope of the accountancy profession, professionally qualified accountants, both as individuals and firms, are increasingly seeking to be recognized in foreign countries, and often see these barriers as unreasonable.

4. The demand for recognition of foreign accountancy qualifications has been given special impetus by the successful completion of the Uruguay Round of trade negotiations, and the General Agreement on Trade in Services (GATS). The GATS addresses regulatory obstacles to international trade and foreign investment in service industries, including the cross-border practice of accountancy and other professions. It sets out a series of rules to discipline government intervention in the marketplace, to ensure that foreign or

internationally-affiliated service providers, firms and professionals enjoy the same privileges as their domestic counterparts or competitors with respect to government regulation and to remove discriminatory obstacles to market entry and practice by persons from other countries. Signatories to the GATS and its provisions bind their national and sub-national regulatory authorities.

5. The Council of IFAC acknowledges that a truly international market for accountancy services, with equal access to all qualified professionals, is consistent with its mission, and it encourages national professional accountancy organizations and regulatory/licensing authorities to provide for recognition of foreign accountancy qualifications. Of more concern, however, is the public interest, and IFAC believes that any mutual recognition efforts must insure that the overriding need for high standards must be scrupulously respected. In this regard, benchmark international standards, such as those promulgated by IFAC and IASC, can be especially useful in meeting this need.

6. Given the above situation, the Council of IFAC has issued this Statement of Policy, to be used by its member bodies and other interested parties. The provisions of this Statement of Policy will assist with the implementation of the provisions of GATS, as well as helping to insure that the proper standards of professional qualifications are also maintained.

THE CHANGING RULES OF RECOGNITION OF ACCOUNTANCY QUALIFICATIONS

7. Traditionally, the mutual recognition of qualifications of professional accountants of one jurisdiction in another has been arranged between professional organizations with close relationships and with similar traditions, goals and objectives. Sometimes such recognition has been extended by licensing authorities where permission to undertake audits/attest or other reserved functions has been extended by a licensing authority rather than by a professional body.

8. Generally, the recognition is conditional upon an applicant satisfying some agreed additional education, experience, examination or residence requirements to recognize differences in the jurisdictions concerned. Because of sometimes conflicting economic, social and political factors, such arrangements were not widespread. Diverse requirements for qualification as an accountant, variances in educational systems and differences in accounting and auditing standards and related laws and regulations, as well as differences in the way the profession is regulated in various countries, has tended to inhibit mobility. Additionally, criteria related to citizenship and residency have added further barriers.

9. The new GATS addresses regulatory obstacles to international trade and foreign investment in service industries, including the cross-border practice of accountancy and other professions, by setting out rules that intend to:

   • ensure that foreign or internationally-affiliated service providers, firms and professionals enjoy the same privileges as their domestic counterparts or competitors with respect to government regulation,

- remove discriminatory obstacles to market entry and practice by persons from other countries, by concentrating solely on those issues that relate to professional qualifications, and

- provide transparency to all service providers as to the rules governing recognition of qualifications.

Although they apply to the full range of service industry and professions, two of the GATS rules have particular relevance to the accountancy profession (Article VI on "Domestic Regulation" and Article VII on the "Recognition of Qualifications and Licenses" which are in Appendix 1).

10. In essence, GATS seeks to ensure that persons from one country wishing to provide services in another enjoy the same privileges as their domestic counterparts. Recognition requirements may not constitute unreasonable barriers to trade in services. It is expected that rules will be developed on a sector by sector basis to ensure that licensing requirements are based on objective and transparent criteria and are not more burdensome than is necessary to ensure the quality of the service.

11. The GATS requires that all countries have adequate procedures in place to verify the qualifications of professionals from other countries seeking the right to offer services within their jurisdictions. This will have implications both for the professional accountancy organizations, as well as for the licensing and regulatory authorities.

12. Although the GATS is multinational in scope, it does provide for bi-lateral implementation. IFAC believes that the most effective way to achieve recognition is through bi-lateral initiatives. There are differences in educational and examination standards, experience requirements, professional issues, regulatory influence and various other matters, all of which make implementing the recognition on a multilateral basis extremely difficult. Bi-lateral negotiations will enable the countries involved to focus on the key issues related to their two environments. Once bi-lateral agreements have been achieved, however, this can lead to other bi-lateral agreements, which will ultimately extend mutual recognition more broadly.

PRINCIPLES OF RECOGNITION

13. The GATS requires that criteria for recognition of qualifications may not exceed what is necessary to ensure the quality of service. Each country is expected to have a methodology for comparing professional qualifications and this must be applied in a fair and consistent manner to all applicants. IFAC recommends that the appraisal process be founded upon the key components of a professional qualification, falling into the following three areas:

- education—entry standards/body of knowledge

- examinations—tests of professional competence

- experience—relevant to the practice function

8

14. In implementing the appraisal process, the following principles are suggested. These parallel the recommendations of International Education Guideline 9 (IEG 9) and are put forward because they have been found to be widely acceptable within the profession in meeting the need to uphold its high standards and protect the public interest. Additionally, they can assist countries that are negotiating mutual recognitions in making informed decisions as to the degree of equivalence in basic educational requirements. This is a crucial procedure, since, when there is sufficient equivalence in the basic education requirements of the two bodies, the negotiating parties can proceed more efficiently.

Education

15. Initially, the subjects and skills covered in their bodies of knowledge should be compared. The theoretical knowledge to be contained in the body of knowledge of persons seeking recognition should include at least the following subjects:

- analysis and critical assessment of financial statements

- audit

- consolidated accounts

- cost and management accounting

- general accounting

- internal control systems

- legal and professional requirements relating to the exercise of the reserved function(s) concerned

- standards relating to financial statements

16. In addition, the body of knowledge should cover at least the following areas insofar as they are relevant to the reserved function(s) concerned:

- basic principles of the financial management of undertakings

- business, general and financial economics

- civil and commercial law

- information technology and systems

- law of insolvency and similar procedures

- mathematics and statistics

- provision of financial services, advice, etc.

- professional conduct and ethics

- social security and law of employment

- tax law

Applicants should have covered these subjects in a breadth and depth sufficient to enable them to perform the relevant function to the expected standard. In order to ensure that this is the case, a detailed review will need to be made of the respective educational programs and their content.

17. Areas of truly substantial difference (in terms of breadth and depth) in subjects which are considered essential to the practice of the profession in the respective countries should be identified. Applicants seeking recognition will accept that they may be required to take further courses, gain local experience or undergo some further assessment in key subject area(s).

18. There is considerable international diversity in the educational backgrounds of professional accountants and sometimes in the quality of education itself. In particular, in many countries, an undergraduate degree in accounting is required, while others accept different education and/or accept experience in lieu of formal education. Educational standards should not be considered in a vacuum. Rather they should be viewed in the overall context of the experience required for recognition and of evaluation of the professional examinations taken by an applicant of his or her professional background.

Examinations

19. Candidates for recognition of professional qualifications should demonstrate that they have passed an examination of professional competence. This examination must assess not only the necessary level of theoretical knowledge but also the ability to apply that knowledge competently in a practical situation. Objective evaluation of professional examinations thus becomes a key component of the recognition process.

20. Member bodies should not only satisfy themselves that the assessment(s) undergone by applicants indeed tests the body of knowledge and the ability to apply it, but that the policies and procedures for its construction, security and marking are adequate to ensure the integrity of the assessment process. Agreement should also be reached on the need for a periodic review of the education and assessment process for qualifications being recognized so as to ensure that the conditions for recognition continue to apply.

21. The content, rigor, scope and length of professional examinations administered by professional bodies or other examining authorities also vary. Some are case study based, while some make extensive use of objective testing. Some are highly computational, others more discursive. The task is to ensure that applicants have been adequately assessed in relevant areas to the extent necessary to enable them to operate competently in the reserved functions of their choice.

Experience

22. It is crucial to any professional to not only have a sound theoretical knowledge but also to be able to apply that knowledge competently in the world of work.

23. It is suggested that, prior to recognition for the purposes of performing a reserved function, an individual should have completed a minimum of two years approved and properly supervised practical experience primarily in the area of the function concerned and in a suitable professional environment.

24. Member bodies, or other authorities considering recognition of other qualifications, should assess the respective experience requirements and determine how to deal with any emerging differences. Differences normally relate to:

- the nature and extent of required experience (e.g., in some countries, experience outside public accounting is not regarded as acceptable for purposes of recognition of practice),

- the length of the period of the experience gained, and

- the procedures required to certify the experience gained (e.g., some countries require employers attestation, while others rely on periodic reports by those gaining the experience).

Any assessment will need to have due regard to the extent of experience relevant to the reserved function which has been obtained by the applicant. The analysis might result in a requirement that, before recognition in the jurisdiction of the host organization, an applicant might be required to undergo further experience.

25. The host country may also seek to impose a period of practical experience in the host country itself to demonstrate competence in the host country laws, practices and/or regulations. In these instances, such a requirement should be for that purpose only. It should not be unreasonably long for an individual who otherwise meets the basic practical experience requirement, as in paragraph 23.

Other Factors to be Considered

26. Although the basic elements of education, examination and experience will be the foundation of any recognition arrangements, there are several other important factors to be addressed:

- Diversity in accounting and auditing standards may cause problems in the matter of recognition. Such standards develop in response to changing social, economic, legal and political environments. Those countries with extensive technical standards may be hesitant to authorize for practice persons from countries with significantly different technical standards, particularly in the area of the reserved function. This difficulty can be resolved if it is generally accepted that applicants may reasonably be expected to demonstrate an adequate knowledge and understanding of the relevant standards as applied in the host country.

- Ethical practices differ between countries. When a professional accountant is recognized in a host country, he/she would ordinarily be subject to the host country ethics. Where differences appear significant, however, the host country may be reluctant to accept foreign accountants. As with accounting and auditing standards above, demonstration of knowledge of host country ethical practices is a reasonable expectation. Additionally, reference to the IFAC Code of Ethics for Professional Accountants can also be helpful in evaluating the significance of differences.

- Clearly, if one is to practice competently one needs reasonable written and oral skill in the generally used business language of the host country.

- Requirements for continuing professional education (CPE), as opposed to pre-qualification education in paragraphs 15-18 above, are becoming more common within the profession as a condition of a right to practice. The effect of a compulsory requirement in this area will need to be addressed since in many countries, CPE is often voluntary. Difficulties will arise where one body has a mandatory CPE policy in place and this is not the case in the jurisdiction of an applicant. In such circumstances, some further qualifications may need to be agreed for persons seeking recognition by the body which has CPE requirements in place. However, any arrangements being made should be reasonable and designed to facilitate applicants in meeting the necessary requirements within a reasonable period.

27. The GATS relates to mutual recognition of professional qualifications. It does not relate to reciprocity of membership in professional organizations. This will be especially important in those countries where the licensing/practice authorization function is separate from the professional accountancy organization. IFAC believes that the spirit of mutual recognition extends to membership. It encourages all professional accountancy bodies to develop membership classifications or other processes by which recognized foreign professionals can also be part of the accountancy organization. Membership for recognized foreign professionals will help those individuals maintain and enhance their competence in host country practices by access to technical publications, contact with local professional accountants, knowledge of ethical practices and other issues. Enhancing technical competence is of direct benefit to the public interest.

PROCESS OF RECOGNITION

28. In attempting to establish procedures for recognition of foreign qualifications, care must be taken to address the differences in the organizational structure for the profession. In a country where the accounting profession/licensing process is not centralized, a national organization might need to negotiate on behalf of its members at provincial or state level with local licensing authorities, which might themselves have widely differing requirements. In some countries, recognition for practice purposes requires membership of the locally recognized accountancy bodies, while in others recognition is gained either through affiliation with such a body or from a governmental licensing authority.

29. The GATS requires that each country establish a process to provide for recognition of foreign qualifications. Moreover, the process must be transparent and be equitable for all those individuals seeking qualification. Some countries and member bodies may already have such processes in place while others have not. In the emerging climate of greater global mobility, the

former will now need to review their systems and to create more formal structures and the latter will need to put appropriate facilities in place without delay. The following matters should be addressed:

- Close lines of contact with professional organizations in other countries, to assess the different standards.

- A process by which the educational system, curricula and degree programs in foreign countries can be assessed vis-à-vis the local requirements; this will be especially important in those instances where pre-qualification education does not always rely on the university system.

- Evaluation of the examination system in foreign countries, both as to the content of the examination and the process.

- Evaluation of the experience requirements and the way in which such experience is monitored and controlled.

- Establishment of an agency review board, or similar structure, which will analyze the results of the processes above and publish and administer the program to facilitate recognition of foreign qualifications; such an agency would use international reference points (e.g., IFAC's IEG 9) and would recommend special examinations and other programs to enable applicants to demonstrate competence in uniquely local requirements.

30. Inevitably, such structures will have cost implications. Administrative and legal expenses are examples. These could be significant. It would be reasonable that applicants for recognition should be prepared to contribute to the costs incurred in dealing with their applications and to be aware from the outset of the extent of the charges involved. In some countries, the cost/charge element may be a matter for the state of which the professional organizations/licensing authority is acting.

BARRIERS CONSIDERED AS UNRELATED TO PROFESSIONAL QUALIFICATIONS

31. The GATS stipulates that qualification requirements should not constitute unnecessary barriers to trade in serves and should not be more burdensome than necessary to ensure the quality of service and to protect the public interest.

32. Countries impose various restrictions that do not necessarily relate specifically to professional qualifications. Examples are:

- requirements that only citizens are eligible to receive professional titles or licenses;

- requirements that candidates for professional titles or licenses must have been resident in the licensing jurisdiction for a period prior to making the application;

- requirements that the licensed professional be permanently resident in or permanently established in the licensing jurisdiction; however, if the applicant is not permanently resident or permanently established, he/she could reasonably be expected to demonstrate that he/she intends to practice the reserved function; and

- requirements that an applicant attend a specified educational institution or requirements that only a university degree (with no consideration of experience or other types of training) will satisfy educational requirements.

IFAC believes that further research is necessary before it can be concluded as to whether or not such restrictions are unnecessarily burdensome. This research should give due regard, inter alia, to the impact on the capacity of the local national profession to develop itself.

KEY PROVISIONS OF THE GATS

Background

The Uruguay Round trade package, negotiated under the auspices of the General Agreement on Tariffs and Trade (GATT) included the first multinational agreement removing obstacles to accountants who wish to practice across borders. Some of these, such as exchange controls and visa restrictions, are faced in common with other service industries and providers. Others, notably difficulties in obtaining certification to practice in foreign jurisdictions, are unique to the professions.

The multilateral agreement, the General Agreement on Trade in Services (GATS), addresses these problems in qualifying to practice in foreign jurisdictions in two ways.

(1) First, its provisions on domestic regulation require countries to administer their licensing or certification rules in a reasonable, objective and impartial manner and forbids using them as disguised barriers to trade. To carry out this broad mandate, the agreement envisions the development of more specific binding disciplines in the future. Countries are also required to establish specific procedures for verifying the competence and credentials of professionals from other countries.

(2) Second, the agreement encourages countries to recognize other professionals, either autonomously or through mutual recognition agreements. It further sets out guidelines to ensure that such agreements are not used simply to discriminate against professionals from countries that are not party to them.

Articles of Special Interest to the Accountancy Profession

There are two articles within the GATS that are of particular interest to the accountancy profession:

• Article VI on domestic regulation is one of the rules that only applies to accountancy in cases where individual governments have made specific commitments in their schedules. It contains three important features:

  – Governments agree to apply regulations affecting service industries and professions in a reasonable, objective and impartial manner so that they do not act as barriers to trade.

  – Qualification requirements and procedures, technical standards and licensing requirements should not constitute unnecessary barriers to trade in services. Further disciplines or rules shall be developed on a sector-by-sector basis to make sure such measures are based on objective and transparent criteria, are not more burdensome than necessary to ensure the quality of the service and, in the case of licensing requirements, do not in themselves serve as restrictions on the supply of the service. International standards should be taken into account in determining compliance with these principles.

- All countries must have adequate procedures in place to verify the qualifications of professional from other countries seeking the right to practice within their jurisdictions.

• Article VII on registration of qualifications and licenses applies across the board to all services and professions in all signatory countries regardless of whether specific commitments have been made. Like Article VI, this article has three features relevant to the accountancy profession:

- Countries may choose their own approach to recognizing foreign qualifications and licenses, through unilateral recognition, bilateral reciprocal arrangements or international harmonization.

- There is no obligation for a country to enter into such arrangements. However, if a country decides to do so, whatever approach is chosen must be applied in a consistent, objective and fair manner to all other countries seeking recognition of their professionals.

- Countries are encouraged to cooperate with intergovernmental and non-governmental organizations toward the establishment and adoption of common international qualifications and standards of practice.

Implementation

The operation of the GATS, as well as the GATT itself and a new agreement on the protection of intellectual property, will be overseen and administered by the new World Trade Organization (WTO). The GATS also creates a Council on Trade in Services made up of representatives from the signatory countries, to continue negotiations on outstanding issues and otherwise to take up questions that arise in the operation of the services agreement.

It is known that, in the context of professional services, the Council on Trade Services will be establishing a working party when the agreement comes into force to oversee the implementation of services agreement and that its work relating to accountancy has been designated as "a matter of priority".

The following three stage agenda has been set for the working party:

1. The additional disciplines and rules envisioned by Article VI should be developed to make sure that national qualification requirements and procedures, technical standards and licensing requirements in accountancy do not constitute unnecessary barriers to trade.

2. The use of international standards with respect to qualifications and the practice of accountancy should be encouraged through cooperation with relevant international governmental and non-governmental organizations. IFAC and the IASC are the obvious non-governmental organizations to be involved in this effort.

3. The cross border recognition of qualifications should be encouraged, in accordance with Article VII, through the development of appropriate guidelines for recognition agreements.

EXAMPLES OF MUTUAL RECOGNITION INITIATIVES

The European Union

The true legal foundation for the philosophy of mutual recognition was the 1957 Treaty of Rome. However, it took several decades to develop the necessary political will. This happened with The Single European Act 1986 which enshrined the philosophy of mutual recognition. The general system of mutual recognition of diplomas seeks to permit professionals in the European Union to circulate more freely and easily from one member state to another. This system concerns only individuals and ignores firms which may be part of the relevant profession. In addition, the directive relates only to establishment-based provision of services and does not address the question of cross-border provision of services.

The end result sought is the right of the professional to practice his/her profession in the host member state or provide services there under the same conditions as those to which professionals in that country are subject. The progressive implementation of the first directive in member states and the effective organizations of local knowledge examinations for the accountancy profession should result in a significant increase in the number of accountants benefiting from the mutual recognition of diplomas.

North America

The North American Free Trade Agreement (NAFTA) establishes basic rules and obligations to facilitate cross-border trade in services. While recognizing the need for regulation, NAFTA encourages broader market access by providing that licensing requirements must be based on objective and transparent criteria, such as professional competence, and must be no more burdensome than is necessary to ensure the quality of service provided.

In 1991, an agreement was entered into between the Canadian Institute of Chartered Accountants, The American Institute of Certified Public Accountants and the National Association of State Boards of Accountancy which became effective in some, but not all US states in November 1993. A holder of one designation may qualify for the other by passing local knowledge examinations and by meeting certain experience requirements. Candidates for reciprocal recognition, who qualify by passing the local knowledge examinations of one of the bodies, will be exempt from the obligation to write the final qualification examination of that body.

INTERNATIONAL PROFESSIONAL PRACTICE STATEMENTS

CONTENTS OF THIS SECTION

Page

Statements:

1. Assuring the Quality of Professional Services 20

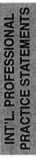

INT'L PROFESSIONAL
PRACTICE STATEMENTS

ASSURING THE QUALITY OF PROFESSIONAL SERVICES

CONTENTS

	Paragraphs
Introduction	1–5
Objectives	6–8
Establishing Quality Control Standards	9–10
Providing Other Quality Control Guidance	11
Establishing a Quality Review Program	12–24
Appendix 1: Quality Control Policies and Procedures	
Appendix 2: Implementation Guide	

August 1999

Assuring the Quality
of Professional Services

Introduction

1. IFAC's Code of Ethics for Professional Accountants notes that "a distinguishing mark of a profession is acceptance of its responsibility to the public." The accountancy profession has acquired a reputation for integrity, objectivity, and competence through its many years of service to clients, employers, and the public. Every professional accountant who fails (or is perceived as failing) to comply with professional standards and legal requirements makes it difficult for the profession to maintain its reputation. IFAC's role is to provide guidance, encourage progress, and promote harmonization. Thus, IFAC believes that member bodies need to demonstrate that there are adequate self-regulatory programs in place to provide reasonable assurance that professional accountants adhere to the highest standards.

2. Regulation of the accountancy profession is carried out cost efficiently and effectively by those dedicated individuals who comprise the profession. It is therefore in the interests of the worldwide accountancy profession, and the public it serves, for member bodies to ensure they carry out and publicize this kind of self-regulatory effort.

3. The duty to adhere to professional requirements rests on the individual professional accountant. However, assessing the extent to which an individual accountant has met this duty is best carried out at the level of the organization for which the professional accountant's work is performed.

4. In the case of employed professional accountants,[1] the implementation of appropriate quality assurance policies and procedures is ordinarily a matter for the organization employing the professional accountant (the employer).

---

[1] The *Code of Ethics for Professional Accountants* defines an employed accountant as *a professional accountant employed in industry, commerce, the public sector or education.*

Accordingly, this Statement of Policy does not deal with employed professional accountants.

5.   In the case of professional accountants in public practice, the implementation of appropriate quality control policies and procedures is the responsibility of each firm of practicing accountants. The task of encouraging and assisting firms of practicing accountants to maintain and improve the quality of professional services is primarily that of the member bodies in each country. IFAC believes that the member bodies have the responsibility to take appropriate steps to achieve that objective in the legal, social, business, and regulatory environment prevailing within their countries. This Statement of Policy discusses the steps that member bodies can take to enhance quality control within accounting firms.

Objectives

6.   IFAC believes that all firms of professional accountants should have quality control policies and procedures for all professional services and that member bodies should ensure that these policies and procedures are subject to external review. Many segments of society when making decisions increasingly depend upon information over which they have no control; they turn to professional accountants for assistance in assessing the credibility of some of that information. In view of the greater degree of reliance that the public places on assurance engagements, it is appropriate for the review of assurance engagements to be more rigorous than the review of other services.

7.   It is not possible for IFAC to outline all of the steps needed to establish effective quality control standards and quality review programs. However, IFAC believes that the following objectives have worldwide applicability and that member bodies should strive to achieve them.

- Member bodies should adopt or develop quality control standards and relevant guidance that require firms of practicing accountants to establish the quality control policies and procedures necessary to provide reasonable assurance of conforming with professional standards in performing services. The nature and extent of a firm's quality control policies and procedures depend on a number of factors, such as the size and nature of its practice, its geographic dispersion, its organization, and appropriate cost/benefit considerations. Accordingly, the policies and procedures adopted by individual firms will vary, as will the manner in which the policies and procedures themselves and compliance with them are documented.

- Member bodies should develop quality review programs designed to evaluate whether firms of practicing accountants have established appropriate quality control policies and procedures and are complying with those policies.

- Member bodies should establish quality review programs designed to evaluate whether firms of practicing accountants have complied with relevant professional standards for assurance engagements.

- Member bodies should require firms of practicing accountants to make appropriate improvements in their quality control policies and procedures, or in their compliance with those policies and procedures, when the need for such improvement is identified. Where firms fail to comply with relevant professional standards, the member body should take appropriate corrective action. Member bodies should also take such educational or disciplinary measures as indicated by the circumstances.

8. As a basic condition, IFAC emphasizes that implementation of an adequate self-regulatory program cannot be effected until firms of practicing accountants in a country are bound by an appropriate code of ethics and also by adequate standards governing accounting principles and engagements to provide professional services. The IFAC Code of Ethics for Professional Accountants, its International Standards on Auditing, and the International Accounting Standards (IASs) issued by the International Accounting Standards Committee (IASC) all provide guidance for such standards.

Establishing Quality Control Standards

9. Member bodies should promulgate or otherwise identify the standards against which it will measure the quality control policies and procedures of firms of practicing accountants. Those standards should set out the objectives of quality controls. It is the responsibility of each firm of practicing accountants to implement policies and procedures that provide reasonable assurance of achieving those objectives. It is also the firm's responsibility to communicate those policies and procedures to its personnel in a manner that provides reasonable assurance that the policies and procedures are understood.

10. General quality control policies and procedures should cover such areas as:

    (*a*) the qualities, skills and competence of the firm's personnel;

    (*b*) the assignment of personnel to engagements and their direction and supervision;

    (*c*) the acceptance of new clients and the retention of existing clients; and

    (*d*) the monitoring of quality control procedures.

    Appendix 1 sets out the objectives and illustrative examples of general quality control policies and procedures. IFAC believes that they are relevant to all services rendered by a firm of practicing accountants.

Providing Other Quality Control Guidance

11. Member bodies should consider whether firms of practicing accountants in their countries need other assistance to understand the objectives of quality control and to implement appropriate quality control policies and procedures. Assistance can be provided in various forms, depending upon the needs within a country. The following are some examples.

    - Mandating Continuing Professional Education (CPE) when it appears that CPE would be effective in assuring that all practicing accountants obtain adequate training. International Education Guideline 2 "Continuing Professional Education" provides further guidance on CPE programs.

- Developing guidelines for comprehensive CPE programs that may be useful to firms in planning, or evaluating the adequacy of, their in-house training.

- Providing CPE programs to firms and sole practitioners that do not have the resources to develop their own internal programs, including programs specifically directed to the implementation of quality control policies and procedures.

- Providing guidelines for the conduct of effective internal inspection programs.

- Implementing voluntary programs that enable firms of practicing accountants to obtain an independent, confidential assessment of their quality control policies and procedures, apart from any formal program of quality review.

Establishing a Quality Review Program

12. Member bodies should establish a quality review program. The program should be mandatory for all firms that provide professional services. The program should cover the firm's quality control policies and procedures for all professional services, and should cover the firm's adherence to relevant professional standards in respect of assurance engagements. The program may be extended, on a voluntary or mandatory basis, to cover adherence to relevant professional standards in respect of other services. Appendix 2 gives assistance on some of the practical aspects of setting up a quality review program.

13. The first consideration is whether the object of the review program will be the individual professional accountant, or the firm of which the accountant is part. Member bodies may chose to do either, but even where the object of the review program is the individual professional accountant, it will usually be necessary to consider the policies and procedures adopted by the firm of which the accountant is part. When reviewing the firm, the work of all partners conducting assurance engagements may be reviewed, or the work of only some of the partners may be reviewed, with the reviews being increased if the standard is unsatisfactory.

14. The next consideration is the scope of the program itself. All firms may be reviewed over an established period of time, or firms of practicing accountants may be selected for quality review on a test basis (for example, upon a random selection or upon the nature and size of their practices). When the quality review program in a country is carried out on a test basis, IFAC believes that it is important that all firms of practicing accountants should face the possibility of being selected for review.

15. In reaching a decision on the scope of a quality review program, member bodies should consider the following.

- The extent to which all firms of practicing accountants conduct assurance engagements.

- Governmental, regulatory, or media criticisms of the quality of professional services.

- The extent to which proposals for quality review programs appear to be supported by the profession or demanded by others.

- The cost of the program in relation to the financial strength of the practicing profession and of the member body itself.

16. When all firms of practicing accountants in a given country are to have quality reviews, it is possible to control the costs without loss of effectiveness. In particular, the program can be implemented over a reasonable number of years, for example, beginning with firms with more extensive assurance engagements, on whom there may be greater public reliance. During that phase-in period, the member body would continue educational efforts to help firms develop effective quality control policies and procedures, and to prepare for review. At the same time, it would be prudent for the member body to use its best efforts to communicate to government and to the public the extent of this commitment by the profession to maintain and improve the quality of service.

17. Where a quality review of a firm's assurance engagements is being undertaken, that review should address the firm's work product as well as its quality control procedures. Quality reviews of other types of work may be limited to a consideration of the quality control policies and procedures.

18. Personal visits to a firm to conduct a quality review should produce the most benefit to the firm and to the public. For this reason, the partners and senior staff members of the firm should be encouraged to participate in a discussion of the review's findings. Accordingly, this approach should be taken wherever possible and appropriate. The member body should set up a committee to consider the findings, and the firm's partners should be permitted to make representations to that committee.

19. The next major consideration is whether the reviews are to be conducted by practicing accountants, by non-practicing accountants engaged by the member body, or by its own employees. The services rendered by firms of practicing accountants require a comprehensive knowledge of professional standards and, in many cases, legal, regulatory, and tax requirements. They usually call for knowledge of the client's business and of matters affecting the industry in which the client operates, such as economic conditions, government regulations, and changes in technology. They may involve special expertise in matters as diverse as, for example, information processing, hedging transactions, and valuation methods. Practicing accountants would ordinarily be expected to have current knowledge of such matters and, therefore, should be well suited to carry out quality reviews of other firms of practicing accountants. The member body should ensure that the review program used by firms is based upon programs it has approved. It should also adopt reasonable oversight procedures to provide added

assurance that quality reviews are carried out in an independent, objective manner.

20. All people conducting reviews should also be instructed in the need to carry out their procedures, whenever possible, in a manner that elicits full cooperation from the firms being reviewed, and to maintain the confidentiality of client information.

21. Where quality reviews are to be carried out by non-practicing accountants engaged by the member body, or by its own professionally qualified employees, it should insure that the individuals involved have a current knowledge of applicable professional and quality control standards and the manner in which firms of practicing accountants implement those standards.

22. The number of alternative approaches that exist make it evident that each member body will have to agree upon the appropriate alternatives. It will also need to publish its program in the form of reasonably detailed standards and procedures. In that connection, IFAC believes that it is important for a successful quality review program to have standards that address at least the following matters.

- Assuring that reviewers receive training in the conduct of reviews.

- Assuring the independence and objectivity of reviewers.

- Assuring that reviewers have the technical skill and knowledge and the specialized experience to perform the review with professional competence.

- Documenting the review procedures followed in a manner that permits an objective assessment of whether the review was performed with due care and in compliance with its standards.

- Reporting the findings of the review in a manner that assists the reviewed firm in identifying and implementing any necessary corrective actions and in making other desirable improvements in its quality control policies and procedures.

- Requiring, where applicable, the imposition of added corrective, educational, or monitoring procedures pursuant to guidelines that assure that firms will be treated fairly and consistently. Examples of such procedures are requirements for changes in quality control policies and procedures, for specified continuing professional education, or for follow up visits by reviewers to obtain assurance that corrective actions planned by the firm have been appropriately implemented.

- Imposing disciplinary measures on firms that either refuse to cooperate in the conduct of the review, fail to take necessary corrective action, or are found to have serious deficiencies that cannot be dealt with in a meaningful way by remedial or educational measures.

- Maintaining the confidentiality of client information.

23. Member bodies establishing a quality review program will also need to develop specific administrative procedures to guide the selection of reviewers, to monitor the progress of reviews, to evaluate the performance of

reviewers, and to deal with the resolution of differences of professional opinion on matters related to the review.

24. Finally, the number of tasks enumerated above (and each member body implementing a quality review program will identify many others) makes it evident that careful advance planning, committed members, qualified staff at the member body, and comprehensive training and communications programs are essential to success.

QUALITY CONTROL POLICIES AND PROCEDURES

Personnel Qualities

1. Personnel in the firm should adhere to the principles of integrity, objectivity, independence, and confidentiality.

2. Quality control standards should encourage firms of practicing accountants to adopt quality control policies and procedures that provide the firm with reasonable assurance that:

    • The firm's policies on matters involving integrity, objectivity, independence, and confidentiality as they relate to the various types of services provided by the firm are communicated to personnel at all levels within the firm.

    • Questions on these matters are identified and resolved by individuals at appropriate management levels.

    • Compliance with the firm's policies and procedures relating to independence is monitored.

Skills and Competence

3. The firm should be staffed by personnel who have attained and maintain the skills and competence required to enable them to fulfill their responsibilities.

4. Quality control standards should encourage firms of practicing accountants to adopt quality control policies and procedures that provide them with reasonable assurance that:

    • The firm's recruiting program will meet the firm's personnel needs and that personnel hired by the firm, both inexperienced and experienced, will have integrity and the other attributes, achievements, and experience necessary to enable them to perform with skill and competence.

    • The firm's continuing professional education (CPE) and training programs are carried out in compliance with guidelines designed to provide personnel with the knowledge required to fulfill their responsibilities and to progress within the firm.

    • Personnel are informed about the responsibilities of their positions, counseled on a timely basis on their performance, progress, and career opportunities, and advanced to positions of greater responsibility in accordance with guidelines that give appropriate recognition to the quality of their work.

Assignment

5. Work should be assigned to personnel who have the degree of technical training and proficiency required in the circumstances.

6. Quality control standards should encourage firms of practicing accountants to adopt quality control policies and procedures that provide them with reasonable assurance that:

- In assigning personnel to engagements, appropriate consideration is given to the workload requirements of an engagement, the skills and competence required by an engagement, the experience and competence of personnel in relation to the complexity or other requirements of an engagement, the extent of supervision to be provided, and other relevant factors.

- Assignment decisions are made by individuals charged with that responsibility, and the decision is approved by the person responsible for the conduct of the specific engagement.

Direction and Supervision

7. There should be sufficient direction and supervision of work at all levels to provide the firm with reasonable assurance that the work performed by the firm meets appropriate standards of quality. Whenever necessary, consultation should be made with those who have appropriate expertise.

8. Quality control standards should encourage firms of practicing accountants to adopt quality control policies and procedures that provide them with reasonable assurance that:

- Work is properly planned by appropriate personnel.

- Work is properly supervised at all organizational levels, considering the training, ability, and experience of the personnel assigned.

- Other appropriate procedures for maintaining the firm's standards of quality are complied with (such as policies and procedures for the conduct of the work, standardized forms, checklists and questionnaires, and procedures for resolving differences of professional opinion).

- Personnel consult with or use authoritative sources on specialized, complex, or unusual matters; to that end, situations requiring consultation and the persons or sources to be consulted should be identified, appropriate reference libraries should be maintained, and the extent to which consultation should be documented should be specified.

- Appropriate on-the-job training is provided.

- Guidelines for the review of the work performed and of the work product are complied with; such guidelines should deal, among other things, with the qualifications of the reviewer, the documentation of the review, and the types of situations that call for a review by an individual having no other responsibility for the engagement.

Acceptance and Retention of Clients

9. The firm should carry out an evaluation of a prospective client prior to acceptance and should review, on an ongoing basis, its association with present clients. In making a decision to accept or retain a client, the firm should consider the nature of the work contemplated by the engagement, circumstances that would cause the firm to regard the engagement as one requiring special attention or presenting special risks, its own independence (where required), its ability to service the client properly, and the integrity of the client's management.

10. Quality control standards should encourage firms of practicing accountants to adopt quality control policies and procedures that provide them with reasonable assurance that:

   - Present and prospective clients are evaluated consistently against guidelines relevant to the firm and its practice by individuals at appropriate management levels.

   - Adequate procedures exist for identifying and addressing conditions that would have caused the firm to reject a client had such conditions existed at the time of initial acceptance and that those procedures are complied with.

   - There is a clear understanding with clients about the objectives, nature, scope and limitations of an engagement, ordinarily through preparation of an engagement letter.

Inspection

11. The firm should monitor the effectiveness of its quality control policies and procedures.

12. Quality control standards should encourage firms of practicing accountants to adopt quality control policies and procedures that provide them with reasonable assurance that:

   - The scope and content of the firm's inspection program are appropriately defined in relation to the size of the firm, the nature of its practice, the degree of operating autonomy allowed to its personnel and operating offices, and other procedures the firm follows to assist it in monitoring compliance with other quality control policies and procedures (such as a "cold" review of working papers and reports).

   - The inspection program is carried out by personnel with the necessary competence and experience.

   - Corrective actions indicated by inspection findings are implemented on a timely basis.

IMPLEMENTATION GUIDE

Introduction

1. This implementation guide is intended to provide assistance to member bodies in their implementation of Council's Statement of Policy on *Assuring the Quality of Professional Services*.

Initial Steps

2. The first point to consider is whether the body's constitution permits it to operate a quality review scheme. If the constitution does not, then it should be altered accordingly. Similarly, the rules on client confidentiality need to be examined to ensure that the operation of a review scheme would not break those rules. Any relevant laws would also need to be considered.

3. Member bodies have to decide at an early stage whether the reviews:

   (*a*) will be carried out by their own employees or by other firms of professional accountants in public practice; and

   (*b*) will be paid for on a "per review basis" by firms that are reviewed or whether the cost of the review system is funded by a general levy on members as a whole or on members in public practice.

4. The scope of the review needs to be established at an early stage. The member body needs to ensure that there are appropriate professional standards against which the practicing firm can be measured.

The Next Stages

5. The member body also needs to set up an appropriate infrastructure internally for considering the results of reviews. For example, a bad review (or a series of bad reviews) should lead to appropriate regulatory and disciplinary action, and may lead to professional accountants having their licenses to practice revoked. An appropriate committee and appeal structure need to be put in place.

6. Where the reviews are to be carried out by employees of the member body, then the body needs to recruit sufficient professional accountants with appropriate experience. Those people need to be integrated into the body's structure.

7. Where the reviews are to be carried out by firms of professional accountants in public practice, criteria for selecting suitable firms need to be prepared. The body also needs to decide whether it will select the firm to carry out a particular review, or whether the firm being reviewed may select its own reviewer. Where firms may select their own reviewers then the body needs to

establish a mechanism to ensure that the firm conducting the review is suitable.

8. Those conducting reviews (whether employees of the member body or firms of professional accountants) need to receive training in review procedures. A mechanism needs to be set up that ensures consistency between reviewers, and allows for the pooling of experience. This will include the design of suitable review programs for those conducting reviews.

9. The body then needs to consider the following further points, which have important implications for the smooth running of the scheme.

   (a) Will the reviews be of individual professional accountants, or of firms of professional accountants? If it is of firms, will each partner be subject to review, or will only a sample of some of the partners be chosen?

   (b) Is it intended that all firms will be reviewed within a given period, or is it intended that only a sample will be chosen each year and that some firms might never be reviewed?

10. The member body will need to establish a mechanism to keep track of those providing professional services to provide a base for the selection of those being reviewed.

Introducing the Scheme

11. It is important that members are informed about the introduction of the scheme and what aspects of their work will fall within the scheme. In some cases member bodies may wish to set up practice advisory schemes whereby professional accountants in public practice can receive confidential assistance on practice management or technical issues.

12. The purpose of a review is to help the firm, and the member body, be sure that work is carried out in accordance with professional standards. The review process should not be confrontational, but should be carried out in a spirit of mutual co-operation. This also helps the review to be carried out speedily and efficiently. This factor should be borne in mind when designing the training programs for those conducting reviews.

13. In most cases it is essential for firms to be given advance warning of the review. This is because they will often need to gather information together and because the partners concerned will need to be available to answer questions when the review is being carried out. Similarly, the reviewers should discuss their findings with the firm being reviewed before issuing the final report.

14. There will need to be a system for monitoring the reviews. Where the outcome of a review is less than satisfactory, then that information needs to be passed on to the appropriate committee. It may also be appropriate to schedule the firm for a follow up visit earlier than would otherwise be the case.

AUDITING

July 1994

CODIFICATION OF INTERNATIONAL STANDARDS ON AUDITING AND INTERNATIONAL AUDITING PRACTICE STATEMENTS

Contents of this Section — Subject Matter

Subject Matter Number and Document Title

Page

100-199 Introductory Matters

100	Preface to ISAs and RSs	37
110	Glossary of Terms	43
120	Framework of ISAs	54

200-299 Responsibilities

200	Objective and General Principles Governing an Audit of Financial Statements	61
210	Terms of Audit Engagements	65
220	Quality Control for Audit Work	72
230	Documentation	90

AUDITING

220	Quality Control for Audit Work	72
230	Documentation	90

**Subject Matter Number
and Document Title** **Page**

240	Fraud and Error	94
250	Consideration of Laws and Regulations in an Audit of Financial Statements	102

300-399 Planning

300	Planning	111
310	Knowledge of the Business	115
320	Audit Materiality	122

400-499 Internal Control

400	Risk Assessments and Internal Control	126
401	Auditing in a Computer Information Systems Environment	140
402	Audit Considerations Relating to Entities Using Service Organizations	145

500-599 Audit Evidence

500	Audit Evidence	150
501	Audit Evidence—Additional Considerations for Specific Items	155
510	Initial Engagements—Opening Balances	163
520	Analytical Procedures	167
530	Audit Sampling and Other Selective Testing Procedures	172
540	Audit of Accounting Estimates	190
550	Related Parties	196
560	Subsequent Events	201
570	Going Concern	206
580	Management Representations	212

600-699 Using Work of Others

600	Using the Work of Another Auditor	218

Subject Matter Number and Document Title	Page

700-799 Audit Conclusions and Reporting

700	The Auditor's Report on Financial Statements	233
710	Comparatives	245
720	Other Information in Documents Containing Audited Financial Statements	258

800-899 Specialized Areas

800	The Auditor's Report on Special Purpose Audit Engagements	262
810	The Examination of Prospective Financial Information	277

900-999 Related Services

910	Engagements to Review Financial Statements	287
920	Engagements to Perform Agreed-Upon Procedures Regarding Financial Information	307
930	Engagements to Compile Financial Information	317

1000-1100 International Auditing Practice Statements

1000	Inter-Bank Confirmation Procedures	327

Supplements #1-3 to Subject Matter 400:

1001	CIS Environments—Stand-Alone Microcomputers	334
1002	CIS Environments—On-Line Computer Systems	344
1003	CIS Environments—Database Systems	353
1004	The Relationship Between Bank Supervisors and External Auditors	361
1005	The Special Considerations in the Audit of Small Entities	377
1006	The Audit of International Commercial Banks	402
1007	Communications With Management	462
1008	Risk Assessments and Internal Control—CIS Characteristics and Considerations	467
1009	Computer-Assisted Audit Techniques	474

AUDITING

**Subject Matter Number
and Document Title**   **Page**

1010   The Consideration of Environmental Matters in the Audit
        of Financial Statements   482

1011   Implications for Management and Auditors of the Year
        2000 Issue   504

Summary of Discussion Paper:

    • The Audit Profession and the Environment   516

**Approved Standards with Future Application Dates – Included
for Informational Purposes Only**

    Going Concern   519

    Communications of Audit Matters with Those Charged
with Governance   531

For additional information on the International Auditing Practices Committee, recent developments, and/or to obtain outstanding exposure drafts, visit the Committee's page at http://www.ifac.org/Committees/IAPC.

CONTENTS

	Paragraphs
Introduction	1-3
The International Auditing Practices Committee	4-6
International Standards on Auditing and Related Services	7-8
The Authority Attaching to International Standards on Auditing	9-16
The Authority Attaching to International Auditing Practice Statements	17
Working Procedures	18-21
Language	22
Application of International Standards on Auditing as National Standards	23
Appendix: Illustrative Wording that a Country May Wish to Use When it Adopts International Standards on Auditing as National Standards	

AUDITING

Introduction

1. This Preface to International Standards on Auditing and Related Services is issued to facilitate understanding of the objectives and operating procedures of the International Auditing Practices Committee (IAPC) and the scope and authority of the documents issued by the Committee. The Preface was approved by the Council of the International Federation of Accountants (IFAC) for publication in July 1994. The approved text of this Preface is that published by IFAC in the English language.

2. The mission of IFAC as set out in its Constitution is "the worldwide development and enhancement of an accountancy profession with harmonized standards, able to provide services of consistently high quality in the public interest." In working toward this mission, the Council of IFAC has established IAPC to develop and issue, on behalf of the Council, standards and statements on auditing and related services. IAPC believes that the issue of such standards and statements will improve the degree of uniformity of auditing practices and related services throughout the world.

3. In accordance with the Constitution of IFAC, member bodies subscribe to the mission set out in paragraph 2 above. In order to assist member bodies in the implementation of International Standards on Auditing (ISAs), IAPC will, with the support of the Council, seek to promote their voluntary acceptance.

The International Auditing Practices Committee

4. IAPC is a standing committee of the Council of IFAC.

5. The members of IAPC are those nominated by the member bodies in the countries selected by the Council to serve on IAPC. The representatives designated by the member body or bodies to serve on IAPC must be a member of one of such bodies.

6. To obtain a broad spectrum of views, subcommittees of IAPC may include individuals from countries which are not represented on IAPC and information may be sought from other organizations.

International Standards on Auditing and Related Services

7. Within each country, local regulations govern, to a greater or lesser degree, the practices followed in the auditing of financial or other information. Such regulations may be either of a statutory nature, or in the form of statements issued by the regulatory or professional bodies in the countries concerned.

8. National standards on auditing and related services published in many countries differ in form and content. IAPC takes cognizance of such documents and differences and, in the light of such knowledge, issues ISAs which are intended for international acceptance.

The Authority Attaching to International Standards on Auditing

9. ISAs are to be applied in the audit of financial statements. ISAs are also to be applied, adapted as necessary, to the audit of other information and to related services.

10. ISAs contain basic principles and essential procedures (identified in bold type black lettering) together with related guidance in the form of explanatory and other material. The basic principles and essential procedures are to be interpreted in the context of the explanatory and other material that provide guidance for their application.

11. To understand and apply the basic principles and essential procedures together with the related guidance, it is necessary to consider the whole text of the ISA including explanatory and other material contained in the ISA not just that text which is black lettered.

12. In exceptional circumstances, an auditor may judge it necessary to depart from an ISA in order to more effectively achieve the objective of an audit. When such a situation arises, the auditor should be prepared to justify the departure.

13. ISAs need only be applied to material matters.

14. Any limitation of the applicability of a specific ISA is made clear in the introductory paragraphs to that ISA.

15. The Public Sector Perspective (PSP) issued by the Public Sector Committee of IFAC is set out at the end of an ISA. Where no PSP is added, the ISA is applicable in all material respects to the public sector.

16. ISAs do not override the local regulations referred to in paragraph 7 above governing the audit of financial or other information in a particular country. To the extent that ISAs conform with local regulations on a particular subject, the audit of financial or other information in that country in accordance with local regulations will automatically comply with the ISA regarding that subject. In the event that the local regulations differ from, or conflict with, ISAs on a particular subject, member bodies should comply with the obligations of membership set forth in the IFAC Constitution as regards these ISAs[1].

The Authority Attaching to International Auditing Practice Statements

17. International Auditing Practice Statements (IAPSs) are issued to provide practical assistance to auditors in implementing the Standards or to promote good practice. These Statements are not intended to have the authority of Standards.

Working Procedures

18. The working procedure of IAPC is to select subjects for detailed study by a subcommittee established for that purpose. IAPC delegates to the

---

[1] The IFAC Constitution states that "Member bodies shall ..... support the work of IFAC by bringing to the notice of their members every pronouncement developed by IFAC and by using their best endeavors:

  i. to work towards implementation, when and to the extent possible under local circumstances, of those pronouncements and

  ii. specifically to incorporate in their national auditing standards the principles on which are based International Standards on Auditing developed by IFAC."

100

AUDITING

subcommittee the initial responsibility for the preparation and drafting of auditing standards and statements. The subcommittee studies background information in the form of statements, recommendations, studies or standards issued by member bodies, regional organizations, or other bodies. As a result of that study, an exposure draft is prepared for consideration by IAPC. If approved, the exposure draft is widely distributed for comment by member bodies of IFAC, and to such international organizations that have an interest in auditing standards as appropriate. Adequate time is allowed for each exposure draft to be considered by the persons and organizations to whom it is sent for comment.

19. The comments and suggestions received as a result of this exposure are then considered by IAPC and the exposure draft is revised as appropriate. Provided that the revised draft is approved, it is issued as a definitive ISA or as an IAPS and becomes operative from the date stated therein.

20. The quorum for a meeting is ten members. Exposure drafts, standards and statements require approval of three quarters of the members present at the meeting with a minimum of ten approving.

21. Each member of IAPC has the right to one vote.

Language

22. The approved text of an exposure draft, standard or statement is that published by IFAC in the English language. Member bodies of IFAC are authorized, after obtaining IFAC approval, to prepare translations of such documents, at their own cost, to be issued in the language of their own countries as appropriate. These translations should indicate the name of the accountancy body that prepared them and that they are translations of the approved text.

Application of International Standards on Auditing as National Standards

23. To assist the member countries that choose to adopt ISAs as their own national standards, IAPC has developed wording which may be used to indicate the authority and applicability in the country concerned. It is attached as the Appendix to this Preface.

Appendix

Illustrative Wording that a Country May Wish to Use When it Adopts International Standards on Auditing as National Standards

Preface to National Standards on
Auditing and Related Services

Statement of Policy of [Council]

This Preface has been approved by the [Council of Member Body] for publication.

1. The [Name of Member Body] as a member of the International Federation of Accountants (IFAC) is committed to the Federation's broad mission of the worldwide development and enhancement of an accountancy profession with harmonized standards, able to provide "services of consistently high quality in the public interest." In working toward this mission, the Council of IFAC has established the International Auditing Practices Committee (IAPC) to develop and issue, on behalf of the Council, standards and statements on auditing and related services. IAPC believes that the issue of such standards and statements will help to improve the degree of uniformity of auditing practices and related services throughout the world.

2. As a condition of its membership, the [Name of Member Body] is obliged to support the work of IFAC by informing its members of every pronouncement developed by IFAC and by using their best endeavors, to work towards implementation, when and to the extent possible under local circumstances, of those pronouncements and specifically to incorporate the principles on which are based IFAC's International Standards on Auditing (ISAs) in national auditing pronouncements.

3. The [Name of Member Body] has determined to adopt the ISAs as the basis for approved standards on auditing and related services in [Name of Country]. Council will prepare an explanatory foreword on the status on each approved ISA that is adopted.

> *Possible wording for such a foreword is:*
>
> *International Standard on Auditing [Number]*
>
> *[Title]*
>
> *Explanatory Foreword*
>
> *The Council of [Name of Member Body] has determined that this International Standard on Auditing should be adopted from [199X].*
>
> *International Standards on Auditing (ISAs) are to be applied in the audit of financial statements. ISAs are also to be applied, adapted as necessary, to the audit of other information and to related services.*
>
> *ISAs contain basic principles and essential procedures (identified in bold type black lettering) together with related guidance in the form of explanatory and other material. The basic principles and*

AUDITING

100

essential procedures are to be interpreted in the context of the explanatory and other material that provide guidance for their application.

To understand and apply the basic principles and essential procedures together with the related guidance, it is necessary to consider the whole text of the ISA including explanatory and other material contained in the ISA not just that text which is black lettered.

In exceptional circumstances, an auditor may judge it necessary to depart from an ISA in order to more effectively achieve the objective of an audit. When such a situation arises, the auditor should be prepared to justify the departure.

ISAs need only be applied to material matters.

Any limitation of the applicability of a specific ISA is made clear in the introductory paragraphs to that ISA.

The Public Sector Perspective (PSP) issued by the Public Sector Committee of the International Federation of Accountants is set out at the end of an ISA. Where no PSP is added, the ISA is applicable in all material respects to the public sector.

4. In the event that an IAPC-issued ISA contains guidance which is significantly different from [Name of Country] law or practice, the explanatory foreword to an approved ISA will provide guidance on such differences.

   An example of such guidance would be:

   "Paragraph 10 and 14
   Under [Name of Country] legislation, management's responsibility to advise the auditor of events affecting financial statements continues beyond date of issue to date of adoption by members of a Company in general meeting."

5. Where the Council deems it necessary, additional standards may be developed on matters of relevance in [Name of Country] not covered by ISAs.

6. Members of [Name of Member Body] are expected to comply with the standards on auditing and related services issued by [Name of Member Body]. Apparent failure to do so may result in an investigation into the member's conduct by [Name of Appropriate Disciplinary Committee of Member Body].

7. It is impractical to establish standards on auditing and related services which universally apply to all situations and circumstances an auditor may encounter. Therefore auditors should consider the adopted standards as the basic principles which they should follow in performing their work. The precise procedures required to apply these standards are left to the professional judgment of the individual auditor and will depend on the circumstances of each case.

8. The date from which members are expected to observe the standard on auditing and related services is set out in the explanatory foreword.

Glossary of Terms at July 1995

Accounting estimate—An accounting estimate is an approximation of the amount of an item in the absence of a precise means of measurement.

Accounting system—An accounting system is the series of tasks and records of an entity by which transactions are processed as a means of maintaining financial records. Such systems identify, assemble, analyze, calculate, classify, record, summarize and report transactions and other events.

Adverse opinion—(see Modified auditor's report)

Agreed-upon procedures engagement—In an engagement to perform agreed-upon procedures, an auditor is engaged to carry out those procedures of an audit nature to which the auditor and the entity and any appropriate third parties have agreed and to report on factual findings. The recipients of the report must form their own conclusions from the report by the auditor. The report is restricted to those parties that have agreed to the procedures to be performed since others, unaware of the reasons for the procedures may misinterpret the results.

Analytical procedures—Analytical procedures consist of the analysis of significant ratios and trends including the resulting investigation of fluctuations and relationships that are inconsistent with other relevant information or deviate from predictable amounts.

Annual report—An entity ordinarily issues on an annual basis a document which includes its financial statements together with the audit report thereon. This document is frequently referred to as the "annual report."

Application controls in computer information systems—The specific controls over the relevant accounting applications maintained by the computer. The purpose of application controls is to establish specific control procedures over the accounting applications in order to provide reasonable assurance that all transactions are authorized and recorded, and are processed completely, accurately and on a timely basis.

Appropriateness—Appropriateness is the measure of the quality of audit evidence and its relevance to a particular assertion and its reliability.

Assertions—Assertions are representations by management, explicit or otherwise, that are embodied in the financial statements. (see Financial statements assertions)

Assistants—Assistants are personnel involved in an individual audit other than the auditor.

Assurance—Assurance refers to the auditor's satisfaction as to the reliability of an assertion being made by one party for use by another party. To provide such assurance, the auditor assesses the evidence collected as a result of procedures conducted and expresses a conclusion. The degree of satisfaction achieved and, therefore, the level of assurance which may be provided is determined by the procedures performed and their results.

> *Reasonable assurance*—In an audit engagement, the auditor provides a high, but not absolute, level of assurance, expressed positively in the audit report as

110

AUDITING

reasonable assurance, that the information subject to audit is free of material misstatement.

Attendance—Attendance consists of being present during all or part of a process being performed by others; for example, attending physical inventory taking will enable the auditor to inspect inventory, to observe compliance of management's procedures to count quantities and record such counts and to test-count quantities.

Audit—The objective of an audit of financial statements is to enable the auditor to express an opinion whether the financial statements are prepared, in all material respects, in accordance with an identified financial reporting framework. The phrases used to express the auditor's opinion are "give a true and fair view" or "present fairly, in all material respects," which are equivalent terms. A similar objective applies to the audit of financial or other information prepared in accordance with appropriate criteria.

Audit evidence—Audit evidence is the information obtained by the auditor in arriving at the conclusions on which the audit opinion is based. Audit evidence will comprise source documents and accounting records underlying the financial statements and corroborating information from other sources.

Audit firm—Audit firm is either a firm or entity providing audit services, including where appropriate its partners, or a sole practitioner.

Audit opinion—(see Opinion)

Audit program—An audit program sets out the nature, timing and extent of planned audit procedures required to implement the overall audit plan. The audit program serves as a set of instructions to assistants involved in the audit and as a means to control the proper execution of the work.

Audit risk—Audit risk is the risk that the auditor gives an inappropriate audit opinion when the financial statements are materially misstated. Audit risk has three components: inherent risk, control risk and detection risk.

> *Control risk*—Control risk is the risk that a misstatement that could occur in an account balance or class of transactions and that could be material, individually or when aggregated with misstatements in other balances or classes, will not be prevented or detected and corrected on a timely basis by the accounting and internal control systems.

> *Detection risk*—Detection risk is the risk that an auditor's substantive procedures will not detect a misstatement that exists in an account balance or class of transactions that could be material, individually or when aggregated with misstatements in other balances or classes.

> *Inherent risk*—Inherent risk is the susceptibility of an account balance or class of transactions to misstatement that could be material, individually or when aggregated with misstatements in other balances of classes, assuming that there were no related internal controls.

Audit sampling—Audit sampling involves the application of audit procedures to less than 100% of the items within an account balance or class of transactions to enable the auditor to obtain and evaluate audit evidence about some characteristic of the items selected in order to form or assist in forming a conclusion concerning the population.

Population—The population is the entire set of data from which the auditor wishes to sample in order to reach a conclusion.

Sampling units—The individual items that make up the population are known as sampling units.

Stratification—Stratification is the process of dividing a population into subpopulations, each of which is a group of sampling units, which have similar characteristics (often monetary value).

Auditor—The auditor is the person with final responsibility for the audit. This term is also used to refer to an audit firm. (For ease of reference, the term "auditor" is used throughout the ISAs when describing both auditing and related services which may be performed. Such reference is not intended to imply that a person performing related services need necessarily be the auditor of the entity's financial statements.)

Continuing auditor—The continuing auditor is the auditor who audited and reported on the prior period's financial statements and continues as the auditor for the current period.

External auditor—Where appropriate the terms "external auditor" and "external audit" are used to distinguish the external auditor from an internal auditor and to distinguish the external audit from the activities of internal auditing.

Incoming auditor—The incoming auditor is a current period's auditor who did not audit the prior period's financial statements.

Other auditor—The other auditor is an auditor, other than the principal auditor, with responsibility for reporting on the financial information of a component which is included in the financial statements audited by the principal auditor. Other auditors include affiliated firms, whether using the same name or not, and correspondents, as well as unrelated auditors.

Personnel—Personnel includes all partners and professional staff engaged in the audit practice of the firm.

Predecessor auditor—The auditor who was previously the auditor of an entity and who has been replaced by an incoming auditor.

Principal auditor—The principal auditor is the auditor with responsibility for reporting on the financial statements of an entity when those financial statements include financial information of one or more components audited by another auditor.

Auditor's association—An auditor is associated with financial information when the auditor attaches a report to that information or consents to the use of the auditor's name in a professional connection.

Comparatives—Comparatives are corresponding amounts and other disclosures for the preceding financial reporting period, or periods, presented for comparative purposes. Comparatives can be presented as either:

AUDITING

Corresponding figures—included as part of the current period financial statements, and which are intended to be read in relation to the amounts and other disclosures relating to the current period. They are an integral part of the current period financial statements intended to be read only in relation to the current period figures and not as complete financial statements capable of standing alone.

Comparative financial statements—the financial statements of the preceding period are included for comparison with the financial statements of the current period, but do not form part of the current period financial statements.

Compilation engagement—In a compilation engagement, the accountant is engaged to use accounting expertise as opposed to auditing expertise to collect, classify and summarize financial information.

Component—Component is a division, branch, subsidiary, joint venture, associated company or other entity whose financial information is included in financial statements audited by the principal auditor.

Comprehensive basis of accounting—A comprehensive basis of accounting comprises a set of criteria used in preparing financial statements which applies to all material items and which has substantial support.

Computation—Computation consists of checking the arithmetical accuracy of source documents and accounting records or of performing independent calculations.

Computer-assisted audit techniques—Applications of auditing procedures using the computer as an audit tool are known as Computer Assisted Audit Techniques (CAATs).

Computer information systems—A computer information systems (CIS) environment exists when a computer of any type or size is involved in the processing by the entity of financial information of significance to the audit, whether that computer is operated by the entity or by a third party.

Confirmation—Confirmation consists of the response to an inquiry to corroborate information contained in the accounting records.

Continuing auditor—(see Auditor)

Control environment—The control environment comprises the overall attitude, awareness and actions of directors and management regarding the internal control system and its importance in the entity.

Control procedures—Control procedures are those policies and procedures in addition to the control environment which management has established to achieve the entity's specific objectives.

Control risk—(see Audit risk)

Database—A collection of data that is shared and used by a number of different users for different purposes.

Detection risk—(see Audit risk)

Disclaimer of opinion—(see Modified auditor's report)

Documentation—Documentation is the material (working papers) prepared by and for, or obtained and retained by the auditor in connection with the performance of the audit.

Emphasis of matter paragraph(s)—(see Modified auditor's report)

Engagement letter—An engagement letter documents and confirms the auditor's acceptance of the appointment, the objective and scope of the audit, the extent of the auditor's responsibilities to the client and the form of any reports.

Error—An error is an unintentional mistake in financial statements.

Expected error—The error that the auditor expects to be present in the population.

Expert—An expert is a person or firm possessing special skill, knowledge and experience in a particular field other than accounting and auditing.

External audit/auditor—(see Auditor)

Financial statements—The balance sheets, income statements or profit and loss accounts, statements of changes in financial position (which may be presented in a variety of ways, for example, as a statement of cash flows or a statement of fund flows), notes and other statements and explanatory material which are identified as being part of the financial statements.

> *Summarized financial statements*—An entity may prepare financial statements summarizing its annual audited financial statements for the purpose of informing user groups interested in the highlights only of the entity's financial performance and position.

Financial statement assertions— Financial statement assertions are assertions by management, explicit or otherwise, that are embodied in the financial statements and can be categorized as follows:

(a) *existence*: an asset or a liability exists at a given date;

(b) *rights and obligations*: an asset or a liability pertains to the entity at a given date;

(c) *occurrence*: a transaction or event took place which pertains to the entity during the period;

(d) *completeness*: there are no unrecorded assets, liabilities, transactions or events, or undisclosed items;

(e) *valuation*: an asset or liability is recorded at an appropriate carrying value;

(f) *measurement*: a transaction or event is recorded at the proper amount and revenue or expense is allocated to the proper period; and

(g) *presentation and disclosure*: an item is disclosed, classified, and described in accordance with the applicable financial reporting framework.

Forecast—A forecast is prospective financial information prepared on the basis of assumptions as to future events which management expects to take place and the

AUDITING

110

actions management expects to take as of the date the information is prepared (best-estimate assumptions).

Fraud—The term "fraud" refers to an intentional act by one or more individuals among management, employees, or third parties, which results in a misrepresentation of financial statements.

General controls in computer information systems—The establishment of a framework of overall control over the computer information systems activities to provide a reasonable level of assurance that the overall objectives of internal control are achieved.

Going concern assumption—The going concern assumption is an assumption that an enterprise will continue in operation for the foreseeable future; and that the enterprise has neither the intention nor the need to liquidate or curtail materially the scale of its operations. As a result assets are valued on the basis of continued use, such as historical cost or replacement cost rather than net realizable value or liquidation value.

Government business enterprises—Government business enterprises are businesses which operate within the public sector ordinarily to meet a political or social interest objective. They are ordinarily required to operate commercially, that is, to make profits or to recoup, through user charges a substantial proportion of their operating costs.

Incoming auditor—(see Auditor)

Inherent risk—(see Audit risk)

Inquiry—Inquiry consists of seeking information of knowledgeable persons inside or outside the entity.

Inspection—Inspection consists of examining records, documents, or tangible assets.

Interim financial information or statements—Financial information (which may be less than full financial statements as defined above) issued at interim dates (usually half-yearly or quarterly) in respect of a financial period.

Internal auditing—Internal auditing is an appraisal activity established within an entity as a service to the entity. Its functions include, amongst other things, examining, evaluating and monitoring the adequacy and effectiveness of the accounting and internal control systems.

Internal control system—An internal control system consists of all the policies and procedures (internal controls) adopted by the management of an entity to assist in achieving management's objective of ensuring, as far as practicable, the orderly and efficient conduct of its business, including adherence to management policies, the safeguarding of assets, the prevention and detection of fraud and error, the accuracy and completeness of the accounting records, and the timely preparation of reliable financial information. The internal control system extends beyond these matters which relate directly to the functions of the accounting system.

Knowledge of the business—The auditor's general knowledge of the economy and the industry within which the entity operates and a more particular knowledge of how the entity operates.

Limitation on scope—A limitation on the scope of the auditor's work may sometimes be imposed by the entity (for example, when the terms of the engagement specify that the auditor will not carry out an audit procedure that the auditor believes is necessary). A scope limitation may be imposed by circumstances (for example, when the timing of the auditor's appointment is such that the auditor is unable to observe the counting of physical inventories). It may also arise when, in the opinion of the auditor, the entity's accounting records are inadequate or when the auditor is unable to carry out an audit procedure believed desirable.

Management—Management comprises officers and others who also perform senior managerial functions. Management includes directors and the audit committee only in those instances when they perform such functions.

Management representations—Representations made by management to the auditor during the course of an audit, either unsolicited or in response to specific inquiries.

Material inconsistency—A material inconsistency exists when other information contradicts information contained in the audited financial statements. A material inconsistency may raise doubt about the audit conclusions drawn from audit evidence previously obtained and, possibly, about the basis for the auditor's opinion on the financial statements.

Material misstatement of fact—A material misstatement of fact in other information exists when such information, not related to matters appearing in the audited financial statements, is incorrectly stated or presented.

Material weaknesses—The weaknesses in internal control that could have a material effect on the financial statements.

Materiality—Information is material if its omission or misstatement could influence the economic decisions of users taken on the basis of the financial statements. Materiality depends on the size of the item or error judged in the particular circumstances of its omission or misstatement. Thus, materiality provides a threshold or cutoff point rather than being a primary qualitative characteristic which information must have if it is to be useful.

Misstatement—A mistake in financial information which would arise from errors and fraud.

Modified auditor's report—An auditor's report is considered to be modified if either an emphasis of matter paragraph(s) is added to the report or if the opinion is other than unqualified:

Matters That Do Not Affect the Auditor's Opinion

Emphasis of matter paragraph(s)—An auditor's report may be modified by adding an emphasis of matter paragraph(s) to highlight a matter affecting the financial statements which is included in a note to the financial statements that more extensively discusses the matter. The addition of such an emphasis of matter paragraph(s) does not affect the auditor's opinion. The auditor may also modify the auditor's report by using an emphasis of matter paragraph(s) to report matters other than those affecting the financial statements.

AUDITING

110

Matters That Do Affect The Auditor's Opinion

Qualified opinion—A qualified opinion is expressed when the auditor concludes that an unqualified opinion cannot be expressed but that the effect of any disagreement with management, or limitation on scope is not so material and pervasive as to require an adverse opinion or a disclaimer of opinion.

Disclaimer of opinion—A disclaimer of opinion is expressed when the possible effect of a limitation on scope is so material and pervasive that the auditor has not been able to obtain sufficient appropriate audit evidence and accordingly is unable to express an opinion on the financial statements.

Adverse opinion—An adverse opinion is expressed when the effect of a disagreement is so material and pervasive to the financial statements that the auditor concludes that a qualification of the report is not adequate to disclose the misleading or incomplete nature of the financial statements.

National practices (auditing)—A set of auditing guidelines not having the authority of standards defined by an authoritative body at a country level and commonly applied by auditors in the conduct of an audit or related services.

National standards (auditing)—A set of auditing standards defined by law or regulations or an authoritative body at a country level, the application of which is mandatory in conducting an audit or related services and which should be complied with in the conduct of an audit or related services.

Noncompliance—The term "noncompliance" is used to refer to acts of omission or commission by the entity being audited, either intentional or unintentional, which are contrary to the prevailing laws or regulations.

Non-sampling risk—(see Sampling risk)

Observation—Observation consists of looking at a process or procedure being performed by others, for example, the observation by the auditor of the counting of inventories by the entity's personnel or the performance of internal control procedures that leave no audit trail.

Opening balances—Opening balances are those account balances which exist at the beginning of the period. Opening balances are based upon the closing balances of the prior period and reflect the effects of transactions of prior periods and accounting policies applied in the prior period.

Opinion—The auditor's report contains a clear written expression of opinion on the financial statements as a whole. An unqualified opinion is expressed when the auditor concludes that the financial statements give a true and fair view (or are presented fairly, in all material respects,) in accordance with the identified financial reporting framework. (See Modified auditor's report)

Other auditor—(see Auditor)

Personnel—(see Auditor)

Planning—Planning involves developing a general strategy and a detailed approach for the expected nature, timing and extent of the audit.

Population—(see Audit sampling)

Post balance sheet events—(see Subsequent events)

Predecessor auditor—(see Auditor)

Principal auditor—(see Auditor)

Projection—A projection is prospective financial information prepared on the basis of:

    (a)   hypothetical assumptions about future events and management actions which are not necessarily expected to take place, such as when some entities are in a start-up phase or are considering a major change in the nature of operations; or

    (b)   a mixture of best-estimate and hypothetical assumptions.

Prospective financial information—Prospective financial information is financial information based on assumptions about events that may occur in the future and possible actions by an entity. Prospective financial information can be in the form of a forecast, a projection or a combination of both. (See Forecast and Projection)

Public sector—The term "public sector" refers to national governments, regional (for example, state, provincial, territorial) governments, local (for example, city, town) governments and related governmental entities (for example, agencies, boards, commissions and enterprises).

Qualified opinion—(see Modified auditor's report)

Quality controls—The policies and procedures adopted by a firm to provide reasonable assurance that all audits done by the firm are being carried out in accordance with the Objective and General Principles Governing an Audit of Financial Statements, as set out in International Standard on Auditing 220 "Quality Control for Audit Work."

Reasonable assurance—(see Assurance)

Related parties—Related parties and related party transaction are defined in International Accounting Standard 24 as:

    Related party—Parties are considered to be related if one party has the ability to control the other party or exercise significant influence over the other party in making financial and operating decisions.

    Related party transaction—A transfer of resources or obligations between related parties, regardless of whether a price is charged.

Related services—Related services comprise reviews, agreed-upon procedures and compilations.

Review engagement—The objective of a review engagement is to enable an auditor to state whether, on the basis of procedures which do not provide all the evidence that would be required in an audit, anything has come to the auditor's attention that causes the auditor to believe that the financial statements are not prepared, in all material respects, in accordance with an identified financial reporting framework.

AUDITING

Sampling risk—Sampling risk arises from the possibility that the auditor's conclusion, based on a sample, may be different from the conclusion that would be reached if the entire population were subjected to the same audit procedure.

> *Non-sampling risk*—Non-sampling risk arises because, for example, most audit evidence is persuasive rather than conclusive, the auditor might use inappropriate procedures or might misinterpret evidence and thus fail to recognize an error.

Sampling units—(see Audit sampling)

Scope of an Audit—The term "scope of an audit" refers to the audit procedures deemed necessary in the circumstances to achieve the objective of the audit.

Scope limitation—(see Limitation on scope)

Segment information—Information in the financial statements regarding distinguishable components or industry and geographical aspects of an entity.

Service organization—A client may use a service organization such as one that executes transactions and maintains related accountability or records transactions and processes related data (e.g., a computer information systems service organization).

Significance—Significance is related to materiality of the financial statement assertion affected.

Special purpose auditor's report—A report issued in connection with the independent audit of financial information other than an auditor's report on financial statements, including:

(a) financial statements prepared in accordance with a comprehensive basis of accounting other than International Accounting Standards or national standards;

(b) specified accounts, elements of accounts, or items in a financial statement;

(c) compliance with contractual agreements; and

(d) summarized financial statements.

Stratification—(see Audit sampling)

Subsequent events—International Accounting Standard 10 identifies two types of events both favorable and unfavorable occurring after period end:

(a) those that provide further evidence of conditions that existed at period end; and

(b) those that are indicative of conditions that arose subsequent to period end.

Substantive procedures—Substantive procedures are tests performed to obtain audit evidence to detect material misstatements in the financial statements, and are of two types:

(a) tests of details of transactions and balances; and

(b) analytical procedures.

Sufficiency—Sufficiency is the measure of the quantity of audit evidence.

Summarized financial statements—(see Financial statements)

Supreme Audit Institution—The public body of a State which, however designated, constituted or organized, exercises by virtue of law, the highest public auditing function of that State.

Tests of control—Tests of control are performed to obtain audit evidence about the effectiveness of the:

(a) design of the accounting and internal control systems, that is, whether they are suitably designed to prevent or detect and correct material misstatements; and

(b) operation of the internal controls throughout the period.

Tolerable error—Tolerable error is the maximum error in the population that the auditor would be willing to accept and still conclude that the result from the sample has achieved the audit objective.

Uncertainty— An uncertainty is a matter whose outcome depends on future actions or events not under the direct control of the entity but that may affect the financial statements.

Unqualified opinion—(see Opinion)

Walk-through test—A walk-through test involves tracing a few transactions through the accounting system.

Working papers—Working papers are a record of the auditor's planning; nature, timing and extent of the auditing procedures performed; and results of such procedures and the conclusions drawn from the evidence obtained. Working papers may be in the form of data stored on paper, film, electronic media or other media.

AUDITING

110

CONTENTS

	Paragraphs
Introduction	1-2
Financial Reporting Framework	3
Framework for Auditing and Related Services	4-5
Levels of Assurance	6-10
Audit	11-13
Related Services	14-18
Auditor Association with Financial Information	19

International Standards on Auditing (ISAs) are to be applied in the audit of financial statements. ISAs are also to be applied, adapted as necessary, to the audit of other information and to related services.

ISAs contain the basic principles and essential procedures (identified in bold type black lettering) together with related guidance in the form of explanatory and other material. The basic principles and essential procedures are to be interpreted in the context of the explanatory and other material that provide guidance for their application.

To understand and apply the basic principles and essential procedures together with the related guidance, it is necessary to consider the whole text of the ISA including explanatory and other material contained in the ISA not just that text which is black lettered.

In exceptional circumstances, an auditor may judge it necessary to depart from an ISA in order to more effectively achieve the objective of an audit. When such a situation arises, the auditor should be prepared to justify the departure.

ISAs need only be applied to material matters.

The Public Sector Perspective (PSP) issued by the Public Sector Committee of the International Federation of Accountants is set out at the end of an ISA. Where no PSP is added, the ISA is applicable in all material respects to the public sector.

Introduction

1. The International Auditing Practices Committee has been authorized to issue International Standards on Auditing (ISAs). The purpose of this document is to describe the framework within which ISAs are issued in relation to the services which may be performed by auditors.

2. For ease of reference, except where indicated, the term "auditor" is used throughout the ISAs when describing both auditing and related services which may be performed. Such reference is not intended to imply that a person performing related services need be the auditor of the entity's financial statements.

Financial Reporting Framework

3. Financial statements are ordinarily prepared and presented annually and are directed toward the common information needs of a wide range of users. Many of those users rely on the financial statements as their major source of information because they do not have the power to obtain additional information to meet their specific information needs. Thus, financial statements need to be prepared in accordance with one, or a combination of:

   (a) International Accounting Standards;

   (b) national accounting standards; and

   (c) another authoritative and comprehensive financial reporting framework which has been designed for use in financial reporting and is identified in the financial statements.

Framework for Auditing and Related Services

4. This Framework distinguishes audits from related services. Related services comprise reviews, agreed-upon procedures and compilations. As illustrated in the diagram below, audits and reviews are designed to enable the auditor to provide high and moderate levels of assurance respectively, such terms being used to indicate their comparative ranking. Engagements to undertake agreed-upon procedures and compilations are not intended to enable the auditor to express assurance.

AUDITING

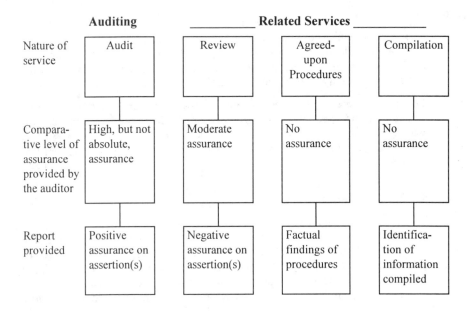

	Auditing		Related Services	
Nature of service	Audit	Review	Agreed-upon Procedures	Compilation
Comparative level of assurance provided by the auditor	High, but not absolute, assurance	Moderate assurance	No assurance	No assurance
Report provided	Positive assurance on assertion(s)	Negative assurance on assertion(s)	Factual findings of procedures	Identification of information compiled

5. The Framework does not apply to other services provided by auditors such as taxation, consultancy, and financial and accounting advice.

Levels of Assurance

6. Assurance in the context of this Framework refers to the auditor's satisfaction as to the reliability of an assertion being made by one party for use by another party. To provide such assurance, the auditor assesses the evidence collected as a result of procedures conducted and expresses a conclusion. The degree of satisfaction achieved and, therefore, the level of assurance which may be provided is determined by the procedures performed and their results.

7. In an audit engagement, the auditor provides a high, but not absolute, level of assurance that the information subject to audit is free of material misstatement. This is expressed positively in the audit report as reasonable assurance.

8. In a review engagement, the auditor provides a moderate level of assurance that the information subject to review is free of material misstatement. This is expressed in the form of negative assurance.

9. For agreed-upon procedures, as the auditor simply provides a report of the factual findings, no assurance is expressed. Instead, users of the report assess for themselves the procedures and findings reported by the auditor and draw their own conclusions from the auditor's work.

10. In a compilation engagement, although the users of the compiled information derive some benefit from the accountant's[1] involvement, no assurance is expressed in the report.

Audit

11. The objective of an audit of financial statements is to enable the auditor to express an opinion whether the financial statements are prepared, in all material respects, in accordance with an identified financial reporting framework. The phrases used to express the auditor's opinion are "give a true and fair view" or "present fairly, in all material respects," which are equivalent terms. A similar objective applies to the audit of financial or other information prepared in accordance with appropriate criteria.

12. In forming the audit opinion, the auditor obtains sufficient appropriate audit evidence to be able to draw conclusions on which to base that opinion.

13. The auditor's opinion enhances the credibility of financial statements by providing a high, but not absolute, level of assurance. Absolute assurance in auditing is not attainable as a result of such factors as the need for judgment, the use of testing, the inherent limitations of any accounting and internal control systems and the fact that most of the evidence available to the auditor is persuasive, rather than conclusive, in nature.

Related Services

Reviews

14. The objective of a review of financial statements is to enable an auditor[2] to state whether, on the basis of procedures which do not provide all the evidence that would be required in an audit, anything has come to the auditor's attention that causes the auditor to believe that the financial statements are not prepared, in all material respects, in accordance with an identified financial reporting framework. A similar objective applies to the review of financial or other information prepared in accordance with appropriate criteria.

15. A review comprises inquiry and analytical procedures which are designed to review the reliability of an assertion that is the responsibility of one party for use by another party. While a review involves the application of audit skills and techniques and the gathering of evidence, it does not ordinarily involve an assessment of accounting and internal control systems, tests of records and of responses to inquiries by obtaining corroborating evidence through inspection, observation, confirmation and computation, which are procedures ordinarily performed during an audit.

AUDITING

---

[1] To distinguish compilation engagements from audits and other related services the term "accountant" (rather than "auditor") has been used to refer to a professional accountant in public practice.

[2] As explained in paragraph 2 the term auditor is used when describing both auditing and related services. Such reference is not intended to imply that a person performing related services need be the auditor of the entity's financial statements.

16. Although the auditor attempts to become aware of all significant matters, the procedures of a review make the achievement of this objective less likely than in an audit engagement, thus the level of assurance provided in a review report is correspondingly less than that given in an audit report.

Agreed-upon Procedures

17. In an engagement to perform agreed-upon procedures, an auditor[3] is engaged to carry out those procedures of an audit nature to which the auditor and the entity and any appropriate third parties have agreed and to report on factual findings. The recipients of the report must form their own conclusions from the report by the auditor. The report is restricted to those parties that have agreed to the procedures to be performed since others, unaware of the reasons for the procedures, may misinterpret the results.

Compilations

18. In a compilation engagement, the accountant[4] is engaged to use accounting expertise as opposed to auditing expertise to collect, classify and summarize financial information. This ordinarily entails reducing detailed data to a manageable and understandable form without a requirement to test the assertions underlying that information. The procedures employed are not designed and do not enable the accountant to express any assurance on the financial information. However, users of the compiled financial information derive some benefit as a result of the accountant's involvement because the service has been performed with due professional skill and care.

Auditor Association with Financial Information

19. An auditor[5] is associated with financial information when the auditor attaches a report to that information or consents to the use of the auditor's name in a professional connection. If the auditor is not associated in this manner, third parties can assume no responsibility of the auditor. If the auditor learns that an entity is inappropriately using the auditor's name in association with financial information, the auditor would require management to cease doing so and consider what further steps, if any, need to be taken, such as informing any known third party users of the information of the inappropriate use of the auditor's name in connection with the information. The auditor may also believe it necessary to take other action, for example, to seek legal advice.

Public Sector Perspective

1. *The Public Sector Committee (PSC) issues pronouncements aimed at developing and harmonizing public sector financial reporting, accounting*

---

[3] See footnote 2.

[4] See footnote 1.

[5] This includes an accountant engaged to perform compilation engagements.

and auditing practices. "Public Sector" refers to national governments, regional (state, provincial, territorial) governments, local (city, town) governments and related governmental entities (agencies, boards, commissions and enterprises). The PSC considers and makes use of pronouncements issued by the International Auditing Practices Committee to the extent they are applicable to the public sector.

2.   Governments, government business enterprises and other non-business public sector entities ordinarily prepare financial statements to report on their financial position (or aspects thereof), results of operations and cash flows, for use by legislators, government departments, outside investors, employees, lenders, the public and other users. The audit of such financial statements may be the responsibility of a Supreme Audit Institution, other bodies appointed by statute or practicing auditors.

3.   Whenever an audit opinion is to be expressed on financial statements, the same audit principles apply regardless of the nature of the entity, because users of audited financial statements are entitled to a uniform quality of audit performance. Since ISAs set out the basic audit principles and related practices and procedures, they apply to audits of the financial statements of governments and other public sector entities. However, the application of certain ISAs may need to be clarified or supplemented to accommodate the public sector circumstances and perspective of individual jurisdictions, particularly as they relate to the audits of governments and other non-business public sector entities. The nature of potential matters for clarification or supplementation is identified in the "Public Sector Perspective (PSP)" included at the end of each ISA.

4.   The financial statements of governments, government business enterprises and other non-business public sector entities may include information that is different from, or in addition to, that contained in the financial statements of private sector entities (for example, comparisons of expenditures in the period with limits established by legislation). In such circumstances, appropriate modifications may be required to the nature, timing and extent of audit procedures, and the auditor's report.

5.   Further, governments and non-business public sector entities, as well as some government business enterprises, are required to achieve service delivery as well as financial objectives. For such entities, the financial statements, by themselves, are unlikely to adequately report on all aspects of the entity's performance. Consequently, these public sector entities may be required to include in their annual report other performance indicators relating to such matters as productivity levels, quality and volume of service and the extent to which particular service delivery objectives have been achieved. The PSPs included in the ISAs are not intended to apply to the audit of such information.

6.   In addition, the auditors of public sector entities may be required to report on:

(a)   compliance with legislative or regulatory requirements and related authorities;

AUDITING

(b)   adequacy of accounting and internal control systems; and

(c)   economy, efficiency and effectiveness of programs, projects and activities.

The PSPs also do not apply to such reports.

7.   If no PSP is added at the end of an ISA, the ISA is applicable in all material respects to the audit of financial statements in the public sector.

CONTENTS

	Paragraphs
Introduction	1
Objective of an Audit	2-3
General Principles of an Audit	4-6
Scope of an Audit	7
Reasonable Assurance	8-11
Responsibility for the Financial Statements	12

International Standards on Auditing (ISAs) are to be applied in the audit of financial statements. ISAs are also to be applied, adapted as necessary, to the audit of other information and to related services.

ISAs contain the basic principles and essential procedures (identified in bold type black lettering) together with related guidance in the form of explanatory and other material. The basic principles and essential procedures are to be interpreted in the context of the explanatory and other material that provide guidance for their application.

To understand and apply the basic principles and essential procedures together with the related guidance, it is necessary to consider the whole text of the ISA including explanatory and other material contained in the ISA not just that text which is black lettered.

In exceptional circumstances, an auditor may judge it necessary to depart from an ISA in order to more effectively achieve the objective of an audit. When such a situation arises, the auditor should be prepared to justify the departure.

ISAs need only be applied to material matters.

The Public Sector Perspective (PSP) issued by the Public Sector Committee of the International Federation of Accountants is set out at the end of an ISA. Where no PSP is added, the ISA is applicable in all material respects to the public sector.

AUDITING

200

Introduction

1. The purpose of this International Standard on Auditing (ISA) is to establish standards and provide guidance on the objective and general principles governing an audit of financial statements. This ISA is to be read in conjunction with ISA 120 "Framework of International Standards on Auditing."

Objective of an Audit

2. **The objective of an audit of financial statements is to enable the auditor to express an opinion whether the financial statements are prepared, in all material respects, in accordance with an identified financial reporting framework.** The phrases used to express the auditor's opinion are "give a true and fair view" or "present fairly, in all material respects," which are equivalent terms.

3. Although the auditor's opinion enhances the credibility of the financial statements, the user cannot assume that the opinion is an assurance as to the future viability of the entity nor the efficiency or effectiveness with which management has conducted the affairs of the entity.

General Principles of an Audit

4. **The auditor should comply with the "Code of Ethics for Professional Accountants" issued by the International Federation of Accountants.** Ethical principles governing the auditor's professional responsibilities are:

    (a) independence;

    (b) integrity;

    (c) objectivity;

    (d) professional competence and due care;

    (e) confidentiality;

    (f) professional behavior; and

    (g) technical standards.

5. **The auditor should conduct an audit in accordance with ISAs.** These contain basic principles and essential procedures together with related guidance in the form of explanatory and other material.

6. **The auditor should plan and perform the audit with an attitude of professional skepticism recognizing that circumstances may exist which cause the financial statements to be materially misstated.** For example, the auditor would ordinarily expect to find evidence to support management representations and not assume they are necessarily correct.

Scope of an Audit

7. The term "scope of an audit" refers to the audit procedures deemed necessary in the circumstances to achieve the objective of the audit. **The procedures required to conduct an audit in accordance with ISAs should be determined by the auditor having regard to the requirements of ISAs, relevant professional bodies, legislation, regulations and, where appropriate, the terms of the audit engagement and reporting requirements.**

Reasonable Assurance

8. An audit in accordance with ISAs is designed to provide reasonable assurance that the financial statements taken as a whole are free from material misstatement. Reasonable assurance is a concept relating to the accumulation of the audit evidence necessary for the auditor to conclude that there are no material misstatements in the financial statements taken as a whole. Reasonable assurance relates to the whole audit process.

9. However, there are inherent limitations in an audit that affect the auditor's ability to detect material misstatements. These limitations result from factors such as:

   - The use of testing.

   - The inherent limitations of any accounting and internal control system (for example, the possibility of collusion).

   - The fact that most audit evidence is persuasive rather than conclusive.

10. Also, the work undertaken by the auditor to form an opinion is permeated by judgment, in particular regarding:

    (a) the gathering of audit evidence, for example, in deciding the nature, timing and extent of audit procedures; and

    (b) the drawing of conclusions based on the audit evidence gathered, for example, assessing the reasonableness of the estimates made by management in preparing the financial statements.

11. Further, other limitations may affect the persuasiveness of evidence available to draw conclusions on particular financial statement assertions (for example, transactions between related parties). In these cases certain ISAs identify specified procedures which will, because of the nature of the particular assertions, provide sufficient appropriate audit evidence in the absence of:

    (a) unusual circumstances which increase the risk of material misstatement beyond that which would ordinarily be expected; or

    (b) any indication that a material misstatement has occurred.

AUDITING

Responsibility for the Financial Statements

12. While the auditor is responsible for forming and expressing an opinion on the financial statements, the responsibility for preparing and presenting the financial statements is that of the management of the entity. The audit of the financial statements does not relieve management of its responsibilities.

Public Sector Perspective

1. *Irrespective of whether an audit is being conducted in the private or public sector, the basic principles of auditing remain the same. What may differ for audits carried out in the public sector is the audit objective and scope. These factors are often attributable to differences in the audit mandate and legal requirements or the form of reporting (for example, public sector entities may be required to prepare additional financial reports).*

2. *When carrying out audits of public sector entities, the auditor will need to take into account the specific requirements of any other relevant regulations, ordinances or ministerial directives which affect the audit mandate and any special auditing requirements, including the need to have regard to issues of national security. Audit mandates may be more specific than those in the private sector, and often encompass a wider range of objectives and a broader scope than is ordinarily applicable for the audit of private sector financial statements. The mandates and requirements may also effect, for example, the extent of the auditor's discretion in establishing materiality, in reporting fraud and error, and in the form of the audit report. Differences in audit approach and style may also exist. However, these differences would not constitute a difference in the basic principles and essential procedures.*

CONTENTS

	Paragraphs
Introduction	1-4
Audit Engagement Letters	5-9
Recurring Audits	10-11
Acceptance of a Change in Engagement	12-19
Appendix: Example of an Audit Engagement Letter	

International Standards on Auditing (ISAs) are to be applied in the audit of financial statements. ISAs are also to be applied, adapted as necessary, to the audit of other information and to related services.

ISAs contain the basic principles and essential procedures (identified in bold type black lettering) together with related guidance in the form of explanatory and other material. The basic principles and essential procedures are to be interpreted in the context of the explanatory and other material that provide guidance for their application.

To understand and apply the basic principles and essential procedures together with the related guidance, it is necessary to consider the whole text of the ISA including explanatory and other material contained in the ISA not just that text which is black lettered.

In exceptional circumstances, an auditor may judge it necessary to depart from an ISA in order to more effectively achieve the objective of an audit. When such a situation arises, the auditor should be prepared to justify the departure.

ISAs need only be applied to material matters.

The Public Sector Perspective (PSP) issued by the Public Sector Committee of the International Federation of Accountants is set out at the end of an ISA. Where no PSP is added, the ISA is applicable in all material respects to the public sector.

AUDITING

Introduction

1. The purpose of this International Standard on Auditing (ISA) is to establish standards and provide guidance on:

    (a) agreeing the terms of the engagement with the client; and

    (b) the auditor's response to a request by a client to change the terms of an engagement to one that provides a lower level of assurance.

2. **The auditor and the client should agree on the terms of the engagement.** The agreed terms would need to be recorded in an audit engagement letter or other suitable form of contract.

3. This ISA is intended to assist the auditor in the preparation of engagement letters relating to audits of financial statements. The guidance is also applicable to related services. When other services such as tax, accounting, or management advisory services are to be provided, separate letters may be appropriate.

4. In some countries, the objective and scope of an audit and the auditor's obligations are established by law. Even in those situations the auditor may still find audit engagement letters informative for their clients.

Audit Engagement Letters

5. It is in the interest of both client and auditor that the auditor sends an engagement letter, preferably before the commencement of the engagement, to help in avoiding misunderstandings with respect to the engagement. The engagement letter documents and confirms the auditor's acceptance of the appointment, the objective and scope of the audit, the extent of the auditor's responsibilities to the client and the form of any reports.

Principal Contents

6. The form and content of audit engagement letters may vary for each client, but they would generally include reference to:

    -   The objective of the audit of financial statements.

    -   Management's responsibility for the financial statements.

    -   The scope of the audit, including reference to applicable legislation, regulations, or pronouncements of professional bodies to which the auditor adheres.

    -   The form of any reports or other communication of results of the engagement.

    -   The fact that because of the test nature and other inherent limitations of an audit, together with the inherent limitations of any accounting and internal control system, there is an unavoidable risk that even some material misstatement may remain undiscovered.

- Unrestricted access to whatever records, documentation and other information requested in connection with the audit.

7. The auditor may also wish to include in the letter:

- Arrangements regarding the planning of the audit.

- Expectation of receiving from management written confirmation concerning representations made in connection with the audit.

- Request for the client to confirm the terms of the engagement by acknowledging receipt of the engagement letter.

- Description of any other letters or reports the auditor expects to issue to the client.

- Basis on which fees are computed and any billing arrangements.

8. When relevant, the following points could also be made:

- Arrangements concerning the involvement of other auditors and experts in some aspects of the audit.

- Arrangements concerning the involvement of internal auditors and other client staff.

- Arrangements to be made with the predecessor auditor, if any, in the case of an initial audit.

- Any restriction of the auditor's liability when such possibility exists.

- A reference to any further agreements between the auditor and the client.

An example of an audit engagement letter is set out in the Appendix.

Audits of Components

9. When the auditor of a parent entity is also the auditor of its subsidiary, branch or division (component), the factors that influence the decision whether to send a separate engagement letter to the component include:

- Who appoints the auditor of the component.

- Whether a separate audit report is to be issued on the component.

- Legal requirements.

- The extent of any work performed by other auditors.

- Degree of ownership by parent.

- Degree of independence of the component's management.

Recurring Audits

10. **On recurring audits, the auditor should consider whether circumstances require the terms of the engagement to be revised and whether there is a need to remind the client of the existing terms of the engagement.**

AUDITING

11. The auditor may decide not to send a new engagement letter each period. However, the following factors may make it appropriate to send a new letter:

- Any indication that the client misunderstands the objective and scope of the audit.

- Any revised or special terms of the engagement.

- A recent change of senior management, board of directors or ownership.

- A significant change in nature or size of the client's business.

- Legal requirements.

Acceptance of a Change in Engagement

12. **An auditor who, before the completion of the engagement, is requested to change the engagement to one which provides a lower level of assurance, should consider the appropriateness of doing so.**

13. A request from the client for the auditor to change the engagement may result from a change in circumstances affecting the need for the service, a misunderstanding as to the nature of an audit or related service originally requested or a restriction on the scope of the engagement, whether imposed by management or caused by circumstances. The auditor would consider carefully the reason given for the request, particularly the implications of a restriction on the scope of the engagement.

14. A change in circumstances that affects the entity's requirements or a misunderstanding concerning the nature of service originally requested would ordinarily be considered a reasonable basis for requesting a change in the engagement. In contrast a change would not be considered reasonable if it appeared that the change relates to information that is incorrect, incomplete or otherwise unsatisfactory.

15. Before agreeing to change an audit engagement to a related service, an auditor who was engaged to perform an audit in accordance with ISAs would consider, in addition to the above matters, any legal or contractual implications of the change.

16. If the auditor concludes, that there is reasonable justification to change the engagement and if the audit work performed complies with the ISAs applicable to the changed engagement, the report issued would be that appropriate for the revised terms of engagement. In order to avoid confusing the reader, the report would not include reference to:

(a) the original engagement; or

(b) any procedures that may have been performed in the original engagement, except where the engagement is changed to an engagement to undertake agreed-upon procedures and thus reference to the procedures performed is a normal part of the report.

17. **Where the terms of the engagement are changed, the auditor and the client should agree on the new terms.**

18. **The auditor should not agree to a change of engagement where there is no reasonable justification for doing so.** An example might be an audit engagement where the auditor is unable to obtain sufficient appropriate audit evidence regarding receivables and the client asks for the engagement to be changed to a review engagement to avoid a qualified audit opinion or a disclaimer of opinion.

19. **If the auditor is unable to agree to a change of the engagement and is not permitted to continue the original engagement, the auditor should withdraw and consider whether there is any obligation, either contractual or otherwise, to report to other parties, such as the board of directors or shareholders, the circumstances necessitating the withdrawal.**

Public Sector Perspective

1. *The purpose of the engagement letter is to inform the auditee of the nature of the engagement and to clarify the responsibilities of the parties involved. The legislation and regulations governing the operations of public sector audits generally mandate the appointment of a public sector auditor and the use of audit engagement letters may not be a widespread practice. Nevertheless, a letter setting out the nature of the engagement or recognizing an engagement not indicated in the legislative mandate may be useful to both parties. Public sector auditors have to give serious consideration to issuing audit engagements letters when undertaking an audit.*

2. *Paragraphs 12 to 19 of this ISA deal with the action a private sector auditor may take when there are attempts to change an audit engagement to one which provides a lower level of assurance. In the public sector specific requirements may exist within the legislation governing the audit mandate; for example, the auditor may be required to report directly to a minister, the legislature or the public if management (including the department head) attempts to limit the scope of the audit.*

AUDITING

Appendix

Example of an Audit Engagement Letter

The following letter is for use as a guide in conjunction with the considerations outlined in this ISA and will need to be varied according to individual requirements and circumstances.

To the Board of Directors or the appropriate representative of senior management:

You have requested that we audit the balance sheet of .... as of ...., and the related statements of income and cash flows for the year then ending. We are pleased to confirm our acceptance and our understanding of this engagement by means of this letter. Our audit will be made with the objective of our expressing an opinion on the financial statements.

We will conduct our audit in accordance with International Standards on Auditing (or refer to relevant national standards or practices). Those Standards require that we plan and perform the audit to obtain reasonable assurance about whether the financial statements are free of material misstatements. An audit includes examining, on a test basis, evidence supporting the amounts and disclosures in the financial statements. An audit also includes assessing the accounting principles used and significant estimates made by management, as well as evaluating the overall financial statement presentation.

Because of the test nature and other inherent limitations of an audit, together with the inherent limitations of any accounting and internal control system, there is an unavoidable risk that even some material misstatements may remain undiscovered.

In addition to our report on the financial statements, we expect to provide you with a separate letter concerning any material weaknesses in accounting and internal control systems which come to our notice.

We remind you that the responsibility for the preparation of financial statements including adequate disclosure is that of the management of the company. This includes the maintenance of adequate accounting records and internal controls, the selection and application of accounting policies, and the safeguarding of the assets of the company. As part of our audit process, we will request from management written confirmation concerning representations made to us in connection with the audit.

We look forward to full cooperation with your staff and we trust that they will make available to us whatever records, documentation and other information are requested in connection with our audit. Our fees, which will be billed as work progresses, are based on the time required by the individuals assigned to the engagement plus out-of-pocket expenses.

Individual hourly rates vary according to the degree of responsibility involved and the experience and skill required.

This letter will be effective for future years unless it is terminated, amended or superseded.

Please sign and return the attached copy of this letter to indicate that it is in accordance with your understanding of the arrangements for our audit of the financial statements.

XYZ & Co.

Acknowledged on behalf of
ABC Company by

(signed)
....
Name and Title
Date

AUDITING

CONTENTS

	Paragraphs
Introduction	1-3
Audit Firm	4-7
Individual Audits	8-17

Appendix: Illustrative Examples of Quality Control Procedures for an Audit Firm[1]

International Standards on Auditing (ISAs) are to be applied in the audit of financial statements. ISAs are also to be applied, adapted as necessary, to the audit of other information and to related services.

ISAs contain the basic principles and essential procedures (identified in bold type black lettering) together with related guidance in the form of explanatory and other material. The basic principles and essential procedures are to be interpreted in the context of the explanatory and other material that provide guidance for their application.

To understand and apply the basic principles and essential procedures together with the related guidance, it is necessary to consider the whole text of the ISA including explanatory and other material contained in the ISA not just that text which is black lettered.

In exceptional circumstances, an auditor may judge it necessary to depart from an ISA in order to more effectively achieve the objective of an audit. When such a situation arises, the auditor should be prepared to justify the departure.

ISAs need only be applied to material matters.

The Public Sector Perspective (PSP) issued by the Public Sector Committee of the International Federation of Accountants is set out at the end of an ISA. Where no PSP is added, the ISA is applicable in all material respects to the public sector.

---

[1] Reference may also be made to the International Professional Practice Statement 1 of the International Federation of Accountants "Assuring the Quality of Professional Services."

Introduction

1. The purpose of this International Standard on Auditing (ISA) is to establish standards and provide guidance on the quality control:

    (a) policies and procedures of an audit firm regarding audit work generally; and

    (b) procedures regarding the work delegated to assistants on an individual audit.

2. **Quality control policies and procedures should be implemented at both the level of the audit firm and on individual audits.**

3. In this ISA the following terms have the meaning attributed below:

    (a) "the auditor" means the person with final responsibility for the audit;

    (b) "audit firm" means either the partners of a firm providing audit services or a sole practitioner providing audit services, as appropriate;

    (c) "personnel" means all partners and professional staff engaged in the audit practice of the firm; and

    (d) "assistants" means personnel involved in an individual audit other than the auditor.

Audit Firm

4. **The audit firm should implement quality control policies and procedures designed to ensure that all audits are conducted in accordance with ISAs or relevant national standards or practices.**

5. The nature, timing and extent of an audit firm's quality control policies and procedures depend on a number of factors such as the size and nature of its practice, its geographic dispersion, its organization and appropriate cost/benefit considerations. Accordingly, the policies and procedures adopted by individual audit firms will vary, as will the extent of their documentation. Illustrative examples of quality control procedures are presented in the Appendix to this ISA.

6. The objectives of the quality control policies to be adopted by an audit firm will ordinarily incorporate the following:

    (a) Professional Requirements[2] :

    Personnel in the firm are to adhere to the principles of independence, integrity, objectivity, confidentiality and professional behavior.

    (b) Skills and Competence[3] :

---

[2] Refer to the "Code of Ethics for Professional Accountants" issued by the International Federation of Accountants and the requirement on auditors to observe these in ISA 200 "Objective and General Principles Governing an Audit of Financial Statements."

[3] See footnote 2.

The firm is to be staffed by personnel who have attained and maintain the technical standards and professional competence required to enable them to fulfill their responsibilities with due care.

(c)   Assignment:

Audit work is to be assigned to personnel who have the degree of technical training and proficiency required in the circumstances.

(d)   Delegation:

There is to be sufficient direction, supervision and review of work at all levels to provide reasonable assurance that the work performed meets appropriate standards of quality.

(e)   Consultation:

Whenever necessary, consultation within or outside the firm is to occur with those who have appropriate expertise.

(f)   Acceptance and Retention of Clients:

An evaluation of prospective clients and a review, on an ongoing basis, of existing clients is to be conducted. In making a decision to accept or retain a client, the firm's independence and ability to serve the client properly and the integrity of the client's management are to be considered.

(g)   Monitoring:

The continued adequacy and operational effectiveness of quality control policies and procedures is to be monitored.

7.   **The firm's general quality control policies and procedures should be communicated to its personnel in a manner that provides reasonable assurance that the policies and procedures are understood and implemented.**

Individual Audits

8.   **The auditor should implement those quality control procedures which are, in the context of the policies and procedures of the firm, appropriate to the individual audit.**

9.   The auditor, and assistants with supervisory responsibilities, will consider the professional competence of assistants performing work delegated to them when deciding the extent of direction, supervision and review appropriate for each assistant.

10.   Any delegation of work to assistants would be in a manner that provides reasonable assurance that such work will be performed with due care by persons having the degree of professional competence required in the circumstances.

Direction

11. Assistants to whom work is delegated need appropriate direction. Direction involves informing assistants of their responsibilities and the objectives of the procedures they are to perform. It also involves informing them of matters, such as the nature of the entity's business and possible accounting or auditing problems that may affect the nature, timing and extent of audit procedures with which they are involved.

12. The audit program is an important tool for the communication of audit directions. Time budgets and the overall audit plan are also helpful in communicating audit directions.

Supervision

13. Supervision is closely related to both direction and review and may involve elements of both.

14. Personnel carrying out supervisory responsibilities perform the following functions during the audit:

 (a) monitor the progress of the audit to consider whether:

  (i) assistants have the necessary skills and competence to carry out their assigned tasks;

  (ii) assistants understand the audit directions; and

  (iii) the work is being carried out in accordance with the overall audit plan and the audit program;

 (b) become informed of and address significant accounting and auditing questions raised during the audit, by assessing their significance and modifying the overall audit plan and the audit program as appropriate; and

 (c) resolve any differences of professional judgment between personnel and consider the level of consultation that is appropriate.

Review

15. The work performed by each assistant needs to be reviewed by personnel of at least equal competence to consider whether:

 (a) the work has been performed in accordance with the audit program;

 (b) the work performed and the results obtained have been adequately documented;

 (c) all significant audit matters have been resolved or are reflected in audit conclusions;

 (d) the objectives of the audit procedures have been achieved; and

 (e) the conclusions expressed are consistent with the results of the work performed and support the audit opinion.

AUDITING

16. The following need to be reviewed on a timely basis:

    (a) the overall audit plan and the audit program;

    (b) the assessments of inherent and control risks, including the results of tests of control and the modifications, if any, made to the overall audit plan and the audit program as a result thereof;

    (c) the documentation of the audit evidence obtained from substantive procedures and the conclusions drawn therefrom, including the results of consultations; and

    (d) the financial statements, proposed audit adjustments and the proposed auditor's report.

17. The process of reviewing an audit may include, particularly in the case of large complex audits, requesting personnel not otherwise involved in the audit to perform certain additional procedures before issuing the auditor's report.

Public Sector Perspective

1. *This ISA refers to the work of private sector audit firms. Many audits of governments and other public sector entities are carried out by Supreme Audit Institutions (SAIs), other bodies appointed by statute or practicing auditors. The general principles in this ISA on quality control apply equally to SAIs. However, some of the specific policies and procedures may not be applicable (for example, acceptance and retention of clients, SAIs organized on a collegial basis) and there may be additional policies relevant to public sector auditors.*

2. *Also, in the public sector of some countries, quality control generally has a different meaning to that adopted in this ISA. Quality assurance is the term applied to internal supervision and review procedures whereas quality control is the term applied to external quality reviews.*

Appendix

Illustrative Examples of Quality Control Procedures for an Audit Firm

A. PROFESSIONAL REQUIREMENTS

Policy

Personnel in the firm are to adhere to the principles of independence, integrity, objectivity, confidentiality and professional behavior.

Procedures

1. Assign an individual or group to provide guidance and to resolve questions on matters of integrity, objectivity, independence and confidentiality.

    (a) Identify circumstances where documentation as to the resolution of questions would be appropriate.

    (b) Require consultation with authoritative sources when considered necessary.

2. Communicate policies and procedures regarding independence, integrity, objectivity, confidentiality and professional behavior to personnel at all levels within the firm.

    (a) Inform personnel of the firm's policies and procedures and advise them that they are expected to be familiar with them.

    (b) Emphasize independence of mental attitude in training programs and in supervision and review of audits.

    (c) Inform personnel on a timely basis of those entities to which independence policies apply.

      (i) Prepare and maintain for independence purposes a list of the firm's clients and of other entities (client's affiliates, parents, associates, and so forth) to which independence policies apply.

      (ii) Make the list available to personnel (including personnel new to the firm or to an office) who need it to determine their independence.

      (iii) Establish procedures to notify personnel of changes in the list.

3. Monitor compliance with policies and procedures relating to independence, integrity, objectivity, confidentiality and professional behavior.

    (a) Obtain from personnel periodic written representations, ordinarily on an annual basis, stating that—

      (i) They are familiar with the firm's policies and procedures.

      (ii) Prohibited investments are not held and were not held during the period.

AUDITING

(iii) Prohibited relationships do not exist, and transactions prohibited by firm policy have not occurred.

(b) Assign responsibility for resolving exceptions to a person or group with appropriate authority.

(c) Assign responsibility for obtaining representations and reviewing independence compliance files for completeness to a person or group with appropriate authority.

(d) Review periodically the firm's association with clients to ascertain whether any areas of involvement may or may be seen to impair the firm's independence.

B. SKILLS AND COMPETENCE

Policy

The firm is to be staffed by personnel who have attained and maintain the technical standards and professional competence required to enable them to fulfill their responsibilities with due care.

Procedures

Hiring

1. Maintain a program designed to obtain qualified personnel by planning for personnel needs, establishing hiring objectives, and setting qualifications for those involved in the hiring function.

   (a) Plan for the firm's personnel needs at all levels and establish quantified hiring objectives based on current clientele, anticipated growth, and retirement.

   (b) Design a program to achieve hiring objectives which provides for—

   (i) Identification of sources of potential hirees.

   (ii) Methods of contact with potential hirees.

   (iii) Methods of specific identification of potential hirees.

   (iv) Methods of attracting potential hirees and informing them about the firm.

   (v) Methods of evaluating and selecting potential hirees for extension of employment offers.

   (c) Inform those persons involved in hiring as to the firm's personnel needs and hiring objectives.

   (d) Assign to authorized persons the responsibility for employment decisions.

   (e) Monitor the effectiveness of the recruiting program.

      (i) Evaluate the recruiting program periodically to determine whether policies and procedures for obtaining qualified personnel are being observed.

      (ii) Review hiring results periodically to determine whether goals and personnel needs are being achieved.

2.   Establish qualifications and guidelines for evaluating potential hirees at each professional level.

   (a) Identify the attributes to be sought in hirees, such as intelligence, integrity, honesty, motivation and aptitude for the profession.

   (b) Identify achievements and experiences desirable for entry level and experienced personnel. For example:

      (i) Academic background.

      (ii) Personal achievements.

      (iii) Work experience.

      (iv) Personal interests.

   (c) Set guidelines to be followed when hiring individuals in situations such as:

      (i) Hiring relatives of personnel or relatives of clients.

      (ii) Rehiring former employees.

      (iii) Hiring client employees.

   (d) Obtain background information and documentation of qualifications of applicants by appropriate means, such as:

      (i) Resumes.

      (ii) Application forms.

      (iii) Interviews.

      (iv) Academic record.

      (v) Personal references.

      (vi) Former employment references.

   (e) Evaluate the qualifications of new personnel, including those obtained from other than the usual hiring channels (for example, those joining the firm at supervisory levels or through merger or acquisition), to determine that they meet the firm's requirements and standards.

3.   Inform applicants and new personnel of the firm's policies and procedures relevant to them.

   (a) Use a brochure or other means to inform applicants and new personnel.

   (b) Prepare and maintain a manual describing policies and procedures for distribution to personnel.

   (c) Conduct an orientation program for new personnel.

AUDITING

Professional Development

4. Establish guidelines and requirements for continuing professional education and communicate them to personnel.

   (a) Assign responsibility for the professional development function to a person or group with appropriate authority.

   (b) Provide that programs developed by the firm be reviewed by qualified individuals. Programs would contain statements of objectives and education and/or experience prerequisites.

   (c) Provide an orientation program relating to the firm and the profession for newly employed personnel.

      (i) Prepare publications and programs designed to inform newly employed personnel of their professional responsibilities and opportunities.

      (ii) Assign responsibility for conducting orientation conferences to explain professional responsibilities and firm policies.

   (d) Establish continuing professional education requirements for personnel at each level within the firm.

      (i) Consider legislative and professional bodies' requirements or voluntary guidelines in establishing firm requirements.

      (ii) Encourage participation in external continuing professional education programs, including self-study courses.

      (iii) Encourage membership in professional organizations. Consider having the firm pay or contribute toward membership dues and expenses.

      (iv) Encourage personnel to serve on professional committees, prepare articles, and participate in other professional activities.

   (e) Monitor continuing professional education programs and maintain appropriate records, both on a firm and an individual basis.

      (i) Review periodically the records of participation by personnel to determine compliance with firm requirements.

      (ii) Review periodically evaluation reports and other records prepared for continuing education programs to evaluate whether the programs are being presented effectively and are accomplishing firm objectives. Consider the need for new programs and for revision or elimination of ineffective programs.

5. Make available to personnel information about current developments in professional technical standards and materials containing the firm's technical policies and procedures and encourage personnel to engage in self-development activities.

   (a) Provide personnel with professional literature relating to current developments in professional technical standards.

    (i) Distribute to personnel material of general interest, such as relevant international and national pronouncements on accounting and auditing matters.

    (ii) Distribute pronouncements on relevant regulations and statutory requirements in areas of specific interest, such as company securities and taxation law, to persons who have responsibility in such areas.

    (iii) Distribute manuals containing firm policies and procedures on technical matters to personnel. Manuals need to be updated for new developments and changing conditions.

(b) For training programs presented by the firm, develop or obtain course materials and select and train instructors.

    (i) State the program objectives and education and/or experience prerequisites in the training programs.

    (ii) Provide that program instructors be qualified as to both program content and teaching methods.

    (iii) Have participants evaluate program content and instructors of training sessions.

    (iv) Have instructors evaluate program content and participants in training sessions.

    (v) Update programs as needed in light of new developments, changing conditions, and evaluation reports.

    (vi) Maintain a library or other facility containing professional, regulatory and firm literature relating to professional technical matters.

6. Provide, to the extent necessary, programs to fill the firm's needs for personnel with expertise in specialized areas and industries.

(a) Conduct firm programs to develop and maintain expertise in specialized areas and industries, such as regulated industries, computer auditing, and statistical sampling methods.

(b) Encourage attendance at external education programs, meetings, and conferences to acquire technical or industry expertise.

(c) Encourage membership and participation in organizations concerned with specialized areas and industries.

(d) Provide technical literature relating to specialized areas and industries.

Advancement

7. Establish qualifications deemed necessary for the various levels of responsibility within the firm.

(a) Prepare guidelines describing responsibilities at each level and expected performance and qualifications necessary for advancement to each level, including:

AUDITING

      (i) Titles and related responsibilities.

     (ii) The amount of experience (which may be expressed as a time period) generally required for advancement to the succeeding level.

  (b) Identify criteria which will be considered in evaluating individual performance and expected proficiency, such as:

      (i) Technical knowledge.

     (ii) Analytical and judgmental abilities.

    (iii) Communication skills.

    (iv) Leadership and training skills.

     (v) Client relations.

    (vi) Personal attitude and professional bearing (character, intelligence, judgment and motivation).

   (vii) Qualification as a professional accountant for advancement to a supervisory position.

  (c) Use a personnel manual or other means to communicate advancement policies and procedures to personnel.

8. Evaluate performance of personnel and advise personnel of their progress.

  (a) Gather and evaluate information on performance of personnel.

      (i) Identify evaluation responsibilities and requirements at each level indicating who will prepare evaluations and when they will be prepared.

     (ii) Instruct personnel on the objectives of personnel evaluation.

    (iii) Utilize forms, which may be standardized, for evaluating performance of personnel.

    (iv) Review evaluations with the individual being evaluated.

     (v) Require that evaluations be reviewed by the evaluator's superior.

    (vi) Review evaluations to determine that individuals worked for and were evaluated by different persons.

   (vii) Determine that evaluations are completed on a timely basis.

  (viii) Maintain personnel files containing documentation relating to the evaluation process.

  (b) Periodically counsel personnel as to their progress and career opportunities.

      (i) Review periodically with personnel the evaluation of their performance, including an assessment of their progress with the firm. Considerations would include the following:

        – Performance.

        – Future objectives of the firm and the individual.

        – Assignment preference.

      – Career opportunities.

  (ii) Evaluate partners periodically by means of senior partner or fellow partner evaluation and counseling as to whether they continue to have the qualifications to fulfill their responsibilities.

  (iii) Review periodically the system of personnel evaluation and counseling to ascertain that:

      – Procedures for evaluation and documentation are being followed on a timely basis.

      – Requirements established for advancement are being achieved.

      – Personnel decisions are consistent with evaluations.

      – Recognition is given to outstanding performance.

9.   Assign responsibility for making advancement decisions.

  (a) Assign responsibility to designated persons for making advancement and termination decisions, conducting evaluation interviews with persons considered for advancement, documenting the results of the interviews, and maintaining appropriate records.

  (b) Evaluate data obtained giving appropriate recognition in advancement decisions to the quality of the work performed.

  (c) Study the firm's advancement experience periodically to ascertain whether individuals meeting stated criteria are assigned increased degrees of responsibility.

C. ASSIGNMENT

Policy

Audit work is to be assigned to personnel who have the degree of technical training and proficiency required in the circumstances.

Procedures

1.   Delineate the firm's approach to assigning personnel, including the planning of overall firm and office needs and the measures employed to achieve a balance of audit manpower requirements, personnel skills, individual development and utilization.

  (a) Plan the personnel needs of the firm on an overall basis and for individual practice offices.

  (b) Identify on a timely basis the staffing requirements of specific audits.

  (c) Prepare time budgets for audits to determine manpower requirements and to schedule audit work.

  (d) Consider the following factors in achieving a balance of audit manpower requirements, personal skills, individual development and utilization—

AUDITING

(i) Audit size and complexity.

(ii) Personnel availability.

(iii) Special expertise required.

(iv) Timing of the work to be performed.

(v) Continuity and periodic rotation of personnel.

(vi) Opportunities for on-the-job training.

2. Assign an appropriate person or persons to be responsible for assigning personnel to audits.

    (a) Consider the following in making assignments of individuals—

        (i) Staffing and timing requirements of the specific audit.

        (ii) Evaluations of the qualifications of personnel as to experience, position, background, and special expertise.

        (iii) The planned supervision and involvement by supervisory personnel.

        (iv) Projected time availability of individuals assigned.

        (v) Situations where possible independence problems and conflicts of interest may exist, such as assignment of personnel to audits for clients who are former employers or are employers of certain kin.

    (b) Give appropriate consideration, in assigning personnel, to both continuity and rotation to provide for efficient conduct of the audit and the perspective of other personnel with different experience and backgrounds.

3. Provide for approval of the scheduling and staffing of the audit by the auditor.

    (a) Submit, where necessary, for review and approval the names and qualifications of personnel to be assigned to an audit.

    (b) Consider the experience and training of the audit personnel in relation to the complexity or other requirements of the audit, and the extent of supervision to be provided.

D. DELEGATION

Policy

There is to be sufficient direction, supervision and review of work at all levels to provide reasonable assurance that the work performed meets appropriate standards of quality.

Procedures

1. Provide procedures for planning audits.

    (a) Assign responsibility for planning an audit. Involve appropriate personnel assigned to the audit in the planning process.

(b) Develop background information or review information obtained from prior audits and update for changed circumstances.

(c) Describe matters to be included in the overall audit plan and the audit program, such as the following:

(i) Development of proposed work programs for particular areas of audit interest.

(ii) Determination of manpower requirements and need for specialized knowledge.

(iii) Development of estimates of time required to complete the audit.

(iv) Consideration of current economic conditions affecting the client or its industry and their potential effect on the conduct of the audit.

2. Provide procedures for maintaining the firm's standards of quality for the work performed.

(a) Provide adequate supervision at all organizational levels, considering the training, ability and experience of the personnel assigned.

(b) Develop guidelines for the form and content of working papers.

(c) Utilize standardized forms, checklists, and questionnaires to the extent appropriate to assist in the performance of audits.

(d) Provide procedures for resolving differences of professional judgment among personnel involved in an audit.

3. Provide on-the-job training during the performance of audits.

(a) Emphasize the importance of on-the-job training as a significant part of an individual's development.

(i) Discuss with assistants the relationship of the work they are performing to the audit as a whole.

(ii) Involve assistants in as many portions of the audit as practicable.

(b) Emphasize the significance of personnel management skills and include coverage of these subjects in firm training programs.

(c) Encourage personnel to train and develop subordinates.

(d) Monitor assignments to determine that personnel.

(i) Fulfill, where applicable, the experience requirements of the relevant legislative, regulatory or professional body.

(ii) Gain experience in various areas of audits and varied industries.

(iii) Work under different supervisory personnel.

AUDITING

E. CONSULTATION

Policy

Whenever necessary, consultation within or outside the firm is to occur with those who have appropriate expertise.

Procedures

1. Identify areas and specialized situations where consultation is required and encourage personnel to consult with or use authoritative sources on other complex or unusual matters.

    (a) Inform personnel of the firm's consultation policies and procedures.

    (b) Specify areas or specialized situations requiring consultation because of the nature or complexity of the subject matter. Examples include—

        (i) Application of newly issued technical pronouncements.

        (ii) Industries with special accounting, auditing or reporting requirements.

        (iii) Emerging practice problems.

        (iv) Filing requirements of legislative and regulatory bodies, particularly those of a foreign jurisdiction.

    (c) Maintain or provide access to adequate reference libraries and other authoritative sources.

        (i) Establish responsibility for maintaining a reference library in each practice office.

        (ii) Maintain technical manuals and issue technical pronouncements, including those relating to particular industries and other specialties.

        (iii) Maintain consultation arrangements with other firms and individuals where necessary to supplement firm resources.

        (iv) Refer problems to a division or group in the professional body established to deal with technical inquiries.

2. Designate individuals as specialists to serve as authoritative sources and define their authority in consultative situations.

    (a) Designate individuals as specialists for filings with legislative and other regulatory bodies.

    (b) Designate specialists for particular industries.

    (c) Advise personnel of the degree of authority to be accorded specialists' opinions and of the procedures to be followed for resolving differences of opinion with specialists.

3. Specify the extent of documentation to be provided for the results of consultation in those areas and specialized situations where consultation is required.

(a) Advise personnel as to the extent of documentation to be prepared and the responsibility for its preparation.

(b) Indicate where consultation documentation is to be maintained.

(c) Maintain subject files containing the results of consultations for reference and research purposes.

F. ACCEPTANCE AND RETENTION OF CLIENTS

Policy

An evaluation of prospective clients and a review, on an ongoing basis, of existing clients is to be conducted. In making a decision to accept or retain a client, the firm's independence and ability to serve the client properly and the integrity of the client's management are to be considered.

Procedures

1. Establish procedures for evaluation of prospective clients and for their approval as clients.

   (a) Evaluation procedures could include the following:

   (i) Obtain and review available financial statements regarding the prospective client, such as annual reports, interim financial statements and income tax returns.

   (ii) Inquire of third parties as to any information regarding the prospective client and its management and principals which may have a bearing on evaluating the prospective client. Inquiries may be directed to the prospective client's bankers, legal advisers, investment banker, and others in the financial or business community who may have such knowledge.

   (iii) Communicate with the predecessor auditor. Inquiries would include questions regarding the facts that might bear on the integrity of management, on disagreements with management as to accounting policies, audit procedures, or other similarly significant matters, and on the predecessor's understanding as to the reasons for the change in auditors.

   (iv) Consider circumstances which would cause the firm to regard the engagement as one requiring special attention or presenting unusual risks.

   (v) Evaluate the firm's independence and ability to serve the prospective client. In evaluating the firm's ability, consider needs for technical skills, knowledge of the industry and personnel.

   (vi) Determine that acceptance of the client would not violate codes of professional ethics.

   (b) Designate an individual or group, at appropriate management levels, to evaluate the information obtained regarding the prospective client and to make the acceptance decision.

    (i) Consider types of engagements that the firm would not accept or which would be accepted only under certain conditions.

    (ii) Provide for documentation of the conclusion reached.

(c) Inform appropriate personnel of the firm's policies and procedures for accepting clients.

(d) Designate responsibility for administering and monitoring compliance with the firm's policies and procedures for acceptance of clients.

2. Evaluate clients upon the occurrence of specified events to determine whether the relationships ought to be continued.

  (a) Events specified for this purpose could include:

    (i) The expiration of a time period.

    (ii) A major change in one or more of the following
- Management
- Directors
- Ownership
- Legal advisers
- Financial condition
- Litigation status
- Scope of the engagement
- Nature of the client's business.

    (iii) The existence of conditions which would have caused the firm to reject a client had such conditions existed at the time of the initial acceptance.

  (b) Designate an individual or group, at appropriate management levels, to evaluate the information obtained and to make retention decisions.

    (i) Consider types of engagements that the firm would not continue or which would be continued only under certain conditions.

    (ii) Provide for documentation of the conclusion reached.

  (c) Inform appropriate personnel of the firm's policies and procedures for retaining clients.

  (d) Designate responsibility for administering and monitoring compliance with the firm's policies and procedures for retention of clients

G. MONITORING

Policy

The continued adequacy and operational effectiveness of quality control policies and procedures is to be monitored.

Procedures

1. Define the scope and content of the firm's monitoring program.

    (a) Determine the monitoring procedures necessary to provide reasonable assurance that the firm's other quality control policies and procedures are operating effectively.

        (i) Determine objectives and prepare instructions and review programs for use in conducting monitoring activities.

        (ii) Provide guidelines for the extent of work and criteria for selection of engagements for review.

        (iii) Establish the frequency and timing of monitoring activities.

        (iv) Establish procedures to resolve disagreements which may arise between reviewers and engagement or management personnel.

    (b) Establish levels of competence, etc., for personnel to participate in monitoring activities and the method of their selection.

        (i) Determine criteria for selecting monitoring personnel, including levels of responsibility in the firm and requirements for specialized knowledge.

        (ii) Assign responsibility for selecting monitoring personnel.

    (c) Conduct monitoring activities.

        (i) Review and test compliance with the firm's general quality control policies and procedures.

        (ii) Review selected engagements for compliance with professional standards and with the firm's quality control policies and procedures.

2. Provide for reporting findings to the appropriate management levels, for monitoring actions taken or planned, and for overall review of the firm's quality control system.

    (a) Discuss general findings with appropriate management personnel.

    (b) Discuss findings on selected engagements with engagement management personnel.

    (c) Report both general and selected engagement findings and recommendations to firm management together with corrective actions taken or planned.

    (d) Determine that planned corrective actions were taken.

    (e) Determine need for modification of quality control policies and procedures in view of results of monitoring activities and other relevant matters.

AUDITING

220

CONTENTS

	Paragraphs
Introduction	1-4
Form and Content of Working Papers	5-12
Confidentiality, Safe Custody, Retention and Ownership of Working Papers	13-14

International Standards on Auditing (ISAs) are to be applied in the audit of financial statements. ISAs are also to be applied, adapted as necessary, to the audit of other information and to related services.

ISAs contain the basic principles and essential procedures (identified in bold type black lettering) together with related guidance in the form of explanatory and other material. The basic principles and essential procedures are to be interpreted in the context of the explanatory and other material that provide guidance for their application.

To understand and apply the basic principles and essential procedures together with the related guidance, it is necessary to consider the whole text of the ISA including explanatory and other material contained in the ISA not just that text which is black lettered.

In exceptional circumstances, an auditor may judge it necessary to depart from an ISA in order to more effectively achieve the objective of an audit. When such a situation arises, the auditor should be prepared to justify the departure.

ISAs need only be applied to material matters.

The Public Sector Perspective (PSP) issued by the Public Sector Committee of the International Federation of Accountants is set out at the end of an ISA. Where no PSP is added, the ISA is applicable in all material respects to the public sector.

Introduction

1. The purpose of this International Standard on Auditing (ISA) is to establish standards and provide guidance regarding documentation in the context of the audit of financial statements.

2. **The auditor should document matters which are important in providing evidence to support the audit opinion and evidence that the audit was carried out in accordance with ISAs.**

3. "Documentation" means the material (working papers) prepared by and for, or obtained and retained by the auditor in connection with the performance of the audit. Working papers may be in the form of data stored on paper, film, electronic media or other media.

4. Working papers:

   (a) assist in the planning and performance of the audit;

   (b) assist in the supervision and review of the audit work; and

   (c) record the audit evidence resulting from the audit work performed to support the auditor's opinion.

Form and Content of Working Papers

5. **The auditor should prepare working papers which are sufficiently complete and detailed to provide an overall understanding of the audit.**

6. **The auditor should record in the working papers information on planning the audit work, the nature, timing and extent of the audit procedures performed, the results thereof, and the conclusions drawn from the audit evidence obtained.** Working papers would include the auditor's reasoning on all significant matters which require the exercise of judgment, together with the auditor's conclusion thereon. In areas involving difficult questions of principle or judgment, working papers will record the relevant facts that were known by the auditor at the time the conclusions were reached.

7. The extent of working papers is a matter of professional judgment since it is neither necessary nor practical to document every matter the auditor considers. In assessing the extent of working papers to be prepared and retained, it may be useful for the auditor to consider what would be necessary to provide another auditor who has no previous experience with the audit with an understanding of the work performed and the basis of the principle decisions taken but not the detailed aspects of the audit. That other auditor may only be able to obtain an understanding of detailed aspects of the audit by discussing them with the auditors who prepared the working papers.

8. The form and content of working papers are affected by matters such as the:

   • Nature of the engagement.

   • Form of the auditor's report.

AUDITING

- Nature and complexity of the business.

- Nature and condition of the entity's accounting and internal control systems.

- Needs in the particular circumstances for direction, supervision and review of work performed by assistants.

- Specific audit methodology and technology used in the course of the audit.

9. Working papers are designed and organized to meet the circumstances and the auditor's needs for each individual audit. The use of standardized working papers (for example, checklists, specimen letters, standard organization of working papers) may improve the efficiency with which such working papers are prepared and reviewed. They facilitate the delegation of work while providing a means to control its quality.

10. To improve audit efficiency, the auditor may utilize schedules, analyses and other documentation prepared by the entity. In such circumstances, the auditor would need to be satisfied that those materials have been properly prepared.

11. Working papers ordinarily include:

- Information concerning the legal and organizational structure of the entity.

- Extracts or copies of important legal documents, agreements and minutes.

- Information concerning the industry, economic environment and legislative environment within which the entity operates.

- Evidence of the planning process including audit programs and any changes thereto.

- Evidence of the auditor's understanding of the accounting and internal control systems.

- Evidence of inherent and control risk assessments and any revisions thereof.

- Evidence of the auditor's consideration of the work of internal auditing and conclusions reached.

- Analyses of transactions and balances.

- Analyses of significant ratios and trends.

- A record of the nature, timing and extent of audit procedures performed and the results of such procedures.

- Evidence that the work performed by assistants was supervised and reviewed.

- An indication as to who performed the audit procedures and when they were performed.

- Details of procedures applied regarding components whose financial statements are audited by another auditor.

- Copies of communications with other auditors, experts and other third parties.

- Copies of letters or notes concerning audit matters communicated to or discussed with the entity, including the terms of the engagement and material weaknesses in internal control.

- Letters of representation received from the entity.

- Conclusions reached by the auditor concerning significant aspects of the audit, including how exceptions and unusual matters, if any, disclosed by the auditor's procedures were resolved or treated.

- Copies of the financial statements and auditor's report.

12. In the case of recurring audits, some working paper files may be classified as "permanent" audit files which are updated with new information of continuing importance, as distinct from current audit files which contain information relating primarily to the audit of a single period.

Confidentiality, Safe Custody, Retention and Ownership of Working Papers

13. **The auditor should adopt appropriate procedures for maintaining the confidentiality and safe custody of the working papers and for retaining them for a period sufficient to meet the needs of the practice and in accordance with legal and professional requirements of record retention.**

14. Working papers are the property of the auditor. Although portions of or extracts from the working papers may be made available to the entity at the discretion of the auditor, they are not a substitute for the entity's accounting records.

AUDITING

CONTENTS

	Paragraphs
Introduction	1-4
Responsibility of Management	5
Responsibility of the Auditor	6-11
Inherent Limitations of an Audit	12-14
Procedures When There is an Indication That Fraud or Error May Exist	15-18
Reporting of Fraud and Error	19-24
Withdrawal from the Engagement	25-26
Appendix: Examples of Conditions or Events which Increase the Risk of Fraud or Error	

International Standards on Auditing (ISAs) are to be applied in the audit of financial statements. ISAs are also to be applied, adapted as necessary, to the audit of other information and to related services.

ISAs contain the basic principles and essential procedures (identified in bold type black lettering) together with related guidance in the form of explanatory and other material. The basic principles and essential procedures are to be interpreted in the context of the explanatory and other material that provide guidance for their application.

To understand and apply the basic principles and essential procedures together with the related guidance, it is necessary to consider the whole text of the ISA including explanatory and other material contained in the ISA not just that text which is black lettered.

In exceptional circumstances, an auditor may judge it necessary to depart from an ISA in order to more effectively achieve the objective of an audit. When such a situation arises, the auditor should be prepared to justify the departure.

ISAs need only be applied to material matters.

The Public Sector Perspective (PSP) issued by the Public Sector Committee of the International Federation of Accountants is set out at the end of an ISA. Where no PSP is added, the ISA is applicable in all material respects to the public sector.

Introduction

1. The purpose of this International Standard on Auditing (ISA) is to establish standards and provide guidance on the auditor's responsibility to consider fraud and error in an audit of financial statements.

2. **When planning and performing audit procedures and in evaluating and reporting the results thereof, the auditor should consider the risk of material misstatements in the financial statements resulting from fraud or error.**

3. The term "fraud" refers to an intentional act by one or more individuals among management, employees, or third parties, which results in a misrepresentation of financial statements. Fraud may involve:

   - Manipulation, falsification or alteration of records or documents.

   - Misappropriation of assets.

   - Suppression or omission of the effects of transactions from records or documents.

   - Recording of transactions without substance.

   - Misapplication of accounting policies.

4. The term "error" refers to unintentional mistakes in financial statements, such as:

   - Mathematical or clerical mistakes in the underlying records and accounting data.

   - Oversight or misinterpretation of facts.

   - Misapplication of accounting policies.

Responsibility of Management

5. The responsibility for the prevention and detection of fraud and error rests with management through the implementation and continued operation of adequate accounting and internal control systems. Such systems reduce but do not eliminate the possibility of fraud and error.

Responsibility of the Auditor

6. The auditor is not and cannot be held responsible for the prevention of fraud and error. The fact that an annual audit is carried out may, however, act as a deterrent.

Risk Assessment

7. **In planning the audit, the auditor should assess the risk that fraud and error may cause the financial statements to contain material misstatements and should inquire of management as to any fraud or significant error which has been discovered.**

AUDITING

8. In addition to weaknesses in the design of the accounting and internal control systems and noncompliance with identified internal controls, conditions or events which increase the risk of fraud and error include:

    • Questions with respect to the integrity or competence of management.

    • Unusual pressures within or on an entity.

    • Unusual transactions.

    • Problems in obtaining sufficient appropriate audit evidence.

    Examples of these conditions or events are set out in the Appendix to this ISA.

Detection

9. **Based on the risk assessment, the auditor should design audit procedures to obtain reasonable assurance that misstatements arising from fraud and error that are material to the financial statements taken as a whole are detected.**

10. Consequently, the auditor seeks sufficient appropriate audit evidence that fraud and error which may be material to the financial statements have not occurred or that, if they have occurred, the effect of fraud is properly reflected in the financial statements or the error is corrected. The likelihood of detecting errors ordinarily is higher than that of detecting fraud, since fraud is ordinarily accompanied by acts specifically designed to conceal its existence.

11. Due to the inherent limitations of an audit (see paragraphs 12-14) there is an unavoidable risk that material misstatements in the financial statements resulting from fraud and, to a lesser extent, error may not be detected. The subsequent discovery of material misstatement of the financial statements resulting from fraud or error existing during the period covered by the auditor's report does not, in itself, indicate that the auditor has failed to adhere to the basic principles and essential procedures of an audit. Whether the auditor has adhered to these principles and procedures is determined by the adequacy of the audit procedures undertaken in the circumstances and the suitability of the auditor's report based on the results of those audit procedures.

Inherent Limitations of an Audit

12. An audit is subject to the unavoidable risk that some material misstatements of the financial statements will not be detected, even though the audit is properly planned and performed in accordance with ISAs.

13. The risk of not detecting a material misstatement resulting from fraud is higher than the risk of not detecting a material misstatement resulting from error, because fraud ordinarily involves acts designed to conceal it, such as collusion, forgery, deliberate failure to record transactions, or intentional misrepresentations being made to the auditor. Unless the audit reveals evidence to the contrary, the auditor is entitled to accept representations as

truthful and records and documents as genuine. **However, in accordance with ISA 200 "Objective and General Principles Governing an Audit of Financial Statements," the auditor should plan and perform the audit with an attitude of professional skepticism, recognizing that conditions or events may be found that indicate that fraud or error may exist.**

14. While the existence of effective accounting and internal control systems reduces the probability of misstatement of financial statements resulting from fraud and error, there will always be some risk of internal controls failing to operate as designed. Furthermore, any accounting and internal control system may be ineffective against fraud involving collusion among employees or fraud committed by management. Certain levels of management may be in a position to override controls that would prevent similar frauds by other employees; for example, by directing subordinates to record transactions incorrectly or to conceal them, or by suppressing information relating to transactions.

Procedures When There is an Indication That Fraud or Error May Exist

15. **When the application of audit procedures designed from the risk assessment indicates the possible existence of fraud or error, the auditor should consider the potential effect on the financial statements. If the auditor believes the indicated fraud or error could have a material effect on the financial statements, the auditor should perform appropriate modified or additional procedures.**

16. The extent of such modified or additional procedures depends on the auditor's judgment as to:

    (a) the types of fraud and error indicated;

    (b) the likelihood of their occurrence; and

    (c) the likelihood that a particular type of fraud or error could have a material effect on the financial statements.

    Unless circumstances clearly indicate otherwise, the auditor cannot assume that an instance of fraud or error is an isolated occurrence. If necessary, the auditor adjusts the nature, timing and extent of substantive procedures.

17. Performing modified or additional procedures would ordinarily enable the auditor to confirm or dispel a suspicion of fraud or error. **Where suspicion of fraud or error is not dispelled by the results of modified or additional procedures, the auditor should discuss the matter with management and consider whether the matter has been properly reflected or corrected in the financial statements. The auditor should consider the possible impact on the auditor's report.**

18. **The auditor should consider the implications of fraud and significant error in relation to other aspects of the audit, particularly the reliability of management representations.** In this regard, the auditor reconsiders the risk assessment and the validity of management representations, in case of fraud and error not detected by internal controls or not included in management representations. The implications of particular instances of

fraud or error discovered by the auditor will depend on the relationship of the perpetration and concealment, if any, of the fraud or error to specific control procedures and the level of management or employees involved.

Reporting of Fraud and Error

To Management

19. **The auditor should communicate factual findings to management as soon as practicable if:**

    (a) **the auditor suspects fraud may exist, even if the potential effect on the financial statements would be immaterial; or**

    (b) **fraud or significant error is actually found to exist.**

20. In determining an appropriate representative of the entity to whom to report occurrences of possible or actual fraud or significant error, the auditor would consider all the circumstances. With respect to fraud, the auditor would assess the likelihood of senior management involvement. In most cases involving fraud, it would be appropriate to report the matter to a level in the organization structure of the entity above that responsible for the persons believed to be implicated. When those persons ultimately responsible for the overall direction of the entity are doubted, the auditor would ordinarily seek legal advice to assist in the determination of procedures to follow.

To Users of the Auditor's Report on the Financial Statements

21. **If the auditor concludes that the fraud or error has a material effect on the financial statements and has not been properly reflected or corrected in the financial statements, the auditor should express a qualified or an adverse opinion.**

22. **If the auditor is precluded by the entity from obtaining sufficient appropriate audit evidence to evaluate whether fraud or error that may be material to the financial statements, has, or is likely to have, occurred, the auditor should express a qualified opinion or a disclaimer of opinion on the financial statements on the basis of a limitation on the scope of the audit.**

23. **If the auditor is unable to determine whether fraud or error has occurred because of limitations imposed by the circumstances rather than by the entity, the auditor should consider the effect on the auditor's report.**

To Regulatory and Enforcement Authorities

24. The auditor's duty of confidentiality would ordinarily preclude reporting fraud or error to a third party. However, in certain circumstances, the duty of confidentiality is overridden by statute, law or by courts of law (for example, in some countries the auditor is required to report fraud or error by financial institutions to the supervisory authorities). The auditor may need to seek

legal advice in such circumstances, giving due consideration to the auditor's responsibility to the public interest.

Withdrawal from the Engagement

25. The auditor may conclude that withdrawal from the engagement is necessary when the entity does not take the remedial action regarding fraud that the auditor considers necessary in the circumstances, even when the fraud is not material to the financial statements. Factors that would affect the auditor's conclusion include the implications of the involvement of the highest authority within the entity, which may affect the reliability of management representations, and the effects on the auditor of continuing association with the entity. In reaching such conclusion, the auditor would ordinarily seek legal advice.

26. **As stated in the "Code of Ethics for Professional Accountants" issued by the International Federation of Accountants, on receipt of an inquiry from the proposed auditor, the existing auditor should advise whether there are any professional reasons why the proposed auditor should not accept the appointment.** The extent to which an existing auditor can discuss the affairs of a client with a proposed auditor will depend on whether the client's permission to do so has been obtained and/or the legal or ethical requirements that apply in each country relating to such disclosure. If there are any such reasons or other matters which need to be disclosed, the existing auditor would, taking account of the legal and ethical constraints including where appropriate permission of the client, give details of the information and discuss freely with the proposed auditor all matters relevant to the appointment. **If permission from the client to discuss its affairs with the proposed auditor is denied by the client, that fact should be disclosed to the proposed auditor.**

Public Sector Perspective

1. *In respect of paragraph 9 of this ISA, it has to be noted that the nature and the scope of the public sector audit may be affected by legislation, regulation, ordinances and ministerial directives relating to the detection of fraud and error. These requirements may lessen the auditor's ability to exercise judgment. In addition to any formally mandated responsibility to detect fraud, the use of "public monies" tends to impose a higher profile on fraud issues, and auditors may need to be responsive to public "expectations" regarding detection of fraud. It also has to be recognized that reporting responsibilities as discussed in paragraphs 19 and 20 of this ISA, may be subject to specific provisions of the audit mandate or related legislation or regulation.*

AUDITING

Appendix

Examples of Conditions or Events which Increase the Risk of Fraud or Error

Questions with respect to the integrity or competence of management

- Management is dominated by one person (or a small group) and there is no effective oversight board or committee.
- There is a complex corporate structure where complexity does not seem to be warranted.
- There is a continuing failure to correct major weaknesses in internal controls where such corrections are practicable.
- There is a high turnover rate of key accounting and financial personnel.
- There is a significant and prolonged understaffing of the accounting department.
- There are frequent changes of legal counsel or auditors.

Unusual pressures within or on an entity

- The industry is declining and failures are increasing.
- There is inadequate working capital due to declining profits or too rapid expansion.
- The quality of earnings is deteriorating, for example, increased risk taking with respect to credit sales, changes in business practice or selection of accounting policy alternatives that improve income.
- The entity needs a rising profit trend to support the market price of its shares due to a contemplated public offering, a takeover or other reason.
- The entity has a significant investment in an industry or product line noted for rapid change.
- The entity is heavily dependent on one or a few products or customers.
- Financial pressure on top managers.
- Pressure is exerted on accounting personnel to complete financial statements in an unusually short time period.

Unusual transactions

- Unusual transactions, especially near the year-end, that have a significant effect on earnings.
- Complex transactions or accounting treatments.
- Transactions with related parties.

- Payments for services (for example, to lawyers, consultants or agents) that appear excessive in relation to the services provided.

Problems in obtaining sufficient appropriate audit evidence

- Inadequate records, for example, incomplete files, excessive adjustments to books and accounts, transactions not recorded in accordance with normal procedures and out of balance control accounts.

- Inadequate documentation of transactions, such as lack of proper authorization, supporting documents not available and alteration to documents (any of these documentation problems assume greater significance when they relate to large or unusual transactions).

- An excessive number of differences between accounting records and third party confirmations, conflicting audit evidence and unexplainable changes in operating ratios.

- Evasive or unreasonable responses by management to audit inquiries.

Some factors unique to a computer information systems environment which relate to the conditions and events in described above include:

- Inability to extract information from computer files due to lack of, or noncurrent, documentation of record contents or programs.

- Large numbers of program changes that are not documented, approved and tested.

- Inadequate overall balancing of computer transactions and data bases to the financial accounts.

AUDITING

CONTENTS

	Paragraphs
Introduction	1-8
Responsibility of Management for the Compliance with Laws and Regulations	9-10
The Auditor's Consideration of Compliance with Laws and Regulations	11-31
Reporting of Noncompliance	32-38
Withdrawal from the Engagement	39-40
Appendix: Indications That Noncompliance May Have Occurred	

International Standards on Auditing (ISAs) are to be applied in the audit of financial statements. ISAs are also to be applied, adapted as necessary, to the audit of other information and to related services.

ISAs contain the basic principles and essential procedures (identified in bold type black lettering) together with related guidance in the form of explanatory and other material. The basic principles and essential procedures are to be interpreted in the context of the explanatory and other material that provide guidance for their application.

To understand and apply the basic principles and essential procedures together with the related guidance, it is necessary to consider the whole text of the ISA including explanatory and other material contained in the ISA not just that text which is black lettered.

In exceptional circumstances, an auditor may judge it necessary to depart from an ISA in order to more effectively achieve the objective of an audit. When such a situation arises, the auditor should be prepared to justify the departure.

ISAs need only be applied to material matters.

The Public Sector Perspective (PSP) issued by the Public Sector Committee of the International Federation of Accountants is set out at the end of an ISA. Where no PSP is added, the ISA is applicable in all material respects to the public sector.

Introduction

1. The purpose of this International Standard on Auditing (ISA) is to establish standards and provide guidance on the auditor's responsibility to consider laws and regulations in an audit of financial statements.

2. **When planning and performing audit procedures and in evaluating and reporting the results thereof, the auditor should recognize that noncompliance by the entity with laws and regulations may materially affect the financial statements.** However, an audit cannot be expected to detect noncompliance with all laws and regulations. Detection of noncompliance, regardless of materiality, requires consideration of the implications for the integrity of management or employees and the possible effect on other aspects of the audit.

3. The term "noncompliance" as used in this ISA refers to acts of omission or commission by the entity being audited, either intentional or unintentional, which are contrary to the prevailing laws or regulations. Such acts, include transactions entered into by, or in the name of, the entity or on its behalf by its management or employees. For the purpose of this ISA, noncompliance does not include personal misconduct (unrelated to the business activities of the entity) by the entity's management or employees.

4. Whether an act constitutes noncompliance is a legal determination that is ordinarily beyond the auditor's professional competence. The auditor's training, experience and understanding of the entity and its industry may provide a basis for recognition that some acts coming to the auditor's attention may constitute noncompliance with laws and regulations. The determination as to whether a particular act constitutes or is likely to constitute noncompliance is generally based on the advice of an informed expert qualified to practice law but ultimately can only be determined by a court of law.

5. Laws and regulations vary considerably in their relation to the financial statements. Some laws or regulations determine the form or content of an entity's financial statements or the amounts to be recorded or disclosures to be made in financial statements. Other laws or regulations are to be complied with by management or set the provisions under which the entity is allowed to conduct its business. Some entities operate in heavily regulated industries (such as banks and chemical companies). Others are only subject to the many laws and regulations that generally relate to the operating aspects of the business (such as those related to occupational safety and health and equal employment). Noncompliance with laws and regulations could result in financial consequences for the entity such as fines, litigation, etc. Generally, the further removed noncompliance is from the events and transactions ordinarily reflected in financial statements, the less likely the auditor is to become aware of it or to recognize its possible noncompliance.

6. Laws and regulations vary from country to country. National accounting and auditing standards are therefore likely to be more specific as to the relevance of laws and regulations to an audit.

AUDITING

7. This ISA applies to audits of financial statements and does not apply to other engagements in which the auditor is specifically engaged to test and report separately on compliance with specific laws or regulations.

8. Guidance on the auditor's responsibility to consider fraud and errors in an audit of financial statements is provided in ISA 240 "Fraud and Error."

Responsibility of Management for the Compliance with Laws and Regulations

9. It is management's responsibility to ensure that the entity's operations are conducted in accordance with laws and regulations. The responsibility for the prevention and detection of noncompliance rests with management.

10. The following policies and procedures, among others, may assist management in discharging its responsibilities for the prevention and detection of noncompliance:

    • Monitoring legal requirements and ensuring that operating procedures are designed to meet these requirements.

    • Instituting and operating appropriate systems of internal control.

    • Developing, publicizing and following a Code of Conduct.

    • Ensuring employees are properly trained and understand the Code of Conduct.

    • Monitoring compliance with the Code of Conduct and acting appropriately to discipline employees who fail to comply with it.

    • Engaging legal advisors to assist in monitoring legal requirements.

    • Maintaining a register of significant laws with which the entity has to comply within its particular industry and a record of complaints.

    In larger entities, these policies and procedures may be supplemented by assigning appropriate responsibilities to:

    • An internal audit function.

    • An audit committee.

The Auditor's Consideration of Compliance with Laws and Regulations

11. The auditor is not, and cannot be held responsible for preventing noncompliance. The fact that an annual audit is carried out may, however, act as a deterrent.

12. An audit is subject to the unavoidable risk that some material misstatements of the financial statements will not be detected, even though the audit is properly planned and performed in accordance with ISAs. This risk is higher with regard to material misstatements resulting from noncompliance with laws and regulations due to factors such as:

    • There are many laws and regulations, relating principally to the operating aspects of the entity, that typically do not have a material effect on the financial statements and are not captured by the accounting and internal control systems.

- The effectiveness of audit procedures is affected by the inherent limitations of the accounting and internal control systems and by the use of testing.

- Much of the evidence obtained by the auditor is persuasive rather than conclusive in nature.

- Noncompliance may involve conduct designed to conceal it, such as collusion, forgery, deliberate failure to record transactions, senior management override of controls or intentional misrepresentations being made to the auditor.

13. **In accordance with ISA 200 "Objective and General Principles Governing an Audit of Financial Statements," the auditor should plan and perform the audit with an attitude of professional skepticism recognizing that the audit may reveal conditions or events that would lead to questioning whether an entity is complying with laws and regulations.**

14. In accordance with specific statutory requirements, the auditor may be specifically required to report as part of the audit of the financial statements whether the entity complies with certain provisions of laws or regulations. In these circumstances, the auditor would plan to test for compliance with these provisions of the laws and regulations.

15. **In order to plan the audit, the auditor should obtain a general understanding of the legal and regulatory framework applicable to the entity and the industry and how the entity is complying with that framework.**

16. In obtaining this general understanding, the auditor would particularly recognize that some laws and regulations may have a fundamental effect on the operations of the entity. That is, noncompliance with certain laws and regulations may cause the entity to cease operations, or call into question the entity's continuance as a going concern. For example, noncompliance with the requirements of the entity's license or other title to perform its operations could have such an impact (for example, for a bank, noncompliance with capital or investment requirements).

17. To obtain the general understanding of laws and regulations, the auditor would ordinarily:

- Use the existing knowledge of the entity's industry and business.

- Inquire of management concerning the entity's policies and procedures regarding compliance with laws and regulations.

- Inquire of management as to the laws or regulations that may be expected to have a fundamental effect on the operations of the entity.

- Discuss with management the policies or procedures adopted for identifying, evaluating and accounting for litigation claims and assessments.

- Discuss the legal and regulatory framework with auditors of subsidiaries in other countries (for example, if the subsidiary is required to adhere to the securities regulations of the parent company).

18. **After obtaining the general understanding, the auditor should perform procedures to help identify instances of noncompliance with those laws and regulations where noncompliance should be considered when preparing financial statements, specifically:**

   - **Inquiring of management as to whether the entity is in compliance with such laws and regulations.**

   - **Inspecting correspondence with the relevant licensing or regulatory authorities.**

19. **Further, the auditor should obtain sufficient appropriate audit evidence about compliance with those laws and regulations generally recognized by the auditor to have an effect on the determination of material amounts and disclosures in financial statements. The auditor should have a sufficient understanding of these laws and regulations in order to consider them when auditing the assertions related to the determination of the amounts to be recorded and the disclosures to be made.**

20. Such laws and regulations would be well established and known to the entity and within the industry; they would be considered on a recurring basis each time financial statements are issued. These laws and regulations, may relate, for example, to the form and content of financial statements, including industry specific requirements; accounting for transactions under government contracts; or the accrual or recognition of expenses for income taxes or pension costs.

21. Other than as described in paragraphs 18, 19 and 20, the auditor does not test or perform other procedures on the entity's compliance with laws and regulations since this would be outside the scope of an audit of financial statements.

22. **The auditor should be alert to the fact that procedures applied for the purpose of forming an opinion on the financial statements may bring instances of possible noncompliance with laws and regulations to the auditor's attention.** For example, such procedures include reading minutes; inquiring of the entity's management and legal counsel concerning litigation, claims and assessments; and performing substantive tests of details of transactions or balances.

23. **The auditor should obtain written representations that management has disclosed to the auditor all known actual or possible noncompliance with laws and regulations whose effects should be considered when preparing financial statements.**

24. In the absence of evidence to the contrary, the auditor is entitled to assume the entity is in compliance with these laws and regulations.

Procedures When Noncompliance is Discovered

25. The Appendix to this ISA sets out examples of the type of information that might come to the auditor's attention that may indicate noncompliance.

26. **When the auditor becomes aware of information concerning a possible instance of noncompliance, the auditor should obtain an understanding of the nature of the act and the circumstances in which it has occurred, and sufficient other information to evaluate the possible effect on the financial statements.**

27. When evaluating the possible effect on the financial statements, the auditor considers:

    • The potential financial consequences, such as fines, penalties, damages, threat of expropriation of assets, enforced discontinuation of operations and litigation.

    • Whether the potential financial consequences require disclosure.

    • Whether the potential financial consequences are so serious as to call into question the true and fair view (fair presentation) given by the financial statements.

28. **When the auditor believes there may be noncompliance, the auditor should document the findings and discuss them with management.** Documentation of findings would include copies of records and documents and making minutes of conversations, if appropriate.

29. If management does not provide satisfactory information that it is in fact in compliance, the auditor would consult with the entity's lawyer about the application of the laws and regulations to the circumstances and the possible effects on the financial statements. When it is not considered appropriate to consult with the entity's lawyer or when the auditor is not satisfied with the opinion, the auditor would consider consulting the auditor's own lawyer as to whether a violation of a law or regulation is involved, the possible legal consequences and what further action, if any, the auditor would take.

30. **When adequate information about the suspected noncompliance cannot be obtained, the auditor should consider the effect of the lack of audit evidence on the auditor's report.**

31. **The auditor should consider the implications of noncompliance in relation to other aspects of the audit, particularly the reliability of management representations.** In this regard, the auditor reconsiders the risk assessment and the validity of management representations, in case of noncompliance not detected by internal controls or not included in management representations. The implications of particular instances of noncompliance discovered by the auditor will depend on the relationship of the perpetration and concealment, if any, of the act to specific control procedures and the level of management or employees involved.

AUDITING

250

Reporting of Noncompliance

To Management

32. **The auditor should, as soon as practicable, either communicate with the audit committee, the board of directors and senior management, or obtain evidence that they are appropriately informed, regarding noncompliance that comes to the auditor's attention.** However, the auditor need not do so for matters that are clearly inconsequential or trivial and may reach agreement in advance on the nature of such matters to be communicated.

33. **If in the auditor's judgment the noncompliance is believed to be intentional and material, the auditor should communicate the finding without delay.**

34. **If the auditor suspects that members of senior management, including members of the board of directors, are involved in noncompliance, the auditor should report the matter to the next higher level of authority at the entity, if it exists, such as an audit committee or a supervisory board.** Where no higher authority exists, or if the auditor believes that the report may not be acted upon or is unsure as to the person to whom to report, the auditor would consider seeking legal advice.

To the Users of the Auditor's Report on the Financial Statements

35. **If the auditor concludes that the noncompliance has a material effect on the financial statements, and has not been properly reflected in the financial statements, the auditor should express a qualified or an adverse opinion.**

36. **If the auditor is precluded by the entity from obtaining sufficient appropriate audit evidence to evaluate whether noncompliance that may be material to the financial statements, has, or is likely to have, occurred, the auditor should express a qualified opinion or a disclaimer of opinion on the financial statements on the basis of a limitation on the scope of the audit.**

37. **If the auditor is unable to determine whether noncompliance has occurred because of limitations imposed by the circumstances rather than by the entity, the auditor should consider the effect on the auditor's report.**

To Regulatory and Enforcement Authorities

38. The auditor's duty of confidentiality would ordinarily preclude reporting noncompliance to a third party. However, in certain circumstances, that duty of confidentiality is overridden by statute, law or by courts of law (for example, in some countries the auditor is required to report noncompliance by financial institutions to the supervisory authorities). The auditor may need to seek legal advice in such circumstances, giving due consideration to the auditor's responsibility to the public interest.

Withdrawal from the Engagement

39. The auditor may conclude that withdrawal from the engagement is necessary when the entity does not take the remedial action that the auditor considers necessary in the circumstances, even when the noncompliance is not material to the financial statements. Factors that would affect the auditor's conclusion include the implications of the involvement of the highest authority within the entity which may affect the reliability of management representations, and the effects on the auditor of continuing association with the entity. In reaching such a conclusion, the auditor would ordinarily seek legal advice.

40. **As stated in the "Code of Ethics for Professional Accountants" issued by the International Federation of Accountants, on receipt of an inquiry from the proposed auditor, the existing auditor should advise whether there are any professional reasons why the proposed auditor should not accept the appointment.** The extent to which an existing auditor can discuss the affairs of a client with a proposed auditor will depend on whether the client's permission to do so has been obtained and/or the legal or ethical requirements that apply in each country relating to such disclosure. If there are any such reasons or other matters which need to be disclosed, the existing auditor would, taking account of the legal and ethical constraints, including where appropriate permission of the client, give details of the information and discuss freely with the proposed auditor all matters relevant to the appointment. **If permission from the client to discuss its affairs with the proposed auditor is denied by the client, that fact should be disclosed to the proposed auditor.**

Public Sector Perspective

1. *Many public sector engagements include additional audit responsibilities with respect to consideration of laws and regulations. Even if the auditor's responsibilities do not extend beyond those of the private sector auditor, reporting responsibilities may be different as the public sector auditor may be obliged to report on instances of noncompliance to governing authorities or to report them in the audit report. In respect to public sector entities, the Public Sector Committee has supplemented the guidance included in this ISA in its Study 3 "Auditing for Compliance with Authorities—A Public Sector Perspective."*

AUDITING

250

Appendix

Indications That Noncompliance May Have Occurred

Examples of the type of information that may come to the auditor's attention that may indicate that noncompliance with laws or regulations has occurred are listed below:

- Investigation by government departments or payment of fines or penalties.

- Payments for unspecified services or loans to consultants, related parties, employees or government employees.

- Sales commissions or agent's fees that appear excessive in relation to those ordinarily paid by the entity or in its industry or to the services actually received.

- Purchasing at prices significantly above or below market price.

- Unusual payments in cash, purchases in the form of cashiers' checks payable to bearer or transfers to numbered bank accounts.

- Unusual transactions with companies registered in tax havens.

- Payments for goods or services made other than to the country from which the goods or services originated.

- Payments without proper exchange control documentation.

- Existence of an accounting system which fails, whether by design or by accident, to provide an adequate audit trail or sufficient evidence.

- Unauthorized transactions or improperly recorded transactions.

- Media comment.

CONTENTS

	Paragraphs
Introduction	1-3
Planning the Work	4-7
The Overall Audit Plan	8-9
The Audit Program	10-11
Changes to the Overall Audit Plan and Audit Program	12

International Standards on Auditing (ISAs) are to be applied in the audit of financial statements. ISAs are also to be applied, adapted as necessary, to the audit of other information and to related services.

ISAs contain the basic principles and essential procedures (identified in bold type black lettering) together with related guidance in the form of explanatory and other material. The basic principles and essential procedures are to be interpreted in the context of the explanatory and other material that provide guidance for their application.

To understand and apply the basic principles and essential procedures together with the related guidance, it is necessary to consider the whole text of the ISA including explanatory and other material contained in the ISA not just that text which is black lettered.

In exceptional circumstances, an auditor may judge it necessary to depart from an ISA in order to more effectively achieve the objective of an audit. When such a situation arises, the auditor should be prepared to justify the departure.

ISAs need only be applied to material matters.

The Public Sector Perspective (PSP) issued by the Public Sector Committee of the International Federation of Accountants is set out at the end of an ISA. Where no PSP is added, the ISA is applicable in all material respects to the public sector.

AUDITING

300

Introduction

1. The purpose of this International Standard on Auditing (ISA) is to establish standards and provide guidance on planning an audit of financial statements. This ISA is framed in the context of recurring audits. In a first audit, the auditor may need to extend the planning process beyond the matters discussed herein.

2. **The auditor should plan the audit work so that the audit will be performed in an effective manner.**

3. "Planning" means developing a general strategy and a detailed approach for the expected nature, timing and extent of the audit. The auditor plans to perform the audit in an efficient and timely manner.

Planning the Work

4. Adequate planning of the audit work helps to ensure that appropriate attention is devoted to important areas of the audit, that potential problems are identified and that the work is completed expeditiously. Planning also assists in proper assignment of work to assistants and in coordination of work done by other auditors and experts.

5. The extent of planning will vary according to the size of the entity, the complexity of the audit and the auditor's experience with the entity and knowledge of the business.

6. Obtaining knowledge of the business is an important part of planning the work. The auditor's knowledge of the business assists in the identification of events, transactions and practices which may have a material effect on the financial statements.

7. The auditor may wish to discuss elements of the overall audit plan and certain audit procedures with the entity's audit committee, management and staff to improve the effectiveness and efficiency of the audit and to coordinate audit procedures with work of the entity's personnel. The overall audit plan and the audit program, however, remain the auditor's responsibility.

The Overall Audit Plan

8. **The auditor should develop and document an overall audit plan describing the expected scope and conduct of the audit.** While the record of the overall audit plan will need to be sufficiently detailed to guide the development of the audit program, its precise form and content will vary depending on the size of the entity, the complexity of the audit and the specific methodology and technology used by the auditor.

9. Matters to be considered by the auditor in developing the overall audit plan include:

Knowledge of the Business

- General economic factors and industry conditions affecting the entity's business.

- Important characteristics of the entity, its business, its financial performance and its reporting requirements including changes since the date of the prior audit.

- The general level of competence of management.

Understanding the Accounting and Internal Control Systems

- The accounting policies adopted by the entity and changes in those policies.

- The effect of new accounting or auditing pronouncements.

- The auditor's cumulative knowledge of the accounting and internal control systems and the relative emphasis expected to be placed on tests of control and substantive procedures.

Risk and Materiality

- The expected assessments of inherent and control risks and the identification of significant audit areas.

- The setting of materiality levels for audit purposes.

- The possibility of material misstatement, including the experience of past periods, or fraud.

- The identification of complex accounting areas including those involving accounting estimates.

Nature, Timing and Extent of Procedures

- Possible change of emphasis on specific audit areas.

- The effect of information technology on the audit.

- The work of internal auditing and its expected effect on external audit procedures.

Coordination, Direction, Supervision and Review

- The involvement of other auditors in the audit of components, for example, subsidiaries, branches and divisions.

- The involvement of experts.

- The number of locations.

- Staffing requirements.

Other Matters

- The possibility that the going concern assumption may be subject to question.

AUDITING

- Conditions requiring special attention, such as the existence of related parties.

- The terms of the engagement and any statutory responsibilities.

- The nature and timing of reports or other communication with the entity that are expected under the engagement.

The Audit Program

10. **The auditor should develop and document an audit program setting out the nature, timing and extent of planned audit procedures required to implement the overall audit plan.** The audit program serves as a set of instructions to assistants involved in the audit and as a means to control and record the proper execution of the work. The audit program may also contain the audit objectives for each area and a time budget in which hours are budgeted for the various audit areas or procedures.

11. In preparing the audit program, the auditor would consider the specific assessments of inherent and control risks and the required level of assurance to be provided by substantive procedures. The auditor would also consider the timing of tests of controls and substantive procedures, the coordination of any assistance expected from the entity, the availability of assistants and the involvement of other auditors or experts. The other matters noted in paragraph 9 may also need to be considered in more detail during the development of the audit program.

Changes to the Overall Audit Plan and Audit Program

12. **The overall audit plan and the audit program should be revised as necessary during the course of the audit.** Planning is continuous throughout the engagement because of changes in conditions or unexpected results of audit procedures. The reasons for significant changes would be recorded.

CONTENTS

	Paragraphs
Introduction	1-3
Obtaining the Knowledge	4-8
Using the Knowledge	9-12
Appendix—Knowledge of the Business—Matters to Consider	

International Standards on Auditing (ISAs) are to be applied in the audit of financial statements. ISAs are also to be applied, adapted as necessary, to the audit of other information and to related services.

ISAs contain the basic principles and essential procedures (identified in bold type black lettering) together with related guidance in the form of explanatory and other material. The basic principles and essential procedures are to be interpreted in the context of the explanatory and other material that provide guidance for their application.

To understand and apply the basic principles and essential procedures together with the related guidance, it is necessary to consider the whole text of the ISA including explanatory and other material contained in the ISA not just that text which is black lettered.

In exceptional circumstances, an auditor may judge it necessary to depart from an ISA in order to more effectively achieve the objective of an audit. When such a situation arises, the auditor should be prepared to justify the departure.

ISAs need only be applied to material matters.

The Public Sector Perspective (PSP) issued by the Public Sector Committee of the International Federation of Accountants is set out at the end of an ISA. Where no PSP is added, the ISA is applicable in all material respects to the public sector.

AUDITING

310

Introduction

1. The purpose of this International Standard on Auditing (ISA) is to establish standards and provide guidance on what is meant by a knowledge of the business, why it is important to the auditor and to members of the audit staff working on an engagement, why it is relevant to all phases of an audit, and how the auditor obtains and uses that knowledge.

2. **In performing an audit of financial statements, the auditor should have or obtain a knowledge of the business sufficient to enable the auditor to identify and understand the events, transactions and practices that, in the auditor's judgment, may have a significant effect on the financial statements or on the examination or audit report.** For example, such knowledge is used by the auditor in assessing inherent and control risks and in determining the nature, timing and extent of audit procedures.

3. The auditor's level of knowledge for an engagement would include a general knowledge of the economy and the industry within which the entity operates, and a more particular knowledge of how the entity operates. The level of knowledge required by the auditor would, however, ordinarily be less than that possessed by management. A list of matters to consider in a specific engagement is set out in the Appendix to this ISA.

Obtaining the Knowledge

4. Prior to accepting an engagement, the auditor would obtain a preliminary knowledge of the industry and of the ownership, management and operations of the entity to be audited, and would consider whether a level of knowledge of the business adequate to perform the audit can be obtained.

5. Following acceptance of the engagement, further and more detailed information would be obtained. To the extent practicable, the auditor would obtain the required knowledge at the start of the engagement. As the audit progresses, that information would be assessed and updated and more information would be obtained.

6. Obtaining the required knowledge of the business is a continuous and cumulative process of gathering and assessing the information and relating the resulting knowledge to audit evidence and information at all stages of the audit. For example, although information is gathered at the planning stage, it is ordinarily refined and added to in later stages of the audit as the auditor and assistants learn more about the business.

7. For continuing engagements, the auditor would update and reevaluate information gathered previously, including information in the prior year's working papers. The auditor would also perform procedures designed to identify significant changes that have taken place since the last audit.

8. The auditor can obtain a knowledge of the industry and the entity from a number of sources. For example:

    • Previous experience with the entity and its industry.

- Discussion with people with the entity (for example, directors and senior operating personnel).

- Discussion with internal audit personnel and review of internal audit reports.

- Discussion with other auditors and with legal and other advisors who have provided services to the entity or within the industry.

- Discussion with knowledgeable people outside the entity (for example, industry economists, industry regulators, customers, suppliers, competitors).

- Publications related to the industry (for example, government statistics, surveys, texts, trade journals, reports prepared by banks and securities dealers, financial newspapers).

- Legislation and regulations that significantly affect the entity.

- Visits to the entity's premises and plant facilities.

- Documents produced by the entity (for example, minutes of meetings, material sent to shareholders or filed with regulatory authorities, promotional literature, prior years' annual and financial reports, budgets, internal management reports, interim financial reports, management policy manual, manuals of accounting and internal control systems, chart of accounts, job descriptions, marketing and sales plans).

Using the Knowledge

9. A knowledge of the business is a frame of reference within which the auditor exercises professional judgment. Understanding the business and using this information appropriately assists the auditor in:

- Assessing risks and identifying problems.

- Planning and performing the audit effectively and efficiently.

- Evaluating audit evidence.

- Providing better service to the client.

10. The auditor makes judgments about many matters throughout the course of the audit where knowledge of the business is important. For example:

- Assessing inherent risk and control risk.

- Considering business risks and management's response thereto.

- Developing the overall audit plan and the audit program.

- Determining a materiality level and assessing whether the materiality level chosen remains appropriate.

- Assessing audit evidence to establish its appropriateness and the validity of the related financial statement assertions.

- Evaluating accounting estimates and management representations.

AUDITING

- Identifying areas where special audit consideration and skills may be necessary.

- Identifying related parties and related party transactions.

- Recognizing conflicting information (for example, contradictory representations).

- Recognizing unusual circumstances (for example, fraud and noncompliance with laws and regulations, unexpected relationships of statistical operating data with reported financial results).

- Making informed inquiries and assessing the reasonableness of answers.

- Considering the appropriateness of accounting policies and financial statement disclosures.

11. **The auditor should ensure that assistants assigned to an audit engagement obtain sufficient knowledge of the business to enable them to carry out the audit work delegated to them.** The auditor would also ensure they understand the need to be alert for additional information and the need to share that information with the auditor and other assistants.

12. **To make effective use of knowledge about the business, the auditor should consider how it affects the financial statements taken as a whole and whether the assertions in the financial statements are consistent with the auditor's knowledge of the business.**

Appendix

Knowledge of the Business—Matters to Consider

This list covers a broad range of matters applicable to many engagements; however, not all matters will be relevant to every engagement and the listing is not necessarily complete.

A. *General economic factors*

- General level of economic activity (for example, recession, growth)
- Interest rates and availability of financing
- Inflation, currency revaluation
- Government policies
  - monetary
  - fiscal
  - taxation—corporate and other
  - financial incentives (for example, government aid programs)
  - tariffs, trade restrictions
- Foreign currency rates and controls

B. *The industry—important conditions affecting the client's business*

- The market and competition
- Cyclical or seasonal activity
- Changes in product technology
- Business risk (for example, high technology, high fashion, ease of entry for competition)
- Declining or expanding operations
- Adverse conditions (for example, declining demand, excess capacity, serious price competition)
- Key ratios and operating statistics
- Specific accounting practices and problems
- Environmental requirements and problems
- Regulatory framework
- Energy supply and cost
- Specific or unique practices (for example, relating to labor contracts, financing methods, accounting methods)

AUDITING

310

C. *The entity*

1. Management and ownership—important characteristics

   - Corporate structure—private, public, government (including any recent or planned changes)

   - Beneficial owners and related parties (local, foreign, business reputation and experience)

   - Capital structure (including any recent or planned changes)

   - Organizational structure

   - Management objectives, philosophy, strategic plans

   - Acquisitions, mergers or disposals of business activities (planned or recently executed)

   - Sources and methods of financing (current, historical)

   - Board of directors

     - composition
     - business reputation and experience of individuals
     - independence from and control over operating management
     - frequency of meetings
     - existence of audit committee and scope of its activities
     - existence of policy on corporate conduct
     - changes in professional advisors (for example, lawyers)

   - Operating Management

     - experience and reputation
     - turnover
     - key financial personnel and their status in the organization
     - staffing of accounting department
     - incentive or bonus plans as part of remuneration (for example, based on profit)
     - use of forecasts and budgets
     - pressures on management (for example, overextended, dominance by one individual, support for share price, unreasonable deadlines for announcing results)
     - management information systems

   - Internal audit function (existence, quality)

   - Attitude to internal control environment

2. The entity's business—products, markets, suppliers, expenses, operations

   - Nature of business(es) (for example, manufacturer, wholesaler, financial services, import/export)

- Location of production facilities, warehouses, offices
- Employment (for example, by location, supply, wage levels, union contracts, pension commitments, government regulation)
- Products or services and markets (for example, major customers and contracts, terms of payment, profit margins, market share, competitors, exports, pricing policies, reputation of products, warranties, order book, trends, marketing strategy and objectives, manufacturing processes)
- Important suppliers of goods and services (for example, long-term contracts, stability of supply, terms of payment, imports, methods of delivery such as "just-in-time")
- Inventories (for example, locations, quantities)
- Franchises, licenses, patents
- Important expense categories
- Research and development
- Foreign currency assets, liabilities and transactions—by currency, hedging
- Legislation and regulation that significantly affect the entity
- Information systems—current, plans to change
- Debt structure, including covenants and restrictions

3. Financial performance—factors concerning the entity's financial condition and profitability

- Key ratios and operating statistics
- Trends

4. Reporting environment—external influences which affect management in the preparation of the financial statements

5. Legislation

- Regulatory environment and requirements
- Taxation
- Measurement and disclosure issues peculiar to the business
- Audit reporting requirements
- Users of the financial statements

AUDITING

CONTENTS

	Paragraphs
Introduction	1-3
Materiality	4-8
The Relationship between Materiality and Audit Risk	9-11
Evaluating the Effect of Misstatements	12-16

International Standards on Auditing (ISAs) are to be applied in the audit of financial statements. ISAs are also to be applied, adapted as necessary, to the audit of other information and to related services.

ISAs contain the basic principles and essential procedures (identified in bold type black lettering) together with related guidance in the form of explanatory and other material. The basic principles and essential procedures are to be interpreted in the context of the explanatory and other material that provide guidance for their application.

To understand and apply the basic principles and essential procedures together with the related guidance, it is necessary to consider the whole text of the ISA including explanatory and other material contained in the ISA not just that text which is black lettered.

In exceptional circumstances, an auditor may judge it necessary to depart from an ISA in order to more effectively achieve the objective of an audit. When such a situation arises, the auditor should be prepared to justify the departure.

ISAs need only be applied to material matters.

The Public Sector Perspective (PSP) issued by the Public Sector Committee of the International Federation of Accountants is set out at the end of an ISA. Where no PSP is added, the ISA is applicable in all material respects to the public sector.

Introduction

1. The purpose of this International Standard on Auditing (ISA) is to establish standards and provide guidance on the concept of materiality and its relationship with audit risk.

2. **The auditor should consider materiality and its relationship with audit risk when conducting an audit.**

3. "Materiality" is defined in the International Accounting Standards Committee's "Framework for the Preparation and Presentation of Financial Statements" in the following terms:

   "Information is material if its omission or misstatement could influence the economic decisions of users taken on the basis of the financial statements. Materiality depends on the size of the item or error judged in the particular circumstances of its omission or misstatement. Thus, materiality provides a threshold or cut-off point rather than being a primary qualitative characteristic which information must have if it is to be useful."

Materiality

4. **The objective of an audit of financial statements is to enable the auditor to express an opinion whether the financial statements are prepared, in all material respects, in accordance with an identified financial reporting framework.** The assessment of what is material is a matter of professional judgment.

5. In designing the audit plan, the auditor establishes an acceptable materiality level so as to detect quantitatively material misstatements. However, both the amount (quantity) and nature (quality) of misstatements need to be considered. Examples of qualitative misstatements would be the inadequate or improper description of an accounting policy when it is likely that a user of the financial statements would be misled by the description, and failure to disclose the breach of regulatory requirements when it is likely that the consequent imposition of regulatory restrictions will significantly impair operating capability.

6. The auditor needs to consider the possibility of misstatements of relatively small amounts that, cumulatively, could have a material effect on the financial statements. For example, an error in a month end procedure could be an indication of a potential material misstatement if that error is repeated each month.

7. The auditor considers materiality at both the overall financial statement level and in relation to individual account balances, classes of transactions and disclosures. Materiality may be influenced by considerations such as legal and regulatory requirements and considerations relating to individual financial statement account balances and relationships. This process may result in different materiality levels depending on the aspect of the financial statements being considered.

AUDITING

8. **Materiality should be considered by the auditor when:**

   (a) **determining the nature, timing and extent of audit procedures; and**

   (b) **evaluating the effect of misstatements.**

The Relationship between Materiality and Audit Risk

9. When planning the audit, the auditor considers what would make the financial statements materially misstated. The auditor's assessment of materiality, related to specific account balances and classes of transactions, helps the auditor decide such questions as what items to examine and whether to use sampling and analytical procedures. This enables the auditor to select audit procedures that, in combination, can be expected to reduce audit risk to an acceptably low level.

10. There is an inverse relationship between materiality and the level of audit risk, that is, the higher the materiality level, the lower the audit risk and vice versa. The auditor takes the inverse relationship between materiality and audit risk into account when determining the nature, timing and extent of audit procedures. For example, if, after planning for specific audit procedures, the auditor determines that the acceptable materiality level is lower, audit risk is increased. The auditor would compensate for this by either:

    (a) reducing the assessed level of control risk, where this is possible, and supporting the reduced level by carrying out extended or additional tests of control; or

    (b) reducing detection risk by modifying the nature, timing and extent of planned substantive procedures.

Materiality and Audit Risk in Evaluating Audit Evidence

11. The auditor's assessment of materiality and audit risk may be different at the time of initially planning the engagement from at the time of evaluating the results of audit procedures. This could be because of a change in circumstances or because of a change in the auditor's knowledge as a result of the audit. For example, if the audit is planned prior to period end, the auditor will anticipate the results of operations and the financial position. If actual results of operations and financial position are substantially different, the assessment of materiality and audit risk may also change. Additionally, the auditor may, in planning the audit work, intentionally set the acceptable materiality level at a lower level than is intended to be used to evaluate the results of the audit. This may be done to reduce the likelihood of undiscovered misstatements and to provide the auditor with a margin of safety when evaluating the effect of misstatements discovered during the audit.

Evaluating the Effect of Misstatements

12. **In evaluating the fair presentation of the financial statements the auditor should assess whether the aggregate of uncorrected misstatements that have been identified during the audit is material.**

13. The aggregate of uncorrected misstatements comprises:

    (a) specific misstatements identified by the auditor including the net effect of uncorrected misstatements identified during the audit of previous periods; and

    (b) the auditor's best estimate of other misstatements which cannot be specifically identified (i.e., projected errors).

14. The auditor needs to consider whether the aggregate of uncorrected misstatements is material. If the auditor concludes that the misstatements may be material, the auditor needs to consider reducing audit risk by extending audit procedures or requesting management to adjust the financial statements. In any event, management may want to adjust the financial statements for the misstatements identified.

15. **If management refuses to adjust the financial statements and the results of extended audit procedures do not enable the auditor to conclude that the aggregate of uncorrected misstatements is not material, the auditor should consider the appropriate modification to the auditor's report in accordance with ISA 700 "The Auditor's Report on Financial Statements."**

16. If the aggregate of the uncorrected misstatements that the auditor has identified approaches the materiality level, the auditor would consider whether it is likely that undetected misstatements, when taken with aggregate uncorrected misstatements could exceed materiality level. Thus, as aggregate uncorrected misstatements approach the materiality level the auditor would consider reducing the risk by performing additional audit procedures or by requesting management to adjust the financial statements for identified misstatements.

Public Sector Perspective

1. *In assessing materiality, the public sector auditor must, in addition to exercising professional judgment, consider any legislation or regulation which may impact that assessment. In the public sector, materiality is also based on the "context and nature" of an item and includes, for example, sensitivity as well as value. Sensitivity covers a variety of matters such as compliance with authorities, legislative concern or public interest.*

AUDITING

320

CONTENTS

	Paragraphs
Introduction	1-10
Inherent Risk	11-12
Accounting and Internal Control Systems	13-20
Control Risk	21-39
Relationship Between the Assessments of Inherent and Control Risks	40
Detection Risk	41-47
Audit Risk in the Small Business	48
Communication of Weaknesses	49
Appendix: Illustration of the Interrelationship of the Components of Audit Risk	

International Standards on Auditing (ISAs) are to be applied in the audit of financial statements. ISAs are also to be applied, adapted as necessary, to the audit of other information and to related services.

ISAs contain the basic principles and essential procedures (identified in bold type black lettering) together with related guidance in the form of explanatory and other material. The basic principles and essential procedures are to be interpreted in the context of the explanatory and other material that provide guidance for their application.

To understand and apply the basic principles and essential procedures together with the related guidance, it is necessary to consider the whole text of the ISA including explanatory and other material contained in the ISA not just that text which is black lettered.

In exceptional circumstances, an auditor may judge it necessary to depart from an ISA in order to more effectively achieve the objective of an audit. When such a situation arises, the auditor should be prepared to justify the departure.

ISAs need only be applied to material matters.

The Public Sector Perspective (PSP) issued by the Public Sector Committee of the International Federation of Accountants is set out at the end of an ISA. Where no PSP is added, the ISA is applicable in all material respects to the public sector.

Introduction

1. The purpose of this International Standard on Auditing (ISA) is to establish standards and provide guidance on obtaining an understanding of the accounting and internal control systems and on audit risk and its components: inherent risk, control risk and detection risk.

2. **The auditor should obtain an understanding of the accounting and internal control systems sufficient to plan the audit and develop an effective audit approach. The auditor should use professional judgment to assess audit risk and to design audit procedures to ensure it is reduced to an acceptably low level.**

3. "Audit risk" means the risk that the auditor gives an inappropriate audit opinion when the financial statements are materially misstated. Audit risk has three components: inherent risk, control risk and detection risk.

4. "Inherent risk" is the susceptibility of an account balance or class of transactions to misstatement that could be material, individually or when aggregated with misstatements in other balances or classes, assuming that there were no related internal controls.

5. "Control risk" is the risk that a misstatement, that could occur in an account balance or class of transactions and that could be material individually or when aggregated with misstatements in other balances or classes, will not be prevented or detected and corrected on a timely basis by the accounting and internal control systems.

6. "Detection risk" is the risk that an auditor's substantive procedures will not detect a misstatement that exists in an account balance or class of transactions that could be material, individually or when aggregated with misstatements in other balances or classes.

7. "Accounting system" means the series of tasks and records of an entity by which transactions are processed as a means of maintaining financial records. Such systems identify, assemble, analyze, calculate, classify, record, summarize and report transactions and other events.

8. "Internal control system" means all the policies and procedures (internal controls) adopted by the management of an entity to assist in achieving management's objective of ensuring, as far as practicable, the orderly and efficient conduct of its business, including adherence to management policies, the safeguarding of assets, the prevention and detection of fraud and error, the accuracy and completeness of the accounting records, and the timely preparation of reliable financial information. The internal control system extends beyond those matters which relate directly to the functions of the accounting system and comprises:

   (a) "the control environment" which means the overall attitude, awareness and actions of directors and management regarding the internal control system and its importance in the entity. The control environment has an effect on the effectiveness of the specific control procedures. A strong control environment, for example, one with tight budgetary controls and

AUDITING

an effective internal audit function, can significantly complement specific control procedures. However, a strong environment does not, by itself, ensure the effectiveness of the internal control system. Factors reflected in the control environment include:

- The function of the board of directors and its committees.

- Management's philosophy and operating style.

- The entity's organizational structure and methods of assigning authority and responsibility.

- Management's control system including the internal audit function, personnel policies and procedures and segregation of duties.

(b) "control procedures" which means those policies and procedures in addition to the control environment which management has established to achieve the entity's specific objectives. Specific control procedures include:

- Reporting, reviewing and approving reconciliations.

- Checking the arithmetical accuracy of the records.

- Controlling applications and environment of computer information systems, for example, by establishing controls over:
  - changes to computer programs
  - access to data files.

- Maintaining and reviewing control accounts and trial balances.

- Approving and controlling of documents.

- Comparing internal data with external sources of information.

- Comparing the results of cash, security and inventory counts with accounting records.

- Limiting direct physical access to assets and records.

- Comparing and analyzing the financial results with budgeted amounts.

9. In the audit of financial statements, the auditor is only concerned with those policies and procedures within the accounting and internal control systems that are relevant to the financial statement assertions. The understanding of relevant aspects of the accounting and internal control systems, together with the inherent and control risk assessments and other considerations, will enable the auditor to:

(a) identify the types of potential material misstatements that could occur in the financial statements;

(b) consider factors that affect the risk of material misstatements; and

(c) design appropriate audit procedures.

10. When developing the audit approach, the auditor considers the preliminary assessment of control risk (in conjunction with the assessment of inherent risk) to determine the appropriate detection risk to accept for the financial statement assertions and to determine the nature, timing and extent of substantive procedures for such assertions.

Inherent Risk

11. **In developing the overall audit plan, the auditor should assess inherent risk at the financial statement level. In developing the audit program, the auditor should relate such assessment to material account balances and classes of transactions at the assertion level, or assume that inherent risk is high for the assertion.**

12. To assess inherent risk, the auditor uses professional judgment to evaluate numerous factors, examples of which are:

At the Financial Statement Level

- The integrity of management.

- Management experience and knowledge and changes in management during the period, for example, the inexperience of management may affect the preparation of the financial statements of the entity.

- Unusual pressures on management, for example, circumstances that might predispose management to misstate the financial statements, such as the industry experiencing a large number of business failures or an entity that lacks sufficient capital to continue operations.

- The nature of the entity's business, for example, the potential for technological obsolescence of its products and services, the complexity of its capital structure, the significance of related parties and the number of locations and geographical spread of its production facilities.

- Factors affecting the industry in which the entity operates, for example, economic and competitive conditions as identified by financial trends and ratios, and changes in technology, consumer demand and accounting practices common to the industry.

At the Account Balance and Class of Transactions Level

- Financial statement accounts likely to be susceptible to misstatement, for example, accounts which required adjustment in the prior period or which involve a high degree of estimation.

- The complexity of underlying transactions and other events which might require using the work of an expert.

- The degree of judgment involved in determining account balances.

- Susceptibility of assets to loss or misappropriation, for example, assets which are highly desirable and movable such as cash.

- The completion of unusual and complex transactions, particularly at or near period end.

AUDITING

129

400

- Transactions not subjected to ordinary processing.

Accounting and Internal Control Systems

13. Internal controls relating to the accounting system are concerned with achieving objectives such as:

   - Transactions are executed in accordance with management's general or specific authorization.

   - All transactions and other events are promptly recorded in the correct amount, in the appropriate accounts and in the proper accounting period so as to permit preparation of financial statements in accordance with an identified financial reporting framework.

   - Access to assets and records is permitted only in accordance with management's authorization.

   - Recorded assets are compared with the existing assets at reasonable intervals and appropriate action is taken regarding any differences.

Inherent Limitations of Internal Controls

14. Accounting and internal control systems cannot provide management with conclusive evidence that objectives are reached because of inherent limitations. Such limitations include:

   - Management's usual requirement that the cost of an internal control does not exceed the expected benefits to be derived.

   - Most internal controls tend to be directed at routine transactions rather than non-routine transactions.

   - The potential for human error due to carelessness, distraction, mistakes of judgment and the misunderstanding of instructions.

   - The possibility of circumvention of internal controls through the collusion of a member of management or an employee with parties outside or inside the entity.

   - The possibility that a person responsible for exercising an internal control could abuse that responsibility, for example, a member of management overriding an internal control.

   - The possibility that procedures may become inadequate due to changes in conditions, and compliance with procedures may deteriorate.

Understanding the Accounting and Internal Control Systems

15. When obtaining an understanding of the accounting and internal control systems to plan the audit, the auditor obtains a knowledge of the design of the accounting and internal control systems, and their operation. For example, an auditor may perform a "walk-through" test, that is, tracing a few transactions through the accounting system. When the transactions selected are typical of those transactions that pass through the system, this procedure

may be treated as part of the tests of control. The nature and extent of walk-through tests performed by the auditor are such that they alone would not provide sufficient appropriate audit evidence to support a control risk assessment which is less than high.

16. The nature, timing and extent of the procedures performed by the auditor to obtain an understanding of the accounting and internal control systems will vary with, among other things:

- The size and complexity of the entity and of its computer system.

- Materiality considerations.

- The type of internal controls involved.

- The nature of the entity's documentation of specific internal controls.

- The auditor's assessment of inherent risk.

17. Ordinarily, the auditor's understanding of the accounting and internal control systems significant to the audit is obtained through previous experience with the entity and is supplemented by:

(a) inquiries of appropriate management, supervisory and other personnel at various organizational levels within the entity, together with reference to documentation, such as procedures manuals, job descriptions and flow charts;

(b) inspection of documents and records produced by the accounting and internal control systems; and

(c) observation of the entity's activities and operations, including observation of the organization of computer operations, management personnel and the nature of transaction processing.

Accounting System

18. **The auditor should obtain an understanding of the accounting system sufficient to identify and understand:**

(a) **major classes of transactions in the entity's operations;**

(b) **how such transactions are initiated;**

(c) **significant accounting records, supporting documents and accounts in the financial statements; and**

(d) **the accounting and financial reporting process, from the initiation of significant transactions and other events to their inclusion in the financial statements.**

Control Environment

19. **The auditor should obtain an understanding of the control environment sufficient to assess directors' and management's attitudes, awareness and actions regarding internal controls and their importance in the entity.**

AUDITING

Control Procedures

20. **The auditor should obtain an understanding of the control procedures sufficient to develop the audit plan.** In obtaining this understanding, the auditor would consider knowledge about the presence or absence of control procedures obtained from the understanding of the control environment and accounting system in determining whether any additional understanding of control procedures is necessary. Because control procedures are integrated with the control environment and the accounting system, as the auditor obtains an understanding of the control environment and the accounting system, some knowledge about control procedures is also likely to be obtained, for example, in obtaining an understanding of the accounting system pertaining to cash, the auditor ordinarily becomes aware of whether bank accounts are reconciled. Ordinarily, development of the overall audit plan does not require an understanding of control procedures for every financial statement assertion in each account balance and transaction class.

Control Risk

Preliminary Assessment of Control Risk

21. The preliminary assessment of control risk is the process of evaluating the effectiveness of an entity's accounting and internal control systems in preventing or detecting and correcting material misstatements. There will always be some control risk because of the inherent limitations of any accounting and internal control system.

22. **After obtaining an understanding of the accounting and internal control systems, the auditor should make a preliminary assessment of control risk, at the assertion level, for each material account balance or class of transactions.**

23. The auditor ordinarily assesses control risk at a high level for some or all assertions when:

     (a)   the entity's accounting and internal control systems are not effective; or

     (b)   evaluating the effectiveness of the entity's accounting and internal control systems would not be efficient.

24. **The preliminary assessment of control risk for a financial statement assertion should be high unless the auditor:**

     (a)   **is able to identify internal controls relevant to the assertion which are likely to prevent or detect and correct a material misstatement; and**

     (b)   **plans to perform tests of control to support the assessment.**

Documentation of Understanding and Assessment of Control Risk

25. **The auditor should document in the audit working papers:**

    (a) **the understanding obtained of the entity's accounting and internal control systems; and**

    (b) **the assessment of control risk.** When control risk is assessed at less than high, the auditor would also document the basis for the conclusions.

26. Different techniques may be used to document information relating to accounting and internal control systems. Selection of a particular technique is a matter for the auditor's judgment. Common techniques, used alone or in combination, are narrative descriptions, questionnaires, check lists and flow charts. The form and extent of this documentation is influenced by the size and complexity of the entity and the nature of the entity's accounting and internal control systems. Generally, the more complex the entity's accounting and internal control systems and the more extensive the auditor's procedures, the more extensive the auditor's documentation will need to be.

Tests of Control

27. Tests of control are performed to obtain audit evidence about the effectiveness of the:

    (a) design of the accounting and internal control systems, that is, whether they are suitably designed to prevent or detect and correct material misstatements; and

    (b) operation of the internal controls throughout the period.

28. Some of the procedures performed to obtain the understanding of the accounting and internal control systems may not have been specifically planned as tests of control but may provide audit evidence about the effectiveness of the design and operation of internal controls relevant to certain assertions and, consequently, serve as tests of control. For example, in obtaining the understanding of the accounting and internal control systems pertaining to cash, the auditor may have obtained audit evidence about the effectiveness of the bank reconciliation process through inquiry and observation.

29. When the auditor concludes that procedures performed to obtain the understanding of the accounting and internal control systems also provide audit evidence about the suitability of design and operating effectiveness of policies and procedures relevant to a particular financial statement assertion, the auditor may use that audit evidence, provided it is sufficient, to support a control risk assessment at less than a high level.

30. Tests of control may include:

    • Inspection of documents supporting transactions and other events to gain audit evidence that internal controls have operated properly, for example, verifying that a transaction has been authorized.

AUDITING

400

- Inquiries about, and observation of, internal controls which leave no audit trail, for example, determining who actually performs each function not merely who is supposed to perform it.

- Reperformance of internal controls, for example, reconciliation of bank accounts, to ensure they were correctly performed by the entity.

31. **The auditor should obtain audit evidence through tests of control to support any assessment of control risk which is less than high. The lower the assessment of control risk, the more support the auditor should obtain that accounting and internal control systems are suitably designed and operating effectively.**

32. When obtaining audit evidence about the effective operation of internal controls, the auditor considers how they were applied, the consistency with which they were applied during the period and by whom they were applied. The concept of effective operation recognizes that some deviations may have occurred. Deviations from prescribed controls may be caused by such factors as changes in key personnel, significant seasonal fluctuations in volume of transactions and human error. When deviations are detected the auditor makes specific inquiries regarding these matters, particularly the timing of staff changes in key internal control functions. The auditor then ensures that the tests of control appropriately cover such a period of change or fluctuation.

33. In a computer information systems environment, the objectives of tests of control do not change from those in a manual environment; however, some audit procedures may change. The auditor may find it necessary, or may prefer, to use computer-assisted audit techniques. The use of such techniques, for example, file interrogation tools or audit test data, may be appropriate when the accounting and internal control systems provide no visible evidence documenting the performance of internal controls which are programmed into a computerized accounting system.

34. **Based on the results of the tests of control, the auditor should evaluate whether the internal controls are designed and operating as contemplated in the preliminary assessment of control risk.** The evaluation of deviations may result in the auditor concluding that the assessed level of control risk needs to be revised. In such cases, the auditor would modify the nature, timing and extent of planned substantive procedures.

Quality and Timeliness of Audit Evidence

35. Certain types of audit evidence obtained by the auditor are more reliable than others. Ordinarily, the auditor's observation provides more reliable audit evidence than merely making inquiries, for example, the auditor might obtain audit evidence about the proper segregation of duties by observing the individual who applies a control procedure or by making inquiries of appropriate personnel. However, audit evidence obtained by some tests of control, such as observation, pertains only to the point in time at which the procedure was applied. The auditor may decide, therefore, to supplement these procedures with other tests of control capable of providing audit evidence about other periods of time.

36. In determining the appropriate audit evidence to support a conclusion about control risk, the auditor may consider the audit evidence obtained in prior audits. In a continuing engagement, the auditor will be aware of the accounting and internal control systems through work carried out previously but will need to update the knowledge gained and consider the need to obtain further audit evidence of any changes in control. **Before relying on procedures performed in prior audits, the auditor should obtain audit evidence which supports this reliance.** The auditor would obtain audit evidence as to the nature, timing and extent of any changes in the entity's accounting and internal control systems since such procedures were performed and assess their impact on the auditor's intended reliance. The longer the time elapsed since the performance of such procedures the less assurance that may result.

37. **The auditor should consider whether the internal controls were in use throughout the period.** If substantially different controls were used at different times during the period, the auditor would consider each separately. A breakdown in internal controls for a specific portion of the period requires separate consideration of the nature, timing and extent of the audit procedures to be applied to the transactions and other events of that period.

38. The auditor may decide to perform some tests of control during an interim visit in advance of the period end. However, the auditor cannot rely on the results of such tests without considering the need to obtain further audit evidence relating to the remainder of the period. Factors to be considered include:

- The results of the interim tests.

- The length of the remaining period.

- Whether any changes have occurred in the accounting and internal control systems during the remaining period.

- The nature and amount of the transactions and other events and the balances involved.

- The control environment, especially supervisory controls.

- The substantive procedures which the auditor plans to carry out.

Final Assessment of Control Risk

39. **Before the conclusion of the audit, based on the results of substantive procedures and other audit evidence obtained by the auditor, the auditor should consider whether the assessment of control risk is confirmed.**

Relationship Between the Assessments of Inherent and Control Risks

40. Management often reacts to inherent risk situations by designing accounting and internal control systems to prevent or detect and correct misstatements and therefore, in many cases, inherent risk and control risk are highly interrelated. In such situations, if the auditor attempts to assess inherent and control risks separately, there is a possibility of inappropriate risk assessment.

135

As a result, audit risk may be more appropriately determined in such situations by making a combined assessment.

Detection Risk

41.   The level of detection risk relates directly to the auditor's substantive procedures. The auditor's control risk assessment, together with the inherent risk assessment, influences the nature, timing and extent of substantive procedures to be performed to reduce detection risk, and therefore audit risk, to an acceptably low level. Some detection risk would always be present even if an auditor were to examine 100 percent of the account balance or class of transactions because, for example, most audit evidence is persuasive rather than conclusive.

42.   **The auditor should consider the assessed levels of inherent and control risks in determining the nature, timing and extent of substantive procedures required to reduce audit risk to an acceptably low level.** In this regard the auditor would consider:

   (a)   the nature of substantive procedures, for example, using tests directed toward independent parties outside the entity rather than tests directed toward parties or documentation within the entity, or using tests of details for a particular audit objective in addition to analytical procedures;

   (b)   the timing of substantive procedures, for example, performing them at period end rather than at an earlier date; and

   (c)   the extent of substantive procedures, for example, using a larger sample size.

43.   There is an inverse relationship between detection risk and the combined level of inherent and control risks. For example, when inherent and control risks are high, acceptable detection risk needs to be low to reduce audit risk to an acceptably low level. On the other hand, when inherent and control risks are low, an auditor can accept a higher detection risk and still reduce audit risk to an acceptably low level. Refer to the Appendix to this ISA for an illustration of the interrelationship of the components of audit risk.

44.   While tests of control and substantive procedures are distinguishable as to their purpose, the results of either type of procedure may contribute to the purpose of the other. Misstatements discovered in conducting substantive procedures may cause the auditor to modify the previous assessment of control risk. Refer to the Appendix to this ISA for an illustration of the interrelationship of the components of audit risk.

45.   The assessed levels of inherent and control risks cannot be sufficiently low to eliminate the need for the auditor to perform any substantive procedures. **Regardless of the assessed levels of inherent and control risks, the auditor should perform some substantive procedures for material account balances and classes of transactions.**

46.   The auditor's assessment of the components of audit risk may change during the course of an audit, for example, information may come to the auditor's

attention when performing substantive procedures that differs significantly from the information on which the auditor originally assessed inherent and control risks. In such cases, the auditor would modify the planned substantive procedures based on a revision of the assessed levels of inherent and control risks.

47. **The higher the assessment of inherent and control risk, the more audit evidence the auditor should obtain from the performance of substantive procedures.** When both inherent and control risks are assessed as high, the auditor needs to consider whether substantive procedures can provide sufficient appropriate audit evidence to reduce detection risk, and therefore audit risk, to an acceptably low level. **When the auditor determines that detection risk regarding a financial statement assertion for a material account balance or class of transactions cannot be reduced to an acceptable level, the auditor should express a qualified opinion or a disclaimer of opinion.**

Audit Risk in the Small Business

48. The auditor needs to obtain the same level of assurance in order to express an unqualified opinion on the financial statements of both small and large entities. However, many internal controls which would be relevant to large entities are not practical in the small business. For example, in small businesses, accounting procedures may be performed by a few persons who may have both operating and custodial responsibilities, and therefore segregation of duties may be missing or severely limited. Inadequate segregation of duties may, in some cases, be offset by a strong management control system in which owner/manager supervisory controls exist because of direct personal knowledge of the entity and involvement in transactions. In circumstances where segregation of duties is limited and audit evidence of supervisory controls is lacking, the audit evidence necessary to support the auditor's opinion on the financial statements may have to be obtained entirely through the performance of substantive procedures.

Communication of Weaknesses

49. As a result of obtaining an understanding of the accounting and internal control systems and tests of control, the auditor may become aware of weaknesses in the systems. **The auditor should make management aware, as soon as practical and at an appropriate level of responsibility, of material weaknesses in the design or operation of the accounting and internal control systems, which have come to the auditor's attention.** The communication to management of material weaknesses would ordinarily be in writing. However, if the auditor judges that oral communication is appropriate, such communication would be documented in the audit working papers. It is important to indicate in the communication that only weaknesses which have come to the auditor's attention as a result of the audit have been reported and that the examination has not been designed to determine the adequacy of internal control for management purposes.

AUDITING

Public Sector Perspective

1. *In respect of paragraph 8 of this ISA, the auditor has to be aware that the "management objectives" of public sector entities may be influenced by concerns regarding public accountability and may include objectives which have their source in legislation, regulations, government ordinances, and ministerial directives. The source and nature of these objectives have to be considered by the auditor in assessing whether the internal control procedures are effective for purposes of the audit.*

2. *Paragraph 9 of this ISA states that, in the audit of financial statements, the auditor is only concerned with those policies and procedures within the accounting and internal control systems that are relevant to the financial statement assertions. Public sector auditors often have additional responsibilities, even in the context of their financial statement audits, with respect to internal controls. Their review of the internal controls may be broader and more detailed than in an audit of financial statements in the private sector.*

3. *Paragraph 49 of this ISA deals with communication of weaknesses. There may be additional reporting requirements for public sector auditors. For example, internal control weaknesses found in the financial statement and other audits may have to be reported to the legislature or other governing body.*

Appendix

Illustration of the Interrelationship of the Components of Audit Risk

The following table shows how the acceptable level of detection risk may vary based on assessments of inherent and control risks.

		Auditor's assessment of control risk is:		
		High	Medium	Low
Auditor's assessment	High	Lowest	Lower	Medium
of inherent risk	Medium	Lower	Medium	Higher
	Low	Medium	Higher	Highest

The shaded areas in this table relate to detection risk.

There is an inverse relationship between detection risk and the combined level of inherent and control risks. For example, when inherent and control risks are high, acceptable levels of detection risk need to be low to reduce audit risk to an acceptably low level. On the other hand, when inherent and control risks are low, an auditor can accept a higher detection risk and still reduce audit risk to an acceptably low level.

AUDITING

CONTENTS

	Paragraphs
Introduction	1-3
Skills and Competence	4
Planning	5-7
Assessment of Risk	8-10
Audit Procedures	11-12

International Standards on Auditing (ISAs) are to be applied in the audit of financial statements. ISAs are also to be applied, adapted as necessary, to the audit of other information and to related services.

ISAs contain the basic principles and essential procedures (identified in bold type black lettering) together with related guidance in the form of explanatory and other material. The basic principles and essential procedures are to be interpreted in the context of the explanatory and other material that provide guidance for their application.

To understand and apply the basic principles and essential procedures together with the related guidance, it is necessary to consider the whole text of the ISA including explanatory and other material contained in the ISA not just that text which is black lettered.

In exceptional circumstances, an auditor may judge it necessary to depart from an ISA in order to more effectively achieve the objective of an audit. When such a situation arises, the auditor should be prepared to justify the departure.

ISAs need only be applied to material matters.

The Public Sector Perspective (PSP) issued by the Public Sector Committee of the International Federation of Accountants is set out at the end of an ISA. Where no PSP is added, the ISA is applicable in all material respects to the public sector.

Introduction

1. The purpose of this International Standard on Auditing (ISA) is to establish standards and provide guidance on procedures to be followed when an audit is conducted in a computer information systems (CIS)[1] environment. For purposes of ISAs, a CIS environment exists when a computer of any type or size is involved in the processing by the entity of financial information of significance to the audit, whether that computer is operated by the entity or by a third party.

2. **The auditor should consider how a CIS environment affects the audit.**

3. The overall objective and scope of an audit does not change in a CIS environment. However, the use of a computer changes the processing, storage and communication of financial information and may affect the accounting and internal control systems employed by the entity. Accordingly, a CIS environment may affect:

    *   The procedures followed by the auditor in obtaining a sufficient understanding of the accounting and internal control systems.

    *   The consideration of inherent risk and control risk through which the auditor arrives at the risk assessment.

    *   The auditor's design and performance of tests of control and substantive procedures appropriate to meet the audit objective.

Skills and Competence

4. **The auditor should have sufficient knowledge of the CIS to plan, direct, supervise and review the work performed. The auditor should consider whether specialized CIS skills are needed in an audit.** These may be needed to:

    *   Obtain a sufficient understanding of the accounting and internal control systems affected by the CIS environment.

    *   Determine the effect of the CIS environment on the assessment of overall risk and of risk at the account balance and class of transactions level.

    *   Design and perform appropriate tests of control and substantive procedures.

    If specialized skills are needed, the auditor would seek the assistance of a professional possessing such skills, who may be either on the auditor's staff or an outside professional. **If the use of such a professional is planned, the auditor should obtain sufficient appropriate audit evidence that such work is adequate for the purposes of the audit, in accordance with ISA 620 "Using the Work of an Expert."**

Planning

5. **In accordance with ISA 400 "Risk Assessments and Internal Control," the auditor should obtain an understanding of the accounting and**

---

[1] This term is used throughout this ISA in place of electronic data processing (EDP) used in prior ISA "Auditing in an EDP Environment."

AUDITING

internal control systems sufficient to plan the audit and develop an effective audit approach.

6. **In planning the portions of the audit which may be affected by the client's CIS environment, the auditor should obtain an understanding of the significance and complexity of the CIS activities and the availability of data for use in the audit.** This understanding would include such matters as:

    - The significance and complexity of computer processing in each significant accounting application. Significance relates to materiality of the financial statement assertions affected by the computer processing. An application may be considered to be complex when, for example:

        - The volume of transactions is such that users would find it difficult to identify and correct errors in processing.

        - The computer automatically generates material transactions or entries directly to another application.

        - The computer performs complicated computations of financial information and/or automatically generates material transactions or entries that cannot be (or are not) validated independently.

        - Transactions are exchanged electronically with other organizations (as in electronic data interchange (EDI) systems) without manual review for propriety or reasonableness.

    - The organizational structure of the client's CIS activities and the extent of concentration or distribution of computer processing throughout the entity, particularly as they may affect segregation of duties.

    - The availability of data. Source documents, certain computer files, and other evidential matter that may be required by the auditor may exist for only a short period or only in machine-readable form. Client CIS may generate internal reporting that may be useful in performing substantive tests (particularly analytical procedures). The potential for use of computer-assisted audit techniques may permit increased efficiency in the performance of audit procedures, or may enable the auditor to economically apply certain procedures to an entire population of accounts or transactions.

7. **When the CIS are significant, the auditor should also obtain an understanding of the CIS environment and whether it may influence the assessment of inherent and control risks.** The nature of the risks and the internal control characteristics in CIS environments include the following:

    - Lack of transaction trails. Some CIS are designed so that a complete transaction trail that is useful for audit purposes might exist for only a short period of time or only in computer readable form. Where a complex application system performs a large number of processing steps, there may not be a complete trail. Accordingly, errors embedded in an application's program logic may be difficult to detect on a timely basis by manual (user) procedures.

- Uniform processing of transactions. Computer processing uniformly processes like transactions with the same processing instructions. Thus, the clerical errors ordinarily associated with manual processing are virtually eliminated. Conversely, programming errors (or other systematic errors in hardware or software) will ordinarily result in all transactions being processed incorrectly.

- Lack of segregation of functions. Many control procedures that would ordinarily be performed by separate individuals in manual systems may be concentrated in CIS. Thus, an individual who has access to computer programs, processing or data may be in a position to perform incompatible functions.

- Potential for errors and irregularities. The potential for human error in the development, maintenance and execution of CIS may be greater than in manual systems, partially because of the level of detail inherent in these activities. Also, the potential for individuals to gain unauthorized access to data or to alter data without visible evidence may be greater in CIS than in manual systems.

  In addition, decreased human involvement in handling transactions processed by CIS can reduce the potential for observing errors and irregularities. Errors or irregularities occurring during the design or modification of application programs or systems software can remain undetected for long periods of time.

- Initiation or execution of transactions. CIS may include the capability to initiate or cause the execution of certain types of transactions, automatically. The authorization of these transactions or procedures may not be documented in the same way as those in a manual system, and management's authorization of these transactions may be implicit in its acceptance of the design of the CIS and subsequent modification.

- Dependence of other controls over computer processing. Computer processing may produce reports and other output that are used in performing manual control procedures. The effectiveness of these manual control procedures can be dependent on the effectiveness of controls over the completeness and accuracy of computer processing. In turn, the effectiveness and consistent operation of transaction processing controls in computer applications is often dependent on the effectiveness of general CIS controls.

- Potential for increased management supervision. CIS can offer management a variety of analytical tools that may be used to review and supervise the operations of the entity. The availability of these additional controls, if used, may serve to enhance the entire internal control structure.

- Potential for the use of computer-assisted audit techniques. The case of processing and analyzing large quantities of data using computers may provide the auditor with opportunities to apply general or specialized computer audit techniques and tools in the execution of audit tests.

Both the risks and the controls introduced as a result of these characteristics of CIS have a potential impact on the auditor's assessment of risk, and the nature, timing and extent of audit procedures.

AUDITING

Assessment of Risk

8. **In accordance with ISA 400 "Risk Assessments and Internal Control," the auditor should make an assessment of inherent and control risks for material financial statement assertions.**

9. The inherent risks and control risks in a CIS environment may have both a pervasive effect and an account-specific effect on the likelihood of material misstatements, as follows:

    -   The risks may result from deficiencies in pervasive CIS activities such as program development and maintenance, systems software support, operations, physical CIS security, and control over access to special-privilege utility programs. These deficiencies would tend to have a pervasive impact on all application systems that are processed on the computer.

    -   The risks may increase the potential for errors or fraudulent activities in specific applications, in specific data bases or master files, or in specific processing activities. For example, errors are not uncommon in systems that perform complex logic or calculations, or that must deal with many different exception conditions. Systems that control cash disbursements or other liquid assets are susceptible to fraudulent actions by users or by CIS personnel.

10. As new CIS technologies emerge, they are frequently employed by clients to build increasingly complex computer systems that may include micro-to-mainframe links, distributed data bases, end-user processing, and business management systems that feed information directly into the accounting systems. Such systems increase the overall sophistication of CIS and the complexity of the specific applications that they affect. As a result, they may increase risk and require further consideration.

Audit Procedures

11. **In accordance with ISA 400 "Risk Assessments and Internal Control," the auditor should consider the CIS environment in designing audit procedures to reduce audit risk to an acceptably low level.**

12. The auditor's specific audit objectives do not change whether accounting data is processed manually or by computer. However, the methods of applying audit procedures to gather evidence may be influenced by the methods of computer processing. The auditor can use either manual audit procedures, computer-assisted audit techniques, or a combination of both to obtain sufficient evidential matter. However, in some accounting systems that use a computer for processing significant applications, it may be difficult or impossible for the auditor to obtain certain data for inspection, inquiry, or confirmation without computer assistance.

CONTENTS

	Paragraphs
Introduction	1-3
Consideration of the Client Auditor	4-10
Service Organization Auditor's Report	11-18

International Standards on Auditing (ISAs) are to be applied in the audit of financial statements. ISAs are also to be applied, adapted as necessary, to the audit of other information and to related services.

ISAs contain the basic principles and essential procedures (identified in bold type black lettering) together with related guidance in the form of explanatory and other material. The basic principles and essential procedures are to be interpreted in the context of the explanatory and other material that provide guidance for their application.

To understand and apply the basic principles and essential procedures together with the related guidance, it is necessary to consider the whole text of the ISA including explanatory and other material contained in the ISA not just that text which is black lettered.

In exceptional circumstances, an auditor may judge it necessary to depart from an ISA in order to more effectively achieve the objective of an audit. When such a situation arises, the auditor should be prepared to justify the departure.

ISAs need only be applied to material matters.

The Public Sector Perspective (PSP) issued by the Public Sector Committee of the International Federation of Accountants is set out at the end of an ISA. Where no PSP is added, the ISA is applicable in all material respects to the public sector.

AUDITING

402

Introduction

1. The purpose of this International Standard on Auditing (ISA) is to establish standards and provide guidance to an auditor whose client uses a service organization. This ISA also describes the service organization auditor's reports which may be obtained by client auditors.

2. **The auditor should consider how a service organization affects the client's accounting and internal control systems so as to plan the audit and develop an effective audit approach.**

3. A client may use a service organization such as one that executes transactions and maintains related accountability or records transactions and processes related data (e.g., a computer systems service organization). If a client uses a service organization, certain policies, procedures and records maintained by the service organization may be relevant to the audit of the financial statements of the client.

Considerations of the Client Auditor

4. A service organization may establish and execute policies and procedures that affect a client organization's accounting and internal control systems. These policies and procedures are physically and operationally separate from the client organization. When the services provided by the service organization are limited to recording and processing client transactions and the client retains authorization and maintenance of accountability, the client may be able to implement effective policies and procedures within its organization. When the service organization executes the client's transactions and maintains accountability, the client may deem it necessary to rely on policies and procedures at the service organization.

5. **The auditor should determine the significance of service organization activities to the client and the relevance to the audit.** In doing so, the client auditor would need to consider the following, as appropriate:

   • Nature of the services provided by the service organization.

   • Terms of contract and relationship between the client and the service organization.

   • The material financial statement assertions that are affected by the use of the service organization.

   • Inherent risk associated with those assertions.

   • Extent to which the client's accounting and internal control systems interact with the systems at the service organization.

   • Client's internal controls that are applied to the transactions processed by the service organization.

   • Service organization's capability and financial strength, including the possible effect of the failure of the service organization on the client.

   • Information about the service organization such as that reflected in user and technical manuals.

- Information available on general controls and computer systems controls relevant to the client's applications.

Consideration of the above may lead the auditor to decide that the control risk assessment will not be affected by controls at the service organization; if so, further consideration of this ISA is unnecessary.

6. The client auditor would also consider the existence of third-party reports from service organization auditors, internal auditors, or regulatory agencies as a means of providing information about the accounting and internal control systems of the service organization and about its operation and effectiveness.

7. **If the client auditor concludes that the activities of the service organization are significant to the entity and relevant to the audit, the auditor should obtain sufficient information to understand the accounting and internal control systems and to assess control risk at either the maximum, or a lower level if tests of control are performed.**

8. If information is insufficient, the client auditor would consider the need to request the service organization to have its auditor perform such procedures as to supply the necessary information, or the need to visit the service organization to obtain the information. A client auditor wishing to visit a service organization may advise the client to request the service organization to give the client auditor access to the necessary information.

9. The client auditor may be able to obtain an understanding of the accounting and internal control systems affected by the service organization by reading the third-party report of the service organization auditor. In addition, when assessing control risk for assertions affected by the systems' controls of the service organization, the client auditor may also use the service organization auditor's report. **If the client auditor uses the report of a service organization auditor, the auditor should consider making inquiries concerning that auditor's professional competence in the context of the specific assignment undertaken by the service organization auditor.**

10. The client auditor may conclude that it would be efficient to obtain audit evidence from tests of control to support an assessment of control risk at a lower level. Such evidence may be obtained by:

- Performing tests of the client's controls over activities of the service organization.

- Obtaining a service organization auditor's report that expresses an opinion as to the operating effectiveness of the service organization's accounting and internal control systems for the processing applications relevant to the audit.

- Visiting the service organization and performing tests of control.

Service Organization Auditor's Reports

11. **When using a service organization auditor's report, the client auditor should consider the nature of and content of that report.**

AUDITING

12. The report of the service organization auditor will ordinarily be one of two types as follows:

Type A—Report on suitability of design

(a) a description of the service organization's accounting and internal control systems, ordinarily prepared by the management of the service organization; and

(b) an opinion by the service organization auditor that:

  (i) the above description is accurate;

  (ii) the systems' controls have been placed in operation; and

  (iii) the accounting and internal control systems are suitably designed to achieve their stated objectives.

Type B—Report on suitability of design and operating effectiveness

(a) a description of the service organization's accounting and internal control systems, ordinarily prepared by the management of the service organization; and

(b) an opinion by the service organization auditor that:

  (i) the above description is accurate;

  (ii) the systems' controls have been placed in operation;

  (iii) the accounting and internal control systems are suitably designed to achieve their stated objectives; and

  (iv) the accounting and internal control systems are operating effectively based on the results from the tests of control. In addition to the opinion on operating effectiveness, the service organization auditor would identify the tests of control performed and related results.

The report of the service organization auditor will ordinarily contain restrictions as to use (generally to management, the service organization and its customers, and client auditors).

13. **The client auditor should consider the scope of work performed by the service organization auditor and should assess the usefulness and appropriateness of reports issued by the service organization auditor.**

14. While Type A reports may be useful to a client auditor in gaining the required understanding of the accounting and internal control systems, an auditor would not use such reports as a basis for reducing the assessment of control risk.

15. In contrast, Type B reports may provide such a basis since tests of control have been performed. When a Type B report is to be used as evidence to support a lower control risk assessment, a client auditor would consider whether the controls tested by the service organization auditor are relevant to the client's transactions (significant assertions in the client's financial statements) and whether the service organization auditor's tests of control

and the results are adequate. With respect to the latter, two key considerations are the length of the period covered by the service organization auditor's tests and the time since the performance of those tests.

16. **For those specific tests of control and results that are relevant, a client auditor should consider whether the nature, timing and extent of such tests provide sufficient appropriate audit evidence about the effectiveness of the accounting and internal control systems to support the client auditor's assessed level of control risk.**

17. The auditor of a service organization may be engaged to perform substantive procedures that are of use to a client auditor. Such engagements may involve the performance of procedures agreed upon by the client and its auditor and by the service organization and its auditor.

18. **When a client auditor uses a report from the auditor of a service organization, no reference should be made in the client auditor's report to the auditor's report on the service organization.**

AUDITING

CONTENTS

	Paragraphs
Introduction	1-6
Sufficient Appropriate Audit Evidence	7-18
Procedures for Obtaining Audit Evidence	19-25

International Standards on Auditing (ISAs) are to be applied in the audit of financial statements. ISAs are also to be applied, adapted as necessary, to the audit of other information and to related services.

ISAs contain the basic principles and essential procedures (identified in bold type black lettering) together with related guidance in the form of explanatory and other material. The basic principles and essential procedures are to be interpreted in the context of the explanatory and other material that provide guidance for their application.

To understand and apply the basic principles and essential procedures together with the related guidance, it is necessary to consider the whole text of the ISA including explanatory and other material contained in the ISA not just that text which is black lettered.

In exceptional circumstances, an auditor may judge it necessary to depart from an ISA in order to more effectively achieve the objective of an audit. When such a situation arises, the auditor should be prepared to justify the departure.

ISAs need only be applied to material matters.

The Public Sector Perspective (PSP) issued by the Public Sector Committee of the International Federation of Accountants is set out at the end of an ISA. Where no PSP is added, the ISA is applicable in all material respects to the public sector.

Introduction

1. The purpose of this International Standard on Auditing (ISA) is to establish standards and provide guidance on the quantity and quality of audit evidence to be obtained when auditing financial statements, and the procedures for obtaining that audit evidence.

2. **The auditor should obtain sufficient appropriate audit evidence to be able to draw reasonable conclusions on which to base the audit opinion.**

3. Audit evidence is obtained from an appropriate mix of tests of control and substantive procedures. In some circumstances, evidence may be obtained entirely from substantive procedures.

4. "Audit evidence" means the information obtained by the auditor in arriving at the conclusions on which the audit opinion is based. Audit evidence will comprise source documents and accounting records underlying the financial statements and corroborating information from other sources.

5. "Tests of control" means tests performed to obtain audit evidence about the suitability of design and effective operation of the accounting and internal control systems.

6. "Substantive procedures" means tests performed to obtain audit evidence to detect material misstatements in the financial statements, and are of two types:

    (a) tests of details of transactions and balances; and
    (b) analytical procedures.

Sufficient Appropriate Audit Evidence

7. Sufficiency and appropriateness are interrelated and apply to audit evidence obtained from both tests of control and substantive procedures. Sufficiency is the measure of the quantity of audit evidence; appropriateness is the measure of the quality of audit evidence and its relevance to a particular assertion and its reliability. Ordinarily, the auditor finds it necessary to rely on audit evidence that is persuasive rather than conclusive and will often seek audit evidence from different sources or of a different nature to support the same assertion.

8. In forming the audit opinion, the auditor does not ordinarily examine all of the information available because conclusions can be reached about an account balance, class of transactions or control by way of using judgmental or statistical sampling procedures.

9. The auditor's judgment as to what is sufficient appropriate audit evidence is influenced by such factors as the:

    • Auditor's assessment of the nature and level of inherent risk at both the financial statement level and the account balance or class of transactions level.

    • Nature of the accounting and internal control systems and the assessment of control risk.

AUDITING

- Materiality of the item being examined.
- Experience gained during previous audits.
- Results of audit procedures, including fraud or error which may have been found.
- Source and reliability of information available.

10. **When obtaining audit evidence from tests of control, the auditor should consider the sufficiency and appropriateness of the audit evidence to support the assessed level of control risk.**

11. The aspects of the accounting and internal control systems about which the auditor would obtain audit evidence are:

   (a) *design*: the accounting and internal control systems are suitably designed to prevent and/or detect and correct material misstatements; and

   (b) *operation*: the systems exist and have operated effectively throughout the relevant period.

12. **When obtaining audit evidence from substantive procedures, the auditor should consider the sufficiency and appropriateness of audit evidence from such procedures together with any evidence from tests of control to support financial statement assertions.**

13. Financial statement assertions are assertions by management, explicit or otherwise, that are embodied in the financial statements. They can be categorized as follows:

   (a) *existence:* an asset or a liability exists at a given date;

   (b) *rights and obligations:* an asset or a liability pertains to the entity at a given date;

   (c) *occurrence:* a transaction or event took place which pertains to the entity during the period;

   (d) *completeness:* there are no unrecorded assets, liabilities, transactions or events, or undisclosed items;

   (e) *valuation:* an asset or liability is recorded at an appropriate carrying value;

   (f) *measurement:* a transaction or event is recorded at the proper amount and revenue or expense is allocated to the proper period; and

   (g) *presentation and disclosure:* an item is disclosed, classified, and described in accordance with the applicable financial reporting framework.

14. Ordinarily, audit evidence is obtained regarding each financial statement assertion. Audit evidence regarding one assertion, for example, existence of inventory, will not compensate for failure to obtain audit evidence regarding another, for example, valuation. The nature, timing and extent of substantive procedures will vary depending on the assertions. Tests can provide audit evidence about more than one assertion, for example, collection of

receivables may provide audit evidence regarding both existence and valuation.

15. The reliability of audit evidence is influenced by its source: internal or external, and by its nature: visual, documentary or oral. While the reliability of audit evidence is dependent on individual circumstance, the following generalizations will help in assessing the reliability of audit evidence:

- Audit evidence from external sources (for example, confirmation received from a third party) is more reliable than that generated internally.

- Audit evidence generated internally is more reliable when the related accounting and internal control systems are effective.

- Audit evidence obtained directly by the auditor is more reliable than that obtained from the entity.

- Audit evidence in the form of documents and written representations is more reliable than oral representations.

16. Audit evidence is more persuasive when items of evidence from different sources or of a different nature are consistent. In these circumstances, the auditor may obtain a cumulative degree of confidence higher than would be obtained from items of audit evidence when considered individually. Conversely, when audit evidence obtained from one source is inconsistent with that obtained from another, the auditor determines what additional procedures are necessary to resolve the inconsistency.

17. The auditor needs to consider the relationship between the cost of obtaining audit evidence and the usefulness of the information obtained. However, the matter of difficulty and expense involved is not in itself a valid basis for omitting a necessary procedure.

18. When in substantial doubt as to a material financial statement assertion, the auditor would attempt to obtain sufficient appropriate audit evidence to remove such doubt. **If unable to obtain sufficient appropriate audit evidence, however, the auditor should express a qualified opinion or a disclaimer of opinion.**

Procedures for Obtaining Audit Evidence

19. The auditor obtains audit evidence by one or more of the following procedures: inspection, observation, inquiry and confirmation, computation and analytical procedures. The timing of such procedures will be dependent, in part, upon the periods of time during which the audit evidence sought is available.

Inspection

20. Inspection consists of examining records, documents, or tangible assets. Inspection of records and documents provides audit evidence of varying degrees of reliability depending on their nature and source and the effectiveness of internal controls over their processing. Three major categories of documentary audit evidence, which provide different degrees of reliability to the auditor, are:

AUDITING

(a)   documentary audit evidence created and held by third parties;

(b)   documentary audit evidence created by third parties and held by the entity; and

(c)   documentary audit evidence created and held by the entity.

Inspection of tangible assets provides reliable audit evidence with respect to their existence but not necessarily as to their ownership or value.

Observation

21.   Observation consists of looking at a process or procedure being performed by others, for example, the observation by the auditor of the counting of inventories by the entity's personnel or the performance of control procedures that leave no audit trail.

Inquiry and Confirmation

22.   Inquiry consists of seeking information of knowledgeable persons inside or outside the entity. Inquiries may range from formal written inquiries addressed to third parties to informal oral inquiries addressed to persons inside the entity. Responses to inquiries may provide the auditor with information not previously possessed or with corroborative audit evidence.

23.   Confirmation consists of the response to an inquiry to corroborate information contained in the accounting records. For example, the auditor ordinarily seeks direct confirmation of receivables by communication with debtors.

Computation

24.   Computation consists of checking the arithmetical accuracy of source documents and accounting records or of performing independent calculations.

Analytical Procedures

25.   Analytical procedures consist of the analysis of significant ratios and trends including the resulting investigation of fluctuations and relationships that are inconsistent with other relevant information or deviate from predicted amounts.

Public Sector Perspective

1.   *When carrying out audits of public sector entities, the auditor will need to take into account the legislative framework and any other relevant regulations, ordinances or ministerial directives which affect the audit mandate and any special auditing requirements. Such requirements might affect, for example, the extent of the auditor's discretion in establishing materiality and judgments on the nature and scope of audit procedures to be applied. Paragraph 9 of this ISA has to be applied only after giving consideration to such restrictions on the auditor's judgment.*

CONTENTS

	Paragraphs
Introduction	1-3
Part A: Attendance at Physical Inventory Counting	4-18
Part B: Confirmation of Accounts Receivable	19-30
Part C: Inquiry Regarding Litigation and Claims	31-37
Part D: Valuation and Disclosure of Long-term Investments	38-41
Part E: Segment Information	42-45

International Standards on Auditing (ISAs) are to be applied in the audit of financial statements. ISAs are also to be applied, adapted as necessary, to the audit of other information and to related services.

ISAs contain the basic principles and essential procedures (identified in bold type black lettering) together with related guidance in the form of explanatory and other material. The basic principles and essential procedures are to be interpreted in the context of the explanatory and other material that provide guidance for their application.

To understand and apply the basic principles and essential procedures together with the related guidance, it is necessary to consider the whole text of the ISA including explanatory and other material contained in the ISA not just that text which is black lettered.

In exceptional circumstances, an auditor may judge it necessary to depart from an ISA in order to more effectively achieve the objective of an audit. When such a situation arises, the auditor should be prepared to justify the departure.

ISAs need only be applied to material matters.

The Public Sector Perspective (PSP) issued by the Public Sector Committee of the International Federation of Accountants is set out at the end of an ISA. Where no PSP is added, the ISA is applicable in all material respects to the public sector.

AUDITING

501

Introduction

1. The purpose of this International Standard on Auditing (ISA) is to establish standards and provide guidance additional to that contained in ISA 500 "Audit Evidence," with respect to certain specific financial statement amounts and other disclosures.

2. Application of the standards and guidance provided in this ISA will assist the auditor in obtaining audit evidence with respect to the specific financial statement amounts and other disclosures addressed.

3. This ISA comprises the following parts:

    Part A: Attendance at Physical Inventory Counting

    Part B: Confirmation of Accounts Receivable

    Part C: Inquiry Regarding Litigation and Claims

    Part D: Valuation and Disclosure of Long-term Investments

    Part E: Segment Information

PART A: Attendance at Physical Inventory Counting

4. Management ordinarily establishes procedures under which inventory is physically counted at least once a year to serve as a basis for the preparation of the financial statements or to ascertain the reliability of the perpetual inventory system.

5. **When inventory is material to the financial statements, the auditor should obtain sufficient appropriate audit evidence regarding its existence and condition by attendance at physical inventory counting unless impracticable.** Such attendance will enable the auditor to inspect the inventory, to observe compliance with the operation of management's procedures for recording and controlling the results of the count and to provide evidence as to the reliability of management's procedures.

6. **If unable to attend the physical inventory count on the date planned due to unforeseen circumstances, the auditor should take or observe some physical counts on an alternative date and, when necessary, perform tests of intervening transactions.**

7. **Where attendance is impracticable, due to factors such as the nature and location of the inventory, the auditor should consider whether alternative procedures provide sufficient appropriate audit evidence of existence and condition to conclude that the auditor need not make reference to a scope limitation.** For example, documentation of the subsequent sale of specific inventory items acquired or purchased prior to the physical inventory count may provide sufficient appropriate audit evidence.

8. In planning attendance at the physical inventory count or the alternative procedures, the auditor would consider:

   - The nature of the accounting and internal control systems used regarding inventory.
   - Inherent, control and detection risks, and materiality related to inventory.
   - Whether adequate procedures are expected to be established and proper instructions issued for physical inventory counting.
   - The timing of the count.
   - The locations at which inventory is held.
   - Whether an expert's assistance is needed.

9. When the quantities are to be determined by a physical inventory count and the auditor attends such a count, or when the entity operates a perpetual system and the auditor attends a count one or more times during the year, the auditor would ordinarily observe count procedures and perform test counts.

10. If the entity uses procedures to estimate the physical quantity, such as estimating a coal pile, the auditor would need to be satisfied regarding the reasonableness of those procedures.

11. When inventory is situated in several locations, the auditor would consider at which locations attendance is appropriate, taking into account the materiality

of the inventory and the assessment of inherent and control risk at different locations.

12. The auditor would review management's instructions regarding:

    (a) the application of control procedures, for example, collection of used stocksheets, accounting for unused stocksheets and count and re-count procedures;

    (b) accurate identification of the stage of completion of work in progress, of slow moving, obsolete or damaged items and of inventory owned by a third party, for example, on consignment; and

    (c) whether appropriate arrangements are made regarding the movement of inventory between areas and the shipping and receipt of inventory before and after the cutoff date.

13. To obtain assurance that management's procedures are adequately implemented, the auditor would observe employees' procedures and perform test counts. When performing counts, the auditor would test both the completeness and the accuracy of the count records by tracing items selected from those records to the physical inventory and items selected from the physical inventory to the count records. The auditor would consider the extent to which copies of such count records need to be retained for subsequent testing and comparison.

14. The auditor would also consider cutoff procedures including details of the movement of inventory just prior to, during and after the count so that the accounting for such movements can be checked at a later date.

15. For practical reasons, the physical inventory count may be conducted at a date other than period end. This will ordinarily be adequate for audit purposes only when control risk is assessed at less than high. The auditor would assess whether, through the performance of appropriate procedures, changes in inventory between the count date and period end are correctly recorded.

16. When the entity operates a perpetual inventory system which is used to determine the period end balance, the auditor would assess whether, through the performance of additional procedures, the reasons for any significant differences between the physical count and the perpetual inventory records are understood and the records are properly adjusted.

17. The auditor would test the final inventory listing to assess whether it accurately reflects actual inventory counts.

18. When inventory is under the custody and control of a third party, the auditor would ordinarily obtain direct confirmation from the third party as to the quantities and condition of inventory held on behalf of the entity. Depending on materiality of this inventory the auditor would also consider:

    • The integrity and independence of the third party.

    • Observing, or arranging for another auditor to observe, the physical inventory count.

- Obtaining another auditor's report on the adequacy of the third party's accounting and internal control systems for ensuring that inventory is correctly counted and adequately safeguarded.

- Inspecting documentation regarding inventory held by third parties, for example, warehouse receipts, or obtaining confirmation from other parties when such inventory has been pledged as collateral.

PART B: Confirmation of Accounts Receivable

19. **When the accounts receivable are material to the financial statements and when it is reasonable to expect debtors will respond, the auditor should ordinarily plan to obtain direct confirmation of accounts receivable or individual entries in an account balance.**

20. Direct confirmation provides reliable audit evidence as to the existence of debtors and the accuracy of their recorded account balances. However, it does not ordinarily provide evidence as to the collectibility of balances or as to the existence of unrecorded receivable balances.

21. **When it is expected that debtors will not respond, the auditor should plan to perform alternative procedures.** An example of such alternative procedures would be examining subsequent cash receipts related to the specific account balance or individual entries at period end.

22. The accounts to be confirmed are selected to enable the auditor to reach an appropriate conclusion as to existence and accuracy of the accounts receivable as a whole, taking into account identified audit risks and other planned procedures.

23. Letters requesting confirmation are sent by the auditor, and debtors are requested to reply direct to the auditor. Such letters contain management's authorization to the debtor to disclose the necessary information to the auditor.

24. The request for confirmation of balances may take a positive form, in which the debtor is asked to confirm agreement or to express disagreement with the recorded balance, or a negative form, in which a reply is requested only in the event of disagreement with the recorded balance.

25. Positive confirmations provide more reliable evidence than negative confirmations. The choice between positive and negative forms will depend upon the circumstances, including the assessment of both inherent and control risks. The positive form is preferred when inherent or control risk is assessed at high since with the negative form, no reply may be due to causes other than agreement with the recorded balance.

26. A combination of positive and negative forms may be used. For example, where the total accounts receivable balance consists of a small number of large balances and a large number of small balances, the auditor may decide that it is appropriate to confirm all or a sample of the large balances with positive confirmation requests and a sample of the small balances using negative confirmation requests.

AUDITING

501

27. When the positive form is used, the auditor would ordinarily send a reminder to those debtors who do not reply within a reasonable time. Replies may contain exceptions which will need to be fully investigated.

28. **If a reply to a positive confirmation is not received, alternative procedures should be applied or the item treated as an error.** An example of such alternative procedure is the examination of subsequent cash receipts or examining sales and dispatch documents. Items for which a reply has not been received and for which alternative procedures have not been performed, would be treated as errors for the purpose of evaluating the audit evidence provided by the audit sample.

29. For practical reasons, when control risk is assessed at less than high, the auditor may decide to confirm accounts receivable balances at a date other than period end, for example, when the audit is to be completed within a short time after the balance sheet date. In such cases, the auditor would review and test intervening transactions as deemed necessary.

30. **When management requests the auditor not to confirm certain accounts receivable balances, the auditor should consider whether there are valid grounds for such a request.** For example, if the particular account is in dispute with the debtor and communication on behalf of the auditor may aggravate sensitive negotiations between the entity and the debtor. **Before accepting a refusal as justified, the auditor should examine any available evidence to support management's explanations. In such cases, the auditor should apply alternative procedures to the accounts receivable not subjected to confirmation.**

PART C: Inquiry Regarding Litigation and Claims

31. Litigation and claims involving an entity may have a material effect on the financial statements and thus may be required to be disclosed and/or provided for in the financial statements.

32. **The auditor should carry out procedures in order to become aware of any litigation and claims involving the entity which may have a material effect on the financial statements.** Such procedures would include:

   - Make appropriate inquiries of management including obtaining representations.
   - Review board minutes and correspondence with the entity's lawyers.
   - Examine legal expense accounts.
   - Use any information obtained regarding the entity's business including information obtained from discussions with any in-house legal department.

33. **When litigation or claims have been identified or when the auditor believes they may exist, the auditor should seek direct communication with the entity's lawyers.** Such communication will assist in obtaining sufficient appropriate audit evidence as to whether potentially material litigation and claims are known and management's estimates of the financial implications, including costs, are reliable.

34. **The letter, which should be prepared by management and sent by the auditor, should request the lawyer to communicate directly with the auditor.** When it is considered unlikely that the lawyer will respond to a general inquiry, the letter would ordinarily specify:

   - A list of litigation and claims.

   - Management's assessment of the outcome of the litigation or claim and its estimate of the financial implications, including costs involved.

   - A request that the lawyer confirm the reasonableness of management's assessments and provide the auditor with further information if the list is considered by the lawyer to be incomplete or incorrect.

35. The auditor considers the status of legal matters up to the date of the audit report. In some instances, the auditor may need to obtain updated information from lawyers.

36. In certain circumstances, for example, where the matter is complex or there is disagreement between management and the lawyer, it may be necessary for the auditor to meet with the lawyer to discuss the likely outcome of litigation and claims. Such meetings would take place with management's permission and, preferably, with a representative of management in attendance.

37. **If management refuses to give the auditor permission to communicate with the entity's lawyers, this would be a scope limitation and should ordinarily lead to a qualified opinion or a disclaimer of opinion.** Where a lawyer refuses to respond in an appropriate manner and the auditor is unable to obtain sufficient appropriate audit evidence by applying alternative procedures, the auditor would consider whether there is a scope limitation which may lead to a qualified opinion or a disclaimer of opinion.

PART D: Valuation and Disclosure of Long-term Investments

38. **When long-term investments are material to the financial statements, the auditor should obtain sufficient appropriate audit evidence regarding their valuation and disclosure.**

39. Audit procedures regarding long-term investments ordinarily include considering evidence as to whether the entity has the ability to continue to hold the investments on a long term basis and discussing with management whether the entity will continue to hold the investments as long-term investments and obtaining written representations to that effect.

40. Other procedures would ordinarily include considering related financial statements and other information, such as market quotations, which provide an indication of value and comparing such values to the carrying amount of the investments up to the date of the auditor's report.

41. If such values do not exceed the carrying amounts, the auditor would consider whether a write-down is required. If there is an uncertainty as to whether the carrying amount will be recovered, the auditor would consider whether appropriate adjustments and/or disclosures have been made.

AUDITING

PART E: Segment Information

42. **When segment information is material to the financial statements, the auditor should obtain sufficient appropriate audit evidence regarding its disclosure in accordance with the identified financial reporting framework.**

43. The auditor considers segment information in relation to the financial statements taken as a whole, and is not ordinarily required to apply auditing procedures that would be necessary to express an opinion on the segment information standing alone. However, the concept of materiality encompasses both quantitative and qualitative factors and the auditor's procedures recognize this.

44. Audit procedures regarding segment information ordinarily consist of analytical procedures and other audit tests appropriate in the circumstances.

45. The auditor would discuss with management the methods used in determining segment information, and consider whether such methods are likely to result in disclosure in accordance with the applicable financial reporting framework and test the application of such methods. The auditor would consider sales, transfers and charges between segments, elimination of inter-segment amounts, comparisons with budgets and other expected results, for example, operating profits as a percentage of sales, and the allocation of assets and costs among segments including consistency with prior periods and the adequacy of the disclosures with respect to inconsistencies.

CONTENTS

	Paragraphs
Introduction	1-3
Audit Procedures	4-10
Audit Conclusions and Reporting	11-14

International Standards on Auditing (ISAs) are to be applied in the audit of financial statements. ISAs are also to be applied, adapted as necessary, to the audit of other information and to related services.

ISAs contain the basic principles and essential procedures (identified in bold type black lettering) together with related guidance in the form of explanatory and other material. The basic principles and essential procedures are to be interpreted in the context of the explanatory and other material that provide guidance for their application.

To understand and apply the basic principles and essential procedures together with the related guidance, it is necessary to consider the whole text of the ISA including explanatory and other material contained in the ISA not just that text which is black lettered.

In exceptional circumstances, an auditor may judge it necessary to depart from an ISA in order to more effectively achieve the objective of an audit. When such a situation arises, the auditor should be prepared to justify the departure.

ISAs need only be applied to material matters.

The Public Sector Perspective (PSP) issued by the Public Sector Committee of the International Federation of Accountants is set out at the end of an ISA. Where no PSP is added, the ISA is applicable in all material respects to the public sector.

AUDITING

Introduction

1. The purpose of this International Standard on Auditing (ISA) is to establish standards and provide guidance regarding opening balances when the financial statements are audited for the first time or when the financial statements for the prior period were audited by another auditor. This ISA would also be considered so the auditor may become aware of contingencies and commitments existing at the beginning of the period. Guidance on the audit and reporting requirements regarding comparatives is provided in ISA 710 "Comparatives."

2. **For initial audit engagements, the auditor should obtain sufficient appropriate audit evidence that:**

   (a) **the opening balances do not contain misstatements that materially affect the current period's financial statements;**

   (b) **the prior period's closing balances have been correctly brought forward to the current period or, when appropriate, have been restated; and**

   (c) **appropriate accounting policies are consistently applied or changes in accounting policies have been properly accounted for and adequately disclosed.**

3. "Opening balances" means those account balances which exist at the beginning of the period. Opening balances are based upon the closing balances of the prior period and reflect the effects of:

   (a) transactions of prior periods; and

   (b) accounting policies applied in the prior period.

   In an initial audit engagement, the auditor will not have previously obtained audit evidence supporting such opening balances.

Audit Procedures

4. The sufficiency and appropriateness of the audit evidence the auditor will need to obtain regarding opening balances depends on such matters as:

   - The accounting policies followed by the entity.
   - Whether the prior period's financial statements were audited, and if so whether the auditor's report was modified.
   - The nature of the accounts and the risk of misstatement in the current period's financial statements.
   - The materiality of the opening balances relative to the current period's financial statements.

5. The auditor will need to consider whether opening balances reflect the application of appropriate accounting policies and that those policies are consistently applied in the current period's financial statements. When there are any changes in the accounting policies or application thereof, the auditor

would consider whether they are appropriate and properly accounted for and adequately disclosed.

6. When the prior period's financial statements were audited by another auditor, the current auditor may be able to obtain sufficient appropriate audit evidence regarding opening balances by reviewing the predecessor auditor's working papers. In these circumstances, the current auditor would also consider the professional competence and independence of the predecessor auditor. If the prior period's auditor's report was modified, the auditor would pay particular attention in the current period to the matter which resulted in the modification.

7. Prior to communicating with the predecessor auditor, the current auditor will need to consider the Code of Ethics for Professional Accountants issued by the International Federation of Accountants.

8. When the prior period's financial statements were not audited or when the auditor is not able to be satisfied by using the procedures described in paragraph 6, the auditor will need to perform other procedures such as those discussed in paragraphs 9 and 10.

9. For current assets and liabilities some audit evidence can ordinarily be obtained as part of the current period's audit procedures. For example, the collection (payment) of opening accounts receivable (accounts payable) during the current period will provide some audit evidence of their existence, rights and obligations, completeness and valuation at the beginning of the period. In the case of inventories, however, it is more difficult for the auditor to be satisfied as to inventory on hand at the beginning of the period. Therefore, additional procedures are ordinarily necessary such as observing a current physical inventory taking and reconciling it back to the opening inventory quantities, testing the valuation of the opening inventory items, and testing gross profit and cutoff. A combination of these procedures may provide sufficient appropriate audit evidence.

10. For noncurrent assets and liabilities, such as fixed assets, investments and long-term debt, the auditor will ordinarily examine the records underlying the opening balances. In certain cases, the auditor may be able to obtain confirmation of opening balances with third parties, for example, for long-term debt and investments. In other cases, the auditor may need to carry out additional audit procedures.

Audit Conclusions and Reporting

11. **If, after performing procedures including those set out above, the auditor is unable to obtain sufficient appropriate audit evidence concerning opening balances, the auditor's report should include:**

    (a) **a qualified opinion,** for example:

    > "We did not observe the counting of the physical inventory stated at XXX as at December 31, 19X1, since that date was prior to our appointment as auditors. We were unable to satisfy ourselves as to the inventory quantities at that date by other audit procedures.

AUDITING

In our opinion, except for the effects of such adjustments, if any, as might have been determined to be necessary had we been able to observe the counting of physical inventory and satisfy ourselves as to the opening balance of inventory, the financial statements give a true and fair view of (or 'present fairly, in all material respects,') the financial position of ... as at December 31, 19X2 and the results of its operations and its cash flows for the year then ended in accordance with ...";

(b) **a disclaimer of opinion; or**

(c) **in those jurisdictions where it is permitted, an opinion which is qualified or disclaimed regarding the results of operations and unqualified regarding financial position,** for example:

"We did not observe the counting of the physical inventory stated at XXX as at December 31, 19X1, since that date was prior to our appointment as auditors. We were unable to satisfy ourselves as to the inventory quantities at that date by other audit procedures.

Because of the significance of the above matter in relation to the results of the Company's operations for the year to December 31, 19X2, we are not in a position to, and do not, express an opinion on the results of its operations and its cash flows for the year then ended.

In our opinion, the balance sheet gives a true and fair view of (or 'presents fairly in all material respects,') the financial position of the Company as at December 31, 19X2, in accordance with ...".

12. If the opening balances contain misstatements which could materially affect the current period's financial statements, the auditor would inform management and, after having obtained management's authorization, the predecessor auditor, if any. **If the effect of the misstatement is not properly accounted for and adequately disclosed, the auditor should express a qualified opinion or an adverse opinion, as appropriate.**

13. **If the current period's accounting policies have not been consistently applied in relation to opening balances and if the change has not been properly accounted for and adequately disclosed, the auditor should express a qualified opinion or an adverse opinion as appropriate.**

14. If the entity's prior period auditor's report was modified, the auditor would consider the effect thereof on the current period's financial statements. For example, if there was a scope limitation, such as one due to the inability to determine opening inventory in the prior period, the auditor may not need to qualify or disclaim the current period's audit opinion. **However, if a modification regarding the prior period's financial statements remains relevant and material to the current period's financial statements, the auditor should modify the current auditor's report accordingly.**

CONTENTS

	Paragraphs
Introduction	1-3
Nature and Purpose of Analytical Procedures	4-7
Analytical Procedures in Planning the Audit	8-9
Analytical Procedures as Substantive Procedures	10-12
Analytical Procedures in the Overall Review at the End of the Audit	13
Extent of Reliance on Analytical Procedures	14-16
Investigating Unusual Items	17-18

International Standards on Auditing (ISAs) are to be applied in the audit of financial statements. ISAs are also to be applied, adapted as necessary, to the audit of other information and to related services.

ISAs contain the basic principles and essential procedures (identified in bold type black lettering) together with related guidance in the form of explanatory and other material. The basic principles and essential procedures are to be interpreted in the context of the explanatory and other material that provide guidance for their application.

To understand and apply the basic principles and essential procedures together with the related guidance, it is necessary to consider the whole text of the ISA including explanatory and other material contained in the ISA not just that text which is black lettered.

In exceptional circumstances, an auditor may judge it necessary to depart from an ISA in order to more effectively achieve the objective of an audit. When such a situation arises, the auditor should be prepared to justify the departure.

ISAs need only be applied to material matters.

The Public Sector Perspective (PSP) issued by the Public Sector Committee of the International Federation of Accountants is set out at the end of an ISA. Where no PSP is added, the ISA is applicable in all material respects to the public sector.

520

Introduction

1. The purpose of this International Standard on Auditing (ISA) is to establish standards and provide guidance on the application of analytical procedures during an audit.

2. **The auditor should apply analytical procedures at the planning and overall review stages of the audit.** Analytical procedures may also be applied at other stages.

3. "Analytical procedures" means the analysis of significant ratios and trends including the resulting investigation of fluctuations and relationships that are inconsistent with other relevant information or deviate from predicted amounts.

Nature and Purpose of Analytical Procedures

4. Analytical procedures include the consideration of comparisons of the entity's financial information with, for example:

    • Comparable information for prior periods.

    • Anticipated results of the entity, such as budgets or forecasts, or expectations of the auditor, such as an estimation of depreciation.

    • Similar industry information, such as a comparison of the entity's ratio of sales to accounts receivable with industry averages or with other entities of comparable size in the same industry.

5. Analytical procedures also include consideration of relationships:

    • Among elements of financial information that would be expected to conform to a predictable pattern based on the entity's experience, such as gross margin percentages.

    • Between financial information and relevant non-financial information, such as payroll costs to number of employees.

6. Various methods may be used in performing the above procedures. These range from simple comparisons to complex analyses using advanced statistical techniques. Analytical procedures may be applied to consolidated financial statements, financial statements of components (such as subsidiaries, divisions or segments) and individual elements of financial information. The auditor's choice of procedures, methods and level of application is a matter of professional judgment.

7. Analytical procedures are used for the following purposes:

    (a) to assist the auditor in planning the nature, timing and extent of other audit procedures;

    (b) as substantive procedures when their use can be more effective or efficient than tests of details in reducing detection risk for specific financial statement assertions; and

    (c) as an overall review of the financial statements in the final review stage of the audit.

Analytical Procedures in Planning the Audit

8. **The auditor should apply analytical procedures at the planning stage to assist in understanding the business and in identifying areas of potential risk.** Application of analytical procedures may indicate aspects of the business of which the auditor was unaware and will assist in determining the nature, timing and extent of other audit procedures.

9. Analytical procedures in planning the audit use both financial and non-financial information, for example, the relationship between sales and square footage of selling space or volume of goods sold.

Analytical Procedures as Substantive Procedures

10. The auditor's reliance on substantive procedures to reduce detection risk relating to specific financial statement assertions may be derived from tests of details, from analytical procedures, or from a combination of both. The decision about which procedures to use to achieve a particular audit objective is based on the auditor's judgment about the expected effectiveness and efficiency of the available procedures in reducing detection risk for specific financial statement assertions.

11. The auditor will ordinarily inquire of management as to the availability and reliability of information needed to apply analytical procedures and the results of any such procedures performed by the entity. It may be efficient to use analytical data prepared by the entity, provided the auditor is satisfied that such data is properly prepared.

12. When intending to perform analytical procedures as substantive procedures, the auditor will need to consider a number of factors such as the:

   - Objectives of the analytical procedures and the extent to which their results can be relied upon (paragraphs 14 - 16).

   - Nature of the entity and the degree to which information can be disaggregated, for example, analytical procedures may be more effective when applied to financial information on individual sections of an operation or to financial statements of components of a diversified entity, than when applied to the financial statements of the entity as a whole.

   - Availability of information, both financial, such as budgets or forecasts, and nonfinancial, such as the number of units produced or sold.

   - Reliability of the information available, for example, whether budgets are prepared with sufficient care.

   - Relevance of the information available for example, whether budgets have been established as results to be expected rather than as goals to be achieved.

   - Source of the information available, for example, sources independent of the entity are ordinarily more reliable than internal sources.

   - Comparability of the information available, for example, broad industry data may need to be supplemented to be comparable to that of an entity that produces and sells specialized products.

AUDITING

- Knowledge gained during previous audits, together with the auditor's understanding of the effectiveness of the accounting and internal control systems and the types of problems that in prior periods have given rise to accounting adjustments.

Analytical Procedures in the Overall Review at the End of the Audit

13. **The auditor should apply analytical procedures at or near the end of the audit when forming an overall conclusion as to whether the financial statements as a whole are consistent with the auditor's knowledge of the business.** The conclusions drawn from the results of such procedures are intended to corroborate conclusions formed during the audit of individual components or elements of the financial statements and assist in arriving at the overall conclusion as to the reasonableness of the financial statements. However, they may also identify areas requiring further procedures.

Extent of Reliance on Analytical Procedures

14. The application of analytical procedures is based on the expectation that relationships among data exist and continue in the absence of known conditions to the contrary. The presence of these relationships provides audit evidence as to the completeness, accuracy and validity of the data produced by the accounting system. However, reliance on the results of analytical procedures will depend on the auditor's assessment of the risk that the analytical procedures may identify relationships as expected when, in fact, a material misstatement exists.

15. The extent of reliance that the auditor places on the results of analytical procedures depends on the following factors:

    (a) materiality of the items involved, for example, when inventory balances are material, the auditor does not rely only on analytical procedures in forming conclusions. However, the auditor may rely solely on analytical procedures for certain income and expense items when they are not individually material;

    (b) other audit procedures directed toward the same audit objectives for example, other procedures performed by the auditor in reviewing the collectibility of accounts receivable, such as the review of subsequent cash receipts, might confirm or dispel questions raised from the application of analytical procedures to an aging of customers' accounts;

    (c) accuracy with which the expected results of analytical procedures can be predicted. For example, the auditor will ordinarily expect greater consistency in comparing gross profit margins from one period to another than in comparing discretionary expenses, such as research or advertising; and

    (d) assessments of inherent and control risks, for example, if internal control over sales order processing is weak and therefore control risk is high, more reliance on tests of details of transactions and balances than on analytical procedures in drawing conclusions on receivables may be required.

16. The auditor will need to consider testing the controls, if any, over the preparation of information used in applying analytical procedures. When such controls are effective, the auditor will have greater confidence in the reliability of the information and, therefore, in the results of analytical procedures. The controls over non-financial information can often be tested in conjunction with tests of accounting-related controls. For example, an entity in establishing controls over the processing of sales invoices may include controls over the recording of unit sales. In these circumstances, the auditor could test the controls over the recording of unit sales in conjunction with tests of the controls over the processing of sales invoices.

Investigating Unusual Items

17. **When analytical procedures identify significant fluctuations or relationships that are inconsistent with other relevant information or that deviate from predicted amounts, the auditor should investigate and obtain adequate explanations and appropriate corroborative evidence.**

18. The investigation of unusual fluctuations and relationships ordinarily begins with inquiries of management, followed by:

   (a) corroboration of management's responses, for example, by comparing them with the auditor's knowledge of the business and other evidence obtained during the course of the audit; and

   (b) consideration of the need to apply other audit procedures based on the results of such inquiries, if management is unable to provide an explanation or if the explanation is not considered adequate.

Public Sector Perspective

1. *The relationships between individual financial statement items traditionally considered in the audit of business entities may not always be appropriate in the audit of governments or other non-business public sector entities; for example, in many such public sector entities there is often little direct relationship between revenues and expenditures. In addition, because expenditure on the acquisition of assets is frequently noncapitalized, there may be no relationship between expenditures on, for example, inventories and fixed assets and the amount of those assets reported in the financial statements. In addition, in the public sector, industry data or statistics for comparative purposes may not be available. However, other relationships may be relevant, for example, variations in the cost per kilometer of road construction or the number of vehicles acquired compared with vehicles retired. Where appropriate, reference has to be made to available private sector industry data and statistics. In certain instances, it may also be appropriate for the auditor to generate an in-house database of reference information.*

AUDITING

CONTENTS

	Paragraphs
Introduction	1–2
Definitions	3–12
Audit Evidence	13
Tests of Control	14–16
Substantive Procedures	17
Risk Considerations in Obtaining Evidence	18–20
Procedures for Obtaining Evidence	21
Selecting Items for Testing to Gather Audit Evidence	22–23
Selecting All Items	24
Selecting Specific Items	25–26
Audit Sampling	27
Statistical versus Non-statistical Sampling Approaches	28–30
Design of the Sample	31–34
Population	35
Stratification	36–38
Value weighted selection	39
Sample Size	40–41
Selecting the Sample	42–43
Performing the Audit Procedure	44–46
Nature and Cause of Errors	47–50
Projecting Errors	51–53
Evaluating the Sample Results	54–56

Appendix 1: Examples of Factors Influencing Sample Size for Tests of Control

Appendix 2: Examples of Factors Influencing Sample Size for Substantive Procedures

Appendix 3: Sample Selection Methods

International Standards on Auditing (ISAs) are to be applied in the audit of financial statements. ISAs are also to be applied, adapted as necessary, to the audit of other information and to related services.

ISAs contain the basic principles and essential procedures (identified in bold type black lettering) together with related guidance in the form of explanatory and other material. The basic principles and essential procedures are to be interpreted in the context of the explanatory and other material that provide guidance for their application.

To understand and apply the basic principles and essential procedures together with the related guidance, it is necessary to consider the whole text of the ISA including explanatory and other material contained in the ISA not just that text which is black lettered.

In exceptional circumstances, an auditor may judge it necessary to depart from an ISA in order to more effectively achieve the objective of an audit. When such a situation arises, the auditor should be prepared to justify the departure.

ISAs need only be applied to material matters.

The Public Sector Perspective (PSP) issued by the Public Sector Committee of the International Federation of Accountants is set out at the end of an ISA. Where no PSP is added, the ISA is applicable in all material respects to the public sector.

AUDITING

Introduction

i. The purpose of this International Standard on Auditing (ISA) is to establish standards and provide guidance on the use of audit sampling procedures and other means of selecting items for testing to gather audit evidence.

2. **When designing audit procedures, the auditor should determine appropriate means for selecting items for testing so as to gather audit evidence to meet the objectives of audit tests.**

Definitions

3. "Audit sampling" (sampling) involves the application of audit procedures to less than 100% of items within an account balance or class of transactions such that all sampling units have a chance of selection. This will enable the auditor to obtain and evaluate audit evidence about some characteristic of the items selected in order to form or assist in forming a conclusion concerning the population from which the sample is drawn. Audit sampling can use either a statistical or a non-statistical approach.

4. For purposes of this ISA, "error" means either control deviations, when performing tests of control, or misstatements, when performing substantive procedures. Similarly, total error is used to mean either the rate of deviation or total misstatement.

5. "Anomalous error" means an error that arises from an isolated event that has not recurred other than on specifically identifiable occasions and is therefore not representative of errors in the population.

6. "Population" means the entire set of data from which a sample is selected and about which the auditor wishes to draw conclusions. For example, all of the items in an account balance or a class of transactions constitute a population. A population may be divided into strata, or sub-populations, with each stratum being examined separately. The term population is used to include the term stratum.

7. "Sampling risk" arises from the possibility that the auditor's conclusion, based on a sample may be different from the conclusion reached if the entire population were subjected to the same audit procedure. There are two types of sampling risk:

   (a) the risk the auditor will conclude, in the case of a test of control, that control risk is lower than it actually is, or in the case of a substantive test, that a material error does not exist when in fact it does. This type of risk affects audit effectiveness and is more likely to lead to an inappropriate audit opinion; and

   (b) the risk the auditor will conclude, in the case of a test of control, that control risk is higher than it actually is, or in the case of a substantive test, that a material error exists when in fact it does not. This type of risk affects audit efficiency as it would usually lead to additional work to establish that initial conclusions were incorrect.

   The mathematical complements of these risks are termed confidence levels.

8.   "Non-sampling risk" arises from factors that cause the auditor to reach an erroneous conclusion for any reason not related to the size of the sample. For example, most audit evidence is persuasive rather than conclusive, the auditor might use inappropriate procedures, or the auditor might misinterpret evidence and fail to recognize an error.

9.   "Sampling unit" means the individual items constituting a population, for example checks listed on deposit slips, credit entries on bank statements, sales invoices or debtors' balances, or a monetary unit.

10. "Statistical sampling" means any approach to sampling that has the following characteristics:

    (a)   random selection of a sample; and

    (b)   use of probability theory to evaluate sample results, including measurement of sampling risk.

    A sampling approach that does not have characteristics (a) and (b) is considered non-statistical sampling.

11. "Stratification" is the process of dividing a population into subpopulations, each of which is a group of sampling units which have similar characteristics (often monetary value).

12. "Tolerable error" means the maximum error in a population that the auditor is willing to accept.

Audit Evidence

13. In accordance with ISA 500 "Audit Evidence", audit evidence is obtained from an appropriate mix of tests of control and substantive procedures. The type of test to be performed is important to an understanding of the application of audit procedures in gathering audit evidence.

Tests of Control

14. In accordance with ISA 400 "Risk Assessments and Internal Control" tests of control are performed if the auditor plans to assess control risk less than high for a particular assertion.

15. Based on the auditor's understanding of the accounting and internal control systems, the auditor identifies the characteristics or attributes that indicate performance of a control, as well as possible deviation conditions which indicate departures from adequate performance. The presence or absence of attributes can then be tested by the auditor.

16. Audit sampling for tests of control is generally appropriate when application of the control leaves evidence of performance (for example, initials of the credit manager on a sales invoice indicating credit approval, or evidence of authorization of data input to a microcomputer based data processing system).

AUDITING

Substantive Procedures

17. Substantive procedures are concerned with amounts and are of two types: analytical procedures and tests of details of transactions and balances. The purpose of substantive procedures is to obtain audit evidence to detect material misstatements in the financial statements. When performing substantive tests of details, audit sampling and other means of selecting items for testing and gathering audit evidence may be used to verify one or more assertions about a financial statement amount (for example, the existence of accounts receivable), or to make an independent estimate of some amount (for example, the value of obsolete inventories).

Risk Considerations in Obtaining Evidence

18. **In obtaining evidence, the auditor should use professional judgment to assess audit risk and design audit procedures to ensure this risk is reduced to an acceptably low level.**

19. Audit risk is the risk that the auditor gives an inappropriate audit opinion when the financial statements are materially misstated. Audit risk consists of inherent risk - the susceptibility of an account balance to material misstatement, assuming there are no related internal controls; control risk - the risk that a material misstatement will not be prevented or detected and corrected on a timely basis by the accounting and internal control systems; and, detection risk - the risk that the material misstatements will not be detected by the auditor's substantive procedures. These three components of audit risk are considered during the planning process in the design of audit procedures in order to reduce audit risk to an acceptably low level.

20. Sampling risk and non-sampling risk can affect the components of audit risk. For example, when performing tests of control, the auditor may find no errors in a sample and conclude that control risk is low, when the rate of error in the population is, in fact, unacceptably high (sampling risk). Or there may be errors in the sample which the auditor fails to recognize (non-sampling risk). With respect to substantive procedures, the auditor may use a variety of methods to reduce detection risk to an acceptable level. Depending on their nature, these methods will be subject to sampling and/or non-sampling risks. For example, the auditor may choose an inappropriate analytical procedure (non-sampling risk) or may find only minor misstatements in a test of details when, in fact, the population misstatement is greater than the tolerable amount (sampling risk). For both tests of control and substantive tests, sampling risk can be reduced by increasing sample size, while non-sampling risk can be reduced by proper engagement planning, supervision, and review.

Procedures for Obtaining Evidence

21. Procedures for obtaining audit evidence include inspection, observation, inquiry and confirmation, computation and analytical procedures. The choice of appropriate procedures is a matter of professional judgment in the circumstances. Application of these procedures will often involve the selection of items for testing from a population.

Selecting Items for Testing to Gather Audit Evidence

22. **When designing audit procedures, the auditor should determine appropriate means of selecting items for testing.** The means available to the auditor are:

(a) Selecting all items (100% examination);

(b) Selecting specific items, and

(c) Audit sampling.

23. The decision as to which approach to use will depend on the circumstances, and the application of any one or combination of the above means may be appropriate in particular circumstances. While the decision as to which means, or combination of means, to use is made on the basis of audit risk and audit efficiency, the auditor needs to be satisfied that methods used are effective in providing sufficient appropriate audit evidence to meet the objectives of the test.

Selecting all items

24. The auditor may decide that it will be most appropriate to examine the entire population of items that make up an account balance or class of transactions (or a stratum within that population). 100% examination is unlikely in the case of tests of control; however, it is more common for substantive procedures. For example, 100% examination may be appropriate when the population constitutes a small number of large value items, when both inherent and control risks are high and other means do not provide sufficient appropriate audit evidence, or when the repetitive nature of a calculation or other process performed by a computer information system makes a 100% examination cost effective.

Selecting Specific Items

25. The auditor may decide to select specific items from a population based on such factors as knowledge of the client's business, preliminary assessments of inherent and control risks, and the characteristics of the population being tested. The judgmental selection of specific items is subject to non-sampling risk. Specific items selected may include:

• *High value or key items.* The auditor may decide to select specific items within a population because they are of high value, or exhibit some other characteristic, for example items that are suspicious, unusual, particularly risk-prone or that have a history of error.

• *All items over a certain amount.* The auditor may decide to examine items whose values exceed a certain amount so as to verify a large proportion of the total amount of an account balance or class of transactions.

• *Items to obtain information.* The auditor may examine items to obtain information about matters such as the client's business, the nature of transactions, accounting and internal control systems.

- *Items to test procedures.* The auditor may use judgment to select and examine specific items to determine whether or not a particular procedure is being performed.

26. While selective examination of specific items from an account balance or class of transactions will often be an efficient means of gathering audit evidence, it does not constitute audit sampling. The results of procedures applied to items selected in this way cannot be projected to the entire population. The auditor considers the need to obtain appropriate evidence regarding the remainder of the population when that remainder is material.

Audit Sampling

27. The auditor may decide to apply audit sampling to an account balance or class of transactions. Audit sampling can be applied using either non-statistical or statistical sampling methods. Audit sampling is discussed in detail in paragraphs 31 through 56.

Statistical versus Non-Statistical Sampling Approaches

28. The decision whether to use a statistical or non-statistical sampling approach is a matter for the auditor's judgment regarding the most efficient manner to obtain sufficient appropriate audit evidence in the particular circumstances. For example, in the case of tests of control the auditor's analysis of the nature and cause of errors will often be more important than the statistical analysis of the mere presence or absence (that is, the count) of errors. In such a situation, non-statistical sampling may be most appropriate.

29. When applying statistical sampling, the sample size can be determined using either probability theory or professional judgment. Moreover, sample size is not a valid criterion to distinguish between statistical and non-statistical approaches. Sample size is a function of factors such as those identified in Appendices 1 and 2. When circumstances are similar, the effect on sample size of factors such as those identified in Appendices 1 and 2 will be similar regardless of whether a statistical or non-statistical approach is chosen.

30. Often, while the approach adopted does not meet the definition of statistical sampling, elements of a statistical approach are used, for example the use of random selection using computer generated random numbers. However, only when the approach adopted has the characteristics of statistical sampling are statistical measurements of sampling risk valid.

Design of the Sample

31. **When designing an audit sample, the auditor should consider the objectives of the test and the attributes of the population from which the sample will be drawn.**

32. The auditor first considers the specific objectives to be achieved and the combination of audit procedures which is likely to best achieve those objectives. Consideration of the nature of the audit evidence sought and possible error conditions or other characteristics relating to that audit

evidence will assist the auditor in defining what constitutes an error and what population to use for sampling.

33.   The auditor considers what conditions constitute an error by reference to the objectives of the test. A clear understanding of what constitutes an error is important to ensure that all, and only, those conditions that are relevant to the test objectives are included in the projection of errors. For example, in a substantive procedure relating to the existence of accounts receivable, such as confirmation, payments made by the customer before the confirmation date but received shortly after that date by the client are not considered an error. Also, a misposting between customer accounts does not affect the total accounts receivable balance. Therefore, it is not appropriate to consider this an error in evaluating the sample results of this particular procedure, even though it may have an important effect on other areas of the audit, such as the assessment of the likelihood of fraud or the adequacy of the allowance for doubtful accounts.

34.   When performing tests of control, the auditor generally makes a preliminary assessment of the rate of error the auditor expects to find in the population to be tested and the level of control risk. This assessment is based on the auditor's prior knowledge or the examination of a small number of items from the population. Similarly, for substantive tests, the auditor generally makes a preliminary assessment of the amount of error in the population. These preliminary assessments are useful for designing an audit sample and in determining sample size. For example, if the expected rate of error is unacceptably high, tests of control will normally not be performed. However, when performing substantive procedures, if the expected amount of error is high, 100% examination or the use of a large sample size may be appropriate.

Population

35.   It is important for the auditor to ensure that the population is:

(a)   *Appropriate* to the objective of the sampling procedure, which will include consideration of the direction of testing. For example, if the auditor's objective is to test for overstatement of accounts payable, the population could be defined as the accounts payable listing. On the other hand, when testing for understatement of accounts payable, the population is not the accounts payable listing but rather subsequent disbursements, unpaid invoices, suppliers' statements, unmatched receiving reports or other populations that provide audit evidence of understatement of accounts payable; and

(b)   *Complete.* For example, if the auditor intends to select payment vouchers from a file, conclusions cannot be drawn about all vouchers for the period unless the auditor is satisfied that all vouchers have in fact been filed. Similarly, if the auditor intends to use the sample to draw conclusions about the operation of an accounting and internal control system during the financial reporting period, the population needs to include all relevant items from throughout the entire period. A different approach may be to stratify the population and use sampling only to

AUDITING

draw conclusions about the control during, say, the first 10 months of a year, and to use alternative procedures or a separate sample regarding the remaining two months.

Stratification

36. Audit efficiency may be improved if the auditor stratifies a population by dividing it into discrete sub-populations which have an identifying characteristic. The objective of stratification is to reduce the variability of items within each stratum and therefore allow sample size to be reduced without a proportional increase in sampling risk. Sub-populations need to be carefully defined such that any sampling unit can only belong to one stratum.

37. When performing substantive procedures, an account balance or class of transactions is often stratified by monetary value. This allows greater audit effort to be directed to the larger value items which may contain the greatest potential monetary error in terms of overstatement. Similarly, a population may be stratified according to a particular characteristic that indicates a higher risk of error, for example, when testing the valuation of accounts receivable, balances may be stratified by age.

38. The results of procedures applied to a sample of items within a stratum can only be projected to the items that make up that stratum. To draw a conclusion on the entire population, the auditor will need to consider risk and materiality in relation to whatever other strata make up the entire population. For example, 20% of the items in a population may make up 90% of the value of an account balance. The auditor may decide to examine a sample of these items. The auditor evaluates the results of this sample and reaches a conclusion on the 90% of value separately from the remaining 10% (on which a further sample or other means of gathering evidence will be used, or which may be considered immaterial).

Value weighted selection

39. It will often be efficient in substantive testing, particularly when testing for overstatements, to identify the sampling unit as the individual monetary units (e.g. dollars) that make up an account balance or class of transactions. Having selected specific monetary units from within the population, for example, the accounts receivable balance, the auditor then examines the particular items, for example, individual balances, that contain those monetary units. This approach to defining the sampling unit ensures that audit effort is directed to the larger value items because they have a greater chance of selection, and can result in smaller sample sizes. This approach is ordinarily used in conjunction with the systematic method of sample selection (described in Appendix 3) and is most efficient when selecting from a computerized database.

Sample Size

40. **In determining the sample size, the auditor should consider whether sampling risk is reduced to an acceptably low level.** Sample size is affected

by the level of sampling risk that the auditor is willing to accept. The lower the risk the auditor is willing to accept, the greater the sample size will need to be.

41. The sample size can be determined by the application of a statistically-based formula or through the exercise of professional judgement objectively applied to the circumstances. Appendices 1 and 2 indicate the influences that various factors typically have on the determination of sample size, and hence the level of sampling risk.

Selecting the Sample

42. **The auditor should select items for the sample with the expectation that all sampling units in the population have a chance of selection.** Statistical sampling requires that sample items are selected at random so that each sampling unit has a known chance of being selected. The sampling units might be physical items (such as invoices) or monetary units. With non-statistical sampling, an auditor uses professional judgment to select the items for a sample. Because the purpose of sampling is to draw conclusions about the entire population, the auditor endeavors to select a representative sample by choosing sample items which have characteristics typical of the population, and the sample needs to be selected so that bias is avoided.

43. The principal methods of selecting samples are the use of random number tables or computer programs, systematic selection and haphazard selection. Each of these methods is discussed in Appendix 3.

Performing the Audit Procedure

44. **The auditor should perform audit procedures appropriate to the particular test objective on each item selected.**

45. If a selected item is not appropriate for the application of the procedure, the procedure is ordinarily performed on a replacement item. For example, a voided check may be selected when testing for evidence of payment authorization. If the auditor is satisfied that the check had been properly voided such that it does not constitute an error, an appropriately chosen replacement is examined.

46. Sometimes however, the auditor is unable to apply the planned audit procedures to a selected item because, for instance, documentation relating to that item has been lost. If suitable alternative procedures cannot be performed on that item, the auditor ordinarily considers that item to be in error. An example of a suitable alternative procedure might be the examination of subsequent receipts when no reply has been received in response to a positive confirmation request.

Nature and Cause of Errors

47. **The auditor should consider the sample results, the nature and cause of any errors identified, and their possible effect on the particular test objective and on other areas of the audit.**

48. When conducting tests of control, the auditor is primarily concerned with the design and operation of the controls themselves and the assessment of control risk. However, when errors are identified, the auditor also needs to consider matters such as:

    (a) the direct effect of identified errors on the financial statements; and

    (b) the effectiveness of the accounting and internal control systems and their effect on the audit approach when, for example, the errors result from management override of an internal control.

49. In analyzing the errors discovered, the auditor may observe that many have a common feature, for example, type of transaction, location, product line or period of time. In such circumstances, the auditor may decide to identify all items in the population that possess the common feature, and extend audit procedures in that stratum. In addition, such errors may be intentional, and may indicate the possibility of fraud.

50. Sometimes, the auditor may be able to establish that an error arises from an isolated event that has not recurred other than on specifically identifiable occasions and is therefore not representative of similar errors in the population (an anomalous error). To be considered an anomalous error, the auditor has to have a high degree of certainty that such error is not representative of the population. The auditor obtains this certainty by performing additional work. The additional work depends on the situation, but is adequate to provide the auditor with sufficient appropriate evidence that the error does not affect the remaining part of the population. One example is an error caused by a computer breakdown that is known to have occurred on only one day during the period. In that case, the auditor assesses the effect of the breakdown, for example by examining specific transactions processed on that day, and considers the effect of the cause of the breakdown on audit procedures and conclusions. Another example is an error that is found to be caused by use of an incorrect formula in calculating all inventory values at one particular branch. To establish that this is an anomalous error, the auditor needs to ensure the correct formula has been used at other branches.

Projecting Errors

51. **For substantive procedures, the auditor should project monetary errors found in the sample to the population, and should consider the effect of the projected error on the particular test objective and on other areas of the audit.** The auditor projects the total error for the population to obtain a broad view of the scale of errors, and to compare this to the tolerable error. For substantive procedures, tolerable error is the tolerable misstatement, and will be an amount less than or equal to the auditor's preliminary estimate of materiality used for the individual account balances being audited.

52. When an error has been established as an anomalous error, it may be excluded when projecting sample errors to the population. The effect of any such error, if uncorrected, still needs to be considered in addition to the projection of the non-anomalous errors. If an account balance or class of

transactions has been divided into strata, the error is projected for each stratum separately. Projected errors plus anomalous errors for each stratum are then combined when considering the possible effect of errors on the total account balance or class of transactions.

53. For tests of control, no explicit projection of errors is necessary since the sample error rate is also the projected rate of error for the population as a whole.

Evaluating the Sample Results

54. **The auditor should evaluate the sample results to determine whether the preliminary assessment of the relevant characteristic of the population is confirmed or needs to be revised.** In the case of a test of controls, an unexpectedly high sample error rate may lead to an increase in the assessed level of control risk, unless further evidence substantiating the initial assessment is obtained. In the case of a substantive procedure, an unexpectedly high error amount in a sample may cause the auditor to believe that an account balance or class of transactions is materially misstated, in the absence of further evidence that no material misstatement exists.

55. If the total amount of projected error plus anomalous error is less than but close to that which the auditor deems tolerable, the auditor considers the persuasiveness of the sample results in the light of other audit procedures, and may consider it appropriate to obtain additional audit evidence. The total of projected error plus anomalous error is the auditor's best estimate of error in the population. However, sampling results are affected by sampling risk. Thus when the best estimate of error is close to the tolerable error, the auditor recognizes the risk that a different sample would result in a different best estimate that could exceed the tolerable error. Considering the results of other audit procedures helps the auditor to assess this risk, while the risk is reduced if additional audit evidence is obtained.

56. If the evaluation of sample results indicates that the preliminary assessment of the relevant characteristic of the population needs to be revised, the auditor may:

(a) request management to investigate identified errors and the potential for further errors, and to make any necessary adjustments; and/or

(b) modify planned audit procedures. For example, in the case of a test of control, the auditor might extend the sample size, test an alternative control or modify related substantive procedures; and/or

(c) consider the effect on the audit report.

57. This ISA is effective for audits of financial statements for periods ending on or after July 1, 1999. Earlier application is permitted.

AUDITING

Appendix 1

Examples of Factors Influencing Sample Size for Tests of Control

The following are factors that the auditor considers when determining the sample size for a test of control. These factors need to be considered together.

FACTOR	EFFECT ON SAMPLE SIZE
An increase in the auditor's intended reliance on accounting and internal control systems	Increase
An increase in the rate of deviation from the prescribed control procedure that the auditor is willing to accept	Decrease
An increase in the rate of deviation from the prescribed control procedure that the auditor expects to find in the population	Increase
An increase in the auditor's required confidence level (or conversely, a decrease in the risk that the auditor will conclude that the control risk is lower than the actual control risk in the population)	Increase
An increase in the number of sampling units in the population	Negligible effect

1. *The auditor's intended reliance on accounting and internal control systems:* The more assurance the auditor intends to obtain from accounting and internal control systems, the lower the auditor's assessment of control risk will be, and the larger the sample size will need to be. For example, a preliminary assessment of control risk as low indicates that the auditor plans to place considerable reliance on the effective operation of particular internal controls. The auditor therefore needs to gather more audit evidence to support this assessment than would be the case if control risk were assessed at a higher level (that is, if less reliance were planned).

2. *The rate of deviation from the prescribed control procedure the auditor is willing to accept (tolerable error).* The lower the rate of deviation that the auditor is willing to accept, the larger the sample size needs to be.

3. *The rate of deviation from the prescribed control procedure the auditor expects to find in the population (expected error).* The higher the rate of deviation that the auditor expects, the larger the sample size needs to be so as to be in a position to make a reasonable estimate of the actual rate of deviation. Factors relevant to the auditor's consideration of the expected error rate include the auditor's understanding of the business (in particular, procedures undertaken to obtain an understanding of the accounting and internal control systems), changes in personnel or in the accounting and internal control systems, the results of audit procedures applied in prior periods and the results of other audit procedures. High expected error rates ordinarily warrant little, if any, reduction of control risk, and therefore in such circumstances tests of controls would ordinarily be omitted.

4. *The auditor's required confidence level.* The greater the degree of confidence that the auditor requires that the results of the sample are in fact indicative of the actual incidence of error in the population, the larger the sample size needs to be.

5. *The number of sampling units in the population.* For large populations, the actual size of the population has little, if any, effect on sample size. For small populations however, audit sampling is often not as efficient as alternative means of obtaining sufficient appropriate audit evidence.

AUDITING

Appendix 2

Examples of Factors Influencing Sample Size for Substantive Procedures

The following are factors that the auditor considers when determining the sample size for a substantive procedure. These factors need to be considered together.

FACTOR	EFFECT ON SAMPLE SIZE
An increase in the auditor's assessment of inherent risk	Increase
An increase in the auditor's assessment of control risk	Increase
An increase in the use of other substantive procedures directed at the same financial statement assertion	Decrease
An increase in the auditor's required confidence level (or conversely, a decrease in the risk that the auditor will conclude that a material error does not exist, when in fact it does exist)	Increase
An increase in the total error that the auditor is willing to accept (tolerable error)	Decrease
An increase in the amount of error the auditor expects to find in the population	Increase
Stratification of the population when appropriate	Decrease
The number of sampling units in the population	Negligible Effect

1. *The auditor's assessment of inherent risk.* The higher the auditor's assessment of inherent risk, the larger the sample size needs to be. Higher inherent risk implies that a lower detection risk is needed to reduce the audit risk to an acceptable low level, and lower detection risk can be obtained by increasing sample size.

2. *The auditor's assessment of control risk.* The higher the auditor's assessment of control risk, the larger the sample size needs to be. For example, an assessment of control risk as high indicates that the auditor cannot place much reliance on the effective operation of internal controls with respect to the particular financial statement assertion. Therefore, in order to reduce audit risk to an acceptably low level, the auditor needs a low detection risk and will rely more on substantive tests. The more reliance that is placed on substantive tests (that is, the lower the detection risk), the larger the sample size will need to be.

3. *The use of other substantive procedures directed at the same financial statement assertion.* The more the auditor is relying on other substantive procedures (tests of detail or analytical procedures) to reduce to an acceptable level the detection risk regarding a particular account balance or class of transactions, the less assurance the auditor will require from sampling and, therefore, the smaller the sample size can be.

4. *The auditor's required confidence level.* The greater the degree of confidence that the auditor requires that the results of the sample are in fact indicative of the actual amount of error in the population, the larger the sample size needs to be.

5. *The total error the auditor is willing to accept (tolerable error).* The lower the total error that the auditor is willing to accept, the larger the sample size needs to be.

6. *The amount of error the auditor expects to find in the population (expected error).* The greater the amount of error the auditor expects to find in the population, the larger the sample size needs to be in order to make a reasonable estimate of the actual amount of error in the population. Factors relevant to the auditor's consideration of the expected error amount include the extent to which item values are determined subjectively, the results of tests of control, the results of audit procedures applied in prior periods, and the results of other substantive procedures.

7. *Stratification.* When there is a wide range (variability) in the monetary size of items in the population. It may be useful to group items of similar size into separate sub-populations or strata. This is referred to as stratification. When a population can be appropriately stratified, the aggregate of the sample sizes from the strata generally will be less than the sample size that would have been required to attain a given level of sampling risk, had one sample been drawn from the whole population.

8. *The number of sampling units in the population.* For large populations, the actual size of the population has little, if any, effect on sample size. Thus, for

small populations, audit sampling is often not as efficient as alternative means of obtaining sufficient appropriate audit evidence. (However, when using monetary unit sampling, an increase in the monetary value of the population increases sample size, unless this is offset by a proportional increase in materiality.)

Appendix 3

Sample Selection Methods

The principal methods of selecting samples are:

(a)   Use of a computerized random number generator or random number tables.

(b)   Systematic selection, in which the number of sampling units in the population is divided by the sample size to give a sampling interval, for example 50, and having determined a starting point within the first 50, each 50th sampling unit thereafter is selected. Although the starting point may be determined haphazardly, the sample is more likely to be truly random if it is determined by use of a computerized random number generator or random number tables. When using systematic selection, the auditor would need to determine that sampling units within the population are not structured in such a way that the sampling interval corresponds with a particular pattern in the population.

(c)   Haphazard selection, in which the auditor selects the sample without following a structured technique. Although no structured technique is used, the auditor would nonetheless avoid any conscious bias or predictability (for example avoiding difficult to locate items, or always choosing or avoiding the first or last entries on a page) and thus attempt to ensure that all items in the population have a chance of selection. Haphazard selection is not appropriate when using statistical sampling.

Block selection involves selecting a block(s) of contiguous items from within the population. Block selection cannot ordinarily be used in audit sampling because most populations are structured such that items in a sequence can be expected to have similar characteristics to each other, but different characteristics from items elsewhere in the population. Although in some circumstances it may be an appropriate audit procedure to examine a block of items, it would rarely be an appropriate sample selection technique when the auditor intends to draw valid inferences about the entire population based on the sample.

AUDITING

CONTENTS

	Paragraphs
Introduction	1-4
The Nature of Accounting Estimates	5-7
Audit Procedures	8-10
Reviewing and Testing the Process Used by Management	11-21
Use of an Independent Estimate	22
Review of Subsequent Events	23
Evaluation of Results of Audit Procedures	24-27

International Standards on Auditing (ISAs) are to be applied in the audit of financial statements. ISAs are also to be applied, adapted as necessary, to the audit of other information and to related services.

ISAs contain the basic principles and essential procedures (identified in bold type black lettering) together with related guidance in the form of explanatory and other material. The basic principles and essential procedures are to be interpreted in the context of the explanatory and other material that provide guidance for their application.

To understand and apply the basic principles and essential procedures together with the related guidance, it is necessary to consider the whole text of the ISA including explanatory and other material contained in the ISA not just that text which is black lettered.

In exceptional circumstances, an auditor may judge it necessary to depart from an ISA in order to more effectively achieve the objective of an audit. When such a situation arises, the auditor should be prepared to justify the departure.

ISAs need only be applied to material matters.

The Public Sector Perspective (PSP) issued by the Public Sector Committee of the International Federation of Accountants is set out at the end of an ISA. Where no PSP is added, the ISA is applicable in all material respects to the public sector.

Introduction

1. The purpose of this International Standard on Auditing (ISA) is to establish standards and provide guidance on the audit of accounting estimates contained in financial statements. This ISA is not intended to be applicable to the examination of prospective financial information, though many of the procedures outlined herein may be suitable for that purpose.

2. **The auditor should obtain sufficient appropriate audit evidence regarding accounting estimates.**

3. "Accounting estimate" means an approximation of the amount of an item in the absence of a precise means of measurement. Examples are:

   - Allowances to reduce inventory and accounts receivable to their estimated realizable value.
   - Provisions to allocate the cost of fixed assets over their estimated useful lives.
   - Accrued revenue.
   - Deferred tax.
   - Provision for a loss from a lawsuit.
   - Losses on construction contracts in progress.
   - Provision to meet warranty claims.

4. Management is responsible for making accounting estimates included in financial statements. These estimates are often made in conditions of uncertainty regarding the outcome of events that have occurred or are likely to occur and involve the use of judgment. As a result, the risk of material misstatement is greater when accounting estimates are involved.

The Nature of Accounting Estimates

5. The determination of an accounting estimate may be simple or complex depending upon the nature of the item. For example, accruing a charge for rent may be a simple calculation, whereas estimating a provision for slow-moving or surplus inventory may involve considerable analyses of current data and a forecast of future sales. In complex estimates, there may be a high degree of special knowledge and judgment required.

6. Accounting estimates may be determined as part of the routine accounting system operating on a continuing basis, or may be nonroutine, operating only at period end. In many cases, accounting estimates are made by using a formula based on experience, such as the use of standard rates for depreciating each category of fixed assets or a standard percentage of sales revenue for computing a warranty provision. In such cases, the formula needs to be reviewed regularly by management, for example, by reassessing the remaining useful lives of assets or by comparing actual results with the estimate and adjusting the formula when necessary.

AUDITING

7. The uncertainty associated with an item, or the lack of objective data may make it incapable of reasonable estimation, in which case, the auditor needs to consider whether the auditor's report needs modification to comply with ISA 700 "The Auditor's Report on Financial Statements."

Audit Procedures

8. **The auditor should obtain sufficient appropriate audit evidence as to whether an accounting estimate is reasonable in the circumstances and, when required, is appropriately disclosed.** The evidence available to support an accounting estimate will often be more difficult to obtain and less conclusive than evidence available to support other items in the financial statements.

9. An understanding of the procedures and methods, including the accounting and internal control systems, used by management in making the accounting estimates is often important for the auditor to plan the nature, timing and extent of the audit procedures.

10. **The auditor should adopt one or a combination of the following approaches in the audit of an accounting estimate:**

    (a) **review and test the process used by management to develop the estimate;**

    (b) **use an independent estimate for comparison with that prepared by management; or**

    (c) **review subsequent events which confirm the estimate made.**

Reviewing and Testing the Process Used by Management

11. The steps ordinarily involved in reviewing and testing of the process used by management are:

    (a) evaluation of the data and consideration of assumptions on which the estimate is based;

    (b) testing of the calculations involved in the estimate;

    (c) comparison, when possible, of estimates made for prior periods with actual results of those periods; and

    (d) consideration of management's approval procedures.

Evaluation of Data and Consideration of Assumptions

12. The auditor would evaluate whether the data on which the estimate is based is accurate, complete and relevant. When accounting data is used, it will need to be consistent with the data processed through the accounting system. For example, in substantiating a warranty provision, the auditor would obtain audit evidence that the data relating to products still within the warranty period at period end agree with the sales information within the accounting system.

13. The auditor may also seek evidence from sources outside the entity. For example, when examining a provision for inventory obsolescence calculated by reference to anticipated future sales, the auditor may, in addition to examining internal data such as past levels of sales, orders on hand and marketing trends, seek evidence from industry-produced sales projections and market analyses. Similarly, when examining management's estimates of the financial implications of litigation and claims, the auditor would seek direct communication with the entity's lawyers.

14. The auditor would evaluate whether the data collected is appropriately analyzed and projected to form a reasonable basis for determining the accounting estimate. Examples are the analysis of the age of accounts receivable and the projection of the number of months of supply on hand of an item of inventory based on past and forecast usage.

15. The auditor would evaluate whether the entity has an appropriate base for the principal assumptions used in the accounting estimate. In some cases, the assumptions will be based on industry or government statistics, such as future inflation rates, interest rates, employment rates and anticipated market growth. In other cases, the assumptions will be specific to the entity and will be based on internally generated data.

16. In evaluating the assumptions on which the estimate is based, the auditor would consider, among other things, whether they are:

- Reasonable in light of actual results in prior periods.
- Consistent with those used for other accounting estimates.
- Consistent with management's plans which appear appropriate.

The auditor would need to pay particular attention to assumptions which are sensitive to variation, subjective or susceptible to material misstatement.

17. In the case of complex estimating processes involving specialized techniques, it may be necessary for the auditor to use the work of an expert, for example, engineers for estimating quantities in stock piles of mineral ores. Guidance on how to use the work of an expert is provided in ISA 620 "Using the Work of an Expert."

18. The auditor would review the continuing appropriateness of formulae used by management in the preparation of accounting estimates. Such a review would reflect the auditor's knowledge of the financial results of the entity in prior periods, practices used by other entities in the industry and the future plans of management as disclosed to the auditor.

Testing of Calculations

19. The auditor would test the calculation procedures used by management. The nature, timing and extent of the auditor's testing will depend on such factors as the complexity involved in calculating the accounting estimate, the auditor's evaluation of the procedures and methods used by the entity in producing the estimate and the materiality of the estimate in the context of the financial statements.

AUDITING

Comparison of Previous Estimates with Actual Results

20. When possible, the auditor would compare accounting estimates made for prior periods with actual results of those periods to assist in:

(a) obtaining evidence about the general reliability of the entity's estimating procedures;

(b) considering whether adjustments to estimating formulae may be required; and

(c) evaluating whether differences between actual results and previous estimates have been quantified and that, where necessary, appropriate adjustments or disclosures have been made.

Consideration of Management's Approval Procedures

21. Material accounting estimates are ordinarily reviewed and approved by management. The auditor would consider whether such review and approval is performed by the appropriate level of management and that it is evidenced in the documentation supporting the determination of the accounting estimate.

Use of an Independent Estimate

22. The auditor may make or obtain an independent estimate and compare it with the accounting estimate prepared by management. When using an independent estimate the auditor would ordinarily evaluate the data, consider the assumptions and test the calculation procedures used in its development. It may also be appropriate to compare accounting estimates made for prior periods with actual results of those periods.

Review of Subsequent Events

23. Transactions and events which occur after period end, but prior to completion of the audit, may provide audit evidence regarding an accounting estimate made by management. The auditor's review of such transactions and events may reduce, or even remove, the need for the auditor to review and test the process used by management to develop the accounting estimate or to use an independent estimate in assessing the reasonableness of the accounting estimate.

Evaluation of Results of Audit Procedures

24. **The auditor should make a final assessment of the reasonableness of the estimate based on the auditor's knowledge of the business and whether the estimate is consistent with other audit evidence obtained during the audit.**

25. The auditor would consider whether there are any significant subsequent transactions or events which affect the data and the assumptions used in determining the accounting estimate.

26. Because of the uncertainties inherent in accounting estimates, evaluating differences can be more difficult than in other areas of the audit. When there is a difference between the auditor's estimate of the amount best supported by the available audit evidence and the estimated amount included in the financial statements, the auditor would determine whether such a difference requires adjustment. If the difference is reasonable, for example, because the amount in the financial statements falls within a range of acceptable results, it may not require adjustment. However, if the auditor believes the difference is unreasonable, management would be requested to revise the estimate. If management refuses to revise the estimate, the difference would be considered a misstatement and would be considered with all other misstatements in assessing whether the effect on the financial statements is material.

27. The auditor would also consider whether individual differences which have been accepted as reasonable are biased in one direction, so that, on a cumulative basis, they may have a material effect on the financial statements. In such circumstances, the auditor would evaluate the accounting estimates taken as a whole.

AUDITING

CONTENTS

	Paragraphs
Introduction	1-6
Existence and Disclosure of Related Parties	7-8
Transactions with Related Parties	9-12
Examining Identified Related Party Transactions	13-14
Management Representations	15
Audit Conclusions and Reporting	16

International Standards on Auditing (ISAs) are to be applied in the audit of financial statements. ISAs are also to be applied, adapted as necessary, to the audit of other information and to related services.

ISAs contain the basic principles and essential procedures (identified in bold type black lettering) together with related guidance in the form of explanatory and other material. The basic principles and essential procedures are to be interpreted in the context of the explanatory and other material that provide guidance for their application.

To understand and apply the basic principles and essential procedures together with the related guidance, it is necessary to consider the whole text of the ISA including explanatory and other material contained in the ISA not just that text which is black lettered.

In exceptional circumstances, an auditor may judge it necessary to depart from an ISA in order to more effectively achieve the objective of an audit. When such a situation arises, the auditor should be prepared to justify the departure.

ISAs need only be applied to material matters.

The Public Sector Perspective (PSP) issued by the Public Sector Committee of the International Federation of Accountants is set out at the end of an ISA. Where no PSP is added, the ISA is applicable in all material respects to the public sector.

Introduction

1. The purpose of this International Standard on Auditing (ISA) is to establish standards and provide guidance on the auditor's responsibilities and audit procedures regarding related parties and transactions with such parties regardless of whether International Accounting Standard (IAS) 24, Related Party Disclosures, or similar requirement, is part of the financial reporting framework.

2. **The auditor should perform audit procedures designed to obtain sufficient appropriate audit evidence regarding the identification and disclosure by management of related parties and the effect of related party transactions that are material to the financial statements.** However, an audit cannot be expected to detect all related party transactions.

3. As indicated in ISA 200 "Objective and General Principles Governing an Audit of Financial Statements," in certain circumstances there are limitations that may affect the persuasiveness of evidence available to draw conclusions on particular financial statement assertions. Because of the degree of uncertainty associated with the financial statement assertions regarding the completeness of related parties, the procedures identified in this ISA will provide sufficient appropriate audit evidence regarding those assertions in the absence of any circumstance identified by the auditor that:

    (a) increases the risk of misstatement beyond that which would ordinarily be expected; or

    (b) indicates that a material misstatement regarding related parties has occurred.

    Where there is any indication that such circumstances exist, the auditor should perform modified, extended or additional procedures as are appropriate in the circumstances.

4. Definitions regarding related parties are given in IAS 24 and are adopted for the purposes of this ISA[1].

5. Management is responsible for the identification and disclosure of related parties and transactions with such parties. This responsibility requires management to implement adequate accounting and internal control systems to ensure that transactions with related parties are appropriately identified in the accounting records and disclosed in the financial statements.

6. The auditor needs to have a level of knowledge of the entity's business and industry that will enable identification of the events, transactions and

---

[1] Definitions of related party and related party transactions from IAS 24 are:

Related party—parties are considered to be related if one party has the ability to control the other party or exercise significant influence over the other party in making financial and operating decisions.

Related party transactions—a transfer of resources or obligations between related parties, regardless of whether a price is charged.

practices that may have a material effect on the financial statements. While the existence of related parties and transactions between such parties are considered ordinary features of business, the auditor needs to be aware of them because:

(a) the financial reporting framework may require disclosure in the financial statements of certain related party relationships and transactions, such as those required by IAS 24;

(b) the existence of related parties or related party transactions may affect the financial statements. For example, the entity's tax liability and expense may be affected by the tax laws in various jurisdictions which require special consideration when related parties exist;

(c) the source of audit evidence affects the auditor's assessment of its reliability. A greater degree of reliance may be placed on audit evidence that is obtained from or created by unrelated third parties; and

(d) a related party transaction may be motivated by other than ordinary business considerations, for example, profit sharing or even fraud.

Existence and Disclosure of Related Parties

7. The auditor should review information provided by the directors and management identifying the names of all known related parties and should perform the following procedures in respect of the completeness of this information:

(a) review prior year working papers for names of known related parties;

(b) review the entity's procedures for identification of related parties;

(c) inquire as to the affiliation of directors and officers with other entities;

(d) review shareholder records to determine the names of principal shareholders or, if appropriate, obtain a listing of principal shareholders from the share register;

(e) review minutes of the meetings of shareholders and the board of directors and other relevant statutory records such as the register of directors' interests;

(f) inquire of other auditors currently involved in the audit, or predecessor auditors, as to their knowledge of additional related parties; and

(g) review the entity's income tax returns and other information supplied to regulatory agencies.

If, in the auditor's judgment, the risk of significant related parties remaining undetected is low, these procedures may be modified as appropriate.

8. **Where the financial reporting framework requires disclosure of related party relationships, the auditor should be satisfied that the disclosure is adequate.**

Transactions with Related Parties

9. **The auditor should review information provided by directors and management identifying related party transactions and should be alert for other material related party transactions.**

10. **When obtaining an understanding of the accounting and internal control systems and making a preliminary assessment of control risk, the auditor should consider the adequacy of control procedures over the authorization and recording of related party transactions.**

11. During the course of the audit, the auditor needs to be alert for transactions which appear unusual in the circumstances and may indicate the existence of previously unidentified related parties. Examples include:

- Transactions which have abnormal terms of trade, such as unusual prices, interest rates, guarantees, and repayment terms.
- Transactions which lack an apparent logical business reason for their occurrence.
- Transactions in which substance differs from form.
- Transactions processed in an unusual manner.
- High volume or significant transactions with certain customers or suppliers as compared with others.
- Unrecorded transactions such as the receipt or provision of management services at no charge.

12. During the course of the audit, the auditor carries out procedures which may identify the existence of transactions with related parties. Examples include:

- Performing detailed tests of transactions and balances.
- Reviewing minutes of meetings of shareholders and directors.
- Reviewing accounting records for large or unusual transactions or balances, paying particular attention to transactions recognized at or near the end of the reporting period.
- Reviewing confirmations of loans receivable and payable and confirmations from banks. Such a review may indicate guarantor relationship and other related party transactions.
- Reviewing investment transactions, for example, purchase or sale of an equity interest in a joint venture or other entity.

Examining Identified Related Party Transactions

13. **In examining the identified related party transactions, the auditor should obtain sufficient appropriate audit evidence as to whether these transactions have been properly recorded and disclosed.**

14. Given the nature of related party relationships, evidence of a related party transaction may be limited, for example, regarding the existence of inventory held by a related party on consignment or an instruction from a parent company to a subsidiary to record a royalty expense. Because of the limited availability of appropriate evidence about such transactions, the auditor would consider performing procedures such as:

- Confirming the terms and amount of the transaction with the related party.
- Inspecting evidence in possession of the related party.
- Confirming or discussing information with persons associated with the transaction, such as banks, lawyers, guarantors and agents.

Management Representations

15. **The auditor should obtain a written representation from management concerning:**

    (a) the completeness of information provided regarding the identification of related parties; and

    (b) the adequacy of related party disclosures in the financial statements.

Audit Conclusions and Reporting

16. **If the auditor is unable to obtain sufficient appropriate audit evidence concerning related parties and transactions with such parties or concludes that their disclosure in the financial statements is not adequate, the auditor should modify the audit report appropriately.**

Public Sector Perspective

1. *In applying the audit principles in this ISA, auditors have to make reference to legislative requirements which are applicable to public sector entities and employees in respect of related party transactions. Such legislation may prohibit entities and employees from entering into transactions with related parties. There may also be a requirement for public sector employees to declare their interests in entities with which they transact on a professional and/or commercial basis. Where such legislative requirements exist, the audit procedures would need to be expanded to detect instances of noncompliance with these requirements.*

2. *While International Public Sector Guideline 1, Financial Reporting by Government Business Enterprises indicates that all International Accounting Standards (IASs) apply to business enterprises in the public sector, IAS 24, Related Party Disclosures does not require that transactions between state controlled enterprises be disclosed. Definitions of related parties included in IAS 24 and this ISA do not address all circumstances relevant to public sector entities. For example, the status, for purposes of application of this ISA, of the relationship between ministers and departments of state, and departments of state and statutory authorities or government agencies is not discussed.*

CONTENTS

	Paragraphs
Introduction	1-3
Events Occurring up to the Date of the Auditor's Report	4-7
Facts Discovered After the Date of the Auditor's Report but Before the Financial Statements are Issued	8-12
Facts Discovered After the Financial Statements Have Been Issued	13-18
Offering of Securities to the Public	19

International Standards on Auditing (ISAs) are to be applied in the audit of financial statements. ISAs are also to be applied, adapted as necessary, to the audit of other information and to related services.

ISAs contain the basic principles and essential procedures (identified in bold type black lettering) together with related guidance in the form of explanatory and other material. The basic principles and essential procedures are to be interpreted in the context of the explanatory and other material that provide guidance for their application.

To understand and apply the basic principles and essential procedures together with the related guidance, it is necessary to consider the whole text of the ISA including explanatory and other material contained in the ISA not just that text which is black lettered.

In exceptional circumstances, an auditor may judge it necessary to depart from an ISA in order to more effectively achieve the objective of an audit. When such a situation arises, the auditor should be prepared to justify the departure.

ISAs need only be applied to material matters.

The Public Sector Perspective (PSP) issued by the Public Sector Committee of the International Federation of Accountants is set out at the end of an ISA. Where no PSP is added, the ISA is applicable in all material respects to the public sector.

AUDITING

560

Introduction

1. The purpose of this International Standard on Auditing (ISA) is to establish standards and provide guidance on the auditor's responsibility regarding subsequent events. In this ISA, the term "subsequent events" is used to refer to both events occurring between period end and the date of the auditor's report, and facts discovered after the date of the auditor's report.

2. **The auditor should consider the effect of subsequent events on the financial statements and on the auditor's report.**

3. International Accounting Standard 10, Contingencies and Events Occurring After the Balance Sheet Date, deals with the treatment in financial statements of events, both favorable and unfavorable, occurring after period end and identifies two types of events:

   (a) those that provide further evidence of conditions that existed at period end; and

   (b) those that are indicative of conditions that arose subsequent to period end.

Events Occurring up to the Date of the Auditor's Report

4. **The auditor should perform procedures designed to obtain sufficient appropriate audit evidence that all events up to the date of the auditor's report that may require adjustment of, or disclosure in, the financial statements have been identified.** These procedures are in addition to routine procedures which may be applied to specific transactions occurring after period end to obtain audit evidence as to account balances as at period end, for example, the testing of inventory cutoff and payments to creditors. The auditor is not, however, expected to conduct a continuing review of all matters to which previously applied procedures have provided satisfactory conclusions.

5. The procedures to identify events that may require adjustment of, or disclosure in, the financial statements would be performed as near as practicable to the date of the auditor's report and ordinarily include the following:

   • Reviewing procedures management has established to ensure that subsequent events are identified.

   • Reading minutes of the meetings of shareholders, the board of directors and audit and executive committees held after period end and inquiring about matters discussed at meetings for which minutes are not yet available.

   • Reading the entity's latest available interim financial statements and, as considered necessary and appropriate, budgets, cash flow forecasts and other related management reports.

   • Inquiring, or extending previous oral or written inquiries, of the entity's lawyers concerning litigation and claims.

- Inquiring of management as to whether any subsequent events have occurred which might affect the financial statements. Examples of inquiries of management on specific matters are:

  - The current status of items that were accounted for on the basis of preliminary or inconclusive data.

  - Whether new commitments, borrowings or guarantees have been entered into.

  - Whether sales of assets have occurred or are planned.

  - Whether the issue of new shares or debentures or an agreement to merge or liquidate has been made or is planned.

  - Whether any assets have been appropriated by government or destroyed, for example, by fire or flood.

  - Whether there have been any developments regarding risk areas and contingencies.

  - Whether any unusual accounting adjustments have been made or are contemplated.

  - Whether any events have occurred or are likely to occur which will bring into question the appropriateness of accounting policies used in the financial statements as would be the case, for example, if such events call into question the validity of the going concern assumption.

6. When a component, such as a division, branch or subsidiary, is audited by another auditor, the auditor would consider the other auditor's procedures regarding events after period end and the need to inform the other auditor of the planned date of the auditor's report.

7. **When the auditor becomes aware of events which materially affect the financial statements, the auditor should consider whether such events are properly accounted for and adequately disclosed in the financial statements.**

Facts Discovered After the Date of the Auditor's Report but Before the Financial Statements are Issued

8. The auditor does not have any responsibility to perform procedures or make any inquiry regarding the financial statements after the date of the auditor's report. During the period from the date of the auditor's report to the date the financial statements are issued, the responsibility to inform the auditor of facts which may affect the financial statements rests with management.

9. **When, after the date of the auditor's report but before the financial statements are issued, the auditor becomes aware of a fact which may materially affect the financial statements, the auditor should consider whether the financial statements need amendment, should discuss the matter with management, and should take the action appropriate in the circumstances.**

10. When management amends the financial statements, the auditor would carry out the procedures necessary in the circumstances and would provide

AUDITING

management with a new report on the amended financial statements. The new auditor's report would be dated not earlier than the date the amended financial statements are signed or approved and, accordingly, the procedures referred to in paragraphs 4 and 5 would be extended to the date of the new auditor's report.

11. **When management does not amend the financial statements in circumstances where the auditor believes they need to be amended and the auditor's report has not been released to the entity, the auditor should express a qualified opinion or an adverse opinion.**

12. When the auditor's report has been released to the entity, the auditor would notify those persons ultimately responsible for the overall direction of the entity not to issue financial statements and the auditor's report thereon to third parties. If the financial statements are subsequently released, the auditor needs to take action to prevent reliance on the auditor's report. The action taken will depend on the auditor's legal rights and obligations and the recommendations of the auditor's lawyer.

Facts Discovered After the Financial Statements Have Been Issued

13. After the financial statements have been issued, the auditor has no obligation to make any inquiry regarding such financial statements.

14. **When, after the financial statements have been issued, the auditor becomes aware of a fact which existed at the date of the auditor's report and which, if known at that date, may have caused the auditor to modify the auditor's report, the auditor should consider whether the financial statements need revision, should discuss the matter with management, and should take the action appropriate in the circumstances.**

15. When management revises the financial statements, the auditor would carry out the audit procedures necessary in the circumstances, would review the steps taken by management to ensure that anyone in receipt of the previously issued financial statements together with the auditor's report thereon is informed of the situation, and would issue a new report on the revised financial statements.

16. **The new auditor's report should include an emphasis of a matter paragraph referring to a note to the financial statements that more extensively discusses the reason for the revision of the previously issued financial statements and to the earlier report issued by the auditor.** The new auditor's report would be dated not earlier than the date the revised financial statements are approved and, accordingly, the procedures referred to in paragraphs 4 and 5 would ordinarily be extended to the date of the new auditor's report. Local regulations of some countries permit the auditor to restrict the audit procedures regarding the revised financial statements to the effects of the subsequent event that necessitated the revision. In such cases, the new auditor's report would contain a statement to that effect.

17. When management does not take the necessary steps to ensure that anyone in receipt of the previously issued financial statements together with the auditor's report thereon is informed of the situation and does not revise the

financial statements in circumstances where the auditor believes they need to be revised, the auditor would notify those persons ultimately responsible for the overall direction of the entity that action will be taken by the auditor to prevent future reliance on the auditor's report. The action taken will depend on the auditor's legal rights and obligations and the recommendations of the auditor's lawyers.

18. It may not be necessary to revise the financial statements and issue a new auditor's report when issue of the financial statements for the following period is imminent, provided appropriate disclosures are to be made in such statements.

Offering of Securities to the Public

19. **In cases involving the offering of securities to the public, the auditor should consider any legal and related requirements applicable to the auditor in all jurisdictions in which the securities are being offered.** For example, the auditor may be required to carry out additional audit procedures to the date of the final offering document. These procedures would ordinarily include carrying out the procedures referred to in paragraphs 4 and 5 up to a date at or near the effective date of the final offering document and reading the offering document to assess whether the other information in the offering document is consistent with the financial information with which the auditor is associated.

AUDITING

CONTENTS

	Paragraphs
Introduction	1-4
Appropriateness of the Going Concern Assumption	5-7
Audit Evidence	8-11
Audit Conclusions and Reporting	12-18

International Standards on Auditing (ISAs) are to be applied in the audit of financial statements. ISAs are also to be applied, adapted as necessary, to the audit of other information and to related services.

ISAs contain the basic principles and essential procedures (identified in bold type black lettering) together with related guidance in the form of explanatory and other material. The basic principles and essential procedures are to be interpreted in the context of the explanatory and other material that provide guidance for their application.

To understand and apply the basic principles and essential procedures together with the related guidance, it is necessary to consider the whole text of the ISA including explanatory and other material contained in the ISA not just that text which is black lettered.

In exceptional circumstances, an auditor may judge it necessary to depart from an ISA in order to more effectively achieve the objective of an audit. When such a situation arises, the auditor should be prepared to justify the departure.

ISAs need only be applied to material matters.

The Public Sector Perspective (PSP) issued by the Public Sector Committee of the International Federation of Accountants is set out at the end of an ISA. Where no PSP is added, the ISA is applicable in all material respects to the public sector.

Introduction

1. The purpose of this International Standard on Auditing (ISA) is to establish standards and provide guidance on the auditor's responsibilities in the audit of financial statements regarding the appropriateness of the going concern assumption as a basis for the preparation of the financial statements.

2. **When planning and performing audit procedures and in evaluating the results thereof, the auditor should consider the appropriateness of the going concern assumption underlying the preparation of the financial statements.**

3. The auditor's report helps establish the credibility of the financial statements. However, the auditor's report is not a guarantee as to the future viability of the entity.

4. An entity's continuance as a going concern for the foreseeable future, generally a period not to exceed one year after period end, is assumed in the preparation of financial statements in the absence of information to the contrary. Accordingly, assets and liabilities are recorded on the basis that the entity will be able to realize its assets and discharge its liabilities in the normal course of business. If this assumption is unjustified, the entity may not be able to realize its assets at the recorded amounts and there may be changes in the amounts and maturity dates of liabilities. As a consequence, the amounts and classification of assets and liabilities in the financial statements may need to be adjusted.

Appropriateness of the Going Concern Assumption

5. **The auditor should consider the risk that the going concern assumption may no longer be appropriate.**

6. Indications of risk that continuance as a going concern may be questionable could come from the financial statements or from other sources. Examples of such indications that would be considered by the auditor are listed below. This listing is not all-inclusive nor does the existence of one or more always signify that the going concern assumption needs to be questioned.

Financial Indications

- Net liability or net current liability position.
- Fixed-term borrowings approaching maturity without realistic prospects of renewal or repayment, or excessive reliance on short-term borrowings to finance long-term assets.
- Adverse key financial ratios.
- Substantial operating losses.
- Arrears or discontinuance of dividends.
- Inability to pay creditors on due dates.
- Difficulty in complying with the terms of loan agreements.
- Change from credit to cash-on-delivery transactions with suppliers.

AUDITING

- Inability to obtain financing for essential new product development or other essential investments.

Operating Indications

- Loss of key management without replacement.
- Loss of a major market, franchise, license, or principal supplier.
- Labor difficulties or shortages of important supplies.

Other Indications

- Noncompliance with capital or other statutory requirements.
- Pending legal proceedings against the entity that may, if successful, result in judgments that could not be met.
- Changes in legislation or government policy.

7. The significance of such indications can often be mitigated by other factors. For example, the effect of an entity being unable to make its normal debt repayments may be counterbalanced by management's plans to maintain adequate cash flows by alternative means, such as by disposal of assets, rescheduling of loan repayments, or obtaining additional capital. Similarly, the loss of a principal supplier may be mitigated by the availability of a suitable alternative source of supply.

Audit Evidence

8. **When a question arises regarding the appropriateness of the going concern assumption, the auditor should gather sufficient appropriate audit evidence to attempt to resolve, to the auditor's satisfaction, the question regarding the entity's ability to continue in operation for the foreseeable future.**

9. During the course of the audit, the auditor carries out audit procedures designed to obtain audit evidence as the basis for the expression of an opinion on the financial statements. When a question arises regarding the going concern assumption, certain of these procedures may take on additional significance or it may be necessary to perform additional procedures or to update information obtained earlier. Procedures that are relevant in this connection may include:

- Analyze and discuss cash flow, profit and other relevant forecasts with management.
- Review events after period end for items affecting the entity's ability to continue as a going concern.
- Analyze and discuss the entity's latest available interim financial statements.
- Review the terms of debentures and loan agreements and determine whether any have been breached.
- Read minutes of the meetings of shareholders, the board of directors and important committees for reference to financing difficulties.
- Inquire of the entity's lawyer regarding litigation and claims.

- Confirm the existence, legality and enforceability of arrangements to provide or maintain financial support with related and third parties and assess the financial ability of such parties to provide additional funds.
- Consider the entity's position concerning unfilled customer orders.

10. When analyzing cash flow, profit and other relevant forecasts, the auditor would consider the reliability of the entity's system for generating such information. The auditor would also consider whether the assumptions underlying the forecast appear appropriate in the circumstances. In addition, the auditor would compare the prospective data for recent prior periods with historical results, and would compare the prospective data for the current period with results achieved to date.

11. The auditor would also consider and discuss with management its plans for future action, such as plans to liquidate assets, borrow money or restructure debt, reduce or delay expenditures, or increase capital. The relevance of such plans to an auditor generally decreases as the time period for planned actions and anticipated events increases. Particular emphasis is ordinarily placed on plans that might have a significant effect on the entity's solvency within the foreseeable future. The auditor would obtain sufficient appropriate audit evidence that these plans are feasible, are likely to be implemented and that the outcome of these plans will improve the situation. The auditor would ordinarily seek written representations from management regarding these plans.

Audit Conclusions and Reporting

12. After the procedures considered necessary have been carried out, all the information required has been obtained, and the effect of any plans of management and other mitigating factors have been considered, the auditor would decide whether the question raised regarding the going concern assumption has been satisfactorily resolved.

Going Concern Assumption Considered Appropriate

13. If, in the auditor's judgment, sufficient appropriate audit evidence has been obtained to support the going concern assumption, the auditor would not modify the auditor's report.

14. If, in the auditor's judgment, the going concern assumption is appropriate because of mitigating factors, in particular management's plans for future action, the auditor would consider whether such plans or other factors need to be disclosed in the financial statements. **If adequate disclosure is not made, the auditor should express a qualified or adverse opinion, as appropriate.**

Going Concern Question not Resolved

15. If, in the auditor's judgment, the going concern question is not satisfactorily resolved, the auditor would consider whether the financial statements:

(a) adequately describe the principal conditions that raise substantial doubt about the entity's ability to continue in operation for the foreseeable future;

(b) state that there is significant uncertainty that the entity will be able to continue as a going concern and, therefore, as appropriate may be unable to realize its assets and discharge its liabilities in the normal course of business; and

(c) state that the financial statements do not include any adjustments relating to the recoverability and classification of recorded asset amounts or to amounts and classification of liabilities that may be necessary if the entity is unable to continue as a going concern.

Provided the disclosure is considered adequate, the auditor would not express a qualified or adverse opinion.

16. **If adequate disclosure is made in the financial statements, the auditor should ordinarily express an unqualified opinion and modify the auditor's report by adding an emphasis of a matter paragraph that highlights the going concern problem by drawing attention to the note in the financial statements that discloses the matters set out in paragraph 15.** The following is an example of such a paragraph:

"Without qualifying our opinion we draw attention to Note X in the financial statements. The Company incurred a net loss of XXX during the year ended December 31, 19X1 and, as of that date, the Company's current liabilities exceeded its current assets by XXX and its total liabilities exceeded its total assets by XXX. These factors, along with other matters as set forth in Note X, raise substantial doubt that the Company will be able to continue as a going concern."

The auditor is not precluded from expressing a disclaimer of opinion for a going concern uncertainty.

17. **If adequate disclosure is not made in the financial statements, the auditor should express a qualified or adverse opinion, as appropriate.** The following is an example of the explanation and opinion paragraphs when a qualified opinion is to be expressed:

"The Company has been unable to renegotiate its borrowings from its bankers. Without such financial support there is substantial doubt that it will be able to continue as a going concern. Consequently adjustments may be required to the recorded asset amounts and classification of liabilities. The financial statements (and notes thereto) do not disclose this fact.

In our opinion, except for the omission of the information included in the preceding paragraph, the financial statements give a true and fair view of ('present fairly, in all material respects,') the financial position of the Company at December 31, 19XX and the results of its operations and its cash flows for the year then ended in accordance with ..."

Going Concern Assumption Considered Inappropriate

18. If, on the basis of the additional procedures carried out and the information obtained, including the effect of mitigating circumstances, the auditor's judgment is that the entity will not be able to continue in operation for the foreseeable future, the auditor would conclude that the going concern assumption used in the preparation of the financial statements is inappropriate. **If the result of the inappropriate assumption used in the preparation of the financial statements is so material and pervasive as to make the financial statements misleading, the auditor should express an adverse opinion.**

Public Sector Perspective

1. *The appropriateness of the going concern assumption is generally not in question when auditing either a central government or those public sector entities having funding arrangements backed by a central government. However, where such arrangements do not exist, or where central government funding of the entity may be withdrawn and the existence of the entity may be at risk, this ISA will provide useful guidance.*

2. *Even where the going concern of a public sector entity is not in question, auditors are expected generally to provide an assessment of the general financial standing of the entity under audit in terms of its ability to meet its commitments and likely future demands.*

AUDITING

CONTENTS

	Paragraphs
Introduction	1-2
Acknowledgment by Management of its Responsibility for the Financial Statements	3
Representations by Management as Audit Evidence	4-9
Documentation of Representations by Management	10-14
Action if Management Refuses to Provide Representations	15
Appendix: Example of a Management Representation Letter	

International Standards on Auditing (ISAs) are to be applied in the audit of financial statements. ISAs are also to be applied, adapted as necessary, to the audit of other information and to related services.

ISAs contain the basic principles and essential procedures (identified in bold type black lettering) together with related guidance in the form of explanatory and other material. The basic principles and essential procedures are to be interpreted in the context of the explanatory and other material that provide guidance for their application.

To understand and apply the basic principles and essential procedures together with the related guidance, it is necessary to consider the whole text of the ISA including explanatory and other material contained in the ISA not just that text which is black lettered.

In exceptional circumstances, an auditor may judge it necessary to depart from an ISA in order to more effectively achieve the objective of an audit. When such a situation arises, the auditor should be prepared to justify the departure.

ISAs need only be applied to material matters.

The Public Sector Perspective (PSP) issued by the Public Sector Committee of the International Federation of Accountants is set out at the end of an ISA. Where no PSP is added, the ISA is applicable in all material respects to the public sector.

Introduction

1. The purpose of this International Standard on Auditing (ISA) is to establish standards and provide guidance on the use of management representations as audit evidence, the procedures to be applied in evaluating and documenting management representations and the action to be taken if management refuses to provide appropriate representations.

2. **The auditor should obtain appropriate representations from management.**

Acknowledgment by Management of its Responsibility for the Financial Statements

3. **The auditor should obtain evidence that management acknowledges its responsibility for the fair presentation of the financial statements in accordance with the relevant financial reporting framework, and has approved the financial statements.** The auditor can obtain evidence of management's acknowledgment of such responsibility and approval from relevant minutes of meetings of the board of directors or similar body or by obtaining a written representation from management or a signed copy of the financial statements.

Representations by Management as Audit Evidence

4. **The auditor should obtain written representations from management on matters material to the financial statements when other sufficient appropriate audit evidence cannot reasonably be expected to exist.** The possibility of misunderstandings between the auditor and management is reduced when oral representations are confirmed by management in writing. Matters which might be included in a letter from management or in a confirmatory letter to management are contained in the example of a management representation letter in the Appendix to this ISA.

5. Written representations requested from management may be limited to matters that are considered either individually or collectively material to the financial statements. Regarding certain items it may be necessary to inform management of the auditor's understanding of materiality.

6. During the course of an audit, management makes many representations to the auditor, either unsolicited or in response to specific inquiries. When such representations relate to matters which are material to the financial statements, the auditor will need to:

    (a) seek corroborative audit evidence from sources inside or outside the entity;

    (b) evaluate whether the representations made by management appear reasonable and consistent with other audit evidence obtained, including other representations; and

AUDITING

(c) consider whether the individuals making the representations can be expected to be well informed on the particular matters.

7. Representations by management cannot be a substitute for other audit evidence that the auditor could reasonably expect to be available. For example, a representation by management as to the cost of an asset is not a substitute for the audit evidence of such cost that an auditor would ordinarily expect to obtain. If the auditor is unable to obtain sufficient appropriate audit evidence regarding a matter which has, or may have, a material effect on the financial statements and such evidence is expected to be available, this will constitute a limitation in the scope of the audit, even if a representation from management has been received on the matter.

8. In certain instances, a representation by management may be the only audit evidence which can reasonably be expected to be available. For example, the auditor would not necessarily expect that other audit evidence would be available to corroborate management's intention to hold a specific investment for long-term appreciation.

9. **If a representation by management is contradicted by other audit evidence, the auditor should investigate the circumstances and, when necessary, reconsider the reliability of other representations made by management.**

Documentation of Representations by Management

10. The auditor would ordinarily include in audit working papers evidence of management's representations in the form of a summary of oral discussions with management or written representations from management.

11. A written representation is better audit evidence than an oral representation and can take the form of:

(a) a representation letter from management;

(b) a letter from the auditor outlining the auditor's understanding of management's representations, duly acknowledged and confirmed by management; or

(c) relevant minutes of meetings of the board of directors or similar body or a signed copy of the financial statements.

Basic Elements of a Management Representation Letter

12. When requesting a management representation letter, the auditor would request that it be addressed to the auditor, contain specified information and be appropriately dated and signed.

13. A management representation letter would ordinarily be dated the same date as the auditor's report. However, in certain circumstances, a separate representation letter regarding specific transactions or other events may also be obtained during the course of the audit or at a date after the date of the auditor's report, for example, on the date of a public offering.

14. A management representation letter would ordinarily be signed by the members of management who have primary responsibility for the entity and its financial aspects (ordinarily the senior executive officer and the senior financial officer) based on the best of their knowledge and belief. In certain circumstances, the auditor may wish to obtain representation letters from other members of management. For example, the auditor may wish to obtain a written representation about the completeness of all minutes of the meetings of shareholders, the board of directors and important committees from the individual responsible for keeping such minutes.

Action if Management Refuses to Provide Representations

15. **If management refuses to provide a representation that the auditor considers necessary, this constitutes a scope limitation and the auditor should express a qualified opinion or a disclaimer of opinion.** In such circumstances, the auditor would evaluate any reliance placed on other representations made by management during the course of the audit and consider if the other implications of the refusal may have any additional effect on the auditor's report.

215

AUDITING

Appendix

Example of a Management Representation Letter

The following letter is not intended to be a standard letter. Representations by management will vary from one entity to another and from one period to the next.

Although seeking representations from management on a variety of matters may serve to focus management's attention on those matters, and thus cause management to specifically address those matters in more detail than would otherwise be the case, the auditor needs to be cognizant of the limitations of management representations as audit evidence as set out in this ISA.

(Entity Letterhead)

(To Auditor)   (Date)

This representation letter is provided in connection with your audit of the financial statements of ABC Company for the year ended December 31, 19X1 for the purpose of expressing an opinion as to whether the financial statements give a true and fair view of (or 'present fairly, in all material respects,') the financial position of ABC Company as of December 31, 19X1 and of the results of its operations and its cash flows for the year then ended in accordance with (indicate relevant financial reporting framework).

[1]We acknowledge our responsibility for the fair presentation of the financial statements in accordance with (indicate relevant financial reporting framework).

We confirm, to the best of our knowledge and belief, the following representations:

Include here representations relevant to the entity. Such representations may include:

- *There have been no irregularities involving management or employees who have a significant role in the accounting and internal control systems or that could have a material effect on the financial statements.*

- *We have made available to you all books of account and supporting documentation and all minutes of meetings of shareholders and the board of directors (namely those held on March 15, 19X1 and September 30, 19X1, respectively).*

- *We confirm the completeness of the information provided regarding the identification of related parties.*

- *The financial statements are free of material misstatements, including omissions.*

---

[1] If required add "On behalf of the board of directors (or similar body)."

- The Company has complied with all aspects of contractual agreements that could have a material effect on the financial statements in the event of noncompliance. There has been no noncompliance with requirements of regulatory authorities that could have a material effect on the financial statements in the event of noncompliance.

  - *The following have been properly recorded and when appropriate, adequately disclosed in the financial statements:*

    a) *The identity of, and balances and transactions with, related parties.*

    b) *Losses arising from sale and purchase commitments.*

    c) *Agreements and options to buy back assets previously sold.*

    d) *Assets pledged as collateral.*

  - *We have no plans or intentions that may materially alter the carrying value or classification of assets and liabilities reflected in the financial statements.*

  - *We have no plans to abandon lines of product or other plans or intentions that will result in any excess or obsolete inventory, and no inventory is stated at an amount in excess of net realizable value.*

  - *The Company has satisfactory title to all assets and there are no liens or encumbrances on the company's assets, except for those that are disclosed in Note X to the financial statements.*

  - *We have recorded or disclosed, as appropriate, all liabilities, both actual and contingent, and have disclosed in Note X to the financial statements all guarantees that we have given to third parties.*

  - *Other than . . . described in Note X to the financial statements, there have been no events subsequent to period end which require adjustment of or disclosure in the financial statements or Notes thereto.*

  - *The . . . claim by XYZ Company has been settled for the total sum of XXX which has been properly accrued in the financial statements. No other claims in connection with litigation have been or are expected to be received.*

  - *There are no formal or informal compensating balance arrangements with any of our cash and investment accounts. Except as disclosed in Note X to the financial statements, we have no other line of credit arrangements.*

  - *We have properly recorded or disclosed in the financial statements the capital stock repurchase options and agreements, and capital stock reserved for options, warrants, conversions and other requirements.*

_____

(Senior Executive Officer)

_____

(Senior Financial Officer)

AUDITING

CONTENTS

	Paragraphs
Introduction	1-5
Acceptance as Principal Auditor	6
The Principal Auditor's Procedures	7-14
Cooperation Between Auditors	15
Reporting Considerations	16-17
Division of Responsibility	18

International Standards on Auditing (ISAs) are to be applied in the audit of financial statements. ISAs are also to be applied, adapted as necessary, to the audit of other information and to related services.

ISAs contain the basic principles and essential procedures (identified in bold type black lettering) together with related guidance in the form of explanatory and other material. The basic principles and essential procedures are to be interpreted in the context of the explanatory and other material that provide guidance for their application.

To understand and apply the basic principles and essential procedures together with the related guidance, it is necessary to consider the whole text of the ISA including explanatory and other material contained in the ISA not just that text which is black lettered.

In exceptional circumstances, an auditor may judge it necessary to depart from an ISA in order to more effectively achieve the objective of an audit. When such a situation arises, the auditor should be prepared to justify the departure.

ISAs need only be applied to material matters.

The Public Sector Perspective (PSP) issued by the Public Sector Committee of the International Federation of Accountants is set out at the end of an ISA. Where no PSP is added, the ISA is applicable in all material respects to the public sector.

Introduction

1. The purpose of this International Standard on Auditing (ISA) is to establish standards and provide guidance when an auditor, reporting on the financial statements of an entity, uses the work of another auditor on the financial information of one or more components included in the financial statements of the entity. This ISA does not deal with those instances where two or more auditors are appointed as joint auditors nor does it deal with the auditor's relationship with a predecessor auditor. Further, when the principal auditor concludes that the financial statements of a component are immaterial, the standards in this ISA do not apply. When, however, several components, immaterial in themselves, are together material, the procedures outlined in this ISA would need to be considered.

2. **When the principal auditor uses the work of another auditor, the principal auditor should determine how the work of the other auditor will affect the audit.**

3. "Principal auditor" means the auditor with responsibility for reporting on the financial statements of an entity when those financial statements include financial information of one or more components audited by another auditor.

4. "Other auditor" means an auditor, other than the principal auditor, with responsibility for reporting on the financial information of a component which is included in the financial statements audited by the principal auditor. Other auditors include affiliated firms, whether using the same name or not, and correspondents, as well as unrelated auditors.

5. "Component" means a division, branch, subsidiary, joint venture, associated company or other entity whose financial information is included in financial statements audited by the principal auditor.

Acceptance as Principal Auditor

6. **The auditor should consider whether the auditor's own participation is sufficient to be able to act as the principal auditor.** For this purpose the principal auditor would consider:

    (a) the materiality of the portion of the financial statements which the principal auditor audits;

    (b) the principal auditor's degree of knowledge regarding the business of the components;

    (c) the risk of material misstatements in the financial statements of the components audited by the other auditor; and

    (d) the performance of additional procedures as set out in this ISA regarding the components audited by the other auditor resulting in the principal auditor having significant participation in such audit.

The Principal Auditor's Procedures

7. **When planning to use the work of another auditor, the principal auditor should consider the professional competence of the other auditor in the context of the specific assignment.** Some of the sources of information for this consideration could be common membership of a professional organization, common membership of, or affiliation, with another firm or reference to the professional organization to which the other auditor belongs. These sources can be supplemented when appropriate by inquiries with other auditors, bankers, etc. and by discussions with the other auditor.

8. **The principal auditor should perform procedures to obtain sufficient appropriate audit evidence, that the work of the other auditor is adequate for the principal auditor's purposes, in the context of the specific assignment.**

9. The principal auditor would advise the other auditor of:

    (a) the independence requirements regarding both the entity and the component and obtain written representation as to compliance with them;

    (b) the use that is to be made of the other auditor's work and report and make sufficient arrangements for the coordination of their efforts at the initial planning stage of the audit. The principal auditor would inform the other auditor of matters such as areas requiring special consideration, procedures for the identification of intercompany transactions that may require disclosure and the timetable for completion of the audit; and

    (c) the accounting, auditing and reporting requirements and obtain written representation as to compliance with them.

10. The principal auditor might also, for example, discuss with the other auditor the audit procedures applied, review a written summary of the other auditor's procedures (which may be in the form of a questionnaire or checklist) or review working papers of the other auditor. The principal auditor may wish to perform these procedures during a visit to the other auditor. The nature, timing and extent of procedures will depend on the circumstances of the engagement and the principal auditor's knowledge of the professional competence of the other auditor. This knowledge may have been enhanced from the review of previous audit work of the other auditor.

11. The principal auditor may conclude that it is not necessary to apply procedures such as those described in paragraph 10 because sufficient appropriate audit evidence previously obtained that acceptable quality control policies and procedures are complied with in the conduct of the other auditor's practice. For example, when they are affiliated firms the principal auditor and the other auditor may have a continuing, formal relationship providing for procedures that give that audit evidence such as periodic inter-firm review, tests of operating policies and procedures and review of working papers of selected audits.

12. **The principal auditor should consider the significant findings of the other auditor.**

13. The principal auditor may consider it appropriate to discuss with the other auditor and the management of the component, the audit findings or other matters affecting the financial information of the component and may also decide that supplementary tests of the records or the financial information of the component are necessary. Such tests may, depending on the circumstances, be performed by the principal auditor or the other auditor.

14. The principal auditor would document in the audit working papers the components whose financial information was audited by other auditors, their significance to the financial statements of the entity as a whole, the names of the other auditors and any conclusions reached that individual components are immaterial. The principal auditor would also document the procedures performed and the conclusions reached. For example, working papers of the other auditor that have been reviewed would be identified and the results of discussions with the other auditor would be recorded. However, the principal auditor need not document the reasons for limiting the procedures in the circumstances described in paragraph 11, provided those reasons are summarized elsewhere in documentation maintained by the principal auditor's firm.

Cooperation Between Auditors

15. **The other auditor, knowing the context in which the principal auditor will use the other auditor's work, should cooperate with the principal auditor.** For example, the other auditor would bring to the principal auditor's attention any aspect of the other auditor's work that cannot be carried out as requested. Similarly, subject to legal and professional considerations, the other auditor will need to be advised of any matters that come to the attention of the principal auditor which may have an important bearing on the other auditor's work.

Reporting Considerations

16. **When the principal auditor concludes that the work of the other auditor cannot be used and the principal auditor has not been able to perform sufficient additional procedures regarding the financial information of the component audited by the other auditor, the principal auditor should express a qualified opinion or disclaimer of opinion because there is a limitation in the scope of the audit.**

17. If the other auditor issues, or intends to issue, a modified auditor's report, the principal auditor would consider whether the subject of the modification is of such a nature and significance, in relation to the financial statements of the entity on which the principal auditor is reporting, that a modification of the principal auditor's report is required.

Division of Responsibility

18. While compliance with the guidance in the preceding paragraphs is considered desirable, the local regulations of some countries permit a principal auditor to base the audit opinion on the financial statements taken as a whole solely upon the report of another auditor regarding the audit of one or more components. **When the principal auditor does so, the principal auditor's report should state this fact clearly and should indicate the magnitude of the portion of the financial statements audited by the other auditor.** When the principal auditor makes such a reference in the auditor's report, audit procedures are ordinarily limited to those described in paragraphs 7 and 9.

Public Sector Perspective

1. *The basic principles in this ISA apply to the audit of financial statements in the public sector, however, supplementary guidance on additional considerations when using the work of other auditors in the public sector is needed. For example, the principal auditor in the public sector has to ensure that, where legislation has prescribed compliance with a particular set of auditing standards, the other auditor has complied with those standards. In respect to public sector entities, the Public Sector Committee has supplemented the guidance included in this ISA in its Study 4 "Using the Work of Other Auditors—A Public Sector Perspective."*

CONTENTS

	Paragraphs
Introduction	1-4
Scope and Objectives of Internal Auditing	5
Relationship Between Internal Auditing and the External Auditor	6-8
Understanding and Preliminary Assessment of Internal Auditing	9-13
Timing of Liaison and Coordination	14-15
Evaluating and Testing the Work of Internal Auditing	16-19

International Standards on Auditing (ISAs) are to be applied in the audit of financial statements. ISAs are also to be applied, adapted as necessary, to the audit of other information and to related services.

ISAs contain the basic principles and essential procedures (identified in bold type black lettering) together with related guidance in the form of explanatory and other material. The basic principles and essential procedures are to be interpreted in the context of the explanatory and other material that provide guidance for their application.

To understand and apply the basic principles and essential procedures together with the related guidance, it is necessary to consider the whole text of the ISA including explanatory and other material contained in the ISA not just that text which is black lettered.

In exceptional circumstances, an auditor may judge it necessary to depart from an ISA in order to more effectively achieve the objective of an audit. When such a situation arises, the auditor should be prepared to justify the departure.

ISAs need only be applied to material matters.

The Public Sector Perspective (PSP) issued by the Public Sector Committee of the International Federation of Accountants is set out at the end of an ISA. Where no PSP is added, the ISA is applicable in all material respects to the public sector.

AUDITING

610

Introduction

1. The purpose of this International Standard on Auditing (ISA) is to establish standards and provide guidance to external auditors in considering the work of internal auditing. This ISA does not deal with instances when personnel from internal auditing assist the external auditor in carrying out external audit procedures. The procedures noted in this ISA need only be applied to internal auditing activities which are relevant to the audit of the financial statements.

2. **The external auditor should consider the activities of internal auditing and their effect, if any, on external audit procedures.**

3. "Internal auditing" means an appraisal activity established within an entity as a service to the entity. Its functions include, amongst other things, examining, evaluating and monitoring the adequacy and effectiveness of the accounting and internal control systems.

4. While the external auditor has sole responsibility for the audit opinion expressed and for determining the nature, timing and extent of external audit procedures, certain parts of internal auditing work may be useful to the external auditor.

Scope and Objectives of Internal Auditing

5. The scope and objectives of internal auditing vary widely and depend on the size and structure of the entity and the requirements of its management. Ordinarily, internal auditing activities include one or more of the following:

   - Review of the accounting and internal control systems. The establishment of adequate accounting and internal control systems is a responsibility of management which demands proper attention on a continuous basis. Internal auditing is ordinarily assigned specific responsibility by management for reviewing these systems, monitoring their operation and recommending improvements thereto.

   - Examination of financial and operating information. This may include review of the means used to identify, measure, classify and report such information and specific inquiry into individual items including detailed testing of transactions, balances and procedures.

   - Review of the economy, efficiency and effectiveness of operations including non-financial controls of an entity.

   - Review of compliance with laws, regulations and other external requirements and with management policies and directives and other internal requirements.

Relationship Between Internal Auditing and the External Auditor

6. The role of internal auditing is determined by management, and its objectives differ from those of the external auditor who is appointed to report independently on the financial statements. The internal audit function's objectives vary according to management's requirements. The external

auditor's primary concern is whether the financial statements are free of material misstatements.

7. Nevertheless some of the means of achieving their respective objectives are often similar and thus certain aspects of internal auditing may be useful in determining the nature, timing and extent of external audit procedures.

8. Internal auditing is part of the entity. Irrespective of the degree of autonomy and objectivity of internal auditing, it cannot achieve the same degree of independence as required of the external auditor when expressing an opinion on the financial statements. The external auditor has sole responsibility for the audit opinion expressed, and that responsibility is not reduced by any use made of internal auditing. All judgments relating to the audit of the financial statements are those of the external auditor.

Understanding and Preliminary Assessment of Internal Auditing

9. **The external auditor should obtain a sufficient understanding of internal audit activities to assist in planning the audit and developing an effective audit approach.**

10. Effective internal auditing will often allow a modification in the nature and timing, and a reduction in the extent of procedures performed by the external auditor but cannot eliminate them entirely. In some cases, however, having considered the activities of internal auditing, the external auditor may decide that internal auditing will have no effect on external audit procedures.

11. **During the course of planning the audit, the external auditor should perform a preliminary assessment of the internal audit function when it appears that internal auditing is relevant to the external audit of the financial statements in specific audit areas.**

12. The external auditor's preliminary assessment of the internal audit function will influence the external auditor's judgment about the use which may be made of internal auditing in modifying the nature, timing and extent of external audit procedures.

13. When obtaining an understanding and performing a preliminary assessment of the internal audit function, the important criteria are:

    (a) Organizational Status: specific status of internal auditing in the entity and the effect this has on its ability to be objective. In the ideal situation, internal auditing will report to the highest level of management and be free of any other operating responsibility. Any constraints or restrictions placed on internal auditing by management would need to be carefully considered. In particular, the internal auditors will need to be free to communicate fully with the external auditor.

    (b) Scope of Function: the nature and extent of internal auditing assignments performed. The external auditor would also need to consider whether management acts on internal audit recommendations and how this is evidenced.

AUDITING

610

(c) Technical Competence: whether internal auditing is performed by persons having adequate technical training and proficiency as internal auditors. The external auditor may, for example, review the policies for hiring and training the internal auditing staff and their experience and professional qualifications.

(d) Due Professional Care: whether internal auditing is properly planned, supervised, reviewed and documented. The existence of adequate audit manuals, work programs and working papers would be considered.

Timing of Liaison and Coordination

14. When planning to use the work of internal auditing, the external auditor will need to consider internal auditing's tentative plan for the period and discuss it at as early a stage as possible. Where the work of internal auditing is to be a factor in determining the nature, timing and extent of the external auditor's procedures, it is desirable to agree in advance the timing of such work, the extent of audit coverage, test levels and proposed methods of sample selection, documentation of the work performed and review and reporting procedures.

15. Liaison with internal auditing is more effective when meetings are held at appropriate intervals during the period. The external auditor would need to be advised of and have access to relevant internal auditing reports and be kept informed of any significant matter that comes to the internal auditor's attention which may affect the work of the external auditor. Similarly, the external auditor would ordinarily inform the internal auditor of any significant matters which may affect internal auditing.

Evaluating and Testing the Work of Internal Auditing

16. **When the external auditor intends to use specific work of internal auditing, the external auditor should evaluate and test that work to confirm its adequacy for the external auditor's purposes.**

17. The evaluation of specific work of internal auditing involves consideration of the adequacy of the scope of work and related programs and whether the preliminary assessment of the internal auditing remains appropriate. This evaluation may include consideration of whether:

(a) the work is performed by persons having adequate technical training and proficiency as internal auditors and the work of assistants is properly supervised, reviewed and documented;

(b) sufficient appropriate audit evidence is obtained to afford a reasonable basis for the conclusions reached;

(c) conclusions reached are appropriate in the circumstances and any reports prepared are consistent with the results of the work performed; and

(d) any exceptions or unusual matters disclosed by internal auditing are properly resolved.

18.   The nature, timing and extent of the testing of the specific work of internal auditing will depend on the external auditor's judgment as to the risk and materiality of the area concerned, the preliminary assessment of internal auditing and the evaluation of the specific work by internal auditing. Such tests may include examination of items already examined by internal auditing, examination of other similar items and observation of internal auditing procedures.

19.   The external auditor would record conclusions regarding the specific internal auditing work that has been evaluated and tested.

Public Sector Perspective

1.   *The basic principles in this ISA apply to the audit of financial statements in the public sector. Supplementary guidance on additional considerations, when considering the work of internal auditing in the public sector is provided in the Public Sector Committee's Study 4 "Using the Work of Other Auditors—A Public Sector Perspective."*

AUDITING

CONTENTS

	Paragraphs
Introduction	1-5
Determining the Need to Use the Work of an Expert	6-7
Competence and Objectivity of the Expert	8-10
Scope of the Expert's Work	11
Assessing the Work of the Expert	12-15
Reference to an Expert in the Auditor's Report	16-17

International Standards on Auditing (ISAs) are to be applied in the audit of financial statements. ISAs are also to be applied, adapted as necessary, to the audit of other information and to related services.

ISAs contain the basic principles and essential procedures (identified in bold type black lettering) together with related guidance in the form of explanatory and other material. The basic principles and essential procedures are to be interpreted in the context of the explanatory and other material that provide guidance for their application.

To understand and apply the basic principles and essential procedures together with the related guidance, it is necessary to consider the whole text of the ISA including explanatory and other material contained in the ISA not just that text which is black lettered.

In exceptional circumstances, an auditor may judge it necessary to depart from an ISA in order to more effectively achieve the objective of an audit. When such a situation arises, the auditor should be prepared to justify the departure.

ISAs need only be applied to material matters.

The Public Sector Perspective (PSP) issued by the Public Sector Committee of the International Federation of Accountants is set out at the end of an ISA. Where no PSP is added, the ISA is applicable in all material respects to the public sector.

Introduction

1. The purpose of this International Standard on Auditing (ISA) is to establish standards and provide guidance on using the work of an expert as audit evidence.

2. **When using the work performed by an expert, the auditor should obtain sufficient appropriate audit evidence that such work is adequate for the purposes of the audit.**

3. "Expert" means a person or firm possessing special skill, knowledge and experience in a particular field other than accounting and auditing.

4. The auditor's education and experience enable the auditor to be knowledgeable about business matters in general, but the auditor is not expected to have the expertise of a person trained for or qualified to engage in the practice of another profession or occupation, such as an actuary or engineer.

5. An expert may be:

   (a) engaged by the entity;

   (b) engaged by the auditor;

   (c) employed by the entity; or

   (d) employed by the auditor.

   When the auditor uses the work of an expert employed by the auditor, that work is used in the employee's capacity as an expert rather than as an assistant on the audit as contemplated in ISA 220 "Quality Control for Audit Work." Accordingly, in such circumstances the auditor will need to apply relevant procedures to the employee's work and findings but will not ordinarily need to assess for each engagement the employee's skills and competence.

Determining the Need to Use the Work of an Expert

6. During the audit the auditor may need to obtain, in conjunction with the entity or independently, audit evidence in the form of reports, opinions, valuations and statements of an expert. Examples are:

   - Valuations of certain types of assets, for example, land and buildings, plant and machinery, works of art, and precious stones.

   - Determination of quantities or physical condition of assets, for example, minerals stored in stockpiles, underground mineral and petroleum reserves, and the remaining useful life of plant and machinery.

   - Determination of amounts using specialized techniques or methods, for example, an actuarial valuation.

   - The measurement of work completed and to be completed on contracts in progress.

AUDITING

- Legal opinions concerning interpretations of agreements, statutes and regulations.

7. When determining the need to use the work of an expert, the auditor would consider:

    (a) the materiality of the financial statement item being considered;

    (b) the risk of misstatement based on the nature and complexity of the matter being considered; and

    (c) the quantity and quality of other audit evidence available.

Competence and Objectivity of the Expert

8. **When planning to use the work of an expert, the auditor should assess the professional competence of the expert.** This will involve considering the expert's:

    (a) professional certification or licensing by, or membership in, an appropriate professional body; and

    (b) experience and reputation in the field in which the auditor is seeking audit evidence.

9. **The auditor should assess the objectivity of the expert.**

10. The risk that an expert's objectivity will be impaired increases when the expert is:

    (a) employed by the entity; or

    (b) related in some other manner to the entity, for example, by being financially dependent upon or having an investment in the entity.

    If the auditor is concerned regarding the competence or objectivity of the expert, the auditor needs to discuss any reservations with management and consider whether sufficient appropriate audit evidence can be obtained concerning the work of an expert. The auditor may need to undertake additional audit procedures or seek audit evidence from another expert (after taking into account the factors in paragraph 7).

Scope of the Expert's Work

11. **The auditor should obtain sufficient appropriate audit evidence that the scope of the expert's work is adequate for the purposes of the audit.** Audit evidence may be obtained through a review of the terms of reference which are often set out in written instructions from the entity to the expert. Such instructions to the expert may cover matters such as:

    - The objectives and scope of the expert's work.

    - A general outline as to the specific matters the auditor expects the expert's report to cover.

- The intended use by the auditor of the expert's work, including the possible communication to third parties of the expert's identity and extent of involvement.

- The extent of the expert's access to appropriate records and files.

- Clarification of the expert's relationship with the entity, if any.

- Confidentiality of the entity's information.

- Information regarding the assumptions and methods intended to be used by the expert and their consistency with those used in prior periods.

In the event that these matters are not clearly set out in written instructions to the expert, the auditor may need to communicate with the expert directly to obtain audit evidence in this regard.

Assessing the Work of the Expert

12. **The auditor should assess the appropriateness of the expert's work as audit evidence regarding the financial statement assertion being considered.** This will involve assessment of whether the substance of the expert's findings is properly reflected in the financial statements or supports the financial statement assertions, and consideration of:

- Source data used.

- Assumptions and methods used and their consistency with prior periods.

- Results of the expert's work in the light of the auditor's overall knowledge of the business and of the results of other audit procedures.

13. When considering whether the expert has used source data which is appropriate in the circumstances, the auditor would consider the following procedures:

    (a) making inquiries regarding any procedures undertaken by the expert to establish whether the source data is sufficient, relevant and reliable; and

    (b) reviewing or testing the data used by the expert.

14. The appropriateness and reasonableness of assumptions and methods used and their application are the responsibility of the expert. The auditor does not have the same expertise and, therefore, cannot always challenge the expert's assumptions and methods. However, the auditor will need to obtain an understanding of the assumptions and methods used and to consider whether they are appropriate and reasonable, based on the auditor's knowledge of the business and the results of other audit procedures.

15. **If the results of the expert's work do not provide sufficient appropriate audit evidence or if the results are not consistent with other audit evidence, the auditor should resolve the matter.** This may involve discussions with the entity and the expert, applying additional procedures, including possibly engaging another expert, or modifying the auditor's report.

AUDITING

Reference to an Expert in the Auditor's Report

16. **When issuing an unmodified auditor's report, the auditor should not refer to the work of an expert.** Such a reference might be misunderstood to be a qualification of the auditor's opinion or a division of responsibility, neither of which is intended.

17. If, as a result of the work of an expert, the auditor decides to issue a modified auditor's report, in some circumstances it may be appropriate, in explaining the nature of the modification, to refer to or describe the work of the expert (including the identity of the expert and the extent of the expert's involvement). In these circumstances, the auditor would obtain the permission of the expert before making such a reference. If permission is refused and the auditor believes a reference is necessary, the auditor may need to seek legal advice.

CONTENTS

	Paragraphs
Introduction	1-4
Basic Elements of the Auditor's Report	5-26
The Auditor's Report	27-28
Modified Reports	29-40
Circumstances That May Result in Other Than an Unqualified Opinion	41-46

International Standards on Auditing (ISAs) are to be applied in the audit of financial statements. ISAs are also to be applied, adapted as necessary, to the audit of other information and to related services.

ISAs contain the basic principles and essential procedures (identified in bold type black lettering) together with related guidance in the form of explanatory and other material. The basic principles and essential procedures are to be interpreted in the context of the explanatory and other material that provide guidance for their application.

To understand and apply the basic principles and essential procedures together with the related guidance, it is necessary to consider the whole text of the ISA including explanatory and other material contained in the ISA not just that text which is black lettered.

In exceptional circumstances, an auditor may judge it necessary to depart from an ISA in order to more effectively achieve the objective of an audit. When such a situation arises, the auditor should be prepared to justify the departure.

ISAs need only be applied to material matters.

The Public Sector Perspective (PSP) issued by the Public Sector Committee of the International Federation of Accountants is set out at the end of an ISA. Where no PSP is added, the ISA is applicable in all material respects to the public sector.

AUDITING

700

Introduction

1. The purpose of this International Standard on Auditing (ISA) is to establish standards and provide guidance on the form and content of the auditor's report issued as a result of an audit performed by an independent auditor of the financial statements of an entity. Much of the guidance provided can be adapted to auditor reports on financial information other than financial statements.

2. **The auditor should review and assess the conclusions drawn from the audit evidence obtained as the basis for the expression of an opinion on the financial statements.**

3. This review and assessment involves considering whether the financial statements have been prepared in accordance with an acceptable financial reporting framework[1] being either International Accounting Standards (IASs) or relevant national standards or practices. It may also be necessary to consider whether the financial statements comply with statutory requirements.

4. **The auditor's report should contain a clear written expression of opinion on the financial statements taken as a whole.**

Basic Elements of the Auditor's Report

5. The auditor's report includes the following basic elements, ordinarily in the following layout:

   (a) title;

   (b) addressee;

   (c) *opening or introductory paragraph*

       (i) identification of the financial statements audited;

       (ii) a statement of the responsibility of the entity's management and the responsibility of the auditor;

   (d) *scope paragraph (describing the nature of an audit)*

       (i) a reference to the ISAs or relevant national standards or practices;

       (ii) a description of the work the auditor performed;

   (e) *opinion paragraph* containing an expression of opinion on the financial statements;

   (f) date of the report;

   (g) auditor's address; and

---

[1] The Framework of International Standards on Auditing also identifies another authoritative and comprehensive financial reporting framework. Reporting in accordance with this third type of framework is covered in ISA 800 "The Auditor's Report on Special Purpose Audit Engagements."

(h)   auditor's signature.

A measure of uniformity in the form and content of the auditor's report is desirable because it helps to promote the reader's understanding and to identify unusual circumstances when they occur.

Title

6.   **The auditor's report should have an appropriate title.**   It may be appropriate to use the term "Independent Auditor" in the title to distinguish the auditor's report from reports that might be issued by others, such as by officers of the entity, the board of directors, or from the reports of other auditors who may not have to abide by the same ethical requirements as the independent auditor.

Addressee

7.   **The auditor's report should be appropriately addressed as required by the circumstances of the engagement and local regulations.**   The report is ordinarily addressed either to the shareholders or the board of directors of the entity whose financial statements are being audited.

Opening or Introductory Paragraph

8.   **The auditor's report should identify the financial statements of the entity that have been audited, including the date of and period covered by the financial statements.**

9.   **The report should include a statement that the financial statements are the responsibility of the entity's management[2] and a statement that the responsibility of the auditor is to express an opinion on the financial statements based on the audit.**

10.   Financial statements are the representations of management. The preparation of such statements requires management to make significant accounting estimates and judgments, as well as to determine the appropriate accounting principles and methods used in preparation of the financial statements. In contrast, the auditor's responsibility is to audit these financial statements in order to express an opinion thereon.

11.   An illustration of these matters in an opening (introductory) paragraph is:

"We have audited the accompanying[3] balance sheet of the ABC Company as of December 31, 19X1, and the related statements of income and cash flows for the year then ended.   These financial statements are the responsibility of the Company's management. Our responsibility is to express an opinion on these financial statements based on our audit."

---

[2] The level of management responsible for the financial statements will vary according to the legal situation in each country.

[3] The reference can be by page numbers.

AUDITING

Scope Paragraph

12. **The auditor's report should describe the scope of the audit by stating that the audit was conducted in accordance with ISAs or in accordance with relevant national standards or practices as appropriate.** "Scope" refers to the auditor's ability to perform audit procedures deemed necessary in the circumstances. The reader needs this as an assurance that the audit has been carried out in accordance with established standards or practices. Unless otherwise stated, the auditing standards or practices followed are presumed to be those of the country indicated by the auditor's address.

13. **The report should include a statement that the audit was planned and performed to obtain reasonable assurance about whether the financial statements are free of material misstatement.**

14. **The auditor's report should describe the audit as including:**

    (a) **examining, on a test basis, evidence to support the financial statement amounts and disclosures;**

    (b) **assessing the accounting principles used in the preparation of the financial statements;**

    (c) **assessing the significant estimates made by management in the preparation of the financial statements; and**

    (d) **evaluating the overall financial statement presentation.**

15. **The report should include a statement by the auditor that the audit provides a reasonable basis for the opinion.**

16. An illustration of these matters in a scope paragraph is:

    "We conducted our audit in accordance with International Standards on Auditing (or refer to relevant national standards or practices). Those Standards require that we plan and perform the audit to obtain reasonable assurance about whether the financial statements are free of material misstatement. An audit includes examining, on a test basis, evidence supporting the amounts and disclosures in the financial statements. An audit also includes assessing the accounting principles used and significant estimates made by management, as well as evaluating the overall financial statement presentation. We believe that our audit provides a reasonable basis for our opinion."

Opinion Paragraph

17. **The auditor's report should clearly state the auditor's opinion as to whether the financial statements give a true and fair view (or are presented fairly, in all material respects,) in accordance with the financial reporting framework and, where appropriate, whether the financial statements comply with statutory requirements.**

18. The terms used to express the auditor's opinion are "give a true and fair view" or "present fairly, in all material respects," and are equivalent. Both

terms indicate, amongst other things, that the auditor considers only those matters that are material to the financial statements.

19.   The financial reporting framework is determined by IASs, rules issued by professional bodies, and the development of general practice within a country, with an appropriate consideration of fairness and with due regard to local legislation. To advise the reader of the context in which "fairness" is expressed, the auditor's opinion would indicate the framework upon which the financial statements are based by using words such as "in accordance with (indicate IASs or relevant national standards)."

20.   In addition to an opinion on the true and fair view (or fair presentation, in all material respects,), the auditor's report may need to include an opinion as to whether the financial statements comply with other requirements specified by relevant statutes or law.

21.   An illustration of these matters in an opinion paragraph is:

> "In our opinion, the financial statements give a true and fair view of (or 'present fairly, in all material respects,') the financial position of the Company as of December 31, 19X1, and of the results of its operations and its cash flows for the year then ended in accordance with ...[4] (and comply with ...[5])."

22.   **In any situation where it is not evident which country's accounting principles have been used, the country should be stated.** When reporting on financial statements that are distributed extensively outside the country of origin, it is recommended that the auditor refer to the standards of the country of origin in the auditor's report, such as:

> "...in accordance with accounting principles generally accepted in country A...."

This designation will help the user to better understand which accounting principles were used in preparing the financial statements. When reporting on financial statements that are prepared specifically for use in another country (e.g., where the statements have been translated into the language and currency of another country in a cross-border financing), the auditor will consider the need to refer to the accounting principles of the country of origin where prepared, and consider whether appropriate disclosure has been made in the statements.

Date of Report

23.   **The auditor should date the report as of the completion date of the audit.** This informs the reader that the auditor has considered the effect on the financial statements and on the report of events and transactions of which the auditor became aware and that occurred up to that date.

---

[4] Indicate IASs or relevant national standards.

[5] Refer to relevant statutes or law.

24. **Since the auditor's responsibility is to report on the financial statements as prepared and presented by management, the auditor should not date the report earlier than the date on which the financial statements are signed or approved by management.**

Auditor's Address

25. **The report should name a specific location, which is ordinarily the city where the auditor maintains the office that has responsibility for the audit.**

Auditor's Signature

26. **The report should be signed in the name of the audit firm, the personal name of the auditor or both, as appropriate.** The auditor's report is ordinarily signed in the name of the firm because the firm assumes responsibility for the audit.

The Auditor's Report

27. **An *unqualified opinion* should be expressed when the auditor concludes that the financial statements give a true and fair view (or are presented fairly, in all material respects,) in accordance with the identified financial reporting framework.** An unqualified opinion also indicates implicitly that any changes in accounting principles or in the method of their application, and the effects thereof, have been properly determined and disclosed in the financial statements.

28. The following is an illustration of the entire auditor's report incorporating the basic elements set forth and illustrated above. This report illustrates the expression of an unqualified opinion.

"AUDITOR'S REPORT

(APPROPRIATE ADDRESSEE)

We have audited the accompanying[6] balance sheet of the ABC Company as of December 31, 19X1, and the related statements of income, and cash flows for the year then ended. These financial statements are the responsibility of the Company's management. Our responsibility is to express an opinion on these financial statements based on our audit.

We conducted our audit in accordance with International Standards on Auditing (or refer to relevant national standards or practices). Those Standards require that we plan and perform the audit to obtain reasonable assurance about whether the financial statements are free of material misstatement. An audit includes examining, on a test basis, evidence supporting the amounts and disclosures in the financial statements. An audit also includes assessing the accounting principles

---

[6] See footnote 3.

used and significant estimates made by management, as well as evaluating the overall financial statement presentation. We believe that our audit provides a reasonable basis for our opinion.

In our opinion, the financial statements give a true and fair view of (or 'present fairly, in all material respects,') the financial position of the Company as of December 31, 19X1, and of the results of its operations and its cash flows for the year then ended in accordance with ...[7] (and comply with ...[8]).

AUDITOR

Date
Address"

Modified Reports

29. An auditor's report is considered to be modified in the following situations:

Matters That Do Not Affect the Auditor's Opinion

(a)   emphasis of matter

Matters That Do Affect the Auditor's Opinion

(a)   qualified opinion,

(b)   disclaimer of opinion, or

(c)   adverse opinion.

Uniformity in the form and content of each type of modified report will further the user's understanding of such reports. Accordingly, this ISA includes suggested wording to express an unqualified opinion as well as examples of modifying phrases for use when issuing modified reports.

Matters That Do Not Affect the Auditor's Opinion

30. In certain circumstances, an auditor's report may be modified by adding an emphasis of matter paragraph to highlight a matter affecting the financial statements which is included in a note to the financial statements that more extensively discusses the matter. The addition of such an emphasis of matter paragraph does not affect the auditor's opinion. The paragraph would preferably be included after the opinion paragraph and would ordinarily refer to the fact that the auditor's opinion is not qualified in this respect.

31. **The auditor should modify the auditor's report by adding a paragraph to highlight a material matter regarding a going concern problem.**

32. **The auditor should consider modifying the auditor's report by adding a paragraph if there is a significant uncertainty (other than a going concern problem), the resolution of which is dependent upon future**

---

[7] See footnote 4.

[8] See footnote 5.

AUDITING

events and which may affect the financial statements. An uncertainty is a matter whose outcome depends on future actions or events not under the direct control of the entity but that may affect the financial statements.

33. An illustration of an emphasis of matter paragraph for a significant uncertainty in an auditor's report follows:

> "In our opinion ... (remaining words are the same as illustrated in the opinion paragraph—paragraph 28 above).

> *Without qualifying our opinion we draw attention to Note X to the financial statements. The Company is the defendant in a lawsuit alleging infringement of certain patent rights and claiming royalties and punitive damages. The Company has filed a counter action, and preliminary hearings and discovery proceedings on both actions are in progress. The ultimate outcome of the matter cannot presently be determined, and no provision for any liability that may result has been made in the financial statements."*

(An illustration of an emphasis of matter paragraph relating to going concern is set out in ISA 570 "Going Concern.")

34. The addition of a paragraph emphasizing a going concern problem or significant uncertainty is ordinarily adequate to meet the auditor's reporting responsibilities regarding such matters. However, in extreme cases, such as situations involving multiple uncertainties that are significant to the financial statements, the auditor may consider it appropriate to express a disclaimer of opinion instead of adding an emphasis of matter paragraph.

35. In addition to the use of an emphasis of matter paragraph for matters that affect the financial statements, the auditor may also modify the auditor's report by using an emphasis of matter paragraph, preferably after the opinion paragraph, to report on matters other than those affecting the financial statements. For example, if an amendment to other information in a document containing audited financial statements is necessary and the entity refuses to make the amendment, the auditor would consider including in the auditor's report an emphasis of matter paragraph describing the material inconsistency. An emphasis of matter paragraph may also be used when there are additional statutory reporting responsibilities.

Matters That Do Affect the Auditor's Opinion

36. An auditor may not be able to express an unqualified opinion when either of the following circumstances exist and, in the auditor's judgment, the effect of the matter is or may be material to the financial statements:

    (a) there is a limitation on the scope of the auditor's work; or

    (b) there is a disagreement with management regarding the acceptability of the accounting policies selected, the method of their application or the adequacy of financial statement disclosures.

    The circumstances described in a) could lead to a qualified opinion or a disclaimer of opinion. The circumstances described in b) could lead to a qualified opinion or an adverse opinion. These circumstances are discussed more fully in paragraphs 41-46.

37.   A *qualified opinion* should be expressed when the auditor concludes that an unqualified opinion cannot be expressed but that the effect of any disagreement with management, or limitation on scope is not so material and pervasive as to require an adverse opinion or a disclaimer of opinion. A qualified opinion should be expressed as being 'except for' the effects of the matter to which the qualification relates.

38.   A *disclaimer of opinion* should be expressed when the possible effect of a limitation on scope is so material and pervasive that the auditor has not been able to obtain sufficient appropriate audit evidence and accordingly is unable to express an opinion on the financial statements.

39.   An *adverse opinion* should be expressed when the effect of a disagreement is so material and pervasive to the financial statements that the auditor concludes that a qualification of the report is not adequate to disclose the misleading or incomplete nature of the financial statements.

40.   Whenever the auditor expresses an opinion that is other than unqualified, a clear description of all the substantive reasons should be included in the report and, unless impracticable, a quantification of the possible effect(s) on the financial statements. Ordinarily, this information would be set out in a separate paragraph preceding the opinion or disclaimer of opinion and may include a reference to a more extensive discussion, if any, in a note to the financial statements.

Circumstances That May Result in Other Than an Unqualified Opinion

Limitation on Scope

41.   A limitation on the scope of the auditor's work may sometimes be imposed by the entity (for example, when the terms of the engagement specify that the auditor will not carry out an audit procedure that the auditor believes is necessary). However, when the limitation in the terms of a proposed engagement is such that the auditor believes the need to express a disclaimer of opinion exists, the auditor would ordinarily not accept such a limited engagement as an audit engagement, unless required by statute. Also, a statutory auditor would not accept such an audit engagement when the limitation infringes on the auditor's statutory duties.

42.   A scope limitation may be imposed by circumstances (for example, when the timing of the auditor's appointment is such that the auditor is unable to observe the counting of physical inventories). It may also arise when, in the opinion of the auditor, the entity's accounting records are inadequate or when the auditor is unable to carry out an audit procedure believed to be desirable. In these circumstances, the auditor would attempt to carry out reasonable alternative procedures to obtain sufficient appropriate audit evidence to support an unqualified opinion.

43.   When there is a limitation on the scope of the auditor's work that requires expression of a qualified opinion or a disclaimer of opinion, the

AUDITING

auditor's report should describe the limitation and indicate the possible adjustments to the financial statements that might have been determined to be necessary had the limitation not existed.

44. Illustrations of these matters are set out below.

Limitation on Scope—Qualified Opinion

"We have audited ... (remaining words are the same as illustrated in the introductory paragraph—paragraph 28 above).

Except as discussed in the following paragraph, we conducted our audit in accordance with ... (remaining words are the same as illustrated in the scope paragraph—paragraph 28 above).

We did not observe the counting of the physical inventories as of December 31, 19X1, since that date was prior to the time we were initially engaged as auditors for the Company. Owing to the nature of the Company's records, we were unable to satisfy ourselves as to inventory quantities by other audit procedures.

In our opinion, except for the effects of such adjustments, if any, as might have been determined to be necessary had we been able to satisfy ourselves as to physical inventory quantities, the financial statements give a true and ... (remaining words are the same as illustrated in the opinion paragraph—paragraph 28 above)."

Limitation on Scope—Disclaimer of Opinion

"We were engaged to audit the accompanying balance sheet of the ABC Company as of December 31, 19X1, and the related statements of income and cash flows for the year then ended. These financial statements are the responsibility of the Company's management. *(Omit the sentence stating the responsibility of the auditor).*

(The paragraph discussing the scope of the audit would either be omitted or amended according to the circumstances.)

(Add a paragraph discussing the scope limitation as follows:)
We were not able to observe all physical inventories and confirm accounts receivable due to limitations placed on the scope of our work by the Company.

Because of the significance of the matters discussed in the preceding paragraph, we do not express an opinion on the financial statements."

Disagreement with Management

45. The auditor may disagree with management about matters such as the acceptability of accounting policies selected, the method of their application, or the adequacy of disclosures in the financial statements. **If such disagreements are material to the financial statements, the auditor should express a qualified or an adverse opinion.**

46.   Illustrations of these matters are set out below.

Disagreement on Accounting Policies-Inappropriate Accounting Method—Qualified Opinion

"We have audited ... (remaining words are the same as illustrated in the introductory paragraph—paragraph 28 above).

We conducted our audit in accordance with ... (remaining words are the same as illustrated in the scope paragraph—paragraph 28 above).

As discussed in Note X to the financial statements, no depreciation has been provided in the financial statements which practice, in our opinion, is not in accordance with International Accounting Standards. The provision for the year ended December 31, 19X1, should be xxx based on the straight-line method of depreciation using annual rates of 5% for the building and 20% for the equipment. Accordingly, the fixed assets should be reduced by accumulated depreciation of xxx and the loss for the year and accumulated deficit should be increased by xxx and xxx, respectively.

In our opinion, *except for the effect on the financial statements of the matter referred to in the preceding paragraph,* the financial statements give a true and ... (remaining words are the same as illustrated in the opinion paragraph—paragraph 28 above)."

Disagreement on Accounting Policies—Inadequate Disclosure—Qualified Opinion

"We have audited ... (remaining words are the same as illustrated in the introductory paragraph—paragraph 28 above).

We conducted our audit in accordance with ... (remaining words are the same as illustrated in the scope paragraph—paragraph 28 above).

On January 15, 19X2, the Company issued debentures in the amount of xxx for the purpose of financing plant expansion. The debenture agreement restricts the payment of future cash dividends to earnings after December 31, 19X1. In our opinion, disclosure of this information is required by ...[9] .

In our opinion, except for the omission of the information included in the preceding paragraph, the financial statements give a true and ... (remaining words are the same as illustrated in the opinion paragraph—paragraph 28 above)."

Disagreement on Accounting Policies—Inadequate Disclosure—Adverse Opinion

"We have audited ... (remaining words are the same as illustrated in the introductory paragraph—paragraph 28 above).

---

[9] See footnotes 4 and 5.

700

We conducted our audit in accordance with ... (remaining words are the same as illustrated in the scope paragraph—paragraph 28 above).

(Paragraph(s) discussing the disagreement).

In our opinion, *because of the effects of the matters discussed in the preceding paragraph(s), the financial statements do not give a true and fair view of (or do not 'present fairly') the financial position of the Company as of December 31, 19X1, and of the results of its operations and its cash flows for the year then ended in accordance with ...*[10] *(and do not comply with ...*[11]*)."*

Public Sector Perspective

1. *While the basic principles contained in this ISA apply to the audit of financial statements in the public sector, the legislation giving rise to the audit mandate may specify the nature, content and form of the auditor's report.*

2. *This ISA does not address the form and content of the auditor's report in circumstances where financial statements are prepared in conformity with a disclosed basis of accounting, whether mandated by legislation or ministerial (or other) directive, and that basis results in financial statements which are misleading.*

---

[10] See footnote 4.

[11] See footnote 5.

CONTENTS

	Paragraphs
Introduction	1-5
Corresponding Figures	6-19
Comparative Financial Statements	20-31
Effective Date	32

Appendix 1: Discussion of Financial Reporting Frameworks for Comparatives

Appendix 2: Example Auditor's Reports

International Standards on Auditing (ISAs) are to be applied in the audit of financial statements. ISAs are also to be applied, adapted as necessary, to the audit of other information and to related services.

ISAs contain the basic principles and essential procedures (identified in bold type black lettering) together with related guidance in the form of explanatory and other material. The basic principles and essential procedures are to be interpreted in the context of the explanatory and other material that provide guidance for their application.

To understand and apply the basic principles and essential procedures together with the related guidance, it is necessary to consider the whole text of the ISA including explanatory and other material contained in the ISA not just that text which is black lettered.

In exceptional circumstances, an auditor may judge it necessary to depart from an ISA in order to more effectively achieve the objective of an audit. When such a situation arises, the auditor should be prepared to justify the departure.

ISAs need only be applied to material matters.

The Public Sector Perspective (PSP) issued by the Public Sector Committee of the International Federation of Accountants is set out at the end of an ISA. Where no PSP is added, the ISA is applicable in all material respects to the public sector.

AUDITING

Introduction

1. The purpose of this International Standard on Auditing (ISA) is to establish standards and provide guidance on the auditor's responsibilities regarding comparatives. It does not deal with situations when summarized financial statements are presented with the audited financial statements (for guidance see ISA 720 "Other Information in Documents Containing Audited Financial Statements," and ISA 800 "The Auditor's Report on Special Purpose Audit Engagements").

2. **The auditor should determine whether the comparatives comply in all material respects with the financial reporting framework relevant to the financial statements being audited.**

3. The existence of differences in financial reporting frameworks between countries results in comparative financial information being presented differently in each framework. Comparatives in financial statements, for example, may present amounts (such as financial position, results of operations, cash flows) and appropriate disclosures of an entity for more than one period, depending on the framework. The frameworks and methods of presentation are referred to in this ISA as follows:

    (a) *Corresponding Figures* where amounts and other disclosures for the preceding period are included as part of the current period financial statements, and are intended to be read in relation to the amounts and other disclosures relating to the current period (referred to as "current period figures" for the purpose of this ISA). These corresponding figures are not presented as complete financial statements capable of standing alone, but are an integral part of the current period financial statements intended to be read only in relationship to the current period figures; and

    (b) *Comparative Financial Statements* where amounts and other disclosures for the preceding period are included for comparison with the financial statements of the current period, but do not form part of the current period financial statements.

    (Refer to Appendix 1 to this ISA for discussion of these different reporting frameworks.)

4. Comparatives are presented in compliance with the relevant financial reporting framework. The essential audit reporting differences are that:

    (a) for corresponding figures, the auditor's report only refers to the financial statements of the current period; whereas

    (b) for comparative financial statements, the auditor's report refers to each period that financial statements are presented.

5. This ISA provides guidance on the auditor's responsibilities for comparatives and for reporting on them under the two frameworks in separate sections.

Corresponding Figures

The Auditor's Responsibilities

6. **The auditor should obtain sufficient appropriate audit evidence that the corresponding figures meet the requirements of the relevant financial reporting framework.** The extent of audit procedures performed on the corresponding figures is significantly less than for the audit of the current period figures and is ordinarily limited to ensuring that the corresponding figures have been correctly reported and are appropriately classified. This involves the auditor assessing whether:

    (a) accounting policies used for the corresponding figures are consistent with those of the current period or whether appropriate adjustments and/or disclosures have been made; and

    (b) corresponding figures agree with the amounts and other disclosures presented in the prior period or whether appropriate adjustments and/or disclosures have been made.

7. When the financial statements of the prior period have been audited by another auditor, the incoming auditor assesses whether the corresponding figures meet the conditions specified in paragraph 6 above and also follows the guidance in ISA 510 "Initial Engagements — Opening Balances."

8. When the financial statements of the prior period were not audited, the incoming auditor nonetheless assesses whether the corresponding figures meet the conditions specified in paragraph 6 above and also follows the guidance in ISA 510 "Initial Engagements — Opening Balances."

9. If the auditor becomes aware of a possible material misstatement in the corresponding figures when performing the current period audit, the auditor performs such additional procedures as are appropriate in the circumstances.

Reporting

10. **When the comparatives are presented as corresponding figures, the auditor should issue an audit report in which the comparatives are not specifically identified because the auditor's opinion is on the current period financial statements as a whole, including the corresponding figures.**

11. The auditor's report would make specific reference to the corresponding figures only in the circumstances described in paragraphs 12, 13, 15(b), and 16 through 19.

12. **When the auditor's report on the prior period, as previously issued, included a qualified opinion, disclaimer of opinion, or adverse opinion and the matter which gave rise to the modification is:**

    (a) **unresolved, and results in a modification of the auditor's report regarding the current period figures, the auditor's report should also be modified regarding the corresponding figures; or**

AUDITING

(b) unresolved, but does not result in a modification of the auditor's report regarding the current period figures, the auditor's report should be modified regarding the corresponding figures.

13. When the auditor's report on the prior period, as previously issued, included a qualified opinion, disclaimer of opinion, or adverse opinion and the matter which gave rise to the modification is resolved and properly dealt with in the financial statements, the current report does not ordinarily refer to the previous modification. However, if the matter is material to the current period, the auditor may include an emphasis of matter paragraph dealing with the situation.

14. In performing the audit of the current period financial statements, the auditor, in certain unusual circumstances, may become aware of a material misstatement that affects the prior period financial statements on which an unmodified report has been previously issued.

15. In such circumstances, the auditor should consider the guidance in ISA 560 "Subsequent Events" and:

(a) if the prior period financial statements have been revised and reissued with a new auditor's report, the auditor should be satisfied that the corresponding figures agree with the revised financial statements; or

(b) if the prior period financial statements have not been revised and reissued, and the corresponding figures have not been properly restated and/or appropriate disclosures have not been made, the auditor should issue a modified report on the current period financial statements modified with respect to the corresponding figures included therein.

16. If, in the circumstances described in paragraph 14, the prior period financial statements have not been revised and an auditor's report has not been reissued, but the corresponding figures have been properly restated and/or appropriate disclosures have been made in the current period financial statements, the auditor may include an emphasis of matter paragraph describing the circumstances and referencing to the appropriate disclosures. In this regard, the auditor also considers the guidance in ISA 560 "Subsequent Events."

Incoming Auditor—Additional Requirements

Prior Period Financial Statements Audited by Another Auditor

17. In some jurisdictions, the incoming auditor is permitted to refer to the predecessor auditor's report on the corresponding figures in the incoming auditor's report for the current period. When the auditor decides to refer to another auditor, the incoming auditor's report should indicate:

(a) that the financial statements of the prior period were audited by another auditor;

(b) the type of report issued by the predecessor auditor and, if the report was modified, the reasons therefor; and

(c) the date of that report.

Prior Period Financial Statements Not Audited

18. **When the prior period financial statements are not audited, the incoming auditor should state in the auditor's report that the corresponding figures are unaudited.** Such a statement does not, however, relieve the auditor of the requirement to perform appropriate procedures regarding opening balances of the current period. Clear disclosure in the financial statements that the corresponding figures are unaudited is encouraged.

19. **In situations where the incoming auditor identifies that the corresponding figures are materially misstated, the auditor should request management to revise the corresponding figures or if management refuses to do so, appropriately modify the report.**

Comparative Financial Statements

The Auditor's Responsibilities

20. **The auditor should obtain sufficient appropriate audit evidence that the comparative financial statements meet the requirements of the relevant financial reporting framework.** This involves the auditor assessing whether:

(a) accounting policies of the prior period are consistent with those of the current period or whether appropriate adjustments and/or disclosures have been made; and

(b) prior period figures presented agree with the amounts and other disclosures presented in the prior period or whether appropriate adjustments and disclosures have been made.

21. When the financial statements of the prior period have been audited by another auditor, the incoming auditor assesses whether the comparative financial statements meet the conditions in paragraph 20 above and also follows the guidance in ISA 510 "Initial Engagements — Opening Balances."

22. When the financial statements of the prior period were not audited, the incoming auditor nonetheless assesses whether the comparative financial statements meet the conditions specified in paragraph 20 above and also follows the guidance in ISA 510 "Initial Engagements — Opening Balances."

23. If the auditor becomes aware of a possible material misstatement in the prior year figures when performing the current period audit, the auditor performs such additional procedures as are appropriate in the circumstances.

Reporting

24. **When the comparatives are presented as comparative financial statements, the auditor should issue a report in which the comparatives**

AUDITING

are specifically identified because the auditor's opinion is expressed individually on the financial statements of each period presented. Since the auditor's report on comparative financial statements applies to the individual financial statements presented, the auditor may express a qualified or adverse opinion, disclaim an opinion, or include an emphasis of matter paragraph with respect to one or more financial statements for one or more periods, while issuing a different report on the other financial statements.

25. **When reporting on the prior period financial statements in connection with the current year's audit, if the opinion on such prior period financial statements is different from the opinion previously expressed, the auditor should disclose the substantive reasons for the different opinion in an emphasis of matter paragraph.** This may arise when the auditor becomes aware of circumstances or events that materially affect the financial statements of a prior period during the course of the audit of the current period.

Incoming Auditor—Additional Requirements

Prior Period Financial Statements Audited by Another Auditor

26. **When the financial statements of the prior period were audited by another auditor,**

    (a) **the predecessor auditor may reissue the audit report on the prior period with the incoming auditor only reporting on the current period; or**

    (b) **the incoming auditor's report should state that the prior period was audited by another auditor and the incoming auditor's report should indicate:**

        (i) **that the financial statements of the prior period were audited by another auditor;**

        (ii) **the type of report issued by the predecessor auditor and if the report was modified, the reasons therefor; and**

        (iii) **the date of that report.**

27. In performing the audit on the current period financial statements, the incoming auditor, in certain unusual circumstances, may become aware of a material misstatement that affects the prior period financial statements on which the predecessor auditor had previously reported without modification.

28. **In these circumstances, the incoming auditor should discuss the matter with management and, after having obtained management's authorization, contact the predecessor auditor and propose that the prior period financial statements be restated. If the predecessor agrees to reissue the audit report on the restated financial statements of the prior period, the auditor should follow the guidance in paragraph 26.**

29. If, in the circumstances discussed in paragraph 27, the predecessor does not agree with the proposed restatement or refuses to reissue the audit report on

the prior period financial statements, the introductory paragraph of the auditor's report may indicate that the predecessor auditor reported on the financial statements of the prior period before restatement. In addition, if the incoming auditor is engaged to audit and applies sufficient procedures to be satisfied as to the appropriateness of the restatement adjustment, the auditor may also include the following paragraph in the report:

> We also audited the adjustments described in Note X that were applied to restate the 19X1 financial statements. In our opinion, such adjustments are appropriate and have been properly applied.

Prior Period Financial Statements Not Audited

30. **When the prior period financial statements are not audited, the incoming auditor should state in the auditor's report that the comparative financial statements are unaudited.** Such a statement does not, however, relieve the auditor of the requirement to carry out appropriate procedures regarding opening balances of the current period. Clear disclosure in the financial statements that the comparative financial statements are unaudited is encouraged.

31. **In situations where the incoming auditor identifies that the prior year unaudited figures are materially misstated, the auditor should request management to revise the prior year's figures or if management refuses to do so, appropriately modify the report.**

Effective Date

32. This ISA is effective for reports issued or reissued on or after July 1, 1997. Earlier application is permitted.

AUDITING

Appendix 1

Discussion of Financial Reporting Frameworks for Comparatives

1. Comparatives covering one or more preceding periods provide the users of financial statements with information necessary to identify trends and changes affecting an entity over a period of time.

2. Under financial reporting frameworks (both implicit and explicit) prevailing in a number of countries, comparability and consistency are desirable qualities for financial information. Defined in broadest terms, comparability is the quality of having certain characteristics in common and comparison is normally a quantitative assessment of the common characteristics. Consistency is a quality of the relationship between two accounting numbers. Consistency (for example, consistency in the use of accounting principles from one period to another, the consistency of the length of the reporting period, etc.) is a prerequisite for true comparability.

3. There are two broad financial reporting frameworks for comparatives: the corresponding figures and the comparative financial statements.

4. Under the corresponding figures framework, the corresponding figures for the prior period(s) are an integral part of the current period financial statements and have to be read in conjunction with the amounts and other disclosures relating to the current period. The level of detail presented in the corresponding amounts and disclosures is dictated primarily by its relevance to the current period figures.

5. Under the comparative financial statements framework, the comparative financial statements for the prior period(s) are considered separate financial statements. Accordingly, the level of information included in those comparative financial statements (including all statement amounts, disclosures, footnotes and other explanatory statements to the extent that they continue to be of significance) approximates that of the financial statements of the current period.

Appendix 2

Example Auditor's Reports

Example A   *Corresponding Figures: Example Report for the circumstances described in paragraph 12a*

AUDITOR'S REPORT

(APPROPRIATE ADDRESSEE)

We have audited the accompanying[1] balance sheet of the ABC Company as of December 31, 19X1, and the related statements of income and cash flows for the year then ended. These financial statements are the responsibility of the Company's management. Our responsibility is to express an opinion on these financial statements based on our audit.

We conducted our audit in accordance with International Standards on Auditing (or refer to relevant national standards or practices). Those Standards require that we plan and perform the audit to obtain reasonable assurance about whether the financial statements are free of material misstatement. An audit includes examining, on a test basis, evidence supporting the amounts and disclosures in the financial statements. An audit also includes assessing the accounting principles used and significant estimates made by management, as well as evaluating the overall financial statement presentation. We believe that our audit provides a reasonable basis for our opinion.

As discussed in Note X to the financial statements, no depreciation has been provided in the financial statements which practice, in our opinion, is not in accordance with International Accounting Standards (or refer to relevant national standards). This is the result of a decision taken by management at the start of the preceding financial year and caused us to qualify our audit opinion on the financial statements relating to that year. Based on the straight-line method of depreciation and annual rates of 5% for the building and 20% for the equipment, the loss for the year should be increased by XXX in 19X1 and XXX in 19X0, the fixed assets should be reduced by accumulated depreciation of XXX in 19X1 and XXX in 19X0, and the accumulated loss should be increased by XXX in 19X1 and XXX in 19X0.

In our opinion, except for the effect on the financial statements of the matter referred to in the preceding paragraph, the financial statements give a true and fair view of (or 'present fairly, in all material respects,') the financial position of the Company as of December 31, 19X1, and of the results of its operations and its cash flows for the year then ended in accordance with ...[2] (and comply with ...[3]).

AUDITOR

Date
Address

---

[1] The reference can be by page numbers.

[2] Indicate International Accounting Standards or relevant national standards.

[3] Reference to relevant statutes or laws.

Example B   *Corresponding Figures: Example Report for the circumstances described in paragraph 12b*

AUDITOR'S REPORT

(APPROPRIATE ADDRESSEE)

We have audited the accompanying[4] balance sheet of the ABC Company as of December 31, 19X1, and the related statements of income and cash flows for the year then ended. These financial statements are the responsibility of the Company's management. Our responsibility is to express an opinion on these financial statements based on our audit.

We conducted our audit in accordance with International Standards on Auditing (or refer to relevant national standards or practices). Those Standards require that we plan and perform the audit to obtain reasonable assurance about whether the financial statements are free of material misstatement. An audit includes examining, on a test basis, evidence supporting the amounts and disclosures in the financial statements. An audit also includes assessing the accounting principles used and significant estimates made by management, as well as evaluating the overall financial statement presentation. We believe that our audit provides a reasonable basis for our opinion.

Because we were appointed auditors of the Company during 19X0, we were not able to observe the counting of the physical inventories at the beginning of that (period) or satisfy ourselves concerning those inventory quantities by alternative means. Since opening inventories enter into the determination of the results of operations, we were unable to determine whether adjustments to the results of operations and opening retained earnings might be necessary for 19X0. Our audit report on the financial statements for the (period) ended (balance sheet date) 19X0 was modified accordingly.

In our opinion, except for the effect on the corresponding figures for 19X0 of the adjustments, if any, to the results of operations for the (period) ended 19X0, which we might have determined to be necessary had we been able to observe beginning inventory quantities as at ..., the financial statements give a true and fair view of (or 'present fairly, in all material respects,') the financial position of the Company as of December 31, 19X1, and of the results of its operations and its cash flows for the year then ended in accordance with ...[5] (and comply with ....[6]).

AUDITOR

Date
Address

---

[4] The reference can be by page numbers.

[5] Indicate International Accounting Standards or relevant national standards.

[6] Reference to relevant statutes or laws.

Example C *Comparative Financial Statements: Example Report for the circumstances described in paragraph 24*

AUDITOR'S REPORT

(APPROPRIATE ADDRESSEE)

We have audited the accompanying[7] balance sheets of the ABC Company as of December 31, 19X1 and 19X0, and the related statements of income and cash flows for the years then ended. These financial statements are the responsibility of the Company's management. Our responsibility is to express an opinion on these financial statements based on our audits.

We conducted our audits in accordance with International Standards on Auditing (or refer to relevant national standards or practices). Those Standards require that we plan and perform the audit to obtain reasonable assurance about whether the financial statements are free of material misstatement. An audit includes examining, on a test basis, evidence supporting the amounts and disclosures in the financial statements. An audit also includes assessing the accounting principles used and significant estimates made by management, as well as evaluating the overall financial statement presentation. We believe that our audits provide a reasonable basis for our opinion.

As discussed in Note X to the financial statements, no depreciation has been provided in the financial statements which practice, in our opinion, is not in accordance with International Accounting Standards (or refer to relevant national standards). Based on the straight-line method of depreciation and annual rates of 5% for the building and 20% for the equipment, the loss for the year should be increased by XXX in 19X1 and XXX in 19X0, the fixed assets should be reduced by accumulated depreciation of XXX in 19X1 and XXX in 19X0, and the accumulated loss should be increased by XXX in 19X1 and XXX in 19X0.

In our opinion, except for the effect on the financial statements of the matter referred to in the preceding paragraph, the financial statements give a true and fair view of (or 'present fairly, in all material respects,') the financial position of the Company as of December 31, 19X1 and 19X0, and of the results of its operations and its cash flows for the years then ended in accordance with ...[8] (and comply with ....[9]).

AUDITOR

Date
Address

---

[7] The reference can be by page numbers.

[8] Indicate International Accounting Standards or relevant national standards.

[9] Reference to relevant statutes or laws.

Example D   *Corresponding Figures: Example Report for the circumstances described in paragraph 17*

AUDITOR'S REPORT

(APPROPRIATE ADDRESSEE)

We have audited the accompanying[10] balance sheet of the ABC Company as of December 31, 19X1, and the related statements of income and cash flows for the year then ended. These financial statements are the responsibility of the Company's management. Our responsibility is to express an opinion on these financial statements based on our audit. The financial statements of the Company as of December 31, 19X0, were audited by another auditor whose report dated March 31, 19X1, expressed an unqualified opinion on those statements.

We conducted our audit in accordance with International Standards on Auditing (or refer to relevant national standards or practices). Those Standards require that we plan and perform the audit to obtain reasonable assurance about whether the financial statements are free of material misstatement. An audit includes examining, on a test basis, evidence supporting the amounts and disclosures in the financial statements. An audit also includes assessing the accounting principles used and significant estimates made by management, as well as evaluating the overall financial statement presentation. We believe that our audit provides a reasonable basis for our opinion.

In our opinion, the financial statements give a true and fair view of (or 'present fairly, in all material respects,') the financial position of the Company as of December 31, 19X1, and of the results of its operations and its cash flows for the year then ended in accordance with ...[11] (and comply with ...[12]).

AUDITOR

Date
Address

---

[10] The reference can be by page numbers.

[11] Indicate International Accounting Standards or relevant national standards.

[12] Reference to relevant statutes or laws.

Example E   *Comparative Financial Statements: Example Report for the circumstances described in paragraph 26b*

AUDITOR'S REPORT

(APPROPRIATE ADDRESSEE)

We have audited the accompanying[13] balance sheet of the ABC Company as of December 31, 19X1, and the related statements of income and cash flows for the year then ended. These financial statements are the responsibility of the Company's management. Our responsibility is to express an opinion on these financial statements based on our audit. The financial statements of the Company as of December 31, 19X0, were audited by another auditor whose report dated March 31, 19X1, expressed a qualified opinion due to their disagreement as to the adequacy of the provision for doubtful receivables.

We conducted our audit in accordance with International Standards on Auditing (or refer to relevant national standards or practices). Those Standards require that we plan and perform the audit to obtain reasonable assurance about whether the financial statements are free of material misstatement. An audit includes examining, on a test basis, evidence supporting the amounts and disclosures in the financial statements. An audit also includes assessing the accounting principles used and significant estimates made by management, as well as evaluating the overall financial statement presentation. We believe that our audit provides a reasonable basis for our opinion.

The receivables referred to above are still outstanding at December 31, 19X1 and no provision for potential loss has been made in the financial statements. Accordingly, the provision for doubtful receivables at December 31, 19X1 and 19X0 should be increased by XXX, the net profit for 19X0 decreased by XXX and the retained earnings at December 31, 19X1 and 19X0 reduced by XXX.

In our opinion, except for the effect on the financial statements of the matter referred to in the preceding paragraph, the 19X1 financial statements referred to above give a true and fair view of (or 'present fairly, in all material respects,') the financial position of the Company as of December 31, 19X1, and of the results of its operations and its cash flows for the year then ended in accordance with ...[14] (and comply with ...[15]).

AUDITOR

Date
Address

---

[13] The reference can be by page numbers.

[14] Indicate International Accounting Standards or relevant national standards.

[15] Reference to relevant statutes or laws.

CONTENTS

	Paragraphs
Introduction	1-8
Access to Other Information	9
Consideration of Other Information	10
Material Inconsistencies	11-13
Material Misstatements of Fact	14-18
Availability of Other Information After the Date of the Auditor's Report	19-23

International Standards on Auditing (ISAs) are to be applied in the audit of financial statements. ISAs are also to be applied, adapted as necessary, to the audit of other information and to related services.

ISAs contain the basic principles and essential procedures (identified in bold type black lettering) together with related guidance in the form of explanatory and other material. The basic principles and essential procedures are to be interpreted in the context of the explanatory and other material that provide guidance for their application.

To understand and apply the basic principles and essential procedures together with the related guidance, it is necessary to consider the whole text of the ISA including explanatory and other material contained in the ISA not just that text which is black lettered.

In exceptional circumstances, an auditor may judge it necessary to depart from an ISA in order to more effectively achieve the objective of an audit. When such a situation arises, the auditor should be prepared to justify the departure.

ISAs need only be applied to material matters.

The Public Sector Perspective (PSP) issued by the Public Sector Committee of the International Federation of Accountants is set out at the end of an ISA. Where no PSP is added, the ISA is applicable in all material respects to the public sector.

Introduction

1. The purpose of this International Standard on Auditing (ISA) is to establish standards and provide guidance on the auditor's consideration of other information, on which the auditor has no obligation to report, in documents containing audited financial statements. This ISA applies when an annual report is involved, however it may also apply to other documents, such as those used in securities offerings.

2. **The auditor should read the other information to identify material inconsistencies with the audited financial statements.**

3. A "material inconsistency" exists when other information contradicts information contained in the audited financial statements. A material inconsistency may raise doubt about the audit conclusions drawn from audit evidence previously obtained and, possibly, about the basis for the auditor's opinion on the financial statements.

4. An entity ordinarily issues on an annual basis a document which includes its audited financial statements together with the auditor's report thereon. This document is frequently referred to as the "annual report." In issuing such a document, an entity may also include, either by law or custom, other financial and non-financial information. For the purpose of this ISA, such other financial and non-financial information is called "other information."

5. Examples of other information include a report by management or the board of directors on operations, financial summaries or highlights, employment data, planned capital expenditures, financial ratios, names of officers and directors and selected quarterly data.

6. In certain circumstances, the auditor has a statutory or contractual obligation to report specifically on other information. In other circumstances, the auditor has no such obligation. However, the auditor needs to give consideration to such other information when issuing a report on the financial statements, as the credibility of the audited financial statements may be undermined by inconsistencies which may exist between the audited financial statements and other information.

7. Some jurisdictions require the auditor to apply specific procedures to certain of the other information, for example, required supplementary data and interim financial information. If such other information is omitted or contains deficiencies, the auditor may be required to refer to the matter in the auditor's report.

8. When there is an obligation to report specifically on other information, the auditor's responsibilities are determined by the nature of the engagement and by local legislation and professional standards. When such responsibilities involve the review of other information, the auditor will need to follow the guidance on review engagements in the appropriate ISAs.

Access to Other Information

9. In order that an auditor can consider other information included in the annual report, timely access to such information will be required. The auditor

therefore needs to make appropriate arrangements with the entity to obtain such information prior to the date of the auditor's report. In certain circumstances, all the other information may not be available prior to such date. In these circumstances, the auditor would follow the guidance in paragraphs 20 to 23.

Consideration of Other Information

10. The objective and scope of an audit of financial statements are formulated on the premise that the auditor's responsibility is restricted to information identified in the auditor's report. Accordingly, the auditor has no specific responsibility to determine that other information is properly stated.

Material Inconsistencies

11. **If, on reading the other information, the auditor identifies a material inconsistency, the auditor should determine whether the audited financial statements or the other information needs to be amended.**

12. **If an amendment is necessary in the audited financial statements and the entity refuses to make the amendment, the auditor should express a qualified or adverse opinion.**

13. **If an amendment is necessary in the other information and the entity refuses to make the amendment, the auditor should consider including in the auditor's report an emphasis of matter paragraph describing the material inconsistency or taking other actions.** The actions taken, such as not issuing the auditor's report or withdrawing from the engagement, will depend upon the particular circumstances and the nature and significance of the inconsistency. The auditor would also consider obtaining legal advice as to further action.

Material Misstatements of Fact

14. While reading the other information for the purpose of identifying material inconsistencies, the auditor may become aware of an apparent material misstatement of fact.

15. For the purpose of this ISA, a "material misstatement of fact" in other information exists when such information, not related to matters appearing in the audited financial statements, is incorrectly stated or presented.

16. **If the auditor becomes aware that the other information appears to include a material misstatement of fact, the auditor should discuss the matter with the entity's management.** When discussing the matter with the entity's management, the auditor may not be able to evaluate the validity of the other information and management's responses to the auditor's inquiries, and would need to consider whether valid differences of judgment or opinion exist.

17. **When the auditor still considers that there is an apparent misstatement of fact, the auditor should request management to consult with a qualified third party, such as the entity's legal counsel and should consider the advice received.**

18. **If the auditor concludes that there is a material misstatement of fact in the other information which management refuses to correct, the auditor should consider taking further appropriate action.** The actions taken could include such steps as notifying those persons ultimately responsible for the overall direction of the entity in writing of the auditor's concern regarding the other information and obtaining legal advice.

Availability of Other Information After the Date of the Auditor's Report

19. When all the other information is not available to the auditor prior to the date of the auditor's report, the auditor would read the other information at the earliest possible opportunity thereafter to identify material inconsistencies.

20. If, on reading the other information, the auditor identifies a material inconsistency or becomes aware of an apparent material misstatement of fact, the auditor would determine whether the audited financial statements or the other information need revision.

21. When revision of the audited financial statements is appropriate, the guidance in ISA 560 "Subsequent Events" would be followed.

22. When revision of the other information is necessary and the entity agrees to make the revision, the auditor would carry out the procedures necessary under the circumstances. The procedures may include reviewing the steps taken by management to ensure that individuals in receipt of the previously issued financial statements, the auditor's report thereon and the other information are informed of the revision.

23. **When revision of the other information is necessary but management refuses to make the revision, the auditor should consider taking further appropriate action.** The actions taken could include such steps as notifying those persons ultimately responsible for the overall direction of the entity in writing of the auditor's concern regarding the other information and obtaining legal advice.

Public Sector Perspective

1. *This ISA is applicable in the context of the audit of financial statements. In the public sector, the auditor may often have a statutory or contractual obligation to report specifically on other information. As paragraph 8 of this ISA indicates, the procedures stated in this ISA would not be adequate to satisfy legislative or other audit requirements related to, for example, the expression of an opinion on the reliability of performance indicators and other information contained in the annual report. It would be inappropriate to apply this ISA in circumstances where the auditor does have an obligation to express an opinion on such information. In the absence of specific auditing requirements in relation to "other information," the broad principles contained in this ISA are applicable.*

AUDITING

720

CONTENTS

	Paragraphs
Introduction	1-2
General Considerations	3-8
Reports on Financial Statements Prepared in Accordance with a Comprehensive Basis of Accounting other than International Accounting Standards or National Standards	9-11
Reports on a Component of Financial Statements	12-17
Reports on Compliance with Contractual Agreements	18-20
Reports on Summarized Financial Statements	21-25

Appendix 1: Examples of Reports on Financial Statements Prepared in Accordance with a Comprehensive Basis of Accounting other than International Accounting Standards or National Standards

Appendix 2: Examples of Reports on Components of Financial Statements

Appendix 3: Examples of Reports on Compliance

Appendix 4: Examples of Reports on Summarized Financial Statements

International Standards on Auditing (ISAs) are to be applied in the audit of financial statements. ISAs are also to be applied, adapted as necessary, to the audit of other information and to related services.

ISAs contain the basic principles and essential procedures (identified in bold type black lettering) together with related guidance in the form of explanatory and other material. The basic principles and essential procedures are to be interpreted in the context of the explanatory and other material that provide guidance for their application.

To understand and apply the basic principles and essential procedures together with the related guidance, it is necessary to consider the whole text of the ISA including explanatory and other material contained in the ISA not just that text which is black lettered.

In exceptional circumstances, an auditor may judge it necessary to depart from an ISA in order to more effectively achieve the objective of an audit. When such a situation arises, the auditor should be prepared to justify the departure.

ISAs need only be applied to material matters.

The Public Sector Perspective (PSP) issued by the Public Sector Committee of the International Federation of Accountants is set out at the end of an ISA. Where no PSP is added, the ISA is applicable in all material respects to the public sector.

Introduction

1. The purpose of this International Standard on Auditing (ISA) is to establish standards and provide guidance in connection with special purpose audit engagements including:

   • Financial statements prepared in accordance with a comprehensive basis of accounting other than International Accounting Standards or national standards;

   • Specified accounts, elements of accounts, or items in a financial statement (hereafter referred to as reports on a component of financial statements);

   • Compliance with contractual agreements; and

   • Summarized financial statements.

   This ISA does not apply to review, agreed-upon procedures or compilation engagements.

2. **The auditor should review and assess the conclusions drawn from the audit evidence obtained during the special purpose audit engagement as the basis for an expression of opinion. The report should contain a clear written expression of opinion.**

General Considerations

3. The nature, timing and extent of work to be performed in a special purpose audit engagement will vary with the circumstances. **Before undertaking a special purpose audit engagement, the auditor should ensure there is agreement with the client as to the exact nature of the engagement and the form and content of the report to be issued.**

4. In planning the audit work, the auditor will need a clear understanding of the purpose for which the information being reported on is to be used, and who is likely to use it. To avoid the possibility of the auditor's report being used for purposes for which it was not intended, the auditor may wish to indicate in the report the purpose for which the report is prepared and any restrictions on its distribution and use.

5. **The auditor's report on a special purpose audit engagement, except for a report on summarized financial statements, should include the following basic elements, ordinarily in the following layout:**

   (a) title[1] ;

   (b) addressee;

   (c) opening or introductory paragraph

      (i) identification of the financial information audited; and

---

[1] It may be appropriate to use the term "Independent Auditor" in the title to distinguish the auditor's report from reports that might be issued by others, such as officers of the entity, or from the reports of other auditors who may not have to abide by the same ethical requirements as the independent auditor.

      (ii) a statement of the responsibility of the entity's management and the responsibility of the auditor;

(d) a scope paragraph (describing the nature of an audit)

      (i) the reference to the ISAs applicable to special purpose audit engagements or relevant national standards or practices; and

      (ii) a description of the work the auditor performed;

(e) opinion paragraph containing an expression of opinion on the financial information;

(f) date of the report;

(g) auditor's address; and

(h) auditor's signature.

A measure of uniformity in the form and content of the auditor's report is desirable because it helps to promote the reader's understanding.

6.   In the case of financial information to be supplied by an entity to government authorities, trustees, insurers and other entities there may be a prescribed format for the auditor's report. Such prescribed reports may not conform to the requirements of this ISA. For example, the prescribed report may require a certification of fact when an expression of opinion is appropriate, may require an opinion on matters outside the scope of the audit or may omit essential wording. **When requested to report in a prescribed format, the auditor should consider the substance and wording of the prescribed report and, when necessary, should make appropriate changes to conform to the requirements of this ISA, either by rewording the form or by attaching a separate report.**

7.   When the information on which the auditor has been requested to report is based on the provisions of an agreement, the auditor needs to consider whether any significant interpretations of the agreement have been made by management in preparing the information. An interpretation is significant when adoption of another reasonable interpretation would have produced a material difference in the financial information.

8.   **The auditor should consider whether any significant interpretations of an agreement on which the financial information is based are clearly disclosed in the financial information.** The auditor may wish to make reference in the auditor's report on the special purpose audit engagement to the note within the financial information that describe such interpretations.

Reports on Financial Statements Prepared in Accordance with a Comprehensive Basis of Accounting other than International Accounting Standards or National Standards

9.   A comprehensive basis of accounting comprises a set of criteria used in preparing financial statements which applies to all material items and which has substantial support. Financial statements may be prepared for a special purpose in accordance with a comprehensive basis of accounting other than

International Accounting Standards or relevant national standards (referred to herein as an "other comprehensive basis of accounting"). A conglomeration of accounting conventions devised to suit individual preference is not a comprehensive basis of accounting. Other comprehensive financial reporting frameworks may include:

- That used by an entity to prepare its income tax return.

- The cash receipts and disbursements basis of accounting.

- The financial reporting provisions of a government regulatory agency.

10. **The auditor's report on financial statements prepared in accordance with another comprehensive basis of accounting should include a statement that indicates the basis of accounting used or should refer to the note to the financial statements giving that information. The opinion should state whether the financial statements are prepared, in all material respects, in accordance with the identified basis of accounting.** The terms used to express the auditor's opinion are "give a true and fair view" or "present fairly, in all material respects," which are equivalent terms. Appendix 1 to this ISA gives examples of auditor's reports on financial statements prepared in accordance with an other comprehensive basis of accounting.

11. The auditor would consider whether the title of, or a note to, the financial statements makes it clear to the reader that such statements are not prepared in accordance with International Accounting Standards or national standards. For example, a tax basis financial statement might be entitled "Statement of Income and Expenses—Income Tax Basis." **If the financial statements prepared on an other comprehensive basis are not suitably titled or the basis of accounting is not adequately disclosed, the auditor should issue an appropriately modified report.**

Reports on a Component of Financial Statements

12. The auditor may be requested to express an opinion on one or more components of financial statements, for example, accounts receivable, inventory, an employee's bonus calculation or a provision for income taxes. This type of engagement may be undertaken as a separate engagement or in conjunction with an audit of the entity's financial statements. However, this type of engagement does not result in a report on the financial statements taken as a whole and, accordingly, the auditor would express an opinion only as to whether the component audited is prepared, in all material respects, in accordance with the identified basis of accounting.

13. Many financial statement items are interrelated, for example, sales and receivables, and inventory and payables. Accordingly, when reporting on a component of financial statements, the auditor will sometimes be unable to consider the subject of the audit in isolation and will need to examine certain other financial information. **In determining the scope of the engagement, the auditor should consider those financial statement items that are interrelated and which could materially affect the information on which the audit opinion is to be expressed.**

14. **The auditor should consider the concept of materiality in relation to the component of financial statements being reported upon.** For example, a particular account balance provides a smaller base against which to measure materiality compared with the financial statements taken as a whole. Consequently, the auditor's examination will ordinarily be more extensive than if the same component were to be audited in connection with a report on the entire financial statements.

15. To avoid giving the user the impression that the report relates to the entire financial statements, the auditor would advise the client that the auditor's report on a component of financial statements is not to accompany the financial statements of the entity.

16. **The auditor's report on a component of financial statements should include a statement that indicates the basis of accounting in accordance with which the component is presented or refers to an agreement that specifies the basis. The opinion should state whether the component is prepared, in all material respects, in accordance with the identified basis of accounting.** Appendix 2 to this ISA gives examples of audit reports on components of financial statements.

17. **When an adverse opinion or disclaimer of opinion on the entire financial statements has been expressed, the auditor should report on components of the financial statements only if those components are not so extensive as to constitute a major portion of the financial statements.** To do otherwise may overshadow the report on the entire financial statements.

Reports on Compliance with Contractual Agreements

18. The auditor may be requested to report on an entity's compliance with certain aspects of contractual agreements, such as bond indentures or loan agreements. Such agreements ordinarily require the entity to comply with a variety of covenants involving such matters as payments of interest, maintenance of predetermined financial ratios, restriction of dividend payments and the use of the proceeds of sales of property.

19. **Engagements to express an opinion as to an entity's compliance with contractual agreements should be undertaken only when the overall aspects of compliance relate to accounting and financial matters within the scope of the auditor's professional competence.** However, when there are particular matters forming part of the engagement that are outside the auditor's expertise, the auditor would consider using the work of an expert.

20. **The report should state whether, in the auditor's opinion, the entity has complied with the particular provisions of the agreement.** Appendix 3 to this ISA gives examples of auditor's reports on compliance given in a separate report and in a report accompanying financial statements.

Reports on Summarized Financial Statements

21. An entity may prepare financial statements summarizing its annual audited financial statements for the purpose of informing user groups interested in the

highlights only of the entity's financial position and the results of its operations. **Unless the auditor has expressed an audit opinion on the financial statements from which the summarized financial statements were derived, the auditor should not report on summarized financial statements.**

22. Summarized financial statements are presented in considerably less detail than annual audited financial statements. Therefore, such financial statements need to clearly indicate the summarized nature of the information and caution the reader that, for a better understanding of an entity's financial position and the results of its operations, summarized financial statements are to be read in conjunction with the entity's most recent audited financial statements which include all disclosures required by the relevant financial reporting framework.

23. Summarized financial statements need to be appropriately titled to identify the audited financial statements from which they have been derived, for example, "Summarized Financial Information Prepared from the Audited Financial Statements for the Year Ended December 31, 19X1."

24. Summarized financial statements do not contain all the information required by the financial reporting framework used for the annual audited financial statements. Consequently, wording such as "true and fair" or "present fairly, in all material respects," is not used by the auditor when expressing an opinion on summarized financial statements.

25. **The auditor's report on summarized financial statements should include the following basic elements ordinarily in the following layout:**

    (a) **title[2] ;**

    (b) **addressee;**

    (c) **an identification of the audited financial statements from which the summarized financial statements were derived;**

    (d) **a reference to the date of the audit report on the unabridged financial statements and the type of opinion given in that report;**

    (e) **an opinion as to whether the information in the summarized financial statements is consistent with the audited financial statements from which it was derived. When the auditor has issued a modified opinion on the unabridged financial statements yet is satisfied with the presentation of the summarized financial statements, the audit report should state that, although consistent with the unabridged financial statements, the summarized financial statements were derived from financial statements on which a modified audit report was issued;**

    (f) **a statement, or reference to the note within the summarized financial statements, which indicates that for a better understanding of an entity's financial performance and position**

AUDITING

---

[2] See footnote 1.

and of the scope of the audit performed, the summarized financial statements should be read in conjunction with the unabridged financial statements and the audit report thereon;

(g)　date of the report;

(h)　auditor's address; and

(i)　auditor's signature.

Appendix 4 to this ISA gives examples of auditor's reports on summarized financial statements.

Public Sector Perspective

1.　*Some of the engagements considered "special purpose audit engagements" in the private sector are not special purpose in the public sector. For example, reports on financial statements prepared in accordance with a comprehensive basis of accounting other than IASs or national standards is ordinarily the norm, not the exception in the public sector. This has to be noted and guidance provided to the auditor on his or her responsibility to assess whether the accounting policies will result in misleading information.*

2.　*A factor that also has to be considered is that public sector audit reports are ordinarily public documents and therefore, it is not possible to restrict the report to specific users.*

Appendix 1

Examples of Reports on Financial Statements Prepared in Accordance with a Comprehensive Basis of Accounting other than International Accounting Standards or National Standards.

A Statement of Cash Receipts and Disbursements

AUDITOR'S REPORT TO .....

We have audited the accompanying statement of ABC Company's cash receipts and disbursements for the year ended December 31, 19X1[3] . This statement is the responsibility of ABC Company's management. Our responsibility is to express an opinion on the accompanying statement based on our audit.

We conducted our audit in accordance with International Standards on Auditing (or refer to relevant national standards or practices). Those Standards require that we plan and perform the audit to obtain reasonable assurance about whether the financial statement is free of material misstatement. An audit includes examining, on a test basis, evidence supporting the amounts and disclosures in the financial statement. An audit also includes assessing the accounting principles used and significant estimates made by management as well as evaluating the overall statement presentation. We believe that our audit provides a reasonable basis for our opinion.

The Company's policy is to prepare the accompanying statement on the cash receipts and disbursements basis. On this basis revenue is recognized when received rather than when earned, and expenses are recognized when paid rather than when incurred.

In our opinion, the accompanying statement gives a true and fair view of (or 'presents fairly, in all material respects,') the revenue collected and expenses paid by the Company during the year ended December 31, 19X1 in accordance with the cash receipts and disbursements basis as described in Note X.

Date   AUDITOR
Address

AUDITING

---

[3] Provide suitable identification, such as by reference to page numbers or by identifying the individual statement.

800

Financial Statements Prepared on the Entity's Income Tax Basis

AUDITOR'S REPORT TO .....

We have audited the accompanying income tax basis financial statements of ABC Company for the year ended December 31, 19X1[4] . These statements are the responsibility of ABC Company's management. Our responsibility is to express an opinion on the financial statements based on our audit.

We conducted our audit in accordance with International Standards on Auditing (or refer to relevant national standards or practices). Those Standards require that we plan and perform the audit to obtain reasonable assurance about whether the financial statements are free of material misstatement. An audit includes examining, on a test basis, evidence supporting the amounts and disclosures in the financial statements. An audit also includes assessing the accounting principles used and significant estimates made by management, as well as evaluating the overall financial statement presentation. We believe that our audit provides a reasonable basis for our opinion.

In our opinion, the financial statements give a true and fair view of (or 'present fairly, in all material respects,') the financial position of the Company as of December 31, 19X1 and its revenues and expenses for the year then ended, in accordance with the basis of accounting used for income tax purposes as described in Note X.

Date   AUDITOR
Address

---

[4] See footnote 3.

Appendix 2

Examples of Reports on Components of Financial Statements

Schedule of Accounts Receivable

AUDITOR'S REPORT TO .....

We have audited the accompanying schedule of accounts receivable of ABC Company for the year ended December 31, 19X1[5]. This schedule is the responsibility of ABC Company's management. Our responsibility is to express an opinion on the schedule based on our audit.

We conducted our audit in accordance with International Standards on Auditing (or refer to relevant national standards or practices). Those Standards require that we plan and perform the audit to obtain reasonable assurance about whether the schedule is free of material misstatement. An audit includes examining, on a test basis, evidence supporting the amounts and disclosures in the schedule. An audit also includes assessing the accounting principles used and significant estimates made by management, as well as evaluating the overall presentation of the schedule. We believe that our audit provides a reasonable basis for our opinion.

In our opinion, the schedule of accounts receivable gives a true and fair view of (or 'presents fairly, in all material respects,') the accounts receivable of the Company as of December 31, 19X1 in accordance with ... [6].

Date   AUDITOR
Address

AUDITING

---

[5] See footnote 3.

[6] Indicate the relevant national standards or refer to International Accounting Standards, the terms of an agreement or any described basis of accounting.

Schedule of Profit Participation

AUDITOR'S REPORT TO .....

We have audited the accompanying schedule of DEF's profit participation for the year ended December 31, 19X1[7]. This schedule is the responsibility of ABC Company's management. Our responsibility is to express an opinion on the schedule based on our audit.

We conducted our audit in accordance with International Standards on Auditing (or refer to relevant national standards or practices). Those Standards require that we plan and perform the audit to obtain reasonable assurance about whether the schedule is free of material misstatement. An audit includes examining, on a test basis, evidence supporting the amounts and disclosures in the schedule. An audit also includes assessing the accounting principles used and significant estimates made by management, as well as evaluating the overall presentation of the schedule. We believe that our audit provides a reasonable basis for our opinion.

In our opinion, the schedule of profit participation gives a true and fair view of (or 'presents fairly, in all material respects,') DEF's participation in the profits of the Company for the year ended December 31, 19X1 in accordance with the provisions of the employment agreement between DEF and the Company dated June 1, 19X0.

Date   AUDITOR
Address

---

[7] See footnote 3.

Appendix 3

Examples of Reports on Compliance

Separate Report

AUDITOR'S REPORT TO .....

We have audited ABC Company's compliance with the accounting and financial reporting matters of sections XX to XX inclusive of the Indenture dated May 15, 19X1 with DEF Bank.

We conducted our audit in accordance with International Standards on Auditing applicable to compliance auditing (or refer to relevant national standards or practices). Those Standards require that we plan and perform the audit to obtain reasonable assurance about whether ABC Company has complied with the relevant sections of the Indenture. An audit includes examining appropriate evidence on a test basis. We believe that our audit provides a reasonable basis for our opinion.

In our opinion, the Company was, in all material respects, in compliance with the accounting and financial reporting matters of the sections of the Indenture referred to in the preceding paragraphs as of December 31, 19X1.

Date   AUDITOR
Address

AUDITING

Report Accompanying Financial Statements

AUDITOR'S REPORT TO .....

We have audited the accompanying balance sheet of the ABC Company as of December 31, 19X1, and the related statements of income, and cash flows for the year then ended (the reference can be by page numbers). These financial statements are the responsibility of the Company's management. Our responsibility is to express an opinion on these financial statements based on our audit. We have also audited ABC Company's compliance with the accounting and financial reporting matters of sections XX to XX inclusive of the Indenture dated May 15, 19X1 with DEF Bank.

We conducted our audits in accordance with International Standards on Auditing (or refer to relevant national standards or practices) applicable to the audit of financial statements and to compliance auditing. Those Standards require that we plan and perform the audits to obtain reasonable assurance about whether the financial statements are free of material misstatement and about whether ABC Company has complied with the relevant sections of the Indenture. An audit includes examining, on a test basis, evidence supporting the amounts and disclosures in the financial statements. An audit also includes assessing the accounting principles used and significant estimates made by management, as well as evaluating the overall financial statement presentation. We believe that our audits provide a reasonable basis for our opinion.

In our opinion:

(a) the financial statements give a true and fair view of (or 'present fairly, in all material respects,') the financial position of the Company as of December 31, 19X1, and of the results of its operations and its cash flows for the year then ended in accordance with ... (and comply with ...); and

(b) the Company was, in all material respects, in compliance with the accounting and financial reporting matters of the sections of the Indenture referred to in the preceding paragraphs as of December 31, 19X1.

Date   AUDITOR

Address

Appendix 4

Examples of Reports on Summarized Financial Statements

When an Unqualified Opinion Was Expressed on the Annual Audited Financial Statements

AUDITOR'S REPORT TO .....

We have audited the financial statements of ABC Company for the year ended December 31, 19X0, from which the summarized financial statements[8] were derived, in accordance with International Standards on Auditing (or refer to relevant national standards or practices). In our report dated March 10, 19X1 we expressed an unqualified opinion on the financial statements from which the summarized financial statements were derived.

In our opinion, the accompanying summarized financial statements are consistent, in all material respects, with the financial statements from which they were derived.

For a better understanding of the Company's financial position and the results of its operations for the period and of the scope of our audit, the summarized financial statements should be read in conjunction with the financial statements from which the summarized financial statements were derived and our audit report thereon.

Date   AUDITOR
Address

---

[8] See footnote 3.

When a Qualified Opinion Was Expressed on the Annual Audited Financial Statements

AUDITOR'S REPORT TO .....

We have audited the financial statements of ABC Company for the year ended December 31, 19X0, from which the summarized financial statements[9] were derived, in accordance with International Standards on Auditing (or refer to relevant national standards or practices). In our report dated March 10, 19X1 we expressed an opinion that the financial statements from which the summarized financial statements were derived gave a true and fair view of (or 'presented fairly, in all material respects,') ... except that inventory had been overstated by ....

In our opinion, the accompanying summarized financial statements are consistent, in all material respects, with the financial statements from which they were derived and on which we expressed a qualified opinion.

For a better understanding of the Company's financial position and the results of its operations for the period and of the scope of our audit, the summarized financial statements should be read in conjunction with the financial statements from which the summarized financial statements were derived and our audit report thereon.

Date   AUDITOR
Address

---

[9] See footnote 3.

CONTENTS

	Paragraphs
Introduction	1-7
The Auditor's Assurance regarding Prospective Financial Information	8-9
Acceptance of Engagement	10-12
Knowledge of the Business	13-15
Period Covered	16
Examination Procedures	17-25
Presentation and Disclosure	26
Report on Examination of Prospective Financial Information	27-33

International Standards on Auditing (ISAs) are to be applied in the audit of financial statements. ISAs are also to be applied, adapted as necessary, to the audit of other information and to related services.

ISAs contain the basic principles and essential procedures (identified in bold type black lettering) together with related guidance in the form of explanatory and other material. The basic principles and essential procedures are to be interpreted in the context of the explanatory and other material that provide guidance for their application.

To understand and apply the basic principles and essential procedures together with the related guidance, it is necessary to consider the whole text of the ISA including explanatory and other material contained in the ISA not just that text which is black lettered.

In exceptional circumstances, an auditor may judge it necessary to depart from an ISA in order to more effectively achieve the objective of an audit. When such a situation arises, the auditor should be prepared to justify the departure.

ISAs need only be applied to material matters.

The Public Sector Perspective (PSP) issued by the Public Sector Committee of the International Federation of Accountants is set out at the end of an ISA. Where no PSP is added, the ISA is applicable in all material respects to the public sector.

AUDITING

810

Introduction

1. The purpose of this International Standard on Auditing (ISA) is to establish standards and provide guidance on engagements to examine and report on prospective financial information including examination procedures for best-estimate and hypothetical assumptions. This ISA does not apply to the examination of prospective financial information expressed in general or narrative terms, such as that found in management's discussion and analysis in an entity's annual report, though many of the procedures outlined herein may be suitable for such an examination.

2. **In an engagement to examine prospective financial information, the auditor should obtain sufficient appropriate evidence as to whether:**

    (a) **management's best-estimate assumptions on which the prospective financial information is based are not unreasonable and, in the case of hypothetical assumptions, such assumptions are consistent with the purpose of the information;**

    (b) **the prospective financial information is properly prepared on the basis of the assumptions;**

    (c) **the prospective financial information is properly presented and all material assumptions are adequately disclosed, including a clear indication as to whether they are best-estimate assumptions or hypothetical assumptions; and**

    (d) **the prospective financial information is prepared on a consistent basis with historical financial statements, using appropriate accounting principles.**

3. "Prospective financial information" means financial information based on assumptions about events that may occur in the future and possible actions by an entity. It is highly subjective in nature and its preparation requires the exercise of considerable judgment. Prospective financial information can be in the form of a forecast, a projection or a combination of both, for example, a one year forecast plus a five year projection.

4. A "forecast" means prospective financial information prepared on the basis of assumptions as to future events which management expects to take place and the actions management expects to take as of the date the information is prepared (best-estimate assumptions).

5. A "projection" means prospective financial information prepared on the basis of:

    (a) hypothetical assumptions about future events and management actions which are not necessarily expected to take place, such as when some entities are in a start-up phase or are considering a major change in the nature of operations; or

    (b) a mixture of best-estimate and hypothetical assumptions.

    Such information illustrates the possible consequences as of the date the information is prepared if the events and actions were to occur (a "what-if" scenario).

6. Prospective financial information can include financial statements or one or more elements of financial statements and may be prepared:

    (a) as an internal management tool, for example, to assist in evaluating a possible capital investment; or

    (b) for distribution to third parties in, for example:

        -   A prospectus to provide potential investors with information about future expectations.

        -   An annual report to provide information to shareholders, regulatory bodies and other interested parties.

        -   A document for the information of lenders which may include, for example, cash flow forecasts.

7. Management is responsible for the preparation and presentation of the prospective financial information, including the identification and disclosure of the assumptions on which it is based. The auditor may be asked to examine and report on the prospective financial information to enhance its credibility whether it is intended for use by third parties or for internal purposes.

The Auditor's Assurance regarding Prospective Financial Information

8. Prospective financial information relates to events and actions that have not yet occurred and may not occur. While evidence may be available to support the assumptions on which the prospective financial information is based, such evidence is itself generally future oriented and, therefore, speculative in nature, as distinct from the evidence ordinarily available in the audit of historical financial information. The auditor is, therefore, not in a position to express an opinion as to whether the results shown in the prospective financial information will be achieved.

9. Further, given the types of evidence available in assessing the assumptions on which the prospective financial information is based, it may be difficult for the auditor to obtain a level of satisfaction sufficient to provide a positive expression of opinion that the assumptions are free of material misstatement. Consequently, in this ISA, when reporting on the reasonableness of management's assumptions the auditor provides only a moderate level of assurance. However, when in the auditor's judgment an appropriate level of satisfaction has been obtained, the auditor is not precluded from expressing positive assurance regarding the assumptions.

Acceptance of Engagement

10. Before accepting an engagement to examine prospective financial information, the auditor would consider, amongst other things:

    -   The intended use of the information.

    -   Whether the information will be for general or limited distribution.

810

- The nature of the assumptions, that is, whether they are best-estimate or hypothetical assumptions.

- The elements to be included in the information.

- The period covered by the information.

11. **The auditor should not accept, or should withdraw from, an engagement when the assumptions are clearly unrealistic or when the auditor believes that the prospective financial information will be inappropriate for its intended use.**

12. **The auditor and the client should agree on the terms of the engagement.** It is in the interests of both entity and auditor that the auditor sends an engagement letter to help in avoiding misunderstandings regarding the engagement. An engagement letter would address the matters in paragraph 10 and set out management's responsibilities for the assumptions and for providing the auditor with all relevant information and source data used in developing the assumptions.

Knowledge of the Business

13. **The auditor should obtain a sufficient level of knowledge of the business to be able to evaluate whether all significant assumptions required for the preparation of the prospective financial information have been identified.** The auditor would also need to become familiar with the entity's process for preparing prospective financial information, for example, by considering:

- The internal controls over the system used to prepare prospective financial information and the expertise and experience of those persons preparing the prospective financial information.

- The nature of the documentation prepared by the entity supporting management's assumptions.

- The extent to which statistical, mathematical and computer-assisted techniques are used.

- The methods used to develop and apply assumptions.

- The accuracy of prospective financial information prepared in prior periods and the reasons for significant variances.

14. **The auditor should consider the extent to which reliance on the entity's historical financial information is justified.** The auditor requires a knowledge of the entity's historical financial information to assess whether the prospective financial information has been prepared on a basis consistent with the historical financial information and to provide a historical yardstick for considering management's assumptions. The auditor will need to establish, for example, whether relevant historical information was audited or reviewed and whether acceptable accounting principles were used in its preparation.

15. If the audit or review report on prior period historical financial information was other than unmodified or if the entity is in a start-up phase, the auditor would consider the surrounding facts and the effect on the examination of the prospective financial information.

Period Covered

16. **The auditor should consider the period of time covered by the prospective financial information.** Since assumptions become more speculative as the length of the period covered increases, as that period lengthens, the ability of management to make best-estimate assumptions decreases. The period would not extend beyond the time for which management has a reasonable basis for the assumptions. The following are some of the factors that are relevant to the auditor's consideration of the period of time covered by the prospective financial information:

- Operating cycle, for example, in the case of a major construction project the time required to complete the project may dictate the period covered.

- The degree of reliability of assumptions, for example, if the entity is introducing a new product the prospective period covered could be short and broken into small segments, such as weeks or months. Alternatively, if the entity's sole business is owning a property under long-term lease, a relatively long prospective period might be reasonable.

- The needs of users, for example, prospective financial information may be prepared in connection with an application for a loan for the period of time required to generate sufficient funds for repayment. Alternatively, the information may be prepared for investors in connection with the sale of debentures to illustrate the intended use of the proceeds in the subsequent period.

Examination Procedures

17. **When determining the nature, timing and extent of examination procedures, the auditor's considerations should include:**

   (a)   the likelihood of material misstatement;

   (b)   the knowledge obtained during any previous engagements;

   (c)   management's competence regarding the preparation of prospective financial information;

   (d)   the extent to which the prospective financial information is affected by the management's judgment; and

   (e)   the adequacy and reliability of the underlying data.

AUDITING

810

18. The auditor would assess the source and reliability of the evidence supporting management's best-estimate assumptions. Sufficient appropriate evidence supporting such assumptions would be obtained from internal and external sources including consideration of the assumptions in the light of historical information and an evaluation of whether they are based on plans that are within the entity's capacity.

19. The auditor would consider whether, when hypothetical assumptions are used, all significant implications of such assumptions have been taken into consideration. For example, if sales are assumed to grow beyond the entity's current plant capacity, the prospective financial information will need to include the necessary investment in the additional plant capacity or the costs of alternative means of meeting the anticipated sales, such as subcontracting production.

20. Although evidence supporting hypothetical assumptions need not be obtained, the auditor would need to be satisfied that they are consistent with the purpose of the prospective financial information and that there is no reason to believe they are clearly unrealistic.

21. The auditor will need to be satisfied that the prospective financial information is properly prepared from management's assumptions by, for example, making clerical checks such as recomputation and reviewing internal consistency, that is, the actions management intends to take are compatible with each other and there are no inconsistencies in the determination of the amounts that are based on common variables such as interest rates.

22. The auditor would focus on the extent to which those areas that are particularly sensitive to variation will have a material effect on the results shown in the prospective financial information. This will influence the extent to which the auditor will seek appropriate evidence. It will also influence the auditor's evaluation of the appropriateness and adequacy of disclosure.

23. When engaged to examine one or more elements of prospective financial information, such as an individual financial statement, it is important that the auditor consider the interrelationship of other components in the financial statements.

24. When any elapsed portion of the current period is included in the prospective financial information, the auditor would consider the extent to which procedures need to be applied to the historical information. Procedures will vary depending on the circumstances, for example, how much of the prospective period has elapsed.

25. **The auditor should obtain written representations from management regarding the intended use of the prospective financial information, the completeness of significant management assumptions and management's acceptance of its responsibility for the prospective financial information.**

Presentation and Disclosure

26. When assessing the presentation and disclosure of the prospective financial information, in addition to the specific requirements of any relevant statutes, regulations or professional standards, the auditor will need to consider whether:

    (a) the presentation of prospective financial information is informative and not misleading;

    (b) the accounting policies are clearly disclosed in the notes to the prospective financial information;

    (c) the assumptions are adequately disclosed in the notes to the prospective financial information. It needs to be clear whether assumptions represent management's best-estimates or are hypothetical and, when assumptions are made in areas that are material and are subject to a high degree of uncertainty, this uncertainty and the resulting sensitivity of results needs to be adequately disclosed;

    (d) the date as of which the prospective financial information was prepared is disclosed. Management needs to confirm that the assumptions are appropriate as of this date, even though the underlying information may have been accumulated over a period of time;

    (e) the basis of establishing points in a range is clearly indicated and the range is not selected in a biased or misleading manner when results shown in the prospective financial information are expressed in terms of a range; and

    (f) any change in accounting policy since the most recent historical financial statements is disclosed, along with the reason for the change and its effect on the prospective financial information.

Report on Examination of Prospective Financial Information

27. The report by an auditor on an examination of prospective financial information should contain the following:

    (a) title;

    (b) addressee;

    (c) identification of the prospective financial information;

    (d) a reference to the International Standards on Auditing or relevant national standards or practices applicable to the examination of prospective financial information;

    (e) a statement that management is responsible for the prospective financial information including the assumptions on which it is based;

    (f) when applicable, a reference to the purpose and/or restricted distribution of the prospective financial information;

AUDITING

810

(g) a statement of negative assurance as to whether the assumptions provide a reasonable basis for the prospective financial information;

(h) an opinion as to whether the prospective financial information is properly prepared on the basis of the assumptions and is presented in accordance with the relevant financial reporting framework;

(i) appropriate caveats concerning the achievability of the results indicated by the prospective financial information;

(j) date of the report which should be the date procedures have been completed;

(k) auditor's address; and

(l) signature.

28. Such a report would:

- State whether, based on the examination of the evidence supporting the assumptions, anything has come to the auditor's attention which causes the auditor to believe that the assumptions do not provide a reasonable basis for the prospective financial information.

- Express an opinion as to whether the prospective financial information is properly prepared on the basis of the assumptions and is presented in accordance with the relevant financial reporting framework.

- State that:

  – actual results are likely to be different from the prospective financial information since anticipated events frequently do not occur as expected and the variation could be material. Likewise, when the prospective financial information is expressed as a range, it would be stated that there can be no assurance that actual results will fall within the range, and

  – in the case of a projection, the prospective financial information has been prepared for (state purpose), using a set of assumptions that include hypothetical assumptions about future events and management's actions that are not necessarily expected to occur. Consequently, readers are cautioned that the prospective financial information is not used for purposes other than that described.

29. The following is an example of an extract from an unmodified report on a forecast:

> We have examined the forecast[1] in accordance with International Standards on Auditing applicable to the examination of prospective financial information. Management is responsible for the forecast including the assumptions set out in Note X on which it is based.

---

[1] Include name of the entity, the period covered by the forecast and provide suitable identification, such as by reference to page numbers or by identifying the individual statements.

Based on our examination of the evidence supporting the assumptions, nothing has come to our attention which causes us to believe that these assumptions do not provide a reasonable basis for the forecast. Further, in our opinion the forecast is properly prepared on the basis of the assumptions and is presented in accordance with ...[2] .

Actual results are likely to be different from the forecast since anticipated events frequently do not occur as expected and the variation may be material.

30. The following is an example of an extract from an unmodified report on a projection:

We have examined the projection[3] in accordance with International Standards on Auditing applicable to the examination of prospective financial information. Management is responsible for the projection including the assumptions set out in Note X on which it is based.

This projection has been prepared for (describe purpose). As the entity is in a start-up phase the projection has been prepared using a set of assumptions that include hypothetical assumptions about future events and management's actions that are not necessarily expected to occur. Consequently, readers are cautioned that this projection may not be appropriate for purposes other than that described above.

Based on our examination of the evidence supporting the assumptions, nothing has come to our attention which causes us to believe that these assumptions do not provide a reasonable basis for the projection, assuming that (state or refer to the hypothetical assumptions). Further, in our opinion the projection is properly prepared on the basis of the assumptions and is presented in accordance with ...[4] .

Even if the events anticipated under the hypothetical assumptions described above occur, actual results are still likely to be different from the projection since other anticipated events frequently do not occur as expected and the variation may be material.

31. **When the auditor believes that the presentation and disclosure of the prospective financial information is not adequate, the auditor should express a qualified or adverse opinion in the report on the prospective financial information, or withdraw from the engagement as appropriate.** An example would be where financial information fails to disclose adequately the consequences of any assumptions which are highly sensitive.

32. **When the auditor believes that one or more significant assumptions do not provide a reasonable basis for the prospective financial information prepared on the basis of best-estimate assumptions or that one or more**

---

[2] Indicate the relevant financial reporting framework.

[3] Include name of the entity, the period covered by the projection and provide suitable identification, such as by reference to page numbers or by identifying the individual statements.

[4] See footnote 2.

810

significant assumptions do not provide a reasonable basis for the prospective financial information given the hypothetical assumptions, the auditor should either express an adverse opinion in the report on the prospective financial information, or withdraw from the engagement.

33. When the examination is affected by conditions that preclude application of one or more procedures considered necessary in the circumstances, the auditor should either withdraw from the engagement or disclaim the opinion and describe the scope limitation in the report on the prospective financial information.

CONTENTS

	Paragraphs
Introduction	1-2
Objective of a Review Engagement	3
General Principles of a Review Engagement	4-7
Scope of a Review	8
Moderate Assurance	9
Terms of Engagement	10-12
Planning	13-15
Work Performed by Others	16
Documentation	17
Procedures and Evidence	18-22
Conclusions and Reporting	23-28

Appendix 1: Example of an Engagement Letter for a Review of Financial Statements

Appendix 2: Illustrative Detailed Procedures that may be Performed in an Engagement to Review Financial Statements

Appendix 3: Form of Unqualified Review Report

Appendix 4: Examples of Review Reports other than Unqualified

---

International Standards on Auditing (ISAs) are to be applied in the audit of financial statements. ISAs are also to be applied, adapted as necessary, to the audit of other information and to related services.

ISAs contain the basic principles and essential procedures (identified in bold type black lettering) together with related guidance in the form of explanatory and other material. The basic principles and essential procedures are to be interpreted in the context of the explanatory and other material that provide guidance for their application.

To understand and apply the basic principles and essential procedures together with the related guidance, it is necessary to consider the whole text of the ISA including explanatory and other material contained in the ISA not just that text which is black lettered.

In exceptional circumstances, an auditor may judge it necessary to depart from an ISA in order to more effectively achieve the objective of an audit. When such a situation arises, the auditor should be prepared to justify the departure.

ISAs need only be applied to material matters.

The Public Sector Perspective (PSP) issued by the Public Sector Committee of International Federation of Accountants is set out at the end of an ISA. Where no PSP is added, the ISA is applicable in all material respects to the public sector.

AUDITING

Introduction

1. The purpose of this International Standard on Auditing (ISA) is to establish standards and provide guidance on the auditor's[1] professional responsibilities when an engagement to review financial statements is undertaken and on the form and content of the report that the auditor issues in connection with such a review.

2. This ISA is directed towards the review of financial statements. However, it is to be applied to the extent practicable to engagements to review financial or other information. This ISA is to be read in conjunction with ISA 120 "Framework of International Standards on Auditing." Guidance in other ISAs may be useful to the auditor in applying this ISA.

Objective of a Review Engagement

3. **The objective of a review of financial statements is to enable an auditor to state whether, on the basis of procedures which do not provide all the evidence that would be required in an audit, anything has come to the auditor's attention that causes the auditor to believe that the financial statements are not prepared, in all material respects, in accordance with an identified financial reporting framework (negative assurance).**

General Principles of a Review Engagement

4. **The auditor should comply with the "Code of Ethics for Professional Accountants" issued by the International Federation of Accountants.** Ethical principles governing the auditor's professional responsibilities are:

    (a) independence;

    (b) integrity;

    (c) objectivity;

    (d) professional competence and due care;

    (e) confidentiality;

    (f) professional behavior; and

    (g) technical standards.

5. **The auditor should conduct a review in accordance with this ISA.**

6. **The auditor should plan and perform the review with an attitude of professional skepticism recognizing that circumstances may exist which cause the financial statements to be materially misstated.**

---

[1] As explained in the Framework of International Standards on Auditing "... the term auditor is used throughout the ISAs when describing both auditing and related services which may be performed. Such reference is not intended to imply that a person performing related services need be the auditor of the entity's financial statements."

7. **For the purpose of expressing negative assurance in the review report, the auditor should obtain sufficient appropriate evidence primarily through inquiry and analytical procedures to be able to draw conclusions.**

Scope of a Review

8. The term "scope of a review" refers to the review procedures deemed necessary in the circumstances to achieve the objective of the review. **The procedures required to conduct a review of financial statements should be determined by the auditor having regard to the requirements of this ISA, relevant professional bodies, legislation, regulation and, where appropriate, the terms of the review engagement and reporting requirements.**

Moderate Assurance

9. A review engagement provides a moderate level of assurance that the information subject to review is free of material misstatement, this is expressed in the form of negative assurance.

Terms of Engagement

10. **The auditor and the client should agree on the terms of the engagement.** The agreed terms would be recorded in an engagement letter or other suitable form such as a contract.

11. An engagement letter will be of assistance in planning the review work. It is in the interests of both the auditor and the client that the auditor send an engagement letter documenting the key terms of the appointment. An engagement letter confirms the auditor's acceptance of the appointment and helps avoid misunderstanding regarding such matters as the objectives and scope of the engagement, the extent of the auditor's responsibilities and the form of reports to be issued.

12. Matters that would be included in the engagement letter include:

    • The objective of the service being performed.

    • Management's responsibility for the financial statements.

    • The scope of the review, including reference to this International Standard on Auditing (or relevant national standards or practices).

    • Unrestricted access to whatever records, documentation and other information requested in connection with the review.

    • A sample of the report expected to be rendered.

    • The fact that the engagement cannot be relied upon to disclose errors, illegal acts or other irregularities, for example, fraud or defalcations that may exist.

AUDITING

- A statement that an audit is not being performed and that an audit opinion will not be expressed. To emphasize this point and to avoid confusion, the auditor may also consider pointing out that a review engagement will not satisfy any statutory or third party requirements for an audit.

An example of an engagement letter for a review of financial statements appears in Appendix 1 to this ISA.

Planning

13. **The auditor should plan the work so that an effective engagement will be performed.**

14. **In planning a review of financial statements, the auditor should obtain or update the knowledge of the business including consideration of the entity's organization, accounting systems, operating characteristics and the nature of its assets, liabilities, revenues and expenses.**

15. The auditor needs to possess an understanding of such matters and other matters relevant to the financial statements, for example, a knowledge of the entity's production and distribution methods, product lines, operating locations and related parties. The auditor requires this understanding to be able to make relevant inquiries and to design appropriate procedures, as well as to assess the responses and other information obtained.

Work Performed by Others

16. **When using work performed by another auditor or an expert, the auditor should be satisfied that such work is adequate for the purposes of the review.**

Documentation

17. **The auditor should document matters which are important in providing evidence to support the review report, and evidence that the review was carried out in accordance with this ISA.**

Procedures and Evidence

18. **The auditor should apply judgment in determining the specific nature, timing and extent of review procedures.** The auditor will be guided by such matters as:

- Any knowledge acquired by carrying out audits or reviews of the financial statements for prior periods.

- The auditor's knowledge of the business including knowledge of the accounting principles and practices of the industry in which the entity operates.

- The entity's accounting systems.

- The extent to which a particular item is affected by management judgment.

- The materiality of transactions and account balances.

19. **The auditor should apply the same materiality considerations as would be applied if an audit opinion on the financial statements were being given.** Although there is a greater risk that misstatements will not be detected in a review than in an audit, the judgment as to what is material is made by reference to the information on which the auditor is reporting and the needs of those relying on that information, not to the level of assurance provided.

20. Procedures for the review of financial statements will ordinarily include:

- Obtaining an understanding of the entity's business and the industry in which it operates.

- Inquiries concerning the entity's accounting principles and practices.

- Inquiries concerning the entity's procedures for recording, classifying and summarizing transactions, accumulating information for disclosure in the financial statements and preparing financial statements.

- Inquiries concerning all material assertions in the financial statements.

- Analytical procedures designed to identify relationships and individual items that appear unusual. Such procedures would include:

  - Comparison of the financial statements with statements for prior periods.

  - Comparison of the financial statements with anticipated results and financial position.

  - Study of the relationships of the elements of the financial statements that would be expected to conform to a predictable pattern based on the entity's experience or industry norm.

In applying these procedures, the auditor would consider the types of matters that required accounting adjustments in prior periods.

- Inquiries concerning actions taken at meetings of shareholders, the board of directors, committees of the board of directors and other meetings that may affect the financial statements.

- Reading the financial statements to consider, on the basis of information coming to the auditor's attention, whether the financial statements appear to conform with the basis of accounting indicated.

- Obtaining reports from other auditors, if any and if considered necessary, who have been engaged to audit or review the financial statements of components of the entity.

- Inquiries of persons having responsibility for financial and accounting matters concerning, for example:

  - Whether all transactions have been recorded.

  - Whether the financial statements have been prepared in accordance with the basis of accounting indicated.

AUDITING

- Changes in the entity's business activities and accounting principles and practices.

- Matters as to which questions have arisen in the course of applying the foregoing procedures.

- Obtaining written representations from management when considered appropriate.

Appendix 2 to this ISA provides an illustrative list of procedures which are often used. The list is not exhaustive, nor is it intended that all the procedures suggested apply to every review engagement.

21. **The auditor should inquire about events subsequent to the date of the financial statements that may require adjustment of or disclosure in the financial statements.** The auditor does not have any responsibility to perform procedures to identify events occurring after the date of the review report.

22. **If the auditor has reason to believe that the information subject to review may be materially misstated, the auditor should carry out additional or more extensive procedures as are necessary to be able to express negative assurance or to confirm that a modified report is required.**

Conclusions and Reporting

23. **The review report should contain a clear written expression of negative assurance. The auditor should review and assess the conclusions drawn from the evidence obtained as the basis for the expression of negative assurance.**

24. **Based on the work performed, the auditor should assess whether any information obtained during the review indicates that the financial statements do not give a true and fair view (or 'are not presented fairly, in all material respects,') in accordance with the identified financial reporting framework.**

25. The report on a review of financial statements describes the scope of the engagement to enable the reader to understand the nature of the work performed and make it clear that an audit was not performed and, therefore, that an audit opinion is not expressed.

26. **The report on a review of financial statements should contain the following basic elements, ordinarily in the following layout:**

   (a) **title [2];**

   (b) **addressee;**

   (c) **opening or introductory paragraph including:**

---

[2] It may be appropriate to use the term "Independent" in the title to distinguish the auditor's report from reports that might be issued by others, such as officers of the entity, or from the reports of other auditors who may not have to abide by the same ethical requirements as an independent auditor.

    (i)   identification of the financial statements on which the review has been performed; and

    (ii) a statement of the responsibility of the entity's management and the responsibility of the auditor;

(d)   scope paragraph, describing the nature of a review, including:

    (i)   a reference to this International Standard on Auditing applicable to review engagements, or to relevant national standards or practices;

    (ii) a statement that a review is limited primarily to inquiries and analytical procedures; and

    (iii) a statement that an audit has not been performed, that the procedures undertaken provide less assurance than an audit and that an audit opinion is not expressed;

(e)   statement of negative assurance;

(f)   date of the report;

(g)   auditor's address; and

(h)   auditor's signature.

Appendices 3 and 4 to this ISA contain illustrations of review reports.

27.   The review report should:

(a)   state that nothing has come to the auditor's attention based on the review that causes the auditor to believe the financial statements do not give a true and fair view (or 'are not presented fairly, in all material respects,') in accordance with the identified financial reporting framework (negative assurance); or

(b)   if matters have come to the auditor's attention, describe those matters that impair a true and fair view ('or a fair presentation, in all material respects,') in accordance with the identified financial reporting framework, including, unless impracticable, a quantification of the possible effect(s) on the financial statements, and either:

    (i)   express a qualification of the negative assurance provided; or

    (ii) when the effect of the matter is so material and pervasive to the financial statements that the auditor concludes that a qualification is not adequate to disclose the misleading or incomplete nature of the financial statements, give an adverse statement that the financial statements do not give a true and fair view (or 'are not presented fairly, in all material respects,') in accordance with the identified financial reporting framework; or

(c)   if there has been a material scope limitation, describe the limitation and either:

      (i)   express a qualification of the negative assurance provided regarding the possible adjustments to the financial statements that might have been determined to be necessary had the limitation not existed; or

     (ii)   when the possible effect of the limitation is so significant and pervasive that the auditor concludes that no level of assurance can be provided, not provide any assurance.

28.   The auditor should date the review report as of the date the review is completed, which includes performing procedures relating to events occurring up to the date of the report. However, since the auditor's responsibility is to report on the financial statements as prepared and presented by management, the auditor should not date the review report earlier than the date on which the financial statements were approved by management.

Appendix 1

Example of an Engagement Letter for a Review of Financial Statements

The following letter is for use as a guide in conjunction with the consideration outlined in paragraph 10 of this ISA and will need to be varied according to individual requirements and circumstances.

To the Board of Directors (or the appropriate representative of senior management):

This letter is to confirm our understanding of the terms and objectives of our engagement and the nature and limitations of the services we will provide.

We will perform the following services:

We will review the balance sheet of ABC Company as of December 31, 19XX, and the related statements of income and cash flows for the year then ended, in accordance with the International Standard on Auditing (or refer to relevant national standards or practices) applicable to reviews. We will not perform an audit of such financial statements and, accordingly, we will not express an audit opinion on them. Accordingly, we expect to report on the financial statements as follows:

(see Appendix 3 to this ISA)

Responsibility for the financial statements, including adequate disclosure, is that of the management of the company. This includes the maintenance of adequate accounting records and internal controls and the selection and application of accounting policies. (As part of our review process, we will request written representations from management concerning assertions made in connection with the review[3].)

This letter will be effective for future years unless it is terminated, amended or superseded (if applicable).

Our engagement cannot be relied upon to disclose whether fraud or errors, or illegal acts exist. However, we will inform you of any material matters that come to our attention.

Please sign and return the attached copy of this letter to indicate that it is in accordance with your understanding of the arrangements for our review of the financial statements.

---

[3] This sentence should be used at the discretion of the auditor.

AUDITING

XYZ & Co

Acknowledged on behalf of
ABC Company by

(signed)
....
Name and Title
Date

Appendix 2

Illustrative Detailed Procedures that may be Performed in an Engagement to Review Financial Statements

1. The inquiry and analytical review procedures carried out in a review of financial statements are determined by the auditor's judgment. The procedures listed below are for illustrative purposes only. It is not intended that all the procedures suggested apply to every review engagement. This Appendix is not intended to serve as a program or checklist in the conduct of a review.

General

2. Discuss terms and scope of the engagement with the client and the engagement team.

3. Prepare an engagement letter setting forth the terms and scope of the engagement.

4. Obtain an understanding of the entity's business activities and the system for recording financial information and preparing financial statements.

5. Inquire whether all financial information is recorded:

    (a) completely;

    (b) promptly; and

    (c) after the necessary authorization.

6. Obtain the trial balance and determine whether it agrees with the general ledger and the financial statements.

7. Consider the results of previous audits and review engagements, including accounting adjustments required.

8. Inquire whether there have been any significant changes in the entity from the previous year (e.g., changes in ownership or changes in capital structure).

9. Inquire about the accounting policies and consider whether:

    (a) they comply with local or international standards;

    (b) they have been applied appropriately; and

    (c) they have been applied consistently and, if not, consider whether disclosure has been made of any changes in the accounting policies.

10. Read the minutes of meetings of shareholders, the board of directors and other appropriate committees in order to identify matters that could be important to the review.

AUDITING

11. Inquire if actions taken at shareholder, board of directors or comparable meetings that affect the financial statements have been appropriately reflected therein.

12. Inquire about the existence of transactions with related parties, how such transactions have been accounted for and whether related parties have been properly disclosed.

13. Inquire about contingencies and commitments.

14. Inquire about plans to dispose of major assets or business segments.

15. Obtain the financial statements and discuss them with management.

16. Consider the adequacy of disclosure in the financial statements and their suitability as to classification and presentation.

17. Compare the results shown in the current period financial statements with those shown in financial statements for comparable prior periods and, if available, with budgets and forecasts.

18. Obtain explanations from management for any unusual fluctuations or inconsistencies in the financial statements.

19. Consider the effect of any unadjusted errors—individually and in aggregate. Bring the errors to the attention of management and determine how the unadjusted errors will influence the report on the review.

20. Consider obtaining a representation letter from management.

Cash

21. Obtain the bank reconciliations. Inquire about any old or unusual reconciling items with client personnel.

22. Inquire about transfers between cash accounts for the period before and after the review date.

23. Inquire whether there are any restrictions on cash accounts.

Receivables

24. Inquire about the accounting policies for initially recording trade receivables and determine whether any allowances are given on such transactions.

25. Obtain a schedule of receivables and determine whether the total agrees with the trial balance.

26. Obtain and consider explanations of significant variations in account balances from previous periods or from those anticipated.

27. Obtain an aged analysis of the trade receivables. Inquire about the reason for unusually large accounts, credit balances on accounts or any other unusual balances and inquire about the collectibility of receivables.

28. Discuss with management the classification of receivables, including noncurrent balances, net credit balances and amounts due from shareholders, directors and other related parties in the financial statements.

29. Inquire about the method for identifying "slow payment" accounts and setting allowances for doubtful accounts and consider it for reasonableness.

30. Inquire whether receivables have been pledged, factored or discounted.

31. Inquire about procedures applied to ensure that a proper cutoff of sales transactions and sales returns has been achieved.

32. Inquire whether accounts represent goods shipped on consignment and, if so, whether adjustments have been made to reverse these transactions and include the goods in inventory.

33. Inquire whether any large credits relating to revenue recorded have been issued after the balance sheet date and whether provision has been made for such amounts.

Inventories

34. Obtain the inventory list and determine whether:

    (a) the total agrees with the balance in the trial balance; and

    (b) the list is based on a physical count of inventory.

35. Inquire about the method for counting inventory.

36. Where a physical count was not carried out on the balance sheet date, inquire whether:

    (a) a perpetual inventory system is used and whether periodic comparisons are made with actual quantities on hand; and

    (b) an integrated cost system is used and whether it has produced reliable information in the past.

37. Discuss adjustments made resulting from the last physical inventory count.

38. Inquire about procedures applied to control cutoff and any inventory movements.

39. Inquire about the basis used in valuing each category of the inventory and, in particular, regarding the elimination of inter-branch profits. Inquire whether inventory is valued at the lower of cost and net realizable value.

40. Consider the consistency with which inventory valuation methods have been applied, including factors such as material, labor and overhead.

41. Compare amounts of major inventory categories with those of prior periods and with those anticipated for the current period. Inquire about major fluctuations and differences.

42. Compare inventory turnover with that in previous periods.

43. Inquire about the method used for identifying slow moving and obsolete inventory and whether such inventory has been accounted for at net realizable value.

AUDITING

44. Inquire whether any of the inventory has been consigned to the entity and, if so, whether adjustments have been made to exclude such goods from inventory.

45. Inquire whether any inventory is pledged, stored at other locations or on consignment to others and consider whether such transactions have been accounted for appropriately.

Investments (including associated companies and marketable securities)

46. Obtain a schedule of the investments at the balance sheet date and determine whether it agrees with the trial balance.

47. Inquire about the accounting policy applied to investments.

48. Inquire from management about the carrying values of investments. Consider whether there are any realization problems.

49. Consider whether there has been proper accounting for gains and losses and investment income.

50. Inquire about the classification of long-term and short-term investments.

Property and depreciation

51. Obtain a schedule of the property indicating the cost and accumulated depreciation and determine whether it agrees with the trial balance.

52. Inquire about the accounting policy applied regarding the provision for depreciation and distinguishing between capital and maintenance items. Consider whether the property has suffered a material, permanent impairment in value.

53. Discuss with management the additions and deletions to property accounts and accounting for gains and losses on sales or retirements. Inquire whether all such transactions have been accounted for.

54. Inquire about the consistency with which the depreciation method and rates have been applied and compare depreciation provisions with prior years.

55. Inquire whether there are any liens on the property.

56. Discuss whether lease agreements have been properly reflected in the financial statements in conformity with current accounting pronouncements.

Prepaid expenses, intangibles and other assets

57. Obtain schedules identifying the nature of these accounts and discuss with management the recoverability thereof.

58. Inquire about the basis for recording these accounts and the amortization methods used.

59. Compare balances of related expense accounts with those of prior periods and discuss significant variations with management.

60. Discuss the classification between long-term and short-term accounts with management.

Loans payable

61. Obtain from management a schedule of loans payable and determine whether the total agrees with the trial balance.

62. Inquire whether there are any loans where management has not complied with the provisions of the loan agreement and, if so, inquire as to management's actions and whether appropriate adjustments have been made in the financial statements.

63. Consider the reasonableness of interest expense in relation to loan balances.

64. Inquire whether loans payable are secured.

65. Inquire whether loans payable have been classified between noncurrent and current.

Trade payables

66. Inquire about the accounting policies for initially recording trade payables and whether the entity is entitled to any allowances given on such transactions.

67. Obtain and consider explanations of significant variations in account balances from previous periods or from those anticipated.

68. Obtain a schedule of trade payables and determine whether the total agrees with the trial balance.

69. Inquire whether balances are reconciled with the creditors' statements and compare with prior period balances. Compare turnover with prior periods.

70. Consider whether there could be material unrecorded liabilities.

71. Inquire whether payables to shareholders, directors and other related parties are separately disclosed.

Accrued and contingent liabilities

72. Obtain a schedule of the accrued liabilities and determine whether the total agrees with the trial balance.

73. Compare major balances of related expense accounts with similar accounts for prior periods.

74. Inquire about approvals for such accruals, terms of payment, compliance with terms, collateral and classification.

75. Inquire about the method for determining accrued liabilities.

76. Inquire as to the nature of amounts included in contingent liabilities and commitments.

77. Inquire whether any actual or contingent liabilities exist which have not been recorded in the accounts. If so, discuss with management whether provisions

AUDITING

need to be made in the accounts or whether disclosure should be made in the notes to the financial statements.

Income and other taxes

78. Inquire from management if there were any events, including disputes with taxation authorities, which could have a significant effect on the taxes payable by the entity.

79. Consider the tax expense in relation to the entity's income for the period.

80. Inquire from management as to the adequacy of the recorded deferred and current tax liabilities including provisions in respect of prior periods.

Subsequent events

81. Obtain from management the latest interim financial statements and compare them with the financial statements being reviewed or with those for comparable periods from the preceding year.

82. Inquire about events after the balance sheet date that would have a material effect on the financial statements under review and, in particular, inquire whether:

    (a) any substantial commitments or uncertainties have arisen subsequent to the balance sheet date;

    (b) any significant changes in the share capital, long-term debt or working capital have occurred up to the date of inquiry; and

    (c) any unusual adjustments have been made during the period between the balance sheet date and the date of inquiry.

    Consider the need for adjustments or disclosure in the financial statements.

83. Obtain and read the minutes of meetings of shareholders, directors and appropriate committees subsequent to the balance sheet date.

Litigation

84. Inquire from management whether the entity is the subject of any legal actions-threatened, pending or in process. Consider the effect thereof on the financial statements.

Equity

85. Obtain and consider a schedule of the transactions in the equity accounts, including new issues, retirements and dividends.

86. Inquire whether there are any restrictions on retained earnings or other equity accounts.

Operations

87. Compare results with those of prior periods and those expected for the current period. Discuss significant variations with management.

88. Discuss whether the recognition of major sales and expenses have taken place in the appropriate periods.

89. Consider extraordinary and unusual items.

90. Consider and discuss with management the relationship between related items in the revenue account and assess the reasonableness thereof in the context of similar relationships for prior periods and other information available to the auditor.

AUDITING

Appendix 3

Form of Unqualified Review Report

REVIEW REPORT TO .....

We have reviewed the accompanying balance sheet of ABC Company at December 31,19XX, and the related statements of income and cash flows for the year then ended. These financial statements are the responsibility of the Company's management. Our responsibility is to issue a report on these financial statements based on our review.

We conducted our review in accordance with the International Standard on Auditing (or refer to relevant national standards or practices) applicable to review engagements. This Standard requires that we plan and perform the review to obtain moderate assurance as to whether the financial statements are free of material misstatement. A review is limited primarily to inquiries of company personnel and analytical procedures applied to financial data and thus provides less assurance than an audit. We have not performed an audit and, accordingly, we do not express an audit opinion.

Based on our review, nothing has come to our attention that causes us to believe that the accompanying financial statements do not give a true and fair view (or 'are not presented fairly, in all material respects,') in accordance with International Accounting Standards[4] .

Date   AUDITOR
Address

---

[4] Or indicate the relevant national accounting standards.

Appendix 4

Examples of Review Reports other than Unqualified

Qualification For a Departure From International Accounting Standards

REVIEW REPORT TO .....

We have reviewed the accompanying balance sheet of ABC Company at December 31, 19XX, and the related statements of income and cash flows for the year then ended. These financial statements are the responsibility of the Company's management. Our responsibility is to issue a report on these financial statements based on our review.

We conducted our review in accordance with the International Standard on Auditing (or refer to relevant national standards or practices) applicable to review engagements. This Standard requires that we plan and perform the review to obtain moderate assurance as to whether the financial statements are free of material misstatement. A review is limited primarily to inquiries of company personnel and analytical procedures applied to financial data and thus provides less assurance than an audit. We have not performed an audit, and, accordingly, we do not express an audit opinion.

Management has informed us that inventory has been stated at its cost which is in excess of its net realizable value. Management's computation, which we have reviewed, shows that inventory, if valued at the lower of cost and net realizable value as required by International Accounting Standards[5], would have been decreased by $X, and net income and shareholders' equity would have been decreased by $Y.

Based on our review, except for the effects of the overstatement of inventory described in the previous paragraph, nothing has come to our attention that causes us to believe that the accompanying financial statements do not give a true and fair view (or 'are not presented fairly, in all material respects,') in accordance with International Accounting Standards[5].

Date   AUDITOR
Address

---

[5] See footnote 4.

Adverse Report For a Departure From International Accounting Standards

REVIEW REPORT TO .....

We have reviewed the balance sheet of ABC Company at December 31, 19XX, and the related statements of income and cash flows for the year then ended. These financial statements are the responsibility of the Company's management. Our responsibility is to issue a report on these financial statements based on our review.

We conducted our review in accordance with the International Standard on Auditing (or refer to relevant national standards or practices) applicable to review engagements. This Standard requires that we plan and perform the review to obtain moderate assurance as to whether the financial statements are free of material misstatement. A review is limited primarily to inquiries of company personnel and analytical procedures applied to financial data and thus provides less assurance than an audit. We have not performed an audit and, accordingly, we do not express an audit opinion.

As noted in footnote X, these financial statements do not reflect the consolidation of the financial statements of subsidiary companies, the investment in which is accounted for on a cost basis. Under International Accounting Standards[6], the financial statements of the subsidiaries are required to be consolidated.

Based on our review, because of the pervasive effect on the financial statements of the matter discussed in the preceding paragraph, the accompanying financial statements do not give a true and fair view (or 'are not presented fairly, in all material respects,') in accordance with International Accounting Standards[6].

Date   AUDITOR
Address

---

[6] See footnote 4.

CONTENTS

	Paragraphs
Introduction	1-3
Objective of an Agreed-upon Procedures Engagement	4-6
General Principles of an Agreed-upon Procedures Engagement	7-8
Defining the Terms of the Engagement	9-12
Planning	13
Documentation	14
Procedures and Evidence	15-16
Reporting	17-18

Appendix 1: Example of an Engagement Letter for an Agreed-upon Procedures Engagement

Appendix 2: Example of a Report of Factual Findings in Connection with Accounts Payable

International Standards on Auditing (ISAs) are to be applied in the audit of financial statements. ISAs are also to be applied, adapted as necessary, to the audit of other information and to related services.

ISAs contain the basic principles and essential procedures (identified in bold type black lettering) together with related guidance in the form of explanatory and other material. The basic principles and essential procedures are to be interpreted in the context of the explanatory and other material that provide guidance for their application.

To understand and apply the basic principles and essential procedures together with the related guidance, it is necessary to consider the whole text of the ISA including explanatory and other material contained in the ISA not just that text which is black lettered.

In exceptional circumstances, an auditor may judge it necessary to depart from an ISA in order to more effectively achieve the objective of an audit. When such a situation arises, the auditor should be prepared to justify the departure.

ISAs need only be applied to material matters.

The Public Sector Perspective (PSP) issued by the Public Sector Committee of International Federation of Accountants is set out at the end of an ISA. Where no PSP is added, the ISA is applicable in all material respects to the public sector.

AUDITING

920

Introduction

1. The purpose of this International Standard on Auditing (ISA) is to establish standards and provide guidance on the auditor's[1] professional responsibilities when an engagement to perform agreed-upon procedures regarding financial information is undertaken and on the form and content of the report that the auditor issues in connection with such an engagement.

2. This ISA is directed toward engagements regarding financial information. However, it may provide useful guidance for engagements regarding non-financial information, provided the auditor has adequate knowledge of the subject matter in question and reasonable criteria exist on which to base findings. This ISA is to be read in conjunction with ISA 120 "Framework of International Standards on Auditing." Guidance in other ISAs may be useful to the auditor in applying this ISA.

3. An engagement to perform agreed-upon procedures may involve the auditor in performing certain procedures concerning individual items of financial data (for example, accounts payable, accounts receivable, purchases from related parties and sales and profits of a segment of an entity), a financial statement (for example, a balance sheet) or even a complete set of financial statements.

Objective of an Agreed-upon Procedures Engagement

4. **The objective of an agreed-upon procedures engagement is for the auditor to carry out procedures of an audit nature to which the auditor and the entity and any appropriate third parties have agreed and to report on factual findings.**

5. As the auditor simply provides a report of the factual findings of agreed-upon procedures, no assurance is expressed. Instead, users of the report assess for themselves the procedures and findings reported by the auditor and draw their own conclusions from the auditor's work.

6. The report is restricted to those parties that have agreed to the procedures to be performed since others, unaware of the reasons for the procedures, may misinterpret the results.

General Principles of an Agreed-upon Procedures Engagement

7. **The auditor should comply with the "Code of Ethics for Professional Accountants" issued by IFAC.** Ethical principles governing the auditor's professional responsibilities for this type of engagement are:

---

[1] As explained in the Framework of International Standards on Auditing "... the term auditor is used throughout the ISAs when describing both auditing and related services which may be performed. Such reference is not intended to imply that a person performing related services need be the auditor of the entity's financial statements."

(a) integrity;

(b) objectivity;

(c) professional competence and due care;

(d) confidentiality;

(e) professional behavior; and

(f) technical standards.

Independence is not a requirement for agreed-upon procedures engagements; however, the terms or objectives of an engagement or national standards may require the auditor to comply with the independence requirements of IFAC's Code of Ethics. Where the auditor is not independent, a statement to that effect would be made in the report of factual findings.

8. **The auditor should conduct an agreed-upon procedures engagement in accordance with this ISA and the terms of the engagement.**

Defining the Terms of the Engagement

9. **The auditor should ensure with representatives of the entity and, ordinarily, other specified parties who will receive copies of the report of factual findings, that there is a clear understanding regarding the agreed procedures and the conditions of the engagement.** Matters to be agreed include the:

- Nature of the engagement including the fact that the procedures performed will not constitute an audit or a review and that accordingly no assurance will be expressed.

- Stated purpose for the engagement.

- Identification of the financial information to which the agreed-upon procedures will be applied.

- Nature, timing and extent of the specific procedures to be applied.

- Anticipated form of the report of factual findings.

- Limitations on distribution of the report of factual findings. When such limitation would be in conflict with the legal requirements, if any, the auditor would not accept the engagement.

10. In certain circumstances, for example, when the procedures have been agreed to between the regulator, industry representatives and representatives of the accounting profession, the auditor may not be able to discuss the procedures with all the parties who will receive the report. In such cases, the auditor may consider, for example, discussing the procedures to be applied with appropriate representatives of the parties involved, reviewing relevant correspondence from such parties or sending them a draft of the type of report that will be issued.

11. It is in the interests of both the client and the auditor that the auditor send an engagement letter documenting the key terms of the appointment. An

engagement letter confirms the auditor's acceptance of the appointment and helps avoid misunderstanding regarding such matters as the objectives and scope of the engagement, the extent of the auditor's responsibilities and the form of reports to be issued.

12. Matters that would be included in the engagement letter include:

- A listing of the procedures to be performed as agreed upon between the parties.

- A statement that the distribution of the report of factual findings would be restricted to the specified parties who have agreed to the procedures to be performed.

In addition, the auditor may consider attaching to the engagement letter a draft of the type of report of factual findings that will be issued. An example of an engagement letter appears in Appendix 1 to this ISA.

Planning

13. **The auditor should plan the work so that an effective engagement will be performed.**

Documentation

14. **The auditor should document matters which are important in providing evidence to support the report of factual findings, and evidence that the engagement was carried out in accordance with this ISA and the terms of the engagement.**

Procedures and Evidence

15. **The auditor should carry out the procedures agreed upon and use the evidence obtained as the basis for the report of factual findings.**

16. The procedures applied in an engagement to perform agreed-upon procedures may include:

- Inquiry and analysis.

- Recomputation, comparison and other clerical accuracy checks.

- Observation.

- Inspection.

- Obtaining confirmations.

Appendix 2 to this ISA is an example report which contains an illustrative list of procedures which may be used as one part of a typical agreed-upon procedures engagement.

Reporting

17. The report on an agreed-upon procedures engagement needs to describe the purpose and the agreed-upon procedures of the engagement in sufficient detail to enable the reader to understand the nature and the extent of the work performed.

18. **The report of factual findings should contain:**

    (a) title;

    (b) addressee (ordinarily the client who engaged the auditor to perform the agreed-upon procedures);

    (c) identification of specific financial or non-financial information to which the agreed-upon procedures have been applied;

    (d) a statement that the procedures performed were those agreed upon with the recipient;

    (e) a statement that the engagement was performed in accordance with the International Standard on Auditing applicable to agreed-upon procedures engagements, or with relevant national standards or practices;

    (f) when relevant a statement that the auditor is not independent of the entity;

    (g) identification of the purpose for which the agreed-upon procedures were performed;

    (h) a listing of the specific procedures performed;

    (i) a description of the auditor's factual findings including sufficient details of errors and exceptions found;

    (j) statement that the procedures performed do not constitute either an audit or a review and, as such, no assurance is expressed;

    (k) a statement that had the auditor performed additional procedures, an audit or a review, other matters might have come to light that would have been reported;

    (l) a statement that the report is restricted to those parties that have agreed to the procedures to be performed;

    (m) a statement (when applicable) that the report relates only to the elements, accounts, items or financial and non-financial information specified and that it does not extend to the entity's financial statements taken as a whole;

    (n) date of the report;

    (o) auditor's address; and

    (p) auditor's signature.

AUDITING

Appendix 2 to this ISA contains an example of a report of factual findings issued in connection with an engagement to perform agreed-upon procedures regarding financial information.

Public Sector Perspective

1. *The report in a public sector engagement may not be restricted only to those parties that have agreed to the procedures to be performed, but made available also to a wider range of entities or people (for example, a parliamentary investigation about a specific public entity or governmental department).*

2. *It also has to be noted that public sector mandates vary significantly and caution has to be taken to distinguish engagements that are truly "agreed upon procedures" from engagements that are expected to be audits of financial information, such as performance reports.*

Appendix 1

Example of an Engagement Letter for an Agreed-upon Procedures Engagement

The following letter is for use as a guide in conjunction with paragraph 9 of this ISA and is not intended to be a standard letter. The engagement letter will need to be varied according to individual requirements and circumstances.

Date

To the Board of Directors or other appropriate representatives of the client who engaged the auditor.

This letter is to confirm our understanding of the terms and objectives of our engagement and the nature and limitations of the services that we will provide. Our engagement will be conducted in accordance with the International Standard on Auditing (or refer to relevant national standards or practices) applicable to agreed-upon procedures engagements and we will indicate so in our report.

We have agreed to perform the following procedures and report to you the factual findings resulting from our work:

(describe the nature, timing and extent of the procedures to be performed, including specific reference, where applicable, to the identity of documents and records to be read, individuals to be contacted and parties from whom confirmations will be obtained.)

The procedures that we will perform are solely to assist you in (state purpose). Our report is not to be used for any other purpose and is solely for your information.

The procedures that we will perform will not constitute an audit or a review made in accordance with International Standards on Auditing (or refer to relevant national standards or practices) and, consequently, no assurance will be expressed.

We look forward to full cooperation with your staff and we trust that they will make available to us whatever records, documentation and other information requested in connection with our engagement.

Our fees, which will be billed as work progresses, are based on the time required by the individuals assigned to the engagement plus out-of-pocket expenses. Individual hourly rates vary according to the degree of responsibility involved and the experience and skill required.

AUDITING

Please sign and return the attached copy of this letter to indicate that it is in accordance with your understanding of the terms of the engagement including the specific procedures which we have agreed will be performed.

XYZ & Co

Acknowledged on behalf of
ABC Company by

(signed)
....
Name and Title
Date

Appendix 2

Example of a Report of Factual Findings in Connection with Accounts Payable

REPORT OF FACTUAL FINDINGS

To (those who engaged the auditor)

We have performed the procedures agreed with you and enumerated below with respect to the accounts payable of ABC Company as at (date), set forth in the accompanying schedules (not shown in this example). Our engagement was undertaken in accordance with the International Standard on Auditing (or refer to relevant national standards or practices) applicable to agreed-upon procedures engagements. The procedures were performed solely to assist you in evaluating the validity of the accounts payable and are summarized as follows:

1. We obtained and checked the addition of the trial balance of accounts payable as at (date) prepared by ABC Company, and we compared the total to the balance in the related general ledger account.

2. We compared the attached list (not shown in this example) of major suppliers and the amounts owing at (date) to the related names and amounts in the trial balance.

3. We obtained suppliers' statements or requested suppliers to confirm balances owing at (date).

4. We compared such statements or confirmations to the amounts referred to in 2. For amounts which did not agree, we obtained reconciliations from ABC Company. For reconciliations obtained, we identified and listed outstanding invoices, credit notes and outstanding checks, each of which was greater than $xxx. We located and examined such invoices and credit notes subsequently received and checks subsequently paid and we ascertained that they should in fact have been listed as outstanding on the reconciliations.

We report our findings below:

a) With respect to item 1 we found the addition to be correct and the total amount to be in agreement.

b) With respect to item 2 we found the amounts compared to be in agreement.

c) With respect to item 3 we found there were suppliers' statements for all such suppliers.

d) With respect to item 4 we found the amounts agreed, or with respect to amounts which did not agree, we found ABC Company had prepared reconciliations and that the credit notes, invoices and outstanding

920

checks over $xxx were appropriately listed as reconciling items with the following exceptions:

(Detail the exceptions)

Because the above procedures do not constitute either an audit or a review made in accordance with International Standards on Auditing (or relevant national standards or practices), we do not express any assurance on the accounts payable as of (date).

Had we performed additional procedures or had we performed an audit or review of the financial statements in accordance with International Standards on Auditing (or relevant national standards or practices), other matters might have come to our attention that would have been reported to you.

Our report is solely for the purpose set forth in the first paragraph of this report and for your information and is not to be used for any other purpose or to be distributed to any other parties. This report relates only to the accounts and items specified above and does not extend to any financial statements of ABC Company, taken as a whole.

Date   AUDITOR
Address

CONTENTS

	Paragraphs
Introduction	1-2
Objective of a Compilation Engagement	3-4
General Principles of a Compilation Engagement	5-6
Defining the Terms of the Engagement	7-8
Planning	9
Documentation	10
Procedures	11-17
Reporting on a Compilation Engagement	18-19

Appendix 1: Example of an Engagement Letter for a Compilation Engagement

Appendix 2: Examples of Compilation Reports

International Standards on Auditing (ISAs) are to be applied in the audit of financial statements. ISAs are also to be applied, adapted as necessary, to the audit of other information and to related services.

ISAs contain the basic principles and essential procedures (identified in bold type black lettering) together with related guidance in the form of explanatory and other material. The basic principles and essential procedures are to be interpreted in the context of the explanatory and other material that provide guidance for their application.

To understand and apply the basic principles and essential procedures together with the related guidance, it is necessary to consider the whole text of the ISA including explanatory and other material contained in the ISA not just that text which is black lettered.

In exceptional circumstances, an auditor may judge it necessary to depart from an ISA in order to more effectively achieve the objective of an audit. When such a situation arises, the auditor should be prepared to justify the departure.

ISAs need only be applied to material matters.

AUDITING

The Public Sector Perspective (PSP) issued by the Public Sector Committee of the International Federation of Accountants is set out at the end of an ISA. Where no PSP is added, the ISA is applicable in all material respects to the public sector.

Introduction

1. The purpose of this International Standard on Auditing (ISA) is to establish standards and provide guidance on the accountant's[1] professional responsibilities when an engagement to compile financial information is undertaken and the form and content of the report the accountant issues in connection with such a compilation.

2. This ISA is directed toward the compilation of financial information. However, it is to be applied to the extent practicable to engagements to compile non-financial information, provided the accountant has adequate knowledge of the subject matter in question. Engagements to provide limited assistance to a client in the preparation of financial statements (for example, on the selection of an appropriate accounting policy), do not constitute an engagement to compile financial information. This ISA is to be read in conjunction with ISA 120 "Framework of International Standards on Auditing."

Objective of a Compilation Engagement

3. **The objective of a compilation engagement is for the accountant to use accounting expertise, as opposed to auditing expertise, to collect, classify and summarize financial information.** This ordinarily entails reducing detailed data to a manageable and understandable form without a requirement to test the assertions underlying that information. The procedures employed are not designed and do not enable the accountant to express any assurance on the financial information. However, users of the compiled financial information derive some benefit as a result of the accountant's involvement because the service has been performed with professional competence and due care.

4. A compilation engagement would ordinarily include the preparation of financial statements (which may or may not be a complete set of financial statements) but may also include the collection, classification and summarization of other financial information.

General Principles of a Compilation Engagement

5. **The accountant should comply with the "Code of Ethics for Professional Accountants" issued by IFAC.** Ethical principles governing the accountant's professional responsibilities for this type of engagement are:

   (a) integrity;

   (b) objectivity;

   (c) professional competence and due care;

---

[1] For the purposes of this ISA and to distinguish between an audit and a compilation engagement the term 'accountant' (rather than 'auditor') has been used throughout to refer to a professional accountant in public practice.

(d)   confidentiality;

(e)   professional behavior; and

(f)   technical standards.

Independence is not a requirement for a compilation engagement. However, where the accountant is not independent, a statement to that effect would be made in the accountant's report.

6.   **In all circumstances when an accountant's name is associated with financial information compiled by the accountant, the accountant should issue a report.**

Defining the Terms of the Engagement

7.   **The accountant should ensure that there is a clear understanding between the client and the accountant regarding the terms of the engagement.** Matters to be considered include the:

- Nature of the engagement including the fact that neither an audit nor a review will be carried out and that accordingly no assurance will be expressed.

- Fact that the engagement cannot be relied upon to disclose errors, illegal acts or other irregularities, for example, fraud or defalcations that may exist.

- Nature of the information to be supplied by the client.

- Fact that management is responsible for the accuracy and completeness of the information supplied to the accountant for the completeness and accuracy of the compiled financial information.

- Basis of accounting on which the financial information is to be compiled and the fact that it, and any known departures therefrom, will be disclosed.

- Intended use and distribution of the information, once compiled.

- Form of report to be rendered regarding the financial information compiled, when the accountant's name is to be associated therewith.

8.   An engagement letter will be of assistance in planning the compilation work. It is in the interests of both the accountant and the entity that the accountant send an engagement letter documenting the key terms of the appointment. An engagement letter confirms the accountant's acceptance of the appointment and helps avoid misunderstanding regarding such matters as the objectives and scope of the engagement, the extent of the accountant's responsibilities and the form of reports to be issued. An example of an engagement letter for a compilation engagement appears in Appendix 1 to this ISA.

AUDITING

Planning

9. The accountant should plan the work so that an effective engagement will be performed.

Documentation

10. The accountant should document matters which are important in providing evidence that the engagement was carried out in accordance with this ISA and the terms of the engagement.

Procedures

11. The accountant should obtain a general knowledge of the business and operations of the entity and should be familiar with the accounting principles and practices of the industry in which the entity operates and with the form and content of the financial information that is appropriate in the circumstances.

12. To compile financial information, the accountant requires a general understanding of the nature of the entity's business transactions, the form of its accounting records and the accounting basis on which the financial information is to be presented. The accountant ordinarily obtains knowledge of these matters through experience with the entity or inquiry of the entity's personnel.

13. Other than as noted in this ISA, the accountant is not ordinarily required to:

    (a) make any inquiries of management to assess the reliability and completeness of the information provided;

    (b) assess internal controls;

    (c) verify any matters; or

    (d) verify any explanations.

14. If the accountant becomes aware that information supplied by management is incorrect, incomplete, or otherwise unsatisfactory, the accountant should consider performing the above procedures and request management to provide additional information. If management refuses to provide additional information, the accountant should withdraw from the engagement, informing the entity of the reasons for the withdrawal.

15. The accountant should read the compiled information and consider whether it appears to be appropriate in form and free from obvious material misstatements. In this sense, misstatements include:

    • Mistakes in the application of the identified financial reporting framework.

    • Nondisclosure of the financial reporting framework and any known departures therefrom.

    • Nondisclosure of any other significant matters of which the accountant has become aware.

The identified financial reporting framework and any known departures therefrom should be disclosed within the financial information, though their effects need not be quantified.

16. If the accountant becomes aware of material misstatements, the accountant should try to agree appropriate amendments with the entity. If such amendments are not made and the financial information is considered to be misleading, the accountant should withdraw from the engagement.

Responsibility of Management

17. The accountant should obtain an acknowledgment from management of its responsibility for the appropriate presentation of the financial information and of its approval of the financial information. Such acknowledgment may be provided by representations from management which cover the accuracy and completeness of the underlying accounting data and the complete disclosure of all material and relevant information to the accountant.

Reporting on a Compilation Engagement

18. Reports on compilation engagements should contain[2] the following:

   (a) title;

   (b) addressee;

   (c) a statement that the engagement was performed in accordance with the ISA applicable to compilation engagements, or with national standards and practices;

   (d) when relevant, a statement that the accountant is not independent of the entity;

   (e) identification of the financial information noting that it is based on information provided by management;

   (f) a statement that management is responsible for the financial information compiled by the accountant;

   (g) a statement that neither an audit nor a review has been carried out and that accordingly no assurance is expressed on the financial information;

   (h) a paragraph, when considered necessary, drawing attention to the disclosure of material departures from the identified financial reporting framework;

   (i) date of the report;

AUDITING

---

[2] It may also be appropriate for the accountant to refer to the special purpose for which or party for whom the information has been prepared. Alternatively, or in addition, the accountant may add some form of caution designed to ensure that it is not used for purposes other than those intended.

(j)   accountant's address; and

(k)   accountant's signature.

Appendix 2 to this ISA contains examples of compilation reports.

19.   **The financial information compiled by the accountant should contain a reference such as "Unaudited," "Compiled without Audit or Review" or "Refer to Compilation Report" on each page of the financial information or on the front of the complete set of financial statements.**

Appendix 1

Example of an Engagement Letter for a Compilation Engagement

The following letter is for use as a guide in conjunction with the considerations outlined in paragraph 7 of this ISA and will need to be varied according to individual requirements and circumstances. This example is for the compilation of financial statements.

(Date)

To the Board of Directors or the appropriate representatives of senior management:

This letter is to confirm our understanding of the terms of our engagement and the nature and limitations of the services we will provide.

You have requested that we perform the following services:

On the basis of information you provide, we will compile, in accordance with the International Standard on Auditing (or refer to relevant national standards or practices) applicable to compilation engagements, the balance sheet of ABC Company as of December 31, 19XX and related statements of income and cash flows for the year then ended on a cash basis. We will not carry out audit or review engagement procedures in relation to such financial statements. Consequently, no assurance on the financial statements will be expressed. Our report on the financial statements of ABC Company is presently expected to read as follows:

(see Appendix 2 to this ISA)

Management is responsible for both the accuracy and completeness of the information supplied to us and is responsible to users for the financial information compiled by us. This includes the maintenance of adequate accounting records and internal controls and the selection and application of appropriate accounting policies. Our engagement cannot be relied upon to disclose whether fraud or errors, or illegal acts exist. However, we will inform you of any such matters which come to our attention.

The information will be prepared in accordance with [identified financial reporting framework]. Any known departures from this framework will be disclosed within the financial statements and when considered necessary will be referred to in our compilation report.

We understand that the intended use and distribution of the information we have compiled is [specify] and that should this change in a material respect, that you will inform us.

We look forward to full cooperation with your staff and we trust that they will make available to us whatever records, documentation and other information requested in connection with our compilation.

AUDITING

Our fees, which will be billed as work progresses, are based on the time required by the individuals assigned to the engagement plus out-of-pocket expenses. Individual hourly rates vary according to the degree of responsibility involved and the experience and skill required.

This letter will be effective for future years unless it is terminated, amended or superseded.

Please sign and return the attached copy of this letter to indicate that it is in accordance with your understanding of the arrangements for our compilation of your financial statements.

XYZ & Co

Acknowledged on behalf of
ABC Company by

(signed)

....
Name and Title
Date

Appendix 2

Examples of Compilation Reports

Example of a Report on an Engagement to Compile Financial Statements

COMPILATION REPORT TO .....

On the basis of information provided by management we have compiled, in accordance with the International Standard on Auditing (or refer to relevant national standards or practices) applicable to compilation engagements, the balance sheet of ABC Company as of December 31, 19XX and statements of income and cash flows for the year then ended. Management is responsible for these financial statements. We have not audited or reviewed these financial statements and accordingly express no assurance thereon[3] .

Date   ACCOUNTANT
Address

---

[3] See footnote 2.

Example of a Report on an Engagement to Compile Financial Statements with an Additional Paragraph that Draws Attention to a Departure from the Identified Financial Reporting Framework

COMPILATION REPORT TO .....

On the basis of information provided by management we have compiled, in accordance with the International Standard on Auditing (or refer to relevant national standards or practices) applicable to compilation engagements, the balance sheet of XYZ Company as of December 31, 19XX and the related statements of income and cash flows for the year then ended. Management is responsible for these financial statements. We have not audited or reviewed these financial statements and accordingly express no assurance thereon[4] .

We draw attention to Note X to the financial statements because management has elected not to capitalize the leases on plant and machinery which is a departure from the identified financial reporting framework.

Date   ACCOUNTANT
Address

---

[4] See footnote 2.

CONTENTS

	Paragraphs
Introduction	1-4
The Need for Confirmation	5
Use of Confirmation Requests	6-9
Preparation and Dispatch of Requests and Receipt of Replies	10-12
Content of Confirmation Requests	13-20
Appendix: Glossary	

This International Auditing Practice Statement was prepared and approved jointly by the International Auditing Practices Committee of the International Federation of Accountants and the Committee on Banking Regulations and Supervisory Practices of the Group of Ten major industrialized countries and Switzerland in November 1983 for publication in February 1984.

This Statement is published to provide practical assistance to external independent auditors and also internal auditors and inspectors on inter-bank confirmation procedures. This statement is not intended to have the authority of an International Standard on Auditing.

AUDITING

1000

Introduction

1. The purpose of this Statement is to provide assistance on inter-bank confirmation procedures to the external independent auditor and also to bank management, such as internal auditors or inspectors. The guidance contained in this Statement should contribute to the effectiveness of inter-bank confirmation procedures and to the efficiency of processing replies.

2. An important audit step in the examination of bank financial statements and related information is to request direct confirmation from other banks of both balances and other amounts which appear in the balance sheet and other information which may not be shown on the face of the balance sheet but which may be disclosed in the notes to the accounts. Off balance sheet items requiring confirmation include, such items as guarantees, forward purchase and sale commitments, repurchase options, and offset arrangements. This type of audit evidence is valuable because it comes directly from an independent source and, therefore, provides greater assurance of reliability than that obtained solely from the bank's own records.

3. The auditor, in seeking to obtain inter-bank confirmations, may encounter difficulties in relation to language, terminology, consistent interpretation and scope of matters covered by the reply. Frequently, these difficulties result from the use of different kinds of confirmation requests or misunderstandings about what they are intended to cover.

4. Audit procedures may differ from country to country, and consequently local practices will have relevance to the way in which inter-bank confirmation procedures are applied. While this Statement does not purport to describe a comprehensive set of audit procedures, nevertheless, it does emphasize some important steps which should be followed in the use of a confirmation request.

The Need for Confirmation

5. An essential feature of management control over business relations, with individuals or groups of financial institutions, is the ability to obtain confirmation of transactions with those institutions and of the resulting positions. The requirement for bank confirmation arises from the need of the bank's management and its auditors to confirm the financial and business relationships between the following:

   • the bank and other banks within the same country;

   • the bank and other banks in different countries; and

   • the bank and its non-bank customers.

   While inter-bank relationships are similar in nature to those between the bank and a non-bank customer, there may be special significance in some inter-bank relationships, for example, in connection with certain types of "off balance sheet" transactions, such as contingencies, forward transactions, commitments and offset agreements.

Use of Confirmation Requests

6. The guidance set out in the following paragraphs is designed to assist banks and their auditors to obtain independent confirmation of financial and business relationships within other banks. However, there may be occasions on which the approach described within this Statement may also be appropriate to confirmation procedures between the bank and its non-bank customers. The procedures described are not relevant to the routine inter-bank confirmation procedures which are carried out in respect to the day to day commercial transactions conducted between banks.

7. The auditor should decide from which bank or banks to request confirmation, have regard to such matters as size of balances, volume of activity, degree of reliance on internal controls, and materiality within the context of the financial statements. Tests of particular activities of the bank may be structured in different ways and confirmation requests may, therefore, be limited solely to inquiries about those activities. Requests for confirmation of individual transactions may either form part of the test of a bank's system of internal control or be a means of verifying balances appearing in a bank's financial statements at a particular date. Therefore, confirmation requests should be designed to meet the particular purpose for which they are required.

8. The auditor should determine which of the following approaches is the most appropriate in seeking confirmation of balances or other information from another bank:

   • listing balances and other information, and requesting confirmation of their accuracy and completeness, or

   • requesting details of balances and other information, which can then be compared with the requesting bank's records.

   In determining which of the above approaches is the most appropriate, the auditor should weigh the quality of audit evidence he requires in the particular circumstances against the practicality of obtaining a reply from the confirming bank.

9. Difficulty may be encountered in obtaining a satisfactory response even where the requesting bank submits information for confirmation to the confirming bank. It is important that a response be sought for all confirmation requests. It is not usual practice to request a response only if the information submitted is incorrect or incomplete.

Preparation and Dispatch of Requests and Receipt of Replies

10. The auditor should determine the appropriate location to which the confirmation request should be sent, for example a department, such as internal audit, inspection and other specialist department, which may be designated by the confirming bank as responsible for replying to confirmation requests. It may be appropriate, therefore, to direct confirmation requests to the head office of the bank (in which such departments are often located) rather than to the location where balances and other relevant

AUDITING

1000

information are held. In other situations, the appropriate location may be the local branch of the confirming bank.

11. Whenever possible, the confirmation request should be prepared in the language of the confirming bank or in the language normally used for business purposes.

12. Control over the content and dispatch of confirmation requests is the responsibility of the auditor. However, it will be necessary for the request to be authorized by the requesting bank. Replies should be returned directly to the auditor and to facilitate such a reply, a pre-addressed envelope should be enclosed with the request.

Content of Confirmation Requests

13. The form and content of a confirmation request letter will depend on the purpose for which it is required, on local practices and on the requesting bank's account procedures, for example, whether or not it makes extensive use of electronic data processing.

14. The confirmation request should be prepared in a clear and concise manner to ensure ready comprehension by the confirming bank.

15. Not all information for which confirmation is usually sought will be required at the same time. Accordingly, request letters may be sent at various times during the year dealing with particular aspects of the inter-bank relationship.

16. The most commonly requested information is in respect of balances due to or from the requesting bank on current, deposit, loan and other accounts. The request letter should provide the account description, number and the type of currency for the account. It may also be advisable to request information about nil balances on correspondent accounts, and correspondent accounts which were closed in the twelve months prior to the chosen confirmation date. The requesting bank may ask for confirmation not only of the balances on accounts but also, where it may be helpful, other information, such as the maturity and interest terms, unused facilities, lines of credit/standby facilities, any offset or other rights or encumbrances, and details of any collateral given or received.

17. An important part of banking business relates to the control of those transactions commonly designated as "off balance sheet." Accordingly, the requesting bank and its auditors are likely to request confirmation of contingent liabilities, such as those arising on guarantees, comfort letters and letters of undertaking, bills, own acceptances, and endorsements. Confirmation may be sought both of the contingent liabilities of the requesting bank to the confirming bank and of the confirming bank to the requesting bank. The details supplied or requested should describe the nature of the contingent liabilities together with their currency and amount.

18. Confirmation of asset repurchase and resale agreements and options outstanding at the relevant date should also be sought. Such confirmation should describe the asset covered by the agreement, the date the transaction was contracted, its maturity date, and the terms on which it was completed.

19. Another category of information, for which independent confirmation is often requested at a date other than the transaction date, concerns forward currency, bullion, securities and other outstanding contracts. It is well established practice for banks to confirm transactions with other banks as they are made. However, it is the practice for audit purposes to confirm independently a sample of transactions selected from a period of time or to confirm all the unmatured transactions with a counterparty. The request should give details of each contract including its number, the deal date, the maturity or value date, the price at which the deal was transacted and the currency and amount of the contract bought and sold, to and from, the requesting bank.

20. Banks often hold securities and other items in safe custody on behalf of customers. A request letter may thus ask for confirmation of such items held by the confirming bank, at a specific date. The confirmation should include a description of the items and the nature of any encumbrances or other rights over them.

AUDITING

Appendix

Glossary

This appendix defines certain terms used in this Statement. The list is not intended to include all terms used in an inter-bank confirmation request. Definitions have been given within a banking context, although usage and legal application may differ.

Collateral

Security given by a borrower to a lender as a pledge for repayment of a loan, rarely given in the case of inter-bank business. Such lenders thus become secured creditors; in the event of default, such creditors are entitled to proceed against collateral in settlement of their claim. Any kind of property may be employed as collateral. Examples of collateral are: real estate, bonds, stocks, notes, acceptances, chattels, bills of lading, warehouse receipts and assigned debts.

Contingent Liabilities

Potential liabilities, which only crystallize upon the fulfillment of or the failure to fulfill certain conditions. They may arise from the sale, transfer, endorsement, or guarantee of negotiable instruments or from other financial transactions. For example, they may result from:

- re-discount of notes receivable, trade and bank acceptances arising under commercial letters of credit;

- guarantees given; or

- letters of support or comfort.

Encumbrance

A claim or lien, such as a mortgage upon real property, which diminishes the owner's equity in the property.

Offset

The right of a bank, normally evidenced in writing, to take possession of any account balances that a guarantor or debtor may have with it to cover the obligations to the bank of the guarantor, debtor or third party.

Options

The right to buy or sell or to both buy and sell securities or commodities at agreed prices, within a fixed duration of time.

Repurchase (or Resale) Agreement

An agreement between seller and buyer that the seller (or buyer) will buy (or sell) back notes, securities, or both property at the expiration of a period of time, or the completion of certain conditions, or both.

Safe Custody

A facility offered by banks to their customers to store valuable property for safe keeping.

Line of Credit/Standby Facility

An agreed maximum amount of funds which a bank has made or undertakes to make available over a specified period of time.

AUDITING

CONTENTS

	Paragraphs
Introduction	1
Microcomputer Systems	2-4
Microcomputer Configurations	5-9
Characteristics of Microcomputers	10-12
Internal Control in Microcomputer Environments	**13-14**
Management Authorization for Operating Microcomputers	15
Physical Security—Equipment	16-17
Physical Security—Removable and Non-Removable Media	18-20
Program and Data Security	21-27
Software and Data Integrity	28-31
Hardware, Software and Data Back-Up	32
The Effect of Microcomputers on the Accounting System and Related Internal Controls	**33-34**
General CIS Controls—Segregation of Duties	35
CIS Application Controls	36
The Effect of a Microcomputer Environment on Audit Procedures	37-41

This International Auditing Practice Statement was approved by the International Auditing Practices Committee in June 1987 for publication in October 1987.

The auditor should understand and consider the characteristics of the CIS environment because they affect the design of the accounting system and related internal controls, the selection of internal controls upon which he intends to rely, and the nature, timing and extent of his procedures.

This Statement is issued as a supplement to ISA 400 "Risk Assessments and Internal Control." It does not form a part of the ISA or International Auditing Practice Statement 1008 "Risk Assessments and Internal Control—CIS Characteristics and Considerations," and is not intended to have the authority of an ISA.

This Statement forms part of a series intended to help the auditor implement the ISA and the Statement referred to above by describing various CIS environments and their effect on the accounting system and related internal controls and on audit procedures.

Introduction

1. The purpose of this Statement is to help the auditor implement ISA 400 "Risk Assessments and Internal Control," and International Auditing Practice Statement 1008 "Risk Assessments and Internal Control—CIS Characteristics and Considerations," by describing microcomputer systems used as stand-alone work-stations. The Statement describes the effects of the microcomputer on the accounting system and related internal controls and on audit procedures.

Microcomputer Systems

2. Microcomputers, often referred to as "personal computers" or "PCs," are economical yet powerful self-contained general purpose computers consisting typically of a processor, memory, video display unit, data storage unit, keyboard and connections for a printer and communications. Programs and data are stored on removable or non-removable storage media.

3. Microcomputers can be used to process accounting transactions and produce reports that are essential to the preparation of financial statements. The microcomputer may constitute the entire computer-based accounting system or merely a part of it.

4. Generally, computer information systems (CIS)[1] environments in which microcomputers are used are different from other CIS environments. Certain controls and security measures that are used for large computer systems may not be practicable for microcomputers. On the other hand, certain types of internal controls need to be emphasized due to the characteristics of microcomputers and the environments in which they are used.

Microcomputer Configurations

5. A microcomputer can be used in various configurations. These include:

    *   a stand-alone workstation operated by a single user or a number of users at different times;

    *   a workstation which is part of a local area network of microcomputers; and

    *   a workstation connected to a central computer.

6. The stand-alone workstation can be operated by a single user or a number of users at different times accessing the same or different programs. The programs and data are stored in the microcomputer or in close proximity and, generally, data are entered manually through the keyboard. The user of the stand-alone workstation who processes accounting applications may be knowledgeable about programming and typically performs a number of functions, (i.e., entering data, operating application programs and, in some cases, writing the computer programs themselves). This programming may

---

[1] This term is used throughout this Statement in place of electronic data processing (EDP) used in prior Statement "EDP Environments—Stand-Alone Microcomputers."

AUDITING

include the use of third-party software packages to develop electronic spreadsheets or database applications.

7. A local area network is an arrangement where two or more microcomputers are linked together through the use of special software and communication lines. Typically, one of the microcomputers will act as the file server which manages the network. A local area network allows the sharing of resources such as storage facilities and printers. Multiple users, for example, can have access to information, data and programs stored in shared files. A local area network may be referred to as a distributed system.

8. Microcomputers can be linked to central computers and used as part of such systems, for example, as an intelligent on-line workstation or as part of a distributed accounting system. Such an arrangement may be referred to as an on-line system. A microcomputer can act as an intelligent terminal because of its logic, transmission, storage and basic computing capabilities.

9. Since control considerations and the characteristics of the hardware and software are different when a microcomputer is linked to other computers, such environments are described in other Supplements to ISA 400 "Risk Assessments and Internal Control." However, to the extent that a micro-computer which is linked to another computer can also be used as a stand-alone workstation, the information in this Statement is relevant.

Characteristics of Microcomputers

10. Although microcomputers provide the user with substantial computing capabilities, they are small enough to be transportable, are relatively inexpensive and can be placed in operation quickly. Users with basic computer skills can learn to operate a microcomputer easily since many operating system software and application programs are "user-friendly" and contain step-by-step instructions. Another characteristic is that operating system software, which is generally supplied by the microcomputer manufacturer, is less comprehensive than that found in larger computer environments; e.g., it may not contain as many control and security features, such as password controls.

11. Software for a wide range of microcomputer applications can be purchased from third-party vendors to perform (e.g., general ledger accounting, receivable accounting and production and inventory control). Such software packages are typically used without modification of the programs. Users can also develop other applications with the use of generic software packages, such as electronic spreadsheets or database, purchased from third-party vendors.

12. The operating system software, application programs and data can be stored on and retrieved from removable storage media, including diskettes, cartridges and removable hard disks. Such storage media, owing to its small size and portability, is subject to accidental erasure, physical damage, misplacement or theft, particularly by persons unfamiliar with such media or by unauthorized users. Software, programs and data can also be stored on hard disks that are not removable.

Internal Control in Microcomputer Environments

13. Generally, the CIS environment in which microcomputers are used is less structured than a centrally-controlled CIS environment. In the former, application programs can be developed relatively quickly by users possessing only basic data processing skills. In such cases, the controls over the system development process (e.g., adequate documentation) and operations (e.g., access control procedures), which are essential to the effective control of a large computer environment, may not be viewed by the developer, the user or management as being as important or cost-effective in a microcomputer environment. However, because the data are being processed on a computer, users of such data may tend to place unwarranted reliance on the financial information stored or generated by a microcomputer. Since microcomputers are oriented to individual end-users, the degree of accuracy and dependability of financial information produced will depend upon the internal controls prescribed by management and adopted by the user. For example, when there are several users of a single microcomputer, without appropriate controls, programs and data stored on non-removable storage media by one user may be susceptible to unauthorized access, use, alteration or theft by other users.

14. In a typical microcomputer environment, the distinction between general CIS controls and CIS application controls may not be easily ascertained. Paragraphs 15-32 describe security and control procedures that can help improve the overall level of internal control.

Management Authorization for Operating Microcomputers

15. Management can contribute to the effective operation of stand-alone microcomputers by prescribing and enforcing policies for their control and use. Management's policy statement may include:

- management responsibilities;
- instructions on microcomputer use;
- training requirements;
- authorization for access to programs and data;
- policies to prevent unauthorized copying of programs and data;
- security, back-up and storage requirements;
- application development and documentation standards;
- standards of report format and report distribution controls;
- personal usage policies;
- data integrity standards;
- responsibility for programs, data and error correction; and
- appropriate segregation of duties.

AUDITING

Physical Security—Equipment

16. Because of their physical characteristics, microcomputers are susceptible to theft, physical damage, unauthorized access or misuse. This may result in the loss of information stored in the microcomputer, for example, financial data vital to the accounting system.

17. One method of physical security is to restrict access to microcomputers when not in use by using door locks or other security protection during non-business hours. Additional physical security over microcomputers can be established, for example, by:

    - locking the microcomputer in a protective cabinet or shell;

    - using an alarm system that is activated any time the microcomputer is disconnected or moved from its location;

    - fastening the microcomputer to a table; or

    - installing a locking mechanism to control access to the on/off switch. This may not prevent microcomputer theft, but many be effective in controlling unauthorized use.

Physical Security—Removable and Non-Removable Media

18. Programs and data used on a microcomputer can be stored on removable storage media or non-removable storage media. Diskettes and cartridges can be removed physically from the microcomputer, while hard disks are normally sealed in the microcomputer or in a stand-alone unit attached to the microcomputer. When a microcomputer is used by many individuals, users may develop a casual attitude toward the storage of the application diskettes or cartridges for which they are responsible. As a result, critical diskettes or cartridges may be misplaced, altered without authorization or destroyed.

19. Control over removable storage media can be established by placing responsibility for such media under personnel whose responsibilities include duties of software custodians or librarians. Control can be further strengthened when a program and data file check-in and check-out system is used and designated storage locations are locked. Such internal controls help ensure that removable storage media are not lost, misplaced or given to unauthorized personnel. Physical control over non-removable storage media is probably best established with locking devices.

20. Depending on the nature of the program and data files, it is appropriate to keep current copies of diskettes, cartridges and hard disks in a fireproof container, either onsite, offsite or both. This applies equally to operating system and utility software and backup copies of hard disks.

Program and Data Security

21. When microcomputers are accessible to many users, there is a risk that programs and data may be altered without authorization.

22. Because microcomputer operating system software may not contain many control and security features, there are several internal control techniques

which can be built into the application programs to help ensure that data are processed and read as authorized and that accidental destruction of data is prevented. These techniques, which limit access to programs and data to authorized personnel, include:

- segregating data into files organized under separate file directories;

- using hidden files and secret file names;

- employing passwords; and

- using cryptography.

23. The use of a file directory allows the user to segregate information on removable and non-removable storage media. For critical and sensitive information, this technique can be supplemented by assigning secret file names and "hiding" the files.

24. When microcomputers are used by multiple users, an effective internal control technique is the use of passwords, which determine the degree of access granted to a user. The password is assigned and monitored by an employee who is independent of the specific system to which the password applies. Password software can be developed by the entity, but in most instances it will be purchased. In either case, internal controls can be strengthened by installing software that has a low likelihood of being thwarted by users.

25. Cryptography can provide an effective control for protecting confidential or sensitive programs and information from unauthorized access and modification by users. It is generally used when sensitive data are transmitted over communication lines, but it can also be used on information processed by a microcomputer. Cryptography is the process of transforming programs and information into an unintelligible form. Encryption and decryption of data require the use of special programs and a code key known only to those users to whom the programs or information is restricted.

26. Directories and hidden files, user authentication software and cryptography can be used for microcomputers that have both removable and non-removable storage media. For microcomputers that have removable storage media, an effective means of program and data security is to remove diskettes and cartridges from the microcomputer and place them in custody of the users responsible for the data or the file librarians.

27. An additional access control for confidential or sensitive information stored on non-removable storage media is to copy the information to a diskette or cartridge and delete the files on the non-removable storage media. Control over the diskette or cartridge can then be established in the same manner as over other sensitive or confidential data stored on diskettes or cartridges. The user should be aware that many software programs include an "erase" or "delete" function, but that such a function may not actually clear erased or deleted files from the hard disk. Such functions may merely clear the file name from the hard disk's directory. Programs and data are in fact removed from the hard disk only when new data are written over the old files or when special utility programs are used to clear the files.

AUDITING

Software and Data Integrity

28. Microcomputers are oriented to end-users for development of application programs, entry and processing of data and generation of reports. The degree of accuracy and dependability of financial information produced will depend on the internal controls prescribed by management and adopted by users, as well as on controls included in the application programs. Software and data integrity controls may ensure that processed information is free of errors and that software is not susceptible to unauthorized manipulation (i.e., that authorized data are processed in the prescribed manner).

29. Data integrity can be strengthened by incorporating internal control procedures such as format and range checks and cross checks of results. A review of purchased software may determine whether it contains appropriate error checking and error trapping facilities. For user developed software, including electronic spreadsheet templates and database applications, management may specify in writing the procedures for developing and testing application programs. For certain critical applications, the person who processes the data may be expected to demonstrate that appropriate data were used and that calculations and other data handling operations were performed properly. The end-user could use this information to validate the results of the application.

30. Adequate written documentation of applications that are processed on the microcomputer can strengthen software and data integrity controls further. Such documentation may include step-by-step instructions, a description of reports prepared, source of data processed, a description of individual reports, files and other specifications, such as calculations.

31. If the same accounting application is used at various locations, application software integrity and consistency may be improved when application programs are developed and maintained at one place rather than by each user dispersed throughout an entity.

Hardware, Software and Data Back-Up

32. Back-up refers to plans made by the entity to obtain access to comparable hardware, software and data in the event of their failure, loss or destruction. In a microcomputer environment, users are normally responsible for processing, including identifying important programs and data files to be copied periodically and stored at a location away from the microcomputers. It is particularly important to establish back-up procedures for users to perform on a regular basis. Purchased software packages from third-party vendors generally come with a back-up copy or with a provision to make a back-up copy.

**The Effect of Microcomputers on the Accounting System
and Related Internal Controls**

33. The effect of microcomputers on the accounting system and the associated risks will generally depend on:

- the extent to which the microcomputer is being used to process accounting applications;

- the type and significance of financial transactions being processed; and

- the nature of files and programs utilized in the applications.

34. The characteristics of microcomputer systems, described earlier in this Statement, illustrate some of the considerations in designing cost-effective control procedures for stand-alone microcomputers. A summary of some of the key considerations and their effects on general CIS and CIS application controls is described below.

General CIS Controls—Segregation of Duties

35. In a microcomputer environment, it is common for users to be able to perform two or more of the following functions in the accounting system:

- initiating and authorizing source documents;

- entering data into the system;

- operating the computer;

- changing programs and data files;

- using or distributing output; and

- modifying the operating systems.

In other CIS environments, such functions would normally be segregated through appropriate general CIS controls. This lack of segregation of functions in a microcomputer environment may:

- allow errors to go undetected; and

- permit the perpetration and concealment of fraud.

CIS Application Controls

36. The existence and use of appropriate access controls over software, hardware and data files, combined with controls over input, processing and output of data may, in coordination with management policies, compensate for some of the weaknesses in general CIS controls in microcomputer environments. Effective controls may include:

- a system of transaction logs and batch balancing;

- direct supervision; and

- reconciliation of record counts or hash totals.

Control may be established by an independent function which would normally:

- receive all data for processing;

- ensure that all data are authorized and recorded;

AUDITING

- follow up all errors detected during processing;

- verify the proper distribution of output; and

- restrict physical access to application programs and data files.

The Effect of a Microcomputer Environment on Audit Procedures

37. In a microcomputer environment, it may not be practicable or cost-effective for management to implement sufficient controls to reduce the risks of undetected errors to a minimum level. Thus, the auditor may often assume that control risk is high in such systems.

38. In this situation, the auditor may find it more cost-effective, after obtaining an understanding of the control environment and flow of transactions, not to make a review of general CIS controls or CIS application controls, but to concentrate the audit efforts on substantive tests at or near the end of the year. This may entail more physical examination and confirmation of assets, more tests of details, larger sample sizes and greater use of computer-assisted audit techniques, where appropriate.

39. Computer-assisted audit techniques may include the use of client software (database, electronic spreadsheet or utility software), which has been subjected to review by the auditor, or the use of the auditor's own software programs. Such software may be used by the auditor, for example, to add transactions or balances in the data files for comparison with control records or ledger account balances, to select accounts or transactions for detail testing or confirmation or to examine databases for unusual items.

40. In certain circumstances, however, the auditor may decide to take a different approach. These circumstances may include microcomputer systems that process a large number of transactions when it would be cost-effective to perform audit work on the data at a preliminary date. For example, an entity processing a large number of sales transactions on a stand-alone microcomputer may establish control procedures which reduce control risk; the auditor may decide, on the basis of a preliminary review of controls, to develop an audit approach which includes testing of those controls on which he intends to rely.

41. The following are examples of control procedures that an auditor may consider when he intends to rely on internal accounting controls related to stand-alone microcomputers:

(a) Segregation of duties and balancing controls:

- Segregation of functions as listed in paragraph 36.

- Rotation of duties among employees.

- Reconciliation of system balances to general ledger control accounts.

- Periodic review by management of the processing schedule and reports which identify individuals that used the system.

(b)   Access to the microcomputer and its files:

- Placement of the microcomputer within sight of the individual responsible for controlling access to it.

- The use of key locks on the computer and terminals.

- The use of passwords for access to the microcomputer's programs and data files.

- Restriction on the use of utility programs.

(c)   Use of third-party software:

- Review of application software prior to purchasing, including functions, capacity and controls.

- Adequate testing of the software and the modifications to it prior to use.

- Ongoing assessment of the adequacy of the software to meet user requirements.

AUDITING

1001

CONTENTS

Paragraphs

Introduction 1

On-Line Computer Systems... 2-6

Types of On-Line Computer Systems... 7-12

Characteristics of On-Line Computer Systems............................... 13-17

Internal Control in an On-Line Computer System 18-19

Effect of On-Line Computer Systems on the Accounting System
    and Related Internal Controls 20-23

Effect of On-Line Computer Systems on Audit Procedures................... 24-28

This International Auditing Practice Statement was approved by the International Auditing Practices Committee in June 1987 for publication in October 1987.

The auditor should understand and consider the characteristics of the CIS environment because they affect the design of the accounting system and related internal controls, the selection of internal controls upon which he intends to rely, and the nature, timing and extent of his procedures.

This Statement is issued as a supplement to ISA 400 "Risk Assessments and Internal Control." It does not form a part of the ISA or International Auditing Practice Statement 1008 "Risk Assessments and Internal Control—CIS Characteristics and Considerations," and is not intended to have the authority of an ISA.

This Statement forms part of a series intended to help the auditor implement the ISA and the Statement referred to above by describing various CIS environments and their effect on the accounting system and related internal controls and on audit procedures.

Introduction

1. The purpose of this Statement is to help the auditor implement ISA 400 "Risk Assessments and Internal Control," and International Auditing Practice Statement 1008 "Risk Assessments and Internal Control—CIS Characteristics and Considerations," by describing on-line computer systems. The Statement describes the effects of an on-line computer system on the accounting system and related internal controls and on audit procedures.

On-Line Computer Systems

2. Computer systems that enable users to access data and programs directly through terminal devices are referred to as on-line computer systems. Such systems may be based on mainframe computers, minicomputers or microcomputers structured in a network environment.

3. On-line systems allow users to initiate various functions directly. Such functions include:

- entering transactions (e.g., sales transactions in a retail store, cash withdrawals in a bank and shipment of goods in a plant);

- making inquiries (e.g., current customer account or balance information);

- requesting reports (e.g., a list of inventory items with negative "on hand" quantities); and

- updating master files (e.g., setting up new customer accounts and changing general ledger codes).

4. Many different types of terminal devices may be used in on-line computer systems. The functions performed by these terminal devices vary widely depending on their logic, transmission, storage and basic computer capabilities. Types of terminal devices include:

(a) General Purpose Terminals, such as:

- Basic keyboard and screen—used for entering data without any validation within the terminal and for displaying data from the computer system on the screen. For example, in entering a sales order, the product code is validated by the main computer and the result of the validation is displayed on the terminal screen.

- Intelligent terminal—used for the functions of the basic keyboard and screen with the additional functions of validating data within the terminal, maintaining transaction logs and performing other local processing. In the above sales order example, the correct number of characters in the product code is verified by the intelligent terminal and existence of the product code master file is verified by the main computer.

- Microcomputers—used for all of the functions of an intelligent terminal with additional local processing and storage capabilities.

AUDITING

Continuing the above example, all verification of the product code may be performed on the microcomputer.

(b) Special Purpose Terminals, such as:

- Point of sale devices—used to record sales transactions as they occur and to transmit them to the main computer. On-line cash registers and optical scanners used in the retail trade are typical point of sale devices.

- Automated teller machines—used to initiate, validate, record, transmit and complete various banking transactions. Depending on the design of the system, certain of these functions are performed by the automated teller machine and others are performed on-line by the main computer.

5. Terminal devices may be located either locally or at remote sites. Local terminal devices are connected directly to the computer through cables, whereas remote terminal devices require the use of telecommunications to link them to the computer. Terminal devices may be used by many users, for different purposes, in different locations, all at the same time. Users may be within the entity or outside, such as customers or suppliers. In such cases, application software and data are kept on-line to meet the needs of the users. These systems also require other software, such as access control software and software which monitors on-line terminal devices.

6. In addition to the users of these systems, programmers may use the on-line capabilities through terminal devices to develop new programs and maintain existing programs. Computer supplier personnel may also have on-line access to provide maintenance and support services.

Types of On-Line Computer Systems

7. On-line computer systems may be classified according to how information is entered into the system, how it is processed and when the results are available to the user. For purposes of this Statement, on-line computer systems functions are classified as follows:

- On-Line/Real Time Processing

- On-Line/Batch Processing

- On-Line/Memo Update (and Subsequent Processing)

- On-Line/Inquiry

- On-Line Downloading/Uploading Processing

On-Line/Real Time Processing

8. In an on-line/real time processing system, individual transactions are entered at terminal devices, validated and used to update related computer files immediately. An example is cash receipts which are applied directly to customers' accounts. The results of such processing are then available immediately for inquiries or reports.

On-Line/Batch Processing

9. In a system with on-line input and batch processing, individual transactions are entered at a terminal device, subjected to certain validation checks and added to a transaction file that contains other transactions entered during the period. Later, during a subsequent processing cycle, the transaction file may be validated further and then used to update the relevant master file. For example, journal entries may be entered and validated on-line and kept on a transaction file, with the general ledger master file being updated on a monthly basis. Inquiries of, or reports generated from, the master file will not include transactions entered subsequent to the last master file update.

On-Line/Memo Update (and Subsequent Processing)

10. On-line input with memo update processing, also known as shadow update, combines on-line/real time processing and on-line/batch processing. Individual transactions immediately update a memo file containing information which has been extracted from the most recent version of the master file. Inquiries are made from this memo file. These same transactions are added to a transaction file for subsequent validation and updating of the master file on a batch basis. For example, the withdrawal of cash through an automated teller machine, where the withdrawal is checked against the customer's balance on the memo file, is immediately posted to the customer's account on that file to reduce the balance by the amount of the withdrawal. From the user's perspective, this system will seem no different than on-line/real time processing since the results of data that are entered are available immediately, even though the transactions have not been subjected to complete validation prior to the master file update.

On-Line/Inquiry

11. On-line inquiry restricts users at terminal devices to making inquiries of master files. In such systems, the master files are updated by other systems, usually on a batch basis. For example, the user may inquire of the credit status of a particular customer, prior to accepting an order from that customer.

On-Line Downloading/Uploading Processing

12. On-line downloading refers to the transfer of data from a master file to an intelligent terminal device for further processing by the user. For example, data at the head office representing transactions of a branch may be downloaded to a terminal device at the branch for further processing and preparation of branch financial reports. The results of this processing and other locally processed data may be uploaded to the head office computer.

Characteristics of On-Line Computer Systems

13. The characteristics of on-line computer systems may apply to a number of the types of on-line systems discussed in the previous section. The most significant characteristics relate to on-line data entry and validation, on-line access to the system by users, possible lack of visible transaction trail and

AUDITING

potential programmer access to the system. The particular characteristics of a specific on-line system will depend on the design of that system.

14. When data are entered on-line, they are usually subject to immediate validation checks. Data failing this validation would not be accepted and a message may be displayed on the terminal screen, providing the user with the ability to correct the data and re-enter the valid data immediately. For example, if the user enters an invalid inventory part number, an error message will be displayed enabling the user to re-enter a valid part number.

15. Users may have on-line access to the system that enables them to perform various functions (e.g., to enter transactions and to read, change or delete programs and data files through the terminal devices). Unlimited access to all of these functions in a particular application is undesirable because it provides the user with the potential ability to make unauthorized changes to the data and programs. The extent of this access will depend upon such things as the design of the particular application and the implementation of software designed to control access to the system.

16. An on-line computer system may be designed in a way that does not provide supporting documents for all transactions entered into the system. However, the system may provide details of the transactions on request or through the use of transaction logs or other means. Illustrations of these types of systems include orders received by a telephone operator who enters them on-line without written purchase orders, and cash withdrawals through the use of automated teller machines.

17. Programmers may have on-line access to the system that enables them to develop new programs and modify existing programs. Unrestricted access provides the programmer with the potential to make unauthorized changes to programs and obtain unauthorized access to other parts of the system. The extent of this access depends on the requirements of the system. For example, in some systems, programmers may have access only to programs maintained in a separate program development and maintenance library; whereas, in emergency situations which require changes to programs that are maintained on-line, programmers may be authorized to change the operational programs. In such cases, formal control procedures would be followed subsequent to the emergency situation to ensure appropriate authorization and documentation of the changes.

Internal Control in an On-Line Computer System

18. Certain general computer information systems (CIS)[1] controls are particularly important to on-line processing. These include:

- Access controls—procedures designed to restrict access to programs and data. Specifically, such procedures are designed to prevent or detect:

    - unauthorized access to on-line terminal devices, programs and data;

---

[1] This term is used throughout this Statement in place of electronic data processing (EDP) used in prior Statement "EDP Environments—On-Line Computer Systems."

- entry of unauthorized transactions;
- unauthorized changes to data files;
- use of operational computer programs by unauthorized personnel; and
- use of computer programs that have not been authorized.

• These access control procedures include the use of passwords and specialized access control software such as on-line monitors that maintain control over menus, authorization tables, passwords, files and programs that users are permitted to access. The procedures also include physical controls such as the use of key locks on terminal devices.

• Controls over passwords—procedures for the assignment and maintenance of passwords to restrict access to authorized users.

• System development and maintenance controls—additional procedures to ensure that controls essential to on-line applications, such as passwords, access controls, on-line data validation and recovery procedures, are included in the system during its development and maintenance.

• Programming controls—procedures designed to prevent or detect improper changes to computer programs which are accessed through on-line terminal devices. Access may be restricted by controls such as the use of separate operational and program development libraries and the use of specialized program library software. It is important for on-line changes to programs to be adequately documented.

• Transaction logs—reports which are designed to create an audit trail for each on-line transaction. Such reports often document the source of a transaction (terminal, time and user) as well as the transaction's details.

19. Certain CIS application controls are particularly important to on-line processing. These include:

• Pre-processing authorization—permission to initiate a transaction, such as the use of a bank card together with a personal identification number before making a cash withdrawal through an automated teller machine.

• Terminal device edit, reasonableness and other validation tests— programmed routines that check the input data and processing results for completeness, accuracy and reasonableness. These routines may be performed on an intelligent terminal device or on the central computer.

• Cut-off procedures—procedures which ensure that transactions are processed in the proper accounting period. These are particularly necessary in systems which have a continuous flow of transactions. For example, in on-line systems where sales orders and shipments are being recorded through the use of on-line terminal devices in various locations, there is a need to coordinate the actual shipment of goods, inventory relief and invoice processing.

• File controls—procedures which ensure that the correct data files are used for on-line processing.

AUDITING

1002

- Master file controls—changes to master files are controlled by procedures similar to those used for controlling other input transaction data. However, since master file data may have a pervasive effect on processing results, more stringent enforcement of these control procedures may be necessary.

- Balancing—the process of establishing control totals over data being submitted for processing through the on-line terminal devices and comparing the control totals during and after processing to ensure that complete and accurate data are transferred to each processing phase.

Effect of On-Line Computer Systems on the Accounting System and Related Internal Controls

20. The effect of an on-line computer system on the accounting system and the associated risks will generally depend on:

- the extent to which the on-line system is being used to process accounting applications;

- the type and significance of financial transactions being processed; and

- the nature of files and programs utilized in the applications.

21. Risk of fraud or error in on-line systems may be reduced in the following circumstances:

- If on-line data entry is performed at or near the point where transactions originate, there is less risk that the transactions will not be recorded.

- If invalid transactions are corrected and re-entered immediately, there is less risk that such transactions will not be corrected and re-submitted on a timely basis.

- If data entry is performed on-line by individuals who understand the nature of the transactions involved, the data entry process may be less prone to errors than when it is performed by individuals unfamiliar with the nature of the transactions.

- If transactions are processed immediately on-line, there is less risk that they will be processed in the wrong accounting period.

22. Risk of fraud or error in on-line computer systems may be increased for the following reasons:

- If on-line terminal devices are located throughout the entity, the opportunity for unauthorized use of a terminal device and the entry of unauthorized transactions may increase.

- On-line terminal devices may provide the opportunity for unauthorized uses such as:

  - modification of previously entered transactions or balances;
  - modification of computer programs; and
  - access to data and programs from remote locations.

- If on-line processing is interrupted for any reason, for example, due to faulty telecommunications, there may be a greater chance that transactions or files may be lost and that the recovery may not be accurate and complete.

- On-line access to data and programs through telecommunications may provide greater opportunity for access to data and programs by unauthorized persons.

23. On-line computer systems may also have an effect on internal controls. The characteristics of on-line computer systems, as described earlier in this Statement, illustrate some of the considerations influencing the effectiveness of controls in on-line computer systems. Such characteristics may have the following consequences:

- There may not be source documents for every input transaction.

- Results of processing may be highly summarized; for example, only totals from individual on-line data entry devices can be traced to subsequent processing.

- The on-line computer system may not be designed to provide printed reports; for example, edit reports may be replaced by edit messages displayed on a terminal device screen.

Effect of On-Line Computer Systems on Audit Procedures

24. The following matters are of particular importance to the auditor in an on-line computer system:

- Authorization, completeness and accuracy of on-line transactions.

- Integrity of records and processing, due to on-line access to the system by many users and programmers.

- Changes in the performance of audit procedures including the use of CAATs (see International Auditing Practice Statement 1009 "Computer-Assisted Audit Techniques") due to matters such as:
  - the need for auditors with technical skills in on-line computer systems;
  - the effect of the on-line computer system on the timing of audit procedures;
  - the lack of visible transaction trails;
  - procedures carried out during the audit planning stage (see paragraph 25);
  - audit procedures performed concurrently with on-line processing (see paragraph 26); and
  - procedures performed after processing has taken place (see paragraph 27).

25. Procedures carried out during the planning stage may include:

- The participation on the audit team of individuals with technical proficiency in on-line computer systems and related controls.

AUDITING

- Preliminary determination during the risk assessment process of the impact of the system on the audit procedures. Generally, in a well-designed and controlled on-line computer system, it is likely that the auditor will place greater reliance on internal controls in the system in determining the nature, timing and extent of audit procedures.

26. Audit procedures performed concurrently with on-line processing may include compliance testing of the controls over the on-line applications. For example, this may be by means of entering test transactions through the on-line terminal devices or by the use of audit software. These tests may be used by the auditor either to confirm his understanding of the system or to test controls such as passwords and other access controls. The auditor would be advised to review such tests with appropriate client personnel and to obtain approval prior to conducting the tests in order to avoid inadvertent corruption of client records.

27. Procedures performed after processing has taken place may include:

- Compliance testing of controls over transactions logged by the on-line system for authorization, completeness and accuracy.

- Substantive tests of transactions and processing results rather than tests of controls, where the former may be more cost-effective or where the system is not well-designed or controlled.

- Re-processing transactions as either a compliance or substantive procedure.

28. The characteristics of on-line computer systems may make it more effective for the auditor to perform a pre-implementation review of new on-line accounting applications than to review the applications after installation. This pre-implementation review may provide the auditor with an opportunity to request additional functions, such as detailed transaction listings, or controls within the application design. It may also provide the auditor with sufficient time to develop and test audit procedures in advance of their use.

CONTENTS

	Paragraphs
Introduction	1
Database Systems	2-5
Database System Characteristics	6-14
Internal Control in a Database Environment	15-21
The Effect of Databases on the Accounting System and Related Internal Controls	22-24
The Effect of Databases on Audit Procedures	25-30

This International Auditing Practice Statement was approved by the International Auditing Practices Committee in June 1987 for publication in October 1987.

The auditor should understand and consider the characteristics of the CIS environment because they affect the design of the accounting system and related internal controls, the selection of internal controls upon which he intends to rely, and the nature, timing and extent of his procedures.

This Statement is issued as a supplement to ISA 400 "Risk Assessments and Internal Control." It does not form a part of the ISA or International Auditing Practice Statement 1008 "Risk Assessments and Internal Control—CIS Characteristics and Considerations," and is not intended to have the authority of an ISA.

This Statement forms part of a series intended to help the auditor implement the ISA and the Statement referred to above by describing various CIS environments and their effect on the accounting system and related internal controls and on audit procedures.

AUDITING

Introduction

1. The purpose of this Statement is to help the auditor implement ISA 400 "Risk Assessments and Internal Control," and International Auditing Practice Statement 1008 "Risk Assessments and Internal Control—CIS Characteristics and Considerations," by describing database systems. The Statement describes the effects of a database system on the accounting system and related internal controls and on audit procedures.

Database Systems

2. Database systems are comprised principally of two essential components— the database and the database management system (DBMS). Database systems interact with other hardware and software aspects of the overall computer system.

3. A database is a collection of data that is shared and used by a number of different users for different purposes. Each user may not necessarily be aware of all the data stored in the database or of the ways that the data may be used for multiple purposes. Generally, individual users are aware only of the data that they use and may view the data as computer files utilized by their applications.

4. The software that is used to create, maintain and operate the database is referred to as DBMS software. Together with the operating system, the DBMS facilitates the physical storage of the data, maintains the interrelationships among the data, and makes the data available to application programs. Usually, the DBMS software is supplied by a commercial vendor.

5. Database systems may reside on any type of computer system, including a microcomputer system. In some microcomputer environments, database systems are used by a single user. Such systems are not considered to be databases for the purposes of this Statement. The contents of this Statement, however, are applicable to all multiple user environments.

Database System Characteristics

6. Database systems are distinguished by two important characteristics: data sharing and data independence. These characteristics require the use of a data dictionary (paragraph 10) and the establishment of a database administration function (paragraphs 11-14).

Data Sharing

7. A database is composed of data which are set up with defined relationships and are organized in a manner that permits many users to use the data in different application programs. Individual applications share the data in the database for different purposes. For example, an inventory item unit cost maintained by the database may be used by one application program to produce a cost of sales report and by another application program to prepare an inventory valuation.

Data Independence From Application Programs

8. Because of the need for data sharing, there is a need for data independence from application programs. This is achieved by the DBMS recording the data once for use by various application programs. In non-database systems, separate data files are maintained for each application and similar data used by several applications may be repeated on several different files. In a database system, however, a single file of data (or database) is used by many applications, with data redundancy kept to a minimum.

9. DBMS's differ in the degree of data independence they provide. The degree of data independence is related to the ease with which personnel can accomplish changes to application programs or to the database. True data independence is achieved when the structure of data in the database can be changed without affecting the application programs, and vice versa.

Data Dictionary

10. A significant implication of data sharing and data independence is the potential for the recording of data only once for use in several applications. Because various application programs need to access this data, a software facility is required to keep track of the location of the data in the database. This software within the DBMS is known as a data dictionary. It also serves as a tool to maintain standardized documentation and definitions of the database environment and application systems.

Database Administration

11. The use of the same data by various application programs emphasizes the importance of centralized coordination of the use and definition of data and the maintenance of its integrity, security, accuracy and completeness. Coordination is usually performed by a group of individuals whose responsibility is typically referred to as "database administration." The individual who heads this function may be referred to as the "database administrator." The database administrator is responsible generally for the definition, structure, security, operational control and efficiency of databases, including the definition of the rules by which data are accessed and stored.

12. Database administration tasks may also be performed by individuals who are not part of a centralized database administration group. Where the tasks of database administration are not centralized, but are distributed among existing organizational units, the different tasks still need to be coordinated.

13. Database administration tasks typically include:

- Defining the database structure—determining how data are defined, stored and accessed by users of the database in order to ensure that all their requirements are met on a timely basis.

- Maintaining data integrity, security and completeness—developing, implementing and enforcing the rules for data integrity, completeness and access. Responsibilities include:

AUDITING

- defining who may access data and how the access is accomplished (i.e., through passwords and authorization tables);
- preventing the inclusion of incomplete or invalid data;
- detecting the absence of data;
- securing the database from unauthorized access and destruction; and
- arranging total recovery in the event of a loss.

- Coordinating computer operations related to the database—assigning responsibility for physical computer resources and monitoring their use relative to the operation of the database.

- Monitoring system performance—developing performance measurements to monitor the integrity of the data and the ability of the database to respond to the needs of users.

- Providing administrative support—coordinating and liaising with the vendor of the DBMS, assessing new releases issued by the vendor of the DBMS and the extent of their impact on the entity, installing new releases and ensuring that appropriate internal education is provided.

14. In some applications, more than one database may be used. In these circumstances, the tasks of the database administration group will need to ensure that:

- adequate linkage exists between databases;

- coordination of functions is maintained; and

- data contained in different databases are consistent.

Internal Control in a Database Environment

15. Generally, internal control in a database environment requires effective controls over the database, the DBMS and the applications. The effectiveness of internal controls depends to a great extent on the nature of the database administration tasks, described in paragraphs 11-14, and how they are performed.

16. Due to data sharing, data independence and other characteristics of data-base systems, general computer information systems (CIS)[2] controls normally have a greater influence than CIS application controls on database systems. General CIS controls over the database, the DBMS and the activities of the database administration function have a pervasive effect on application processing. The general CIS controls of particular importance in a database environment can be classified into the following groups:

- standard approach for development and maintenance of application programs;

- data ownership;

---

[2] This term is used throughout this Statement in place of electronic data processing (EDP) used in prior Statement "EDP Environments—Database Systems."

- access to the database; and

- segregation of duties.

Standard Approach for Development and Maintenance of Application Programs

17. Since data are shared by many users, control may be enhanced when a standard approach is used for developing each new application program and for application program modification. This includes following a formalized, step-by-step approach that requires adherence by all individuals developing or modifying an application program. It also includes performing an analysis of the effect of new and existing transactions on the database each time a modification is required. The resulting analysis would indicate the effects of the changes on the security and integrity of the database. Implementing a standard approach to develop and modify application programs is a technique that can help improve the accuracy, integrity and completeness of the database.

Data Ownership

18. In a database environment, where many individuals may use programs to input and modify data, a clear and definite assignment of responsibility is required from the database administrator for the accuracy and integrity of each item of data. A single data owner should be assigned responsibility for defining access and security rules, such as who can use the data (access) and what functions they can perform (security). Assigning specific responsibility for data ownership helps to ensure the integrity of the database. For example, the credit manager may be the designated "owner" of a customer's credit limit and would therefore be responsible for determining the authorized users of that information. If several individuals are able to make decisions affecting the accuracy and integrity of given data, the likelihood increases of the data becoming corrupted or improperly used.

Access to the Database

19. User access to the database can be restricted through the use of passwords. These restrictions apply to individuals, terminal devices and programs. For passwords to be effective, adequate procedures are required for changing passwords, maintaining secrecy of passwords and reviewing and investigating attempted security violations. Relating passwords to defined terminal devices, programs and data helps to ensure that only authorized users and programs can access, amend or delete data. For example, the credit manager may give salesmen authority to refer to a customer's credit limit, whereas a warehouse clerk may not have such authorization.

20. User access to the various elements of the database may be further controlled through the use of authorization tables. Improper implementation of access procedures can result in unauthorized access to the data in the database.

Segregation of Duties

21. Responsibilities for performing the various activities required to design, implement and operate a database are divided among technical, design, administrative and user personnel. Their duties include system design, database design, administration and operation. Maintaining adequate segregation of these duties is necessary to ensure the completeness, integrity and accuracy of the database. For example, those persons responsible for modifying personnel database programs should not be the same persons who are authorized to change individual pay rates in the database.

The Effect of Databases on the Accounting System and Related Internal Controls

22. The effect of a database system on the accounting system and the associated risks will generally depend on:

- the extent to which databases are being used by accounting applications;

- the type and significance of financial transactions being processed;

- the nature of the database, the DBMS (including the data dictionary), the database administration tasks and the applications (e.g., batch or on-line update); and

- the general CIS controls which are particularly important in a database environment.

23. Database systems typically provide the opportunity for greater reliability of data than non-database systems. This can result in reduced risk of fraud or error in the accounting system where databases are used. The following factors, combined with adequate controls, contribute to this improved reliability of data:

- Improved consistency of data is achieved because data are recorded and updated only once, rather than in non-database systems, where the same data are stored in several files and updated at different times and by different programs.

- Integrity of data will be improved by effective use of facilities included in the DBMS, such as recovery, restart routines, generalized edit and validation routines, and security and control features.

- Other functions available with the DBMS can facilitate control and audit procedures. These functions include report generators, which may be used to create balancing reports, and query languages, which may be used to identify inconsistencies in the data.

24. Alternatively, risk of fraud or error may be increased if database systems are used without adequate controls. In a typical non-database environment, controls exercised by individual users may compensate for weaknesses in general CIS controls. However, in a database system, this may not be possible, as inadequate database administration controls cannot always be compensated for by the individual users. For example, accounts receivable personnel cannot effectively control accounts receivable data if other

personnel are not restricted from modifying accounts receivable balances in the database.

The Effect of Databases on Audit Procedures

25. Audit procedures in a database environment will be affected principally by the extent to which the data in the database are used by the accounting system. Where significant accounting applications use a common database, the auditor may find it cost-effective to utilize some of the procedures in the following paragraphs.

26. In order to obtain an understanding of the database control environment and the flow of transactions, the auditor may consider the effect of the following on audit risk in planning the audit:

- the DBMS and the significant accounting applications using the database;

- the standards and procedures for development and maintenance of application programs using the database;

- the database administration function;

- job descriptions, standards and procedures for those individuals responsible for technical support, design, administration and operation of the database;

- the procedures used to ensure the integrity, security and completeness of the financial information contained in the database; and

- the availability of audit facilities within the DBMS.

27. During the risk assessment process, in determining the extent of reliance on internal controls related to the use of databases in the accounting system, the auditor may consider how the controls described in paragraphs 17-21 are used in the system. If he subsequently decides to rely on these controls, he would design and perform appropriate compliance tests.

28. Where the auditor decides to perform compliance or substantive tests related to the database system, audit procedures may include using the functions of the DBMS (see paragraph 23) to:

- generate test data;

- provide an audit trail;

- check the integrity of the database;

- provide access to the database or a copy of relevant parts of the database for the purpose of using audit software (see International Auditing Practice Statement 1009 "Computer-Assisted Audit Techniques"); or

- obtain information necessary for the audit.

When using the facilities of the DBMS, the auditor will need to obtain reasonable assurance regarding their correct functioning.

AUDITING

29. Where the auditor determines he cannot rely on the controls in the database system, he would consider whether performing additional substantive tests on all significant accounting applications which use the database would achieve his audit objective, as inadequate database administration controls cannot always be compensated for by the individual users.

30. The characteristics of database systems may make it more effective for the auditor to perform a pre-implementation review of new accounting applications rather than to review the applications after installation. This pre-implementation review may provide the auditor with an opportunity to request additional functions, such as built-in audit routines, or controls within the application design. It may also provide the auditor with sufficient time to develop and test audit procedures in advance of their use.

CONTENTS

	Paragraphs
Introduction	1-6
The Responsibility of the Bank's Management	7-10
The Role of the Banking Supervisor	11-22
The Role of the Bank's External Auditor	23-33
The Relationship Between the Supervisor and the Auditor	34-42
Criteria for a Possible Extension of the Auditor's Role as a Contribution to the Supervisory Process	43-50
Specific Directions in Which the Auditor's Role Can Be Extended	51-55
The Need for a Continuing Dialogue Between Supervisory Authorities and the Auditing Profession	56-58

This International Auditing Practice Statement has been prepared in association with the Committee on Banking Regulations and Supervisory Practices[*] ("the Basle Supervisors' Committee"). It was approved for publication by the International Auditing Practices Committee and by the Basle Supervisors' Committee at their respective meetings in March 1989. It has a common release date of July 1989.

Banks play a vital role in economic life and the continued strength and stability of the banking system is a matter of general public concern. The separate roles of bank supervisors and external auditors are important in this regard. The growing complexity of banking makes it necessary that there be greater mutual understanding and, where appropriate, more communication between the bank supervisors and external auditors.

The purpose of this Statement is to provide information and guidance on how the relationship between bank auditors and supervisors can be strengthened to mutual advantage. However, as the nature of this relationship varies significantly from country to country the guidance may not be applicable in its entirety to all countries. The International Auditing Practices Committee and the Basle Supervisors' Committee hope, however, that it will provide a useful clarification of the respective roles of the two professions in the many countries where the links are close or where the relationship is currently under study.

AUDITING

---

[*]The Basle Supervisors' Committee comprises representatives of the central banks and supervisory authorities of the Group of Ten countries (Belgium, Canada, France, Germany, Italy, Japan, Netherlands, Sweden, Switzerland, United Kingdom, United States) and Luxembourg.

1004

Introduction

1. Banks play a central role in the economy. They hold the savings of the public, provide a means of payment for goods and services and finance the development of business and trade. To perform these functions securely and efficiently, individual banks must command the confidence of the public and those with whom they do business. The stability of the banking system, national and international, has therefore come to be recognized as a matter of general public interest. This public interest is reflected in the way banks in all countries, unlike most other commercial companies, are subject to supervision of their financial soundness (usually referred to as prudential supervision) by central banks and other official agencies. Banks' financial statements are also subject to examination by external auditors. The auditor's opinion lends credibility to such statements and thereby assists in promoting confidence in the banking system.

2. As the business of banking grows in complexity, both nationally and internationally, the tasks of both bank supervisors and external auditors are becoming more and more demanding. In many respects bank supervisors and external auditors face a similar challenge and increasingly their roles are being perceived as complementary. Not only are supervisors relying to a greater extent on the results of the auditors' work, but they are increasingly turning to the accounting profession to undertake additional tasks which contribute to the performance of their supervisory responsibilities. At the same time, auditors, in carrying out their functions, are looking to the supervisors for information which can help in discharging their functions more effectively.

3. The International Auditing Practices Committee and the Basle Supervisors' Committee share the view that greater mutual understanding and, where appropriate, communication would improve the effectiveness of bank audit and supervision to the benefit of both disciplines.

4. Three parties have roles and responsibilities in relation to the prudent conduct of a bank's business, namely, management of the bank itself, the bank's external auditors and the supervisory authorities. The roles and responsibilities of each participant in different countries derive from both law and custom. This Statement is not concerned with challenging or changing these roles or responsibilities. Rather, it is intended to provide a better understanding of the precise nature of the role of bank auditors and supervisors, since a misconception of such roles could lead to inappropriate reliance being placed by one on the work of the other.

5. This Statement seeks to remove these possible misconceptions and to suggest how each might make more effective use of the work performed by the other. The Statement accordingly:

    - defines the primary responsibility of management (paragraphs 7-10);

    - examines the essential features of the roles of supervisors and auditors (paragraphs 11-33);

    - reviews the extent to which the roles overlap (paragraphs 34-42); and

- suggests a mechanism for more effective co-ordination between supervisors and auditors in the fulfillment of their separate tasks (paragraphs 43-58).

6. The Statement has been drawn up in full awareness of the significant differences that exist in national institutional frameworks, notably in accounting standards, in supervisory techniques and in the extent to which, in some countries, the auditors currently perform tasks at the request of the supervisory authorities. It recognizes that in some countries bank supervisors and auditors already have closer relationships than are indicated in the Statement. The arrangements suggested in the Statement should be considered as being complementary to and not as replacing existing relationships. While the Statement is not intended to be prescriptive, it is hoped that the views expressed herein will have relevance for all situations, although they will obviously address the situations in some countries more directly than those in others.

The Responsibility of the Bank's Management

7. The primary responsibility for the conduct of the business of a bank is vested in the board of directors and management appointed by it. This responsibility includes ensuring.

- that those entrusted with banking tasks are professionally competent and that there are sufficiently experienced staff in key positions;

- that proper control systems exist and are functioning;

- that the operations of the bank are conducted with due regard to prudence including the assurance that adequate provisions are maintained for losses;

- that statutory and regulatory directives, including directives regarding solvency and liquidity, are observed; and

- that the interests not only of the shareholders but also of the depositors and other creditors are adequately protected.

8. Management is responsible for preparing financial statements in accordance with national law; such statements must give "a true and fair view of" (or "present fairly") the bank's financial position and the results of its operations in accordance with generally accepted national accounting principles as they apply to banks. This responsibility includes ensuring that the auditor who examines and reports on such statements is provided with all necessary information that can materially affect the financial statements and consequently his opinion thereon. The management also has the responsibility to provide all information to the supervisory agencies which such agencies are entitled by law or regulation to obtain. The information provided to supervisory agencies normally includes the financial statements which are often used by supervisors in their appraisal of the financial condition of the bank.

9. Management is responsible for the establishment and the efficient operation of an internal audit function in a bank appropriate to its size and to the nature of its operations. This function constitutes a separate component of internal

AUDITING

control undertaken by specially assigned staff within the bank with the objective of determining whether, amongst other things, internal controls are well designed and properly operated. Management is responsible for ensuring that the internal audit function is adequately staffed with persons of the appropriate skills and technical competence who are free from operating responsibilities and who report to top management, and that timely and appropriate action is taken on their findings.

10. These responsibilities of the management are in no way diminished by the existence of a system for the supervision of banks by central banks or other official agencies or by a requirement for a bank's financial statements to be subject to audit by independent auditors.

The Role of the Banking Supervisor

11. The customary role of the supervisor, and one that is often written into statute, is to protect the interests of bank depositors. In practice, however, this role has increasingly combined with a wider duty to safeguard the soundness and stability of the banking system. In some countries, supervision may also be directed towards ensuring compliance with monetary or exchange rate policies. However, in this Statement the focus is on the prudential aspect of the supervisor's role.

12. The ultimate power on which the authority of most supervisors is based is the power to authorize or license an entity to conduct a banking business and to withdraw such authorization or license. In order to qualify for and retain a banking license, entities must observe certain prudential requirements. These requirements may differ from country to country in their precise specification; some may be closely defined in regulation and others may be more broadly drawn, allowing the supervisory authority a measure of discretion in their interpretation. However, the following basic requirements for authorization are generally to be found in most systems of supervision:

   • persons who control and manage the business of a bank must be honest and trustworthy and must possess appropriate skills and experience;

   • the bank must have adequate capital to withstand the risks inherent in the nature and size of its business; and

   • the bank must have sufficient liquidity to meet outflows of funds.

   Further and more detailed requirements are often prescribed, including minimum numerical ratios for capital and liquidity adequacy. Whatever the precise form of the regulations, however, their objective is to set conditions to ensure that banks' managements conduct their business prudently and have adequate financial resources to overcome adverse circumstances and protect depositors from loss.

13. Failure by a bank to observe the various conditions or requirements for authorization will provide grounds for the supervisor to consider withdrawing the license. But withdrawal of a license, effectively terminating the business, may well precipitate insolvency and, therefore, is generally a sanction of last resort, to be used only when it is clear that no other possibilities for

corrective action remain. As a less drastic procedure, in order to remedy incipient weaknesses, supervisors generally have powers to issue formal directives to a bank requiring it to take action to strengthen some aspect of its business, for example, by injecting additional capital or improving internal controls. However, recourse to legal powers is rarely necessary and ongoing supervision is generally conducted on the basis of informal guidance and persuasion.

14. One of the main pillars of prudential supervision is capital adequacy. In most countries there are minimum capital requirements for the establishment of new banks and capital adequacy tests are a regular element in ongoing supervision. In line with the method agreed among the supervisory authorities represented on the Basle Supervisors' Committee, capital adequacy is measured in most countries by comparing the capital resources of a bank with its total assets and off-balance-sheet engagements, weighted to reflect the relative risk inherent in the various categories of assets or off-balance-sheet items. For major international banks the members of the Basle Supervisors' Committee have agreed that a minimum standard for this ratio of 8% should apply. Capital is also often used as a standard against which to measure or to limit the risks inherent in the types of transactions undertaken by banks.

15. Banks are subject to a variety of risks. The most significant of these, in terms of historical loss experience, is credit risk—the risk that a borrower will not be able to repay his loan when due. It is not the supervisor's role to direct banks' lending policies, but he has an interest in seeing that banks have effective credit review procedures which are applied consistently. He also seeks to ensure that credit risk is adequately diversified by means of rules to limit exposures, whether in terms of individual borrowers, industrial or commercial sectors or particular countries. Supervisors also seek to monitor and limit a range of other banking risks, such as liquidity and funding risk, interest rate and investment risk, foreign exchange risk and off-balance-sheet risk. Increasingly, supervisors are attempting to develop systems of measurement which will capture the extent of exposure to specific risks. These systems often form the basis for specific controls or limits on the various categories of exposure.

16. One of the most important determinants of a bank's stability, though one of the most difficult to assess, is the quality of its assets. It is therefore essential for the supervisor to be confident that adequate provisions have been made, for example in relation to bad and doubtful debts. While the correct valuation of assets is the primary responsibility of management, it is often a matter of judgment and supervisors seek to satisfy themselves that this judgment is properly and reasonably exercised. For example, supervisors may seek to ensure that banks adequately recognize the risk arising from their loans to heavily-indebted countries, perhaps by laying down guidelines or requirements for adequate levels of provisions.

17. Accurate and prudent valuation of assets is of great importance for supervisors because it has a direct bearing on the determination of the amount of net assets held by a bank and the amount of shareholders' equity (capital plus retained earnings). As already indicated, capital is widely used as the

AUDITING

supervisory standard against which exposures are measured or limited. In general, unless he makes his own independent examination, the supervisor relies in large part on the management's judgment of the correct valuation of assets and on the auditor's examination of that valuation.

18. Supervisors attach considerable importance to the need for banks to have a well-designed organizational structure and to operate efficient information and control systems for the management of risk. Similarly, supervisors are concerned to ensure that accounting records are properly maintained and that standard accounting procedures are followed so that:

- the whole banking operation is effectively and efficiently handled;

- management has a sound basis for monitoring, controlling and planning the different exposures undertaken; and

- the possibility of staff, management or customer fraud is reduced.

The growth in the complexity of financial markets has created a matching need for systems of internal control designed to meet the needs of a growing number of new types of transactions. The development of sophisticated real-time electronic data processing systems has greatly improved the potential for control, but in turn has brought with it additional risks arising from the possibility of computer failure or fraud.

19. Supervisors are concerned to ensure that the quality of management is adequate for the nature and scope of the business. In regulatory environments in which on-site inspections are regularly carried out, the examiners have an opportunity to notice signs of management failing. Elsewhere, the supervisor normally arranges to interview management on a regular basis and pursues other opportunities for contacts where they arise. Whatever the nature of the regulatory environment, the supervisor tries to use these opportunities to form an opinion about the competence of management and to ensure that it has a clear idea of its strategy. Similarly, he seeks to discover whether the bank is properly equipped to carry out its functions in terms of the skills and competence of its staff and the equipment and facilities at its disposal.

20. According to the nature of the supervisory rules, the method of ensuring that they are followed tends to vary from country to country. In essence, there are two main techniques which can be used:

- on-site examinations; and

- the collection and interpretation of regular reporting returns and other statistical data.

Supervisory systems make use of both techniques, although the degree of reliance placed on one or the other will vary from country to country.

21. On-site examination is demanding in terms of supervisory resources and cannot, except in the case of very small banks, regularly address more than a small part of the institution's activities. In some countries, examination techniques tend to concentrate on the quality of the loan assets and the documentation supporting them and the adequacy of internal controls set by management. In other countries, examination focuses not only on loan assets,

but also on other types of exposure referred to in paragraph 15. Where loan quality classification systems are in use, the inspectors will routinely examine a sample of loans to check whether they have been correctly classified. Inspectors will also pay attention to policies with regard to provisions for bad and doubtful debts and will judge whether provisions are adequate in the light of the perceived quality of the loan-book. In the case of banks with wide-ranging activities or complex networks, attention will also be focused on the extent to which control is exercised and the risk managed on a global basis. In special circumstances, where the supervisory authority is already aware of particular problems, the examination would be more narrowly focused.

22. The examination of reporting returns and statistical data is less costly and the expense is shared more evenly between the banks (whose own internal information systems must be adapted to provide data) and the supervisory authority (which is responsible for designing the returns and interpreting the data). The reporting returns will normally provide a detailed breakdown of the composition of the balance sheet (including off-balance-sheet items) and of the profit and loss account. The information should, in principle, be sufficient to enable the supervisor to form a view of a bank's exposure to the various categories of risk. Examination of reporting returns submitted at regular intervals allows the supervisor to monitor developments in the business in a more frequent and timely manner than is the case with on-site inspection. However, reporting returns have the following limitations:

- they are generally designed for completion by the banking system as a whole and may not capture adequately new types of risk or the particular activities of an individual institution;

- their usefulness in providing early warning to the supervisor depends on the quality of banks' own internal information systems and the accuracy with which the returns are completed; and

- even with reliable, comprehensive data, experienced judgment is needed to interpret the results.

The Role of the Bank's External Auditor

23. The primary objective of an audit of a bank by an external auditor is to enable the auditor to express an opinion as to whether the published financial statements of the bank give a "true and fair view of" (or "present fairly") the bank's financial position and the results of its operations for the period for which such statements are prepared. The auditor's report is normally addressed to the shareholders, but is used by many other parties, such as depositors, other creditors and supervisors. The auditor's opinion helps to establish the credibility of the financial statements. The user, however, should not interpret the auditor's opinion as an assurance as to the future viability of the bank or an opinion as to the efficiency or effectiveness with which the management has conducted the affairs of the bank, since these are not the objectives of the audit.

AUDITING

24. To form an opinion on the financial statements, the auditor seeks to obtain reasonable assurance as to whether the information contained in the underlying accounting records and other source data is reliable and sufficient as the basis for the preparation of financial statements and also whether the relevant information is properly communicated in the financial statements. For this purpose, the auditor:

- makes a study and evaluation of the accounting systems and internal controls on which he wishes to rely;

- tests the operation of those controls to assist in determining the nature, extent and timing of other auditing procedures; and

- carries out such tests, inquiries and other verification procedures of accounting transactions and account balances as he considers appropriate in the circumstances.

25. In carrying out the audit of a bank, the independent auditor recognizes that certain features of banks may cause special problems. Thus:

- banks have custody of large volumes of money, including cash and negotiable instruments, whose physical security has to be assured. This applies both to the storage and the transfer of money and makes banks vulnerable to misappropriation or fraud. They therefore need to establish formal operating procedures, well defined limits for individual discretion and rigorous systems of internal control;

- banks engage in a large volume and variety of transactions both in terms of number and value. This necessarily requires complex accounting and internal control systems and widespread use of electronic data processing;

- banks in most countries normally operate through a wide network of branches and departments which are geographically dispersed. This necessarily involves a greater decentralization of authority and dispersal of accounting and control functions with consequent difficulties in maintaining uniform operating practices and accounting systems, particularly when the branch network transcends national boundaries;

- banks usually assume significant commitments without any transfer of funds. These items, normally called "off-balance-sheet" items, may not involve accounting entries and consequently the failure to record such items may be difficult to detect; and

- banks are regulated by governmental authorities and regulatory requirements often influence generally accepted accounting and auditing practices within the industry. Non-compliance with regulatory requirements, e.g., concerning special valuation rules for substandard assets, could have implications for the bank's financial statements.

26. A detailed audit of all transactions of a bank would not only be time-consuming and extremely expensive but also wholly impracticable. The auditor therefore bases his examination on the testing and evaluation of the internal control systems designed to ensure the accuracy of the accounting records and security of the assets, on the use of sampling techniques and analytical review procedures and on the verification and assessment of the

assets and liabilities. In particular, he is concerned about the recoverability and consequently the carrying value of loans, investments and related assets and about the identification and adequate disclosure in the financial statements of all material commitments and liabilities, contingent or otherwise.

27. While the auditor has sole responsibility for his report and for determining the nature, timing and extent of his procedures, much of the work of the internal audit department can be useful to the auditor in his examination of the financial information. The auditor, therefore, as part of his audit evaluates the internal audit function insofar as he believes that it will be relevant in determining the nature, timing and extent of his procedures.

28. Judgment permeates the auditor's work. The auditor has to use his judgment, inter alia, in:

- deciding upon the nature, timing and extent of his audit procedures;

- evaluating the results of those procedures; and

- assessing the reasonableness of the judgments and estimates made by management in preparing the financial statements.

29. An auditor plans and conducts the audit to have a reasonable expectation of detecting misstatements in the bank's financial statements which, individually or in aggregate, are material in relation to the financial information presented by those statements. The auditor considers materiality at both an overall level and in relation to individual account balances and disclosures. The assessment of what is material is a matter for the auditor's professional judgment, but it is influenced by his perception of the needs of the user of the bank's financial statements and by his assessment of the risk that material misstatements in such information may remain undetected and of the consequences thereof. Materiality may also be influenced by other considerations such as legal and regulatory requirements, whether relating to the financial information as a whole or to individual items thereof. Therefore, an auditor may apply different levels of materiality for different components of the financial statements. Similarly, the level of materiality used by an auditor when reporting on a bank's financial statements may be different from the level used when making special reports to a bank's supervisor.

30. In forming his opinion on the financial statements, the auditor carries out procedures designed to obtain reasonable assurance that the financial statements are properly stated in all material respects. Because of the test nature and other inherent limitations of an audit, together with the inherent limitations of any system of internal control, there is an unavoidable risk that even some material misstatements may remain undiscovered. The risk of not detecting a material misstatement resulting from fraud is greater than the risk of not detecting a material misstatement resulting from error, because fraud usually involves acts designed to conceal it, such as collusion, forgery, deliberate failure to record transactions or intentional misrepresentation being made to the auditor. Unless the auditor's examination reveals evidence to the contrary, the auditor feels entitled to accept representations as truthful and records and documents as genuine. However, the auditor plans and performs

AUDITING

his audit with an attitude of professional skepticism, accepting that he may encounter conditions or events during his examination that would lead him to question whether fraud or error exist.

31. A matter of particular concern to the auditor is obtaining assurance that appropriate accounting policies have been followed by the bank and that these have been consistently employed. The financial statements of banks are prepared in the context of the legal and regulatory requirements prevailing in different countries and accounting policies are influenced by such regulations.

32. When the auditor discovers an error material to the financial statements, including the use of an inappropriate accounting policy, an asset valuation with which he does not agree or a failure to disclose essential information, he requires that the financial statements be adjusted to correct the error. If management refuses to make the correction the auditor issues a qualified or an adverse opinion on the financial statements. Such a report would have a serious impact on the credibility and even stability of the bank, and management therefore usually takes the steps necessary to avoid it. Likewise, an auditor would not issue an unqualified opinion if he has not been provided with all the information or explanations he requires.

33. As a supplementary but not necessarily integral part of his role, the auditor usually furnishes management with a management letter. This letter customarily contains comments on such matters as deficiencies in internal control or other errors or omissions which have come to the auditor's attention during the course of the audit, but which do not warrant a qualification in his audit report because he has been able to carry out additional procedures to compensate for a weakness in control or because the errors have been corrected in the financial statements or are immaterial in this context. In some countries, an auditor also submits, either as part of a statutory requirement or by convention, a long-form report to management or to the supervisory authorities on specified matters such as the composition of accounting balances or of the loan portfolio, liquidity and earnings, ratios, the adequacy of internal control systems, an analysis of banking risks, or compliance with legal or supervisory requirements.

The Relationship Between the Supervisor and the Auditor

34. In many respects the supervisor and the auditor have complementary concerns regarding the same matters though the focus of their concerns may be different. Thus:

- the supervisor is primarily concerned with the stability of the bank in order to protect the interests of the depositors. Therefore, he monitors its present and future viability and uses financial statements to assist in assessing its developing activities. The auditor, on the other hand, is primarily concerned with reporting on the financial position of the bank and on the results of its operations. In doing so, he also considers the bank's continuing viability (generally for a period not to exceed one year from the balance-sheet date) in order to support the "going concern" basis on which the financial statements are prepared;

- the supervisor is concerned with the maintenance of a sound system of internal control as a basis for safe and prudent management of the bank's business. The auditor, in most situations, is concerned with the assessment of internal control to determine the degree of reliance he can place on the system in planning and carrying out his work; and

- the supervisor is concerned with the existence of a proper accounting system as a prerequisite for obtaining reliable information for the measurement and control of risk. The auditor is concerned to obtain assurance that the accounting records from which financial statements are prepared have been properly maintained.

35. It is therefore necessary that, when a supervisor uses audited financial statements in the course of his supervisory activities, he recognizes that the statements have been prepared for a purpose which is different from the purpose for which he may wish to use them. In particular, he needs to bear in mind:

- the accounting policies used in the preparation of the statements and their appropriateness for the purposes for which he wishes to use them;

- the "going concern" basis on which the financial statements are drawn up and according to which asset and liability values are determined;

- that financial statements are prepared on the basis of judgments and estimates made by the management and assessed by the auditor, which makes the information contained, to some extent, subjective;

- that the financial position of the bank may have been affected by subsequent events since the financial statements were drawn up; and

- that, given the different purposes for which internal control is evaluated and tested by the supervisor and the auditor, he cannot assume that the auditor's evaluation of internal control for the purposes of his audit will necessarily be adequate for the purposes for which the supervisor needs an evaluation.

36. Nonetheless, there are many areas where the work of the supervisor and of the auditor can be useful to each other. Management letters and long-form reports submitted by auditors can provide supervisors with valuable insight into various aspects of bank's operations. It is the practice in many countries for such reports to be made available to the supervisors.

37. Similarly, auditors can obtain helpful insights from information originating from the supervisory authority. When a supervisory inspection or a management interview takes place, the conclusions drawn from the inspection or interview are customarily communicated to the bank. These communications can be useful to auditors inasmuch as they provide an independent assessment in important areas such as the adequacy of provisions for bad and doubtful debts and focus attention on specific areas of supervisory concern. Supervisory authorities may also develop certain informal prudential ratios or guidelines which are made available to the banks and which can be of assistance to auditors in performing analytical reviews.

AUDITING

38. When communicating with management, both supervisors and auditors need to be aware of the benefits which can flow to each other from knowledge of the matters contained in such communications. It would therefore be advantageous for communications of this nature to be made in writing, so that they would form part of the bank's records to which the other party should have access.

39. There may be circumstances in which either the auditor or the supervisor becomes aware of important information which he believes is not available to, and which needs to be communicated to, the other party. Such circumstances may, for example, arise:

   - where the auditor becomes aware of facts which might endanger the existence of a bank;

   - where either the auditor or the supervisor detects an indication of fraud at a senior level;

   - where the auditor intends to resign in the course of an audit;

   - where the auditor has an irreconcilable difference of view with management over a material aspect of the financial statements, as a result of which he is intending to issue an audit opinion which is not unqualified;

   - where the supervisor has information which can materially affect the financial statements or the auditor's report; and

   - where the auditor believes a matter should be communicated to the supervisor and management has failed to make such communication when requested to do so.

40. In order to preserve the concerns of both parties regarding the confidentiality of information acquired while carrying out their respective functions, it is normal that, when contacts between the supervisor and the auditor become necessary, management of the bank is also present or at least informed, though in a few countries procedures for bilateral contacts between the supervisor and the auditor exist. However, even where they do not exist, rare and exceptional circumstances may arise which justify direct communication between supervisors and auditors. The primary condition for excluding the management of the bank from discussions would be that its presence would compromise their purpose. Some countries have therefore removed the confidentiality constraints from both parties to enable important and otherwise confidential information to be exchanged. Where there is an Audit Committee, a supervisory board or a similar body, the party initiating bilateral consultation should consider whether it needs simultaneously to inform that body of the substance of the problem under discussion.

41. It is becoming common in a number of countries for the auditor to carry out specific assignments or to issue special reports in accordance with statutes or at the request of the supervisor to assist the supervisor in discharging his functions. These duties may, inter alia, include reporting upon whether, in his opinion:

   - specified cover ratios or other prudential requirements included in reporting returns have been accurately completed;

- licensing conditions have been complied with;

- the transactions of the bank which have come to the auditor's attention in the course of the audit are in accordance with specified laws applicable to banks; and

- the systems for maintenance of accounting and other records and/or the systems of internal control are adequate.

42. The supervisor has a clear interest in ensuring high standards of bank auditing. Accordingly, he will seek to maintain close contact with the professional auditing bodies. In some countries, the supervisor has statutory powers over the appointment of auditors, such as the right of approval or removal, and the right to commission an independent audit. These powers are intended to ensure that auditors appointed by banks have the experience, resources and skills necessary in the circumstances. Where there is no obvious reason for a change of auditor, supervisors would also normally wish to investigate the circumstances in which a bank has failed to reappoint an auditor.

Criteria for a Possible Extension of the Auditor's Role as a Contribution of the Supervisory Process

43. It is necessary that requests to auditors to assist in specific supervisory tasks be made in the context of a well defined framework, perhaps even written into national legislation. It is considered that the following criteria need to be established.

44. Firstly, the basic responsibility for supplying complete and accurate information to the supervisor must remain with the bank management. The auditor's role is to verify and to lend additional credibility to that information. As such he does not assume any of the responsibilities of the supervisor but assists the supervisor to make his judgments more effectively.

45. Secondly, the normal relationship between the auditor and his client needs to be safeguarded. There must thus be either a statutory basis for the work or a contractual agreement between the bank and the supervisory authority. If there are no other statutory requirements or contractual arrangements, all information flows between supervisors and auditors need to be channelled through the bank except in exceptional circumstances. Thus, the supervisory authority would request the bank to arrange to obtain the information it requires from the auditor and such information would be submitted to the supervisor through the bank. Any meetings between the auditors and supervisors would, except as indicated in paragraph 40 above, be attended by representatives of the bank; and the bank's approval would be required for transmitting to the supervisory authority copies of management letters and long-form reports.

46. Thirdly, before concluding any arrangements with the supervisor, the auditor should consider whether any conflicts of interest may arise. If so, these should be satisfactorily resolved before the commencement of the work, normally by obtaining the prior approval of the bank's management to undertake the assignment.

AUDITING

1004

47. Fourthly, the supervisory requirements must be specific and clearly defined in relation to the information required. This means that the supervisor needs as far as possible to describe in quantitative terms the standard against which the bank's performance can be measured, e.g., by giving minimum levels or ratios which banks should meet so that the auditor can report whether or not they have been achieved. If, for example, information is required on the quality of loan assets, the supervisor has to specify what criteria are to be used in classifying the audited loans according to risk category. Similarly, wherever possible, some understanding must be reached between supervisors and auditors regarding the concept of materiality.

48. Fifthly, the tasks which the auditor is asked by the supervisor to perform need to be within his competence, both technical and practical. He may, for example, be requested to assess the extent of a bank's exposure to a particular borrower or country, but he would not without clear and specific guidance be in a position to judge whether any particular exposures are excessive. In addition, audits are carried out at intervals and not continuously, so that, for example, it is not reasonable to expect the auditor to carry out a complete evaluation of internal control or to monitor a bank's compliance with all supervisory rules except through an ongoing program of work over a period of time.

49. Sixthly, the auditor's task for the supervisor must have a rational basis. This means that except in special circumstances the task must be complementary to his regular audit work and can be performed more economically or more expeditiously than by the supervisor, either because of the auditor's specialized skills or because duplication is thereby avoided.

50. Finally, certain aspects of confidentiality need to be protected, in particular the confidentiality of information obtained by the auditor through his professional relationships with other clients and not available to the bank or the public.

Specific Directions in Which the Auditor's Role Can Be Extended

51. The way in which the auditor's role can be extended depends on the nature of the national supervisory environment. For example, if an active approach is followed by the supervisor, with frequent and rigorous inspection, the assistance which might be asked of the auditor would normally be minimal. If, on the other hand, there is a history of less direct supervision, primarily based on the analysis of reporting returns provided by bank's management, as opposed to inspection, or if supervisory resources are limited, the supervisor can profit from the assistance which the auditor can offer in providing his opinion on the reliability of the information obtained.

52. Nowadays, however, few countries are practicing a supervisory approach which does not contain elements of both approaches. As banking develops in complexity, inspection is proving more and more demanding in terms of supervisory resources. Many supervisory authorities which practice on-site inspection are thus being driven to place greater reliance on reporting returns and to look to the auditors for assistance in those areas for which their skills are particularly suited.

53.   Where supervisors have hitherto relied solely on the analysis of prudential returns, it is found that a certain degree of on-the-spot examination is a desirable safeguard. In these countries, therefore, the supervisors are relying more than before on the auditors to assist them by performing specific tasks.

54.   Examples of the specific supervisory tasks to which auditors are specifically suited are:

- the verification of prudential returns. In a number of countries, supervisors find it helpful to require banks to obtain the auditor's opinion that selected returns have been properly extracted from the bank's records;

- the evaluation of a bank's information and control systems on the basis of criteria provided by the supervisor. With the increase in the complexity and volume of transactions and increasing reliance on electronic data processing systems, the need for adequate control systems becomes even more imperative;

- the expression of an opinion on adherence to appropriate accounting policies, particularly with regard to provisions against potential losses. Supervisors are increasingly looking to auditors for advice as to whether accounting policies followed are appropriate and whether policies for providing for bad and doubtful debts are adequate; and

- the examination of the accounting records and control systems regarding the bank's fiduciary (including safe custody) activities, in countries where these are not considered as part of the normal audit function. Where the volume of fiduciary activities is material in the context of a bank's size, supervisors are concerned to ensure that these activities are properly segregated from the bank's own operations and that adequate controls are in place to ensure against possible fraud or misappropriation.

55.   In those countries where contacts between the auditors and the supervisors have been close over a long period, a bond of mutual trust has been built up and extended experience has enabled each to benefit from the other's work. Experience in those countries indicates that the conflicts of interest that auditors may in principle perceive as preventing close collaboration with supervisors assume less importance in practice and do not present an obstacle to a fruitful dialogue.

The Need for a Continuing Dialogue Between Supervisory Authorities and the Auditing Profession

56.   If supervisors are to derive benefit from the work of auditors on a continuing basis, supervisors need to take the auditing profession as a whole into their confidence in relation to current areas of supervisory concern. This can probably be achieved most effectively through periodic discussions at the national level between the supervisory authorities and the professional accounting bodies. Such discussions could cover areas of mutual concern, for example the treatment of claims on heavily-indebted countries. It would be of considerable assistance to auditors in making informed judgments if they were to have as clear an understanding as possible of the supervisory authorities' knowledge and attitude on such matters. In the course of such

AUDITING

discussions, supervisors should also have an opportunity to express their views on accounting policies and auditing standards generally and on specific audit procedures in particular. This would assist in improving the standard of auditing generally for banks. It may well be advisable for the banks' own associations to be involved in discussions on some of these topics to ensure that the views of all parties are taken into account.

57. Discussions between supervisory authorities and the professional accounting bodies could also usefully range over major auditing issues and topical accounting problems, such as the appropriate accounting techniques for newly developed instruments and other aspects of financial innovation and securitization. These discussions could assist in the evolution of the most appropriate accounting policies in the circumstances.

58. Both supervisory agencies and the accountancy profession are concerned to ensure that there is uniformity between different banks in the application of appropriate accounting policies. Supervisory agencies are often able to exercise a more persuasive influence over banks in achieving uniform policies because of their regulatory powers, while auditors are often better placed to monitor the actual application of such policies. A continuing dialogue between supervisory agencies and the profession could therefore significantly contribute towards the harmonization of accounting standards at the national level.

CONTENTS

	Paragraphs
Introduction	1–4
The Characteristics of Small Entities	5–18
Commentary on the Application of International Standards on Auditing	
Responsibilities: ISA 200–299	19–35
Planning: ISA 300–399	36–47
Internal Control: ISA 400–499	48–59
Audit Evidence: ISA 500–599	60–89
Audit Conclusions and Reporting: ISA 700–799	90–94
The Provision of Accounting Services to Audit Clients	95–117

This International Auditing Practice Statement (IAPS) has been prepared by the International Auditing Practices Committee (IAPC) of the International Federation of Accountants (IFAC). It was approved by the IAPC in March 1999 for publication in March 1999.

The purpose of this IAPS is to provide practical assistance to auditors in applying International Standards on Auditing (ISAs) in the audit of financial statements of small entities. It does not affect the basic principles and essential procedures of ISAs.

The Public Sector Perspective (PSP) issued by the Public Sector Committee of the International Federation of Accountants is set out at the end of an IAPS. Where no PSP is added, the IAPS is applicable in all material respects to the public sector.

AUDITING

1005

Introduction

1. International Standards on Auditing (ISAs) contain basic principles and essential procedures together with related guidance that apply to the audit of the financial statements of any entity, irrespective of its size, its legal form, ownership or management structure, or the nature of its activities. The IAPC recognizes that small entities give rise to a number of special audit considerations. This IAPS does not establish any new requirements for the audit of small entities; nor does it establish any exemptions from the requirements of ISAs. All audits of small entities are to be conducted in accordance with ISAs.

2. The objective of this IAPS is to describe the characteristics commonly found in small entities and indicate how they may affect the application of ISAs. This IAPS includes:

    (*a*) discussion of the characteristics of small entities;

    (*b*) guidance on the application of ISAs to the audit of small entities; and

    (*c*) guidance on the impact on the auditor's work where the auditor also provides accounting services to the small entity.

3. The provision of accounting services by auditors is prohibited by law in some jurisdictions. In others, the provision of accounting services by auditors is permitted both by law and professional ethics[3]. Section 3 of this IAPS deals with the special factors to be taken into account by auditors who also provide accounting services to small entities.

4. In determining the nature and extent of the guidance provided in this IAPS, the IAPC has aimed to provide a level of guidance that will be of general applicability to all audits of small entities and that will assist the auditor in exercising professional judgment with respect to the application of ISAs. However, detailed guidance of a procedural nature has not been provided, as the issue of such guidance may undermine the proper exercise of professional judgment in auditing.

THE CHARACTERISTICS OF SMALL ENTITIES

5. The auditor of any entity adapts the audit approach to the circumstances of the entity and the engagement. The audit of a small entity differs from the audit of a large entity as documentation may be unsophisticated, and audits of small entities are ordinarily less complex and may be performed using fewer assistants.

6. The meaning of "small entity" in this context gives consideration not only to the size of an entity but also to its typical qualitative characteristics. Quantitative indicators of the size of an entity may include balance sheets totals, revenue and the number of employees, but such indicators are not

---

[3] The IFAC Code of Ethics permits the provision of accounting and other services to audit clients, provided that independence is safeguarded.

definitive. Therefore it is not possible to give an adequate definition of a small entity solely in quantitative terms.

7.   For the purposes of this IAPS, a small entity is any entity in which:

    (*a*)   there is concentration of ownership and management in a small number of individuals (often a single individual[4]); and

    (*b*)   one or more of the following are also found:

- few sources of income;

- unsophisticated record-keeping;

- limited internal controls together with the potential for management override of controls.

8.   The qualitative characteristics described above are not exhaustive, they are not exclusive to small entities and small entities do not necessarily display all of those characteristics. For the purposes of this IAPS, small entities will ordinarily display characteristic (*a*), and one or more of the characteristics included under (*b*).

Concentration of Ownership and Management

9.   Small business entities ordinarily have few owners; often there is a single proprietor. The owner may employ a manager to run the entity but is in most cases directly involved in running the entity on a day-to-day basis. Likewise, in the case of small not-for-profit organizations and public sector entities, although there are often several individuals charged with formal responsibility for the entity, there may be few people involved in managing the entity on a day-to-day basis.

10.   This IAPS uses the term "owner-manager" to indicate the proprietors of entities who are involved in the running of the entity on a day-to-day basis. Where proprietors are not involved on a day-to-day basis, the term "owner-manager" is used to refer to both the proprietors, and to any managers hired to run the entity.

Few Sources of Income

11.   Small entities often have a limited range of products or services and operate from a single or limited number of locations. Such characteristics may make it easier for the auditor to acquire, record, and maintain a knowledge of the entity than would be the case with a larger entity. The application of a wide range of audit procedures may be straightforward in such circumstances. For example, effective predictive models for use in analytical procedures can sometimes be constructed. Analytical procedures may provide useful evidence, sometimes reducing the need for other substantive procedures. In

---

[4] The word "individual" denotes ownership by a natural person, rather than by another entity. An entity owned by another enterprise may, however, be regarded as a "small entity" for the purpose of this IAPS if the owner exhibits the relevant characteristics.

addition, in many small entities, accounting populations are often small and easily analyzed.

Unsophisticated Record-Keeping

12. Small entities need to keep sufficient accounting records to comply with any relevant statutory or regulatory requirements and to meet the needs of the entity, including the preparation and audit of financial statements. Therefore, the accounting system needs to be designed in such a manner so as to provide reasonable assurance that:

    (*a*) all the transactions and other accounting information that should have been recorded have in fact been recorded;

    (*b*) assets and liabilities recorded in the accounting system exist and are recorded at the correct amounts; and

    (*c*) fraud or error in processing accounting information will be detected.

13. Most small entities employ few, if any, personnel who are solely engaged in record-keeping. Consequently the bookkeeping functions and accounting records are often unsophisticated. Record keeping may be unsophisticated or poor, which results in a greater risk that the financial statements may be inaccurate or incomplete. Many small entities outsource some of or all their record keeping.

14. Small entities often find it convenient to use branded accounting software packages designed for use on a personal computer. Many of these packages have been widely tested and accredited and can, if chosen and implemented with care, provide a reasonable basis for a reliable and cost-effective accounting system.

Limited Internal Controls

15. Size and economic considerations in small entities mean that sophisticated internal controls are often neither necessary nor desirable, the fact that there are few employees limits the extent to which segregation of duties is practicable. However, for key areas, even in the very small entity, it can be practicable to implement some degree of segregation of duties or other form of unsophisticated but effective controls. Supervisory controls exercised on a day-to-day basis by the owner-manager may also have a significant beneficial effect as the owner-manager has a personal interest in safeguarding the assets of the entity, measuring its performance and controlling its activities

16. The owner-manager occupies a dominant position in a small entity. The owner-manager's direct control over all decisions, and the ability to intervene personally at any time to ensure an appropriate response to changing circumstances, are often important features of the management of small entities. The exercise of this control can also compensate for otherwise weak internal control procedures. For example, in cases where there is limited segregation of duties in the area of purchasing and cash disbursements, internal control is improved when the owner-manager personally signs all

checks. When the owner manager is not involved, there is a greater risk that employee fraud or error may occur and not be detected.

17. While a lack of sophistication in internal controls does not, of itself, indicate a high risk of fraud or error, an owner-manager's dominant position can be abused: management override of controls may have a significant adverse effect on the control environment in any entity, leading to an increased risk of management fraud or material misstatement in the financial statements. For example, the owner-manager may direct personnel to make disbursements that they would otherwise not make in the absence of supporting documentation.

18. The impact of the owner-manager and the potential for management override of internal controls on the audit depend to a great extent on the integrity, attitude, and motives of the owner-manager. As in any other audit, the auditor of a small entity exercises professional skepticism. The auditor neither assumes that the owner-manager is dishonest nor assumes unquestioned honesty. This is an important factor to be considered by the auditor when assessing audit risk, planning the nature and extent of audit work, evaluating audit evidence, and assessing the reliability of management representations.

COMMENTARY ON THE APPLICATION OF INTERNATIONAL STANDARDS ON AUDITING

19. The commentary that follows provides guidance on the application of ISAs to the audit of a small entity. This guidance is a supplement to, and not a substitute for, the guidance contained in the relevant ISA and takes account of the special considerations relevant to the audit of small entities. For the specific requirements of ISAs, the auditor refers to the ISA concerned. Where an ISA is, in principle, applicable to the audit of the financial statements of small entities and there are no special considerations applicable to the audit of a small entity, no guidance is given in respect of that ISA.

ISA 210: Terms of Audit Engagements

20. In many cases, owner-managers of small entities are not fully aware of their own responsibilities or those of their auditors. In particular, owner-managers may not appreciate that the financial statements are their responsibility, particularly where the owner-manager has outsourced the preparation of the financial statements. One of the purposes of an engagement letter is to communicate clearly the respective responsibilities of the owner-manager and the auditor. The Appendix to ISA 210 provides an example of an audit engagement letter.

21. In some cases the auditor may determine that it will not be possible to obtain sufficient evidence to form an opinion on the financial statements because of weaknesses that may arise from the characteristics of the small entity. In these circumstances, and where permitted by the relevant jurisdiction, the auditor may decide not to accept the engagement, or to withdraw from the engagement after acceptance. Alternatively, the auditor may decide to continue with the engagement but qualify or disclaim the audit opinion. The

AUDITING

auditor has regard to paragraph 41 of ISA 700 "The Auditor's Report on Financial Statements" which states that the auditor would not ordinarily accept an audit engagement in which the terms of the engagement are such that the auditor believes that the need to express a disclaimer of opinion exists.

ISA 220: Quality Control for Audit Work

22. The primary objective of quality control is to provide assurance that audits are conducted in accordance with generally accepted auditing standards. The auditor of a small entity keeps this objective in mind when determining the nature, timing, and extent of the policies and procedures appropriate to the circumstances.

23. Paragraph 5 of ISA 220 states: "The nature, timing and extent of an audit firm's quality control policies and procedures depend on a number of factors such as the size and nature of the practice..." Many audits of small entities are undertaken by small audit firms. Such firms, in determining appropriate policies and procedures, consider the areas listed in paragraph 6 of ISA 220 which are:

(*a*) professional requirements;

(*b*) skills and competence;

(*c*) assignment;

(*d*) delegation;

(*e*) consultation;

(*f*) acceptance and retention of clients; and

(*g*) monitoring.

24. With the possible exception of "assignment" and "delegation" (which may not be relevant to sole practitioners with no assistants), each of these will ordinarily be reflected in the arrangements established by firms auditing small entities.

25. The requirements of ISA 220 relating to quality control on individual audits are mostly relevant to engagements where some of the work is delegated to one or more assistants. Many small entity audits are carried out entirely by the audit engagement partner (who may be a sole practitioner). In such situations, questions of direction and supervision of assistants and review of their work do not arise as the audit engagement partner, having personally conducted all significant aspects of the work, is aware of all material issues.

26. The audit engagement partner (or sole practitioner) nevertheless needs to be satisfied that the audit has been conducted in accordance with ISAs. Developing or obtaining a suitably designed form of audit completion checklist may provide a useful tool for testing the completeness and adequacy of the process followed in an audit. Forming an objective view on the appropriateness of the judgments made in the course of the audit can present practical problems when the same individual also performed the

entire audit. When particularly complex or unusual issues are involved, and the audit is performed by a sole practitioner, it may be desirable to consult with other suitably-experienced auditors or the auditor's professional body, on a confidential basis.

ISA 230: Documentation

27. The auditor may have an in-depth understanding of the entity and its business, because of the close relationship between the auditor and the owner-manager, or because of the size of the entity being audited, or the size of the audit team and the audit firm. However, that understanding does not eliminate the need for the auditor to maintain adequate working papers. Working papers assist in the planning, performance, supervision and review of the audit, and they record the evidence obtained to support the audit opinion.

28. The discipline imposed by the requirement to record the reasoning and conclusions on significant matters requiring the exercise of judgment can often, in practice, add to the clarity of the auditor's understanding of the issues in question and enhance the quality of the conclusions. This is so for all audits, even in the case of a sole practitioner with no assistants.

29. Different techniques may be used to document the entity's accounting and internal control systems, depending on their complexity. However in small entities the use of flowcharts or narrative descriptions of the system are often the most efficient techniques. These can be kept as permanent information and are reviewed and updated as necessary in subsequent years.

30. Paragraph 11 of ISA 230 provides examples of the contents of working papers. These examples are not intended to be used as a checklist of matters to be included in all cases. The auditor of a small entity uses judgment in determining the contents of working papers in any particular case.

31. Nevertheless, the auditor of a large or a small entity, records in the working papers:

    (a) the audit planning;

    (b) an audit program setting out the nature, timing, and extent of the audit procedures performed;

    (c) the results of those procedures; and

    (d) the conclusions drawn from the audit evidence obtained together with the reasoning and conclusions on all significant matters requiring the exercise of judgment.

ISA 240: Fraud and Error

32. Paragraphs 13 and 14 of ISA 240 illustrate certain conditions or events that may increase the risk of fraud or error. Examples of these conditions or events are given in Appendix 1 to the ISA. A relevant example applicable to small entities is "management is dominated by one person (or a small group) and there is no effective oversight board or committee..." Although this

AUDITING

situation applies to most small entities, the guidance in ISA 240 is not intended to imply that all small entities are to be regarded by the auditor as necessarily involving a higher risk of fraud or error than larger entities.

33. The presence of a dominant owner-manager is an important factor in the overall control environment, as the need for management authorization can compensate for otherwise weak control procedures and reduce the risk of employee fraud and error. However, this can be a potential weakness since there is the opportunity for management override of controls. The owner-manager's attitude to control issues in general and to the personal exercise of supervisory controls can have a significant influence on the auditor's approach. The auditor's assessment of the effect of such matters is conditioned by knowledge of that particular entity and the integrity of its owner-manager. Matters that auditors take into account in this assessment include the following.

- Whether the owner-manager has a specific identifiable motive (for example, dependence of the owner-manager on the success of the entity) to distort the financial statements, combined with the opportunity to do so.

- Whether the owner-manager makes no distinction between personal and business transactions.

- Whether the owner-manager's life-style is materially inconsistent with the level of his or her remuneration (this includes other sources of income of which the auditor may be aware by completing the owner-manager's tax return, for example).

- Frequent changes of professional advisers.

- Whether the start date for the audit has been repeatedly delayed or there are unexplained demands to complete the audit in an unreasonably short period of time.

- Unusual transactions around the year-end that have a material effect on profit.

- Unusual related party transactions.

- Payments of fees or commissions to agents and consultants that appear excessive.

- Disputes with tax authorities.

ISA 250: Consideration of Laws and Regulations in an Audit of Financial Statements

34. ISA 250 requires the auditor to obtain a general understanding of the legal and regulatory framework to which the entity is subject. Apart from those laws and regulations that relate directly to the preparation of the financial statements, there may also be laws and regulations that provide a legal framework for the conduct of the entity and that are central to the entity's ability to conduct its business. As most small entities have uncomplicated activities, the legal and regulatory environment to which they are subject is

less complicated than the environment in which larger more diversified entities operate.

35. Once the auditor of a small entity has identified any relevant industry-specific laws and regulations, this information is recorded as permanent information as part of the knowledge of the entity and is reviewed and updated as necessary in subsequent years.

ISA 300: Planning

36. Audits of small entities are conducted by very small audit teams, many involve the audit engagement partner (or sole practitioner) working with one audit assistant (or without audit assistants). With a smaller team, co-ordination and communication between team members is easier. Planning the audit of a small entity need not be a complex or time-consuming exercise, it varies according to the size of the entity and the complexity of the audit. For example, on some small audits, planning may be carried out at a meeting with the owner-manager of the entity or when the entity's records become available to the auditor for audit. Planning the audit can, however, start at the completion of the previous period's audit as the auditor will be well placed to plan for the next period. A brief file note prepared at this time, based on a review of the working papers and highlighting issues identified in the audit just completed can be particularly helpful. This file note, amended for changes arising during the subsequent period, could then be the initial basis for planning the next audit. Discussion with the owner-manager is a very important part of planning, especially in a first-year audit. Such discussions do not need a special meeting they can often take place as a part of other meetings, conversations or correspondence.

37. In principle, planning comprises developing a general strategy (reflected in an overall audit plan) and a detailed approach for implementing the strategy in terms of the nature, timing and extent of the audit work (reflected in an audit program). However, a practical approach to the audit of a small entity need not involve excessive documentation. In the case of a small entity where, because of the size or nature of the entity, the details of the overall plan can be adequately documented in the audit program, or vice versa, separate documentation of each may not be necessary. When standard audit programs are used, these are appropriately modified and tailored to the particular client circumstances.

ISA 310: Knowledge of the Business

38. The Appendix to ISA 310 gives a list of matters that the auditor may consider in relation to knowledge of the business. This list is illustrative only, it is not exhaustive, nor are all the matters listed relevant to every audit. In particular, the auditor of a small entity will often find that many of the points in this list are simply not relevant. It would therefore be inappropriate to regard this Appendix as a form of checklist to be applied routinely in all audits. It may, however, be sufficient for the auditor to use a checklist that has been appropriately tailored to the particular small entity; such a checklist can be reviewed and updated in subsequent years.

AUDITING

39. The auditor of a small entity is often in a position to have a wide and up-to-date knowledge of the business by virtue of the fact that there may be regular close contact with the owner-manager. This relationship often provides information on matters such as the following.

- The activities of the small entity, its main products and services, and the industry in which it operates.

- The management style, aims, and attitudes of the owner-manager.

- Any plans for changes to the nature, management or ownership of the entity.

- Trends in profitability or liquidity and the adequacy of working capital.

- Legal or regulatory issues facing the entity, including its relationship with the taxation authorities.

- The accounting records.

- The control environment.

40. Documenting the auditor's knowledge of the business is equally important in all audits, irrespective of the size of the entity. However, the extent of the documentation depends on the complexity of the entity and the number of persons who will be engaged on the audit. Small entities are ordinarily not complex and their audit rarely involves large teams of assistants. In many cases the audit may be performed by the partner and, perhaps, a single assistant. Therefore, whilst the auditor of a small entity will prepare documentation to a level sufficient to:

(*a*) facilitate proper planning of the audit; and

(*b*) provide for any change of responsibility within the audit firm, such as changes of audit engagement partner or the departure, illness or incapacity of assistants.

Such documentation will ordinarily be unsophisticated in format and as brief as circumstances allow.

ISA 320: Audit Materiality

41. "Materiality" is defined in the International Accounting Standards Committee's "Framework for the Preparation and Presentation of Financial Statements" as follows: "Information is material if its omission or misstatement could influence the economic decisions of users taken on the basis of the financial statements. Materiality depends on the size of the item or error judged in the particular circumstances of its omission or misstatement. Thus, materiality provides a threshold or cut-off point rather than being a primary qualitative characteristic which information must have if it is to be useful".

Planning Stage

42. For audit planning purposes, it is generally necessary to assess materiality from a qualitative and quantitative perspective. One purpose of this

preliminary judgment about materiality is to focus the auditor's attention on the more significant financial statement items while determining the audit strategy. As there are no authoritative pronouncements on how materiality is assessed in quantitative terms, the auditor in each case applies professional judgment in the light of the circumstances. One approach to the assessment of quantitative materiality is to use a percentage of a key figure in the financial statements such as one of the following.

- Profit or loss before tax (adjusted, if appropriate, for the effect of any abnormal levels of items of expenditure such as the owner-manager's remuneration).

- Revenue.

- Balance sheet total.

43. Often in the case of small entities, draft financial statements are not available to the auditor at the commencement of the audit. When this is the case, the auditor uses the best information available at the time. The current year's trial balance may be used, if available. Often an estimate of revenue for the current period can be more readily obtained than of profit (or loss) or of a balance sheet total. A common approach in the preliminary judgment of materiality is to calculate materiality on the previous year's audited financial statements as amended for known circumstances in relation to the year subject to audit.

44. Assessing materiality as a percentage of pre-tax results may be inappropriate when the entity is at or near the break-even point as it may give an inappropriately low level of materiality, leading to unnecessarily extensive audit procedures. In such cases, the auditor may apply the percentage method to, for example, revenue or balance sheet totals. Alternatively, materiality may be assessed having regard to assessed levels of materiality in prior years and the normal level of results. In addition to considering materiality at the overall financial statement level, the auditor considers materiality in relation to individual account balances, classes of transactions, and disclosures.

Assessment of Materiality when Evaluating the Results of Audit Procedures

45. Whatever basis may be used to assess materiality for audit planning purposes, the auditor reassesses materiality when evaluating the results of audit procedures. This reassessment takes account of the final version of the draft financial statements, incorporating all agreed adjustments and information obtained during the course of the audit.

46. Although materiality at the reporting stage is considered in quantitative terms, there is no clear threshold value but rather a range of values within which the auditor exercises judgment. Amounts above the upper limit of the range may be presumed material and amounts below the lower limit may be presumed not material, although either presumption may be rebutted by applying qualitative considerations.

47. In addition, although planning may have been based on a quantitative assessment of materiality, the auditor's opinion will take into account not

only the amount but also the qualitative nature of unadjusted misstatements within the financial statements.

ISA 400: Risk Assessments and Internal Control

Inherent Risk

48. In the audit of a small entity, control risk is often assumed or assessed as high, at least for certain financial statement assertions. The assessment of inherent risk for those assertions takes on a particular significance, as it has a direct impact on the extent of substantive procedures. There are difficulties in the assessment of the inherent risk of a small entity, for example there may be increased risk as a result of the concentration of ownership and control. However, the auditor's assessment of inherent risk in a small entity depends on its particular characteristics. A careful assessment of inherent risk for material financial statement assertions, rather than an assumption that it is high, may enable the auditor to conduct a more efficient and effective audit.

Control Risk

49. An understanding of the control environment is essential to the understanding of control risk. The auditor considers the overall influence of the owner-manager and other key personnel. For example, the auditor considers whether the owner-manager displays a positive control consciousness and considers the extent to which the owner-manager and other key personnel are actively involved in day-to-day operations.

50. After obtaining an understanding of the accounting and internal control systems, the auditor makes a preliminary assessment of control risk, at the assertion level, for each material account balance or class of transactions. Substantive procedures may be reduced if reliance on these controls is warranted after investigation and testing. However, many internal controls relevant to large entities are not practical in the small entity, and as a result it may not be possible to rely on internal control to detect fraud or errors. For example, segregation of duties may be severely limited in small entities because accounting procedures may be performed by few persons who may have both operating and custodial responsibilities. Similarly, when there are few employees, it may not be possible to set up a system of independent checking of their work.

51. Inadequate segregation of duties and the risk of error may, in some cases, be offset by other control procedures such as the exercise of strong supervisory controls by the owner-manager means of direct personal knowledge of the entity and involvement in transactions. However this, in itself, may introduce other risks such as the potential for management override and fraud. Particular difficulties include the possible understatement of income by the non-recording or misrecording of sales. In circumstances where segregation of duties is limited and evidence of supervisory controls is lacking, the audit evidence necessary to support the auditor's opinion on the financial statements may have to be obtained entirely through the performance of substantive procedures.

52. The auditor of a small entity may decide, based on the auditor's understanding of the accounting system and control environment, to assume that control risk is high without planning or performing any detailed procedures (such as tests of controls) to support that assessment. Even where there appear to be effective controls it may be more efficient for the auditor to confine audit procedures to those of a substantive nature.

53. The auditor makes management aware of material weaknesses in the design or operation of the accounting and internal control systems that have come to the auditor's attention. Recommendations for improvement may also be made in this communication. Such recommendations are particularly valuable for the development of the small entity's accounting and internal control systems.

Detection Risk

54. The auditor uses the assessments of inherent and control risk to determine the substantive procedures that will provide the audit evidence to reduce detection risk, and therefore audit risk, to an acceptable level. In some small entities, such as those where most transactions are for cash and there is no regular pattern of costs and margins, the available evidence may be inadequate to support an unqualified opinion on the financial statements.

ISA 401: Auditing in a Computer Information Systems Environment

55. The increasing availability of computer-based accounting systems that are capable of meeting both functional and economic circumstances of even the smallest entity impacts on the audits of those entities. Small entities' accounting systems often make use of personal computers. International Auditing Practice Statement 1001, "CIS Environments—Stand-Alone Microcomputers" gives additional guidance regarding the special considerations of such an environment.

56. Small entities are likely to use less sophisticated hardware and software packages than large entities (often "packaged" rather than developed "in house"). Nevertheless, the auditor has sufficient knowledge of the computer information system to plan, direct, supervise, and review the work performed. The auditor may consider whether specialized skills are needed in an audit.

57. Because of the limited segregation of duties, the use of computer facilities by a small entity may have the effect of increasing control risk. For example, it is common for users to be able to perform two or more of the following functions in the accounting system.

- Initiating and authorizing source documents.

- Entering data into the system.

- Operating the computer.

- Changing programs and data files.

- Using or distributing output.

AUDITING

- Modifying the operating systems.

58. The use of computer information systems by small entities may assist the auditor in obtaining assurance as to the accuracy and appropriateness of accounting records by reducing control risk. Computerized information systems may be better organized, less dependent upon the skills of people using them, and less susceptible to manipulation than non-computerized systems. The ability of the auditor to obtain relevant reports and other information may also be enhanced. Good computerized systems facilitate accurate double entry and the reconciliation of subsidiary ledgers with control accounts. Report generation and the production of bank reconciliations may be more disciplined and effective, and the availability of reports and other information to the auditor is often improved. The assurance provided by such features, providing they are properly evaluated and tested, may permit the auditor limit the volume of substantive testing of transactions and balances.

59. The general principles outlined in International Auditing Practice Statement 1009 "Computer-Assisted Audit Techniques" (CAATs) are also applicable in small entity computer environments and give additional guidance regarding the special considerations in such an environment. However, in many cases where smaller volumes of data are processed, manual methods may be more cost-effective.

ISA 500: Audit Evidence

60. ISA 500 recognizes that, although audit evidence may be obtained in a number of ways, including from an appropriate mix of tests of control and substantive procedures, in some circumstances evidence may be obtained entirely from substantive procedures. A typical example of such circumstances would be where segregation of duties is limited and evidence of supervisory control is lacking, as is the case in many small entities.

61. In the audit of small entities, there are particular problems in obtaining audit evidence to support the assertion of completeness. There are two principal reasons for this:

   (a) the owner-manager occupies a dominant position and may be able to ensure that some transactions are not recorded; and

   (b) the entity may not have internal control procedures that provide documentary evidence that all transactions are recorded.

62. The auditor plans and conducts the audit with an attitude of professional skepticism. In the absence of evidence to the contrary, the auditor is entitled to accept representations as truthful and records as genuine.

63. The auditor of a small entity need not assume that there will be limited internal controls over the completeness of important populations such as revenue. Many small entities have some form of numerically based system to control the dispatch of goods or the provision of services. Where there is such a system to ensure completeness, the auditor may obtain audit evidence of its operation, by means of tests of control, to assist in determining whether

control risk can be assessed at less than high in order to justify a reduction in the extent of substantive testing.

64. Where there are no internal controls relevant to the assertion, the auditor may be able to obtain sufficient evidence from substantive procedures alone. Such procedures may include the following.

- Comparing recorded amounts with amounts calculated on the basis of separately recorded data, for example, goods issues recorded in physical stock records may be expected to give rise to sales income, and job sheets or time records may be expected to give rise to charges to clients.

- Reconciling total quantities of goods bought and sold.

- Analytical procedures.

- External confirmation.

- A Review of transactions after the balance sheet date.

ISA 520: Analytical Procedures

Analytical Procedures in Planning the Audit

65. The auditor applies analytical procedures at the planning stage of the audit. The nature and extent of analytical procedures at the planning stage of the audit of a small entity may be limited by the timeliness of processing of transactions by the small entity and the lack of reliable financial information at that point in time. Small entities may not have interim or monthly financial information that can be used in analytical procedures at the planning stage. The auditor may, as an alternative, conduct a brief review of the general ledger or such other accounting records as may be readily available. In many cases, there may be no documented information that can be used for this purpose, and the auditor may obtain the required information through discussion with the owner-manager.

Analytical Procedures as Substantive Procedures

66. Analytical procedures can often be a cost-effective means of obtaining evidence required by the auditor. The auditor assesses the controls over the preparation of information used in applying analytical procedures. When such controls are effective, the auditor will have greater confidence in the reliability of the information and, therefore, in the results of analytical procedures.

67. An unsophisticated predictive model can sometimes be effective. For example, where a small entity has employed a known number of staff at fixed rates of pay throughout the period, it will ordinarily be possible for the auditor to use this data to estimate the total payroll costs for the period with a high degree of accuracy, thereby providing audit evidence for a significant item in the financial statements and reducing the need to perform tests of details on the payroll. The use of widely recognized trade ratios (such as profit margins for different types of retail entities) can often be used effectively in analytical procedures to provide evidence to support the reasonableness of recorded items. The extent of analytical procedures in the

AUDITING

audit of a small entity may be limited because of the non-availability of information on which the analytical procedures are based.

68.   Predictive analytical procedures can often be an effective means of testing for completeness, provided the results can be predicted with a reasonable degree of precision and confidence. Variations from expected results may indicate possible omissions that have not been detected by other substantive tests.

69.   However, different types of analytical procedure provide different levels of assurance. Analytical procedures involving, for example, the prediction of total rental income on a building divided into apartments, taking the rental rates, the number of apartments and vacancy rates into consideration, can be a very persuasive source of evidence and may eliminate the need for further verification by means of tests of details. In contrast, calculation and comparison of gross margin percentages as a means of confirming a revenue figure may be a less persuasive source of evidence, but may provide useful corroboration if used in combination with other audit procedures.

Analytical Procedures as Part of the Overall Review

70.   The analytical procedures ordinarily performed at this stage of the audit are very similar to those that would be used at the planning stage of the audit. These include the following.

- Comparing the financial statements for the current year to those of previous years.

- Comparing the financial statements to any budgets, forecasts, or management expectations.

- Reviewing trends in any important financial statement ratios.

- Considering whether the financial statements adequately reflect any changes in the entity of which the auditor is aware.

- Inquiring into unexplained or unexpected features of the financial statements.

ISA 530: Audit Sampling and Other Selective Testing Procedures

71.   There are a variety of methods of selecting items for testing, the auditor's choice of an appropriate method will be guided by considerations of effectiveness and efficiency. The means available to the auditor are:

    (*a*)   selecting all items (100% examination);

    (*b*)   selecting specific items; or

    (*c*)   audit sampling.

72.   The small populations ordinarily encountered in small entities may make it feasible to test:

    (*a*)   100% of the population; or

(*b*) 100% of some part of the population, for example, all items above a given amount, applying analytical procedures to the balance of the population, if it is material.

73. When the above methods of obtaining audit evidence are not adopted, the auditor considers the use of procedures involving audit sampling. When the auditor decides to use audit sampling, the same underlying principles apply in both large and small entities. The auditor selects sample items in such a way that the sample can be expected to be representative of the population.

ISA 550: Related Parties

74. Significant transactions are often entered into between the small entity and the owner-manager, or between the small entity and entities related to the owner-manager. Small entities seldom have sophisticated policies and codes of conduct on related party transactions. Indeed, related party transactions are a regular feature of many entities that are owned and managed by an individual or by a family. Further, the owner-manager may not fully understand the definition of a related party, especially where relevant accounting standards deem certain relationships to be related and others not. The provision of management representations in respect of the completeness of disclosure may entail some explanation by the auditor of the technical definition of a related party.

75. The auditor of a small entity ordinarily performs substantive procedures on the identification of related parties and related party transactions. However, if the auditor assesses the risk of undisclosed related party transactions as low, such substantive procedures need not be extensive. The auditor often acts as the auditor of other entities related to the small entity, which may assist in identifying related parties.

76. The auditor's in-depth knowledge of the small entity may be of assistance in the identification of related parties, which in many instances, will be with entities controlled by the owner-manager. This knowledge can also help the auditor assess whether related party transactions might have taken place without recognition in the entity's accounting records.

ISA 560: Subsequent Events

Subsequent Events Between the Period end and the Date of the Auditor's Report

77. It is not common for small entities to be required to report shortly after their period-end. It is often the case that more time elapses between the period end and the approval or signature of the financial statements by the owner-manager in the case of small entities, than in the case of large entities. The period to be covered by the auditor's subsequent events procedures is therefore often longer in the audit of a small entity, allowing more opportunity for the occurrence of subsequent events that can affect the financial statements. ISA 560 requires the auditor to perform procedures to cover the entire period from the period-end up to the date of the audit report.

AUDITING

78. The subsequent events procedures that the auditor of a small entity performs will depend on the information that is available and, in particular, the extent to which the accounting records have been written up since the period-end. When the accounting records are not up-to-date and minutes of meetings of the directors have not been prepared, relevant procedures can take the form of inquiry of the owner-manager, recording the owner-manager's responses and inspection of bank statements. Paragraph 5 of ISA 560 gives examples of some of the matters that it may be appropriate for the auditor to consider in the course of these inquiries.

79. The auditor may, depending on the circumstances, consider that the letter of representation should cover subsequent events. The letter of representation is ordinarily dated on the same day as the audit report, thus covering the entire period since the period end.

80. Guidance on the auditor's procedures relating to subsequent events (if any) in the period between the approval of the financial statements and the date of the auditor's report is given in the guidance provided in this IAPS on ISA 700 "The Auditor's Report on Financial Statements."

Subsequent Events Between the Date of the Auditor's Report and the Financial Statements Being Issued

81. Where, as in many small entities, the meeting at which the financial statements are approved or signed is immediately followed by the annual general meeting, the interval between the two does not to require any separate consideration by the auditor as it is so short.

82. If the auditor becomes aware of a fact that materially affects the financial statements, the auditor considers whether the financial statements require amendment, discusses the matter with management, and takes action appropriate in the circumstances.

ISA 570: Going Concern

83. The size of an entity affects its ability to withstand adverse conditions. Small entities can respond quickly to exploit opportunities, but their lack of reserves limits their ability to sustain operations.

84. ISA 570 requires that auditors consider the risk that the going concern assumption may not be appropriate. Risk factors of particular relevance to small entities include the risk that banks and other lenders may cease to support the entity, the risk of the loss of a major customer or key employee, and the risk of the loss of the right to operate under a license, franchise or other legal agreement.

85. ISA 570 gives guidance on the evidence to be obtained when a question arises as to the appropriateness of the going concern basis. Such evidence may include a review of documentation such as budgets, cash flow and profit forecasts In the audit of a small entity, the auditor does not ordinarily expect to find detailed budgets and forecasts relevant to the consideration of going concern. Nevertheless, the auditor discusses with the owner-manager the going concern status of the entity and in particular, the financing of the entity

in the medium and long-term. The auditor considers these discussions in the light of corroborative documentation and the auditor's knowledge of the business. The auditor considers the need to obtain written management representations.

86. Where the small entity is largely financed by a loan from the owner-manager, it may be important that these funds are not withdrawn. For example, the continuance of a small entity in financial difficulty may be dependent on the owner-manager subordinating his loan to the entity in favor of banks or other financial institutions. In such circumstances the auditor inspects appropriate, documentary evidence of the subordination of the owner-manager's loan. Where an entity is dependent on additional support from the owner-manager, the auditor considers the owner-manager's ability to meet the obligation under the support arrangement. In addition, the auditor may ask for a written representation confirming the owner-manager's intention or understanding.

ISA 580: Management Representations

87. Paragraph 6 of ISA 580 states that, when representations relate to matters that are material to the financial statements, the auditor:

   (a) seeks corroborative audit evidence from sources inside or outside the entity;

   (b) evaluates whether the representations made by management appear reasonable and are consistent with other audit evidence obtained, including other representations; and

   (c) considers whether the individuals making the representations can be expected to be well-informed on the particular matters.

88. Paragraph 7 of ISA 580 states that representations from management cannot be a substitute for other audit evidence that the auditor expects to be available. If such audit evidence cannot be obtained, this may constitute a limitation on the scope of the audit and the auditor considers the implications for the audit report. However, in certain instances, a representation by management may be the only audit evidence that the auditor can reasonably expect to be available.

89. In view of the particular characteristics of small entities, the auditor may judge it appropriate to obtain written representations from the owner-manager as to the completeness and accuracy of the accounting records and of the financial statements (for example, that all income has been recorded). Such representations, on their own, do not provide sufficient audit evidence. The auditor assesses the representations in conjunction with the results of other relevant audit procedures, the auditor's knowledge of the business and of its owner-manager, and considers whether, in the particular circumstances, it would be reasonable to expect other audit evidence to be available. The possibility of misunderstandings between the auditor and the owner-manager is reduced when oral representations are confirmed by the owner-manager in writing.

AUDITING

ISA 700: The Auditor's Report on Financial Statements

90.   The objective of any audit is for the auditor to obtain sufficient appropriate audit evidence to be able to express an opinion on the financial statements. In many cases the auditor will be able to express an unqualified opinion on the financial statements of small entities. However there may be circumstances that necessitate a modification of the auditor's report.

Scope Limitations

91.   When the auditor is unable to design or carry out procedures to obtain sufficient appropriate audit evidence as to the completeness of accounting records, this may constitute a limitation in the scope of the auditor's work. The limitation would lead to a qualification of the opinion or, in circumstances where the possible effects of the limitation are so significant that the auditor is unable to express an opinion on the financial statements, a disclaimer of opinion.

92.   The following illustrative paragraphs may be used for this purpose.

Example of paragraphs for an auditor's report qualified when completeness of accounting records is not substantiated—scope limitation that does not prevent the auditor from expressing an opinion

The company's recorded sales include $X in respect of cash sales. There was no system of control over such sales on which we could rely for the purpose of our audit and there were no satisfactory audit procedures that we could perform to obtain reasonable assurance that all cash sales were properly recorded.

In our opinion, except for the effects of such adjustments, if any, as might have been determined to be necessary had we been able to satisfy ourselves as to the completeness and accuracy of the accounting records in respect of sales, the financial statements give a true and fair view of (or 'present fairly, in all material respects,') the financial position of the company as of...and the results of its operations and its cash flows for the year then ended in accordance with...(and comply with...).

Example of paragraphs for an auditor's report with disclaimer of opinion when completeness of accounting records is not substantiated—scope limitation that is so significant that the auditor is unable to express an opinion.

The company's sales were made entirely on a cash basis. There was no system of control over such sales on which we could rely for the purpose of our audit and there were no satisfactory audit procedures that we could perform to obtain reasonable assurance that all cash sales were properly recorded.

Because of the significance of the matter discussed in the preceding paragraph, we do not express an opinion on the financial statements.

Date and Signature of the Auditor's Report

93.   The auditor dates the audit report as of the completion date of the audit. This date should not be earlier than the date on which the owner-manager

approves or signs the financial statements Approval may be in the form of a management representation. In the audit of small entities, for practical reasons, the auditor may actually sign the report on a date later than that on which the owner-manager approves or signs the financial statements. Prior planning by the auditor, and discussion with the management of their procedures for finalizing the financial statements will often prevent this situation from arising. Where it cannot be avoided, there is a possibility that some event during the intervening period could materially affect the financial statements. Therefore, the auditor takes such steps as are appropriate:

(*a*) to obtain assurance that, on that later date, the owner-manager would have acknowledged responsibility for the financial statements or the items appearing therein; and

(*b*) to ensure that their procedures for reviewing subsequent events cover the period up to that date.

ISA 720: Other Information in Documents Containing Audited Financial Statements

94. The auditor reads the other information to identify material inconsistencies with the audited financial statements. Examples of "other information" often included with the financial statements of a small entity are the detailed income and expenditure statement, that is often attached with audited financial statements for taxation purposes, and the management report.

THE PROVISION OF ACCOUNTING SERVICES TO THE SMALL ENTITY BEING AUDITED

95. This section is relevant to jurisdictions in which auditors are legally and professionally permitted to provide accounting services to their audit clients.

96. In some jurisdictions, auditors are permitted to provide accounting and other services to audit clients The owner-manager of a small entity often needs assistance with the preparation of the financial statements, and other accounting services, and may seek such assistance from the auditor.

97. Examples of accounting services that the auditor may be engaged to perform include the following.

- Assisting with the keeping of accounting records.

- Advising on the selection and application of accounting policies.

- Assisting with the preparation of financial statements.

98. In performing accounting services, the auditor may obtain useful information about the entity and its owner-manager's aims, management style, and ethos. The auditor also acquires an in-depth knowledge of the entity, which assists in planning and conducting the audit. The auditor nevertheless remembers that assistance provided to the entity does not relieve the auditor from obtaining sufficient and appropriate audit evidence.

AUDITING

Ethical Considerations

99. The auditor bears in mind the overriding ethical requirement for independence and objectivity when forming and expressing an opinion on the financial statements and exercises care to ensure that the relationship with the entity does not prejudice the ability to form an objective opinion.

100. Paragraph 8.5 of the IFAC Code of Professional Ethics for Public Accountants permits the provision of other services, but states:

"When a professional accountant in public practice, in addition to carrying out an audit or other reporting function, provides other services to a client, care should be taken not to perform management functions or make management decisions, responsibility for which remains with the board of directors and management."

101. The commentary on paragraph 8.5 states that the provision of other services does not mean that the professional accountant has ceased to be independent. However, with respect to the preparation of accounting records, the commentary provides further advice as follows:

"The preparation of accounting records is a service which is frequently requested of a professional accountant in public practice, particularly by smaller clients, whose businesses are not sufficiently large to employ an adequate internal accounting staff…In all cases in which independence is required and in which a professional accountant in public practice is concerned in the preparation of accounting records for a client, the following requirements should be observed:

(*a*) The professional accountant in public practice should not have any relationship or combination of relationships with the client or any conflict of interest which would impair integrity or independence.

(*b*) The client should accept responsibility for the statements.

(*c*) The professional accountant in public practice should not assume the role of employee or of management conducting the operations of an entity.

(*d*) Staff assigned to the preparation of accounting records ideally should not participate in the examination of such records. The fact that the professional accountant in public practice has processed or maintained certain records does not eliminate the need to make sufficient audit tests."

COMMENTARY ON THE APPLICATION OF INTERNATIONAL STANDARDS ON AUDITING WHEN THE AUDITOR ALSO PROVIDES ACCOUNTING SERVICES TO THE SMALL ENTITY

Where the auditor provides accounting services to the small entity, the following additional matters may be relevant in the application of the ISAs by the auditor.

ISA 210: Terms of Audit Engagements

102. Where the auditor has assisted with the preparation of the financial statements, owner-managers of small entities may not be fully aware of their own legal responsibilities or those of the auditor. Owner-managers may not appreciate that the financial statements are their responsibility, or that the audit of the financial statements is legally quite distinct from any accounting services that the auditor provides. One of the purposes of an engagement letter is to avoid any such misunderstandings.

103. Paragraph 3 of ISA 210 states that the auditor may agree terms of engagement for other services by means of separate letters of engagement. However, there is no requirement for separate letters and, in the case of a small entity, there may be practical reasons why a single combined letter may be more appropriate.

ISA 230: Documentation

104. When the auditor provides accounting services to a small entity, such services are not audit work and so the requirements of ISA 230 do not ordinarily apply to, for example, documentation of the work done in assisting with the preparation of the financial statements.

105. A consideration when establishing a retention policy for the working papers of a small entity is that owner-managers often request copies of the working papers containing accounting information to assist them in the administration of their entity. Paragraph 14 of ISA 230 states that working papers are the property of the auditor. Although portions of, or extracts from, the working papers may be made available to the entity at the discretion of the auditor, they are not a substitute for the entity's accounting records. It may be helpful for the engagement letter to set out these requirements regarding the accounting records.

ISA 240: Fraud and Error

106. The auditor may have obtained knowledge of the owner-manager's personal financial position and lifestyle through the provision of other services to the entity or the owner manager. This knowledge may enhance the quality of the auditor's assessment of the inherent risk of fraud. Unexplained demands to prepare the financial statements and complete the audit in an unreasonably short period of time may indicate that there is a increased risk of fraud or error occurring.

ISA 250: Consideration of Laws and Regulations in an Audit of Financial Statements

107. Most entities are subject to requirements relating directly to the preparation of financial statements, including the relevant companies legislation. The accounting expertise of the auditor as regards the legislation relating to the preparation of the financial statements helps the owner-manager ensure that the relevant statutory obligations have been complied with.

AUDITING

ISA 300: Planning

108. When the auditor assists in the preparation of the financial statements, sufficient flexibility is required in the overall audit plan to take account of any areas of audit risk identified, and evidence obtained in performing those services. The auditor of a small entity therefore plans to take into consideration knowledge obtained from the accounting services so that the approach to obtaining evidence is properly co-ordinated and that efficiency of work and cost can be secured.

ISA 400: Risk Assessments and Internal Control

109. In performing accounting services, the auditor may obtain an understanding of the accounting and internal control system. This may indicate that there are certain internal controls that the auditor may wish to assess and test, which may in turn affect the nature, timing and extent of substantive procedures required for the audit.

ISA 500: Audit Evidence

110. The auditor of a small entity when providing accounting services, applies professional judgment in considering whether the other services rendered result in a reduction in the audit work necessary to support the auditor's opinion. Accounting services will seldom provide all, and may not even provide any, of the audit evidence required by the auditor. In particular, accounting services will ordinarily do no more than provide *some* of the necessary evidence regarding the completeness of a population, or the value at which items are stated in the financial statements. However, audit evidence can often be obtained at the same time that the accounting work is done. Specific audit work will ordinarily be required, for example, on the recoverability of debtors, the valuation and ownership of inventories, the carrying value of fixed assets and investments and the completeness of creditors.

ISA 520: Analytical procedures

111. In small entities where the auditor has been engaged to perform accounting services, analytical procedures carried out at the planning stage of the audit will be more effective if some of the accounting services to be performed by the auditor have been completed before the audit planning is finalized.

ISA 540: Audit of Accounting Estimates

112. Although the owner-manager is responsible for determining the amount of the estimate to be included in the financial statements, the auditor of a small entity is often asked to assist with or advise on the preparation of any accounting estimates. By assisting with the process of preparing the accounting estimate, the auditor at the same time gains evidence relevant to meeting the requirements of ISA 540. However, assisting with this process does not relieve the auditor from obtaining sufficient and appropriate audit

evidence regarding the reasonableness and appropriateness of the underlying assumptions used in arriving at the estimates.

ISA 550: Related parties

113. When assessing the risk of undisclosed related party transactions, the auditor takes account of any related party matters arising when providing any assistance on matters such as the following.

- Keeping the accounting records.

- Preparing the financial statements (in particular any statutory disclosures required concerning loans and other transactions with directors and connected persons).

- Personal and corporate tax matters.

- Compiling and reviewing owner-manager's current accounts.

114. This, taken together with information obtained through discussion with the owner-manager, assists in the assessment of the risk in this area and may provide a reasonable basis for the risk to be assessed as low.

115. This assistance and the close relationship between the auditor and the owner-manager can assist in the identification of related parties, which, in most instances, will be with entities controlled by the owner-manager.

ISA 570: Going Concern

116. In some small entities, the auditor may be asked to assist the owner-manager with the assessment of going concern and sometimes with the preparation of any necessary budgets or forecasts. In all cases, the owner-manager remains responsible for the assessment of going concern for any information prepared (even if the auditor assisted in its compilation), and for the reasonableness of the assumptions on which it is based. In such circumstances, the auditor takes appropriate steps to obtain the owner-manager's agreement, and acknowledgment of responsibility.

ISA 580: Management Representations

117. In the audit of a small entity, it is particularly important for the auditor to obtain management representations in which the owner-manager acknowledges responsibility for the fair presentation of the financial statements. This is particularly necessary where the auditor has assisted in drafting the financial statements, because of the danger of the auditor's role and responsibility in relation to the financial statements being misunderstood. In order to ensure that the representations are meaningful, the auditor considers explaining these matters to management before the representations are obtained.

AUDITING

CONTENTS

Paragraphs

1. Introduction 1.1–1.7

2. **Audit Objectives and the Audit Process**

   The objectives 2.1–2.3
   The process 2.4–2.5

3. **Defining the Terms of the Engagement** 3.1–3.3

4. **Planning the Audit**

   Introduction 4.1–4.2
   Gaining a knowledge of the client 4.3–4.12
   Development of an overall audit plan 4.13–4.26
   Co-ordinating the work to be performed 4.27–4.28

5. **Establishing the Degree of Reliance on Internal Control**

   Introduction 5.1
   Identifying, documenting and testing control procedures 5.2–5.12
   Examples of controls 5.13
   Inherent limitations of internal control 5.14
   Considering the influence of environmental factors 5.15
   Determining the nature, timing and extent of substantive
      tests 5.16–5.19

6. **Performing Substantive Procedures**

   Introduction 6.1–6.2
   Audit techniques 6.3–6.10
   Specific substantive procedure considerations 6.11–6.29

7. **Reporting on the Financial Statements** 7.1–7.3

Appendices

Examples of Internal Control Checklists to Assist in Assessing
   Three Typical Areas of a Bank's Operations   I

Examples of Financial Ratios Commonly Used in the Analysis of
   Bank Financial Condition and Performance   II

Examples of Substantive Audit Procedures for the Evaluation of
   Loan Loss Provisions   III

This Statement has been prepared by the International Auditing Practices Committee (IAPC) of the International Federation of Accountants after consultation with the Basle Committee on Banking Supervision* (formerly known as the Committee on Banking Regulations and Supervisory Practices). It was approved for publication by the IAPC at its meeting in November 1989. It has a common release date of February 1990.

The purpose of this Statement is to provide practical assistance to auditors in the audit of international commercial banks. It is not intended to have the authority of an International Standard on Auditing.

---

*The Basle Committee on Banking Supervision comprises representatives of the central banks and supervisory authorities of the Group of Ten countries (Belgium, Canada, France, Germany, Italy, Japan, Netherlands, Sweden, Switzerland, United Kingdom and United States) and Luxembourg. The supervisory authorities of the countries represented on the Basle Committee attach considerable importance to thorough and reliable standards of external audit. However, there are considerable differences in the way in which individual supervisory authorities use the work of auditors in their supervisory arrangements. Some authorities have specific regulations relating to the scope of the audit and the suggestions made in this Statement are not intended to limit or alter those arrangements but it is hoped that they will be helpful guidance where auditors and supervisors are involved together in the supervisory process.

1. Introduction

1.1 The International Auditing Practices Committee (IAPC) of the International Federation of Accountants (IFAC) issues standards (ISAs) on generally accepted auditing practices and on related services and on the form and content of the auditor's reports. These standards are intended to improve the degree of uniformity of auditing practices and related services throughout the world. The purpose of this Statement is to provide additional guidance to auditors by amplifying and interpreting these standards in the context of the audit of international commercial banks. It is not, however, intended to be an exhaustive listing of the procedures and practices to be used in such an audit.

1.2 For the purpose of this Statement:

- a bank is a type of financial institution that is recognized as a bank by the regulatory authorities in the countries in which it operates and usually has the exclusive right to use the term "bank" as part of its name;

- a commercial bank is a bank whose primary function is the acceptance of deposits and the making of loans. A commercial bank will often also offer other financial services such as the purchase and sale of precious metals, foreign currencies and a wide range of financial instruments, the issuance and acceptance of bills of exchange and the issuance of guarantees; and

- an international commercial bank is a commercial bank which has operating offices in countries other than the country of its incorporation or whose activities transcend national boundaries.

1.3 While this Statement is primarily directed to the audits of international commercial banks, it has relevance also to the audits of commercial banks which operate solely in one country. The term "bank" is henceforth used in this Statement to mean an international commercial bank.

1.4 Banks have the following characteristics which generally distinguish them from most other commercial enterprises:

- They have custody of large volumes of monetary items, including cash and negotiable instruments, whose physical security has to be assured. This applies both to the storage and the transfer of monetary items and makes banks vulnerable to misappropriation and fraud. They therefore need to establish formal operating procedures, well defined limits for individual discretion and rigorous systems of internal control.

- They engage in a large volume and variety of transactions both in terms of number and value. This necessarily requires complex accounting and internal control systems and widespread use of electronic data processing.

- They normally operate through a wide network of branches and departments which are geographically dispersed. This necessarily involves a greater decentralization of authority and dispersal of accounting and control functions, with consequent difficulties in maintaining uniform operating practices and accounting systems, particularly when the branch network transcends national boundaries.

- They often assume significant commitments without any transfer of funds. These items, normally called "off-balance-sheet" items, may not involve accounting entries and consequently the failure to record such items may be difficult to detect.

- They are regulated by governmental authorities and the resultant regulatory requirements often influence generally accepted accounting principles and auditing practices within the industry.

1.5   Special audit considerations arise in the audits of banks because of:

- the particular nature of the risks associated with the transactions undertaken by banks;

- the scale of banking operations and the resultant significant exposures which can arise within short periods of time;

- the extensive dependence on computerized systems to process transactions;

- the effect of the regulations in the various jurisdictions in which they operate; and

- the continuing development of new products and banking practices which may not be matched by the concurrent development of accounting principles and auditing practices.

1.6   In many countries banks undertake activities which are not strictly banking activities and which may not be restricted to banks. These activities include insurance, securities brokerage and leasing services. This Statement is not intended to provide guidance in the audit of such activities.

1.7   This Statement is organized into a discussion of the various stages of the audit of a bank with emphasis being given to those matters which are either peculiar to or of particular importance in such an audit. Also included for illustrative purposes are appendices which contain examples of:

- typical internal control procedures likely to exist in three of the major operating areas of a bank, being the lending, foreign exchange trading and trust activities;

- financial ratios commonly used in the analysis of a bank's financial condition and performance; and

- substantive audit procedures for the evaluation of loan loss provisions.

2.   Audit Objectives and the Audit Process

The objectives

2.1   ISA 200 "Objective and General Principles Governing an Audit of Financial Statements" states:

> The objective of an audit of financial statements is to enable the auditor to express an opinion whether the financial statements are prepared, in all material respects,

in accordance with an identified financial reporting framework.

2.2 The basic objective of the audit of a bank is therefore to render an opinion based on ISAs or relevant national standards or practices established within the country ("relevant auditing standards") on the bank's annual financial statements which are prepared in accordance with IASs or relevant national standards ("relevant accounting principles"), to the extent they are applicable to banks.

2.3 The auditor of a bank is also often required to make special purpose reports to banking supervisory and other regulatory authorities. The requirements for such reports vary significantly between countries and this Statement is not intended to provide guidance in the discharge of the auditor's responsibilities for such reports.

The process

2.4 In carrying out the work required to form an opinion on a bank's financial statements, the auditor's work will be divided into several distinct phases, as contemplated in the ISAs.

2.5 A schematic representation of these phases is as follows:

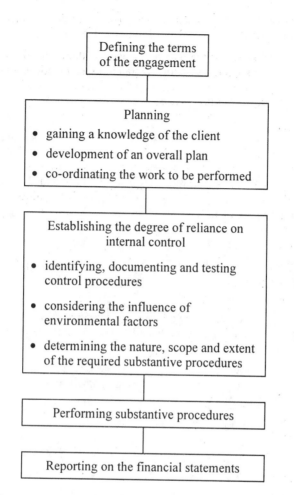

3. Defining the Terms of the Engagement

3.1 As stated in ISA 210 "Terms of Audit Engagements":

> The engagement letter documents and confirms the auditor's acceptance of the appointment, the objective and scope of the audit, the extent of the auditor's responsibilities to the client and the form of any reports.

3.2 In considering the objective and scope of the audit and the extent of his responsibilities, the auditor needs to assess his own skills and competence and that of his staff to conduct the engagement. In making such an assessment, the auditor should consider the following factors:

- the availability of sufficient expertise in the aspects of banking relevant to the audit of the business activities of the bank;

AUDITING

- the adequacy of expertise in the context of the computer information systems (CIS) and electronic funds transfer (EFT) systems used by the bank; and

- the adequacy of resources and/or inter-firm arrangements to carry out the work necessary at the number of domestic and international locations of the bank at which audit procedures are likely to be required.

3.3 In issuing an engagement letter, the auditor should, in addition to the general factors set out in ISA 210 "Terms of Audit Engagements," consider including comments on the following:

- the use and source of specialized accounting principles, with particular reference to:

  - any requirements contained in the law or regulations applicable to banks;

  - pronouncements of the banking supervisory and other regulatory authorities and relevant professional accounting bodies; and

  - industry practice;

- the contents and format of any special purpose reports required in addition to the annual financial statements, including the application of special purpose accounting principles and/or special purpose auditing procedures; and

- the nature of any special reporting relationships that may exist between the auditor and the banking supervisory and other regulatory authorities.

4. Planning the Audit

Introduction

4.1 ISA 300 "Planning" states:

> The auditor should plan the audit work so that the audit will be performed in an effective manner.

Plans should be made to cover, among other things:

- obtaining a sufficient knowledge of the client's business and a sufficient understanding of the accounting and internal control systems;

- assessing the level of audit risk which includes the risk that material misstatements will occur (inherent risk), the risk that the client's system of internal control will not prevent or detect such misstatements (control risk), and the risk that any remaining material misstatements will not be detected by the auditor (detection risk);

- determining and programming the nature, timing and extent of the audit procedures to be performed; and

- considering of the going concern assumption regarding the entity's ability to continue in operation for the foreseeable future, generally for a period not exceed one year after the balance sheet date.

Plans should be further developed and revised as necessary during the course of the audit.

4.2   ISA 300 "Planning" and ISA 310 "Knowledge of the Business," amplify that principle, primarily in the context of recurring audits.

Gaining a knowledge of the client

4.3   Acquiring a knowledge of the bank's business will require the auditor to understand:

- the economic and regulatory environment prevailing for each of the countries in which the bank operates; and

- the market conditions existing in each of the sectors in which the bank operates.

4.4   Similarly the auditor will need to acquire and maintain a good working knowledge of the products and services offered by the bank. In acquiring and maintaining that knowledge, the auditor needs to be aware of the many variations in the basic deposit, loan and treasury services that are offered and continue to be developed by banks in response to market conditions. To do so, the auditor needs to understand the nature of services rendered through instruments such as letters of credit, acceptances, interest rate future, forward and swap contracts, and other similar instruments in order to understand the inherent risks and accounting implications thereof.

4.5   Often a bank's loan portfolio has large concentrations of credits to highly specialized industries such as real estate, shipping and natural resources. Evaluating the nature of these may require a knowledge of the business and reporting practices of those industries.

4.6   There are a number of risks associated with banking activities which, while not unique to banking, are sufficiently important in that they serve to shape banking operations. An understanding of the nature of these risks is fundamental to the auditors' planning process as it enables the auditor to evaluate the inherent risk associated with different aspects of a bank's operations and assists in determining the degree of reliance on internal control and the nature, timing and extent of his audit procedures.

AUDITING

4.7   The risks associated with banking activities can be broadly grouped into:

- product and service risks; and

- operating risks.

Some of the important risks in both categories are discussed in subsequent paragraphs.

Product and service risks

4.8   The most significant product and service risk in a bank is usually credit risk, which is the risk that a customer or counterparty will not settle an obligation for full value, either when due or at any time thereafter. Credit risk also includes:

• country or transfer risk	— the risk of foreign customers and counterparties failing to settle their obligations due to economic, political and social factors of the foreign country and external to the customer or counterparty;
• replacement risk	— the risk of failure of a customer or counterparty to perform the terms of a contract. This failure creates the need to replace the failed transaction with another at the current market price. This may result in a loss to the bank equivalent to the difference between the contract price and the current market price; and
• settlement risk	— the risk that one side of a transaction will be settled without value being received from the customer or counterparty. This will result in the loss to the bank of the full principal amount.

To address credit risk, banks have complex and comprehensive systems and procedures devoted to the various aspects of the credit function, including those activities relating to:

- origination and disbursement;

- monitoring;

- collection; and

- periodic review and evaluation.

4.9   A large portion of the audit effort will typically be devoted to assessing credit risk and in this regard, the auditor needs to be aware that credit risk will also exist in assets other than loans, such as investments and balances due from other banks and also in off-balance sheet commitments.

4.10 Other product and service risks include:

- interest rate risk — the risk of loss arising from the sensitivity of earnings to future movements in interest rates.

  It comprises two elements, being:

  a. income risk, which is the risk of loss arising when movements in borrowing and lending rates are not perfectly synchronized; and

  b. investment risk, which is the risk of loss arising from a change in the value of fixed income securities as a result of interest rate changes.

- liquidity risk — the risk of loss arising from the possibility of the bank not having sufficient funds to meet its obligations;

- currency risk — the risk of loss arising from movements in the exchange rates applicable to foreign currency assets, liabilities, rights and obligations;

- market risk — the risk of loss arising from movements in market prices of investments; and

- fiduciary risk — the risk of loss arising from factors such as failure to maintain safe custody or negligence in the management of assets on behalf of other parties.

4.11 Banking product and service risks increase with the degree of concentration of a bank's exposure to any one customer, industry, geographic area or country.

Operating risks

4.12 Operating risks, primarily arise out of:

- the need to process high volumes of transactions accurately within short time-frames. This need is almost always addressed through the use of large-scale CIS, with the resultant risks of:

  – failure to process executed transactions within required time-frames, causing an inability to receive or make payments for those transactions;

  – wide-scale error arising from a breakdown in internal control;

  – loss of data arising from system failure;

  – corruption of data arising from unauthorized interference with the system; and

AUDITING

411

- exposure to market risks arising from lack of reliable up-to-date financial information.

- the need to use EFT systems to transfer ownership of large volumes of money, with the resultant risk of exposure to loss arising from mispayments through fraud or error;

- the conduct of operations in a number of locations with a resultant geographic dispersion of transaction processing and internal controls. As a result:

  - there is a risk that the bank's worldwide exposure by customer and by product may not be adequately aggregated and monitored; and

  - control breakdowns may occur and remain undetected and uncorrected because of the physical separation between management and those who handle the transactions.

- the need to monitor and manage significant exposures which can arise over short time-frames. The process of clearing transactions may cause a significant build-up of receivables and payables during a day, most of which are completed by the end of the day. This is usually referred to as intra-day payment risk. The nature of these exposures can arise from transactions with customers and counterparties and can include interest rate, currency and market risks;

- the dealing in large volumes of monetary items, including cash, negotiable instruments and transferable customer balances, with the resultant risk of loss arising from theft and fraud by employees or other parties;

- the use of high gearing (i.e., high debt-to-equity ratios), which results in the exposure to:

  - the risk of significant erosion of capital resources as a result of a relatively small percentage loss in asset value;

  - the risk of being unable to obtain the funds required to maintain operations at a reasonable cost as a result of a loss of depositor confidence; and

- the inherent complexity and volatility of the environment in which banks operate, resulting in the risk of inappropriate risk management strategies in relation to such matters as the development of new products and services.

- the need to adhere to laws and regulations. The failure to do so could result in exposure to sanctions in the nature of fines or operating restrictions.

Development of an overall audit plan

4.13 In developing an overall plan for the audit, the auditor needs to give particular attention to:

- the assessment of materiality;

- the assessment of audit risk;

- the expected degree of reliance on internal control;

- the extent of CIS and EFT systems used by the bank;

- the work of internal audit;

- the complexity of the transactions undertaken by the bank and the documentation in respect thereof;

- the existence of significant areas of audit concern not readily apparent from the bank's financial statements;

- the existence of related party transactions;

- the involvement of other auditors;

- management's representations; and

- the work of supervisors.

These matters are discussed in subsequent paragraphs.

Materiality

4.14 In making an assessment of materiality, in addition to the considerations set out in ISA 320 "Audit Materiality," the auditor must keep in mind that:

- because of high gearing, relatively small errors may have a significant effect on the statement of earnings and on capital, though they may have an insignificant effect on the balance sheet itself;

- as the net income of a bank is low when compared to its gross assets and liabilities and its off balance sheet commitments, errors which relate only to assets, liabilities and commitments may be less significant than those which could also relate to the statement of earnings; and

- banks are often subject to regulatory requirements, such as the requirement to maintain minimum levels of capital. It would therefore be necessary to set materiality levels which should identify errors and audit differences which, if uncorrected, would result in a significant contravention of such regulatory requirements.

Audit Risk

4.15 The three components of audit risk as defined in ISA 400 "Risk Assessments and Internal Control," and as amplified in ISA 320 "Audit Materiality" are:

- inherent risk (the risk that material errors will occur);

- control risk (the risk that the bank's system of internal control will not prevent or correct such errors); and

- detection risk (the risk that any remaining material errors will not be detected by the auditor).

413

The risks associated with banking activities as discussed in paragraphs 4.7 to 4.12 indicate that the inherent risk in most cases will be fairly high. It is therefore necessary to ensure through an adequate system of internal control that the control risk is kept at a low level.

Inherent and control risks exist independently of the audit of financial information and cannot be controlled by the auditor. However, he can assess these risks and so design his substantive procedures as to produce an acceptable level of detection risk.

The extent of CIS and EFT systems

4.16   The high volume of transactions and the short time-frames in which they must be processed typically result in the extensive use by most banks of CIS and EFT systems.

The characteristics and control concerns arising from the use of CIS by a bank are similar to those arising when such systems are used by other organizations. However, the matters which are of particular concern to the auditor of a bank include:

- the use of CIS to calculate and record substantially all the interest income and interest expense, which are normally the two most important elements in the determination of a bank's earnings;

- the use of CIS to determine the foreign exchange and security trading positions and to calculate and record the gains and losses arising therefrom; and

- the extensive, almost total, dependence on the records produced by the CIS because they represent the only readily accessible source of detailed up-to-date information on the bank's assets and liability positions, such as customer loan and deposit balances.

EFT systems are used by banks both internally, for example, for transfers between branches and between automated banking machines and the central computerized file which records account activity, and externally between the bank and other financial institutions, for example, through the SWIFT network.

In order to properly evaluate the system of internal control and to determine the nature, timing and extent of the substantive audit procedures, the auditor needs to be aware of the extent and manner in which CIS and EFT systems are used by the banks.

Reliance on internal control

4.17   In forming his audit opinion, the auditor generally cannot rely solely on the results of his substantive tests because of:

- the high volume of transactions entered into by banks;

- the manner in which transactions are entered into by banks;

- the geographic dispersion of banks' operations; and

- the extensive use of CIS and EFT systems.

In most situations the auditor will therefore need to place significant reliance on the bank's system of internal control. To do so he will need to make a careful evaluation of the system to assess the degree of reliance he can place upon the same in determining the nature, timing and extent of his other audit procedures.

The work of internal audit

4.18   While the scope and objectives of internal audit can vary widely depending upon the size and structure of the bank and the requirements of the board of directors and its management, its role normally includes the review of the accounting system and related internal controls and monitoring their operation and recommending improvements thereto. It also generally includes a review of the means used to identify, measure and report financial and operating information and specific inquiry into individual items including detailed testing of transactions, balances and procedures. The factors which often require the auditor to place significant reliance on the bank's system of internal control, will also often require the auditor to use the work of the internal auditor. This is especially relevant in the case of banks which have a large geographic dispersion of branches. Often, as a part of the internal audit department or as a separate component, a bank has a loan review department which reports to management on the quality of loans and the adherence to established procedures in respect thereof. In either case, the auditor will often wish to make use of the work of this department. Detailed guidance on the use of the work of an internal auditor is provided in ISA 610 "Considering the Work of Internal Auditing."

The complexity of transactions undertaken

4.19   Banks undertake transactions which have complex and important underlying features which may not be apparent from the documentation which is used to process the transactions and to enter them into the bank's accounting records. This results in the risk that all aspects of a transaction may not be fully or correctly recorded, with the resultant risks of:

- loss due to the failure to take timely corrective action;

- failure to record adequate provisions for loss on a timely basis; and

- inadequate or improper disclosure in the financial statements and other reports.

Accordingly, the auditor needs to acquire a good understanding of the nature of the transactions and the types of documentation he will need to examine.

The existence of significant areas of audit concern not readily apparent

4.20   Banks also typically engage in transactions which:

AUDITING

- have a low fee revenue or profit element as a percentage of the principal exposure; and
- may not be required by local regulations to be disclosed in the balance sheet, or even in the notes to the financial statements.

Examples of such transactions are guarantees, comfort letters and letters of credit, interest rate and currency swaps and commitments and options to purchase and sell foreign exchange.

4.21   The auditor should review the bank's sources of revenue, assess the related systems of internal control and perform sufficient procedures to obtain reasonable assurance regarding:

- the completeness of the accounting records relating to such transactions;
- the existence of proper controls to limit the banking risks arising from such transactions;
- the adequacy of any provisions for loss which may be required; and
- the adequacy of any financial statement disclosures which may be required.

Related party transactions

4.22   The auditor needs to be particularly aware of the risk that where transactions with related parties exist, normal measures of banking prudence, such as credit assessment and the taking of security, may not be appropriately exercised. Management is responsible for the identification and disclosure of related parties. The auditor needs to perform procedures to obtain reasonable assurance that:

- all significant related parties and related party transactions are identified;
- all such transactions, including their terms and conditions, are properly authorized and appropriately recorded and disclosed in the bank's financial statements; and
- the resultant balances outstanding are collectible.

The auditor also needs to be aware of any regulatory guidance or restrictions on related party transactions. ISA 550 "Related Parties," defines related parties and provides detailed guidance as to the issues to be considered and the procedures to be performed in respect of related parties.

Involvement of other auditors

4.23   As a result of the wide geographic dispersion of offices in most banks, it will often be necessary for the auditor to employ the services of other auditors in a number of the locations in which the bank operates. This is most likely to be achieved through the use of other offices of the auditor's firm or through the use of other auditing firms in those locations.

4.24   Where the auditor is relying on the work of another auditor, he will need to:

- be satisfied as to the independence of those auditors and their competence to undertake the necessary work (including their knowledge of banking);

- ensure that the terms of the engagement, the accounting principles to be applied and the reporting arrangements are clearly communicated; and

- perform procedures to obtain reasonable assurance that the work performed by the other auditor is adequate for his purpose by discussion with the other auditor, by a review of a written summary of the procedures applied and findings, by a review of the working papers of the other auditor, or in any other manner appropriate to the circumstances.

ISA 600 "Using the Work of Another Auditor" provides more detailed guidance on the issues to be addressed and procedures to be performed in such situations.

Management's representations

4.25   Management's representations are relevant in the context of a bank audit to assist the auditor in determining whether the information and evidence produced to him is complete for the purposes of his examination. This is particularly true of the bank's transactions which are not normally reflected in the accounts, but which may be evidenced by other records of which the auditor may not be aware. It is often also necessary for the auditor to obtain from the management representations regarding significant changes in the bank's business and its risk profile and also to identify areas of a bank's operations where audit evidence likely to be obtained may need to be supplemented by management's representations. ISA 580 "Management Representations" provides guidance as to the use of management representations as audit evidence, the procedures that the auditor should apply in evaluating and documenting them, and the circumstances in which representations should be obtained in writing.

The work of supervisors

4.26   There are many tasks performed by auditors and bank supervisors which are common in nature, including:

- the performance of analytical procedures;

- the obtaining of assurance regarding the existence of a satisfactory internal control structure; and

- the review of the quality of a bank's assets and the assessment of banking risks.

The auditor would therefore find it advantageous to interact with the supervisors and to have access to communications which the supervisors may have addressed to the bank management on the results of their work. The assessment made by the supervisors in important areas such as the adequacy of provisions for bad and doubtful loans and the prudential ratios used by the supervisors can be of assistance to the auditor in performing analytical reviews and in focusing attention on specific areas of supervisory concern.

AUDITING

The International Auditing Practice Statement 1004 "The Relationship Between Bank Supervisors and External Auditors" issued in July 1989 by the IAPC in association with the Basle Committee provides information and guidance on the relationship between bank auditors and supervisors.

Co-ordinating the work to be performed

4.27 Given the size and geographic dispersion of most banks, the co-ordination of the work to be performed will be important in achieving an efficient and effective audit. The co-ordination required should take into account the following factors:

- the work to be performed by:

  - various members of the auditor's staff;
  - other offices of the auditor's firm; and
  - other audit firms;

- the extent to which it is proposed to use the work of the internal auditor;

- required reporting dates to shareholders and the regulatory authorities; and

- the need for any special analyses and other documentation to be provided by bank management.

4.28 The best level of co-ordination between senior staff involved in the audit can often be achieved by audit planning and regular audit-status meetings. However, given the number of staff involved in the audit and the number of locations at which they will be involved, the auditor will usually find it most effective to communicate all or relevant portions of the audit plan in writing. When setting out his requirements in writing, the auditor should consider including commentary on the following matters:

- the financial statements and other information which is to be subjected to audit (and if considered necessary, the authority under which the audit is being conducted);

- details of any additional information needed by the auditor [e.g., information on certain loans, portfolio composition, narrative commentary on the audit work performed (especially on the areas of risk described in paragraphs 4.7 to 4.12 which are important to the bank) and on the results of the operation, points for inclusion in letters to management on internal control, local regulatory concerns, income tax assessment status reports], and if relevant, the formats of any required reports;

- the relevant auditing standards to be applied to the work conducted (and, if considered necessary, information on those standards);

- the relevant accounting principles to be followed in the preparation of the financial statements and other information (and, if considered necessary, the details of those principles);

- interim audit status reporting requirements and deadlines;

- particulars of clients' officials to be contacted;

- fee and billing arrangements; and

- any concerns of a regulatory, internal control, accounting or audit nature of which the local auditor should be aware.

5. Establishing the Degree of Reliance on Internal Control

Introduction

5.1 Management's responsibilities include the maintenance of adequate accounting records and internal controls, the selection and application of accounting policies, and the safeguarding of the assets of the entity.

The auditor should obtain a sufficient understanding of the accounting and internal control systems to plan the audit and develop an effective audit approach. After obtaining the understanding, the auditor should consider the assessment of control risk to determine the appropriate detection risk to accept for the financial statement assertions and to determine the nature, timing and extent of substantive procedures for such assertions.

Where the auditor assesses control risk at a lower level, substantive procedures would normally be less extensive than would otherwise be required and may also differ as to their nature and timing.

Identifying, documenting and testing control procedures

5.2 ISA 400 "Risk Assessments and Internal Control" sets out four objectives of internal controls, as follows:

- transactions are executed in accordance with management's general or specific authorization;

- all transactions and other events are promptly recorded in the correct amount, in the appropriate accounts and in the proper accounting period so as to permit preparation of financial statements in accordance with an identified financial reporting framework;

- access to assets is permitted only in accordance with management's authorization; and

- recorded assets are compared with the existing assets at reasonable intervals and appropriate action is taken regarding any differences.

In the case of banks, a further objective is to ensure that the bank adequately fulfills its fiduciary responsibilities arising out of its trustee activities.

The audit considerations in relation to each of these objectives are discussed in the subsequent paragraphs.

"Transactions are executed in accordance with management's general or specific authorization."

5.3 The primary responsibility for the control structure in a bank rests with the board of directors and its committees which are responsible for governing the

AUDITING

bank's operations. However, since the operations of banks are generally large and geographically dispersed, decision-making functions need to be decentralized and the authority to commit the bank to material transactions is usually dispersed geographically and delegated among the various levels of management and staff. Such dispersion and delegation will almost always be found in the lending, treasury and funds transfer functions, where, for example, payment instructions are sent via a tested message. This feature of banking operations creates the need for a structured system of delegation of authority, resulting in the formal identification and documentation of:

- employees who can authorize specific transactions;

- procedures to be followed in granting that authorization; and

- limitations on the amounts that can be authorized, by individual employee and/or by staff level, as well as any requirements that may exist for concurring authorization.

It also creates the need to ensure that appropriate procedures exist for monitoring the level of exposures. This will usually involve the aggregation of exposures, not only within, but across the different activities, departments and offices of the bank.

5.4   An examination of the authorization controls will be important to the auditor in satisfying himself that transactions have been entered into in accordance with the bank's policies and, for example, in the case of the lending function, that they have been subject to appropriate credit assessment procedures prior to the disbursement of funds. The auditor will typically find that limits for levels of exposures will exist in respect of various transaction types. The auditor will wish to ensure that these limits are reasonable, are being adhered to and that positions in excess of these limits are reported to the appropriate level of management on a timely basis.

5.5   From an audit perspective, the proper functioning of a bank's authorization controls will be particularly important in respect of transactions entered into near the date of the financial statements, where aspects of the transaction will have yet to be fulfilled, or where there is a lack of evidence on which to assess the value of the asset acquired or liability incurred. Examples of such transactions are commitments to purchase or sell specific securities after the year-end and loans, where principal and interest payments from the borrower have yet to fall due.

"All transactions and other events are promptly recorded in the correct amount, in the appropriate accounts and in the proper accounting period so as to permit preparation of financial statements in accordance with an identified financial reporting framework."

5.6   In assessing the appropriateness of the individual internal controls used to ensure that all transactions are properly recorded, the auditor will need to take into account a number of factors which are especially important in a banking environment. These are as follows:

- Banks deal in large volumes of transactions, which can individually and cumulatively involve large amounts of money. Accordingly, the bank will need to have balancing and reconciliation procedures which are operated within a time-frame that provides the ability to detect errors and discrepancies so that they can be investigated and corrected with a minimal risk of loss to the bank. Such procedures may be operated hourly, daily, weekly, or monthly, depending on the volume, nature of the transaction, level of risk, and transaction settlement time-frame.

- Many of the transactions entered into by banks are subject to specialized accounting rules. It will therefore be necessary to have control procedures in place to ensure those rules are applied in a manner and in a time-frame which results in the generation of accounting entries that may be required for the preparation of appropriate financial information for management and external reporting. Examples of such control procedures are those which result in the market revaluation of foreign exchange and security purchase and sale commitments so as to ensure that all unrealized profits and losses are recorded.

- Many transactions entered into by banks are not disclosed in the balance sheet or even in the notes to the financial statements. Accordingly, control procedures must be in place to ensure that such transactions are recorded and monitored in a manner which provides management with the required degree of control over them and which allows for the prompt determination of any change in their status which needs to result in the recording of a profit or loss.

- New financial products and services are constantly being developed by banks. The auditor needs to obtain reasonable assurance that necessary revisions are made in accounting procedures and related internal controls.

- End of day balances may not be indicative of the volume of transactions processed through the systems or of the maximum exposure to loss during the course of a business day. This is particularly relevant in executing and processing foreign exchange and securities transactions. Assessment of controls in these areas must take into account the ability to maintain control during the period of maximum volumes or maximum financial exposure.

- The majority of banking transactions must be recorded in a manner which is capable of being verified both internally and by the bank's customers and counterparties. The level of detail to be recorded and maintained on individual transactions must allow for bank management, transaction counterparties, and the bank's customers to verify the accuracy of the amounts. An example of such a control is the continuous verification of foreign exchange trade tickets by having an independent employee match them to incoming confirmations from counterparties.

5.7　The extensive use of CIS and EFT systems will have a significant effect on how the auditor evaluates a bank's accounting system and related internal controls. ISA 400 "Risk Assessments and Internal Control," and International Auditing Practice Statement 1008 "Risk Assessments and Internal Control—CIS Characteristics and Considerations," provide guidance on the CIS aspects of such an evaluation. In carrying out his study and evaluation of the CIS, the auditor will need to ensure that his procedures include an assessment of those controls which affect system development and modifications, system access and data entry, the security of communications networks, and contingency planning. To the extent that the use of EFT is within the bank, similar considerations will apply. To the extent that the EFT systems are external to the bank, the auditor will need to give additional emphasis to the assessment of the integrity of pre-transaction supervisory controls and post-transaction confirmation and reconciliation procedures.

"Access to assets is permitted only in accordance with management's authorization."

5.8   The assets of a bank are often readily transferable, of high value and of a form which cannot be safeguarded solely by physical procedures. In order, therefore, to ensure that access to assets is permitted only in accordance with management's authorization, a bank generally uses controls such as:

- passwords and joint access arrangements to limit CIS and EFT system access to authorized employees;

- segregation of the record-keeping and access functions (including the use of computer generated transaction confirmation reports available immediately and only to the employee in charge of the record-keeping functions); and

- frequent third-party confirmation and reconciliation of asset positions by an independent employee.

5.9   The auditor will need to obtain reasonable assurance that each of these controls is operating effectively. However, given the materiality and transferability of the amounts involved, he will also usually wish to review and/or participate in the confirmation and reconciliation procedures that occur in connection with the preparation of the year-end financial statements.

"Recorded assets are compared with the existing assets at reasonable intervals and appropriate action is taken regarding any differences."

5.10   The large amounts of assets handled by banks, the volumes of transactions undertaken, the potential for changes in the value of those assets due to fluctuations in market prices and the importance of confirming the continued operation of access and authorization controls will necessitate the frequent operation of reconciliation controls. This will have particular importance in regard to:

- assets in negotiable form, such as cash, bearer securities and assets in the form of deposit and security positions with other institutions where failure to detect errors and discrepancies on a timely basis (which may be daily where money market transactions are involved) could lead to an irrecoverable loss. The reconciliation procedures used to achieve this control objective will normally be based on physical counting and third party confirmation; and

- assets whose value is determined with reference to external market prices, such as securities and foreign exchange contracts.

5.11　In designing an audit strategy to assess the effectiveness of a bank's reconciliation controls, the following factors should be considered:

- Because of the number of accounts requiring reconciliation and the frequency with which these reconciliations need to be performed:

  - a large portion of the audit effort will need to be directed to the documentation, testing and evaluation of the reconciliation controls; and

  - the work of the internal auditor will also be similarly directed. The auditor therefore can usually make use of the work of the internal auditor.

- Since reconciliations are cumulative in their effect, most reconciliations can be satisfactorily audited at the year-end date, assuming that they are prepared as at that date, within a time-frame useful to the auditor and that the auditor is satisfied that the reconciliation control procedures are effective.

- The auditor needs to obtain reasonable assurance in examining a reconciliation that items have not been improperly transferred to other accounts which are not subject to reconciliation and investigation in the same time-frame.

"Fiduciary duties are adequately fulfilled"

5.12　The main objectives of internal control with regard to the fiduciary activities of a bank are to ensure that:

- all duties arising from fiduciary relationships are adequately fulfilled; and

- all assets in the bank's custody, arising from fiduciary relationships are adequately safeguarded and properly recorded.

An essential feature of the system is the proper segregation of fiduciary assets from the bank's own assets and the discharge of fiduciary responsibilities by a separate department or by a subsidiary of the bank.

Examples of controls

5.13　Appendix 1 to this Statement contains examples of controls over authorization, recording, access and reconciliation normally found in the credit, foreign exchange trading and trust activities of a bank.

Inherent limitations of internal control

5.14　ISA 400 "Risk Assessments and Internal Control" describes the procedures to be followed by the auditor in identifying, documenting and testing internal controls. In doing so, the auditor should be aware of the inherent limitations of internal control and of the fact that in the context of a bank's operations there may be transactions which are of such a size and importance to the bank's financial statements that reliance on the results of testing internal control alone cannot replace the need to have actual inspection of the underlying documentation.

AUDITING

Considering the influence of environmental factors

5.15 In assessing the effectiveness of specific control procedures, the auditor should consider the environment in which internal control operates. Some of the factors which may be considered are:

- the organizational structure of the bank and the manner in which it provides for the delegation of authority and responsibilities;

- the quality of management supervision;

- the extent and effectiveness of the internal audit system;

- the quality of key personnel; and

- the degree of inspection by supervisory authorities.

Determining the nature, timing and extent of substantive tests

5.16 As a result of his evaluation of the system of internal control, the auditor should be in a position to determine the nature, timing and extent of the substantive tests to be performed on individual account balances and other information contained in the bank's financial statements. The risks and factors that served to shape the bank's systems of internal control will need to be considered by the auditor in designing these substantive tests. In addition, there are a number of audit considerations significant to these risk areas to which the auditor should direct his attention. These are discussed in subsequent paragraphs.

5.17 In addressing the audit considerations affecting product and service risks, the auditor should consider the need to:

- physically examine, confirm and reconcile negotiable items as of the year-end date;

- specifically test balances which are individually significant through procedures such as examinations of underlying documentation and third-party confirmations; and

- examine post year-end transactions and events for evidence of impairment of value at the year-end date.

5.18 In addressing the audit considerations affecting operating risks, the auditor should consider the need to:

- carry out certain tests prior to the year-end in order to complete the audit on a timely basis;

- use computer-assisted audit techniques such as the use of interrogation software to achieve the desired extent of testing in the time-frame available;

- use statistical sampling techniques where there are a large number of homogeneous accounts or transactions of which the auditor wishes to examine a representative sample;

- use analytical review techniques to detect conditions of audit concern. This may be more cost efficient than to test a satisfactory sample of items;

- be satisfied as to the appropriate reconciliation of asset and liability accounts with counterparties (i.e., nostro and vostro accounts with other banks) so as to provide assurance on the propriety and accuracy of completed transactions with those counterparties;

- establish a basis of reliance on the work of the internal auditor as a means of obtaining satisfactory coverage both geographically and in terms of the extent of transaction and account balance coverage;

- ensure that audit staff and representatives conducting examinations at other locations of the bank are appropriately instructed and that the results of their work are properly reviewed;

- ensure that all significant principal positions and related unrealized profits and losses have been recorded;

- be satisfied as to the viability of the bank by considering evidence of factors such as funding difficulties which could call into question the going-concern assumption;

- assess the implications on the bank's financial position of non-compliance with regulatory rules and guidelines; and

- assess the implications on the bank's position of non-compliance with its fiduciary duties, with particular reference to those duties relating to the safekeeping of assets held in trust.

5.19   The above considerations generally determine the specific substantive procedures to be carried out by the auditor. These are further discussed in Section 6.

6.   Performing Substantive Procedures

Introduction

6.1   The nature, timing and extent of the specific substantive procedures to be performed on the financial statement balances will be based on the auditor's assessment of inherent and control risk.

6.2   As stated in ISA 500 "Audit Evidence":

> Substantive procedures means tests performed to obtain audit evidence to detect material misstatements in the financial statements and are of two types:
>
> (a)   tests of details of transactions and balances; and
>
> (b)   analytical procedures.

425

1006

ISA 500 "Audit Evidence" goes on to state:

> When obtaining audit evidence from substantive procedures, the auditor should consider the sufficiency and appropriateness of audit evidence from such procedures together with any evidence from tests of control to support financial statement assertions.
>
> Financial statement assertions are assertions by management, explicit or otherwise, that are embodied in the financial statements. They can be categorized as follows:

Existence	— an asset or a liability exists at a given date
Rights and Obligations	— an asset or a liability pertains to the entity at a given date
Occurrence	— a transaction or event took place which pertains to the entity during the period
Completeness	— there are no unrecorded assets, liabilities, transactions or events, or undisclosed items
Valuation	— an asset or liability is recorded at an appropriate carrying value
Measurement	— a transaction or event is recorded at the proper amount and revenue or expense is allocated to the proper period
Presentation and Disclosure	— an item is disclosed, classified, and described in accordance with the applicable, financial reporting framework

Audit techniques

6.3 To address the assertions discussed above, the auditor will find that the procedures particularly important to the examination of a bank's accounts are:

- analytical procedures;

- inspection; and

- inquiry and confirmation.

A discussion of their application in a bank audit context is contained in the following paragraphs:

Analytical Procedures

6.4   As defined by ISA 500 "Audit Evidence," analytical procedures consist of the analysis of significant ratios and trends including the resulting investigation of fluctuations and relationships that are inconsistent with other relevant information or deviate from predicted amounts.

6.5   A bank will invariably have individual assets (e.g., loans and, possibly, investments) which are of such a size that the auditor will wish to examine their documentation individually. However, in respect of most items, the use of analytical procedures techniques will prove to be a particularly important and useful procedure for the following reasons:

- Normally the two most important elements in the determination of a bank's earnings are interest income and interest expense. These have direct relationships to interest bearing assets and interest bearing liabilities, respectively. To establish the reasonableness of these relationships, the auditor can examine the degree to which the reported income and expense vary from the amounts calculated on the basis of average balances outstanding and the bank's stated rates during the year. This examination would usually be made in respect of the categories of assets and liabilities used by the bank in the management of its business. Such a study could, for example, highlight the existence of significant amounts of non-performing loans. In addition, the auditor may also wish to assess the reasonableness of the stated rates to those prevailing in the market during the year for similar classes of loans and deposits. Evidence of rates charged or allowed above market rates may, in the case of loan assets, indicate the existence of excessive risk, or, in the case of deposit liabilities, may indicate liquidity or funding difficulties. Similarly, fee income which is also a large component of a bank's earnings, will often bear a direct relationship to the volume of obligations on which the fees have been earned.

- The accurate processing of the high volume of transactions entered into by a bank and the need for the auditor to rely on the continued and appropriate operation of the bank's internal controls can benefit from the review of ratios and trends and of the extent to which they vary from previous periods, budgets and the results of other similar entities.

- The analytical review of account composition is an important method by which the auditor can detect certain conditions of audit concern, such as undue concentration of risk of particular industries or geographic areas and potential exposure to interest rate, currency and maturity mismatches.

AUDITING

- In most countries there is widespread availability of statistical and financial information available from regulatory and other sources which the auditor can use to conduct an in-depth analytical review of trends and peer group analyses.

Appendix 2 to this Statement contains examples of the most frequently used ratios in the banking industry.

Inspection

6.6   As defined by ISA 500 "Audit Evidence," inspection consists of examining records, documents, or tangible assets. The auditor inspects in order to:

- satisfy himself as to the physical existence of negotiable assets available with the bank; and

- ensure he has the necessary understanding of the terms and conditions of agreements which are significant individually or in the aggregate in order to:

    – assess their enforceability; and

    – be satisfied as to the appropriateness of the accounting treatment they have been given.

6.7   Examples of areas where inspection is used as an audit technique are:

- bullion;

- securities;

- loan agreements;

- commitment agreements, such as:

    – asset sales and repurchases

    – guarantees.

6.8   In carrying out inspection procedures, the auditor should be particularly vigilant regarding the existence of assets held in a fiduciary capacity. He needs to obtain reasonable assurance that adequate internal controls exist for the proper segregation of such assets from those which are the property of the bank.

Inquiry and Confirmation

6.9   As defined by ISA 500 "Audit Evidence," inquiry consists of seeking information of knowledgeable persons inside or outside the entity. Confirmation consists of the response to an inquiry to corroborate information contained in the accounting records. The auditor inquires and confirms in order to:

- obtain evidence of the operation of internal controls;

- obtain evidence of the recognition by the bank's customers and counterparties of amounts, terms and conditions of certain transactions; and

- obtain information not immediately available from the bank's accounting records.

Due to the existence in a bank of significant amounts of monetary assets and liabilities and of off-balance-sheet commitments, confirmation of balances often proves to be relatively the safest and most practical method of determining the existence and completeness of the amounts of assets and liabilities disclosed in the financial statements.

6.10   Examples of areas for which the auditor may use confirmation, either as a compliance or a substantive audit procedure, are:

- collateral security positions on specific loans;
- asset, liability and forward purchase and sale positions with customers and counterparties such as:
    - outstanding foreign exchange transactions;
    - nostro and vostro accounts;
    - securities held by third parties;
    - loan accounts;
    - deposit accounts;
    - guarantees; and
    - letters of credit.

Specific substantive procedure considerations

6.11   Paragraphs 6.13 to 6.29 identify the audit objectives which are usually of particular importance in relation to the typical items in a bank's financial statements. They also describe some of the audit considerations which would be helpful to the auditor in planning his substantive procedures and suggest some of the techniques which could be used in relation to the items selected by the auditor for his examination.

6.12   In addition to the specific financial statement items addressed in paragraph 6.13 to 6.29, the auditor will need to consider the audit procedures required in connection with the bank's fiduciary activities in the context of their effect on the bank's financial statements. In conducting such procedures, the auditor will need to obtain reasonable assurance that:

- all the bank's income from such activities has been recorded and is fairly stated in the bank's financial statements;
- the bank has not incurred any material liability from a breach of its fiduciary duties, including the safekeeping of assets; and
- in the event that the bank discloses the nature and extent of its fiduciary activities in the notes to its financial statements, that such information is fairly stated.

AUDITING

Financial Statement Item	Audit Objectives and Considerations of Particular Importance

6.13

Bullion

Existence

Because bullion is generally similar in appearance and hence easily interchangeable, the auditor should consider the need for confirmation or physical inspection and tests of reconciliations of the results of physical counts to the accounting records of the amounts held by the bank on its own account and on behalf of customers. As an understanding of the circumstances under which bullion may be held by a bank is necessary to an understanding of how it is accounted for, the audit considerations that relate to the verification of its existence are commented on in conjunction with the discussion below of Rights and Obligations.

Rights and Obligations

Where a bank holds bullion on behalf of customers, the auditor will encounter two possible sets of circumstances, being;

1. The bullion held on behalf of customers is "allocated" (i.e., the bullion received on deposit is specifically identified and the depositor is entitled to have the identified bullion returned—this is equivalent to a fiduciary arrangement); or

2. the bullion held on behalf of customers is "unallocated" (i.e., the bullion received on deposit is not specifically identified but the bank acknowledges receipt of the bullion by general description, specification and weight and the depositor is not entitled to have the specific bullion returned—this is equivalent to a deposit of money, which the bank will in turn attempt to lend to customers requiring loans denominated in bullion).

Where the bank holds bullion on its own account (i.e., as a result of its own dealing position) and also on behalf of customers, the auditor will be concerned to ensure that the bullion of each party has been appropriately segregated and accounted for.

When the bullion held on behalf of customers is held in common custody with the bank's own bullion, the bank will need to ensure there has been a physical count of the bullion on hand and a reconciliation of the results of that count to the accounting records of the amounts held by the bank on its own account and on behalf of customers.

When the bullion held on behalf of customers is held in separate custody, the auditor will need to obtain reasonable assurance as to the adequacy of the system of internal control, failing which, he will need to ensure there has been a physical count and reconciliation as described above.

Where the bank has a dealing position in bullion, the audit considerations will be generally similar to those discussed with respect to foreign exchange (see 6.17).

However, in establishing the physical existence of the bank's bullion position, the auditor needs to be aware that some portion of the bank's "long" positions may be in the custody of other banks or bullion dealers and that the bank may have itself "borrowed" and sold bullion from the unallocated bullion deposits of customers, thereby creating "short" positions.

6.14

Balances with other banks

Existence

The auditor should consider the need for third-party confirmation of the balance. Because the balances held with other banks will usually be the result of large volumes of transactions, the receipt of confirmations from those other banks is likely to provide more conclusive evidence as to the existence of the transactions and of the resultant inter-bank balances than is the testing of the related internal controls. Guidance on inter-bank confirmation procedures, including terminology and the content of confirmation requests, can be found in the International Auditing Practice Statement 1000 "Inter-Bank Confirmation Procedures."

Valuation

The auditor should consider whether there is a need to assess the collectability of the deposit in light of the credit-worthiness of the depository bank. The procedures required in such an assessment will be similar to those used in the audit of loan valuation, discussed later.

AUDITING

Presentation and Disclosure

The auditor should consider whether the balances with other banks as at the date of the financial statements are representative of bona-fide commercial transactions or whether any significant variation from normal or expected levels is indicative of transactions entered into primarily to give a misleading impression of the financial position of the bank and/or to improve liquidity and asset ratios (often known as "window-dressing").

Where window-dressing occurs in a magnitude which may distort the true and fair view of the financial statements, the auditor may consider the need for the adjustment of the balances shown on the financial statements, additional disclosure in the notes, or qualification in the audit report.

6.15

Money market paper

Existence

The auditor should consider the need for physical inspection and confirmation with external custodians and the reconciliation of these related amounts with the accounting records.

Rights and Obligations

The auditor should consider the feasibility of checking for receipt of the related income as a means of establishing ownership.

The auditor should examine for the existence of sale and forward repurchase agreements for evidence of unrecorded liabilities and losses.

Valuation

The auditor should consider the appropriateness of the valuation techniques employed, in light of the creditworthiness of the issuer.

Measurement

The auditor should consider whether there is a need to ensure that income earned on money market instruments, which in some cases will be through the amortization of a purchase discount, has been accrued.

6.16

Trading securities

Existence

The auditor should consider the need for physical inspection of securities and confirmation with external custodians and the reconciliation of these amounts with the accounting records.

Rights and Obligations

The auditor should consider the feasibility of checking for receipt of the related income as a means of establishing ownership. The auditor should examine for the existence of sale and forward repurchase agreements for evidence of unrecorded liabilities and losses.

Valuation

Since trading securities are normally carried at market value or at the lower of cost and market value, the auditor should ensure that securities whose market value has increased are not arbitrarily transferred from the Investment Account (see 6.18) primarily so that an unrealized gain can be taken into income.

6.17

Other financial assets

(a) **those involving a current investment of funds** (e.g., blocks of loans purchased for resale, purchases of securitized assets such as mortgage backed securities)

Rights and Obligations

The auditor should examine the underlying documentation supporting the purchase of such assets in order to ensure that all rights and obligations, such as warranties and options, have been properly accounted for.

Completeness

Due to the continuing development of new financial instruments, there is often a lack of established procedures between participants and within the bank. Many of these transactions are entered into orally, with written documentation being completed subsequently, and therefore, the auditor should assess the adequacy of the system of internal control, particularly with respect to:

AUDITING

- the adequacy of the procedures and the division of duties regarding the matching of documentation received from counterparties and reconciliation of accounts with counterparties; and

- the adequacy of internal audit review.

The auditor will also find it useful to examine post year-end transactions for evidence of items that should have been recorded in the year-end financial statements.

Valuation

The auditor should consider the appropriateness of the valuation techniques employed. Since there may not be established markets for such assets, it may be difficult to obtain independent evidence of value. Additionally, even where such evidence exists, there may be a question as to whether there is sufficient depth to existing markets to rely on quoted values for the asset in question and for any related offsetting hedge transactions which the bank has entered into in those markets.

Presentation and Disclosure

Since many of the items included in this category of assets could, in accordance with relevant accounting principles, also be included in other asset categories, the auditor should consider whether such assets have been included in the appropriate financial statement item.

(b) those not involving the current investment of funds, being:

those involving the option or commitment to purchase an asset (e.g., securities and foreign currencies)

Rights and Obligations

The auditor should examine the underlying documentation supporting such transactions in order to ensure that all rights and obligations, such as warranties and options, have been properly accounted for.

Completeness

Similar considerations as applicable to item a) above will arise.

Valuation

In addition to the audit considerations mentioned in a) above, which are also applicable to this item,

those involving the option or commitment to deposit funds

– those involving the option or commitment to exchange future payments or receipts (e.g., interest rate swaps)

the following additional considerations would arise:

- Where market values need to be considered, but are not available, the auditor should ensure that appropriate alternative valuation techniques have been employed, based, where appropriate, on current interest or foreign exchange rates.

- As many of these instruments have been developed only recently, the auditor should examine their valuation with a special degree of caution, and in doing so should bear in mind the following factors:

  – in most cases the enforceability of the terms in the underlying agreements cannot be evaluated against legal precedents, as such precedents may not have been established;

  – as there are normally relatively few employees involved in managing the portfolio of such instruments, there will be a relatively small number of management personnel who are familiar with the inherent risks of these instruments; and

  – most of these instruments will not have existed through a full economic cycle (bull and bear markets, high and low interest rates, high and low trading and price volatility) and it may therefore be more difficult to assess their value with the same degree of certainty as for more established instruments. Additionally, for the same reason, it may be difficult to predict with any degree of certainty the price correlation with other offsetting instruments used by the bank to hedge its positions.

Measurement

The auditor should satisfy himself as to the purpose for which the transaction resulting in the instrument was entered into, namely whether the bank was dealing as principal to create a dealing position or as principal, intermediary or broker for hedge purposes. The purpose will determine the appropriate accounting treatment.

Since settlement of such transactions is at a future date, the auditor should consider whether a profit or loss has arisen to date.

The auditor should be particularly vigilant for reclassification of hedging and trading trans-

AUDITING

actions/positions which may have been made primarily with a view to taking advantage of differences in the timing of profit and loss recognition.

Presentation and Disclosure

In some countries the relevant accounting principles will require the recording of accrued gains and losses on open positions, whether or not these positions are recorded on the balance sheet. In other countries there is only an obligation to disclose the commitment. Where the latter is the case, the auditor should consider whether the unrecorded amounts are of such significance as to require a disclosure in the financial statements and/or qualification in the audit report.

6.18	**Presentation and Disclosure**
Investments (long-term)	The auditor should consider whether the stated objectives at the time such securities are purchased and subsequent trading activity in those securities provides support for their classification as long-term investments or whether they should more properly be classified as "trading securities."

(a) Marketable

Valuation

Where securities have been transferred from the Trading Account, the auditor should ensure that any unrealized losses in market value are recorded if so required by relevant accounting principles.

(b) Non-marketable

Valuation

The auditor should examine the value of the assets supporting the security value.

The auditor also should consider the implications of any legal or practical requirement for the bank to provide future financial support to ensure the maintenance of operations (and hence the value of the investment) of subsidiaries and associated companies. In certain cases there will be a need to ensure that the related financial obligations are recorded as liabilities of the bank.

The auditor should ensure that appropriate adjustments are made when the accounting policies of companies which are accounted for on an equity basis or are consolidated do not conform to those of the bank.

6.19

Loans

(comprising advances, bills of exchange, letters of credit, acceptances, guarantees, and all other lines of credit extended to customers, including those in connection with foreign exchange and money market activities)
- personal
- commercial
- government

   – domestic
   – foreign

Valuation

The major audit concern is the adequacy of the recorded provision for loan losses.

In establishing the nature, extent and timing of the work to be performed, the auditor should consider the following factors:

- The degree of reliance it is reasonable to place on the bank's system of loan quality classification, on its procedure for ensuring that all documentation is properly completed, on its internal loan review procedures and on the work of the internal auditor.

- Given the relative importance of foreign lending, there is also usually a need for the auditor to examine:

  – the information on the basis of which the bank assesses and monitors the country risk and the criteria (e.g., specific classifications and valuation ratios) it uses for this purpose;

  – whether and, if so, by whom credit limits are set for the individual countries, what they are and the extent to which they are being utilized; and

  – how the foreign loans are distributed by country.

- The composition of the loan portfolio, with particular attention to:

  – the concentration of loans to specific:

    • borrowers and parties connected to them (including the procedures in place to identify such "connections");

    • commercial and industrial sectors;

    • geographic regions; and

    • countries;

  – the size of individual credit exposures (few large loans versus numerous small loans);

  – the trends in loan volume by major categories, especially categories having exhibited rapid

AUDITING

growth, and in delinquencies, non-accrual and restructured loans; and

– related party lending.

- Identified potential problem loans, with particular attention to:

    – the previous loss and recovery experience, including the adequacy and timeliness of provisions and charge-offs; and

    – results of regulatory examinations.

- Local, national and international economic and environmental conditions, including restrictions on the transfer of foreign currency which may affect the repayment of loans by borrowers.

In addition to those problem loans identified by management and, where applicable, by bank regulators, the auditor should consider additional sources of information to determine those loans which may not have been so identified. These include:

- various internally generated listings, such as "watchlist" loans, past due loans, loans on non-accrual status, loans by risk classification, loans to insiders (including directors and officers), and loans in excess of approved limits;

- historical loss experience by types of loan; and

- those loan files lacking current information on borrowers, guarantors or collateral.

6.20

Accounts with depositors, including:

(a) General deposits

Completeness

Given the volume and value of deposit transactions, the auditor should assess the adequacy of the related system of internal control and perform confirmation and analytical review procedures on average balances and on interest expense to assess the reasonableness of the recorded deposit balances.

Presentation and Disclosure

The auditor should ensure that deposit liabilities are classified in accordance with regulations and relevant accounting principles.

Where deposit liabilities have been secured by specific assets, the auditor should consider the need for appropriate disclosure.

The auditor should also consider the need for disclosure where the bank has a funding risk due to economic dependence on a few large depositors or where there is an excessive concentration of deposits due within a specific time-frame.

(b) Items in transit

Existence

The auditor should ensure that items in transit between branches, between the bank and its consolidated subsidiaries and between the bank and counterparties are eliminated and that reconciling items have been appropriately addressed and accounted for.

Additionally, the auditor should examine individual items comprising the balance which have not been cleared within a reasonable time period and should also consider whether the related internal control procedures are adequate to ensure that such items have not been temporarily transferred to other accounts in order to avoid their detection.

6.21

Capital and reserves

Presentation and Disclosure

The auditor should ensure that capital and reserves are adequate for regulatory purposes (e.g., to meet capital adequacy requirements) and that disclosure is both appropriate and in accordance with legal requirements.

In addition, where applicable regulations provide for restrictions on the distribution of retained earnings, the auditor should assess whether they are adequately disclosed.

The auditor should also determine whether the requirements of the International Accounting Standards or local regulations with respect to the disclosure of hidden reserves have been complied with (see also paragraph 7.3).

AUDITING

439

6.22

Contingencies and Commitments

(e.g., commitments to lend funds and to guarantee repayment of funds by customers to third parties)

Completeness

Because most commitments and contingencies are often not recorded in the bank's accounting records, the auditor should:

- identify those activities which have the potential to generate contingent liabilities;

- ascertain, with regard to these activities whether the bank's system of internal control is adequate, particularly with regard to the records maintained for such obligations to ensure that contingent liabilities arising out of such activities are properly identified and recorded and that evidence is retained of the customer's agreement to the related terms and conditions;

- perform substantive audit tests to establish the completeness of the recorded obligations. Such tests could include confirmation procedures as well as examination of related fee income in respect of such activities and would be determined having regard to the degree of risk attached to the particular type of contingency being considered;

- review the reasonableness of the year-end contingency figures in the light of his experience and his knowledge of the current year's activities; and

- obtain representation from management that all contingent liabilities have been recorded.

Valuation

As many of these transactions are either credit substitutes or depend for their completion on the credit-worthiness of the counterparty, the risks associated with such transactions are in principle no different from those associated with "Loans." The audit objectives and considerations of particular importance discussed in paragraph 6.19 would be equally relevant in respect of such transactions.

Presentation and Disclosure

Although relevant accounting principles will usually require disclosure of such obligations in the notes to the financial statements rather than in the balance sheet, the auditor should nevertheless consider the potential financial impact on the bank's capital, funding and profitability of the need to honor such obligations and whether this needs to be specifically disclosed in the financial statements.

6.23

Interest income and interest expense

Measurement

Given the large volume of loans and deposits on which interest income and expense are calculated as well as the variations in interest rates between various categories of loans and deposits and over time, there is a need to:

- obtain reasonable assurance that satisfactory procedures exist for the proper accounting of accrued income and expenditure at the year-end;

- assess the adequacy of the related system of internal control; and

- utilize analytical review techniques in assessing the reasonableness of the reported amounts.

Such techniques include comparison of reported interest yields in percentage terms:

- to market rates;

- to prime rates;

- to advertised rates (by type of loan or deposit); and

- between portfolios.

In making such comparisons, it is important to ensure that average rates in effect (e.g., by month) are used in order to avoid distortions caused by interest rate volatility.

The auditor also needs to assess the reasonableness of the policy applied to income recognition on troubled loans, especially where such income is not being received on a current basis.

6.24

Income from securities, including: gains and losses interest dividends

Measurement

The audit procedures in this area should be carried out in conjunction with Money Market Instruments, Trading Securities, Other Financial Instruments and Investments to ensure that:

- the correlation between securities owned and the related income is reasonable; and

- all significant gains and losses from sales and revaluations have been reported in accordance

AUDITING

with relevant accounting principles (e.g., where gains and losses on trading securities are treated differently from those on investment securities).

6.25

Provisions for loan losses

Measurement

The major audit concerns in this area are discussed above under "Loans." Usually, provisions will take two forms, namely specific provisions in respect of identified losses on individual accounts and general provisions to cover losses which are thought to exist but which have not been specifically identified. In those countries where levels of general provisions are prescribed by local regulations, the auditor should ensure that the reported provision expense is calculated in accordance with such regulations. In other countries the auditor should assess the adequacy of such general provisions based on such factors as past experience and other relevant information. Appendix 3 to this Statement contains examples of substantive audit procedures for the evaluation of loan loss provisions.

6.26

Gains and losses on foreign exchange

Measurement

Given the volume of transactions that are typically undertaken in this area, the auditor should assess:

- the adequacy of the related system of internal control, including the period-end reconciliation procedures, particularly in respect of the completeness and accuracy of the recording of outstanding positions as at the financial statement date (which will necessitate a familiarity by the auditor with the standard inter-bank transaction confirmation procedures);

- the appropriateness of the exchange rates used at the financial statement date to calculate accrued gains and losses; and

- the appropriateness of the accounting policies used having regard to relevant accounting principles particularly with regard to the distinction between realized and unrealized profits and losses.

Additionally, the auditor should ensure that individual foreign exchange contracts have been revalued, rather than foreign exchange positions, as such positions can include contracts maturing on varying dates at varying rates.

6.27

Fee and commission income

Measurement

The auditor should consider whether the fee and commission income recorded:

- relates to the period covered by the financial statements and that those amounts relating to future periods have been deferred;

- is collectible (this should be considered as part of the loan review audit procedures where the fee has been added to a loan balance outstanding);

- is accounted for in accordance with applicable regulatory instructions and relevant accounting principles; and

- is complete (i.e., all individual items have been recorded). In this respect, there may be a need to utilize analytical review techniques in assessing the reasonableness of the reported amounts.

6.28

Provision for taxes on income

Measurement

The auditor should be familiar with special taxation rules applicable to banks in the jurisdiction in which the bank on which he is reporting is located and also needs to ensure that any auditors on whose work he is relying in respect of the bank's foreign operations are similarly familiar with the rules in their jurisdiction. An awareness of the taxation treaties between the various jurisdictions in which the bank operates is also required.

6.29

Notes to the financial statements
(including, where applicable, a Statement of Accounting Policies)

Presentation and Disclosure

The auditor should ensure that the notes to the bank's financial statements are in accordance with both regulatory instructions and with relevant accounting principles, including International Accounting Standards.

Where such notes include information in respect of foreign operations of the bank, the auditor should ensure that appropriate audit procedures have been applied to that information and that the necessary adjustments have been made to ensure it conforms to the accounting principles followed by the preparation of the bank's financial statements.

AUDITING

7. Reporting on the Financial Statements

7.1 ISA 700 "The Auditor's Report on Financial Statements," states:

> The auditor should review and assess the conclusions drawn from the audit evidence obtained as the basis for the expression of an opinion on the financial statements. This review and assessment involves forming an overall conclusion as to whether:
>
> - the financial statements have been prepared using acceptable accounting policies, which have been consistently applied;
>
> - the financial statements comply with regulations and statutory requirements relating to the preparation of financial statements;
>
> - the view presented by the financial statements as a whole is consistent with the auditor's knowledge of the business of the entity; and
>
> - there is adequate disclosure of all material matters relevant to the proper presentation of the financial statements.

7.2 In rendering his opinion on the bank's financial statements, the auditor should consider the need to:

- adhere to specific formats, terminology and accounting principles as specified by the law, the regulatory authorities, professional bodies and industry practice; and

- ensure that adjustments have been made to the accounts of foreign branches and subsidiaries which are included in the consolidated financial statements of the bank to bring them into conformity with the accounting principles under which the bank is reporting. This is particularly relevant in the case of banks because of the large number of countries in which such branches and subsidiaries may be located and the fact that in most countries local regulations prescribe specialized accounting principles applicable primarily to banks. This could lead to a greater divergence in the accounting principles followed by branches and subsidiaries, than would be the case in respect of other business entities.

7.3 In some countries, local regulations permit banks to maintain hidden reserves. Where the existence of hidden reserves is not disclosed in the financial statements, the auditor should disclose this fact in his audit report. It is suggested that this may be accomplished by reference to the relevant statutes or law which permit the existence of hidden reserves.

Appendix 1

Examples of Internal Control Checklists to Assist in Assessing Three Typical Areas of a Bank's Operations:

• Foreign Exchange Trading
• Credit
• Trust Activities

A.   Foreign Exchange Trading

Operational controls

Does the bank have written policies which are in the hands of all dealers in respect of the following:

* prohibiting dealers from trading on their own account;

* identification of approved counterparties; and

* procedures for the review of dealers' activities by management?

Limits & Trading Activity

Does the bank have written policies established for intra-day and end-of-day limits:

* by currency;

* by counterparty;

* by maturity date; and

* by trader?

Recording

Does the bank have written policies in use to:

* spotlight unusually heavy dealing by a customer who may be experiencing financial difficulties;

* adequately disclose sudden increases in trading volume by any one trader, customer or counterparty; and

* adequately disclose transactions at unusual contract rates?

Does the bank have written procedures which require:

* prenumbered trade tickets to be allocated to each dealer;

* the accounting for all used and unused trade tickets;

AUDITING

- the prompt recording into the accounting records by an independent party of all transactions, including procedures to identify and correct rejected transactions;

- the daily reconciliation of dealer's positions and profits with the accounting records and the prompt investigation of all differences; and

- regular reports to management in appropriate detail to allow the monitoring of the limits referred to above?

Confirmations

Does the bank have written procedures in use:

- for the independent dispatch of prenumbered outward confirmations to counterparties for all trades entered into by the dealers;

- for the independent receipt of all incoming confirmations and their matching to pre-numbered copies of internal trade tickets;

- for independent comparison of signatures on incoming confirmations to specimen signatures;

- for the independent confirmation of all deals for which no inward confirmation has been received; and

- for the independent follow-up of discrepancies on confirmations received?

Position account maintenance

Does the bank have accounting records which allow it to prepare reports which show its spot, forward and net open and overall positions:

- by purchase and sale, by currency;

- by maturity dates, by currency; and

- by counterparty, by currency?

Are foreign exchange positions revalued periodically (e.g., daily) to current values based on quoted foreign exchange rates?

Settlement of transactions

Are settlement instructions exchanged in writing with counterparties by the use of inward and outward confirmations?

Are settlement instructions compared to the contracts?

Are settlements made only by appropriate authorized employees independent of the initiation and recording of transactions and only on the basis of authorized, written instructions?

Are all scheduled settlements (receipts and payments) notified daily in writing to the settlements department so that duplicate requests and failures to receive payments can be promptly detected and followed-up?

Are accounting entries either prepared from or checked to supporting documentation by operational employees, other than those who maintain records of uncompleted contracts or perform cash functions?

Account reconciliations

Are all nostro and vostro account reconciliations performed frequently and by employees independent of the settlement function?

B.   Credit

The credit function may conveniently be divided into the following categories:

(a)   origination and disbursement;

(b)   monitoring;

(c)   collection; and

(d)   periodic review and evaluation.

Within these categories, the key internal controls are as follows:

(a)   origination and disbursement:

- does the bank obtain complete and informative loan applications, including financial statements of the borrower and the intended use of proceeds;

- does the bank have written guidelines as to the criteria to be used in assessing loan applications (e.g., interest coverage, margin requirements, debt-to-equity ratios);

- does the bank obtain credit reports or have independent investigations conducted on prospective borrowers;

- does the bank have procedures in use to ensure that connected party lending has been identified;

- is there an appropriate analysis of customer credit information, including projected sources of loan servicing and repayments;

- are loan approval limits based on the lending officer's expertise;

- is appropriate lending committee or board of director approval required for loans exceeding prescribed limits;

- is there appropriate segregation of duties between the loan approval function and the loan disbursement monitoring, collection and review functions;

- is the ownership of loan collateral and priority of the security interest verified;

- is the documentation supporting the loan application reviewed and approved by an employee independent of the lending officer;

- is there a control to ensure the appropriate registration of security (e.g., recording of liens with governmental authorities);

- is there adequate physical protection of notes, collateral and supporting documents;

- is there a control to ensure that loan disbursements are recorded immediately; and

- is there a control to ensure that to the extent possible, loan proceeds are used by the borrower for the intended purpose?

(b) monitoring:

- are ledger trial balances prepared and reconciled with control accounts by employees who do not process or record loan transactions;

- are reports prepared on a timely basis of loans on which principal or interest payments are in arrears;

- are these reports reviewed by employees independent of the lending function;

- are there procedures in use to monitor the borrower's compliance with any loan restrictions (e.g., covenants) and requirements to supply information to the bank;

- are there procedures in place that require the periodic reassessment of collateral values;

- are there procedures in place to ensure that the borrower's financial position and results of operations are reviewed on a regular basis; and

- are there procedures in place to ensure that key administrative dates, such as the renewal of security registrations, are accurately recorded and acted upon as they arise?

(c) collection:

- are the records of principal and interest collections and the updating of loan account balances maintained by employees independent of the credit granting function;

- is there a control to ensure that loans in arrears are followed up for payment on a timely basis;

- are there written procedures in place to define the bank's policy for recovering outstanding principal and interest through legal proceedings, such as foreclosure or repossession; and

- are there procedures in place to provide for the regular confirmation of loan balances by direct written communication with the borrower by employees independent of the credit granting and loan recording functions, as well as the independent investigation of reported differences?

(d) periodic review and evaluation:

- are there procedures in place for the independent review of all loans on a regular basis, including:
  - the review of the results of the monitoring procedures referred to above; and
  - the review of current issues affecting borrowers in relevant geographic and industrial sectors?

- are there appropriate written policies in effect to establish the criteria for:
  - the establishment of loan loss provisions;
  - the cessation of interest accruals (or the establishment of offsetting provisions);
  - the valuation of collateral security for loss provisioning purposes;
  - the reversals of previously established provisions; and
  - the resumption of interest accruals?

- are the procedures in place to ensure that all required provisions are entered into the accounting records on a timely basis?

C. Trust Activities

Account Initiation and Authorization

Does the bank:

- have a committee in place to determine criteria for acceptance of new accounts and to set the fees thereon;

- utilize standard trust agreements to the extent possible and obtain legal advice, where necessary; and

- review the initial deposit of assets to ensure compliance with the trust agreement?

Does the bank have written policies available to all employees responsible for administration of trust assets in respect of the following:

- guidelines for investment decisions;

- listing of brokers and dealers with whom the trust is prepared to deal;

AUDITING

- conflict of interest and self-dealing;
- organizational charts and job descriptions of all employees within the trust function; and
- compliance with regulatory rules?

Monitoring

Does the bank have written procedures in use:

- to ensure on a periodic basis that the customer and the bank have complied with their obligations under the trust agreement;
- to ensure that assets acquired on behalf of a trust adhere to the trust agreement and relevant laws;
- to ensure appropriate approval of all investment decisions;
- to ensure the timely investment or distribution of trust funds;
- to ensure that any principal or income receivable by the trust has been collected, is in the process of collection or requires follow-up;
- to ensure that fees are calculated and charged at regular intervals in accordance with the trust agreement; and
- to ensure adequate review and supervision of the above procedures?

Safeguarding of Trust Assets

Does the bank have written procedures in use in respect of the following:

- joint custody and control over trust assets;
- adequate physical security over trust assets, including storage in locked, fireproof vaults;
- safeguarding of unissued stock or bond certificates;
- existence of an accurate and up-to-date listing of all assets under administration;
- periodic reconciliation of physical holdings of assets in the vault with accounting records, by employees independent of the recording or custody of trust assets; and
- adequate insurance coverage in relation to level of assets under administration?

Accounting

Does the bank:

- ensure that staff engaged on trust operations are distinct from staff engaged in other operations of the bank;
- ensure that trust records are adequately segregated from the records for transactions which the bank enters into on its own account;

- ensure the segregation of duties within the trust operations relating to initiation of transactions, authorization of transactions, custody of assets and maintenance of accounting records;

- maintain control accounts for cash balances relating to principal and income for each trust;

- ensure periodic reconciliations of all control and suspense accounts are performed by an employee independent of the receipts and disbursements functions;

- ensure daily posting of journals including detailed descriptions of principal and income transactions;

- have procedures to ensure appropriate classification of trust assets and income by trust account and nature of assets;

- have procedures in use to ensure appropriate classification of cash receipts between capital and income;

- regularly report the value of assets and income earned to the customer;

- monitor the receipt of income with that expected and follow-up on any differences; and

- have procedures in place to record accurately rights and bonus issues, stock dividends and stock splits?

Appendix 2

Examples of Financial Ratios Commonly Used in the Analysis of Bank Financial Condition and Performance

There are a large number of financial ratios which are used to analyze a bank's financial condition and performance. While these ratios vary somewhat between countries and between banks, their basic purpose tends to remain the same, that is, to provide measures of performance in relation to prior years, to budget and to other banks.

These ratios generally fall into the following categories:

- Asset quality;

- Liquidity;

- Earnings; and

- Capital adequacy.

Set out below are those overall ratios which the auditor is likely to encounter. Many other, more detailed ratios will usually be prepared by management to assist in the analysis of the condition and performance of the bank and its various categories of assets and liabilities, departments and market segments.

(a)   Asset quality ratios:

- loan losses to total loans

- non-performing loans to total loans

- loan loss reserves to non-performing loans

- earnings coverage to loan losses

- increase in loan loss reserves to gross income

(b)   Liquidity ratios:

- cash and liquid securities (e.g., those due within 30 days) to total assets

- inter-bank and money market deposit liabilities to total assets

(c)   Earnings ratios:

- return on average total assets

- return on average total equity

- net interest margin as a percentage of average total assets and average earning assets

- interest income as a percentage of average interest bearing assets

- interest expense as a percentage of average interest bearing liabilities

- non-interest income as a percentage of average commitments
- non-interest income as a percentage of average total assets
- non-interest expense as a percentage of average total assets

(d) Capital adequacy ratios:
- equity as a percentage of total assets
- equity as a percentage of risk assets

AUDITING

Appendix 3

Examples of Substantive Audit Procedures for the Evaluation of Loan Loss Provisions

1. The Examination of Loans, Individually and by Category

A. Introductory Comments

The review of individual loans is generally the most difficult task in the completion of a bank audit. It is also the most critical due to the level of risk and the effect of the provision for loan losses upon the financial position of the bank. In addition, the task of assessing loan collectability is one which demands the greatest amount of judgment and diligence from the auditor. It is therefore essential that the auditor be well prepared prior to commencing such a review.

The auditor must:

- Obtain an understanding of the bank's method of controlling risk. Such risks will arise from factors such as:

  - currency of the loan;
  - creditworthiness of the borrower;
  - purpose of the loan;
  - security for the loan;
  - nature of borrower's business activities; and
  - country of operation of the borrower.

- Obtain a knowledge and understanding of:

  - the bank's loan monitoring process, and its system for ensuring that all connected party lending has been identified and aggregated;
  - the bank's method for appraising the value of loan collateral and for identifying potential and definite losses;
  - the loan portfolio and the various features and characteristics of the loans;
  - the loan documentation used by the bank;
  - what constitutes appropriate loan documentation for different types of loans;
  - the bank's lending practices and customer base; and
  - the bank's procedures and authority levels for granting a loan.

The governing statutes and regulations under which the bank operates may specify the extent of the loan review process and any special reporting requirements to the regulatory authority. Consequently, these should be reviewed to identify any special reporting requirements which may affect the audit.

B. Audit Objectives

Within the context of the overall audit objective, the principal objective of the loan review is to ensure that loans receivable are appropriately valued and that loans requiring a provision for loss have been completely identified and provided for as necessary.

C. Audit Approach

The approach will generally be based upon year-end substantiation although the loan review is often performed before the year-end, with a review of the intervening period being performed at the year-end.

The procedures to be applied should apply not only to loans, but also extend to all other items for which the bank is at risk, whether recorded on or off balance sheet.

In addition to the provisions required against individual loans, a bank will normally need to consider the requirement for provisions in respect to certain categories of loans. Such provisions may be required, either in addition to specific provisions that may have been made against individual loans in the category, or in lieu of such specific provisions. Examples of categories in which an additional provision for loss may be required would be those relating to geographic or industry sectors, where overall concerns as to collectability exist but are not felt to be fully quantified by the provisions against the individual loans. Examples of categories in which a provision for loss may be required in lieu of specific provisions against the individual loans would be those relating to:

(a) categories of homogeneous loans, such as credit card loans and, perhaps, residential mortgages, where the small size of the individual loans may not warrant an item by item evaluation and historical experience may be deemed a satisfactory basis on which to provide for likely losses; and categories of loans, such as those to countries which are experiencing foreign exchange problems, where there is insufficient information available on which to establish specific provisions and where there may be alternative sources of guidance. Such guidance may be provided by:

– the bank's previous provisioning practice and loss experience;

– available information from the supervisors; or

– where such loans are held for disposal, secondary market prices.

In each of the above situations, the auditor will need to assess whether the provisions made in respect of each category are adequate in the light of the information available.

D. Sample substantive procedures

SAMPLE SUBSTANTIVE PROCEDURES

General

1. Record on the audit program the nature, extent and timing of the audit procedures, as determined by the degree of reliance that can be placed on internal controls, the materiality and volume of accounts, and the frequency of transactions, and the proposed degree of coordination of loan review procedures with those of internal audit. Consider performing the following procedures at an early validation date, with an update review to the year-end.

2. Obtain a copy of the bank's complete listing of loans as examined in the loans section of the working paper file.

3. Obtain a listing of definite and potential loan losses identifying the borrower, principal amount outstanding, accrued interest receivable and assessment of the amount of definite and potential loss. (This should be the same listing used in the loans section of the working paper file.) Consider requesting the assistance of an insolvency specialist in completing the review of selected loans.

Sample Selection Criteria

4. Before commencing the loan review, the following general factors should be reviewed for their effect on the sample selection criteria:

   - any change in the level of risk highlighted by a review of the bank's liquidity, interest rate and maturity mis-match and capital adequacy ratios over a longer period of time (e.g., 4 years) and a comparison to other similar financial institutions; and

   - any change in the bank's reliance on inter-bank deposits versus customer deposits, which may be indicative of a decline in external confidence and an over-dependence on more volatile money markets.

5. Consider any special requirements of the regulatory authorities (e.g., maximum limits on individual or connected exposures) and determine the sample selection criteria appropriate in the circumstances. Selection criteria should be applied to all connected party lending and should include the following (the sample size selected below in each case will vary with the selection criteria):

   - accounts with an outstanding balance equal to or greater than (sample size selected);

   - accounts on a "Watch List" with an outstanding balance in excess of (sample size selected);

   - accounts with a provision in excess of (sample size selected);

- accounts which are handled by the department that manages the bank's problem or higher risk accounts;
- accounts where principal or interest is in arrears for more than a specified period (sample size selected);
- accounts where the amount outstanding is in excess of the authorized credit line;
- problem accounts identified by the bank regulatory authorities and problem accounts selected in the prior year;
- degree of exposure to other financial institutions on inter-bank lines; and
- amount of participation in syndicated loans.

In addition, where the bank's personnel have been requested to summarize characteristics of all loans over a specified size grouped on a connection basis, review the summaries for loans with the following characteristics which may indicate a need for a more detailed review:

- large operating loss in the most recent fiscal year;
- sustained operating losses (e.g., 2 or more years);
- a high debt/equity ratio (e.g., in excess of 2:1 — the ratio will vary by industry, however);
- failure to comply with terms of agreement on covenants;
- negative comments by account manager as to:
  - trends and factors affecting performance;
  - company prospects; and
  - significant events such as restructuring of loans or failure to comply with debt covenants;
- qualified audit report;
- information provided not current or complete;
- advances significantly unsecured or secured substantially by a guarantee;
- accounts where reviews not performed by bank management on a timely basis in accordance with laid-down procedures; and
- groupings of accounts that may result in increased exposure (e.g., by currency, country, geographic location, connected group and industry).

Loan Review

6. Select the loans for detailed review from the loan listings above using the sample selection criteria determined in steps 4 and 5.

7. Obtain the documents necessary to assess the collectability of the loans. These may include:

    (a) the loan and security documentation files;

    (b) arrears listings or reports;

    (c) activity summaries;

1006

(d) previous doubtful accounts listings;

(e) the non-current loan report;

(f) financial statements of the borrower; and

(g) security valuation reports.

8. Using the loan documentation file, ascertain the loan type, interest rate, maturity date, repayment terms, security and purpose of the loan.

9. Ensure that security documents bear evidence of registration as appropriate, and that security has been obtained in a legally enforceable form. Determine whether the fair value of the security appears adequate (particularly for those loans where a provision may be required) to secure the loan and that where applicable, the security has been properly insured. Critically evaluate the collateral appraisals, including the appraiser's methods and assumptions.

10. Ensure that the loan application or renewal has been approved by the appropriate authority levels within the bank.

11. Review prior arrears listings and activity summaries and ascertain that the operating history of the loan is in accordance with the original terms of the loans.

12. Review periodic financial statements of the borrower and note significant amounts and operating ratios (i.e., working capital, earnings, shareholders' equity and debt-to-equity ratios).

13. Review any notes and correspondence contained in the loan review file. Note the frequency of review performed by the bank's staff and ensure that it is within bank guidelines.

14. Consider where applicable, the reports of the bank's internal loan review department.

15. Review correspondence and agreements for loans sold or participated by the bank. Ensure that there is no recourse to the bank, or if there is recourse, consider the loans for further review.

Loan Provisions

16. Based upon the information obtained in the preceding steps, evaluate the collectability of loans receivable and determine the need for a provision against the account.

17. Quantify the amount of the provision, identifying the specific loan where a provision is required. Provide details of the calculation of the provision.

18. Compare the amount of the provision to the amount established by the bank and quantify the difference. Summarize the amounts identified.

19. Obtain a listing of provisions established at the previous year-end and ensure all significant movements have been reviewed during the course of the loan review.

20. In addition to assessing the adequacy of the provisions against individual loans, consider whether any additional provisions need to be established

against particular categories or classes of loans (e.g., credit card loans and country risk loans) and assess the adequacy of any provisions that the bank may have established.

21. Discuss the results of the above procedures with management.

Conclusions

22. Based upon the preceding procedures, determine the appropriateness of the bank's provision for loan losses.

23. (a) Confirm that the accounting policies applied for determining loan loss provisions are consistent with those applied in the previous year, are in accordance with relevant accounting principles and are appropriately disclosed in the bank's financial statements.

    (b)   i)   State whether any exceptions were noted in steps 1 to 21 above;

        ii)   If so, confirm that they have been recorded on the working papers and that the nature and level of substantive procedures have been amended as necessary; and

        iii)   Confirm that all exceptions have been carried forward to the summary of unadjusted differences.

    (c)   i)   Consider whether the above substantive procedures have provided any evidence that the bank's loan loss provisions are not fairly stated in its accounts; and

        ii)   If there is such evidence, draw it to the attention of the audit manager and partner, along with the appropriate working paper references.

2. The Evaluation of the Overall Loan Loss Provision

After completing the examination of individual loans, the auditor should evaluate the adequacy of the overall loan loss provision in light of trends noted;

- in the examination of individual loans; and
- in the loan portfolio as a whole and in its components.

These trends can be categorized between those relating to quantitative information and those relating to qualitative information. Using these categorizations, the trends which the auditor may wish to consider are as follows:

(a) trends in quantitative information

    1. Information specifically relating to the bank:

        i) financial and statistical information for the current and prior years, compared to the loan portfolio as a whole and, where appropriate, to individual categories of loans (portfolios):

459

1006

- the level of provisions
- the actual loan loss experience.
- the level of non-accrual loans
- the level of work-outs
- the level of write-offs
- the level of loans in each of the bank's risk rating categories
- recoveries of prior years' provisions
- concentration of loans:
  - by industry
  - by geographic region
  - to specific borrowers and their related parties
- the level of differences in judgement on individual loans between management and the auditor

ii) information which may not be gathered by the bank in a quantitative manner:

- the absence of current financial data on the loan files (e.g., financial statements, appraisals of collateral)
- level of loans to borrowers experiencing financial difficulties
- level of dependence for collectability or relatively illiquid collateral
- frequency of increases in credit lines to troubled borrowers
- level of loans to borrowers exceeding approved credit lines
- frequency of extensions granted for the repayment of principal and interest.

2. Information which may be compared to data available for other banks:

the level of loan loss experience

the level of loan loss provisions in the statement of earnings.

3. Information on the countries in which the bank has credit risk:

gross national product

commodity (e.g., oil and foodstuff) prices

real estate prices/housing starts/commercial construction permits

interest rates

foreign exchange rates.

(b) trends in qualitative information

An outline of the factors the auditor might consider in an assessment of qualitative trends noted in the examination of individual loans is set out below:

- the expertise of credit management, including their industry knowledge;

- the extent of reliance by credit management on external evidence and expertise, particularly in the valuation of collateral; and

- the criteria used for classifying loans as non-accrual and for establishing provisions (e.g., the assumed "loan work-out" success ratio).

In practice, the specific trends which the auditor will consider and the extent to which they are considered and documented will depend on:

- the overall financial condition of the bank;

- the auditor's initial and ongoing assessment of risk (which will be influenced by factors such as the auditor's assessment of the inherent risk in the loan portfolio, the results of the examination of internal control and the review of the work of the internal auditor);

- the results of the examination of individual loans; and

- the degree of comfort the auditor has with management's judgments (usually as a result of previous audits and the above mentioned examinations of individual loans and, in some cases, on the results of the auditor's examination of other financial statement balances).

AUDITING

CONTENTS

	Paragraphs
Introduction	1-3
Legal and Professional Requirements	
Ethical Considerations	4-5
Terms of Audit Engagements	6-9
Management Representations	10-11
Communications With Management During the Audit	12-15
Communications With Management at the End of the Audit	16-18
Communications on Internal Control	19-23

The International Auditing Practices Committee approved this International Auditing Practice Statement in March 1994 for publication in July 1994.

This Statement is published to provide practical guidance to auditors with respect to the auditor's relationship with management. This document discusses that relationship, summarizes certain matters already contained

Introduction

1. A number of International Standards on Auditing (ISAs) refer to the auditor's relationship with management. This document, (which is an International Auditing Practice Statement, rather than an ISA) discusses that relationship, summarizes certain matters already contained in ISAs, and provides additional guidance.

2. Some aspects of the auditor's relationship with management are determined by legal and professional requirements. Others are governed by the auditor's internal procedures and practices. Auditors should have regard to such requirements, procedures and practices.

3. For the purposes of this Statement, 'management' comprises officers and others who also perform senior managerial functions. Management includes directors and the audit committee only in those instances where they perform such functions.

Legal and Professional Requirements

Ethical Considerations

4. During the audit of financial statements, it is necessary for an auditor to establish a constructive working relationship with management to achieve an effective and efficient audit. This should be achieved whilst observing certain ethical principles set by professional standards. These principles are contained in the Code of Ethics for Professional Accountants issued by the International Federation of Accountants. Such principles governing the auditor's professional responsibilities are:

    (a) independence:

    (b) integrity;

    (c) objectivity;

    (d) professional competence and due care;

    (e) confidentiality;

    (f) professional behavior; and

    (g) technical standards.

5. An auditor needs to be free, in fact and in appearance, of any interest in the performance of a professional assignment, which might be regarded as incompatible with ethical principles.

Terms of Audit Engagements

6. It is the interest of both client and auditor that the auditor sends an engagement letter which documents and confirms the auditor's acceptance of the appointment. The ISA 210 "Terms of Audit Engagements" provides guidance to auditors on this subject.

7. The engagement letter helps to avoid misunderstanding of the engagement terms, and forms the basis of a relationship between the auditor and client.

The form and content of audit engagement letters may vary for each client, but they generally include the following:

- The objective of the audit of financial statements.

- Management's responsibility for the financial statements.

- The scope of the audit, including reference to applicable legislation, regulations, or pronouncements of professional bodies to which the auditor adheres.

- The form of any reports or other communication of results of the engagement.

- The fact that because of the test nature and other inherent limitations of an audit, together with the inherent limitations of any accounting and internal control system, there is an unavoidable risk that some material misstatement may remain undiscovered.

- Access to whatever records, documentation and other information requested in connection with the audit.

There may be other matters to be included in the engagement letter; there are illustrations in ISA 210 "Terms of Audit Engagements" together with an example of such a letter.

8. Because agreement on the terms of the engagement and the extent of the auditor's responsibility are important, the auditor would normally request that an appropriate client representative confirm the terms by acknowledging receipt of the engagement letter.

9. On recurring audits the auditor may decide not to send a new engagement letter each period. It may be appropriate to remind the client of the original letter when the auditor decides a new engagement letter is unnecessary.

Management Representations

10. The ISA 580 "Management Representations" contains the standards and professional guidance dealing with management representations.

11. A management representation letter can provide:

- Evidence that management acknowledges its responsibility for the fair presentation of the financial statements in accordance with the relevant financial reporting framework, and has approved such financial statements.

- Written confirmation by management of significant representations made during the course of the audit, thus reducing the possibility of misunderstanding of oral representations made to the auditor.

- Written audit evidence when management representations would be the only evidence the auditor could reasonably be expected to obtain (for example, to corroborate management intention to hold a specific investment for long-term appreciation).

Communications With Management During the Audit

12. During the audit, the auditor will wish to discuss with management various matters including the following:

    - an understanding of the business;

    - the audit plan;

    - the effect of new legislation or professional standards on the audit;

    - information necessary for audit risk assessments;

    - explanations, evidence and representations from management or from a lower level in the organization;

    - any observations and suggestions arising from the audit on such matters as operational or administrative efficiencies, business strategies and other items of interest; and

    - unaudited information management is intending to publish with the audited financial statements which the auditor considers is inconsistent or appears to be misleading.

13. Such discussions are normally conducted during audit visits to the client, but may take place at other times.

14. When discussions are held for the purpose of obtaining audit evidence, the auditor needs to identify carefully the most appropriate person from whom to obtain audit evidence.

15. All important discussions with management should be documented in the auditor's working papers. Such documentation would include explanations and representations regarding material transactions.

Communications With Management at the End of the Audit

16. At the end of the audit the auditor will need to discuss with management matters such as:

    - any practical difficulties encountered in performing the audit;

    - any disagreements with management relating to the financial statements;

    - significant audit adjustments whether or not reflected in the financial statements;

    - significant concerns or problems relating to accounting policies and the disclosure of items in the financial statements that might lead to a modification of the audit report;

    - any irregularities or suspected noncompliance with laws and regulations which came to the attention of the auditor;

    - significant risks or exposures faced by the entity such as matters that have the potential to jeopardize the ability of the entity to continue as a going concern; and

AUDITING

- recommendations (for example, regarding internal control matters) that the auditor wishes to make as a result of the audit.

17. The auditor needs to communicate such matters to the appropriate level of management. The communication may be oral or written. If the communication is oral, the auditor documents communication in the working papers.

18. A specific meeting will usually take place at the end of the audit with the Board of Directors, audit committee or other senior management.

Communications on Internal Control

19. Recommendations regarding internal control are a byproduct of the financial statement audit, not a primary objective, but nonetheless should be of value to a client. The auditor needs to make management aware, on a timely basis, of material weaknesses in the design or operation of the accounting and internal control systems which have come to the auditor's attention.

20. When an auditor prepares a written communication on internal control matters, it is suggested that the communication:

- not include language that has the effect of being in conflict with the opinion expressed in the audit report;

- state that the accounting and internal control systems were considered only to the extent necessary to determine the auditing procedures to report on the financial statements and not to determine the adequacy of internal control for management purposes or to provide assurances on the accounting and internal control systems;

- state that it discusses only weaknesses in internal control which have come to the auditor's attention as a result of the audit and that other weaknesses in internal control may exist; and

- include a statement that the communication is provided for use only by management (or another specific named party).

21. After the above items and the auditor's suggestions for corrective action are communicated to management, the auditor usually ascertains the actions taken, including the reasons for those suggestions rejected. The auditor may encourage management to respond to the auditor's comments in which case any response can be included in the report.

22. The significance of findings relating to the accounting and internal control systems may change with the passage of time. Suggestions from previous years audits which have not been adopted, if any, should normally be repeated or referred to.

23. Communication with management by the auditor regarding internal control, or any other matter, does not remove the need for the auditor to consider any effect on the financial statements or the audit, nor is it an adequate substitute for an emphasis of matter or qualification.

CONTENTS

	Paragraphs
Introduction	1
Organizational Structure	2
Nature of Processing	3
Design and Procedural Aspects	4
Internal Controls in a CIS Environment	5
General CIS Controls	6-7
CIS Application Controls	8
Review of General CIS Controls	9
Review of CIS Application Controls	10
Evaluation	11

The International Auditing Practices Committee approved this International Auditing Practice Statement for publication in October 1991.

The auditor should understand and consider the characteristics of the CIS environment because they affect the design of the accounting system and related internal controls, the selection of internal controls upon which the auditor intends to rely, and the nature, timing and extent of the procedures.

This Statement is issued as a supplement to ISA 400 "Risk Assessments and Internal control." It does not form a part of the ISA, and is not intended to have the authority of an ISA.

AUDITING

1008

Introduction

1. A computer information systems (CIS)[5] environment is defined in International Standard on Auditing (ISA) 401 "Auditing in a Computer Information Systems Environment," as follows:

> For purposes of International Standards on Auditing, a CIS environment exists when a computer of any type or size is involved in the processing by the entity of financial information of significance to the audit, whether that computer is operated by the entity or by a third party.

The introduction of all desired CIS controls may not be practicable when the size of the business is small or when microcomputers are used irrespective of the size of the business. Also, where data is processed by a third party, the consideration of the CIS environment characteristics may vary depending on the degree of access to third party processing. A series of International Auditing Practice Statements has been developed to supplement the following paragraphs. This series describes various CIS environments and their effect on the accounting and internal control systems and on auditing procedures.

Organizational Structure

2. In a CIS environment, an entity will establish an organizational structure and procedures to manage the CIS activities. Characteristics of a CIS organizational structure include:

   a. *Concentration of functions and knowledge*—although most systems employing CIS methods will include certain manual operations, generally the number of persons involved in the processing of financial information is significantly reduced. Furthermore, certain data processing personnel may be the only ones with a detailed knowledge of the interrelationship between the source of data, how it is processed and the distribution and use of the output. It is also likely that they are aware of any internal control weaknesses and, therefore, may be in a position to alter programs or data while stored or during processing. Moreover, many conventional controls based on adequate segregation of incompatible functions may not exist, or in the absence of access and other controls, may be less effective.

   b. *Concentration of programs and data*—transaction and master file data are often concentrated, usually in machine-readable form, either in one computer installation located centrally or in a number of installations distributed throughout an entity. Computer programs which provide the ability to obtain access to and alter such data are likely to be stored at the same location as the data. Therefore, in the absence of appropriate

---

[5] This term is used throughout this Statement in place of electronic data processing (EDP) used in prior Statement "Risk Assessments and Internal Control—EDP Characteristics and Considerations."

controls, there is an increased potential for unauthorized access to, and alteration of, programs and data.

Nature of Processing

3. The use of computers may result in the design of systems that provide less visible evidence than those using manual procedures. In addition, these systems may be accessible by a larger number of persons. System characteristics that may result from the nature of CIS processing include:

   a. *Absence of input documents*—data may be entered directly into the computer system without supporting documents. In some on-line transaction systems, written evidence of individual data entry authorization (e.g., approval for order entry) may be replaced by other procedures, such as authorization controls contained in computer programs (e.g., credit limit approval).

   b. *Lack of visible transaction trail*—certain data may be maintained on computer files only. In a manual system, it is normally possible to follow a transaction through the system by examining source documents, books of account, records, files and reports. In a CIS environment, however, the transaction trail may be partly in machine-readable form, and furthermore it may exist only for a limited period of time.

   c. *Lack of visible output*—certain transactions or results of processing may not be printed. In a manual system, and in some CIS, it is normally possible to examine visually the results of processing. In other CIS, the results of processing may not be printed, or only summary data may be printed. Thus, the lack of visible output may result in the need to access data retained on files readable only by the computer.

   d. *Ease of access to data and computer programs*—data and computer programs may be accessed and altered at the computer or through the use of computer equipment at remote locations. Therefore, in the absence of appropriate controls, there is an increased potential for unauthorized access to, and alteration of, data and programs by persons inside or outside the entity.

Design and Procedural Aspects

4. The development of CIS will generally result in design and procedural characteristics that are different from those found in manual systems. These different design and procedural aspects of CIS include:

   a. *Consistency of performance*—CIS perform functions exactly as programmed and are potentially more reliable than manual systems, provided that all transaction types and conditions that could occur are anticipated and incorporated into the system. On the other hand, a computer program that is not correctly programmed and tested may consistently process transactions or other data erroneously.

b. *Programmed control procedures*—the nature of computer processing allows the design of internal control procedures in computer programs. These procedures can be designed to provide controls with limited visibility (e.g., protection of data against unauthorized access may be provided by passwords). Other procedures can be designed for use with manual intervention, such as review of reports printed for exception and error reporting, and reasonableness and limit checks of data.

c. *Single transaction update of multiple or data base computer files*—a single input to the accounting system may automatically update all records associated with the transaction (e.g., shipment of goods documents may update the sales and customers' accounts receivable files as well as the inventory file). Thus, an erroneous entry in such a system may create errors in various financial accounts.

d. *Systems generated transactions*—certain transactions may be initiated by the CIS itself without the need for an input document. The authorization of such transactions may not be evidenced by visible input documentation nor documented in the same way as transactions which are initiated outside the CIS (e.g., interest may be calculated and charged automatically to customers' account balances on the basis of pre-authorized terms contained in a computer program).

e. *Vulnerability of data and program storage media*—large volumes of data and the computer programs used to process such data may be stored on portable or fixed storage media, such as magnetic disks and tapes. These media are vulnerable to theft, loss, or intentional or accidental destruction.

Internal Controls in a CIS Environment

5. The internal controls over computer processing, which help to achieve the overall objectives of internal control, include both manual procedures and procedures designed into computer programs. Such manual and computer control procedures comprise the overall controls affecting the CIS environment (general CIS controls) and the specific controls over the accounting applications (CIS application controls).

General CIS Controls

6. The purpose of general CIS controls is to establish a framework of overall control over the CIS activities and to provide a reasonable level of assurance that the overall objectives of internal control are achieved. General CIS controls may include:

a. *Organization and management controls*—designed to establish an organizational framework over CIS activities, including:

- Policies and procedures relating to control functions.

- Appropriate segregation of incompatible functions (e.g., preparation of input transactions, programming and computer operations).

b. *Application systems development and maintenance controls*—designed to provide reasonable assurance that systems are developed and maintained in an authorized and efficient manner. They also typically are designed to establish control over:

- Testing, conversion, implementation and documentation of new or revised systems.

- Changes to application systems.

- Access to systems documentation.

- Acquisition of application systems from third parties.

c. *Computer operation controls*—designed to control the operation of the systems and to provide reasonable assurance that:

- The systems are used for authorized purposes only.

- Access to computer operations is restricted to authorized personnel.

- Only authorized programs are used.

- Processing errors are detected and corrected.

d. *Systems software controls*—designed to provide reasonable assurance that system software is acquired or developed in an authorized and efficient manner, including:

- Authorization, approval, testing, implementation and documentation of new systems software and systems software modifications.

- Restriction of access to systems software and documentation to authorized personnel.

e. *Data entry and program controls*—designed to provide reasonable assurance that:

- An authorization structure is established over transactions being entered into the system.

- Access to data and programs is restricted to authorized personnel.

7. There are other CIS safeguards that contribute to the continuity of CIS processing. These may include:

- Offsite back-up of data and computer programs.

- Recovery procedures for use in the event of theft, loss or intentional or accidental destruction.

- Provision for offsite processing in the event of disaster.

CIS Application Controls

8. The purpose of CIS application controls is to establish specific control procedures over the accounting applications in order to provide reasonable assurance that all transactions are authorized and recorded, and are processed

AUDITING

completely, accurately and on a timely basis. CIS application controls include:

A. *Controls over input*—designed to provide reasonable assurance that:

- Transactions are properly authorized before being processed by the computer.

- Transactions are accurately converted into machine readable form and recorded in the computer data files.

- Transactions are not lost, added, duplicated or improperly changed.

- Incorrect transactions are rejected, corrected and, if necessary, resubmitted on a timely basis.

B. *Controls over processing and computer data files*—designed to provide reasonable assurance that:

- Transactions, including system generated transactions, are properly processed by the computer.

- Transactions are not lost, added, duplicated or improperly changed.

- Processing errors are identified and corrected on a timely basis.

C. *Controls over output*—designed to provide reasonable assurance that:

- Results of processing are accurate.

- Access to output is restricted to authorized personnel.

- Output is provided to appropriate authorized personnel on a timely basis.

Review of General CIS Controls

9. The general CIS controls which the auditor may wish to test are described in paragraph 6. The auditor should consider how these general CIS controls affect the CIS applications significant to the audit. General CIS controls that relate to some or all applications are typically interdependent controls in that their operation is often essential to the effectiveness of CIS application controls. Accordingly, it may be more efficient to review the design of the general controls before reviewing the application controls.

Review of CIS Application Controls

10. Control over input, processing, data files and output may be carried out by CIS personnel, by users of the system, by a separate control group, or may be programmed into application software. CIS application controls which the auditor may wish to test include:

A. *Manual controls exercised by the user*—if manual controls exercised by the user of the application system are capable of providing reasonable assurance that the system's output is complete, accurate and authorized, the auditor may decide to limit tests of control to these manual controls (e.g., the manual controls exercised by the user over a computerized payroll system for salaried employees could include an anticipatory input control total for gross pay, the test checking of net salary output computations, the approval of the payments and transfer of funds, comparison to payroll register amounts, and prompt bank reconciliation). In this case, the auditor may wish to test only the manual controls exercised by the user.

B. *Controls over system output*—if, in addition to manual controls exercised by the user, the controls to be tested use information produced by the computer or are contained within computer programs, it may be possible to test such controls by examining the system's output using either manual or computer-assisted audit techniques. Such output may be in the form of magnetic media, microfilm or printouts (e.g., the auditor may test controls exercised by the entity over the reconciliation of report totals to the general ledger control accounts and may perform manual tests of those reconciliations). Alternatively, where the reconciliation is performed by computer, the auditor may wish to test the reconciliation by reperforming the control with the use of computer-assisted audit techniques (see International Auditing Practice Statement 1009 "Computer-Assisted Audit Techniques").

C. *Programmed control procedures*—in the case of certain computer systems, the auditor may find that it is not possible or, in some cases, not practical to test controls by examining only user controls or the system's output (e.g., in an application that does not provide printouts of critical approvals or overrides to normal policies, the auditor may want to test control procedures contained within the application program). The auditor may consider performing tests of control by using computer-assisted audit techniques, such as test data, reprocessing transaction data or, in unusual situations, examining the coding of the application program.

Evaluation

11. The general CIS controls may have a pervasive effect on the processing of transactions in application systems. If these controls are not effective, there may be a risk that misstatements might occur and go undetected in the application systems. Thus, weaknesses in general CIS controls may preclude testing certain CIS application controls; however, manual procedures exercised by users may provide effective control at the application level.

AUDITING

1008

CONTENTS

	Paragraphs
Introduction	1-3
Description of Computer-Assisted Audit Techniques (CAATs)	4-6
Uses of CAATs	7
Considerations in the Use of CAATs	8-16
Using CAATs	17-23
Using CAATs in Small Business Computer Environments	24

The International Auditing Practices Committee approved this International Auditing Practice Statement for publication in October 1984.

The purpose of this Statement is to provide guidance in the use of Computer-Assisted Audit Techniques, which are techniques that use the computer as an audit tool. This Statement applies to all uses of Computer-Assisted Audit Techniques involving a computer of any type or size. This Statement is not intended to have the authority of an International Standard on Auditing.

Introduction

1. The overall objectives and scope of an audit do not change when an audit is conducted in a computer information systems (CIS) environment as defined in International Standard on Auditing (ISA) 401 "Auditing in a Computer Information Systems Environment"; however, the application of auditing procedures may require the auditor to consider techniques that use the computer as an audit tool. These various uses of the computer are known as Computer-Assisted Audit Techniques (CAATs).

2. ISA 401 "Auditing in a Computer Information Systems Environment" discusses some of the uses of CAATs as follows:

   • The absence of input documents or the lack of a visible audit trail may require the use of CAATs in the application of compliance and substantive procedures.

   • The effectiveness and efficiency of auditing procedures may be improved through the use of CAATs.

3. The purpose of this Statement is to provide guidance in the use of CAATs. It applies to all uses of CAATs involving a computer of any type or size. Special considerations relating to small business computer environments are discussed in paragraph 24.

Description of Computer-Assisted Audit Techniques (CAATs)

4. This Statement describes two of the more common types of CAATs; audit software and test data used for audit purposes. However, the guidance provided in this Statement applies to all types of CAATs.

Audit Software

5. Audit software consists of computer programs used by the auditor, as part of his auditing procedures, to process data of audit significance from the entity's accounting system. It may consist of package programs, purpose-written programs, and utility programs. Regardless of the source of the programs, the auditor should substantiate their validity for audit purposes prior to use.

   • *Package programs* are generalized computer programs designed to perform data processing functions which include reading computer files, selecting information, performing calculations, creating data files and printing reports in a format specified by the auditor.

   • *Purpose-written programs* are computer programs designed to perform audit tasks in specific circumstances. These programs may be prepared by the auditor, by the entity or by an outside programmer engaged by the auditor. In some cases, existing entity programs may be used by the auditor in their original or in a modified state because it may be more efficient than developing independent programs.

   • *Utility programs* are used by the entity to perform common data processing functions, such as sorting, creating and printing files. These

AUDITING

programs are generally not designed for audit purposes and, therefore, may not contain such features as automatic record counts or control totals.

Test Data

6. Test data techniques are used in conducting audit procedures by entering data (e.g., a sample of transactions) into an entity's computer system, and comparing the results obtained with predetermined results. Examples of such uses are:

   - Test data used to test specific controls in computer programs, such as on-line password and data access controls.

   - Test transactions selected from previously processed transactions or created by the auditor to test specific processing characteristics of an entity's computer system. Such transactions are generally processed separately from the entity's normal processing.

   - Test transactions used in an integrated test facility where a "dummy" unit (e.g., a department or employee) is established, and to which test transactions are posted during the normal processing cycle.

   When test data is processed with the entity's normal processing, the auditor should ensure that the test transactions are subsequently eliminated from the entity's accounting records.

Uses of CAATs

7. CAATs may be used in performing various auditing procedures, including:

   - Tests of details of transactions and balances-for example, the use of audit software to test all (or a sample) of the transactions in a computer file.

   - Analytical review procedures-for example, the use of audit software to identify unusual fluctuations or items.

   - Compliance tests of general CIS controls-for example, the use of test data to test access procedures to the program libraries.

   - Compliance tests of CIS application controls-for example, the use of test data to test the functioning of a programmed procedure.

Considerations in the Use of CAATs

8. When planning the audit, the auditor should consider an appropriate combination of manual and computer-assisted audit techniques. In determining whether to use CAATs, the factors to be considered include:

   - Computer knowledge, expertise and experience of the auditor.

   - Availability of CAATs and suitable computer facilities.

   - Impracticability of manual tests.

   - Effectiveness and efficiency.

- Timing.

Computer Knowledge, Expertise, and Experience of the Auditor

9. ISA 401 "Auditing in a Computer Information Systems Environment" deals with the level of skill and competence the auditor should have when conducting an audit in a CIS environment and provides guidance when delegating work to assistants with CIS skills or when using work performed by other auditors or experts with such skills. Specifically, the auditor should have sufficient knowledge to plan, execute and use the results of the particular CAAT adopted. The level of knowledge required depends on the complexity and nature of the CAAT and of the entity's accounting system. Accordingly, the auditor should be aware that the use of CAATs in certain circumstances may require significantly more computer knowledge and expertise than in others.

Availability of CAATs and Suitable Computer Facilities

10. The auditor should consider the availability of CAATs, suitable computer facilities and the necessary computer-based accounting systems and files. The auditor may plan to use other computer facilities when the use of CAATs on the entity's computer is uneconomical or impractical-for example, because of an incompatibility between the auditor's package program and the entity's computer. The auditor should have a reasonable expectation that the computer facilities will be controlled as described in paragraphs 18-21.

11. The cooperation of the entity's personnel may be required to provide processing facilities at a convenient time, to assist with activities such as loading and running of the CAATs on the entity's system, and to provide copies of data files in the format required by the auditor.

Impracticability of Manual Tests

12. Many computerized accounting systems perform tasks for which no visible evidence is available and, in these circumstances, it may be impracticable for the auditor to perform tests manually. The lack of visible evidence may occur at different stages in the accounting process-for example:

- Input documents may be non-existent where sales orders are entered on-line. In addition, accounting transactions, such as discounts and interest calculations, may be generated by computer programs with no visible authorization of individual transactions.

- The system may not produce a visible audit trail of transactions processed through the computer. Delivery notes and suppliers' invoices may be matched by a computer program. In addition, programmed control procedures, such as checking customer credit limits, may provide visible evidence only on an exception basis. In such cases, there may be no visible evidence that all transactions have been processed.

- Output reports may not be produced by the system. In addition, a printed report may only contain summary totals while supporting details are retained in computer files.

AUDITING

Effectiveness and Efficiency

13. The effectiveness and efficiency of auditing procedures may be improved through the use of CAATs in obtaining and evaluating audit evidence-for example:

    - Some transactions may be tested more effectively for a similar level of cost by using the computer to examine all or a greater number of transactions than would otherwise be selected.

    - In applying analytical review procedures, transaction or balance details may be reviewed and reports printed of unusual items more efficiently by using the computer than by manual methods.

    - The use of CAATs may make additional substantive procedures more efficient than reliance on controls and related compliance procedures.

14. Matters relating to efficiency which may need to be considered by the auditor include:

    - The time to plan, design, execute and evaluate the CAAT.

    - Technical review and assistance hours.

    - Designing and printing of forms (e.g., confirmations).

    - Keying and verification of input.

    - Computer time.

    In evaluating the effectiveness and efficiency of a CAAT, the auditor may consider the life cycle of the CAAT application. The initial planning, design and development of a CAAT will usually benefit audits in subsequent periods.

Timing

15. Certain computer files, such as detailed transaction files, are often retained only for a short time, and may not be available in machine-readable form when required by the auditor. Thus, the auditor will need to make arrangements for the retention of data required by him, or he may need to alter the timing of his work which requires this data.

16. Where the time available to perform an audit is limited, the auditor may plan to use a CAAT because it will meet his time requirement better than other procedures.

Using CAATs

17. The major steps to be undertaken by the auditor in the application of a CAAT are to:

    (a) Set the objective of the CAAT application.

    (b) Determine the content and accessibility of the entity's files.

    (c) Define the transaction types to be tested.

(d) Define the procedures to be performed on the data.

(e) Define the output requirements.

(f) Identify the audit and computer personnel who may participate in the design and application of the CAAT.

(g) Refine the estimates of costs and benefits.

(h) Ensure that the use of the CAAT is properly controlled and documented.

(i) Arrange the administrative activities, including the necessary skills and computer facilities.

(j) Execute the CAAT application.

(k) Evaluate the results.

Controlling the CAAT Application

18. The use of a CAAT should be controlled by the auditor to provide reasonable assurance that the audit objectives and the detailed specifications of the CAAT have been met, and that the CAAT is not improperly manipulated by the entity's staff. The specific procedures necessary to control the use of a CAAT will depend on the particular application. In establishing audit control, the auditor should consider the need to:

(a) Approve the technical specifications, and carry out a technical review of the work involving the use of the CAAT.

(b) Review the entity's general CIS controls which may contribute to the integrity of the CAAT—for example, controls over program changes and access to computer files. When such controls cannot be relied upon to ensure the integrity of the CAAT, the auditor may consider processing the CAAT application at another suitable computer facility.

(c) Ensure appropriate integration of the output by the auditor into the audit process.

19. Procedures carried out by the auditor to control audit software applications may include:

(a) Participating in the design and testing of the computer programs.

(b) Checking the coding of the program to ensure that it conforms with the detailed program specifications.

(c) Requesting the entity's computer staff to review the operating system instructions to ensure that the software will run in the entity's computer installation.

(d) Running the audit software on small test files before running on the main data files.

(e) Ensuring that the correct files were used-for example, by checking with external evidence, such as control totals maintained by the user.

AUDITING

(f) Obtaining evidence that the audit software functioned as planned-for example, reviewing output and control information.

(g) Establishing appropriate security measures to safeguard against manipulation of the entity's data files.

The presence of the auditor is not necessarily required at the computer facility during the running of a CAAT to ensure appropriate control procedures. However, it may provide practical advantages, such as being able to control distribution of the output and ensuring the timely correction of errors-for example, if the wrong input file were to be used.

20. Procedures carried out by the auditor to control test data applications may include:

(a) Controlling the sequence of submissions of test data where it spans several processing cycles.

(b) Performing test runs containing small amounts of test data before submitting the main audit test data.

(c) Predicting the results of the test data and comparing it with the actual test data output, for the individual transactions and in total.

(d) Confirming that the current version of the programs was used to process the test data.

(e) Obtaining reasonable assurance that the programs used to process the test data were used by the entity throughout the applicable audit period.

21. When using a CAAT, the auditor may require the cooperation of the entity's staff who have extensive knowledge of the computer installation. In such circumstances, the auditor should have reasonable assurance that the entity's staff did not improperly influence the results of the CAAT.

Documentation

22. The standard of working papers and retention procedures for a CAAT should be consistent with that on the audit as a whole (see ISA 230 "Documentation"). It may be convenient to keep the technical papers relating to the use of the CAAT separate from the other audit working papers.

23. The working papers should contain sufficient documentation to describe the CAAT application, such as:

(a) *Planning*

- CAAT objectives.

- Specific CAAT to be used.

- Controls to be exercised.

- Staffing, timing and cost.

(b) *Execution*

- CAAT preparation and testing procedures and controls.

- Details of the tests performed by the CAAT.

- Details of input, processing and output.

- Relevant technical information about the entity's accounting system, such as computer file layouts.

(c) *Audit Evidence*

- Output provided.

- Description of the audit work performed on the output.

- Audit conclusions.

(d) *Other*

- Recommendations to entity management.

In addition, it may be useful to document suggestions for using the CAAT in future years.

Using CAATs in Small Business Computer Environments

24. The general principles outlined in this Statement are applicable in small business computer environments. However, the following points should be given special consideration in these environments:

(a) The level of general CIS controls may be such that the auditor will place less reliance on the system of internal control. This will result in:

- Greater emphasis on tests of details of transactions and balances and analytical review procedures, which may increase the effectiveness of certain CAATs, particularly audit software.

- The application of audit procedures to ensure the proper functioning of the CAAT and validity of the entity's data.

(b) In cases where smaller volumes of data are processed, manual methods may be more cost effective.

(c) Adequate technical assistance may not be available to the auditor from the entity, thus making the use of CAATs impracticable.

(d) Certain audit package programs may not operate on small computers, thus restricting the auditor's choice of CAATs. However, the entity's data files may be copied and processed on another suitable computer.

AUDITING

CONTENTS

	Paragraphs
Introduction	1-12
Guidance on the Application of ISA 310 Knowledge of the Business	13-16
Guidance on the Application of ISA 400 Risk Assessments and Internal Control	17-29
Guidance on the Application of ISA 250 Consideration of Laws and Regulations in an Audit of Financial Statements	30-34
Substantive Procedures	35-47
Management Representations	48
Reporting	49-50
Appendix 1: Obtaining Knowledge of the Business from an Environmental Point of View—Illustrative Questions	
Appendix 2: Substantive Procedures to Detect a Material Misstatement due to Environmental Matters	

International Auditing Practices Statements ("Statements") are issued by the International Auditing Practices Committee ("IAPC") of the International Federation of Accountants to provide practical assistance to auditors in implementing the International Standards on Auditing ("ISAs") or to promote good practice. Statements do not have the authority of ISAs.

This Statement does not establish any new basic principles or essential procedures: its purpose is to assist auditors, and the development of good practice, by providing guidance on the application of the ISAs in cases when environmental matters are significant to the financial statements of the entity. The extent to which any of the audit procedures described in this Statement may be appropriate in a particular case requires the exercise of the auditor's judgment in the light of the requirements of the ISAs and the circumstances of the entity.

This Statement was approved by the IAPC in March 1998 for publication in March 1998.

The Public Sector Perspective (PSP) issued by the Public Sector Committee of the International Federation of Accountants is set out at the end of an IAPS. Where no PSP is added, the IAPS is applicable in all material respects to the public sector.

Introduction

The Purpose of this Statement

1. Environmental matters are becoming significant to an increasing number of entities and may, in certain circumstances, have a material impact on their financial statements. These issues are of growing interest to the users of financial statements. The recognition, measurement, and disclosure of these matters is the responsibility of management.

2. For some entities, environmental matters are not significant. However, when environmental matters are significant to an entity, there may be a risk of material misstatement (including inadequate disclosure) in the financial statements arising from such matters: in these circumstances, the auditor needs to give consideration to environmental matters in the audit of the financial statements.

3. Environmental matters can be complex and may therefore require additional consideration by auditors. This Statement provides practical assistance to auditors by describing:

   (a) the auditor's main considerations in an audit of financial statements with respect to environmental matters;

   (b) examples of possible impacts of environmental matters on financial statements; and

   (c) guidance that the auditor may consider when exercising professional judgment in this context to determine the nature, timing, and extent of audit procedures with respect to:

   - knowledge of the business (ISA 310);

   - risk assessments and internal control (ISA 400);

   - consideration of laws and regulations (ISA 250); and

   - other substantive procedures (ISA 620 and some others).

   The guidance under (c) reflects the typical sequence of the audit process. Having acquired a sufficient knowledge of the business the auditor assesses the risk of a material misstatement in the financial statements. This assessment includes consideration of environmental laws and regulations that may pertain to the entity, and provides a basis for the auditor to decide whether there is a need to pay attention to environmental matters in the course of the audit of financial statements.

   Appendix 1 provides illustrative questions that an auditor may consider when obtaining a knowledge of the business, including an understanding of the entity's control environment and control procedures from an environmental point of view. Appendix 2 provides examples of substantive procedures that an auditor may perform to detect a material misstatement in the financial statements due to environmental matters. These appendices are included for illustrative purposes only. It is not intended that all, or even any, of the questions or examples will necessarily be appropriate in any particular case.

AUDITING

1010

4. This Statement does not establish any new basic principles or essential procedures: its purpose is to assist auditors, and the development of good practice, by providing guidance on the application of the ISAs in cases when environmental matters are significant to the financial statements of the entity. The extent to which any of the audit procedures described in this Statement may be appropriate in a particular case requires the exercise of the auditor's judgment in the light of the requirements of the ISAs and the circumstances of the entity.

5. The Statement does not provide guidance on the audit of the financial statements of insurance companies with regard to claims incurred under insurance policies relating to environmental matters affecting policyholders.

The Auditor's Main Considerations with respect to Environmental Matters

6. The objective of an audit of financial statements is:

    "...to enable the auditor to express an opinion whether the financial statements are prepared, in all material respects, in accordance with an identified financial reporting framework." (ISA 200, paragraph 2).

7. The auditor's opinion relates to the financial statements taken as a whole and not to any specific aspect. When planning and performing audit procedures and in evaluating and reporting the results thereof, the auditor should recognize that noncompliance by the entity with laws and regulations may materially affect the financial statements. However, an audit can not be expected to detect noncompliance with all laws and regulations (ISA 250, paragraph 2). In particular, with respect to the entity's compliance with environmental laws and regulations, the auditor's purpose is not to plan the audit to detect possible breaches of environmental laws and regulations; nor are the auditor's procedures sufficient to draw a conclusion on the entity's compliance with environmental laws and regulations or the adequacy of its controls over environmental matters.

8. In all audits, when developing the overall audit plan, the auditor assesses inherent risk at the financial statement level (ISA 400, paragraph 11). The auditor uses professional judgment to evaluate the factors relevant to this assessment. In certain circumstances these factors may include the risk of material misstatement of the financial statements due to environmental matters. The need to consider, and extent of the consideration of, environmental matters in an audit of financial statements depends on the auditor's judgment as to whether environmental matters give rise to a risk of material misstatement in the financial statements. In some cases, no specific audit procedures may be judged necessary. In other cases, however, the auditor uses professional judgment to determine the nature, timing and extent of the specific procedures considered necessary in order to obtain sufficient appropriate audit evidence that the financial statements are not materially misstated. If the auditor does not have the professional competence to perform these procedures, technical advice may be sought from specialists, such as lawyers, engineers, or other environmental experts.

9. To conclude that an entity operates in compliance with existing environmental laws or regulations ordinarily requires the technical skills of

environmental experts, which the auditor cannot be expected to possess. Also, whether a particular event or condition that comes to the attention of the auditor is a breach of environmental laws and regulations is a legal determination that is ordinarily beyond the auditor's professional competence. However, as with other laws and regulations:

"...the auditor's training, experience and understanding of the entity and its industry may provide a basis for recognition that some acts coming to the auditor's attention may constitute noncompliance with laws and regulations. The determination as to whether a particular act constitutes or is likely to constitute noncompliance is generally based on the advice of an informed expert qualified to practice law but ultimately can only be determined by a court of law." (ISA 250, paragraph 4.)

Environmental Matters and their Impact on the Financial Statements

10. For the purpose of this Statement, "environmental matters" are defined as:

   (a) initiatives to prevent, abate, or remedy damage to the environment, or to deal with conservation of renewable and non-renewable resources (such initiatives may be required by environmental laws and regulations or by contract, or they may be undertaken voluntarily);

   (b) consequences of violating environmental laws and regulations;

   (c) consequences of environmental damage done to others or to natural resources; and

   (d) consequences of vicarious liability imposed by law (for example, liability for damages caused by previous owners).

11. Some examples of environmental matters affecting the financial statements are the following:

   • the introduction of environmental laws and regulations may involve an impairment of assets and consequently a need to write down their carrying value;

   • failure to comply with legal requirements concerning environmental matters, such as emissions or waste disposal, or changes to legislation with retrospective effect, may require accrual of remediation, compensation or legal costs;

   • some entities, for example in the extraction industries (oil and gas exploration or mining), chemical manufacturers or waste management companies may incur environmental obligation as a direct by-product of their core businesses;

   • constructive obligations that stem from a voluntary initiative, for example an entity may have identified contamination of land and, although under no legal obligation, it may have decided to remedy the contamination,

AUDITING

because of its concern for its long-term reputation and its relationship with the community;[6]

- an entity may need to disclose in the notes the existence of a contingent liability where the expense relating to environmental matters cannot be reasonably estimated; and

- in extreme situations, noncompliance with certain environmental laws and regulations may affect the continuance of an entity as a going concern and consequently may affect the disclosures and the basis of preparation of the financial statements.

12.   As of the date of publication of this Statement there are few authoritative accounting standards, whether International Accounting Standards or national standards, that explicitly address the recognition, measurement, and disclosure of the consequences for the financial statements arising from environmental matters. However, existing accounting standards generally do provide appropriate general considerations that also apply to the recognition, measurement and disclosure of environmental matters in financial statements.[7]

Guidance on the Application of ISA 310 Knowledge of the Business

13.   In all audits a sufficient knowledge of the client's business is needed to enable the auditor to identify and understand matters that may have a significant effect on the financial statements, the audit process and the audit report (ISA 310, paragraph 2). In obtaining a sufficient knowledge of the business, the auditor considers important conditions affecting the entity's business and the industry in which it operates, such as environmental requirements and problems.

14.   The auditor's level of knowledge with regard to environmental matters, appropriate for a particular engagement is less than that ordinarily possessed by management or by environmental experts. However, the auditor's level of knowledge needs to be sufficient to enable the auditor to identify and obtain an understanding of the events, transactions, and practices related to environmental matters that may have a material effect on the financial statements and on the audit.

---

[6] The term "constructive obligations" (as opposed to "present legal obligations") has been clarified by the International Accounting Standards Committee as follows: "Sometimes the actions or representations of the enterprise's management, or changes in the economic environment, directly influence the reasonable expectations or actions of those outside the enterprise and, although they have no legal entitlement, they have other sanctions that leave the enterprise with no realistic alternative to certain expenditures. Such obligations are sometimes called "constructive obligations" (IASC: ED 59 Proposed International Accounting Standard on "Provisions, Contingent Liabilities and Contingent Assets", paragraph 16).

[7] For example, International Accounting Standard No.10, on "Contingencies and Events Occurring After the Balance Sheet Date", provides the general considerations which apply to the recognition and disclosure of contingent losses, including losses as a consequence of environmental matters. IAS 10 is currently under review by IASC: ED 59 Proposed International Accounting Standard, on "Provisions, Contingent Liabilities and Contingent Assets", contains some examples of environmental liabilities.

15. The auditor considers the industry in which the entity operates, as it may be indicative of the possible existence of environmental liabilities and contingencies. Certain industries, by their nature, tend to be exposed to significant environmental risk.[8] These include the chemical, oil and gas, pharmaceutical, metallurgical, mining, and utility industries.

16. An entity does not, however, need to operate in one of these industries to be exposed to significant environmental risk. Potential exposure to significant environmental risk may in general arise for any entity that:

(a) is subject to environmental laws and regulations to a substantial degree;

(b) owns, or holds security over, sites contaminated by previous owners ("vicarious liability"); or

(c) has business processes that:

- may cause contamination of soil and groundwater, contamination of surface water, or air pollution;

- use hazardous substances;

- generate or process hazardous waste; or

- may have an adverse impact on customers, employees, or people that live in the neighborhood of the company's sites.

Guidance on the Application of ISA 400 Risk Assessments and Internal Control

17. This section of the Statement provides additional guidance on the application of certain aspects of ISA 400 by explaining the relationship between environmental matters and the audit risk model. More specifically, it provides examples of the auditor's possible consideration of environmental matters with respect to the:

- inherent risk assessment;

- accounting and internal control systems;

- control environment; and

- control procedures.

Inherent Risk

18. The auditor uses professional judgment to evaluate the factors relevant to the assessment of inherent risk for the development of the overall audit plan. In certain circumstances these factors may include the risk of material misstatement of the financial statements due to environmental matters ("environmental risk"). Thus, environmental risk may be a component of inherent risk.

19. Examples of environmental risk at financial statement level are:

---

[8] "Environmental risk" is defined in paragraph 18 of this Statement as a possible component of inherent risk.

- the risk of compliance costs arising from legislation or from contractual requirements;

- the risk of noncompliance with environmental laws and regulations; and

- the possible effects of specific environmental requirements of customers and their possible reactions to the entity's environmental conduct.

20. If the auditor considers that environmental risk is a significant component in the inherent risk assessment, the auditor relates this assessment to material account balances and classes of transactions at the assertion level when developing the audit program (ISA 400, paragraph 11).

21. Examples of environmental risk at the level of account balances or classes of transactions are:

- the extent to which an account balance is based on complex accounting estimates with respect to environmental matters (for example, the measurement of an environmental provision for the removal of contaminated land and future site restoration). ISA 540 "Audit of Accounting Estimates" provides guidance to the auditor for these situations. Inherent risk may be high if there is a lack of data upon which to base a reasonable estimate, for example because of complex technologies for removal and site restoration; and

- the extent to which an account balance is affected by unusual or non-routine transactions involving environmental matters.

Accounting and Internal Control Systems

22. It is management's responsibility to design and operate internal controls to assist in achieving, as far as practicable, the orderly and efficient conduct of the business, including any environmental aspects. The way in which management achieves control over environmental matters differs in practice:

- entities with low exposure to environmental risk, or smaller entities, will probably monitor and control their environmental matters as part of their normal accounting and internal control systems;

- some entities that operate in industries with a high exposure to environmental risk may design and operate a separate internal control sub-system for this purpose, that conforms with existing standards for Environmental Management Systems (EMS);[9] and

- other entities design and operate all of their controls in an integrated control system, encompassing policies and procedures related to

---

[9] Standards for an EMS have been issued by the International Organization for Standardization (ISO 14001: "Environmental management systems—Specification with guidance for use" International Organization for Standardization, Geneva, Switzerland, First edition 1996–09–01). The specification requires participating organizations to develop and implement a systematic approach to managing significant environmental aspects. It also includes a commitment to continual improvement. When in certain countries or regions other standards for an EMS are in use, such as the standards issued by the European Commission on behalf of an entity's participation in the Eco-Management and Audit Scheme (EMAS), those national or regional standards can be used by the entity as benchmarks also.

accounting, environmental and other matters (for example, quality, health and safety).

23.   For the auditor's purposes it makes no difference how management actually achieves control over environmental matters. In particular, the lack of an EMS does not in itself mean that the auditor has to conclude that there is inadequate control over the environmental aspects of the business.

24.   Only if, in the auditor's judgment, environmental matters may have a material effect on the financial statements of an entity, does the auditor need to obtain an understanding of the entity's significant policies and procedures with respect to its monitoring of, and control over these environmental matters (the entity's "environmental controls"), in order to plan the audit and develop an effective audit approach. In such cases the auditor is only concerned with those environmental controls (within or outside the accounting and internal control systems) that are considered relevant to the audit of the financial statements.

Control Environment

25.   In all audits, the auditor obtains an understanding of the control environment sufficient to assess directors' and management's attitudes, awareness, and actions regarding internal controls and their importance in the entity (ISA 400, paragraph 19). Similar conditions as described in paragraph 24 of this Statement apply to the auditor's need to obtain an understanding of the control environment. Factors in obtaining an understanding of the control environment with respect to environmental matters may include:

- the functioning of the board of directors and its committees, with respect to the entity's environmental controls;

- management's philosophy and operating style and its approach to environmental issues, such as any efforts to improve the environmental performance of the entity, participation in certification programs for the entity's EMS, and the voluntary publication of environmental performance reports.[10] This also encompasses management's reaction to external influences such as those relating to monitoring and compliance requirements imposed by regulatory bodies and enforcement agencies;

- the entity's organizational structure and methods of assigning authority and responsibility to deal with environmental operating functions and regulatory requirements; and

- management's control system, including the internal auditing function, the performance of "environmental audits" (see paragraph 45 of this Statement), personnel policies, and procedures and appropriate segregation of duties.

---

[10] An "environmental performance report" is a report, separate from the financial statements, in which an entity provides third parties with qualitative information on the entity's commitments towards the environmental aspects of the business, its policies and targets in that field, its achievement in managing the relationship between its business processes and environmental risk, and quantitative information on its environmental performance.

AUDITING

Control Procedures

26. Applying the considerations and conditions mentioned in paragraphs 18–20 the auditor may come to the conclusion that there is a need to obtain an understanding of environmental controls. Examples of environmental controls are policies and procedures:

    - to monitor compliance with the entity's environmental policy, as well as with relevant environmental laws and regulations;

    - to maintain an appropriate environmental information system, which may include recording of, for example, physical quantities of emissions and hazardous waste, environmental characteristics of products, complaints from stakeholders, results of inspections performed by enforcement agencies, occurrence and effects of incidents, etc;

    - to provide for the reconciliation of environmental information with relevant financial data, for example, physical quantities of waste production in relation to cost of waste disposal; and

    - to identify potential environmental matters and related contingencies affecting the entity.

27. If the entity has established environmental controls, the auditor also inquires of those persons overseeing such controls as to whether any environmental matters have been identified that may have a material effect on the financial statements.

28. One of the possibilities for the auditor to obtain an understanding of the entity's control over environmental matters may be to read the entity's environmental performance report, if available. That report often discloses the entity's environmental commitments and policies, and its major environmental controls.

Control Risk

29. After obtaining an understanding of the accounting and internal control systems, the auditor may need to consider the effect of environmental matters in the assessment of control risk and in any tests of control that may be necessary to support that assessment. (The auditor's assessment of control risk is described in paragraphs 21–39 of ISA 400.)

Guidance on the Application of ISA 250 Consideration of Laws and Regulations in an Audit of Financial Statements

30. It is management's responsibility to ensure that the entity's operations are conducted in accordance with laws and regulations. The responsibility for the prevention and detection of noncompliance rests with management (ISA 250, paragraph 9). In this context, management has to take into account:

    - laws and regulations that impose liability for remediation of environmental pollution arising from past events; this liability may not be limited to the entity's own actions but may also be imposed on the current owner of a property where the damage was incurred by a previous owner ("vicarious liability");

- pollution control and pollution prevention laws that are directed at identifying or regulating sources of pollution, or reducing emissions or discharges of pollutants;

- environmental licenses that, in certain jurisdictions, specify the entity's operating conditions from an environmental point of view, for example, a specification of the maximum levels of emissions; and

- the requirements of regulatory authorities with respect to environmental matters.

31. Changes in environmental legislation could have significant consequences for the operations of the entity and may even result in liabilities that relate to past events which, at the time, were not governed by legislation. An example of the first category is a change in noise regulations that could curtail future use of plant or machinery. An example of the latter is an increase in standards that could render a waste generator liable for waste disposed of in previous years, even though disposal of the waste was in compliance with the then existing practice.

32. The auditor is not, and cannot be held responsible for preventing noncompliance with environmental laws and regulations. Also, as stated in paragraph 9, the detection of possible breaches of environmental laws and regulations is ordinarily beyond the auditor's professional competence. However, an audit carried out in accordance with ISAs is planned and performed with an attitude of professional skepticism, recognizing that the audit may reveal conditions or events that would lead to questioning whether the entity is complying with relevant environmental laws and regulations in so far as noncompliance could result in a material misstatement of the financial statements.

33. As part of the planning process of the audit, the auditor obtains a general understanding of such environmental laws and regulations which, if violated, could reasonably be expected to result in a material misstatement in the financial statements, and of the policies and procedures used by the entity to comply with those laws and regulations. In obtaining this general understanding, the auditor recognizes that noncompliance with some environmental laws and regulations may severely impact the operations of the entity.

34. To obtain a general understanding of relevant environmental laws and regulations, the auditor ordinarily:

- uses existing knowledge of the entity's industry and business;

- inquires of management (including key officers for environmental matters) concerning the entity's policies and procedures regarding compliance with relevant environmental laws and regulations;

- inquires of management as to the environmental laws and regulations that may be expected to have a fundamental effect on the operations of the entity. Noncompliance with these requirements might cause the entity to

491

1010

AUDITING

cease operations, or call into question the entity's continuance as a going concern; and

- discusses with management the policies or procedures adopted for identifying, evaluating and accounting for litigation, claims and assessments.

Substantive Procedures

35. This section of the Statement provides guidance on substantive procedures, including the application of ISA 620 "Using the Work of an Expert".

36. The auditor considers the assessed levels of inherent and control risk in determining the nature, timing and extent of substantive procedures required to reduce the risk of not detecting a material misstatement in the financial statements to an acceptable level, including any material misstatements if the entity fails to properly recognize, measure or disclose the effects of environmental matters.

37. Substantive procedures include obtaining evidence through inquiry of both management responsible for the preparation of the financial statements and key officers responsible for environmental matters. The auditor considers the need to gather corroborative audit evidence for any environmental assertions from sources inside or outside the entity. In certain situations, the auditor may need to consider using the work of environmental experts.

38. Examples of substantive procedures that an auditor may perform to detect a material misstatement in the financial statements due to environmental matters, are provided in Appendix 2.

39. Most of the audit evidence available to the auditor is persuasive rather than conclusive. Therefore, the auditor needs to use professional judgment in determining whether the planned substantive procedures, either individually or in combination, are appropriate. The use of professional judgment may become even more important because of a number of difficulties with respect to the recognition and measurement of the consequences of environmental matters in the financial statements, for example:

- often there is a considerable time delay between the activity that basically causes an environmental issue, and the identification of it by the entity or regulators;

- accounting estimates may not have an established historical pattern or may have wide ranges of reasonableness because of the number and nature of assumptions underlying the determination of these estimates;

- environmental laws or regulations are evolving, and interpretation may be difficult or ambiguous. Consultation of an expert may be necessary to assess the impact of these laws and regulations on the valuation of certain assets (for example, assets that contain asbestos). Making a reasonable estimate of liabilities for known obligations may also appear to be difficult in practice; or

- liabilities may arise other than as a result of legal or contractual obligations.

40. In the course of the audit process, for example in gathering knowledge of the business, in the assessments of inherent and control risk, or in performing certain substantive procedures, evidence may come to the attention of the auditor that indicates the existence of a risk that the financial statements may be materially misstated due to environmental matters. Examples of such circumstances include:

- the existence of reports outlining material environmental problems prepared by environmental experts, internal auditors or environmental auditors;

- violations of environmental laws and regulations cited in correspondence with, or in reports issued by regulatory agencies;

- inclusion of the entity's name in a publicly available register, or plan, for the restoration of soil contamination (if one exists);

- media comment about the entity related to major environmental matters;

- comments relating to environmental matters made in lawyers' letters;

- evidence indicating purchases of goods and services relating to environmental matters that are unusual in relation to the nature of the entity's business; and

- increased or unusual legal or environmental consultants' fees, or payments of penalties as a result of violation of environmental laws and regulations.

In these circumstances the auditor considers the need to re-assess inherent and control risk and the resulting impact on detection risk. If necessary, the auditor may decide to consult an environmental expert.

Environmental Experts

41. Management is responsible for accounting estimates included in the financial statements. Management may require technical advice from specialists such as lawyers, engineers or other environmental experts to assist in developing accounting estimates and disclosures related to environmental matters. Such experts may be involved in many stages in the process of developing accounting estimates and disclosures, including assisting management in:

- identifying situations where the recognition of liabilities and related estimates is required (for example, an environmental engineer may make a preliminary investigation of a site to determine if contamination has occurred, or a lawyer may be used to determine the entity's legal responsibility to restore the site);

- gathering the necessary data on which to base estimates and providing details of information that needs to be disclosed in the financial statements (for example, an environmental expert may test a site in order to assist in quantifying the nature and extent of contamination and considering acceptable alternative methods of site restoration); and

- designing the appropriate remedial action plan and calculating related financial consequences.

42. If the auditor intends to use the results of such work as part of the audit, the auditor considers the adequacy of the work performed by environmental experts for the purposes of the audit, as well as the expert's competence and objectivity, in accordance with ISA 620 "Using the Work of an Expert". The auditor may need to engage another expert in considering such work, to apply additional procedures, or to modify the auditor's report.

43. As the environmental area is an emerging specialty, the expert's professional competence may be more difficult to assess than is the case with some other experts, because there may be no certification or licensing by, or membership of, an appropriate professional body. In this situation, it may be necessary for the auditor to give particular consideration to the experience and reputation of the environmental expert.

44. Timely and ongoing communication with the expert may assist the auditor to understand the nature, scope, objective and limitations of the expert's report. The report might deal with only one aspect of the entity's operations. For example, the expert's report may be based on cost estimates related to only one element of a particular issue (for example, soil contamination), rather than on cost estimates of all relevant issues (for example, contamination of soil and groundwater, including vicarious liability imposed by law). It is also necessary for the auditor to discuss the assumptions, methods, procedures, and source data used by the expert.

Environmental Audit

45. "Environmental audits" are becoming increasingly common in certain industries.[11] The term "environmental audit" has a wide variety of meanings. They can be performed by external or internal experts (sometimes including internal auditors), at the discretion of the entity's management. In practice, persons from various disciplines can qualify to perform "environmental audits". Often the work is performed by a multi-disciplinary team. Normally, "environmental audits" are performed at the request of management and are for internal use. They may address various subject matters, including site contamination, or compliance with environmental laws and regulations. However, an "environmental audit" is not necessarily an equivalent to an audit of an environmental performance report.

46. The auditor of the entity's financial statements may consider using the findings of "environmental audits" as appropriate audit evidence. In that situation the auditor has to decide whether the "environmental audit" meets the evaluation criteria included in ISA 610 "Considering the Work of Internal Auditing" or ISA 620 "Using the Work of an Expert". Important criteria to be considered are:

---

[11] Guidelines for "environmental auditing" have been issued by the International Organization for Standardization (ISO), "Guidelines for environmental auditing—General principles" (International Organization for Standardization, Geneva, Switzerland, First Edition 1996–10–01).

(a) the impact of the results of the environmental audit on the financial statements;

(b) the competency and skill of the environmental audit team and the objectivity of the auditors, specially when chosen from the entity's staff;

(c) the scope of the environmental audit, including management's reactions to the recommendations that result from the environmental audit and how this is evidenced;

(d) the due professional care exercised by the team in the performance of the environmental audit; and

(e) the proper direction, supervision, and review of the audit.

Internal Audit

47. If the entity has an internal auditing function, the auditor considers whether the internal auditors address environmental aspects of the entity's operations as part of their internal auditing activities. If this is the case, the auditor considers the appropriateness of using such work for the purpose of the audit, applying the criteria set out in ISA 610 "Considering the Work of Internal Auditing".

Management Representations

48. ISA 580 "Management Representations" requires that the auditor obtain written representations from management on matters material to the financial statements when other sufficient appropriate audit evidence cannot reasonably be expected to exist. Much of the evidence available to the auditor with respect to the impact of environmental matters on the financial statements will be persuasive in nature rather than conclusive. The auditor may therefore wish to obtain specific representation that management:

(a) is not aware of any material liabilities or contingencies arising from environmental matters, including those resulting from illegal or possibly illegal acts;

(b) is not aware of any other environmental matters that may have a material impact on the financial statements; or

(c) if aware of such matters, has disclosed them properly in the financial statements.

Reporting

49. When forming an opinion on the financial statements, the auditor considers whether the effects of environmental matters are adequately treated or disclosed in accordance with the appropriate financial reporting framework. In addition, the auditor reads any other information to be included with the financial statements in order to identify any material inconsistencies, for example, regarding environmental matters.

50. Management's assessment of uncertainties and the extent of their disclosure in the financial statements are key issues in determining the impact on the auditor's report. The auditor may conclude that there are significant uncertainties, or inappropriate disclosures, due to environmental matters. There may even be circumstances when, in the auditor's judgment, the going concern assumption is no longer appropriate. ISA 700 "The Auditor's Report on Financial Statements" and ISA 570 "Going Concern" provide detailed guidance to auditors in these circumstances.

Public Sector Perspective

1. *As stated in paragraph 3, this Statement provides practical assistance to auditors in identifying and addressing environmental matters in the context of an audit of financial statements. This guidance would generally be equally applicable to public sector auditors in their audit of the financial statements of governments and other public sector entities. However, it should be noted that the nature and scope of public sector audit engagements may be affected by legislation, regulation, ordinances and ministerial directives that impose additional audit and/or reporting responsibilities with respect to environmental issues.*

2. *As in the private sector, auditors of financial statements of governments and other public sector entities may need to consider the recognition, measurement and disclosure of any liabilities or contingencies for environmental damage. Liabilities or contingencies may arise through damage caused by the reporting entity or one of its agencies. However, in the public sector, liability or contingencies may also arise when the government accepts responsibility for clean-up or other costs associated with damage caused by others, if, for example, responsibility is unresolved or cannot be attributed to others.*

3. *Public sector auditors may, in some countries, be obliged to report instances of non compliance with environmental regulations found in the course of a financial statement audit, regardless of whether or not those instances of non-compliance have a material impact on the entity's financial statements.*

4. *A government's responsibilities may also include the monitoring of compliance with laws and regulations in relation to environmental matters. More specifically, this monitoring role will be the responsibility of a particular public sector agency or agencies. In performing the financial statement audit of such an agency or agencies the auditor may need to consider, for example, controls covering the imposing of appropriate charges/fines and the collection of fines. For unresolved cases consideration may also need to be given to the recognition, measurement and disclosure of any liabilities or contingencies.*

Appendix 1

Obtaining Knowledge of the Business from an Environmental Point of View— Illustrative Questions

The purpose of this appendix is to provide examples of questions that an auditor may consider when obtaining a knowledge of the business, including an understanding of the entity's control environment and control procedures, from an environmental point of view.

These examples are included for illustrative purposes only. It is not intended that all of the questions illustrated will be appropriate in any particular case. The questions need to be tailored to fit the particular circumstances of each engagement. In some cases, the auditor may judge it unnecessary to address any of these questions.

It may be necessary for the auditor to consult an environmental expert when evaluating the answers received from the entity's officers in response to any inquiries with regard to environmental matters.

Knowledge of the business

1. Does the entity operate in an industry that is exposed to significant environmental risk that may adversely affect the financial statements of the entity?

2. What are the environmental issues in the entity's industry in general?

3. Which environmental laws and regulations are applicable to the entity?

4. Are there any substances used in the entity's products or production processes that are part of a phase-out scheme required by legislation, or adopted voluntarily by the industry in which the client operates?

5. Do enforcement agencies monitor the entity's compliance with the requirements of environmental laws, regulations or licenses?

6. Have any regulatory actions been taken or reports been issued by enforcement agencies that may have a material impact on the entity and its financial statements?

7. Have initiatives been scheduled to prevent, abate or remedy damage to the environment, or to deal with conservation of renewable and non-renewable resources?

8. Is there a history of penalties and legal proceedings against the entity or its directors in connection with environmental matters? If so, what were the reasons for such actions?

9. Are any legal proceedings pending with regard to compliance with environmental laws and regulations?

10. Are environmental risks covered by insurance?

AUDITING

Control environment and control procedures

11. What is management's philosophy and operating style with respect to environmental control in general (to be assessed by the auditor, based on his knowledge of the entity in general)?

12. Does the entity's operating structure include assigning responsibility, including segregation of duties, to specified individuals for environmental control?

13. Does the entity maintain an environmental information system, based on requirements by regulators or the entity's own evaluation of environmental risks? This system may provide, for example, information about physical quantities of emissions and hazardous waste, eco-balances, environmental characteristics of the entity's products and services, results from inspections performed by enforcement agencies, information about the occurrence and effects of incidents, and the number of complaints made by stakeholders.

14. Does the entity operate an Environmental Management System (EMS)? If so, has the EMS been certified by an independent certification body? Examples of recognized standards for an EMS are the international standard ISO 14001 and the European Commission's Eco-Management and Audit Scheme (EMAS).

15. Has the entity (voluntarily) published an environmental performance report? If so, has it been verified by an independent third party?

16. Are control procedures in place to identify and assess environmental risk, to monitor compliance with environmental laws and regulations, and to monitor possible changes in environmental legislation likely to impact the entity?

17. Does the entity have control procedures to deal with complaints about environmental matters, including health problems, from employees or third parties?

18. Does the entity operate control procedures for handling and disposal of hazardous waste, in compliance with legal requirements?

19. Are control procedures in place to identify and assess environmental hazards associated with the entity's products and services and the proper communication of information to customers about required preventive measures, if necessary?

20. Is management aware of the existence, and the potential impact on the entity's financial statements, of:

    • any risk of liabilities arising as a result of contamination of soil, groundwater, or surface water;

    • any risk of liabilities arising as a result of air pollution; or

    • unresolved complaints about environmental matters from employees or third parties?

Appendix 2

Substantive Procedures to Detect a Material Misstatement due to Environmental Matters

The purpose of this appendix is to provide examples of substantive procedures that an auditor may perform to detect a material misstatement due to environmental matters.

These examples are included for illustrative purposes only. It is not intended that all of the procedures illustrated will be appropriate in any particular case. The procedures need to be tailored to fit the particular circumstances of each engagement. In some cases, the auditor may judge it unnecessary to perform any of these procedures.

It may be necessary for the auditor to consult an environmental expert when evaluating the results of substantive procedures with regard to environmental matters. The decision to involve an expert is a matter of professional judgment, governed by the circumstances and matters such as the technological situation, complexity and materiality of the items concerned.

General

Documentary review in general

1. Consider minutes from board of directors' meetings, audit committees, or any other subcommittees of the board specifically responsible for environmental matters.

2. Consider publicly available industry information to consider any existing or possible future environmental matters. Also consider general available media comment, if any.

3. Where available, consider:

   - reports issued by environmental experts about the entity, such as site assessments or environmental impact studies;
   - internal audit reports;
   - "environmental audit" reports;
   - reports on due diligence investigations
   - reports issued by and correspondence with regulatory agencies;
   - (publicly available) registers or plans for the restoration of soil contamination;
   - environmental performance reports issued by the entity;
   - correspondence with enforcement agencies; and
   - correspondence with the entity's lawyers.

AUDITING

Using the work of others

4. If an environmental expert is involved (for example, an expert has quantified the nature and extent of contamination, considering alternative methods of site restoration) and the outcome has been recognized or disclosed in the financial statements:

    (a) consider the impact of the results of the expert's work on the financial statements;

    (b) assess the professional competence and the objectivity of the environmental expert;

    (c) obtain sufficient appropriate audit evidence that the scope of the work of the environmental expert is adequate for the purposes of the audit of the financial statements; and

    (d) assess the appropriateness of the expert's work as audit evidence.

5. If the internal auditor has addressed certain environmental aspects of the entity's operations as part of the internal audit, consider the appropriateness of the work of the internal auditors for the purpose of the audit of the financial statements, applying the criteria set out in ISA 610 "Considering the Work of Internal Auditing"

6. If an "environmental audit" has been performed and the findings of that audit could qualify as audit evidence in the audit of the financial statements:[12]

    (a) consider the impact of the results of the "environmental audit" on the financial statements;

    (b) assess the professional competence and the objectivity of the "environmental auditor"/audit team;

    (c) obtain sufficient appropriate audit evidence that the scope of "environmental audit" is adequate for the purposes of the audit of the financial statements; and

    (d) assess the appropriateness of the work of the "environmental auditor" as audit evidence.

Insurance

7. Inquire about existing (and earlier) insurance cover for environmental risk and discuss this with management.

Representations from management

8. Obtain written representations from management that it has considered the effects of environmental matters on the financial statements, and that it:

    (a) is not aware of any material liabilities or contingencies arising from environmental matters, including those resulting from illegal or possibly illegal acts;

---

[12] "Environmental audit": see paragraph 45.

(b) is not aware of environmental matters that may result in a material impairment of assets; or

(c) if aware of such matters, has disclosed to the auditor all facts related to them.

Subsidiaries

9. Inquire of auditors of subsidiaries as to the subsidiary's compliance with relevant local environmental laws and regulations and their possible effects on their financial statements.

Assets

Purchases of land, plant and machinery

10. For purchases of land, plant, and machinery made during the period (either directly by the entity, or indirectly through the acquisition of a subsidiary), inquire about the due diligence procedures management conducted to consider the effects of environmental matters in establishing a purchase price, taking into account the findings of remedial investigations and site restoration obligations.

Long-term investments

11. Read, and discuss with those responsible, financial statements underlying long-term investments and consider the effect of any environmental matters discussed in these statements on the valuation of the investments.

Asset impairment

12. Inquire about any planned changes in capital assets, for example, in response to changes in environmental legislation or changes in business strategy, assess their influences on the valuation of these assets or the company as a whole.

13. Inquire about policies and procedures to assess the need to write-down the carrying amount of an asset in situations where an asset impairment has occurred due to environmental matters.

14. Inquire about data gathered on which to base estimates and assumptions developed about the most likely outcome to determine the write-down due to the asset impairment.

15. Inspect the documentation supporting the amount of possible asset impairment and discuss such documentation with management.

16. For any asset impairments related to environmental matters that existed in previous periods, consider whether the assumptions underlying a write-down of related carrying values continue to be appropriate.

Recoverability of claims

17. Review the recoverability of claims with respect to environmental matters that are included in the financial statements.

AUDITING

Liabilities, Provisions and Contingencies

Completeness of Liabilities, Provisions and Contingencies

18. Inquire about policies and procedures implemented to help identify liabilities, provisions or contingencies arising from environmental matters.

19. Inquire about events or conditions that may give rise to liabilities, provisions or contingencies arising from environmental matters, for example,

    • Violations of environmental laws and regulations;

    • Citations or penalties arising from violations of environmental laws and regulations; or

    • Claims and possible claims for environmental damage.

20. If site clean-up costs, future removal or site restoration costs or penalties arising from noncompliance with environmental laws and regulations have been identified, inquire about any related claims or possible claims.

21. Inquire about, read, and evaluate correspondence from regulatory authorities relating to matters dealing with environmental matters and consider whether such correspondence indicates liabilities, provisions or contingencies.

22. For property abandoned, purchased, or closed during the period, inquire about requirements for site clean-up or intentions for future removal and site restoration.

23. For property sold during the period (and in prior periods), inquire about any liabilities relating to environmental matters retained by contract or by law.

24. Perform analytical procedures and consider, as far as practicable, the relationships between financial information and quantitative information included in the entity's environmental records (for example, the relationship between raw materials consumed or energy used, and waste production or emissions, taking into account the entity's liabilities for proper waste disposal or maximum emission levels).

Accounting estimates

25. Review and test the process used by management to develop accounting estimates and disclosures:

    (a) consider the adequacy of the work performed by environmental experts engaged by management, if any, applying the criteria set out in ISA 620 "Using the Work of an Expert;

    (b) review the data gathered on which estimates have been based;

    (c) consider whether the data are relevant, reliable and sufficient for the purpose;

    (d) evaluate whether the assumptions are consistent with each other, the supporting data, relevant historical data, and industry data;

    (e) consider whether changes in the business or industry may cause other factors to become significant to the assumptions;

(f) consider the need to engage an environmental expert regarding the review of certain assumptions;

(g) test the calculations made by management to translate the assumptions into the accounting estimate; and

(h) consider whether top-management has reviewed and approved material accounting estimates with respect to environmental matters.

26. If management's estimates are not appropriate, obtain an independent estimate to corroborate the reasonableness of management's estimate.

27. For liabilities, provisions, or contingencies related to environmental matters consider whether the assumptions underlying the estimates continue to be appropriate.

28. Compare estimates of liabilities relating to one location (for example, estimates for site restoration or future removal and site restoration costs at a specific location) with:

(a) estimates of liabilities for other locations with similar environmental problems;

(b) actual costs incurred for other similar locations; or

(c) estimates of costs of environmental liabilities reflected in the sales price for similar locations sold during the period.

Documentary review

29. Inspect and evaluate the documentation supporting the amount of the environmental liability, provision or contingency and discuss such documentation with those responsible for it, such as:

• site clean-up or restoration studies;

• quotes obtained for site clean-up or future removal and site restoration costs; and

• correspondence with legal counsel as to the amount of a claim or the amount of penalties.

Disclosure

30. Review the adequacy of the disclosure of the effects of environmental matters on the financial statements.

AUDITING

CONTENTS

Paragraphs

Introduction 1

Purpose of the Statement 2-4

Clarifying Responsibilities 5-18

Making Appropriate Inquiries of Management 19-32

Reporting to Management and Those Charged with Governance 33-36

Potential Impact on the Audit Report 37-44

This International Auditing Practice Statement (IAPS) has been prepared by the International Auditing Practices Committee (IAPC) of the International Federation of Accountants (IFAC). It was approved by the IAPC in June 1998 for publication in July 1998.

The purpose of this IAPS is to provide practical assistance to auditors in considering Year 2000 issues in the audit of financial statements. It does not affect the basic principles and essential procedures of International Standards on Auditing (ISAs).

The Public Sector Perspective (PSP) issued by the Public Sector Committee of the International Federation of Accountants is set out at the end of an IAPS. Where no PSP is added, the IAPS is applicable in all material respects to the public sector.

Introduction

1. The Year 2000 issue has had much publicity, but although all entities should be aware of it, responses are varied, with some entities still doing little. The issue is simple to explain; it has arisen because where computerized systems identify the year using two digits only, the digits 00 may be misinterpreted, for example, as 1900 or a special code or an error condition, potentially causing errors or operational failure of computerized systems. In addition, some computerized systems do not properly perform calculations with dates beginning in 1999, because these systems use the digits 99 in date fields to represent something other than the year 1999. It is also important to recognize that the Year 2000 is a leap year and that not all systems recognize February 29, 2000 as a valid date. The impact of these issues is not simple to predict, because even though the basic Year 2000 issue is well publicized, there are new issues emerging and, as a result, appropriate further guidance may need to be developed. The Year 2000 issue may manifest itself before, on or after January 1, 2000 and its effects on financial reporting and operations may range from inconsequential errors to business failure. Accordingly it is appropriate for auditors to consider this guidance immediately in the audits of financial statements.

Purpose of the Statement

2. This guidance is intended to clarify the impact of this issue on a financial statement audit and is based on the following principles:

   (a) it is management's responsibility to ensure the entity adequately addresses the issue;

   (b) the auditor's responsibilities outlined in International Standards on Auditing (ISAs) have not changed; and

   (c) the auditor obtains a sufficient understanding of any material impact on the financial statements subject to audit.

3. There is a risk of an "expectation gap" developing between auditors, and preparers and users of financial statements about what the auditor is expected to do in regard to the Year 2000 issue. The effects of the Year 2000 date change can be widespread throughout an entity and may be far removed from the recording of transactions normally reflected in the financial statements. The most significant effects may relate to the operating functions of an entity and may not have any direct impact on the process for recording transactions. Nevertheless, any significant potential disruption to, or failure of operating systems may impact the recognition, measurement and disclosure of items of the current period, for example, the reporting of assets and liabilities reflecting benefits or sacrifices of future economic benefits reflecting entity operating activities.

4. The objectives of this guidance are therefore:

   • To assist in clarifying the respective responsibilities of the auditor and management.

AUDITING

- To suggest inquiries for the auditor to make of management.

- To suggest matters that might be reported to management.

- To provide assistance in the application of ISAs to this issue.

- To outline circumstances where the auditor may issue a modified report.

- To assist in overcoming the risk of an audit expectation gap arising.

Clarifying Responsibilities

5.   In addressing the responsibilities of auditors and management for the Year 2000 issue, it is important to recognize that it is not, and will not, be possible for any entity to represent that it has achieved complete Year 2000 compliance and to guarantee its remediation efforts. The problem is simply too complex for such a claim to have legitimacy. The nature and complexity of the issue means that efforts to deal with Year 2000 problems are effectively risk mitigation.

General Responsibilities of Auditors

6.   To avoid doubt or misunderstanding, the auditor explains to management that the Year 2000 issue does not create any new responsibilities for the auditor, and that the Year 2000 issue will be addressed by the auditor only in so far as it affects existing audit responsibilities. Those responsibilities relate to the auditor expressing an opinion whether the financial statements are prepared, in all material respects, in accordance with the appropriate financial reporting framework. An audit of financial statements does not provide assurance that the entity's systems, or any other systems, such as those of suppliers or vendors, are, or will be, Year 2000 compliant.

7.   This explanation can be by discussion, but is ordinarily confirmed in writing. Accordingly, it is preferable that the auditor informs management in an engagement letter or other communication that the Year 2000 issue will be considered only to the extent of the auditor's responsibility to express an opinion on the financial statements and that management, not the auditor, is responsible for ensuring that the entity is prepared for the Year 2000 date change. The auditor also considers informing those with governance responsibilities of these matters.

8.   Because of the inherent risks that an entity may face, which could be impacted by both internal and external factors, the auditor will not be able to provide assurance that an entity's remediation efforts will be successful, as this is not within the scope of an audit of financial statements. Nevertheless, the auditor may be able to comment on the client's process for identifying, managing and remediating its Year 2000 problem that come to the auditor's attention during the normal course of the audit.

9.   If, in addition to the audit, the auditor is asked to assist the client with preparations for the Year 2000 date change, this is a separate engagement and a separate engagement letter is appropriate. This statement is not intended to provide guidance for such engagements, which may need to be undertaken together with appropriate specialists or experts. In deciding whether to

undertake such an engagement, the auditor considers whether doing so would be in accordance with the Code of Ethics for Professional Accountants issued by the International Federation of Accountants.

General Responsibilities of Management

10. Management's responsibility for running its business implicitly requires it to take reasonable steps to ensure that the entity is prepared for the Year 2000 date change and the business will not be materially affected. Some of the business risk implications of the Year 2000 issue include:

- The substantial cost of updating or replacing operating and information systems.

- Insurers' exclusions for losses/damages attributable to the Year 2000 issue.

- Operating losses or business failure, if there is extensive disruption to an entity's ability to conduct business because of a Year 2000 problem.

- Reliance on third party systems.

- The ability of suppliers, customers and service providers to meet their obligations to the entity.

- The potential for litigation and regulatory intervention.

Management needs to assess the impact on the entity and make plans to address these types of risks. Management also needs to consider any specific impacts on the financial statements. The review needs to encompass all significant business units, including other group entities, if applicable.

Assessing the Effect on the Entity's Computer Systems

11. The approach to the assessment that an entity takes will depend on its use of and dependence on computers and the type of systems it has. To consider the impact on the business, management will need to compile information on the nature, extent, business significance and likely earliest impact dates of Year 2000 on the entity's computer systems and other date sensitive systems and equipment. This could include:

- The computer environment including hardware, system software, network and communications software.

- Application software developed in-house by an IT function.

- User developed application software.

- Packaged software, considering not just the base package but the way in which it has been implemented.

- Software provided and operated by third parties under outsourcing arrangements or on a computer bureau basis.

- Embedded systems in computer controlled equipment used in the entity, for example in manufacturing processes and environment/process control, or in the products sold.

AUDITING

Management's Plans to Address the Issues Identified

12. In entities that do not have complex computer systems formal plans may not need to be prepared, but management has a responsibility to address the Year 2000 issue. In other entities, management needs to have prepared plans for remediation. For example, depending on the circumstances, management's plans may need to address:

    - Establishing an overall steering committee structure.

    - Defining individual projects for replacing or amending systems.

    - Establishing a timetable and appropriate milestones.

    - Resourcing the projects.

    - Developing and testing an implementation strategy.

    - Identifying constraints.

    - Establishing a process for monitoring implementation.

    - Establishing a contingency plan.

    Management may need to consider obtaining external help to plan and to address the issues identified. This could include extensive reliance on the entity's software suppliers especially where the usage of computers is confined to a few functions and simple, unmodified packages are used.

Management's Assessment of the Impact on the Financial Statements

13. It is also management's responsibility to ensure that the financial statements reflect any impact caused by the Year 2000 issue that has a material effect on the financial statements. Matters to consider will include:

    - The impact with respect to forward looking financial information used as a basis for financial reporting.

    - The establishment of an entity-wide definition of a Year 2000 cost and how such costs will be treated in the financial statements.

    - The write-down of assets such as software or computer controlled equipment that may be rendered inoperable.

    - Changes in amortization rates due to changes in estimates of useful life.

    - The evaluation and disclosure of commitments.

    - Disclosure of contingent liabilities such as for rectifications under warranties, litigation or compensation where the entity is a supplier of equipment requiring modification.

    - Disclosure of measurement uncertainty such as the recoverable amount of operating assets which are dependent upon successful Year 2000 remediation plans.

    - Any impact on the assessment of going concern particularly an evaluation of the magnitude of the costs and/or impact on operations.

Management needs to consider specific requirements for the disclosure of Year 2000 issues, particularly those required by regulatory bodies and the relevant financial reporting framework.

14. Management's consideration of the impact on the financial statements also needs to include an assessment of the possibility that account balances or accounting estimates have been misstated, noting that the Year 2000 issue can, in some cases, cause error in systems before the Year 2000 arrives. For example, where the system carries out calculations involving future dates, errors may start arising as soon as dates beyond December 31, 1999 are included in the calculations.

15. As part of the assessment of the applicability of the going concern basis as required by IAS 1 "Presentation of Financial Statements", management needs to consider whether the issue raises any uncertainty as to the continuing applicability of the underlying going concern assumption. Matters raising uncertainty concerns include significant remediation costs in relationship to net worth, insufficient funds to cover remediation costs, the lack of time or skills to address issues, ability of customers to meet their obligations because of the Year 2000 issue, dependency on suppliers, contractors and public sector entities to meet their commitments to the entity and the continuing functioning of critical operating systems on which the entity is dependent.

Risk of Error and Fraud

16. Management needs to assess the risk of error and opportunities for fraud that could arise where an entity has to make major adaptations to its systems or where the systems are functioning incorrectly. The extent of change and the urgency may cause a relaxation of formal testing and program change control procedures. Manual intervention may occur as problems arise or are identified. Because of the urgency of the issue and consequent demands on manpower, proper supervision and control may not be exercised during the process. Entities may use sub-contractors to identify and implement the program changes. Controls over these sub-contractors may not be stringent, nor may the entity have the necessary knowledge to supervise them properly. This situation increases the risk of processing errors that could result in a material misstatement in the financial statements and the opportunity for managers and/or staff to take advantage of system errors and failures.

Management's Statements to Shareholders and Others

17. The disclosure by management of uncertainties in relation to the impact of the Year 2000 issue or about the plans to address such issues is becoming more common. Views are changing rapidly in regard to the Year 2000 issue and accepted practices may develop in relation to the nature and extent of disclosures by management about the potential impacts of the Year 2000 issue.

18. Management may make statements to shareholders and others in documents containing audited financial information about its assessment of the impact of the Year 2000 issue on the entity and on the planned response. The auditor considers these statements having regard to ISA 720 "Other Information in

AUDITING

Documents Containing Audited Financial Statements" (see paragraphs 31 and 32).

Making Appropriate Inquiries of Management

Planning Considerations and Assessment of Audit Risk

19. To understand the likely significance of the issue to the auditor's responsibilities under International Standards on Auditing, the auditor, in accordance with ISA 310 "Knowledge of the Business", confirms the knowledge of the client's businesses by inquiry of management about:

    - The significance of computers and date sensitive embedded technologies in business operations.

    - The nature of the key computer systems which generate specific accounting information.

    - The dependence of the entity's systems and activities on third parties (for example, outsourcers, customers, suppliers, public sector entities) where failure of the third party systems would have a direct impact on amounts or disclosures in the financial statements.

20. Recognizing the nature of the Year 2000 issue, in accordance with ISA 620 "Using the Work of an Expert", the auditor considers the need to use the work of a computer specialist in obtaining sufficient appropriate audit evidence.

21. The auditor directs inquiries more specifically in order to understand management's views on:

    - Any increased risk of fraud or error in accounting information or other information supporting items in the financial statements.

    - The possible impact on specific financial statement amounts or disclosures, including regulatory disclosure requirements.

    - The potential impact, if any, on the going concern basis.

22. Based on existing knowledge of the client and its systems and supplemented as necessary with inquiries of management, the auditor considers whether the financial statements being audited will be misstated because of the effects of the Year 2000 issue. If the risk of a material misstatement is not considered significant, no further audit work is necessary unless information to the contrary comes to the auditor's attention during the audit.

    On the other hand, if the risk is significant, the auditor:

    (a) considers management's plan to control the risk;

    (b) assesses the impact on the financial statements; and

    (c) designs audit procedures to address the risk

    in accordance with ISA 320 "Materiality" and ISA 400 "Risk Assessments and Internal Control".

23. ISA 401 "Auditing in a Computer Information Systems Environment", paragraph 5 requires the auditor to obtain an understanding of the accounting and internal control systems sufficient to plan the audit and develop an effective audit approach. Where the auditor's preliminary assessment is that control risk is less than high and that therefore reliance on controls is planned, ISA 400, paragraph 31 requires the auditor to obtain audit evidence through tests of those controls being relied upon. On the other hand, where the auditor assesses control risk as high and the Year 2000 issue has been identified as being of potential financial statement significance, the auditor considers modifying the approach taken to obtaining evidence that the information has not been misstated by undertaking specific substantive procedures.

24. ISA 500 "Audit Evidence" requires that the auditor obtains sufficient appropriate audit evidence on which to base the audit opinion on the financial statements, based on the auditor's assessment of materiality and audit risk. The adequacy of evidence is a matter of professional judgment. In circumstances where the client has analyzed the impact or has plans to address the impact of the Year 2000 issue on the financial statements under audit, the auditor obtains information about management's plans in relation to the risk of material misstatement and assesses whether any adverse effects of the Year 2000 issue on the financial statements under audit have been addressed.

25. In considering management's analysis, the auditor may inquire about general factors such as:

- Whether the impact analysis was carried out systematically and the quality of records documenting that process.

- Whether all significant business units were involved in the process.

- Information (or test results) obtained from IT suppliers on packaged systems and outsourced systems.

- The skills, knowledge and experience of the staff involved in the impact analysis.

26. In considering management's plans and progress monitoring, the auditor may consider inquiring as to how management has satisfied itself that:

- Systems replacement or modification projects are being led by staff with experience of such projects (either internal or provided by external suppliers or advisors).

- Sufficient resources have been committed to the systems projects identified.

- Appropriate timescales have been allocated for the systems projects identified and adequate time and resources have been allocated to test modified or replaced systems.

- Progress against plans is being monitored rigorously and regularly.

- Slippage against the plan has resulted in positive action or reprioritization.

AUDITING

- Contingency planning is being addressed.

27. Where Year 2000 modifications affect an entity's systems that produce information for the financial statements, for example accounting estimates, the auditor tests management's plans in accordance with ISA 401 "Auditing in a Computer Information Systems Environment" and ISA 402 "Audit Considerations Relating to Entities Using Service Organizations".

Auditors of Subsidiary Entities

28. Taking into account knowledge of the activities of subsidiary entities, the principal auditor considers whether other auditors have made inquiries about the Year 2000 issue in relation to the entities they are auditing, in the same way as suggested in this guidance, particularly in those subsidiaries that comprise major parts of the group's business.

Internal Auditing

29. In some entities, the internal audit function will be involved in reviewing management's Year 2000 processes, and the external auditor may find that Year 2000 related information can be obtained through inquiries of the internal audit function and the review of its working papers. Where the external auditor decides to use specific internal audit work in determining the nature, timing and extent of audit procedures, the work that the internal audit function has performed is evaluated by the external auditor to confirm its adequacy for the external auditor's purposes in accordance with ISA 610 "Using the Work of Internal Auditing".

Management Representations

30. For information included in the financial statements or in the notes to the financial statements, the auditor considers obtaining management representations on Year 2000 issues in accordance ISA 580 "Management Representations".

Auditor's Considerations of Management Statements

31. Other information included in documents containing audited financial statements may discuss the effects of the Year 2000 issue. For example, management may make qualitative statements about the adequacy of its Year 2000 mitigation efforts and/or the likelihood of their success in information about performance, operations and risk management. In accordance with ISA 720, the auditor reads the other information to identify material inconsistencies with the audited financial statements.

32. The auditor may become aware of other information about the Year 2000 issue that, although not necessarily inconsistent with the audited financial statements, appears to be a material misstatement of fact, such as the entity's description of its efforts to mitigate the effects of the Year 2000 issue. In that case the auditor discusses the concern with management. If the auditor concludes that the matter has not been satisfactorily addressed, the auditor takes further action which could include notifying those persons with

governance responsibilities in writing of the auditor's concern regarding the other information and obtaining legal advice.

Reporting to Management and Those Charged with Governance Responsibilities

33. To avoid misunderstandings about the auditor's responsibilities with respect to Year 2000 matters, the auditor explains these responsibilities under ISAs dealing with communications on these issues during audits leading up to the Year 2000.

34. During the audit, the auditor may identify Year 2000 related matters that represent material weaknesses in the design or operation of the accounting and internal control systems relevant to financial statement assertions that need to be formally communicated to management. In addition, the auditor may also identify other conditions arising from the Year 2000 issue that may be of interest to management in discharging its responsibilities, and may consider reporting these matters to management so that they can be addressed.

35. In making any such reports, the auditor communicates to management the limits of the work on which the comments are based (which would only be that work necessary to fulfil the audit responsibilities), and that consequently, failure to report does not mean that there are no deficiencies.

36. The auditor may similarly report issues to those charged with governance responsibilities, such as a supervisory board or the board of directors including the audit committee where one exists. Any comments are to be made in the context of the auditor's responsibility for giving an opinion on the financial statements.

Potential Impact on the Auditor's Report

37. While this guidance does not repeat the general principles of audit reporting under ISAs, it is important to recognize that situations requiring a modified report in respect of financial statements currently being audited under ISAs may be encountered in relation to Year 2000 issues:

   (a) an emphasis of matter paragraph may be required where the notes to the financial statements include information relating to a significant uncertainty;

   (b) an emphasis of matter paragraph is required where there is a going concern problem relating to Year 2000 issues;

   (c) a qualified or adverse opinion may be required where there is a disagreement with management about the manner in which Year 2000 issues such as those in paragraph 13 are dealt with in the financial statements;

   (d) a qualified or disclaimer of opinion may be required where there is a limitation on scope where necessary evidence that does, did or should

AUDITING

exist in relation to the impact of Year 2000 issues is not available to the auditor.

There are some particular areas that warrant further consideration. The significance of the paragraphs that follow will be greater as the Year 2000 approaches.

Lack of Information from the Entity

38. The auditor obtains sufficient appropriate evidence that the financial statements are not materially misstated. A modified report is appropriate where the auditor has a reasonable basis for considering that the possible impact of Year 2000 issues is material and has not been able to obtain sufficient appropriate evidence.

39. For some entities, management's assessment of the impact on the entity, and any plans to address the issues may be insufficient, for example, because the entity may not have the expertise or resources to carry out a detailed and rigorous analysis of its systems. In some cases, management may not have even considered whether the problem could affect the entity. It is not the auditor's responsibility to attempt to rectify any lack of analysis or planning by management, and a modification based on a limitation on scope is appropriate, but only if the lack of analysis or planning affects the financial statements being audited.

40. In some cases evidence cannot reasonably be expected to be available. This may be because of the scale of the tasks, or the extent to which much of the relevant information is based on management proposals and intentions. In this case it is unlikely that the auditor can independently perform an assessment of the impact. If management is unwilling to provide a written representation of its significant proposals and intentions, then a scope limitation exists. If the only evidence that can reasonably be expected to be available to the auditor is a written representation, and such a representation is provided, the auditor considers whether there is a significant uncertainty with respect to the financial statement issues associated with the Year 2000.

41. A major impact on an entity's financial statements could be caused by problems that are external to the entity itself (e.g. suppliers, customers or EDI interfaces). Evidence about the impact may also be external to the entity. In these circumstances the auditor considers the impact, if any, on the audit report and considers the guidance in paragraph 37 above.

Considerations in Respect of Going Concern

42. Paragraph 5 of ISA 570 "Going Concern" requires the auditor to consider the risk that the going concern assumption may no longer be appropriate. As the Year 2000 approaches, going concern considerations become increasingly significant.

43. In some cases, management's assessment of the impact of the Year 2000 issue may cause the going concern assumption of the entity to be called into question unless management can take effective action to address the impacts identified. For example:

- Business critical systems may become inoperable beyond a certain date and cannot be changed or new systems cannot be installed in time.

- Embedded technologies may cause vital machinery to be rendered similarly inoperable and the entity cannot afford or obtain replacement machinery.

- Key suppliers or customers of the entity, or public sector entities on whom it is dependent, may suffer problems that disrupt the supply chain so that the entity goes out of business.

- A supplier of either computer hardware or software, or of computer controlled machinery which is not Year 2000 compliant may be threatened by the costs of product liability and of legal suits.

44. In considering management's assessment of the impact of the Year 2000 and the appropriateness of the going concern assumption underlying the preparation of the financial statements for the foreseeable future the auditor refers to the requirements of ISA 570 "Going Concern".

AUDITING

SUMMARY OF DISCUSSION PAPER

The Committee has issued one discussion paper, as summarized below.

Discussion Paper
The Audit Profession and the Environment
Issued May 1995

The audit profession can contribute its expertise and services to business and society in making progress towards sustainable development, and towards management of and accountability for environmental stewardship. The profession has the strength, reputation and skills needed to expand its role and contribute to:

- the development of standards and guidance for audit and review of financial statements regarding environmental matters;

- arrangements necessary for obtaining audit evidence that requires the co-operation or use of the work of other professions and disciplines in areas outside the normal competence of financial auditors; and

- the development of standards and guidance needed to respond to the expectations of stakeholders for emerging new services.

IFAC, in its role of representing the worldwide audit profession, is interested in collaborating with other associations, organizations, professions and disciplines, since sustainable development and environmental issues are inherently multi-disciplinary issues, and no single discipline or profession is likely to provide all the solutions. Some member bodies already have authoritative literature on the subject in place or under development. This document seeks to summarize the topics and promote discussion on an international level. The document does not discuss accounting matters.

The preparation of this discussion paper serves three purposes:

- to generate ideas and views on issues to be dealt with by the auditing profession as a whole with regard to 'environmental auditing';

- to gather views of practitioners on the more important implications of environmental issues in relation to the audit of financial statements; and

- to promote discussion amongst both practitioners and a wider audience on reporting on environmental performance, the audit of such reports and on possible future engagements (reporting on, and audits of, environmental management systems and compliance engagements),

To serve these purposes, questions for discussion are included at the end of each chapter. The document is also distributed outside the auditing community.

The following standards have
been approved for release by
the International Auditing
Practices Committee. They are
effective for financial periods
ended after 31 December 2000.
They are included here for
informational purposes.

CONTENTS

	Paragraphs
Introduction	1-2
Management's Responsibility	3-8
Auditor's Responsibility	9-10
Planning Considerations	11-16
Evaluating Management's Assessment	17-21
Period Beyond Management's Assessment	22-25
Additional Audit Procedures When Events or Conditions are Identified	26-29
Audit Conclusions and Reporting	30-38
Significant Delay in the Signature or Approval of Financial Statements	39
Effective Date	40

International Standards on Auditing (ISAs) are to be applied in the audit of financial statements. ISAs are also to be applied, adapted as necessary, to the audit of other information and to related services.

ISAs contain the basic principles and essential procedures (identified in bold type black lettering) together with related guidance in the form of explanatory and other material. The basic principles and essential procedures are to be interpreted in the context of the explanatory and other material that provide guidance for their application.

To understand and apply the basic principles and essential procedures together with the related guidance, it is necessary to consider the whole text of the ISA including explanatory and other material contained in the ISA, not just that text which is black lettered.

In exceptional circumstances, an auditor may judge it necessary to depart from an ISA in order to more effectively achieve the object of an audit. When such a situation arises, the auditor should be prepared to justify the departure.

ISAs need only be applied to material matters.

The Public Sector Perspective (PSP) issued by the Public Sector Committee of the International Federation of Accountants is set out at the end of an ISA. Where no PSP is added, the ISA is applicable in all material respects to the public sector.

AUDITING

Introduction

1. The purpose of this International Standard on Auditing (ISA) is to establish standards and-provide guidance on the auditor's responsibility in the audit of financial statements with respect to the going concern assumption used in the preparation of the financial statements, including considering management's assessment of the entity's ability to continue as a going concern.

2. **When planning and performing audit procedures and in evaluating the results thereof, the auditor should consider the appropriateness of management's use of the going concern assumption in the preparation of the financial statements.**

Management's Responsibility

3. The going concern assumption is a fundamental principle in the preparation of financial statements. Under the going concern assumption, an entity is ordinarily viewed as continuing in business for the foreseeable future with neither the intention nor the necessity of liquidation, ceasing trading or seeking protection from creditors pursuant to laws or regulations. Accordingly, assets and liabilities are recorded on the basis that the entity will be able to realize its assets and discharge its liabilities in the normal course of business.

4. Some financial reporting frameworks contain an explicit requirement[1] for management to make a specific assessment of the entity's ability to continue as a going concern, and standards regarding matters to be considered and disclosures to be made in connection with going concern. For example, International Accounting Standard 1 (revised 1997), "Presentation of Financial Statements" requires management to make an assessment of an enterprise's ability to continue as a going concern[2].

---

1 The detailed requirements regarding management's responsibility to assess the entity's ability to continue as a going concern and related financial statement disclosures may be set out in accounting standards, legislation or regulation.

2 IAS 1, "Presentation of Financial Statements", paragraphs 23 and 24 state: "When preparing financial statements, management should make an assessment of an enterprise's ability to continue as a going concern. Financial statements should be prepared on a going concern basis unless management intends to liquidate the enterprise or to cease trading, or has no realistic alternative but to do so. When management is aware, in making its assessment, of material uncertainties related to events or conditions which may cast significant doubt upon the enterprise's ability to continue as a going concern, those uncertainties should be disclosed. When the financial statements are not prepared on a going concern basis, that fact should be disclosed, together with the basis on which the financial statements are prepared and the reasons why the enterprise is not considered to be a going concern."

In assessing whether the going concern assumption is appropriate, management takes into account all available information for the foreseeable future, which should be at least, but is not limited to, twelve months from the balance sheet date. The degree of consideration depends on the facts in each case. When an enterprise has a history of profitable operations and ready access to financial resources, a conclusion that the going concern basis of accounting is appropriate can be reached without detailed analysis. In other cases, management may need to consider a wide range of factors surrounding current and expected profitability, debt repayment schedules and potential sources of replacement financing before it can satisfy itself that the going concern basis is appropriate."

5. In other financial reporting frameworks, there may be no explicit requirement for management to make a specific assessment of the entity's ability to continue as a going concern. Nevertheless, since the going concern assumption is a fundamental principle in the preparation of the financial statements, management has a responsibility to assess the entity's ability to continue as a going concern even if the financial reporting framework does not include an explicit responsibility to do so.

6. When there is a history of profitable operations and a ready access to financial resources, management may make its assessment without detailed analysis.

7. Management's assessment of the going concern assumption involves making a judgment, at a particular point in time, about the future outcome of events or conditions which are inherently uncertain. The following factors are relevant:

    •   In general terms, the degree of uncertainty associated with the outcome of an event or condition increases significantly the further into the future a judgment is being made about the outcome of an event or condition. For that reason, most financial reporting frameworks that require an explicit management assessment specify the period for which management is required to take into account all available information.

    •   Any judgment about the future is based on information available at the time at which the judgment is made. Subsequent events can contradict a judgment which was reasonable at the time it was made.

    •   The size and complexity of the entity, the nature and condition of its business and the degree to which it is affected by external factors all affect the judgment regarding the outcome of events or conditions.

8. Examples of events or conditions, which individually or collectively, may cast significant doubt about the going concern assumption are set out below. This listing is not all-inclusive nor does the existence of one or more of the items always signify that a material uncertainty[3] exists.

Financial

•   Net liability or net current liability position.

•   Fixed-term borrowings approaching maturity without realistic prospects of renewal or repayment; or excessive reliance on short-term borrowings to finance long-term assets.

•   Indications of withdrawal of financial support by debtors and other creditors.

•   Negative operating cash flows indicated by historical or prospective financial statements.

•   Adverse key financial ratios.

---

[3] The phrase "material uncertainty" is used in IAS 1 in discussing the uncertainties related to events or conditions which may cast significant doubt on the enterprise's ability to continue as a going concern that should be disclosed in the financial statements. In other financial reporting frameworks, and elsewhere in the ISA's, the phrase "significant uncertainties" is used in similar circumstances.

- Substantial operating losses or significant deterioration in the value of assets used to generate cash flows.
- Arrears or discontinuance of dividends.
- Inability to pay creditors on due dates.
- Inability to comply with the terms of loan agreements.
- Change from credit to cash-on-delivery transactions with suppliers.
- Inability to obtain financing for essential new product development or other essential investments.

Operating

- Loss of key management without replacement.
- Loss of a major market, franchise, license, or principal supplier.
- Labor difficulties or shortages of important supplies.

Other

- Non-compliance with capital or other statutory requirements.
- Pending legal or regulatory proceedings against the entity that may, if successful, result in claims that are unlikely to be satisfied.
- Changes in legislation or government policy expected to adversely affect the entity.

The significance of such events or conditions often can be mitigated by other factors. For example, the effect of an entity being unable to make its normal debt repayments may be counter-balanced by management's plans to maintain adequate cash flows by alternative means, such as by disposal of assets, rescheduling of loan repayments, or obtaining additional capital. Similarly, the loss of a principal supplier may be mitigated by the availability of a suitable alternative source of supply.

Auditor's Responsibility

9. The auditor's responsibility is to consider the appropriateness of management's use of the going concern assumption in the preparation of the financial statements, and consider whether there are material uncertainties about the entity's ability to continue as a going concern that need to be disclosed in the financial statements. The auditor considers the appropriateness of management's use of the going concern assumption even if the financial reporting framework used in the preparation of the financial statements does not include an explicit requirement for management to make a specific assessment of the entity's ability to continue as a going concern.

10. The auditor cannot predict future events or conditions that may cause an entity to cease to continue as a going concern. Accordingly, the absence of any reference to going concern uncertainty in an auditor's report cannot be viewed as a guarantee as to the entity's ability to continue as a going concern.

Planning Considerations

11. **In planning the audit, the auditor should consider whether there are events or conditions which may cast significant doubt on the entity's ability to continue as a going concern.**

12. **The auditor should remain alert for evidence of events or conditions which may cast significant doubt on the entity's ability to continue as a going concern throughout the audit. If such events or conditions are identified, the auditor should, in addition to performing the procedures in paragraph 26, consider whether they affect the auditor's assessments of the components of audit risk.**

13. The auditor considers events and conditions relating to the going concern assumption during the planning process, because this consideration allows for more timely discussions with management, review of management's plans and resolution of any identified going concern issues.

14. In some cases, management may have already made a preliminary assessment at the early stages of the audit. If so, the auditor reviews that assessment to determine whether management has identified events or conditions, such as those discussed in paragraph 8, and management's plans to address them.

15. If management has not yet made a preliminary assessment, the auditor discusses with management the basis for their intended use of the going concern assumption, and inquires of management whether events or conditions, such as those discussed in paragraph 8, exist. The auditor may request management to begin making its assessment, particularly when the auditor has already identified events or conditions relating to the going concern assumption.

16. The auditor considers the effect of identified events or conditions when making preliminary assessments of the components of audit risk and, therefore, their existence may affect the nature, timing and extent of the auditor's procedures.

Evaluating Management's Assessment

17. **The auditor should evaluate management's assessment of the entity's ability to continue as a going concern.**

18. The auditor should consider the same period as that used by management in making its assessment under the financial reporting framework. If management's assessment of the entity's ability to continue as a going concern covers less than twelve months from the balance sheet date, the auditor should ask management to extend its assessment period to twelve months from the balance sheet date.

19. Management's assessment of the entity's ability to continue as a going concern is a key part of the auditor's consideration of the going concern assumption. As noted in paragraph 7, most financial reporting frameworks

AUDITING

requiring an explicit management assessment specify the period for which management is required to take into account all available information.[4]

20.   In evaluating management's assessment, the auditor considers the process management followed to make its assessment, the assumptions on which the assessment is based and management's plans for future action. The auditor considers whether the assessment has taken into account all relevant information of which the auditor is aware as a result of the audit procedures.

21.   As noted in paragraph 6, when there is a history of profitable operations and a ready access to financial resources, management may make its assessment without detailed analysis. In such circumstances, the auditor's conclusion about the appropriateness of this assessment normally is also made without the need for performing detailed procedures. When events or conditions have been identified which may cast significant doubt about the entity's ability to continue as a going concern, however, the auditor performs additional audit procedures, as described in paragraph 26.

Period Beyond Management's Assessment

22.   The auditor should inquire of management as to its knowledge of events or conditions beyond the period of assessment used by management that may cast significant doubt on the entity's ability to continue as a going concern.

23.   The auditor is alert to the possibility that there may be known events, scheduled or otherwise, or conditions that will occur beyond the period of assessment used by management that may bring into question the appropriateness of management's use of the going concern assumption in preparing the financial statements. The auditor may become aware of such known events or conditions during the planning and conduct of the audit, including subsequent events procedures.

24.   Since the degree of uncertainty associated with the outcome of an event or condition increases as the event or condition is further into the future, in considering such events or conditions, the indications of going concern issues will need to be significant before the auditor considers taking further action. The auditor may need to ask management to determine the potential significance of the event or condition on their going concern assessment.

25.   The auditor does not have a responsibility to design procedures other than inquiry of management to test for indications of events or conditions which cast significant doubt on the entity's ability to continue as a going concern beyond the period assessed by management which, as discussed in paragraph 18, would be at least twelve months from the balance sheet date.

---

[4] For example, IAS 1 defines this as a period that should be at least, but is not limited to, twelve months from the balance sheet date.

Additional Audit Procedures When Events or Conditions are Identified

26. **When events or conditions have been identified which may cast significant doubt on the entity's ability to continue as a going concern, the auditor should:**

   (a) **review management's plans for future actions based on its going concern assessment;**

   (b) **gather sufficient appropriate audit evidence to confirm or dispel whether or not a material uncertainty exists through carrying out procedures considered necessary, including considering the effect of any plans of management and other mitigating factors; and**

   (c) **seek written representations from management regarding its plans for future action.**

27. Events or conditions which may cast significant doubt on the entity's ability to continue as a going concern may be identified during the planning of the engagement or in the course of performing audit procedures. The process of considering events or conditions continues as the audit progresses. When the auditor believes such events or conditions may cast significant doubt on the entity's ability to continue as a going concern, certain procedures may take on added significance. The auditor inquires of management as to its plans for future action, including its plans to liquidate assets, borrow money or restructure debt, reduce or delay expenditures, or increase capital. The auditor also considers whether any additional facts or information are available since the date on which management made its assessment. The auditor obtains sufficient appropriate audit evidence that management's plans are feasible and that the outcome of these plans will improve the situation.

28. Procedures that are relevant in this regard may include:

   - Analyzing and discussing cash flow, profit and other relevant forecasts with management.

   - Analyzing and discussing the entity's latest available interim financial statements.

   - Reviewing the terms of debentures and loan agreements and determining whether any have been breached.

   - Reading minutes of the meetings of shareholders, the board of directors and important committees for reference to financing difficulties.

   - Inquiring of the entity's lawyer regarding the existence of litigation and claims and the reasonableness of management's assessments of their outcome and the estimate of their financial implications.

   - Confirming the existence, legality and enforceability of arrangements to provide or maintain financial support with related and third parties and assessing the financial ability of such parties to provide additional funds.

   - Considering the entity's plans to deal with unfilled customer orders.

   - Reviewing events after period end to identify those that either mitigate or otherwise affect the entity's ability to continue as a going concern.

AUDITING

29. When analysis of cash flow is a significant factor in considering the future outcome of events or conditions the auditor considers:

the reliability of the entity's system for generating such information, and

whether there is adequate support for the assumptions underlying the forecast.

In addition the auditor compares:

(a) the prospective financial information for recent prior periods with historical results, and

(b) the prospective financial information for the current period with results achieved to date.

Audit Conclusions and Reporting

30. **Based on the audit evidence obtained, the auditor should determine if, in the auditor's judgment, a material uncertainty exists related to events or conditions that alone or in aggregate, may cast significant doubt on the entity's ability to continue as a going concern.**

31. A material uncertainty exists when the magnitude of its potential impact is such that, in the auditor's judgment, clear disclosure of the nature and implications of the uncertainty is necessary for the presentation of the financial statements not to be misleading.

Going Concern Assumption Appropriate but a Material Uncertainty Exists

32. If the use of the going concern assumption is appropriate but a material uncertainty exists, the auditor considers whether the financial statements:

(a) adequately describe the principal events or conditions that give rise to the significant doubt on the entity's ability to continue in operation and management's plans to deal with these events or conditions.

(b) state clearly that there is a material uncertainty related to events or conditions which may cast significant doubt on the entity's ability to continue as a going concern and, therefore, that it may be unable to realize its assets and discharge its liabilities in the normal course of business.

33. **If adequate disclosure is made in the financial statements, the auditor should express an unqualified opinion but modify the auditor's report by adding an emphasis of matter paragraph that highlights the existence of a material uncertainty relating to the event or condition that may cast significant doubt on the entity's ability to continue as a going concern and draws attention to the note in the financial statements that discloses the matters set out in paragraph 32.** In assessing the adequacy of the financial statement disclosure, the auditor considers whether the information explicitly draws the reader's attention to the possibility that the entity may be unable to continue realizing its assets and discharging its liabilities in the normal course of business. The following is an example of such a paragraph when the auditor is satisfied as to the adequacy of the note disclosure:

"Without qualifying our opinion, we draw attention to Note X in the financial statements which indicates that the Company incurred a net loss of ZZZ during the year ended December 31, 20X1 and, as of that date, the Company's current liabilities exceeded its total assets by ZZZ. These conditions, along with other matters as set forth in Note X, indicate the existence of a material uncertainty which may cast significant doubt about the Company's ability to continue as a going concern."

In extreme cases, such as situations involving multiple material uncertainties that are significant to the financial statements, the auditor may consider it appropriate to express a disclaimer of opinion instead of adding an emphasis of matter paragraph.

34. **If adequate disclosure is not made in the financial statements, the auditor should express a qualified or adverse opinion, as appropriate (ISA 700, "The Auditor's Report on Financial Statements", paragraphs 45-46). The report should include specific reference to the fact that there is a material uncertainty that may cast significant doubt about the entity's ability to continue as a going concern.** The following is an example of the relevant paragraphs when a qualified opinion is to be expressed:

"The Company's financing arrangements expire and amounts outstanding are payable on March 19, 20X1. The Company has been unable to re-negotiate or obtain replacement financing. This situation indicates the existence of a material uncertainty which may cast significant doubt on the Company's ability to continue as a going concern and therefore it may be unable to realize its assets and discharge its liabilities in the normal course of business. The financial statements (and notes thereto) do not disclose this fact.

In our opinion, except for the omission of the information included in the preceding paragraph, the financial statements give a true and fair view of (present fairly, in all material respects,) the financial position of the Company at December 31, 20X0 and the results of its operations and its cash flows for the year then ended in accordance with ..."

The following is an example of the relevant paragraphs when an adverse opinion is to be expressed:

"The Company's financing arrangements expired and the amount outstanding was payable on December 31, 20X0. The Company has been unable to re-negotiate or obtain replacement financing and is considering filing for bankruptcy. These events indicate a material uncertainty which may cast significant doubt on the Company's ability to continue as a going concern and therefore it may be unable to realize its assets and discharge its liabilities in the normal course of business. The financial statements (and notes thereto) do not disclose this fact.

In our opinion, because of the omission of the information mentioned in the preceding paragraph, the financial statements do not give a true and fair view of (or do not present fairly) the financial position of the Company as at December 31, 20X0, and of its results of operations and its cash flows for the year then ended in accordance with....(and do not comply with...)..."

AUDITING

Going Concern Assumption Inappropriate

35.   If, in the auditor's judgment, the entity will not be able to continue as a going concern, the auditor should express an adverse opinion if the financial statements have been prepared on a going concern basis. If, on the basis of the additional procedures carried out and the information obtained, including the effect of management's plans, the auditor's judgment is that the entity will not be able to continue as a going concern, the auditor concludes, regardless of whether or not disclosure has been made, that the going concern assumption used in the preparation of the financial statements is inappropriate and expresses an adverse opinion.

36.   When the entity's management has concluded that the going concern assumption used in the preparation of the financial statements is not appropriate, the financial statements need to be prepared on an alternative authoritative basis. If on the basis of the additional procedures carried out and the information obtained the auditor determines the alternative basis is appropriate, the auditor can issue an unqualified opinion if there is adequate disclosure but may require an emphasis of matter in the auditor's report to draw the user's attention to that basis.

Management Unwilling to Make or Extend its Assessment

37.   **If management is unwilling to make or extend its assessment when requested to do so by the auditor, the auditor should consider the need to modify the auditor's report as a result of the limitation on the scope of the auditor's work.** In certain circumstances, such as those described in paragraphs 15, 18 and 24, the auditor may believe that it is necessary to ask management to make or extend its assessment. If management is unwilling to do so, it is not the auditor's responsibility to rectify the lack of analysis by management, and a modified report may be appropriate because it may not be possible for the auditor to obtain sufficient appropriate evidence regarding the use of the going concern assumption in the preparation of the financial statements.

38.   In some circumstances, the lack of analysis by management may not preclude the auditor from being satisfied about the entity's ability to continue as a going concern. For example, the auditor's other procedures may be sufficient to assess the appropriateness of management's use of the going concern assumption in the preparation of the financial statements because the entity has a history of profitable operations and a ready access to financial resources. In other circumstances, however, the auditor may not be able to confirm or dispel, in the absence of management's assessment, whether or not events or conditions exist which indicate there may be a significant doubt on the entity's ability to continue as a going concern, or the existence of plans management has put in place to address them or other mitigating factors. In these circumstances, the auditor modifies the auditor's report as discussed in ISA 700 "The Auditor's Report on Financial Statements" paragraphs 36 – 44.

Significant Delay in the Signature or Approval of Financial Statements

39.   When there is significant delay in the signature or approval of the financial statements by management after the balance sheet date, the auditor considers

the reasons for the delay. When the delay could be related to events or conditions relating to the going concern assessment, the auditor considers the need to perform additional audit procedures, as described in paragraph 26, as well as the effect on the auditor's conclusion regarding the existence of a material uncertainty, as described in paragraph 30.

Effective Date

40. This ISA is effective for audits of financial statements for periods ending on or after December 31, 2000.

Public Sector Perspective

1. *The appropriateness of the use of the going concern assumption in the preparation of the financial statements is generally not in question when auditing either a central government or those public sector entities having funding arrangements backed by a central government. However, where such arrangements do not exist, or where central government funding of the entity may be withdrawn and the existence of the entity may be at risk, this ISA will provide useful guidance. As governments corporatize and privatize government entities, going concern issues will become increasingly relevant to the public sector.*

CONTENTS

	Paragraphs
Introduction	1-4
Relevant Persons	5-10
Audit Matters of Governance Interest to be Communicated	11-12
Timing of Communications	13-14
Forms of Communications	15-17
Other Matters	18-19
Confidentiality	20
Laws and Regulations	21
Effective Date	22

International Standards on Auditing (ISAs) are to be applied in the audit of financial statements. ISAs are also to be applied, adapted as necessary, to the audit of other information and to related services.

ISAs contain the basic principles and essential procedures (identified in bold type black lettering) together with related guidance in the form of explanatory and other material. The basic principles and essential procedures are to be interpreted in the context of the explanatory and other material that provide guidance for their application.

To understand and apply the basic principles and essential procedures together with the related guidance, it is necessary to consider the whole text of the ISA including explanatory and other material contained in the ISA, not just that text which is black lettered.

In exceptional circumstances, an auditor may judge it necessary to depart from an ISA in order to more effectively achieve the object of an audit. When such a situation arises, the auditor should be prepared to justify the departure.

ISAs need only be applied to material matters.

The Public Sector Perspective (PSP) issued by the Public Sector Committee of the International Federation of Accountants is set out at the end of an ISA. Where no PSP is added, the ISA is applicable in all material respects to the public sector.

AUDITING

Introduction

1. The purpose of this International Standard on Auditing (ISA) is to establish standards and provide guidance on communication of audit matters arising from the audit of financial statements between the auditor and those charged with governance of an entity. These communications relate to audit matters of governance interest as defined in this ISA. This ISA does not provide guidance on communications by the auditor to parties outside the entity, for example, external regulatory or supervisory agencies.

2. **The auditor should communicate audit matters of governance interest arising from the audit of financial statements with those charged with governance of an entity.**

3. For the purposes of this ISA, "governance" is the term used to describe the role of persons entrusted with the supervision, control and direction of an entity.[5] Those charged with governance ordinarily are accountable for ensuring that the entity achieves its objectives, financial reporting, and reporting to interested parties. Those charged with governance include management only when it performs such functions.

4. For the purpose of this ISA, "audit matters of governance interest" are those that arise from the audit of financial statements and, in the opinion of the auditor, are both important and relevant to those charged with governance in overseeing the financial reporting and disclosure process. Audit matters of governance interest include only those matters that have come to the attention of the auditor as a result of the performance of the audit. The auditor is not required, in an audit in accordance with ISAs, to design procedures for the specific purpose of identifying matters of governance interest.

Relevant Persons

5. **The auditor should determine the relevant persons who are charged with governance and with whom audit matters of governance interest are communicated.**

6. The structures of governance vary from country to country reflecting cultural and legal backgrounds. For example, in some countries, the supervision function, and the management function are legally separated into different bodies, such as a supervisory (wholly or mainly non-executive) board and a management (executive) board. In other countries, both functions are the legal responsibility of a single, unitary board, although there may be an audit committee that assists that board in its governance responsibilities with respect to financial reporting.

---

[5] Principles of corporate governance have been developed by many countries as a point of reference for the establishment of good corporate behavior. Such principles generally focus on publicly traded companies; however, they may also serve to improve governance in other forms of entities. There is no single model of good corporate governance. Board structures and practices vary from country to country. A common principle is that the entity should have in place a governance structure which enables the board to exercise objective judgment on corporate affairs, including financial reporting, independent in particular from management.

7. This diversity makes it difficult to establish a universal identification of the persons who are charged with governance and with whom the auditor communicates audit matters of governance interest. The auditor uses judgment to determine those persons with whom audit matters of governance interest are communicated, taking into account the governance structure of the entity, the circumstances of the engagement and any relevant legislation. The auditor also considers the legal responsibilities of those persons. For example, in entities with supervisory boards or with audit committees, the relevant persons may be those bodies. However, in entities where a unitary board has established an audit committee, the auditor may decide to communicate with the audit committee, or with the whole board, depending on the importance of the audit matters of governance interest.

8. When the entity's governance structure is not well defined, or those charged with governance are not clearly identified by the circumstances of the engagement, or by legislation, the auditor comes to an agreement with the entity about with whom audit matters of governance interest are to be communicated. Examples include some owner-managed entities, some not for profit organizations, and some government agencies.

9. To avoid misunderstandings, an audit engagement letter may explain that the auditor will communicate only those matters of governance interest that come to attention as a result of the performance of an audit and that the auditor is not required to design procedures for the specific purpose of identifying matters of governance interest. The engagement letter may also:

- Describe the form in which any communications on audit matters of governance interest will be made;

- Identify the relevant persons with whom such communications will be made;

- Identify any specific audit matters of governance interest which it has been agreed are to be communicated.

10. The effectiveness of communications is enhanced by developing a constructive working relationship between the auditor and those charged with governance. This relationship is developed while maintaining an attitude of professional independence and objectivity.

Audit Matters of Governance Interest to be Communicated

11. **The auditor should consider audit matters of governance interest that arise from the audit of the financial statements and communicate them with those charged with governance.** Ordinarily such matters include:

- The general approach and overall scope of the audit, including any expected limitations thereon, or any additional requirements;

- The selection of, or changes in, significant accounting policies and practices that have, or could have, a material effect on the entity's financial statements;

- The potential effect on the financial statements of any significant risks and exposures, such as pending litigation, that are required to be disclosed in the financial statements;

- Audit adjustments, whether or not recorded by the entity that have, or could have, a significant effect on the entity's financial statements;

- Material uncertainties related to events and conditions that may cast significant doubt on the entity's ability to continue as a going concern;

- Disagreements with management about matters that, individually or in aggregate, could be significant to the entity's financial statements or the auditor's report. These communications include consideration of whether the matter has, or has not, been resolved and the significance of the matter;

- Expected modifications to the auditor's report;

- Other matters warranting attention by those charged with governance, such as material weaknesses in internal control, questions regarding management integrity, and fraud involving management;

- Any other matters agreed upon in the terms of the audit engagement.

12. As part of the auditor's communications, those charged with governance are informed that:

- The auditor's communications of matters include only those audit matters of governance interest that have come to the attention of the auditor as a result of the performance of the audit;

- an audit of financial statements is not designed to identify all matters that may be relevant to those charged with governance. Accordingly, the audit does not ordinarily identify all such matters.

Timing of Communications

13. **The auditor should communicate audit matters of governance interest on a timely basis.** This enables those charged with governance to take appropriate action.

14. In order to achieve timely communications, the auditor discusses with those charged with governance the basis and timing of such communications. In certain cases, because of the nature of the matter, the auditor may communicate that matter sooner than previously agreed.

Forms of Communications

15. The auditor's communications with those charged with governance may be made orally or in writing. The auditor's decision whether to communicate orally or in writing is affected by factors such as:

- The size, operating structure, legal structure, and communications processes of the entity being audited;

- The nature, sensitivity and significance of the audit matters of governance interest to be communicated;

- The arrangements made with respect to periodic meetings or reporting of audit matters of governance interest;
- The amount of on-going contact and dialogue the auditor has with those charged with governance.

16.   When audit matters of governance interest are communicated orally, the auditor documents in the working papers the matters communicated and any responses to those matters. This documentation may take the form of a copy of the minutes of the auditor's discussion with those charged with governance. In certain circumstances, depending on the nature, sensitivity, and significance of the matter, it may be advisable for the auditor to confirm in writing with those charged with governance any oral communications on audit matters of governance interest.

17.   Ordinarily, the auditor initially discusses audit matters of governance interest with management, except where those matters relate to questions of management competence or integrity. These initial discussions with management are important in order to clarify facts and issues, and to give management an opportunity to provide further information. If management agrees to communicate a matter of governance interest with those charged with governance, the auditor may not need to repeat the communications, provided that the auditor is satisfied that such communications have effectively and appropriately been made.

Other Matters

18.   If the auditor considers that a modification of the auditor's report on the financial statements is required, as described in ISA 700, "The Auditor's Report on Financial Statements," communications between the auditor and those charged with governance cannot be regarded as a substitute.

19.   The auditor considers whether audit matters of governance interest previously communicated may have an effect on the current year's financial statements. The auditor considers whether the point continues to be a matter of governance interest and whether to communicate the matter again with those charged with governance.

Confidentiality

20.   The requirements of national professional accountancy bodies, legislation or regulation may impose obligations of confidentiality that restrict the auditor's communications of audit matters of governance interest. The auditor refers to such requirements, laws and regulations before communicating with those charged with governance. In some circumstances, the potential conflicts with the auditor's ethical and legal obligations of confidentiality and reporting may be complex. In these cases, the auditor may wish to consult with legal counsel.

AUDITING

Laws and Regulations

21. The requirements of national professional accountancy bodies, legislation or regulation may impose obligations on the auditor to make communications on governance related matters. These additional communications requirements are not covered by this ISA; however, they may affect the content, form and timing of communications with those charged with governance.

Effective Date

22. This ISA is effective for audits of financial statements for periods ending on or after 31 December 2000.

Public Sector Perspective

1. *While the basic principles contained in this ISA apply to the audit of financial statements in the public sector, the legislation giving rise to the audit mandate may specify the nature, content and form of the communications with those charged with governance of the entity.*

2. *For public sector audits, the types of matters that may be of interest to the governing body may be broader than the types of matters discussed in the ISA, which are directly related to the audit of financial statements. Public sector auditors' mandates may require them to report matters that come to their attention that relate to:*

   - *Compliance with legislative or regulatory requirements and related authorities;*
   - *Adequacy of accounting and control systems;*
   - *Economy, efficiency and effectiveness of programs, projects and activities.*

3. *For public sector auditors, the auditors' written communications may be placed on the public record. For that reason, the public sector auditor needs to be aware that their written communications may be distributed to a wider audience than solely those persons charged with governance of the entity.*

ETHICS

CONTENTS

	Page
Code of Ethics for Professional Accountants	538
Statements of Policy of Council:	
• Preface to Ethical Requirements of (Name of Member Body)	583
• Implementation and Enforcement of Ethical Requirements	587

For additional information on the Ethics Committee, recent developments, and/ or to obtain outstanding exposure drafts, visit the Committee's page at http://www.ifac.org/Committees/Ethics.

ETHICS

July 1996
Revised January 1998

Code of Ethics for

Professional Accountants

CONTENTS

	Page
DEFINITIONS	540
INTRODUCTION	542
THE PUBLIC INTEREST	543
OBJECTIVES	544
FUNDAMENTAL PRINCIPLES	545
THE CODE	546

PART A—APPLICABLE TO ALL
PROFESSIONAL ACCOUNTANTS

1	Integrity and Objectivity	547
2	Resolution of Ethical Conflicts	548
3	Professional Competence	550
4	Confidentiality	551
5	Tax Practice	553
6	Cross Border Activities	555
7	Publicity	556

PART B—APPLICABLE TO PROFESSIONAL
ACCOUNTANTS IN PUBLIC PRACTICE

| 8 | Independence | 557 |
| 9 | Professional Competence and Responsibilities regarding the Use of Non-Accountants | 565 |

10	Fees and Commissions	566
11	Activities Incompatible with the Practice of Public Accountancy	569
12	Clients' Monies	570
13	Relations with Other Professional Accountants in Public Practice	571
14	Advertising and Solicitation	576

PART C—APPLICABLE TO EMPLOYED PROFESSIONAL ACCOUNTANTS

15	Conflict of Loyalties	581
16	Support for Professional Colleagues	582
17	Professional Competence	582
18	Presentation of Information	582

ETHICS

Definitions

In this Code of Ethics for Professional Accountants the following expressions appear in **bold type** when they are first used and have the following meanings assigned to them:

Advertising	The communication to the public of information as to the services or skills provided by professional accountants in public practice with a view to procuring professional business.
Client Account	Any bank account which is used solely for the banking of clients' monies.
Clients' Monies	Any monies—including documents of title to money e.g., bills of exchange, promissory notes, and documents of title which can be converted into money e.g., bearer bonds— received by a professional accountant in public practice to be held or paid out on the instruction of the person from whom or on whose behalf they are received.
Company	Any entity or person(s), whether organized for profit or not, including a parent company and all of its subsidiaries.
Employed professional accountant	A professional accountant employed in industry, commerce, the public sector or education.
Existing accountant	A professional accountant in public practice currently holding an audit appointment or carrying out accounting, taxation, consulting or similar professional services for a client.
Investee	A subsidiary or an entity subject to the significant influence of an investor.
Investor	A parent, general partner, or natural person or corporation that has the ability to exercise significant influence on an investee.
Objectivity	A combination of impartiality, intellectual honesty and a freedom from conflicts of interest.
Practice	A sole practitioner, a partnership or a corporation of professional accountants which offers professional services to the public.
Professional accountant	Those persons, whether they be in public practice, (including a sole practitioner, partnership or corporate body), industry, commerce, the public sector or education, who are members of an IFAC member body.

Professional accountant in public practice	Each partner or person occupying a position similar to that of a partner, and each employee in a practice providing professional services to a client irrespective of their functional classification (e.g., audit, tax or consulting) and professional accountants in a practice having managerial responsibilities. This term is also used to refer to a firm of professional accountants in public practice.
Professional services	Any service requiring accountancy or related skills performed by a professional accountant including accounting, auditing, taxation, management consulting and financial management services.
Publicity	The communication to the public of facts about a professional accountant which are not designed for the deliberate promotion of that professional accountant.
Receiving accountant	A professional accountant in public practice to whom the existing accountant or client of the existing accountant has referred audit, accounting, taxation, consulting or similar appointments, or who is consulted in order to meet the needs of the client.
Reporting assignment	An engagement which requires the expression of an opinion by a professional accountant in public practice on financial information.
Solicitation	The approach to a potential client for the purpose of offering professional services.

ETHICS

IFAC Code of Ethics for

Professional Accountants

Introduction

1. The International Federation of Accountants (IFAC) believes that due to national differences of culture, language, legal and social systems, the task of preparing detailed ethical requirements is primarily that of the member bodies in each country concerned and that they also have the responsibility to implement and enforce such requirements.

2. However, IFAC believes that the identity of the accountancy profession is characterized worldwide by its endeavor to achieve a number of common objectives and by its observance of certain fundamental principles for that purpose.

3. IFAC, therefore, recognizing the responsibilities of the accountancy profession as such, and considering its own role to be that of providing guidance, encouraging continuity of efforts, and promoting harmonization, has deemed it essential to establish an international Code of Ethics for Professional Accountants to be the basis on which the ethical requirements (code of ethics, detailed rules, guidelines, standards of conduct, etc.) for **professional accountants*** in each country should be founded.

4. This international Code is intended to serve as a model on which to base national ethical guidance. It sets standards of conduct for professional accountants and states the fundamental principles that should be observed by professional accountants in order to achieve common objectives. The accountancy profession throughout the world operates in an environment with different cultures and regulatory requirements. The basic intent of the Code, however, should always be respected. It is also acknowledged that, in those instances where a national requirement is in conflict with a provision in the Code, the national requirement would prevail. For those countries that wish to adopt the Code as their own national Code, IFAC has developed wording which may be used to indicate the authority and applicability in the country concerned. The wording is contained in the IFAC Statement of Policy of Council *Preface to Ethical Requirements of (Name of Member Body)*.

5. Further, the Code is established on the basis that unless a limitation is specifically stated the objectives and fundamental principles are equally valid

---

* For definitions see pages 540-541.

for all professional accountants, whether they be in public practice, industry, commerce, the public sector or education.

6. A profession is distinguished by certain characteristics including:

  - mastery of a particular intellectual skill, acquired by training and education;[1]

  - adherence by its members to a common code of values and conduct established by its administrating body, including maintaining an outlook which is essentially objective; and

  - acceptance of a duty to society as a whole (usually in return for restrictions in use of a title or in the granting of a qualification).

7. Members' duty to their profession and to society may at times seem to conflict with their immediate self interest or their duty of loyalty to their employer.

8. Against this background it is beholden on member bodies to lay down ethical requirements for their members to ensure the highest quality of performance and to maintain public confidence in the profession.

The Public Interest

9. A distinguishing mark of a profession is acceptance of its responsibility to the public. The accountancy profession's public consists of clients, credit grantors, governments, employers, employees, investors, the business and financial community, and others who rely on the **objectivity*** and integrity of professional accountants to maintain the orderly functioning of commerce. This reliance imposes a public interest responsibility on the accountancy profession. The public interest is defined as the collective well-being of the community of people and institutions the professional accountant serves.

10. A professional accountant's responsibility is not exclusively to satisfy the needs of an individual client or employer. The standards of the accountancy profession are heavily determined by the public interest, for example:

  - independent auditors help to maintain the integrity and efficiency of the financial statements presented to financial institutions in partial support for loans and to stockholders for obtaining capital;

  - financial executives serve in various financial management capacities in organizations and contribute to the efficient and effective use of the organization's resources;

  - internal auditors provide assurance about a sound internal control system which enhances the reliability of the external financial information of the employer;

---

[1] For details of the education requirements recommended by IFAC, reference should be made to the International Education Guidelines prepared by the Education Committee of IFAC.

* **For definitions see pages 540-541.**

- tax experts help to establish confidence and efficiency in, and the fair application of, the tax system; and

- management consultants have a responsibility toward the public interest in advocating sound management decision making.

11. Professional accountants have an important role in society. Investors, creditors, employers and other sectors of the business community, as well as the government and the public at large rely on professional accountants for sound financial accounting and reporting, effective financial management and competent advice on a variety of business and taxation matters. The attitude and behavior of professional accountants in providing such services have an impact on the economic well-being of their community and country.

12. Professional accountants can remain in this advantageous position only by continuing to provide the public with these unique services at a level which demonstrates that the public confidence is firmly founded. It is in the best interest of the worldwide accountancy profession to make known to users of the services provided by professional accountants that they are executed at the highest level of performance and in accordance with ethical requirements that strive to ensure such performance.

13. In formulating their national code of ethics, member bodies should therefore consider the public service and user expectations of the ethical standards of professional accountants and take their views into account. By doing so, any existing "expectation gap" between the standards expected and those prescribed can be addressed or explained.

Objectives

14. The Code recognizes that the objectives of the accountancy profession are to work to the highest standards of professionalism, to attain the highest levels of performance and generally to meet the public interest requirement set out above. These objectives require four basic needs to be met:

- *Credibility*

  In the whole of society there is a need for credibility in information and information systems.

- *Professionalism*

  There is a need for individuals who can be clearly identified by clients, employers and other interested parties as professional persons in the accountancy field.

- *Quality of Services*

  There is a need for assurance that all services obtained from a professional accountant are carried out to the highest standards of performance.

- *Confidence*

    Users of the services of professional accountants should be able to feel confident that there exists a framework of professional ethics which governs the provision of those services.

Fundamental Principles

15. In order to achieve the objectives of the accountancy profession, professional accountants have to observe a number of prerequisites or fundamental principles.

16. The fundamental principles are:

- *Integrity*

    A professional accountant should be straightforward and honest in performing **professional services.***

- *Objectivity*

    A professional accountant should be fair and should not allow prejudice or bias, conflict of interest or influence of others to override objectivity.

- *Professional Competence and Due Care*

    A professional accountant should perform professional services with due care, competence and diligence and has a continuing duty to maintain professional knowledge and skill at a level required to ensure that a client or employer receives the advantage of competent professional service based on up-to-date developments in practice, legislation and techniques.

- *Confidentiality*

    A professional accountant should respect the confidentiality of information acquired during the course of performing professional services and should not use or disclose any such information without proper and specific authority or unless there is a legal or professional right or duty to disclose.

- *Professional Behavior*

    A professional accountant should act in a manner consistent with the good reputation of the profession and refrain from any conduct which might bring discredit to the profession. The obligation to refrain from any conduct which might bring discredit to the profession requires IFAC member bodies to consider, when developing ethical requirements, the responsibilities of a professional accountant to clients, third parties, other members of the accountancy profession, staff, employers, and the general public.

---

* **For definitions see pages 540-541.**

- *Technical Standards*

  A professional accountant should carry out professional services in accordance with the relevant technical and professional standards. Professional accountants have a duty to carry out with care and skill, the instructions of the client or employer insofar as they are compatible with the requirements of integrity, objectivity and, in the case of **professional accountants in public practice**,* independence (see Section 8 below). In addition, they should conform with the technical and professional standards promulgated by:

    – IFAC (e.g., International Standards on Auditing);

    – International Accounting Standards Committee;

    – the member's professional body or other regulatory body; and

    – relevant legislation.

The Code

17. The objectives as well as the fundamental principles are of a general nature and are not intended to be used to solve a professional accountant's ethical problems in a specific case. However, the Code provides some guidance as to the application in practice of the objectives and the fundamental principles with regard to a number of typical situations occurring in the accountancy profession.

18. The Code set out below is divided into three parts:

    - Part A applies to all professional accountants unless otherwise specified.

    - Part B applies only to those accountants in public practice.

    - Part C applies to **employed professional accountants**,* and may also apply, in appropriate circumstances, to accountants employed in public practice.

---

* **For definitions see pages 540-541.**

PART A — APPLICABLE TO ALL PROFESSIONAL ACCOUNTANTS

SECTION 1

Integrity and Objectivity

1.1 Integrity implies not merely honesty but fair dealing and truthfulness. The principle of objectivity imposes the obligation on all professional accountants to be fair, intellectually honest and free of conflicts of interest.

1.2 Professional accountants serve in many different capacities and should demonstrate their objectivity in varying circumstances. Professional accountants in public practice undertake reporting assignments, and render tax and other management advisory services. Other professional accountants prepare financial statements as a subordinate of others, perform internal auditing services, and serve in financial management capacities in industry, commerce, the public sector and education. They also educate and train those who aspire to admission into the profession. Regardless of service or capacity, professional accountants should protect the integrity of their professional services, and maintain objectivity in their judgment.

1.3 In selecting the situations and practices to be specifically dealt within ethics requirements relating to objectivity, adequate consideration should be given to the following factors:

   (a) Professional accountants are exposed to situations which involve the possibility of pressures being exerted on them. These pressures may impair their objectivity.

   (b) It is impracticable to define and prescribe all such situations where these possible pressures exist. Reasonableness should prevail in establishing standards for identifying relationships that are likely to, or appear to, impair a professional accountant's objectivity.

   (c) Relationships should be avoided which allow prejudice, bias or influences of others to override objectivity.

   (d) Professional accountants have an obligation to ensure that personnel engaged on professional services adhere to the principle of objectivity.

   (e) Professional accountants should neither accept nor offer gifts or entertainment which might reasonably be believed to have a significant and improper influence on their professional judgment or those with whom they deal. What constitutes an excessive gift or offer of entertainment varies from country to country but professional accountants should avoid circumstances which would bring their professional standing into disrepute.

ETHICS

547

SECTION 2

Resolution of Ethical Conflicts

2.1   From time to time professional accountants encounter situations which give rise to conflicts of interest. Such conflicts may arise in a wide variety of ways, ranging from the relatively trivial dilemma to the extreme case of fraud and similar illegal activities. It is not possible to attempt to itemize a comprehensive check list of potential cases where conflicts of interest might occur. The professional accountant should be constantly conscious of and be alert to factors which give rise to conflicts of interest. It should be noted that an honest difference of opinion between a professional accountant and another party is not in itself an ethical issue. However, the facts and circumstances of each case need investigation by the parties concerned.

2.2   It is recognized, however, that there can be particular factors which occur when the responsibilities of a professional accountant may conflict with internal or external demands of one type or another. Hence:

- There may be the danger of pressure from an overbearing supervisor, manager, director or partner; or when there are family or personal relationships which can give rise to the possibility of pressures being exerted upon them (see paragraph 8.6 below). Indeed, relationships or interests which could adversely influence, impair or threaten a professional accountant's integrity should be discouraged.

- A professional accountant may be asked to act contrary to technical and/or professional standards.

- A question of divided loyalty as between the professional accountant's superior and the required professional standards of conduct could occur.

- Conflict could arise when misleading information is published which may be to the advantage of the employer or client and which may or may not benefit the professional accountant as a result of such publication.

2.3   In applying standards of ethical conduct professional accountants may encounter problems in identifying unethical behavior or in resolving an ethical conflict. When faced with significant ethical issues, professional accountants should follow the established policies of the employing organization to seek a resolution of such conflict. If those policies do not resolve the ethical conflict, the following should be considered:

- Review the conflict problem with the immediate superior. If the problem is not resolved with the immediate superior and the professional accountant determines to go to the next higher managerial level, the immediate superior should be notified of the decision. If it appears that the superior is involved in the conflict problem, the professional accountant should raise the issue with the next higher level of management. When the immediate superior is the Chief Executive Officer (or equivalent) the next higher reviewing level may be the Executive Committee, Board of Directors, Non-Executive Directors, Trustees, Partners' Management Committee or Shareholders.

- Seek counseling and advice on a confidential basis with an independent advisor or the applicable professional accountancy body to obtain an understanding of possible courses of action.

- If the ethical conflict still exists after fully exhausting all levels of internal review, the professional accountant as a last resort may have no other recourse on significant matters (e.g., fraud) than to resign and to submit an information memorandum to an appropriate representative of that organization.

2.4 Furthermore, in some countries local laws, regulations or professional standards may require certain serious matters to be reported to an external body such as an enforcement or supervisory authority.

2.5 Any professional accountant in a senior position should endeavor to ensure that policies are established within his or her employing organization to seek resolution of conflicts.

2.6 Member bodies are urged to ensure that confidential counseling and advice is available to members who experience ethical conflicts.

SECTION 3

Professional Competence

3.1   Professional accountants should not portray themselves as having expertise or experience they do not possess.

3.2   Professional competence may be divided into two separate phases:

(a)   Attainment of professional competence

The attainment of professional competence requires initially a high standard of general education followed by specific education, training and examination in professionally relevant subjects, and whether prescribed or not, a period of work experience. This should be the normal pattern of development for a professional accountant.

(b)   Maintenance of professional competence

(i)   The maintenance of professional competence requires a continuing awareness of developments in the accountancy profession including relevant national and international pronouncements on accounting, auditing and other relevant regulations and statutory requirements.

(ii) A professional accountant should adopt a program designed to ensure quality control in the performance of professional services consistent with appropriate national and international pronouncements.

Confidentiality

4.1 Professional accountants have an obligation to respect the confidentiality of information about a client's or employer's affairs acquired in the course of professional services. The duty of confidentiality continues even after the end of the relationship between the professional accountant and the client or employer.

4.2 Confidentiality should always be observed by a professional accountant unless specific authority has been given to disclose information or there is a legal or professional duty to disclose.

4.3 Professional accountants have an obligation to ensure that staff under their control and persons from whom advice and assistance is obtained respect the principle of confidentiality.

4.4 Confidentiality is not only a matter of disclosure of information. It also requires that a professional accountant acquiring information in the course of performing professional services does neither use nor appear to use that information for personal advantage or for the advantage of a third party.

4.5 A professional accountant has access to much confidential information about a client's or employer's affairs not otherwise disclosed to the public. Therefore, the professional accountant should be relied upon not to make unauthorized disclosures to other persons. This does not apply to disclosure of such information in order properly to discharge the professional accountant's responsibility according to the profession's standards.

4.6 It is in the interest of the public and the profession that the profession's standards relating to confidentiality be defined and guidance given on the nature and extent of the duty of confidentiality and the circumstances in which disclosure of information acquired during the course of providing professional services shall be permitted or required.

4.7 It should be recognized, however, that confidentiality of information is part of statute or common law and therefore detailed ethical requirements in respect thereof will depend on the law of the country of each member body.

4.8 The following are examples of the points which should be considered in determining whether confidential information may be disclosed:

    (a) When disclosure is authorized. When authorization to disclose is given by the client or the employer the interests of all the parties including those third parties whose interests might be affected should be considered.

    (b) When disclosure is required by law. Examples of when a professional accountant is required by law to disclose confidential information are:

        (i) to produce documents or to give evidence in the course of legal proceedings; and

ETHICS

      (ii) to disclose to the appropriate public authorities infringements of the law which come to light.

(c) When there is a professional duty or right to disclose:

      (i) to comply with technical standards and ethics requirements; such disclosure is not contrary to this section;

      (ii) to protect the professional interests of a professional accountant in legal proceedings;

      (iii) to comply with the quality (or peer) review of a member body or professional body; and

      (iv) to respond to an inquiry or investigation by a member body or regulatory body.

4.9   When the professional accountant has determined that confidential information can be disclosed, the following points should be considered:

- whether or not all the relevant facts are known and substantiated, to the extent it is practicable to do so; when the situation involves unsubstantiated fact or opinion, professional judgment should be used in determining the type of disclosure to be made, if any

- what type of communication is expected and the addressee; in particular, the professional accountant should be satisfied that the parties to whom the communication is addressed are appropriate recipients and have the responsibility to act on it, and

- whether or not the professional accountant would incur any legal liability having made a communication and the consequences thereof.

In all such situations, the professional accountants should consider the need to consult legal counsel and/or the professional organization(s) concerned.

SECTION 5

Tax Practice

5.1   A professional accountant rendering professional tax services is entitled to put forward the best position in favor of a client, or an employer, provided the service is rendered with professional competence, does not in any way impair integrity and objectivity, and is in the opinion of the professional accountant consistent with the law. Doubt may be resolved in favor of the client or the employer if there is reasonable support for the position.

5.2   A professional accountant should not hold out to a client or an employer the assurance that the tax return prepared and the tax advice offered are beyond challenge. Instead, the professional accountant should ensure that the client or the employer are aware of the limitations attaching to tax advice and services so that they do not misinterpret an expression of opinion as an assertion of fact.

5.3   A professional accountant who undertakes or assists in the preparation of a tax return should advise the client or the employer that the responsibility for the content of the return rests primarily with the client or employer. The professional accountant should take the necessary steps to ensure that the tax return is properly prepared on the basis of the information received.

5.4   Tax advice or opinions of material consequence given to a client or an employer should be recorded, either in the form of a letter or in a memorandum for the files.

5.5   A professional accountant should not be associated with any return or communication in which there is reason to believe that it:

(a)   contains a false or misleading statement;

(b)   contains statements or information furnished recklessly or without any real knowledge of whether they are true or false; or

(c)   omits or obscures information required to be submitted and such omission or obscurity would mislead the revenue authorities.

5.6   A professional accountant may prepare tax returns involving the use of estimates if such use is generally acceptable or if it is impractical under the circumstances to obtain exact data. When estimates are used, they should be presented as such in a manner so as to avoid the implication of greater accuracy than exists. The professional accountant should be satisfied that estimated amounts are reasonable under the circumstances.

5.7   In preparing a tax return, a professional accountant ordinarily may rely on information furnished by the client or employer provided that the information appears reasonable. Although the examination or review of documents or other evidence in support of the information is not required, the professional accountant should encourage, when appropriate, such supporting data to be provided.

ETHICS

In addition, the professional accountant:

(a) should make use of the client's returns for prior years whenever feasible;

(b) is required to make reasonable inquiries when the information presented appears to be incorrect or incomplete; and

(c) is encouraged to make reference to the books and records of the business operations.

5.8 When a professional accountant learns of a material error or omission in a tax return of a prior year (with which the professional accountant may or may not have been associated), or of the failure to file a required tax return, the professional accountant has a responsibility to:

(a) Promptly advise the client or employer of the error or omission and recommend that disclosure be made to the revenue authorities. Normally, the professional accountant is not obligated to inform the revenue authorities, nor may this be done without permission.

(b) If the client or the employer does not correct the error the professional accountant:

(i) should inform the client or the employer that it is not possible to act for them in connection with that return or other related information submitted to the authorities; and,

(ii) should consider whether continued association with the client or employer in any capacity is consistent with professional responsibilities.

(c) If the professional accountant concludes that a professional relationship with the client or employer can be continued, all reasonable steps should be taken to ensure that the error is not repeated in subsequent tax returns.

(d) Professional or statutory requirements in some countries may also make it necessary for the professional accountant to inform the revenue authorities that there is no longer any association with the return or other information involved and that acting for the client or employer has ceased. In these circumstances, the professional accountant should advise the client or employer of the position before informing the authorities and should give no further information to the authorities without the consent of the client or employer unless required to do so by law.

SECTION 6

Cross Border Activities

6.1   When considering the application of ethical requirements in cross border activities a number of situations may arise. Whether a professional accountant is a member of the profession in one country only or is also a member of the profession in the country where the services are performed should not affect the manner of dealing with each situation.

6.2   A professional accountant qualifying in one country may reside in another country or may be temporarily visiting that country to perform professional services. In all circumstances, the professional accountant should carry out professional services in accordance with the relevant technical standards and ethical requirements. The particular technical standards which should be followed are not dealt within this section. In all other respects, however, the professional accountant should be guided by the ethical requirements set out below.

6.3   When a professional accountant performs services in a country other than the home country and differences on specific matters exist between ethical requirements of the two countries the following provisions should be applied:

(a)   When the ethical requirements of the country in which the services are being performed are less strict than the IFAC Code of Ethics, then the IFAC Code of Ethics should be applied.

(b)   When the ethical requirements of the country in which services are being performed are stricter than the IFAC Code of Ethics, then the ethical requirements in the country where services are being performed should be applied.

(c)   When the ethical requirements of the home country are mandatory for services performed outside that country and are stricter than set out in (a) and (b) above, then the ethical requirements of the home country should be applied. (In the case of cross border advertising and solicitation see also section 14 paragraph 14.4 and 14.5 below.)

SECTION 7

Publicity[*]

In the marketing and promotion of themselves and their work, professional accountants should:

(a) not use means which brings the profession into disrepute;

(b) not make exaggerated claims for the services they are able to offer, the qualifications they possess, or experience they have gained; and

(c) not denigrate the work of other accountants.

---

[*] **For definitions see pages 540-541.**

SECTION 8

Independence

8.1 Professional accountants in public practice when undertaking a **reporting assignment,** should be and appear to be free of any interest which might be regarded, whatever its actual effect, as being incompatible with integrity, objectivity and independence.

8.2 The following paragraphs indicate some of those situations which, because of the actual or apparent lack of independence, would give a reasonable observer grounds for doubting the independence of a professional accountant in public practice.[2]

Financial Involvement with, or in the Affairs of, Clients

8.3 Financial involvement with a client affects independence and may lead a reasonable observer to conclude that it has been impaired. Such involvement can arise in a number of ways such as:

(a) By direct financial interest in a client.

(b) By indirect material financial interest in a client, e.g., by being a trustee of any trust or executor or administrator of any estate if such trust or estate has a financial interest in a client **company.**

(c) By loans to or from the client or any officer, director or principal shareholder of a client company.

(d) By holding a financial interest in a joint venture with a client or employee(s) of a client.

(e) By having a financial interest in a nonclient that has an **investor** or **investee** relationship with the client.

Commentary

Independence is impaired when a professional accountant in public practice has or is committed to acquire a direct or indirect material financial interest in a company for which the professional accountant in public practice provides professional services requiring independence. A direct financial interest

---

*For definitions see pages 540-541.

[2] For the purposes of Paragraph 8.3 the term "professional accountant in public practice" is restricted to:
an individual performing professional services requiring independence;
all partners or proprietors in the practice;
all professional employees engaged in the reporting assignment; and
all managerial employees located in an office participating in a significant part of the reporting assignment.

ETHICS

includes an interest held by the spouse or dependent child of the professional accountant in public practice and in some countries may be extended to include other close relatives.

When the professional accountant in public practice holds or advises on investing in shares in an audit client on behalf of a third party, e.g., a trust, the appearance of independence is at risk. This is because responsibilities to the third party may conflict with responsibilities to the audit client.

In the case of trustee shareholdings, if a sole practitioner or a partner in a **practice*** or spouse or dependent child of that sole practitioner or partner is a trustee of a trust with a holding in shares material to the size of the issued share capital of the company or the total assets of the trust, the practice should not accept a reporting assignment on that company. The same rule should be applied in the case of those who serve as executors and administrators of any estate.

Shares in a client may be involuntarily acquired as when a professional accountant in public practice inherits such shares or marries a shareholder or in a take-over situation. In these cases, the shares should be disposed of at the earliest practicable date or the professional accountant in public practice should decline any further reporting assignment on that company.

Neither a professional accountant in public practice nor his or her spouse or dependent child should make a loan to a client or guarantee a client's borrowings or accept a loan from a client or have borrowings guaranteed by a client. This latter proscription does not apply to loans to or from banks or other similar financial institutions when made under normal lending procedures, terms and requirements; to home mortgages or to current or deposit accounts with banks, building societies, etc.

When a nonclient investee is material to a client investor, any direct or material indirect financial interest of the professional accountant in the nonclient investee would be considered to impair the professional accountant's independence with respect to the client. Likewise, where a client investee is material to a nonclient investor, any direct or material indirect financial interest of the professional accountant in the nonclient investor would be considered to impair the professional accountant's independence with respect to the client.

Other relationships, such as client-nonclient joint ventures, may affect the appearance of independence. In general, in a joint venture situation, an immaterial financial interest of the professional accountant in the nonclient investor would not impair the independence of the professional accountant with respect to the client investor provided that the professional accountant could not significantly influence the nonclient investor. If the professional accountant does not and could not reasonably be expected to have knowledge of the financial interests or relationships involving the joint ventures, the professional accountant's independence would not be considered to be impaired.

Generally, the professional accountant should be independent of a client and all its parents, subsidiaries and affiliates.

Appointments in Companies

8.4   When professional accountants in public practice are or were, within the period under current review or immediately preceding an assignment:

(a)   a member of the board, an officer or employee of a company; or

(b)   a partner of, or in the employment of, a member of the board or an officer or employee of a company;

they would be regarded as having an interest which could detract from independence when reporting on that company.

Commentary

It is common practice to prohibit professional accountants in public practice in such situations being appointed as auditors of the companies concerned. It is also clearly desirable that they should not accept from such companies other assignments on which an opinion is required. In the situation described above, it is suggested that the period immediately preceding the assignment should be no less than two years or as required by appropriate legislation.

Provision of Other Services to Audit Clients

8.5   When a professional accountant in public practice, in addition to carrying out an audit or other reporting function, provides other services to a client, care should be taken not to perform management functions or make management decisions, responsibility for which remains with the board of directors and management.

Commentary

It is economic in terms of skill and effort for professional accountants in public practice to be able to offer other financial and management consultancy services to their clients since they already have a close familiarity with the clients' businesses. Many companies (particularly the smaller ones) would be adversely affected if they were denied the right to obtain other services from their auditors. In the course of performing their professional services, professional accountants in public practice offer advice. For example, particularly in the case of smaller businesses, the audit of the accounts and advice on the provision to be made for taxes are often so inextricably linked that they cannot be separated. Moreover, one key concept in auditing involves examination of the system of internal control which necessarily involves suggestions for improvement. For these reasons it is impracticable to define the limitations on the advice which a professional accountant in public practice may give.

The services provided by a professional accountant in public practice in the fields of management consultancy and taxation are advisory services. Such services should not usurp the management functions of client companies. The independence of a professional accountant in public practice is not impaired by offering advisory services, provided there is no involvement in or responsibility assumed for management decisions. The provision of other professional services is not in principle a factor in determining whether the professional accountant in public practice is independent. Nevertheless, the professional accountant in public practice should be careful not to go beyond the advisory function into the management sphere. A professional accountant in public practice who has advised on the installation of a stock recording system, should carry out a normal audit review on the working of the system, as failure to take all normal audit steps in relation to that system has an adverse impact on competence and independence.

The preparation of accounting records is a service which is frequently requested of a professional accountant in public practice, particularly by smaller clients, whose businesses are not sufficiently large to employ an adequate internal accounting staff. It is unlikely that larger clients need this service other than in exceptional circumstances. In all cases in which independence is required and in which a professional accountant in public practice is concerned in the preparation of accounting records for a client, the following requirements should be observed:

(a) The professional accountant in public practice should not have any relationship or combination of relationships with the client or any conflict of interest which would impair integrity or independence.

(b) The client should accept responsibility for the statements.

(c) The professional accountant in public practice should not assume the role of employee or of management conducting the operations of an enterprise.

(d) Staff assigned to the preparation of accounting records ideally should not participate in the examination of such records. The fact that the professional accountant in public practice has processed or maintained certain records does not eliminate the need to make sufficient audit tests.

Personal and Family Relationships

8.6   Personal and family relationships can affect independence. There is a particular need to ensure that an independent approach to any assignment is not endangered as a consequence of any personal or family relationship.

Commentary

It is recognized that it would be impracticable to attempt to prescribe in detail in ethical requirements the permissible extent of a personal relationship between a professional accountant in public practice and a client,[3] or those occupying responsible executive positions (e.g., director, chief executive, financial officer or another employee in a similar position) with a client. Nevertheless, member bodies should advise their members on the kinds of

---

[3] In this context "client" includes the owner of the business, the principal shareholders, the executive directors and the financial officer.

situations which can give rise to the possibility of pressures being exerted upon them.

For example, these may arise when a professional accountant in public practice has a mutual business interest with an officer or employee of a client or has a material interest in a joint venture with a client.

With respect to family relationships, it is for each member body to decide, in the light of the social conditions existing in its own country, what degree of relationship with a client should be regarded as too close to ensure that an independent approach to professional services for that client does not suffer.

Family relationships which always pose an unacceptable threat to independence are those in which a sole practitioner or a partner in a practice, or an employee engaged on the assignment relating to the client, is the spouse, dependent child or relative living in a common household, of the client. In some countries, the range of relationships may be wider, e.g., the child, or its spouse, the parent or grandparent, parent-in-law, brother, sister, or brother-in-law or sister-in-law, of the client.

Fees

8.7　When the receipt of recurring fees from a client or group of connected clients, represents a large proportion of the total gross fees of a professional accountant in public practice or of the practice as a whole, the dependence on that client or group of clients should inevitably come under scrutiny and could raise doubts as to independence.

Commentary

It is desirable that member bodies should prescribe rules or issue guidance to their members on this subject. It is clear that these rules or guidance will need to be related to the economic conditions of each country and to the state of development of the accountancy profession.

It is not possible to state precisely what constitutes an unacceptable proportion of total fees emanating from one client or group of connected clients. However, if such fees are the only or the substantial part of the gross income, the professional accountant in public practice should carefully consider whether independence has been impaired. A similar situation may arise if fees due from a client for professional services remain unpaid for an extended period of time, especially if a substantial part is not paid before the issue of the report of the professional accountant in public practice for the following year. Allowances should be made for new practices seeking to establish themselves or practices which are planning to cease operations. Exemptions should be made for a branch office which is reliant upon one client or group of connected clients. For example, this might be the case if the branch office is auditing the financial statements of a client of the practice as a whole and that client forms a major part of the business of the branch office. In such circumstances, professional services for that client or group should be the subject of review by a partner from another office.

Contingency Fees

8.8 Subject to paragraph 8.9, professional services should not be offered or rendered to a client under an arrangement whereby no fee will be charged unless a specified finding or result is obtained or when the fee is otherwise contingent upon the findings or results of such services.

Commentary

Fees should not be regarded as being contingent if fixed by a court or other public authority.

Fees charged on a percentage or similar basis should be regarded as contingent fees.

8.9 In those countries where charging contingent fees is permitted either by statute or by a member body, such engagements should be limited to those for which independence is not required.

Goods and Services

8.10 Acceptance of goods and services from a client may be a threat to independence. Acceptance of undue hospitality poses a similar threat.

Commentary

Goods and services should not be accepted by professional accountants in public practice, their spouses or dependent children except on business terms no more favorable than those generally available to others. Hospitality and gifts on a scale which is not commensurate with the normal courtesies of social life should not be accepted.

Ownership of the Capital

8.11 Ideally, the capital of a practice should be owned entirely by professional accountants in public practice. However, ownership of capital by others may be permitted provided that the majority of both the ownership of the capital and the voting rights lies only with the professional accountants in public practice.

Commentary

As a principle the total equity capital of a practice should be owned by the professional accountants in public practice. If all or a proportion of the capital were owned by others, they could be in a position to influence professional accountants in public practice in the performance of professional services. A similar situation could exist if a practice owned by professional accountants in public practice were substantially financed by borrowings from others in a way that might constitute an evasion of the rule concerning ownership of the capital.

In some countries, professional accountants in public practice are permitted by law to practice as a corporation without any special restrictions as to the ownership or voting rights of the capital of the corporation. In all circumstances safeguards should be provided either by legislation or ethical requirements, which should not conflict with the legislation, of the member body to preserve the independence of the professional accountant in public practice. Member bodies should consider making representations to government to the effect that the interests of the profession and the public are best served when existing or proposed legislation provides that the majority of both the ownership of the capital and the voting rights rests with professional accountants in public practice.

Former Partners

8.12 A partner in a practice may leave the practice by resignation, termination, retirement, or sale of the practice. Such a partner may accept an appointment with a client of the practice, of which he or she is a former partner when an audit or other reporting function is being performed by that practice of which he or she is a former partner. In such circumstances, the independence of the practice would not be impaired.

(a) Payments of the amounts due to a former partner for his or her interest in the practice and for unfunded, vested retirement benefits are made in accordance with a schedule that is fixed as to both payment dates and amounts. In addition, the amounts owed should be such that they do not cause a substantial doubt about the practices' ability to continue as a going concern.

(b) The former partner does not participate or appear to participate in the practices' business or professional activities whether or not compensated. Indications of participation include the provision of office space and related amenities to the former partner by the practice.

Actual or Threatened Litigation

8.13 Litigation involving the professional accountant in public practice and a client may cause concern that the normal relationship with the client is affected to the extent that the professional accountant's independence and objectivity may be impaired.

Commentary

The commencement by a client or other of proceedings against the professional accountant in public practice, or the commencement of litigation by the professional accountant in public practice alleging, e.g., fraud or deceit by the officers of a company, or substandard performance of the client's audit by the accountant would be considered to impair independence. Such commencement or a credible threat to commence or a declared intention to commence legal action against a professional accountant in public practice relating to the affairs of the company, or vice versa, may cause the professional accountant in public practice and the company to be placed in positions which may affect the objectivity of the professional accountant in public practice. Thus, the ability to report fairly and impartially on the company's financial statements may be affected. At the same time, the existence of such action (or threat of action) may affect the willingness of the

ETHICS

563

management of the company to disclose relevant information to the professional accountant in public practice.

It is not possible to specify precisely the point at which it would become improper for the professional accountant to continue to report. However, the professional accountant in public practice should have regard to circumstances when litigation might be perceived by the public as likely to affect the accountant's independence.

Long Association of Senior Personnel with Audit Clients

8.14   The use of the same senior personnel on an audit engagement over a prolonged period of time may pose a threat to independence. The professional accountant in public practice should take steps to ensure that objectivity and independence are maintained on the engagement.

Commentary

Professional relationships take time to develop, but once developed, they usually lead to maximum efficiency and effectiveness. Continuity of senior personnel on audit engagements is ordinarily to be encouraged both from the standpoint of the client and the professional accountant in public practice. As with personal and family relationships in 8.6 above, there is a concern that a long involvement by a single individual with an audit client could lead to the formation of a close relationship which could be perceived to be a threat to objectivity and independence. Additionally, questions of quality control are affected, in that the professional accountant with continued familiarity may overly rely on that familiarity when carrying out audit procedures and making judgments on key audit decisions.

The professional accountant in public practice should take steps to provide for an orderly rotation of senior personnel serving on the engagement. When rotation is impractical, review procedures should be designed to achieve the same objectives. The timing and nature of rotation of engagement personnel, especially the engagement partner, depends on many practical considerations. Such a rotation should, however, provide for an orderly blend of experienced and replacement personnel as well as an orderly transition. Rotation may be impractical in small offices or when there are specializations relating to assignments. In such cases, alternative safeguards should be applied, such as the setting up of standing arrangements to consult externally with another suitably experienced professional accountant or with any available service provided by the professional body for such purpose.

SECTION 9

Professional Competence and Responsibilities Regarding the Use of Non-Accountants

9.1   Professional accountants in public practice should refrain from agreeing to perform professional services which they are not competent to carry out unless competent advice and assistance is obtained so as to enable them to satisfactorily perform such services. If a professional accountant does not have the competence to perform a specific part of the professional service, technical advice may be sought from experts such as other professional accountants, lawyers, actuaries, engineers, geologists, valuers.

9.2.   In such situations, although the professional accountant is relying on the technical competence of the expert, the knowledge of the ethical requirements cannot be automatically assumed. Since the ultimate responsibility for the professional service rests with the professional accountant, the professional accountant should see that the requirements of ethical behavior are followed.

9.3.   When using the services of experts who are not professional accountants, the professional accountant must take steps to see that such experts are aware of ethical requirements. Primary attention should be paid to the fundamental principles in paragraph 16 of the Introduction to this Code. These principles would extend to any assignment in which such experts would participate.

9.4.   The degree of supervision and the amount of guidance that will be needed will depend upon the individuals involved and the nature of the engagement. Examples of such guidance and supervision might include:

- asking individuals to read the appropriate ethical codes

- requiring written confirmation of understanding of the ethical requirements, and

- providing consultation when potential conflicts arise.

9.5   The professional accountant should also be alert to specific independence requirements or other risks unique to the engagement. Such situations will require special attention and guidance/supervision to see that ethical requirements are met.

9.6   If at any time the professional accountant is not satisfied that proper ethical behavior can be respected or assured, the engagement should not be accepted; or, if the engagement has commenced, it should be terminated.

ETHICS

SECTION 10

Fees and Commissions

10.1 Professional accountants in public practice who undertake professional services for a client, assume the responsibility to perform such services with integrity and objectivity and in accordance with the appropriate technical standards. That responsibility is discharged by applying the professional skill and knowledge which professional accountants in public practice have acquired through training and experience. For the services rendered, the professional accountant in public practice is entitled to remuneration.

Professional Fees

10.2 Professional fees should be a fair reflection of the value of the professional services performed for the client, taking into account:

(a) The skill and knowledge required for the type of professional services involved.

(b) The level of training and experience of the persons necessarily engaged in performing the professional services.

(c) The time necessarily occupied by each person engaged in performing the professional services.

(d) The degree of responsibility that performing those services entails.

10.3 Professional fees should normally be computed on the basis of appropriate rates per hour or per day for the time of each person engaged in performing professional services. These rates should be based on the fundamental premise that the organization and conduct of the professional accountant in public practice and the services provided to clients are well planned, controlled and managed. They should take into account the factors set out in paragraph 10.2 and are influenced by the legal, social and economic conditions of each country. It is for each professional accountant in public practice to determine the appropriate rates.

10.4 A professional accountant in public practice should not make a representation that specific professional services in current or future periods will be performed for either a stated fee, estimated fee, or fee range if it is likely at the time of the representation that such fees will be substantially increased and the prospective client is not advised of that likelihood.

10.5 When performing professional services for a client it may be necessary or expedient to charge a pre-arranged fee, in which event the professional accountant in public practice should estimate a fee taking into account the matters referred to in paragraphs 10.2 through 10.4.

10.6 It is not improper for a professional accountant in public practice to charge a client a lower fee than has previously been charged for similar services, provided the fee has been calculated in accordance with the factors referred to in paragraphs 10.2 through 10.4.

Commentary

The fact that a professional accountant in public practice secures work by quoting a fee lower than another is not improper. However, professional accountants in public practice who obtain work at fees significantly lower than those charged by an existing accountant, or quoted by others, should be aware that there is a risk of a perception that the quality of work could be impaired.

Accordingly, when deciding on a fee to be quoted to a client for the performance of professional services, a professional accountant should be satisfied that, as a result of the fee quoted:

- the quality of work will not be impaired and that due care will be applied to comply with all professional standards and quality control procedures in the performance of those services, and

- the client will not be misled as to the precise scope of services that a quoted fee is intended to cover and the basis on which future fees will be charged.

10.7   As stated in paragraph 8.8:

Professional services should not be offered or rendered to a client under an arrangement whereby no fee will be charged unless a specified finding or result is obtained or when the fee is otherwise contingent upon the findings or results of such services.

Commentary

Fees should not be regarded as being contingent if fixed by a court or other public authority. Fees charged on a percentage or similar basis, except when authorized by statute or approved by a member body as generally accepted practice for certain professional services, should be regarded as contingent fees.

10.8   The foregoing paragraphs relate to fees as distinct from reimbursement of expenses. Out-of-pocket expenses, in particular traveling expenses, attributable directly to the professional services performed for a particular client would normally be charged to that client in addition to the professional fees.

10.9   It is in the best interests of both the client and the professional accountant in public practice that the basis on which fees are computed and any billing arrangements are clearly defined, preferably in writing, before the commencement of the engagement to help in avoiding misunderstandings with respect to fees. (For further guidance refer to International Standard on Auditing 210 "Terms of Audit Engagements".)

Commissions

10.10   The payment or receipt of a commission by a professional accountant in public practice could impair objectivity and independence. Subject to paragraph 10.13, a professional accountant in public practice should not, therefore, pay a commission to obtain a client nor should a commission be accepted for referral of a client to a third party. A professional accountant in public practice should not accept a commission for the referral of the products or services of others.

10.11 Payment and receipt of referral fees between professional accountants in public practice when no services are performed by the referring accountant are regarded as commissions for the purpose of paragraph 10.10.

10.12 A professional accountant in public practice may enter into an arrangement for the purchase of the whole or part of an accounting practice requiring payments to individuals formerly engaged in the practice or payments to their heirs or estates. Such payments are not regarded as commissions for the purpose of paragraph 10.10.

10.13 In those countries where payment and receipt of commissions are permitted, either by statute or by a member body, such engagements should be limited to those for which independence is not required and the professional accountant in public practice should nonetheless disclose the facts to the client.

SECTION 11

Activities Incompatible with the Practice of Public Accountancy

11.1   A professional accountant in public practice should not concurrently engage in any business, occupation or activity which impairs or might impair integrity, objectivity or independence, or the good reputation of the profession and therefore would be incompatible with the rendering of professional services.

11.2   The rendering of two or more types of professional services concurrently does not by itself impair integrity, objectivity or independence.

11.3   The simultaneous engagement in another business, occupation or activity unrelated to professional services which has the effect of not allowing the professional accountant in public practice properly to conduct a professional practice in accordance with the fundamental ethical principles of the accountancy profession should be regarded as inconsistent with the practice of public accountancy.

ETHICS

SECTION 12

Clients' Monies

12.1 It is recognized that in some countries the law does not permit a professional accountant in public practice to hold **clients' monies;**[*] in other countries there are legal duties imposed on professional accountants in public practice who do hold such monies. The professional accountant in public practice should not hold clients' monies if there is reason to believe that they were obtained from, or are to be used for, illegal activities.

12.2 A professional accountant in public practice entrusted with monies belonging to others should:

(a) keep such monies separately from personal or firm monies;

(b) use such monies only for the purpose for which they are intended; and

(c) at all times, be ready to account for those monies to any persons entitled to such accounting.

12.3 A professional accountant in public practice should maintain one or more bank accounts for clients' monies. Such bank accounts may include a general **client account**[*] into which the monies of a number of clients may be paid.

12.4 Clients' monies received by a professional accountant in public practice should be deposited without delay to the credit of a client account, or—if in the form of documents of title to money and documents of title which can be converted into money—be safeguarded against unauthorized use.

12.5 Monies may only be drawn from the client account on the instructions of the client.

12.6 Fees due from a client may be drawn from client's monies provided the client, after being notified of the amount of such fees, has agreed to such withdrawal.

12.7 Payments from a client account shall not exceed the balance standing to the credit of the client.

12.8 When it seems likely that the client's monies remain on client account for a significant period of time, the professional accountant in public practice should, with the concurrence of the client, place such monies in an interest bearing account within a reasonable time.

12.9 All interest earned on clients' monies should be credited to the client account.

12.10 Professional accountants in public practice should keep such books of account as will enable them, at any time, to establish clearly their dealings with clients' monies in general and the monies of each individual client in particular. A statement of account should be provided to the client at least once a year.

---

[*] **For definitions see pages 540-541.**

SECTION 13

Relations with Other Professional Accountants in Public Practice

Accepting New Assignments

13.1 The extension of the operations of a business undertaking frequently results in the formation of branches or subsidiary companies at locations where an **existing accountant*** does not practice. In these circumstances, the client or the existing accountant in consultation with the client may request a **receiving accountant*** practicing at those locations to perform such professional services as necessary to complete the assignment.

13.2 Referral of business may also arise in the area of special services or special tasks. The scope of the services offered by professional accountants in public practice continues to expand and the depth of knowledge which is needed to serve the public often calls for special skills. Since it is impracticable for any one professional accountant in public practice to acquire special expertise or experience in all fields of accountancy, some professional accountants in public practice have decided that it is neither appropriate nor desirable to develop within their firms the complete range of special skills which may be required.

13.3 Professional accountants in public practice should only undertake such services which they can expect to complete with professional competence. It is essential therefore for the profession in general and in the interests of their clients that professional accountants in public practice be encouraged to obtain advice when appropriate from those who are competent to provide it.

13.4 An existing accountant without a particular skill may however be reluctant to refer a client to another professional accountant in public practice who may possess that skill, because of the fear of losing existing business to the other professional accountant in public practice. As a result, clients may be deprived of the benefit of advice which they are entitled to receive.

13.5 The wishes of the client should be paramount in the choice of professional advisers, whether or not special skills are involved. Accordingly, a professional accountant in public practice should not attempt to restrict in any way the client's freedom of choice in obtaining special advice, and when appropriate should encourage a client to do so.

13.6 The services or advice of a professional accountant in public practice having special skills may be sought in one or other of the following ways:

    (a) by the client

        (i) after prior discussion and consultation with the existing accountant;

---

* For definitions see pages 540-541.

(ii) on the specific request or recommendation of the existing accountant; and

(iii) without reference to the existing accountant; or

(b) by the existing accountant with due observance of the duty of confidentiality.

13.7 When a professional accountant in public practice is asked to provide services or advice, inquiries should be made as to whether the prospective client has an existing accountant. In cases where there is an existing accountant who will continue to provide professional services, the procedures set out in paragraphs 13.8-13.14 should be observed. If the appointment will result in another professional accountant in public practice being superseded, the procedures set out in paragraphs 13.15-13.26 should be followed.

13.8 The receiving accountant should limit the services provided to the specific assignment received by referral from the existing accountant or the client unless otherwise requested by the client. The receiving accountant also has the duty to take reasonable steps to support the existing accountant's current relationship with the client and should not express any criticism of the professional services of the existing accountant without giving the latter an opportunity to provide all relevant information.

13.9 A receiving accountant who is asked by the client to undertake an assignment of a type which is clearly distinct from that being carried out by the existing accountant or from that initially received by referral from the existing accountant or from the client, should regard this as a separate request to provide services or advice. Before accepting any appointments of this nature, the receiving accountant should advise the client of the professional obligation to communicate with the existing accountant and should immediately do so preferably in writing, advising of the approach made by the client and the general nature of the request as well as seeking all relevant information, if any, necessary to perform the assignment.

13.10 Circumstances sometimes arise when the client insists that the existing accountant should not be informed. In this case, the receiving accountant should decide whether the client's reasons are valid. In the absence of special circumstances a mere disinclination by the client for communication with the existing accountant would not be a satisfactory reason.

13.11 The receiving accountant should:

(a) comply with the instructions received from the existing accountant or the client to the extent that they do not conflict with relevant legal or other requirements; and

(b) ensure, insofar as it is practicable to do so, that the existing accountant is kept informed of the general nature of the professional services being performed.

13.12 When there are two or more other professional accountants in public practice performing professional services for the client concerned it may be appropriate to notify only the relevant professional accountant in public practice depending on the specific services being performed.

13.13 When appropriate the existing accountant, in addition to issuing instructions concerning referred business, should maintain contact with the receiving accountants and cooperate with them in all reasonable requests for assistance.

13.14 When the opinion of a professional accountant, other than the existing accountant, is sought on the application of accounting, auditing, reporting or other standards or principles to specific circumstances or transactions, the professional accountant should be alert to the possibility of the opinion creating undue pressure on the judgment and objectivity of the accountant. An opinion given without full and proper facts can cause difficulty to the receiving accountant if the opinion is challenged or the receiving accountant is subsequently appointed by the company. Accordingly, the professional accountant should seek to minimize the risk of giving inappropriate guidance by ensuring that he or she has access to all relevant information. When there is a request for an opinion in the above circumstances there is a requirement for communication with the existing accountant. It is important that the existing accountant, with the permission of the client, provide the receiving accountant with all requested relevant information about the client. With the permission of the client, the receiving accountant should also provide a copy of the final report to the existing accountant. If the client does not agree to these communications, then the engagement should ordinarily not be performed.

Superseding Another Professional Accountant in Public Practice

13.15 The proprietors of a business have an indisputable right to choose their professional advisers and to change to others should they so desire. While it is essential that the legitimate interests of the proprietors are protected, it is also important that a professional accountant in public practice who is asked to replace another professional accountant in public practice has the opportunity to ascertain if there are any professional reasons why the appointment should not be accepted. This cannot effectively be done without direct communication with the existing accountant. In the absence of a specific request, the existing accountant should not volunteer information about the client's affairs.

13.16 Communication enables a professional accountant in public practice to ascertain whether the circumstances in which a change in appointment is proposed are such that the appointment can properly be accepted and also whether there is a wish to undertake the engagement. In addition, such communication helps to preserve the harmonious relationships which should exist between all professional accountants in public practice on whom clients rely for professional advice and assistance.

13.17 The extent to which an existing accountant can discuss the affairs of the client with the proposed professional accountant in public practice depend on:

(a)   whether the client's permission to do so has been obtained; and/or

(b)   the legal or ethical requirements relating to such disclosure which may vary by country.

13.18 The proposed professional accountant in public practice should treat in the strictest confidence and give due weight to any information provided by the existing accountant.

13.19 The information provided by the existing accountant may indicate, for example, that the ostensible reasons given by the client for the change are not in accordance with the facts. It may disclose that the proposal to make a change in professional accountants in public practice was made because the existing accountants stood their ground and properly carried out the duties as professional accountants in public practice despite opposition or evasion on an occasion on which important differences of principles or practice have arisen with the client.

13.20 Communication between the parties therefore serves:

(a) To protect a professional accountant in public practice from accepting an appointment in circumstances where all the pertinent facts are not known.

(b) To protect the minority proprietors of a business who may not be fully informed of the circumstances in which the change is proposed.

(c) To protect the interests of the existing accountant when the proposed change arises from, or is an attempt to interfere with, the conscientious exercise of the existing accountant's duty to act as an independent professional.

13.21 Before accepting an appointment involving recurring professional services hitherto carried out by another professional accountant in public practice, the proposed professional accountant in public practice should:

(a) Ascertain if the prospective client has advised the existing accountant of the proposed change and has given permission, preferably in writing, to discuss the client's affairs fully and freely with the proposed professional accountant in public practice.

(b) When satisfied with the reply received from prospective client, request permission to communicate with the existing accountant. If such permission is refused or the permission referred to in a) above is not given, the proposed professional accountant in public practice should, in the absence of exceptional circumstances of which there is full knowledge, and unless there is satisfaction as to necessary facts by other means, decline the appointment.

(c) On receipt of permission, ask the existing accountant, preferably in writing:

(i) to provide information on any professional reasons which should be known before deciding whether or not to accept the appointment and, if there are such matters; and

(ii) to provide all the necessary details to be able to come to a decision.

13.22 The existing accountant, on receipt of the communication referred to in paragraph 13.21 (c) should forthwith:

(a) Reply, preferably in writing, advising whether there are any professional reasons why the proposed professional accountant in public practice should not accept the appointment.

(b) If there are any such reasons or other matters which should be disclosed, ensure that the client has given permission to give details of this information to the proposed professional accountant in public practice. If permission is not granted, the existing accountant should report that fact to the proposed professional accountant in public practice.

(c) On receipt of permission from the client, disclose all information needed by the proposed professional accountant in public practice to be able to decide whether or not to accept the appointment, and discuss freely with the proposed professional accountant in public practice all matters relevant to the appointment of which the latter should be aware.

13.23 If the proposed professional accountant in public practice does not receive, within a reasonable time, a reply from the existing accountant and there is no reason to believe that there are any exceptional circumstances surrounding the proposed change, the proposed professional accountant in public practice should endeavor to communicate with the existing accountant by some other means. If unable to obtain a satisfactory outcome in this way, the proposed professional accountant in public practice should send a further letter, stating that there is an assumption that there is no professional reason why the appointment should not be accepted and that there is an intention to do so.

13.24 The fact that there may be fees owing to the existing accountant is not a professional reason why another professional accountant in public practice should not accept the appointment.

13.25 The existing accountant should promptly transfer to the new professional accountant in public practice all books and papers of the client which are or may be held after the change in appointment has been effected and should advise the client accordingly, unless the professional accountant in public practice has a legal right to withhold them.

13.26 Certain organizations, either because of legislative requirements or otherwise, call for submissions or tenders, e.g., competitive bids, in relation to professional services offered by accountants in public practice. In reply to a public advertisement or an unsolicited request to make a submission or submit a tender, a professional accountant in public practice should, if the appointment may result in the replacement of another professional accountant in public practice, state in the submission or tender that before acceptance the opportunity to contact the other professional accountant in public practice is required so that inquiries may be made as to whether there are any professional reasons why the appointment should not be accepted. If the submission or tender is successful, the existing accountant should then be contacted.

SECTION 14

Advertising and Solicitation

14.1 Whether or not **advertising*** and **solicitation*** by individual professional accountants in public practice are permitted is a matter for member bodies to determine based upon the legal, social and economic conditions in each country.

14.2 When permitted, such advertising and solicitation should be aimed at informing the public in an objective manner and should be decent, honest, truthful and in good taste. Solicitation by the use of coercion or harassment should be prohibited.

14.3 Examples of activities which may be considered not to meet the above criteria include those that:

(a) create false, deceptive or unjustified expectations of favorable results;

(b) imply the ability to influence any court, tribunal, regulatory agency or similar body or official;

(c) consist of self-laudatory statements that are not based on verifiable facts;

(d) make comparisons with other professional accountants in public practice;

(e) contain testimonials or endorsements;

(f) contain any other representations that would be likely to cause a reasonable person to misunderstand or be deceived; and

(g) make unjustified claims to be an expert or specialist in a particular field of accountancy.

14.4 A professional accountant in public practice in a country where advertising is permitted should not seek to obtain an advantage by advertising in newspapers or magazines published or distributed in a country where advertising is prohibited. Similarly, a professional accountant in public practice in a country where advertising is prohibited should not advertise in a newspaper or magazine published in a country where advertising is permitted.

14.5 In situations where professional accountants in public practice in their international cross border activities violate the provisions of paragraph 14.4, contact should take place between the member body in the country in which the violation takes place and the member body of the home country of the professional accountant in public practice to ensure that the member body in the home country is made aware of such violation.

---

* For definitions see pages 540-541.

14.6 It is clearly desirable that the public should be aware of the range of services available from a professional accountant. Accordingly there is no objection to a member body communicating such information to the public on an institutional basis, i.e., in the name of the member body.

Publicity by Professional Accountants in Public Practice in a Non-Advertising Environment

14.7 When advertising is not permitted, publicity by individual professional accountants in public practice is acceptable provided:

(a) it has as its object the notification to the public or such sectors of the public as are concerned, of matters of fact in a manner that is not false, misleading or deceptive;

(b) it is in good taste;

(c) it is professionally dignified; and

(d) it avoids frequent repetition of, and any undue prominence being given to the name of the professional accountant in public practice.

14.8 The examples which follow are illustrative of circumstances in which publicity is acceptable and the matters to be considered in connection therewith subject always to the overriding requirements mentioned in the preceding paragraph.

Appointments and Awards

It is in the interests of the public and the accountancy profession that any appointment or other activity of a professional accountant in a matter of national or local importance, or the award of any distinction to a professional accountant, should receive publicity and that membership of the professional body should be mentioned. However, the professional accountant should not make use of any of the aforementioned appointments or activities for personal professional advantage.

Professional Accountants Seeking Employment or Professional Business

A professional accountant may inform interested parties through any medium that a partnership or salaried employment of an accountancy nature is being sought. The professional accountant should not, however, publicize for subcontract work in a manner which could be interpreted as seeking to procure professional business. Publicity seeking subcontract work may be acceptable if placed only in the professional press and provided that neither the professional accountant's name, address or telephone number appears in the publicity. A professional accountant may write a letter or make a direct approach to another professional accountant when seeking employment or professional business.

Directories

A professional accountant may be listed in a directory provided neither the directory itself nor the entry could reasonably be regarded as a promotional advertisement for those listed therein. Entries should be limited to name, address, telephone number, professional description and any other information necessary to enable the user of the directory to make contact with the person or organization to which the entry relates.

Books, Articles, Interviews, Lectures, Radio and Television Appearances

Professional accountants who author books or articles on professional subjects, may state their name and professional qualifications and give the name of their organization but shall not give any information as to the services that firm provides.

Similar provisions are applicable to participation by a professional accountant in a lecture, interview or a radio or television program on a professional subject. What professional accountants write or say, however, should not be promotional of themselves or their firm but should be an objective professional view of the topic under consideration. Professional accountants are responsible for using their best endeavors to ensure that what ultimately goes before the public complies with these requirements.

Training Courses, Seminars, etc.

A professional accountant may invite clients, staff or other professional accountants to attend training courses or seminars conducted for the assistance of staff. Other persons should not be invited to attend such training courses or seminars except in response to an unsolicited request. The requirement should in no way prevent professional accountants from providing training services to other professional bodies, associations or educational institutions which run courses for their members or the public. However, undue prominence should not be given to the name of a professional accountant in any booklets or documents issued in connection therewith.

Booklets and Documents Containing Technical Information

Booklets and other documents bearing the name of a professional accountant and giving technical information for the assistance of staff or clients may be issued to such persons or to other professional accountants.

Other persons should not be issued with such booklets or documents except in response to an unsolicited request.

Staff Recruitment

Genuine vacancies for staff may be communicated to the public through any medium in which comparable staff vacancies normally appear. The fact that a job specification necessarily gives some detail as to one or more of the services provided to clients by the professional accountant in public practice is acceptable but it should not contain any promotional element. There should not be any suggestion that the services offered are superior to those offered by other professional accountants in public practice as a consequence of size, associations, or for any other reason.

In publications such as those specifically directed to schools and other places of education to inform students and graduates of career opportunities in the profession, services offered to the public may be described in a businesslike way.

More latitude may also be permissible in a section of a newspaper devoted to staff vacancies than would be allowed if the vacancy appeared in a prominent position elsewhere in a newspaper on the grounds that it would be most unlikely that a potential client would use such media to select a professional adviser.

Publicity on Behalf of Clients

A professional accountant in public practice may publicize on behalf of clients, primarily for staff. However, the professional accountant in public practice should ensure that the emphasis in the publicity is directed towards the objectives to be achieved for the client.

Brochures and Firm Directories

A professional accountant in public practice may issue to clients or, in response to an unsolicited request, to a non-client:

(a)   a factual and objectively worded account of the services provided; and

(b)   a directory setting out names of partners, office addresses and names and addresses of associated firms and correspondents.

Stationery and Nameplates

Stationery of professional accountants in public practice should be of an acceptable professional standard and comply with the requirements of the law and of the member body concerned as to names of partners, principals and others who participate in the practice, use of professional descriptions and designatory letters, cities or countries where the practice is represented, logotypes, etc. The designation of any services provided by the practice as being of specialist nature should not be permitted. Similar provisions, where applicable, should apply to nameplates.

Newspaper Announcements

Appropriate newspapers or magazines may be used to inform the public of the establishment of a new practice, of changes in the composition of a partnership of professional accountants in public practice, or of any alteration in the address of a practice.

Such announcements should be limited to a bare statement of facts and consideration given to the appropriateness of the area of distribution of the newspaper or magazine and number of insertions.

ETHICS

Inclusion of the Name of a Professional Accountant in Public Practice in a Document Issued by a Client

When a client proposes to publish a report by a professional accountant in public practice dealing with the client's existing business affairs or in connection with the establishment of a new business venture, the professional accountant in public practice should take steps to ensure that the context in which the report is published is not such as might result in the public being misled as to the nature and meaning of the report. In these circumstances, the professional accountant in public practice should advise the client that permission should first be obtained before publication of the document.

Similar consideration should be given to other documents proposed to be issued by a client containing the name of a professional accountant in public practice acting in an independent professional capacity. This does not preclude the inclusion of the name of a professional accountant in public practice in the annual report of a client.

When professional accountants in their private capacity are associated with, or hold office in, an organization, the organization may use their name and professional status on stationery and other documents. The professional accountant in public practice should ensure that this information is not used in such a way as might lead the public to believe that there is a connection with the organization in an independent professional capacity.

PART C — APPLICABLE TO EMPLOYED PROFESSIONAL ACCOUNTANTS

The following sections contain guidance which is particularly relevant to professional accountants working in industry, commerce, the public sector or education. Professional accountants employed in public practice should be aware they may find that the principles set out below are also of application to their particular circumstances. If professional accountants employed in practice are in doubt as to the applicability of any particular guidance, they should seek assistance from their professional body.

SECTION 15

Conflict of Loyalties

15.1 Employed professional accountants owe a duty of loyalty to their employer as well as to their profession and there may be times when the two are in conflict. An employee's normal priority should be to support his or her organization's legitimate and ethical objectives and the rules and procedures drawn up in support of them. However, an employee cannot legitimately be required to:

(a) break the law;

(b) breach the rules and standards of their profession;

(c) lie to or mislead (including misleading by keeping silent) those acting as auditors to the employer; or

(d) put their name to or otherwise be associated with a statement which materially misrepresents the facts.

15.2 Differences in view about the correct judgment on accounting or ethical matters should normally be raised and resolved within the employee's organization, initially with the employee's immediate superior and possibly thereafter, where disagreement about a significant ethical issue remains, with higher levels of management or non executive directors.

15.3 If employed accountants cannot resolve any material issue involving a conflict between their employers and their professional requirements they may, after exhausting all other relevant possibilities, have no other recourse but to consider resignation. Employees should state their reasons for doing so to the employer but their duty of confidentiality normally precludes them from communicating the issue to others (unless legally or professionally required to do so).

15.4 For further guidance as to the considerations involved see Section 2— Resolution of Ethical Conflicts.

ETHICS

SECTION 16

Support for Professional Colleagues

A professional accountant, particularly one having authority over others, should give due weight for the need for them to develop and hold their own judgment in accounting matters and should deal with differences of opinion in a professional way.

SECTION 17

Professional Competence

A professional accountant employed in industry, commerce, the public sector or education may be asked to undertake significant tasks for which he or she has not had sufficient specific training or experience. When undertaking such work the professional accountant should not mislead the employer as to the degree of expertise or experience he or she possesses, and where appropriate expert advice and assistance should be sought.

SECTION 18

Presentation of Information

18.1   A professional accountant is expected to present financial information fully, honestly and professionally and so that it will be understood in its context.

18.2   Financial and non-financial information should be maintained in a manner that describes clearly the true nature of business transactions, assets or liabilities and classifies and records entries in a timely and proper manner, and professional accountants should do everything that is within their powers to ensure that this is the case.

Preface to Ethical Requirements of

(Name of Member Body)

Statement of Policy of Council

This Preface has been approved by the Council of the [Name of Member Body] for publication.

1. The [Name of Member Body] as a member of the International Federation of Accountants (IFAC) is committed to the IFAC's broad objective of developing and enhancing a coordinated worldwide accountancy profession with harmonized standards. In working toward this objective, IFAC develops guidance on ethics for professional accountants. IFAC believes that issuing such guidance will improve the degree of uniformity of professional ethics throughout the world.

2. As a condition of its membership, the [Name of Member Body] is obliged to support the work of IFAC by informing its members of every pronouncement developed by IFAC, and to work towards implementation, when and to the extent possible under local circumstances, of those pronouncements.

3. The (name of Member Body) has determined to (either 1 or 2)

    1. adopt the IFAC Code of Ethics for Professional Accountants as the ethical requirements in [Name of Country]. The Council of [Name of Member Body] has prepared an explanatory foreword (attachment A) which sets out the status and effective date of this decision.

    2. adopt the IFAC Code of Ethics for Professional Accountants as the basis for approved ethical requirements in [Name of Country]. The Council of [Name of Member Body] has prepared an explanatory foreword (attachment B) which sets out the status and effective date of this decision along with significant differences between the IFAC guidance and the law or practice in [Name of Country] and how such differences have been resolved.

An explanatory foreword will be issued on the status of each additional IFAC pronouncement on Ethics that is adopted by the Council of [Name of the Member

ETHICS

Body]. Where the Council of [Name of Member Body] deems it necessary, additional ethical requirements may be developed on matters of relevance in [Name of Country] not covered by an IFAC pronouncement.

4. Members of [Name of Member Body] are expected to comply with the ethical requirements issued by [Name of Member Body]. Apparent failure to do so may result in an investigation into the member's conduct by [Name of Appropriate Disciplinary Committee of Member Body].

5. It is not practical to establish ethical requirements which apply to all situations and circumstances that professional accountants may encounter. Therefore, professional accountants should consider the ethical requirements as the basic principles which they should follow in performing their work.

6. The date from which members are expected to observe pronouncements on ethics is set out in the explanatory foreword.

Code of Ethics for Professional Accountants

[Title]

<u>Explanatory Foreword</u>

The Council of [Name of Member Body] has determined that this Code should be adopted. This Code is mandatory for all members of [Name of Member Body] to observe in respect of professional services performed in [Name of Country] after [Month, Day, Year].

Code of Ethics for Professional Accountants

[Title]

<u>Explanatory Foreword</u>

The Council of [Name of Member Body] has determined that this Code should be adopted with the explanatory notes below. This Code is mandatory for all members of [Name of Member Body] to observe in respect of the performance of professional services in [Name of Country] after [Month, Day, Year].

Section 8.11   Under [Name of Country] legislation, shares in an accounting practice may not be held by those who are not members of the [Name of Member Body]. This section is therefore not relevant in [Name of Country].

Section 14   Under [Name of Country] legislation, professional accountants are not permitted to advertise their services. Thus paragraphs 14.2 and 14.3 are not relevant in [Name of Country].

Implementation and Enforcement of

Ethical Requirements

Statement of Policy of Council

Introduction

1. The mission of the International Federation of Accountants (IFAC) as set out in paragraph 2 of its Constitution is "the worldwide development and enhancement of an accountancy profession with harmonized standards, able to provide services of consistently high quality in the public interest." In working towards this objective, the Council of IFAC has established committees to develop and issue pronouncements on behalf of the Council on a wide variety of professional issues.

2. IFAC believes that the issue of such pronouncements will help improve the degree of uniformity of the accountancy profession throughout the world. However, it should be recognized that in order to develop such pronouncements the legal, social and economic conditions prevailing in each country will affect the extent and manner in which the pronouncements are applied. Notwithstanding this condition, it is important that each national profession have a set of clearly articulated pronouncements and technical standards to cover the professional practice of accounting.

3. Once the relevant pronouncements are implemented they should be governed by a policy which ensures that the ethical requirements (which includes compliance with technical standards) are followed.

4. The Council of IFAC wishes to draw the attention of member bodies to the following Statement of Policy on Implementation and Enforcement of Ethical Requirements.

Implementation of Ethical Requirements

5. The task of preparing detailed ethical requirements is primarily that of the professional bodies of each country concerned, even if the responsibility for promulgating those requirements is assumed, partly or wholly by the legislative body of that country.

ETHICS

6. The adoption of ethical requirements by member bodies will not necessarily ensure that the standard of conduct laid down will be maintained; if it is to be effective, provision must be made by the appropriate bodies in each country for their implementation.

7. Each member body has the responsibility to promote high standards of professional conduct and to ensure that ethical requirements are observed and failure to observe them will be investigated and appropriate action taken.

   As noted in paragraph 2.6 of the *Code of Ethics for Professional Accountants*, member bodies are urged to ensure that counseling and advice is available to help resolve ethical conflicts. This function is an important part of implementation and can be fulfilled by such means as providing a service to respond to questions raised by individual members on interpretations of ethical requirements or by the formation of appropriate committees within member bodies which would monitor the ethical requirements of those bodies.

   Provision of an interpretation/advice/counseling service should offer the following features:

   - its purposes and operating procedures should be transparent and widely promoted to the membership;

   - the operating procedures should provide safeguards such that only reasonable questions from members are considered and that the questioner is responsible for clearly setting out the facts and circumstances;

   - the individuals charged with responsibility for providing the advice must be at a level commensurate with such authority and have sufficient technical expertise to provide such advice;

   - inquiries would ordinarily be made on a totally confidential basis; and

   - results of any interpretation/ counseling/advice questions could be subject to publication (on a "no-name" basis) to the general membership as an educational method.

8. Implementation of ethical requirements will be assisted by the introduction of a program designed to ensure that individual members are aware of all ethical requirements and the consequences of non-compliance with those requirements. This information may be communicated to individual members in such ways as members' handbooks, technical releases, professional journals, reports on disciplinary hearings and activities, programs of continuing professional education, newsletters, financial and business press, and responses from the appropriate committee to requests for advice.

9. Most accountants will respect the ethical requirements to which they are subject without any necessity for compulsion or sanctions. Nevertheless, cases may occur where such requirements are flagrantly ignored or where accountants through error, oversight or lack of understanding, fail to observe them. It is in the interest of the profession and all its members in any country that the general public should have confidence that failure to observe the ethical requirements of the profession in that country will be investigated and, where appropriate, disciplinary action taken.

10. Members of member bodies should therefore be prepared to justify any departures from the ethical requirements. Failure to comply with ethical requirements or the inability to justify departures therefrom may constitute professional misconduct that could give rise to disciplinary action.

Enforcement of Ethical Requirements

11. The power for disciplinary action may be provided by legislation or by the constitution of the professional body. In many countries, disciplinary action may be provided by legislatory agencies other than the professional body. Such regulatory agencies may be jointly or solely responsible for the disciplinary action or provide a review process over disciplinary action already taken.

12. Disciplinary action ordinarily arises from such issues as:

- Failure to observe the required standard of professional care, skills or competence.

- Non-compliance with rules of ethics.

- Discreditable or dishonorable conduct.

13. Disciplinary investigations will ordinarily commence as a result of a complaint. Member bodies should consider all complaints. Investigations may, however, be initiated by the member body or regulatory agency without a complaint being made. Investigations can be carried out on a verbal or correspondence basis. Reference should always be made to the member against whom the complaint is being made as well as to the complainant. When there is a dispute, conciliation may be attempted. Setting time limits on the investigatory process may be difficult, particularly when the circumstances involve other legal processes.

14. Arising from the investigatory process, the member body or regulatory agency will decide as to whether to commence disciplinary proceedings. There may be a right to appeal, within a set time frame, against the decision.

15. The disciplinary proceedings will ordinarily be carried out by the disciplinary committee or similar tribunal. Consideration should be given to the inclusion of nonmembers in the disciplinary committee or similar tribunal. The proceedings should be held in a manner which is consistent with the legal requirements of the country concerned. This will ordinarily involve legal representation, taking evidence and keeping records of the proceedings. The case against the defendant may be presented by a lawyer, a representative of the investigation committee or the secretariat of the member body.

16. Sanctions commonly imposed by disciplinary bodies include the following:

- Reprimand.

- Fine.

- Payment of costs.

- Withdrawal of practicing rights.

ETHICS

- Suspension.

- Expulsion from membership.

Other sanctions can include a warning, the refund of the fee charged to the client, additional education and the work to be completed by another member at the disciplined member's expense.

17. Ordinarily there is a right to appeal by both sides within fixed time limits. Such a right of appeal may be to a body not connected with the member body. Consideration should be given to the inclusion of nonmembers in the body of appeal and the appointment of a nonmember as the chairman. The appeal body should review all the evidence considered at the disciplinary proceedings. Additional evidence may also be called for and taken either orally or in writing.

18. It may be appropriate for publicity to be given to the disciplinary and appeal proceedings. In this way, both members and the general public are informed. However, the aspects of confidentiality and the type of violation have to be considered in deciding the method of publicity. There may also be a need to communicate the decision to an appropriate regulatory body or vice versa where the regulatory body has carried out the disciplinary hearing.

EDUCATION

CONTENTS OF THIS SECTION

	Page
Introduction to the Education Committee of the International Federation of Accountants	592

Guidelines:*

2.	Continuing Professional Education	595
9.	Prequalification Education, Assessment of Professional Competence and Experience Requirements of Professional Accountants	606
10.	Professional Ethics for Accountants: The Educational Challenge and Practical Application	623
11.	Information Technology in the Accounting Curriculum	628

Summary of Discussion Papers and Studies:

• Specialization in the Accounting Profession	688
• Minimum Skill Levels in Information Technology for Professional Accountants	688
• 2000 AND BEYOND A Strategic Framework for Prequalification Education for the Accountancy Profession in the Year 2000 and Beyond	689
• INTEGRATING INFORMATION TECHNOLOGY ACROSS THE ACCOUNTING CURRICULUM: The Experience of the Certified General Accountants' Association of Canada	689
• IMPLEMENTING INTERNATIONAL EDUCATION GUIDELINE 11: Strategies of the American Institute of Certified Public Accountants	690
• Competence-Based Approaches to the Professional Preparation of Accountants	691
• Practical Experience	692
• Study 1—An Advisory on Examination Administration	692
• Study 2—An Advisory on Education and Training of Technical Accounting Staff..	693

*Guidelines 1, 3, 4, 5, 6 and 8 were consolidated into Guideline 9. Guideline 7 has been replaced by Study 2.

Introduction to the Education Committee of the International Federation of Accountants

CONTENTS

	Paragraphs
Objectives and Terms of Reference	1-4
International Education Standards and Guidelines	5-9
Language	10

For additional information on the Education Committee, recent developments, and/or to obtain outstanding exposure drafts, visit the Committee's page at http://www.ifac.org/Committees/Education.

INTRODUCTION TO THE EDUCATION COMMITTEE OF THE INTERNATIONAL FEDERATION OF ACCOUNTANTS

Objectives and Terms of Reference

1. The mission of the International Federation of Accountants (IFAC) as set out in paragraph 2 of its Constitution is "the worldwide development and enhancement of an accountancy profession with harmonized standards, able to provide services of consistently high quality in the public interest."

2. The Education Committee is a standing committee of the Council of IFAC, formed to develop standards, guidelines, discussion papers and other information documents on both prequalification education and training of accountants and on continuing professional education for members of the accountancy profession. In addition, the Education Committee is expected to act as a catalyst in bringing together the developed and developing nations and to assist in the advancement of accounting education programs worldwide, particularly where this will assist economic development.

3. The members of the Education Committee are nominated by the member bodies in the countries selected by the Council of IFAC to serve on the committee. Members are appointed for an initial term of two and a half years which may be renewed for further two and a half year terms. For voting purposes, each country and organization represented on the committee has one vote.

4. In accordance with the Constitution of IFAC, member bodies subscribe to the mission set out in paragraph 1 above. In order to assist member bodies in the implementation of International Education Standards and Guidelines, the Education Committee will seek to promote an understanding and acceptance of such standards and guidelines.

International Education Standards and Guidelines

5. International Education Standards establish essential methods and techniques which have the potential for international recognition, acceptance and application. Although they cannot override authoritative local pronouncements, they are essentially prescriptive in nature. International Education Guidelines promote good practice and/or provide advice. They are based on careful study of the best practices and most effective methods for dealing with the issues being addressed.

6. The Committee is conscious of the wide diversity of educational systems and social and economic conditions in the countries of the member bodies and of the variety of functions performed by accountants. Consequently, the recommendations contained in International Education Standards and Guidelines are intended to establish the essential elements on which education and training programs, both prequalification and post-qualification, for all accountants should be founded.

7. International Education Standards and Guidelines are not intended to override the requirements of individual member bodies. They set out the basic, essential elements which education and training programs may be expected to contain. It is for each individual member body to determine the detailed requirements of the prequalification and postqualification education and training programs. However, member bodies should consider the recommendations in the standards and guidelines in developing their education and training programs.

8. While the Education Committee is responsible for selecting the subject matter to be addressed by International Education Standards and Guidelines, suggestions and proposals from interested individuals and organizations are encouraged. The work of carrying out the necessary research and of preparing pronouncements may be delegated by the committee to subcommittees or individuals.

9. Education pronouncements may be issued if approved by at least three-quarters of the total voting rights of the Education Committee. Guidelines and Standards must be issued first as exposure drafts, which are widely distributed for comment by member bodies of IFAC. This process provides an opportunity for those interested in the education and training of accountant to present their views before the drafts are finalized. The Education Committee welcomes and considers all comments received on exposure drafts and makes such modifications as it considers appropriate before issuing the International Education Standard or Guideline.

Language

10. The approved text of a pronouncement is that published by the Education Committee in the English language. Member bodies of IFAC are authorized after obtaining IFAC approval to prepare translations of such pronouncements at their own cost to be issued in the language of their own countries as appropriate. These translations should indicate the name of the body that prepared the translation and that it is a translation of the approved text.

First Issued February 1982
Revised May 1998

Continuing Professional Education

CONTENTS

	Paragraphs
Introduction	1-9
Objectives of a CPE Program	10-15
Appropriate Subject Areas	16-19
Minimum Individual Commitment to CPE	20-28
Mandatory CPE as a Requirement	29-35
Monitoring CPE	36-41
Responding to Noncompliance	42-45
Conclusion	46-47

INTRODUCTION

1. This Guideline sets forth recommendations, indicated in **boldface** print, for the establishment and operation by member bodies of an effective program of continuing professional education (CPE) to maintain and improve the professional competence of accountants and to meet public expectations about the quality of their work. The "Discussion" sections represent elaboration and rationale for the recommendations.

2. The recommendations:

   - address the objectives of CPE; the subject areas that should be viewed as consistent with those objectives; and the extent of the CPE commitment appropriate for professional accountants in public practice, industry, commerce, education and the public service

   - establish the goal of mandatory CPE as a requirement of all member bodies on a worldwide basis

   - explain the necessity of appropriate disciplinary mechanisms to assure compliance with CPE requirements

3. This Guideline is a revision of International Education Guideline 2, which was issued in February 1982. Since then, the knowledge needed to function effectively as an accountant in public practice, industry, commerce, education and the public service has expanded and changed at a rapid rate. That trend is certain to continue.

4. For example, there have been significant changes in the environment in which the accountant must operate. These include changes in accounting and auditing standards, new legislation and regulation affecting the profession and the people and organizations it serves, increasingly complex tax systems and rules, and the on-going development and greater use of sophisticated financial instruments. These changes have been accompanied by the widespread use of new tools, such as personal computers and related electronic communications systems, the resources on the Internet, and the everyday use of quantitative methods.

5. Not only are accountants faced with increased knowledge requirements, but they and their professional associations are also faced with increased public expectations about the quality of financial statements and of independent audits. Related pressures for disclosure of more information and for greater use of forecasts have had an impact on management accountants and independent auditors alike. In addition, the need to be competitive in a worldwide economy has led to more attention being paid to the role and responsibilities of the management accountant in entities of all types. All of this places a special responsibility on accountants in education. Finally, there is an increasing interest around the world in the public accountability of the business and financial community and that of the governmental sector, and accountants in all occupations have important contributions to make to that process.

6. The changes made in this revision of IEG 2 are intended to keep the Federation's recommendations in step with this changing environment, in which the individual member's commitment to CPE has become even more important and the role of member bodies in promoting effective CPE has taken on a correspondingly greater significance.

7. The Federation recognizes that in recent years many member bodies have addressed some or all of the issues considered in this Guideline, and it also recognizes that some member bodies may find it very challenging to implement some of its recommendations. However, the Federation believes that it is important for all member bodies to reassess their CPE programs in the light of these recommendations and consider, where necessary, how to move towards their implementation. By acting on the recommendations in this Guideline, member bodies will help significantly in the furtherance of the broad objective of IFAC, which is "the development and enhancement of a coordinated worldwide accountancy profession with harmonized standards."

8. In making that suggestion, the Federation has noted that the maintenance of career-long competence is already a requirement of the profession. (Paragraph 16 of the IFAC Code of Ethics for Professional Accountants indicates that a professional accountant has "a continuing duty to maintain knowledge and skill at a level required to ensure that a client or employer receives the advantage of competent professional service based on up-to-date developments in practice, legislation and techniques.") Also, it has concluded that the effectiveness of national CPE programs are and will continue to be a significant factor in any dialogues related to international reciprocity.

9. When working towards implementing the recommendations in this Guideline on CPE, a member body may find it useful to draw attention to its statements on ethics and to the IFAC Code of Ethics for Professional Accountants concerning the continuing duty to maintain professional competence, noting that an effective CPE program will help members comply with that existing obligation and thus help maintain public confidence in the profession.

OBJECTIVES OF A CPE PROGRAM

10. Member bodies should establish and operate or otherwise make available CPE programs that:

   a) maintain and improve the technical knowledge and professional skills possessed by their members;

   b) assist members of the profession to apply new techniques, to understand economic developments and evaluate their impact on their clients or employers and on their own work, and to meet changing responsibilities and expectations; and

   c) provide reasonable assurance to society at large that members of the profession have the technical knowledge and professional skills required to perform the services they undertake to provide.

Discussion

11. In many countries, the profession is granted the privilege of self-regulation and, in some cases, of reserved functions. These privileges are implicitly granted on the assumption that the organized profession in a country is best able to maintain and improve the professional competence of its members and the quality of the services they provide to clients and employers. Even in those countries where such privileges are not granted to the accounting profession, the profession must accept a similar responsibility. Indeed, meeting that responsibility is the raison d'être of any professional association of accountants.

12. In today's changing and increasingly complex environment, accountants cannot possess the knowledge required to render professional services of a high quality if they do not recognize the need for, and obtain, continuing professional education (CPE) appropriate to their circumstances. Thus, to fulfill their responsibilities to their members and to the public, member bodies should strive to establish and operate an effective CPE program that assists their members in obtaining the CPE they need and provides reasonable assurance to the public that their members can and will perform their work with professional competence.

13. It is not suggested that CPE on its own provides assurance to society at large that all members will provide every professional service with high quality. Doing so involves more than maintaining and updating technical and general knowledge; it involves applying that knowledge with professional judgment and an objective attitude in the real-life situations found in today's environment of socio-economic change. Also, there cannot be complete assurance that every person who participates in a CPE program will obtain the full benefits of that program, because of variances in individual commitment and capability. Nevertheless, it is certain that members who are not up-to-date with current technical and general knowledge applying to their work cannot provide professional services competently. Therefore, notwithstanding the inherent limitations of any CPE program, an effective program of continuing professional education can and should be an important element in preserving the standards of the profession and maintaining public confidence.

14. It is the professional duty of members of any profession not only to maintain professional competence, but also to strive continually to improve their competence. Thus, the objective of a program of CPE established by a member body should be focused on continual improvement, not on maintaining some minimum knowledge level. A CPE program that sets its objectives too low will be viewed with disdain by members who seek to provide the highest quality professional services and will be ineffective in motivating and enabling other members to improve the quality of their services.

15. Maintaining and improving technical knowledge (e.g., knowledge about accounting and auditing standards, taxation matters, budgetary control systems, computer techniques) is an important objective of a program of CPE. However, clients and employers expect accountants to perform their

work not only effectively but efficiently, and they often expect accountants to be able to advise them as to the impact of changes in the economic and business environment. Even when that is not the case, accountants must be aware of these matters to perform their work competently. For example, changed circumstances or the desire to improve efficiency may call for the use of new techniques which involve new risks that must be recognized and addressed by the accountant. Similarly, changes in the economic and business environment may affect the judgments and estimates made by the accountant in the process of preparing financial statements as well as the nature, timing and extent of procedures applied by the auditor. For these reasons, a program of CPE established and operated by a member body should give appropriate consideration to educational needs that go beyond basic technical knowledge.

APPROPRIATE SUBJECT AREAS

16. **CPE should contribute to the professional ability of the individual member and, therefore, acceptable CPE courses or activities should be relevant to the work of the member concerned. It is not necessary for member bodies to go beyond that general guideline by mandating specific topics for a program of CPE. It is reasonable to rely on members to select subject areas from the body of knowledge for accountants that are appropriate for them.**

Discussion

17. Continuing professional education carries a cost to members in terms of both time and money. The vast majority of members, trained in accountancy and schooled in business matters, are not likely to select CPE activities whose costs are not outweighed or at least balanced by their benefits.

18. Moreover, given the diverse activities in which members of the accountancy profession engage, it would be difficult to define a common CPE curriculum that all members should be required to follow. Any attempt to do so would be likely to result in too rigid an approach and one which might serve as a disincentive to many members. A preferable approach for member bodies is to establish as a general rule that the subjects selected by members should be relevant to the work of the member concerned, and not merely useful in, for example, the personal or financial affairs of the member.

19. In considering whether a CPE course or activity is relevant to the work of a member, member bodies are encouraged to recognize the changing nature of the environment and not to inhibit participation in courses simply because they do not bear immediately upon the member's daily work, e.g., programs dealing with social, economic and environmental trends likely to have a future impact upon the work environment of the accountancy profession.

MINIMUM INDIVIDUAL COMMITMENT TO CPE

20. **Member bodies should establish reasonable norms for the extent of CPE that their members should obtain in the form of structured learning activities.**

Discussion

21. "Structured learning activities" are measurable, verifiable activities that are designed to impart specific technical and general knowledge. Examples would include courses presented by educational institutions, member bodies or employers; individual study programs (correspondence courses, audiotape or videotape packages, computerized learning programs) that require some evidence of successful completion by the member; and participation as a speaker or attendee in conferences, briefing sessions or discussion groups.

22. The Federation suggests that each member who is active as an accounting professional should participate in a minimum of 30 hours per year, or a minimum of 90 hours in every three-year period,[1] of structured learning activity, whether compliance with that norm is voluntary or mandatory. (The recommended period of structured learning need not be taken in one block of time. It can also be made up by participation in a number of shorter programs throughout the period.) In making this recommendation, the Federation recognizes that the effectiveness of CPE is best measured in terms of what has been learned and has no intention to discourage efforts to establish other measurement criteria that can be broadly and cost-effectively applied within the accounting profession. However, it seems likely that hours will continue to be the measurement criterion that is commonly used and accepted for the near future.

23. Although the Federation's recommendation is applicable to all active accounting professionals, a member body may reasonably conclude, based on an assessment of public expectations (which may focus on the independent auditor) and the circumstances in the country (e.g., the occupational classification of members, existing CPE requirements or guidance, and the availability of local educational facilities, qualified instructors, and appropriate instructional materials), that the norm should be applicable only to members in public practice or that it should be different for members working in industry, commerce, education and the public service. A member body that draws a distinction between members based upon their occupations should periodically review the continuing appropriateness of such a distinction in the light of future developments within the country and in the international accounting profession. Also, member bodies should consider what additional CPE, if any, should be obtained by members who decide to move into or return to public practice.

24. It is for each member body to determine what activities would qualify for recognition as structured learning. In that connection, member bodies should focus on the need for an activity to be measurable and verifiable, as well as the need to meet appropriate learning objectives. For example, acting as a lecturer, instructor or discussion leader on a structured course would normally meet these criteria (but repeat presentations of the course should not be considered for this purpose). Service as a member of a technical

---

[1] Spreading the CPE requirement over a three-year period permits greater flexibility in the application of the guidelines and enables members to adapt their CPE activities to their particular circumstances.

committee of a professional body or individual firm may be deemed to be a structured learning activity to the extent a specific portion of the meeting is formally designed to impart specific knowledge in preparation for committee debate or discussion. Writing technical articles, papers or books may also be deemed to be a structured learning activity, within reasonable limits, since the output is clearly verifiable. There may also be special circumstances under which member bodies permit the substitution of an intensive, measurable and verifiable "on the job" experience for structured learning, for a finite period of time. In general, however, one single, repetitive activity - for example, writing - should not comprise the entire extent of someone's CPE activity.

25. Apart from participation in structured learning activities, there is a continuing need for members of the profession to keep abreast of a wide range of developments affecting their profession, clients and employers. This is done through unstructured learning activities, such as regularly reading professional journals and the financial and business press, discussing current developments with colleagues, accessing relevant data bases on the Internet and other activities.

26. Unstructured learning activities are important to every professional and the Federation recognizes that some member bodies may wish to emphasize their importance by covering them in the norms they adopt. However, the Federation believes that any norm for unstructured learning should be an addition to, not a substitute for, the norm set for structured learning. There are several reasons for this, and they are all related to the need to be able to provide reasonable assurance to the public that the objectives of the member body's CPE program are being achieved. First, structured learning activities can be efficiently monitored and measured, while unstructured learning activities cannot. Second, structured learning activities are usually designed to achieve specific learning objectives, while unstructured learning activities are usually general and unplanned in nature. Third, structured learning activities usually depend on approved instructors and/or instructional materials, while unstructured learning activities depend on the individual accountant.

27. As they develop their programs of CPE, member bodies should keep under review the adequacy of the minimum recommended period in relation to the needs of their members.

28. Some member bodies may find that adequate educational resources are not yet available to meet the needs of members wishing to observe the recommendations on CPE as outlined above. In these circumstances it may be necessary to adopt a program of CPE which is commensurate with immediately available resources and increases gradually to 30 hours per year (or 90 hours in every three-year period) over a reasonable period. Such a gradual but firm plan is preferred because it is likely to stimulate the development of necessary educational resources, while making a norm contingent on the development of those resources is likely only to delay implementation of the plan.

MANDATORY CPE AS A REQUIREMENT

29. **Member bodies should require their members to comply with norms established for participation in structured learning activities.**

Discussion

30. As is stated in paragraph 8, professional accountants have a continuing duty to maintain their professional competence. The importance attached to this duty by a professional body can best be demonstrated if the professional body requires its members to participate in a certain amount of structured learning activities. Such a requirement will be referred to in this guideline as "mandatory CPE".

31. The case for mandatory CPE now is the same as it was when IEG 2 was first issued:

    - The profession must be seen to be taking practical steps to ensure that its members maintain their technical knowledge.

    - Reliance on competition and market forces is unacceptable since it is likely that detection of incompetence or inadequate service will take place only after the damage has been suffered.

    - This is the only way to ensure participation in CPE by accountants whose knowledge is badly out of date and who are unlikely to respond to a voluntary program.

32. Under a voluntary system of CPE, it is entirely at the discretion of each individual as to whether and to what extent he or she participates in structured learning. Such an approach avoids the administrative burden of a system of mandatory CPE. It acknowledges that many members of the profession, recognizing their professional duty and their own self-interest, participate diligently, regularly and voluntarily in CPE with a view to maintaining and improving their technical knowledge. However, it does not deal with those members of the profession who do not now obtain adequate CPE and whose participation in a voluntary program would be desultory, lacking in discipline and not seen as a professional priority. Moreover, a voluntary program is not effective in persuading society at large of the profession's commitment to continuing professional education and professional competence.

33. Under a system of monitored voluntary CPE, members would have guidance, added motivation, and an agreed norm under which to plan and measure their participation in CPE. For its part, the individual member body would have a measure of the extent to which its members were observing its guidelines and adhering to the established norm. However, a system of monitored voluntary CPE is essentially an interim step that does not adequately achieve the objectives of a CPE program set forth in paragraph 10.

34. A system of mandatory CPE does not, in and of itself, pose administrative burdens substantially different from or greater than those necessitated by a system of monitored voluntary CPE. It does not require members eager to maintain and improve their professional competence to participate in

structured learning activities to an extent greater than that which they would be likely to do voluntarily. At the same time, it deals effectively with the problem of the less committed member; it provides reasonable assurance to society at large that members of the profession have the technical knowledge and professional skills required to perform the services they undertake to provide; and it contributes to the Federations' objective of "the development and enhancement of a coordinated worldwide accountancy profession with harmonized standards".

35. In making this recommendation, the Federation recognizes that some member bodies do not, because of legal or other environmental constraints, presently have the ability to implement a system of mandatory CPE and/or enforce compliance with it. As noted in the Introduction, those member bodies are encouraged to consider how to move towards the implementation of the recommendations in this Guideline.

MONITORING CPE

36. **In developing their programs of CPE, member bodies should adopt systems which will enable them to monitor effectively the extent to which members are observing their guidelines on CPE.**

Discussion

37. A member body would need to set up its own system for monitoring participation by individual members in structured learning activities and for evaluating the quality of those activities. It is suggested that a member body consider setting up a board or committee under its control that would be charged with those responsibilities.

38. The monitoring of participation in structured learning activities can be done in a number of ways. One approach is to require the member to submit an annual report of CPE activities. Individual reports submitted by a representative sample of the members should be checked against attendance or completion documents provided to the member by the individual or entity responsible for the CPE course or activity. It would be desirable to require these annual reports to identify the specific structured learning activities in which the member has engaged, rather than to accept a simple representation as to compliance with the requirement. This allows the member body to skim the reports for overall reasonableness and facilitates checking reports to supporting information. Another approach to monitoring is one in which the individuals are required to maintain documentation on their CPE activities which the member body "audits" on a selective sampling basis.

39. Evaluating the quality of structured learning activities offered to members of the profession at large, and the CPE credit to be granted for participation, can be done by approving the providers of those programs or by approving individual programs. Approving program providers is often more efficient, and would focus on the procedures and controls instituted by the providers to insure that programs are prepared, reviewed and conducted by qualified individuals, that the learning objectives are appropriate for the intended

participants and achievable within the time allotted for the program, and that the instructional materials, including case studies, are sufficiently comprehensive and properly designed. Whichever approach is taken, the member body should subsequently monitor offerings of actual programs on a test basis. Member bodies have a right to expect to be compensated by these providers for the costs incurred in making these evaluations.

40. Evaluating the quality of structured learning activities presented by accounting firms or other employers may be more difficult because the documentation of the program may be more informal because the program may be presented only once or a few times to a limited number of people. Evaluating the CPE content of other activities such as service on technical committees and writing articles (see paragraph 24) may pose different difficulties. When the approaches discussed in paragraph 39 do not appear relevant in situations like these, the member body would usually be able to make a reasonable evaluation by requesting copies of outlines and/or other available materials from the individual member claiming credit for participation.

41. The Federation recognizes that in establishing the norms and procedures for a system of mandatory CPE each member body will have regard to such matters as the occupational classification of its members, its existing CPE requirements or guidance, and the availability of local educational facilities, qualified instructors, and appropriate instructional materials.

RESPONDING TO NONCOMPLIANCE

42. **Member bodies should establish appropriate mechanisms to respond to instances of noncompliance with CPE requirements. Such mechanisms should focus on bringing a member into compliance, but should explicitly provide for disciplinary action when necessary.**

Discussion

43. A system of mandatory CPE will operate effectively and in the public interest only if members who willfully fail to comply with the requirement are brought into compliance on a timely basis or, if they persist in willful noncompliance, promptly disciplined. Accordingly, the monitoring procedures adopted by a member body should require timely reporting by the members and should result in effective follow-up by the member body if noncompliance is not cured by the member within a reasonable established period.

44. The sanctions initially applied for noncompliance should focus on bringing the member into compliance within a reasonable period of time. However, in deciding on the amount of CPE that should be obtained by the member, care should be taken to strike a balance between an amount that is too small (e.g., a sanction that in substance amounts to permitting a member to defer obtaining the CPE he or she should have obtained in the first place) and one that is excessively punitive. Punitive sanctions should be determined by member bodies after consideration of legal and environmental conditions in

their countries (in some countries they might include expulsion from membership and/or denial of the right to practice). They should be reserved for members who have made it clear through a pattern of noncompliance or through their response to the member body's inquiries that they are likely to continue to disregard the importance of participation in structured learning activities and of compliance with the requirements of their member body.

45. Imposing sanctions on colleagues is not an action that should be taken lightly. However, a willful failure to maintain and improve one's professional competence is a violation of a significant professional duty that justifies disciplinary action by a member body. Moreover, it is unfair to the majority of members who do and will continue to participate in required CPE programs at a cost in time and money to allow others who do not do so to escape any penalty.

CONCLUSION

46. This Guideline has set forth the recommendations for the establishment and operation by member bodies of an effective program of continuing professional education which will assist their members to maintain and improve their professional competence. It has recommended the goal of mandatory CPE, to be earned through participation in structured learning activities. It should be recognized, however, that each professional body will need to determine how best to accomplish this.

47. The accounting profession is a dynamic one, operating in an environment of change. Guidelines developed today are unlikely to meet the needs of tomorrow. It is for this reason that the Federation recommends that every member body should make formal arrangements to keep its CPE arrangements under regular review so as to ensure that they accord with the needs of the profession at any particular time.

9

First Issued July 1991
Revised October 1996

Prequalification Education, Assessment of Professional Competence and Experience Requirements of Professional Accountants

CONTENTS

Paragraphs

Preface

Introduction 1-6

GOAL OF ACCOUNTING EDUCATION
  AND EXPERIENCE 7-9

KNOWLEDGE, SKILLS, AND PROFESSIONAL VALUES 10-21

    Knowlege 11-15

    Skills 16-19

    Professional Values 20-21

ELEMENTS OF ACCOUNTING EDUCATION
  AND EXPERIENCE 22-56

    Entry Requirements 26-28

    General Education 29-30

    Professional Education 31-43

    Assessment of Professional Competence 44-48

    Experience Requirements 49-56

Conclusion 57

Preface

This Guideline sets forth recommendations, indicated in **boldface** print, as to the education and experience needed by prospective professional accountants to become qualified and to exercise their profession effectively and responsibly. The "Discussion" sections represent elaboration and rationale for the recommendations.

The recommendations are directed toward establishing:

- the goal of accounting education and experience; its components of knowledge, skills and professional values; and the elements on which education and experience for all professional accountants should be founded;

- the minimum benchmarks of professional education and experience that professional accountants should meet in order to obtain membership in their professional body and to exercise their profession; and

- the criteria for the assessment of professional competence.

In this Guideline the term 'professional accountants' refers to those individuals — whether they be in public practice, industry, commerce, the public sector or education — who are members of an International Federation of Accountants (IFAC) member body. It is appreciated that the education and experience needs — as well as the institutional and cultural environment — of persons in these various spheres will differ and that those responsible for the formation of accountants will need to adapt the recommendations to meet their particular requirements.

Qualification/admission to membership is recognition that, at a given point in time, persons are deemed to have met the requirements for recognition in their own environment. In a time of constant change, however, such persons must be advised that continuing competence is a hallmark of the professional accountant and that the maintenance of career-long competence is a requirement of the profession. The issue of continuing professional education is addressed in International Education Guideline 2.

IFAC also recognizes that member bodies are at different stages in their development. Some may already have addressed a number or all of the issues considered in the Guideline. Others may find them very challenging. Irrespective of the stage at which member bodies find themselves, IFAC suggests that, in the current time of change, all should now review their arrangements for the formation of their future members.

The area of assessment is one of great change at the current time. Much work is being done on the emerging concept of competence assessment. In addressing the recommendations of the Guideline in this area, member bodies should have regard to this emerging concept and as to how it could be adopted over time within their structures. Here again, it will be up to those responsible for policy formulation to address the Guideline in the light of their own circumstances.

Users of the Guideline will be aware of the growing movement towards international reciprocity and the comparability of standards. Some member bodies may find it helpful to use the Guideline as a benchmark appraising their structures and those of other bodies with which they may be in dialogue.

Introduction

1. Historically, accountancy has been looked upon as a profession that plays an important role in all societies. As the world moves toward market economies, and with investments and operations crossing borders to a greater extent, the professional accountant must have a broad-based global perspective to understand the context in which business and other organizations operate.

2. Rapid change is the predominant characteristic of the environment in which professional accountants work. Businesses and other organizations are engaging in more complex arrangements and transactions. Information technology is advancing at a rapid pace. Trade and commerce have become more international. Privatization has become an increasingly important goal in many countries. Many societies have become more litigious. Concern for the environment has grown. Because of these trends, the need for accountability and the resulting demand on the profession is high in all cultures and continues to increase. It is the profession's capacity for satisfying this demand that determines its value to society.

3. These trends challenge professional accountants to make greater contributions to society than ever before, but they also present a challenge to maintaining their competence. The viability of accountancy as a profession depends on the ability and willingness of its individual members to accept responsibility for meeting these challenges. It is the responsibility of the professional bodies to equip their members for fulfilling these responsibilities.

4. To meet the challenges brought about by change, the competence of individuals becoming professional accountants must be enhanced. Since the means by which individuals obtain competence is through education and experience, the profession must aspire to increasingly higher standards in both of these areas.

5. The recommendations in this Guideline are intended to advance the profession of accountancy by establishing benchmarks for the education and experience of qualified accountants.

6. The following sections set forth:

   - the goal of accounting education and experience leading to qualification;

   - the knowledge, skills, and professional values necessary to achieve that goal; and

   - the elements that underlie the education and experience of the professional accountant.

The relationship among these sections is shown in Figure 1.

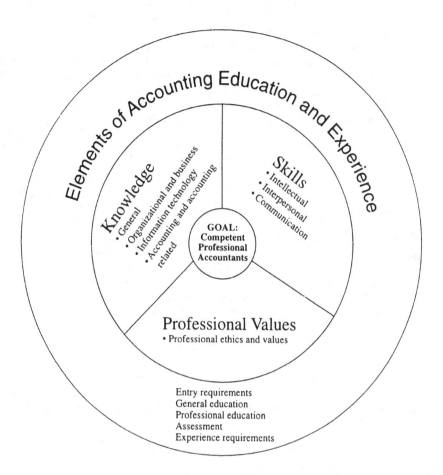

Figure 1 Goal and Structure of Prequalification Education and Experience of Professional Accountants

GOAL OF ACCOUNTING EDUCATION AND EXPERIENCE

7. The goal of accounting education and experience must be to produce competent professional accountants capable of making a positive contribution over their lifetimes to the profession and society in which they work. The maintenance of professional competence in the face of the increasing changes they encounter makes it imperative that accountants develop and maintain an attitude of learning to learn. The education and experience of professional accountants must provide a foundation of knowledge, skills, and professional values that enables them to continue to learn and adapt to change throughout their professional lives.

Discussion

8. All cultures exist in an environment of significant change. Increasingly, today's professional accountants, in addition to acquiring accounting skills and knowledge, must have skills to enable them to be entrepreneurs, financial analysts, excellent sales persons, good communicators, capable negotiators and public relations specialists, as well as good managers. A program of accounting education and experience must go beyond the traditional approach to accounting education, which has emphasized "transfer of knowledge," with learning defined and measured strictly in terms of knowledge of principles, standards, concepts, facts, and procedures at a point in time. Emphasis must be placed on a set of knowledge, skills, and professional values broad enough to enable adaption to change. Individuals who become professional accountants should be characterized by a constant striving to learn and apply what is new.

9. During prequalification, education teaching methods should be used that provide students with the tools for self-directed learning after qualification. To this end, educators may need to be trained and must be encouraged to use a broad range of learner-centered teaching methods that include:

    - Use of case studies and other means to simulate actual work situations;

    - Working in groups;

    - Adapting instructional methods and materials to the ever-changing environment in which the professional accountant works;

    - Pursuing a curriculum that encourages students to learn on their own;

    - Using technology creatively;

    - Encouraging students to be active participants in the learning process;

    - Using measurement and evaluation methods that reflect the changing knowledge, skills, and values required of professional accountants;

    - Integration of knowledge and skills across topics and disciplines to address multifaceted and complex situations typical of professional demands; and

    - Emphasis on problem-solving which encourages identifying relevant information, making logical assessments and communication clear conclusions.

KNOWLEDGE, SKILLS, AND PROFESSIONAL VALUES

10. Achieving the goal of providing a foundation for lifelong learning requires a grounding in the knowledge, skills, and professional values essential to professional competency. Providing students with that grounding must be the focus of a program of accounting education and experience.

Knowledge

11. **The knowledge that individuals must gain prior to qualification falls into four categories:**

    - **general knowledge**

    - **organizational and business knowledge**

    - **information technology knowledge**

    - **accounting and accounting related knowledge**

Discussion

12. *General knowledge* — Broad-based individuals, who think and communicate effectively and who have the basis for conducting inquiry, carrying out abstract logical thinking, and undertaking critical analysis must have a good foundation of general education. This foundation enables them to place decisions in the larger context of society, to exercise good judgment and professional competence, to interact with diverse groups of people, and to begin the process of professional growth. See paragraph 29 for the suggested content of general education.

13. *Organizational and business knowledge* — Organizational and business knowledge provides the context in which professional accountants work. A broad knowledge of business, government, and non-profit organizations, how they are organized, financed, and managed, and the global environment in which they operate is essential to the functioning professional accountant. See paragraph 32 for the suggested content of the organization and business knowledge core.

14. *Information technology knowledge* — Information technology has transformed the role of the professional accountant. The professional accountant not only must use and evaluate information systems, but also must play an important role in the design and management of such systems. See paragraph 34 for the suggested content of the information technology knowledge core.

15. *Accounting knowledge and accounting related knowledge* — Accounting knowledge provides the strong technical background essential to a successful career as a professional accountant. See paragraph 42 for the suggested content of the accounting and accounting related knowledge core.

Skills

16. Skills enable the professional accountant to make successful use of the knowledge gained through education. They are not usually acquired from specific courses devoted to them but from the total effect of the educational program and professional experience. The skills that the individual must acquire are:

   • intellectual skills

   • interpersonal skills

   • communication skills

Discussion

17. *Intellectual skills* — Intellectual skills enable a professional accountant to solve problems, make decisions, and exercise good judgement in complex organizational situations. Capabilities that collectively comprise an individual's intellectual skills are:

   • the capacity for inquiry, research, abstract logical thinking, inductive and deductive reasoning and critical analysis;

   • the ability to identify and solve unstructured problems in unfamiliar settings and to apply problem-solving skills;

   • the ability to select and assign priorities within restricted resources and to organize work to meet tight deadlines; and

   • the ability to adapt to change.

18. *Interpersonal skills* — Interpersonal skills enable professional accountants to work with others for the common good of the organization. The components of interpersonal skills are:

   • the ability to work with others in a consultative process, particularly in groups, to organize and delegate tasks, to motivate and develop people, to withstand and resolve conflict, and, at appropriate times, to lead them;

   • the ability to interact with culturally and intellectually diverse people;

   • the ability to negotiate acceptable solutions and agreements in professional situations; and

   • the ability to work effectively in a cross-cultural setting.

19. *Communication skills* — Communication skills enable the professional accountant to receive and transmit information, form reasoned judgments, and make decisions effectively. The components of communications skills are:

   • the ability to present, discuss, and defend views effectively through formal and informal, written and spoken, language;

   • the ability to listen and read effectively, including a sensitivity to cultural and language differences; and

- the ability to locate, obtain, organize, report, and use information from human, print, and electronic sources.

Professional Values

20. **The program of education and experience must provide potential professional accountants with a framework of professional values for exercising good judgment and for acting in an ethical manner that is in the best interest of society and the profession.**

Discussion

21. Professional values comprise the attitudes that identify professional accountants as members of a profession. They are essential to making a continuing contribution to the development of the profession and the society in which it operates. The attributes which collectively comprise the values and attitudes of professional accountants are:

- a commitment to act with integrity and objectivity and to be independent under applicable professional standards;

- a knowledge of the standards of professional ethics of the member body to which an individual aspires;

- a concern for the public interest and sensitivity to social responsibilities; and

- a commitment to lifelong learning.

ELEMENTS OF ACCOUNTING EDUCATION AND EXPERIENCE

22. **To achieve the goal of accounting education and experience and its components of knowledge, skills, and professional values various elements must be considered. These include:**

- **entry requirements**

- **general education**

- **professional education**

- **assessment**

- **experience requirements**

Discussion

23. Although the elements are discussed in the paragraphs below in the order listed above, it is understood that they are not necessarily sequential. For example, professional education may be gained concurrently with general education while pursuing a university degree or it may be obtained in advanced study after completing another program of study at the collegiate level. Experience may be obtained after a program of study, or concurrently with a program of study.

24. The aim of the benchmarks presented below is to identify the subject areas which should be covered rather than to suggest actual courses that would be taken, because the subjects identified are covered under different descriptions in different parts of the world. It is also recognized that some bodies require a greater range of subjects; others might place greater emphasis on some subjects in order to meet the purposes for which their students are being trained. The required level of understanding may vary in different professional bodies and over different time periods. An important determinant of the curriculum should be the set of knowledge, skills, and values relevant to a particular country or professional body while continuing to recognize the broader global perspective required of today's professional accountant.

25. Where the educational process is conducted on a part-time basis concurrently with the acquisition of practical work experience, the responsible member body or government organization should be satisfied that the extent of the part-time study is equivalent to the required full-time study.

Entry Requirements

26. **An individual must bring to a program of education and experience in accounting at least a minimum level of prior education to provide the foundation necessary to acquire the knowledge, skills, and professional values needed to become a professional accountant. The minimum entry requirement for an individual seeking to begin a program of study leading to membership as a professional accountant in an accountancy body should be at least equivalent to that which would entitle one to admission into a recognized university degree program or its equivalent.**

Discussion

27. The intent of this requirement is to ensure that students aspiring to become professional accountants have an educational background which enables them to have a reasonable possibility of achieving success in their studies, qualifying examinations, and professional experience. For this requirement, the member bodies, if so desired, may require the entrants to take pre-entry proficiency tests.

28. Fundamentally, the quality of a profession cannot be maintained and improved if the capability of the individuals that enter it does not meet high standards. All professional bodies should attempt to attract outstanding individuals to the study of accounting.

General Education

29. **Although general education requirements vary greatly from program to program and from country to country, a portion of the education must focus on the development of general knowledge, intellectual skills, interpersonal skills, and communication skills through a broad range of subjects that provide students with a grounding in arts, sciences and humanities.**

Discussion

30. A broad-based general education is critical to lifelong learning and provides the foundation on which to build professional and accounting studies. Its purpose is to provide students with:

* an understanding of the flow of ideas and events in history, the different cultures in today's world, and an international perspective;

* basic knowledge of human behavior;

* a sense of the breadth of ideas, issues and contrasting economic, political, and social forces in the world;

* experience in inquiry and evaluation of quantitative data;

* the ability to conduct inquiry, carry out abstract logical thinking, and understand critical thinking;

* an appreciation of art, literature, and science;

* an awareness of personal and social values and of the process of inquiry and judgment; and

* experience in making value judgments.

Professional Education

31. **The professional education component must consist of at least two years of full-time study (or the equivalent) and must build on and develop further the intellectual, interpersonal, and communication skills provided in general education. Professional education consists of the:**

* **organizational and business knowledge core**

* **information technology knowledge core**

* **accounting and accounting related knowledge core**

32. *Organizational and business knowledge core* — **The organizational and business knowledge core must include coverage of the following subjects:**

* **economics**

* **quantitative methods and statistics for business**

* **organizational behavior**

* **operations management**

* **marketing**

* **international business**

Discussion

33. Organizational and business education provides prospective professional accountants with knowledge of the environments in which the employers or

clients work. It further develops and provides the context for the application of the intellectual, interpersonal, and communication skills acquired during the overall prequalification process. It provides:

- a knowledge of the activities of business, government, and non-profit organizations, and of the environments in which they operate, including the major economic, legal, political, social, international, and cultural forces and their influences and values;

- a knowledge of macro- and micro-economics;

- the application of quantitative methods and statistics to business problems;

- an understanding of interpersonal and group dynamics in organizations, including the methods for creating and managing change in organizations;

- an understanding of personnel issues, operations management, organizational strategy and governance and marketing;

- a basic knowledge of international trade and finance and the ways in which international business is conducted; and

- an ability to integrate the above components in accomplishing strategic objectives.

34. *Information technology knowledge core* — **The requirements of the information technology knowledge core for professional accountants are addressed in the International Education Guideline** *Information Technology in the Accounting Curriculum — IEG 11.*

Discussion

35. The information technology knowledge core provides students with the knowledge and skills they need to use and evaluate information technology and systems and to provide input into the design and management of those systems. It provides the prospective accountant with a knowledge of hardware and software products, information system operations and management processes, and the skills required to apply these products and processes to the task of information production and information system development, management and control.

36. At the prequalification stage, all professional accountants must obtain the general IT knowledge and skills outlined in the section on General Information Technology Education Requirements, as represented by the following basic content categories:

- information technology contents for business systems;

- internal control in computer-based systems;

- management of information technology adoption, implementation, and use;

- development standards and practices for business systems; and

- evaluation of computer-based business systems.

37. In addition, all professional accountants must obtain the knowledge and skills outlined in the section on The Professional Accountant as a User of Information Technology. This includes the background knowledge and familiarity with information systems concepts and terminology that would enable them to make reasonable decisions in connection with simple systems such as:

- defining their needs and identifying alternatives;

- deciding whether to purchase a particular set of hardware or software, and whether to acquire a pre-packaged system or develop the system using end-user tools such as spreadsheet packages or database packages, or outsourcing the development to another branch of the organization or an outside consultant;

- knowledge of how to test and assess the acceptability of a particular system being acquired or developed for their use and how to operate and manage such a system and keep it up to date; and

- knowledge of basic processes used to keep system resources organized, and of control processes and practices for safeguarding their systems and data against theft, unauthorized use, software piracy, virus attacks and system failure.

38. Accountants must also have prior to qualification the ability to use a wordprocessing package, a spreadsheet package, a database package and at least one entry level accounting package.

39. Where feasible, the professional accountant should have experience with at least two different types of systems architecture, for example, a single user standalone micro computer in a business context and a multi-user local area network system. In addition, the aspiring professional accountant should be able to use electronic mail and to access and retrieve information from an on-line data base.

40. Furthermore, all professional accountants are expected to concentrate on at least one of the roles identified in IEG 11 and to acquire the knowledge and skills identified for that role depending on the requirements of the professional body. These roles are: manager of information systems, designer of business systems and evaluator of information systems. Detailed information on the knowledge and skill requirements related to information technology may be found in IEG 11.

41. The information technology knowledge core may be obtained in a variety of ways. These include separate courses or by integrating the subject into the organizational and business knowledge core and/or into the accounting and accounting related knowledge core.

42. *Accounting and accounting related knowledge core* — **This core must include coverage of at least the following subjects:**

- **financial accounting and reporting**

- **management accounting**

- **taxation**

617

- business and commercial law

- auditing

- finance and financial management

- professional ethics

Discussion

43. The accounting and accounting related knowledge core further develops and integrates the knowledge, skills and professional values from general education and other core areas into the subject areas to which all accountants should be exposed. It provides students with the theoretical and technical accounting knowledge and professional ethics and values sufficient to pursue careers as professional accountants. Ideally, it should include:

    - history of the accounting profession and accounting thought;

    - content, concepts, structure, and meaning of reporting for organizational operations, both for internal and external use, including the information needs of financial decision makers and a critical assessment of the role of accounting information in satisfying those needs;

    - national and international accounting and auditing standards;

    - financial management including managing resources, planning and budgeting, cost management, quality control and benchmarking;

    - environmental factors, and the regulation of accounting;

    - ethical and professional responsibilities of an accountant;

    - the concepts, methods and processes of control that provide for the accuracy and integrity of financial data and safeguarding of business assets;

    - taxation and its impact on financial and managerial decisions;

    - a knowledge of the business legal environment including securities and companies law, appropriate for the role of the profession in the particular country;

    - the nature of auditing and other attest services and the conceptual and procedural bases for performing them in manual and electronic environments; and

    - a knowledge of finance, including financial statement analysis, financial instruments, and capital markets, both domestic and international.

Assessment of Professional Competence

44. **An appropriate process of assessment of professional competence must exist or be established. A required component of the assessment process for individuals seeking to become qualified is a final examination, administered by, or with substantive input from, the professional body**

or regulatory authority. The examination must be comprehensive, require a significant portion of responses to be in writing, and be administered near the end of the educational and, where appropriate, experience requirement.

Discussion

45. The assessment process, which may take a variety of forms, should be appropriate to the knowledge, skills and professional values being evaluated. This assessment process must include as a component an examination of professional competence, for several reasons. First, professional organizations, particularly those that are self-regulatory, have a responsibility to ensure that their members have the competence expected from them by society. Second, individuals who assume responsibility for certain aspects of the well-being of others need to demonstrate their ability to discharge them in a competent manner. Third, the well-being of society and the credibility of the profession are enhanced by ensuring that only those who meet the competency standards are able to hold themselves out as professionals.

46. It is acknowledged that the nature of an examination of professional competence is the responsibility of the member bodies and that there is no single preferred method for testing professional competence. Due to the diversity of competencies being evaluated, a variety of assessment methods is encouraged. These methods should be appropriate to the competencies being evaluated. The method(s) adopted will also depend on factors specific to each member body, including geographical location, educational and other resources available, the number of candidates being tested and their backgrounds, experience and training. The examination of professional competence should contain a significant weighting assigned to answers in writing to provide an independent basis for assessment of the individual's knowledge and skills. The examination may include elements of oral and group assessments. Appropriate assessment techniques are critical to the credibility of the final examination.

47. Examinations of professional competence may consist of a series of components or parts over the individual's education and experience period. The timing of the final or ultimate component or part of the examination of professional competence should be at or near the end of the individual's education and experience programs. It should also be comprehensive enough to cover the entire body of knowledge necessary to become qualified.

48. Assessment of professional competence should measure more than just theoretical knowledge. For example, candidates should be able to demonstrate that they:

- have a sound technical knowledge of the specific subjects of the curriculum;

- have an ability to apply technical knowledge in an analytical and practical manner;

- are able to extract from various subjects the knowledge required to solve multiple topic problems;

- can identify information relevant to a particular problem by distinguishing the relevant from the irrelevant in a given body of data;

- are able, in multi-problem situations, to identify the problems and rank them in the order in which they need to be addressed;

- appreciate that there can be alternative solutions and understand the role of judgment in dealing with these;

- have an ability to integrate diverse areas of knowledge and skills;

- can communicate effectively to the user by formulating realistic recommendations in a concise and logical fashion; and

- have knowledge of the ethical requirements of the profession.

Experience Requirements

49. **An appropriate period of relevant experience in performing the work of professional accountants must be a component of a prequalification program. The period of experience may vary due to differences in the environment in which professional accountants offer their services. However, this period should be long enough to permit prospective accountants to demonstrate they have gained the knowledge, skills, and professional values sufficient for performing with professional competence and for continuing to grow throughout their careers. This objective cannot normally be met in a period of less than three years.**

Discussion

50. The term "relevant experience," as used in this Guideline, refers to participation in work activities in an environment appropriate to the application of professional knowledge, skills, and values. Relevant experience provides a professional environment in which the accountant:

- enhances his or her understanding of the organization and functioning of business;

- is able to relate accounting work to other business functions and activities;

- becomes aware of the environment in which services will be provided;

- develops the appropriate professional ethics and values in practical, real-life situations;

- has an opportunity to work at progressive levels of responsibility; and

- obtains the specialized accountancy training needed to ensure professional competence.

51. Prospective professional accountants should gain their relevant experience in accounting positions deemed appropriate by the professional body to which they are applying.

52. Experience leading to qualification should be conducted under the direction and supervision of experienced members of the professional body as

identified by the body or regulatory agency.

53. Given the variety of circumstances which exist among professional accountancy bodies, the requirements for relevant experience may vary from one to another. However, the professional body or regulatory agency should ensure that the experience gained is acceptable. Among the steps it might take are the following:

- Establish a monitoring system that provides for the monitoring and reporting of the experience actually obtained by the student;

- Provide detailed written guidance in the form of manuals for employers and students;

- Establish a mechanism for approving employers as suitable for providing the appropriate experience for the students (This may be in the form of a committee that reviews the reputation and nature of practice of any applicant employer to ensure that the employment situation is satisfactory.);

- Assess and approve the work experience environment before the commencement of employment (To this end, the nature and scope of relevant experience and the organizational structure of the employer should be considered to ensure that the student receives proper direction, supervision, counseling and evaluation.);

- Assess the experience gained on the basis of a written and/or oral submission made by the student, appropriately supported by employers, etc., at the point of application for membership;

- Review employers previously approved. The review may advise an employer on areas that need improvement or may recommend that approval be withdrawn if conditions have changed to the extent that relevant experience criteria are not being met; and

- Establish a system of periodic reporting to cover changes, if any, in the nature, scope, and content of the practical experience provided to the prospective professional accountant in cases where it may be impractical to visit all approved employers.

54. For a program of relevant experience to be effective, close collaboration is necessary between the professional body or regulatory authority, the prospective professional accountant and the employer providing the experience, whether it be in industry, commerce, government or public practice.

55. The program of relevant experience should be designed and implemented to be mutually beneficial to the prospective professional accountant and the employer. It should meet the relevant experience requirements set by the professional body and be cost-effective for the employer.

56. A record of the actual experience provided for each prospective professional accountant should be maintained either by the employer or by the prospective accountant and reviewed by the professional body. The record should be compared regularly with the overall experience program established for the

prospective professional accountant to ensure that the requirements established by the professional body or regulatory agency are being met, and that the prospective professional accountant is being adequately counseled when progress within the program does not match the anticipated development rate. It will also provide an opportunity for the prospective professional accountant to comment on the work experience and contribute to its further development.

Conclusion

57. This Guideline has set forth the elements of education and experience needed in a preaccreditation program of a professional accountancy organization. It has recommended the goal of accounting education and experience, together with its components of knowledge, skills, and professional values and the elements on which education and experience for all professional accountants must be founded. It should be recognized, however, that each professional body will need to determine not only how best to accomplish this, but what emphasis to place on the various components. Furthermore, since the profession is never static, care must be taken to continuously monitor the environment in which it operates to ensure that the educational process remains relevant.

Professional Ethics for Accountants: The Educational Challenge and Practical Application

CONTENTS

	Paragraphs
Introduction	1-2
Purpose of this Guideline	3-6
Prequalification Education	7-15
Continuing Professional Education	16-19
Recommendation	20-21

Introduction

1. In July 1990, the International Federation of Accountants (IFAC) published its "Guideline on Ethics for Professional Accountants," which was subsequently re-titled the "Code of Ethics for Professional Accountants." Its objective was to provide a basis on which ethical requirements for professional accountants in each country should be founded.[1]

    Pursuant to the publication of 1990 and in furtherance of its work in the area of ethics and the promotion of harmonisation, IFAC now publishes this Guideline. Its aim is to encourage member bodies to review their arrangements for the education of their members and future members in the area of professional ethics and their application.

2. IFAC appreciates that systems for the education and training of professional accountants vary in different countries and between different member bodies. It recognizes too that ethical standards are time and context specific. The situation can change in a period of time or in a particular location. It will be a matter for member bodies in their review of the teaching of professional ethics to adapt the guidance herein to their own needs and circumstances.

Purpose of this Guideline

3. Society has high expectations of the profession. An essential prerequisite for any group of professional accountants is the acceptance and observance of professional ethical standards regulating their relationships with users of accounts, employers, employees, fellow members of the group and the public generally.

    Given this, it is incumbent on member bodies to ensure that their members have an adequate understanding of the principles of professional ethics and the underlying rationale of the constraints that professional ethics place on professional accountants.

4. Professional accountants need to have a thorough appreciation of the potential ethical implications of professional and management decisions. They need too an awareness of the pressures of observing and upholding ethical standards which may fall on those involved in the decision making process. As professionals, accountants today have an increasing role in decision making. This applies whether they are working in public practice, in industry or commerce, in the public sector or in education. They operate in a world of change in which corporate collapse, business impropriety, regulatory failure and environmental disaster are on the increase. In such an environment a clear understanding of, and education in, ethical standards is essential.

5. IFAC believes that member bodies owe it to their members and future

---

[1] The term "professional accountant" as used in the Guideline follows on the definition set out in the IFAC Code of Ethics for Professional Accountants which reads "those individuals, whether they be in public practice, industry, commerce, the public sector or education, who are members of an IFAC member body."

members and to society at large, to ensure that their members have a continuing understanding at all times of professional values and ethics adequate to enable them to operate effectively and with integrity and discernment in an environment of change.

6. This Guideline is intended to assist member bodies in this task.

Prequalification Education

Teaching Professional Ethics

7. If future members are to perceive ethical values and standards as important to the work of the profession, it is vital that they do not perceive the treatment of ethics in their education as peripheral to their main program. For this reason, ethics should be treated as an important topic in its own right within the education framework.

8. Students will perceive and evaluate the weighting attached by educators and examiners to ethics as a measure of the true importance placed by the profession and educators on ethics for the professional accountant.

9. Because of its importance to the future professional accountant, ideally the presentation of the topic of professional ethics should be treated initially as a separate subject. As students progress, and gain a wider knowledge of other curriculum subjects, it will be appropriate to integrate treatments. This will encourage them to look for and consider the possible ethical implications of problems being discussed in their study of other subjects.

10. While the approach of each program to the teaching of ethics will reflect its own context and objectives, it is suggested that initial coverage might include:

- the nature of ethics; differentiation between philosophical and professional approach;

- concepts of integrity, obligation, independence, public expectations;

- ethics and the professions: social responsibility;

- ethics and the law;

- consequences of unethical behavior to the individual, to the profession and to society at large;

- ethics in business; and

- ethics and the accountant, ethical dilemmas and their resolution.

Subsequent treatment might address the particular ethical issues likely to be faced by all professional accountants and those more likely to be encountered by accountants in public practice.

11. In the presentation of the topic of ethics and the professional accountant, the student should be encouraged to study the role of, and critically appraise, relevant codes of ethics. Students should be invited to view the pronouncements of the profession in this area as a positive effort by it to

create a framework of trust and integrity within which professional accountants should operate. Students should be encouraged to examine the ethical pronouncements of other professions and, in their light, to examine and discuss alternative approaches for the accounting profession. Rote learning of codes will not produce the desired effect.

12. The presentation of professional ethics to accounting students can be enhanced greatly through the use of participative approaches. These may include: the use of facilities such as multi-dimensional case studies, role playing, discussion of selected readings and video tapes, analysis of real life business situations involving ethical dilemmas, discussion of disciplinary pronouncements and findings and seminars using external speakers with experience of corporate or professional decision making. Such participative work will lead those involved to a greater awareness of the ethical implications and potential conflicts for individuals and corporations which may arise from involvement in complex management decisions.

Application in the work environment

13. Most member bodies require intending members to gain appropriate training and practical experience prior to admission to membership. Professional ethics pervades the work of accountants, wherever they may be engaged. Proper ethical behavior is of equal importance to technical competence. Accordingly, this period of practical experience and training should be structured to provide the future member with an opportunity to observe the application of ethics in the work situation. Those responsible for the direction of the training of intending members have an opportunity here. They can enhance the awareness of their subordinates of the ethical dimensions of the role of the professional accountant in the workplace by encouraging them to seek to identify any apparent ethical implications/conflicts in their work, to form a preliminary view thereon and to discuss this with their superiors.

14. Intending members, and those in their early years in the profession, would benefit too from exposure to, and involvement in, discussions on relevant issues relating to the work of their employers which are perceived to have potential ethical implications.

15. Planned exposure by superiors to their subordinates of ethical problems and potential dilemmas should be the norm. This will help the aspiring accountant to appreciate that expediency may not always be ethical. Subordinates should be advised that, where there is doubt about the ethical aspects of a course of action or situation, a query to some recognized ethical reference point, e.g., their professional body, may be the appropriate course of action.

Continuing Professional Education

16. Learning about professional ethics should continue after admission to membership. The professional accountant should see it as a career-long process.

17. The profession operates in an environment of change. As corporate structures evolve, as business practices change, as new financial instruments and techniques are developed and as there is greater public scrutiny of government and management decisions, so too attitudes change and these may be reflected in more demanding expectations of the professional.

18. In such an environment, it is important that professional accountants are sensitive to change, are aware of potential new ethical dimensions/conflicts in their work and are informed about and understand the views and expectations of their professional body and the public relating to the application of professional ethics in a time of change.

19. Member bodies can assist their members here. They should endeavor to keep them informed. This can be done through:

- seminars on their ethical codes and their application to emerging situations;

- sessions at conferences, preferably involving speakers, from both inside and outside the profession known for their involvement in major corporate decisions; and

- regular discussion of ethical issues in journals and other publications.

The involvement of educators in some or all of these activities would ensure that they too were in touch with, and able to input to, the evolving approach of the profession to the treatment of professional ethics in a dynamic environment.

Recommendation

20. Each member body has a duty to inform and educate its members and future members of its ethical requirements and its expectations of members in this regard. The expectation of the user of the services of professional accountants is that the accountants will exercise their responsibilities and obligations in accordance with high ethical standards.

21. IFAC recommends that member bodies review their arrangements for the education of their members and future members in the area of professional ethics, an area vital to the public perception of the accounting profession.

11

First Issued December 1995
Revised June 1998

Information Technology In The

Accounting Curriculum

CONTENTS

Paragraphs

Preface

Introduction 1-10

SCOPE OF THE GUIDELINE

Work Domains 11-12

Roles 13-18

Prequalification and Postqualification 19-23

Knowledge and Skill 24-31

Prequalification Tests of Professional Competence 32-33

Postqualification Tests of Professional Competence 34-35

PREQUALIFICATION IT KNOWLEDGE
AND SKILL REQUIREMENTS

Introduction 36-39

General Information Technology Education Requirements 40-49

The USER Role 50-62

The MANAGER Role 63-71

The DESIGNER Role 72-84

The EVALUATOR Role 85-97

POSTQUALIFICATION IT KNOWLEDGE
AND SKILL REQUIREMENTS

Introduction 98-100

Continuing Professional Education 101-104

Specialization.. 105-108

The USER Role 109-111

The MANAGER Role 112-117

The DESIGNER Role 118-123

The EVALUATOR Role 124-129

**Appendices—Core IT Knowledge and Skill Areas
for Professional Accountants by Role**

General Information Technology Education Requirements-

    Information Technology Concepts for Business Systems   1

General Information Technology Education Requirements-

    Internal Control in Computer Based Systems   2

The Professional Accountant as a User of Information
    Technology   3

The Professional Accountant as a Manager of Information
    Systems   4

The Professional Accountant as a Designer of Business
    Systems   5

The Professional Accountant as an Evaluator of Information
    Systems   6

EDUCATION

Preface

Information Technology (IT) is pervasive in the world of business. Competence with this technology is an imperative for the professional accountant.

This Guideline has been developed by the Education Committee to provide further guidance to member bodies in developing programs to enhance the competence in IT of their present and future members. It is in a format which both recognizes the different competencies needed for key roles undertaken in the IT area by the professional accountant and distinguishes between pre- and postqualification needs.

The guideline defines the broad content areas and specific knowledge and skills required by all professional accountants in connection with IT applied in a business context.

Because many of the education requirements involve practical skills, they would be best met through a combination of formal education and practical application of skills in a professional work environment.

For the formal education component, the coverage of some of the topics identified in this Guideline could be provided through courses specifically designed to develop IT knowledge and skills or spread over and integrated into courses which are not specifically identified as IT courses. For example, coverage of some aspects of computer-based business systems could be integrated within a financial accounting course; coverage of some aspects of management information systems could be integrated within a management accounting course; coverage of some aspects of internal control in a computer environment could be integrated within an auditing course; and so on.

For the formal IT education, case studies, interactions with experienced professionals, and similar techniques should be used to enhance the presentation of subject matter and to help students develop practical skills.

Some member bodies may wish to offer their own distance education courses, or to supplement courses at post-secondary institutions with their own training programs or employer-provided training programs. This might be necessary where there are not sufficient resources at post-secondary institutions to offer some parts of the required program of studies or to supplement theoretical knowledge obtained at post-secondary institutions with practical experience.

On-the-job training can provide valuable practical exposure to these topics. Member bodies must ensure that prequalification education and experience requirements are designed to provide aspiring professional accountants with opportunities to obtain both theoretical knowledge and practical skills in connection with the topics identified in this guideline.

The Committee recognizes that member bodies will be adopting different approaches to education in the IT area in the light of their own particular circumstances. Already some will have made much progress, others less so. Recognizing that further developments in IT will not wait on the profession, the Committee advises each member body to review the Guideline promptly and consider how it can best address its recommendations.

The Committee is conscious of the diverse circumstances and resources of member bodies and the significant development costs involved in the implementation of programs of education in IT. It would remind users that this is an area wherein there is significant potential for co-operation between member bodies and consequently avoidance of duplication of development costs.

The IT scene is one of constant change and development. It is the intention of the Committee to review this Guideline every two years in the light of emerging changes in information technology and its uses. In the meantime, it will welcome comment and suggestions from users of the Guideline.

Introduction

1. Information technology plays a vital role in supporting the activities of profit-oriented and not-for-profit organizations. Professional accountants, in addition to extensively using various types of information technologies, often play important managerial, advisory, and evaluative roles in connection with the adoption and use of various information technologies by organizations of all types and sizes.

2. The term "information technology" or IT, as used in this Guideline, encompasses hardware and software products, information system operations and management processes, and the skills required to apply those products and processes to the task of information production and information system development, management and control.

3. Society expects that professional accountants who accept an engagement or occupation have the required level of knowledge and can apply it to practical problems. The accountancy profession as a whole has the obligation to ensure that candidates for membership possess the required breadth and depth of knowledge and skill and the credibility of the accountancy profession depends on its success in fulfilling this obligation. In addition, the accountancy profession has an obligation to ensure that, after qualifying, members keep abreast of relevant developments through continuing professional education.

4. The body of knowledge and skill required of professional accountants includes a variety of important areas. IT is one of the core competencies of professional accountants and requires special attention due to its explosive growth and its rapid rate of change.

5. The following IT trends are particularly noteworthy:

   - wide availability of powerful yet inexpensive computer hardware, including the widespread incorporation, through miniaturization, of powerful computing capabilities in numerous devices designed for personal and professional use;

   - wide availability of powerful, inexpensive and relatively user-friendly software with graphical user interfaces;

   - shift from custom-tailored systems to pre-packaged software;

   - shift from mainframes to small computers used alone, or increasingly, as part of networks devoted to information sharing and co-operative computing with corresponding changes in the nature, organization and location of key information system activity, such as the shift to end user computing;

   - increasing availability of computerized data for access in real or delayed time both locally and through remote access facilities, including via the Internet;

   - new data capture and mass storage technologies leading to increasing computerization of data/information in text, graphic, audio and video formats and emphasis on managing, presenting and communicating information using multi-media approaches;

- convergence of information and communication technologies, affecting how people work and shop;

- increasing use of networks to link individuals, intra-organizational units and inter-organizational units through systems such as electronic mail (e-mail) and the Internet, including the World Wide Web;

- increasing use of the Internet for conducting commerce between organizations and individuals and between organizations and other organizations through electronic commerce systems such as electronic data interchange (EDI) and electronic funds transfer systems (EFTS);

- mass marketing and distribution of IT products and services such as computers, pre-packaged software, on-line data retrieval services, electronic mail, and financial services;

- reduction of barriers to systems use, encouraging wider penetration of information systems into profit-oriented and not-for-profit organizations of all sizes for accounting and broader management and strategic purposes and increasing the role of end-user computing;

- wider penetration of information technologies such as computer-assisted design and computer-assisted manufacturing (CAD/CAM), computer imaging systems, executive information systems (EIS), and electronic meeting systems (EMS);

- new system development techniques based around information technologies such as computer-assisted software engineering (CASE), object-oriented programming, and workflow technologies;

- continuing development of intelligent support systems incorporating expert systems, neural networks, intelligent agents, and other problem solving aids; and

- new business re-engineering approaches based on effective integration of information technologies and business processes.

6. The growth and change that has come about as a result of these trends has created a number of important challenges which the accountancy profession must address:

- **Information technologies are affecting the way in which organizations are structured, managed and operated.** In some cases the changes are dramatic. While there is a continuing need for sound business system design practices and effective financial and management controls, the business planning and design processes and internal control requirements will, of necessity, change with changes in information technologies. Traditionally, professional accountants have been entrusted with the tasks of evaluating investments in business systems, evaluating business system designs and reporting on potential weaknesses. Increasingly, information technology deployments are supported by extensive organizational restructuring around such technologies. To maintain the accountancy profession's credibility and capability in supporting new information technology initiatives, the competence of professional accountants must be maintained and enhanced so that public trust and confidence in professional accountancy bodies is maintained.

- **Information technologies are changing the nature and economics of accounting activity.** The career plans of professional accountants and related training systems must be based on a realistic view of the changing nature of accounting, the accountancy profession's changing role in providing services to business, government and the community at large, and the knowledge and skills required for future success as a professional accountant. Some IT skills, such as the ability to use an electronic spreadsheet, are now indispensable and professional accounting bodies must ensure that candidates possess core IT skills before they qualify as members of those bodies. In addition, since an increasing number of professional accountants are engaged in providing IT-related advisory and evaluative services, it is important that professional accountancy bodies maintain the quality and credibility of these services through both prequalification and postqualification education requirements.

- **Information technologies are changing the competitive environment in which professional accountants participate.** Information technologies are eliminating some areas of practice which were once the exclusive domain of professional accountants or are reducing their economic attractiveness. For example:

  - Accounting and accounting system development were once the virtually exclusive domain of professional accountants. Today, inexpensive, easy-to-use and powerful pre-packaged accounting software is reducing the demand for those activities or enabling non-accountants to offer those services. At the same time there is an increasing demand for professionals with a combination of business and IT skills to help organizations structure their systems to provide effective and efficient support for their primary objectives and activities.

  - Tax planning and tax return preparation have traditionally represented important activities for many professional accountants. Today, inexpensive, easy-to-use and powerful pre-packaged software is reducing the demand for tax return preparation services. The professional tax planning expertise that was once the private domain of individual practitioners is increasingly being embedded within these same tax packages, reducing the demand for such services as well.

  - In the past, accountants engaged in internal and external auditing activities were needed in great numbers in order to vouch and trace documents, to perform a variety of analyses, and to document audit work. Today, due to the computerization of business records and the availability of computer-assisted auditing tools, these activities can be performed faster and more thoroughly with the assistance of computer-based tools, reducing the demand for such activities.

7. IT changes have created many new opportunities for professional accountants in areas such as information development and information system design,

information system management and control, and information system evaluation. For example:

- **information development and information system design:** professional accountants have a tradition of producing information to enhance management decision-making. With the advent of new information technologies and expanded sources and means of access to information, professional accountants can help bring richer sets of information to bear on specific managerial decisions or help screen out essential information from the potentially overwhelming proliferation of information that is now available. One of the implications of the growth of such services is the need to expand professional accountants' perspectives beyond their traditional focus on accounting information to other important types of information and performance indicators, including non-financial information.

Information systems are increasingly viewed as a potential means to achieve competitive advantage. Professional accountants, by virtue of their broad business backgrounds, financial skills and objectivity, can provide valuable advisory services related to assessing investments in strategic information technologies and advising about control systems required to meet the needs of management and, in some cases, the requirements of legislators and regulators.

Multiple objectives exist within most information systems installations. They will invariably lead to cost vs. quality vs. control trade-offs; i.e., information systems personnel may resist implementing additional controls if they perceive them to detract from the ease-of-use or efficiency of a system, since these criteria may be important in their performance evaluations. Professional accountants can provide a valuable advisory service by bridging communications gaps, adding a sound business perspective to the consideration of IT control issues and vice versa.

- **information system management and control:** Information system management skills are not primarily technological, but rather, include an understanding of strategic and operational business planning and associated IT issues, the ability to perform appropriate analyses of IT investments, an understanding of IT related benefits and risks, the ability to stimulate and manage organizational change, and the ability to communicate effectively about IT topics.

- Information system management has been characterized by a communication gap between top management or functional managers lacking IT skills and technologists lacking in business backgrounds. Professional accountants can provide a valuable service by bridging such communications gaps, adding a sound business perspective to the consideration of IT issues and vice versa.

- **information system evaluation:** professional accountants have traditionally provided evaluative services in their roles as internal and external auditors. As information technologies proliferate, there are increasing demands for objective assessments of information system controls such as controls over information privacy and integrity, and controls over system changes. In addition, there are concerns about information system failure and the reliability of information processing continuity provisions in the event of system failure. Other areas of concern are the proliferation of incompatible subsystems and inefficient use of systems resources.

8. All of the areas identified above represent important work domains in which significant numbers of professional accountants participate. Some of these areas are not the exclusive domain of professional accountants and are not commonly associated with the accountancy profession. However, they all represent important opportunities for professional accountants.

9. Professional and academic accountancy bodies throughout the world are grappling with the need to define the body of knowledge and skill that must be possessed by their members. Attempts at defining a common body of knowledge and skill are complicated by several important factors which must be recognized, including the fact that the accountancy profession is a diverse profession whose members operate in several domains, that within each of these domains professional accountants may be engaged in a variety of roles, and that the spread of IT and related accounting services is not uniform throughout the world.

10. Nevertheless, it is evident that IT is fundamentally changing professional accounting whatever the accountant's work domain or role. Consequently, professional accountancy bodies throughout the world must address these changes through their educational processes, by including coverage of important IT concepts and skills in prequalification education programs, prequalification work experience, and postqualification professional education in both general work domains and specialty areas.

SCOPE OF THE GUIDELINE

Work Domains

11. The accountancy profession is a diverse profession whose members operate in several work domains, such as:

- industry and commerce

- public practice

- public sector (government and other not-for-profit organizations)

12. This Guideline is intended to apply to all work domains. The use of an organizing framework built around roles, as discussed in the next section, provides a framework that is sufficiently broad to address the needs of all three of the work domains identified above.

Roles

13. Within each of the work domains, professional accountants may be engaged in a variety of roles, such as:

- user

- financial manager (accountant, controller)

- designer of financial information systems (member of business system design team or task force, producer of financial information, analyst)

- internal financial or operational auditor

- external "advisor" (accountant, auditor, tax practitioner, consultant, insolvency practitioner)

14. In different environments, specific needs and opportunities will vary; however, many aspects of IT are common and it is possible and desirable to set out some of the broad elements of an educational background that all professional accountants can be legitimately expected to share.

15. This Guideline establishes a framework for organizing IT-oriented education for professional accountants, and the core areas of knowledge and skill to be covered. This Guideline identifies the IT education requirements for professional accountants under five main headings:

- general IT education requirements

- the accountant as *user* of information technology

- the accountant as *manager* of information systems

- the accountant as *designer* of business systems (alone or as part of a team)

- the accountant as *evaluator* of information systems

16. While the four broad roles of user, manager, designer and evaluator are not as specific as the areas in which many professional accountants actually work, they represent the key elements of knowledge and skill required by professional accountants and provide a useful framework by which an educational approach can be organized.

17. The education requirements may be viewed as building blocks in the sense that the general IT education requirements form the foundation for the user-oriented education requirements and these, in turn, form a foundation for the other role-related education requirements. In addition, the education requirements related to the roles of user, manager, designer and evaluator may be viewed as building blocks for one another, in the sense that the accountant's design role may be enhanced by the skills developed as a user, the accountant's managerial role may be enhanced by the skills and insights obtained through a combination of user and design roles, and the accountant's role as evaluator can be enhanced by skills developed in the user, designer, and manager roles. Thus, an aspiring management accountant would be guided by the portions of the Guideline dealing with the general IT education requirements, user-oriented education requirements and education requirements related to the manager role. An aspiring public accountant would be guided by the portions of the Guideline dealing with the general IT education requirements, user-oriented education requirements and education requirements related to the evaluator role.

18. It is acknowledged that a professional accountant may operate in more than one of these roles during a given time period and throughout his or her career. However, this Guideline does not presume that all professional accountants will work through these roles in a sequential fashion.

Prequalification and postqualification

19. This Guideline distinguishes between the prequalification and postqualification IT related education requirements. The Guideline assumes that at the time of qualification, all professional accountants will operate in at least two roles - the user role and one of the other three roles, depending on the member's work domain. After qualification, professional accountants' careers and their IT education requirements may evolve in many diverse ways. Thus, the postqualification IT education requirements are not based on the same assumptions as the prequalification requirements and have a separate section of the Guideline devoted to them.

20. Member bodies should monitor prequalification experience to ensure that it includes IT-related training opportunities in the knowledge and skill areas related to their members' activities.

21. After qualification professional accountants are expected to continue their professional education activities in connection with IT. It is likely that some members' specific activities and related educational requirements will be relatively specialized. The continuing professional education requirements in connection with IT for both specialist and non-specialist accountants at the postqualification stage must be relevant to their current field(s) of activity.

22. IFAC recommends that member bodies work towards developing continuing professional education (CPE) requirements related to IT for their members' postqualification work domains to ensure that a minimum level of service quality is maintained.

23. Member bodies may wish to recognize the qualifications of members who have achieved specialist status in a recognized domain of IT activity by granting them specialist designations or other appropriate recognition.

Knowledge and Skill

24. The field of IT is both conceptual and concrete. In considering IT education requirements it is easy to blur the distinction between conceptual knowledge and practical skills. However, it is important to emphasize the need for both relevant theoretical knowledge of IT and practical IT skills on the part of the professional accountant.

25. Practical experience consists of knowledge and skills acquired from participation in activities performed by professional accountants. It is distinct from the theoretical knowledge obtained from studies of a conceptual nature.

26. Conceptual education generally aims at knowledge and comprehension of specified subject matter. Practical skills include the abilities to apply conceptual knowledge, analyze, synthesize and evaluate information. An education approach that consists solely of conceptual material will not be

sufficient for professional accountants in any work domain or for any role. However, it is also generally recognized that the development of practical skills is facilitated by the prior development of knowledge and comprehension. Thus conceptual material must form the foundation for practical skills development.

27. This Guideline simplifies several stages of skills development into two main categories - theoretical knowledge and practical skills. Member bodies may wish to refine the classification used here into more specific knowledge and skill requirements corresponding to more specific education objectives.

28. The inculcation of skills in solving practical problems through the application of theoretical knowledge is one of the prime objectives of professional education. This ability is best developed through relevant practical experience in which conceptual knowledge can be applied to specific problems. To ensure that professional accountants possess entry level competence in core IT knowledge and skill areas, all prospective members must receive training and work experience sufficient to develop core IT knowledge and skills prior to qualifying for membership in their respective member bodies. Member bodies must monitor candidates' prequalification experience to ensure that it includes such training opportunities.

29. Core IT knowledge and skill requirements may be viewed from the perspectives of both breadth and depth. In this Guideline, the breadth requirements are addressed by using work domains as a way of categorizing knowledge and skill areas.

30. The depth requirements are addressed by distinguishing two levels of depth — a prequalification level, requiring only general familiarity with topics, and a postqualification level, requiring mastery of those topics. Requirements pertaining to depth of knowledge and skill are further addressed by dividing the education requirements into three building blocks aimed at providing increasing depth of coverage of core IT knowledge and skill sets:

- a set of general IT education requirements;

- a set of user-oriented education requirements; and

- a set of role-related education requirements associated with the manager, designer, and evaluator roles.

31. During the prequalification program there will be comparatively more emphasis on fundamental conceptual knowledge and comparatively less emphasis on practical skills, whereas in the postqualification curriculum there will be comparatively greater emphasis on practical skills tied to the specific needs of the work domain and role of the professional accountant, and comparatively less emphasis on conceptual knowledge. Nevertheless, to be effective, both prequalification and postqualification parts of the professional accountant's education program must incorporate both knowledge and practical skills development.

Prequalification Tests of Professional Competence

32. Prequalification tests of professional competence must include coverage of

639

IT concepts and skills appropriate to the primary roles in which accountants striving for qualification in a given membership body will be expected to function at an entry level.

33. Tests of professional competence in connection with IT must go beyond testing knowledge and comprehension and focus primarily on testing higher level skills such as application, analysis, synthesis and evaluation, applied in a context representative of the work domain in which the entry level professional accountant is likely to work.

Postqualification Tests of Professional Competence

34. Postqualification tests of competence in a specialty area must include coverage of IT concepts and skills appropriate to the area.

35. At the postqualification stage, tests of professional competence must be relatively specialized. Their main purpose is to validate that a professional accountant possesses specialist level skills in a particular domain.

PREQUALIFICATION IT KNOWLEDGE AND SKILL REQUIREMENTS

Introduction

36. This part of the Guideline addresses each of the four roles identified earlier and identifies broad IT knowledge and skill requirements for professional accountants. This broad statement of requirements is supplemented by more detailed Appendices to this Guideline breaking down the knowledge and skill requirements into detailed topics.

37. During the prequalification stage, all professional accountants must obtain the general IT knowledge and skills summarized in paragraphs 40-49 dealing with General Information Technology Education Requirements.

38. In addition, all professional accountants must obtain the knowledge and skills summarized in paragraphs 50-62 and Appendix 3 to this Guidline dealing with The Professional Accountant as a User of Information Technology.

39. Furthermore, as part of their prequalification education, all professional accountants are expected to concentrate on at least one of the three other roles identified in this Guideline and acquire the knowledge and skills identified for the role(s) in which they are expected to function at an entry level. These roles are discussed as follows:

- Manager of information systems — paragraphs 63-71 and Appendix 4 to this Guideline

- Designer of business systems — paragraphs 72-84 and Appendix 5 to this Guideline

- Evaluator of information systems — paragraphs 85-97 and Appendix 6 to this Guideline

General Information Technology Education Requirements

40. All professional accountants, irrespective of their primary work domain or role, must acquire the following essential body of IT knowledge related to business systems:

- information technology concepts for business systems (Appendix 1 to this Guideline)

  - general systems concepts
  - management use of information
  - hardware
  - system software
  - application software
  - data organization and access methods
  - networks and electronic data transfer
  - transaction processing in typical business and accounting applications

- internal control in computer-based business systems (Appendix 2 to this Guideline)

  - control objectives
  - control framework
  - control environment
  - risk assessment
  - control activities
  - monitoring of control compliance

- management of IT adoption, implementation, and use (Appendix 4 to this Guideline)

  - strategic considerations in IT development
  - administrative issues
  - financial control over IT
  - operational issues
  - security, backup and recovery
  - management of system acquisition, development and implementation
  - management of system maintenance and change
  - management of end-user computing

- development standards and practices for business systems (Appendix 5 to this Guideline)

- role of information in organization design and behavior
- system design techniques
- system acquisition/development life cycle phases, tasks, and practices and maintaining control over system development processes

- evaluation of computer-based business systems (Appendix 6 to this Guideline)

  - legal, ethical, auditing and information system control standards
  - evaluation objectives
  - evaluation methods and techniques
  - communicating results of evaluations
  - following up
  - specific types of evaluations
  - computer-assisted audit techniques (CAATs)

41. Prior to qualification, all professional accountants must have at least a general level of knowledge of each of the content areas identified in paragraph 40.

42. Of particular importance to all professional accountants, regardless of their specific domain of professional activity, is the issue of internal control. Because this topic is of central importance to all professional accountants, it must be given particular emphasis.

43. Professional accountants must have effective practical skills as well as theoretical knowledge. Case studies, interactions with experienced professionals, and similar techniques can be used to help develop practical skills. On-the-job training could also provide valuable practical exposure to these topics. Member bodies must ensure that prequalification education and on-the-job training are designed to provide aspiring professional accountants with opportunities to obtain both theoretical knowledge and practical skills in connection with the topics identified in paragraph 40.

44. Appendices 1 and 2 to this Guideline provide a further breakdown of the specific topics that make up the general IT education to be acquired by all professional accountants prior to qualification. It is acknowledged that specific topics may change over time as IT evolves; however, the broad knowledge and skill areas identified in the Appendices represent the topics widely regarded as the minimum coverage required in an IT curriculum for accounting professionals.

45. It is anticipated that coverage of the knowledge and skill areas identified in paragraph 40 at a general introductory level will require, at a minimum, the equivalent of two post-secondary level courses, although the coverage may be spread over and integrated into a number of courses.

46. As contemplated in this Guideline, a post-secondary course is considered to consist of approximately 40 hours of in-class instruction, as well as an additional 80 hours spent on preparation for class, doing homework assignments, and engaging in other relevant study activities.

47. The amount of time devoted to the knowledge and skill areas identified in this Guideline and the level of material presented should be equivalent to

those which would be provided through formal courses at a university. However, it is not necessary for the specified education to be provided through separate IT-oriented courses or exclusively in a university setting.

48. The coverage of some of the topics identified in this Guideline could be spread over and integrated into courses which are not specifically identified as IT courses. For example, coverage of some aspects of computer-based business systems could be integrated within a financial accounting course; coverage of some aspects of management information systems could be integrated within a management accounting course; coverage of some aspects of internal control in a computer environment could be integrated within an auditing course; and so on.

49. Some member bodies may wish to offer their own courses, or to supplement courses at post-secondary institutions with their own training programs or employer-provided training programs. This might be necessary where there are not sufficient resources at post-secondary institutions to offer some parts of the required program of studies or to supplement theoretical knowledge obtained at post-secondary institutions with practical experience.

The USER Role

50. Users of various information technologies employ information systems tools and techniques to help them meet their objectives or to help others meet their objectives. These objectives, and hence the types and uses made of IT tools and techniques, can be infinite in their variety. Some typical tasks that users carry out with the help of IT include gathering and summarizing data, choosing alternative courses of action on the basis of analyses applied to data, devising strategies and tactics, planning and scheduling operational activities in an organizational unit, directing the allocation of resources, implementing operations, evaluating performance, documenting observations, judgments and decisions, and communicating with others.

51. All professional accountants must be familiar with these broad tasks and the way in which information technologies and systems can be applied to their completion.

52. In addition to knowledge of broad uses of IT, candidates for membership in professional accountancy bodies require specific knowledge of key concepts and practical skills relevant to the tools and techniques that are widely used by professional accountants and must meet these educational requirements prior to qualification.

Theoretical Content

53. Professional accountants as users of IT are exposed to a wide array of information systems architectures, hardware, software and data organization methods. Information systems come in a variety of forms because they are designed to suit the needs of specific organizations. While no user could be an expert in every type of information system architecture, hardware, software or data organization, there are nevertheless fundamental knowledge and skill sets that all accountants must have.

54. In addition to the general education requirements outlined in paragraphs 40-49, professional accountants, as users of IT, must have the background knowledge and familiarity with information systems concepts and terminology that would enable them to make reasonable decisions in connection with simple systems such as defining their needs, identifying alternatives, deciding whether to acquire a pre-packaged system or develop the system using end-user tools such as spreadsheet packages or database packages, or outsource the development to another branch of the organization or an outside consultant, and selecting the appropriate hardware, software, and supplier.

55. As users of IT, professional accountants must also know how to test and assess the acceptability of a particular system being acquired or being developed for their use and how to operate and manage such a system and keep it up to date.

56. Professional accountants must have the knowledge of basic processes used to keep their system resources organized, and of control processes and practices for safeguarding their systems and data against errors, theft, unauthorized use, software piracy, virus attacks, vandalism and system failure.

Practical Content

57. Professional accountants may use information systems in a variety of contexts. They may be exposed to systems ranging from centralized to decentralized systems, from mainframe to micro platforms, from simple end-user-oriented pre-packaged software to complex custom-tailored software, and from simple data files to complex multi-user, geographically distributed databases. Given this reality, it is impractical and undesirable to prescribe a fixed comprehensive set of user skills for the practical content of a recommended accounting curriculum for all aspiring professional accountants.

58. Nevertheless, there are certain fundamental skills that are widely regarded as the minimum set of skills that all professional accountants must have prior to qualification:

- ability to use a word processing package;
- ability to use a spreadsheet package;
- ability to use e-mail software and a web browser;
- ability to use a database package; and
- ability to use at least one basic accounting package.

Ideally, these skills would be developed in an accounting context, such as through their use in connection with an accounting course or an assignment in the work place.

59. As well, where feasible, the professional accountant should have experience with at least two different types of systems architectures, for example, a single-user standalone micro computer in a business context and a multi-user local area network system.

60. In addition, the aspiring professional accountant should be able to access and retrieve information from an on-line or local database such as a professional research tool utilizing CD-ROM or other data storage medium and have experience in using the Internet for information retrieval.

61. Appendix 3 to this Guideline outlines a number of additional knowledge and skill areas which would be desirable, depending on the accountant's work domain.

62. It is estimated that the equivalent of one course, as described in paragraph 46, would be required to enable an aspiring accountant to develop the user skills outlined in paragraphs 53-61. The development of user-oriented knowledge and skills could be spread over and integrated into courses which are not specifically identified as IT courses. Because many of the user-oriented education requirements involve practical skills, they would be best met through a combination of in-class instruction and practical application of skills in a professional work environment.

The MANAGER Role

63. Many professional accountants are involved in financial management roles which bring them into contact with information systems. Although the growth of IT has spawned many new groups of professionals, including professional information system managers, many accountants in small and medium organizations fulfill information system management functions, in partnership with other managers, or as part of their overall responsibilities.

64. In this capacity, the professional accountant's responsibilities may include participation in strategic planning for use of information systems to support entity objectives, membership on an information systems steering committee, evaluating potential investments in information technologies, developing operational priorities, exercising control over information system productivity, service quality, and economy of information system use.

Theoretical Content

65. To support their role as managers of information systems, professional accountants must have a sound understanding of the business functions that information systems can fulfill and the related managerial processes of planning and co-ordinating, organizing and staffing, directing and leading, controlling and communicating in an IT context.

66. The professional accountant must, therefore, have a conceptual understanding of information system technology issues of importance to different types of entities and environments, and in particular, the following:

- strategic considerations in IT development;

- administrative issues;

- financial control over IT;

- operational issues;

- security, backup and recovery;

- management of system acquisition, development and implementation;

- management of system maintenance and change; and

- management of end-user computing.

67. Appendix 4 to this Guideline addresses these topics. At the prequalification stage, these concepts would be covered at a general level, focusing on the acquisition of general knowledge and understanding of information system management principles and practices related to issues such as those outlined in the previous paragraph.

68. At the prequalification stage, only general familiarity would be required in connection with the topics listed under the column headed "Key sub-topics" in Appendix 4 to this Guideline.

Practical Content

69. To support their role as managers of information systems, professional accountants must have effective practical skills in planning and co-ordinating, organizing and staffing, directing and leading, and monitoring and controlling. Both the educational material and the prequalification job content should provide aspiring professional accountants with opportunities to obtain the requisite practical IT skills prior to qualification. Education programs could use case studies, interactions with experienced professionals, and similar techniques to help develop practical skills. On-the-job training in a junior managerial capacity could also provide hands on experience with the topics listed in Appendix 4 to this Guideline.

70. In addition to the IT skills listed in Appendix 4 to this Guideline, the professional accountant's skills must include the communication skills and interpersonal skills required to support the manager's interactions with top management, users, steering committees, and suppliers of information system services, both internal employees and external contractors. In contrast with general communication and interpersonal skill requirements, these skills must be developed in an IT context.

71. It is estimated that, in addition to the general education requirements and the user-oriented requirements, the equivalent of one course, as described in paragraph 46, would be required to enable an aspiring accountant to develop the knowledge and skills outlined in paragraphs 65-70.

The DESIGNER Role

72. Professional accountants, as employees or external advisors, have been involved in the design of financial systems for decades. In the past, such design roles have been in the context of manual record-keeping systems. Today, accountants are expected to continue to provide similar services, albeit in an IT context. This may be as a member of an in-house team or task force working to establish business system requirements, as a member of an in-house system development team for an employer, or as an external advisor helping to design a business system for a client.

73. Professional accountants' design activities will often emphasize the

identification of user needs, consideration of costs and benefits of proposed solutions, the appropriate selection and combination of hardware, pre-packaged software, essential control features, and other system components, and the effective implementation and integration of acquired or developed systems with business processes. In this capacity, professional accountants need a sound understanding of business systems and the capabilities of various information technologies to support an organization's objectives, whether it is a profit-oriented, not-for-profit or public sector organization.

Theoretical Content

74. In their design role, professional accountants must know the basic steps to be followed in the design of a system such as:

    - role of information in organization design and behavior;

    - system analysis and design techniques; and

    - system development life cycle phases, tasks and practices, particularly maintaining control over system development processes, incorporating controls within systems, and maintaining controls over system changes.

75. The professional accountant must be aware of standards and preferred practices, particularly internal control practices, that could guide information system design practices.

76. A professional accountant's knowledge of information systems must be developed in the context of gaining an understanding of organizations' business and service objectives and their environments. Thus, education programs and courses aimed at developing system design knowledge must have a managerial rather than a technical orientation.

Practical Content

77. It is generally not sufficient for a professional accountant to be familiar solely with the concepts relating to the major phases of system development and the specific tasks required in each phase. A number of important practical skills are also part of the required preparation for this role.

78. While at the prequalification level the depth of practical skill that a candidate could acquire in connection with the design role would, of necessity, be limited, it is nevertheless desirable for candidates to have practical exposure to some of the important techniques that are used in key phases of system design. Both the educational material and the prequalification job content should provide aspiring professional accountants with opportunities to obtain the requisite practical IT skills prior to qualification. Education programs could use case studies, interactions with experienced professionals, and similar techniques to help develop practical skills. On-the-job training could also provide hands on design experience prior to qualification.

79. Since system design skills are generally applied in an interactive context, interpersonal and communication skills in an IT context are an essential ingredient of the skill set required to support the professional accountant's information system design role.

80. A professional accountant's information system design skills must be developed in the context of designing systems to meet organizations' business and service objectives. Thus, IT education programs and courses aimed at developing practical system design skills must have a managerial rather than a technical orientation.

81. While some practical exposure to specific techniques is desirable, the main emphasis in IT education programs aimed at developing system design skills must be on higher order skills necessary to provide effective advisory services such as the ability to analyze design problems, synthesize user information and control requirements and evaluate alternative designs in light of an entity's business or service objectives.

82. Appendix 5 to this Guideline addresses the knowledge and skill requirements related to the designer role. At the prequalification stage, the coverage of these topics would be aimed at developing general knowledge and understanding of the key tasks that must be accomplished, the documentation requirements, the risks that are inherent in each of these phases and the related control requirements. The risks may be economic, technological, operational or behavioral and all of these risks must be addressed in the education program.

83. At the prequalification stage, only general familiarity would be required in connection with the topics listed under the column headed "Key sub-topics" in Appendix 5 to this Guideline.

84. It is estimated that, in addition to the general education requirements and the user-oriented requirements, the equivalent of one course, as described in paragraph 46, would be required to enable an aspiring accountant to develop the knowledge and skills outlined in paragraphs 74-83.

The EVALUATOR Role

85. The role of the accountant as evaluator encompasses the functions of internal audit, external audit and other evaluative roles filled by accountants, whether or not formally identified as audit roles.

86. In these capacities, professional accountants may be engaged for a variety of purposes, including determining the degree of information system effectiveness in achieving organizational objectives, determining the degree of information system efficiency in achieving organizational objectives, determining the fairness of financial representations and the accuracy and completeness of related accounting records, determining the degree of compliance with management policy, statutes or other relevant authoritative regulations, and evaluating internal control strengths and weaknesses, in particular with respect to financial reporting processes, asset safeguarding, data integrity, information security and privacy, and continuity provisions for information system processing.

Theoretical Content

87. In their evaluator role, professional accountants must possess knowledge of legal, ethical, auditing and control standards relevant to IT and must be able

to distinguish between various information systems evaluation objectives and approaches such as:

- evaluation of efficiency/effectiveness/economy of IT use;

- evaluation of compliance with management policy, statutes and regulations;

- evaluation of internal control in computer-based systems; and

- evaluation of the fairness of financial representations and the accuracy and completeness of related accounting records.

88. Appendix 6 to this Guideline addresses these topics. At the prequalification stage, these concepts would be covered at a general level, focusing on the acquisition of general knowledge and understanding of the key phases and related IT evaluation techniques that could be used for carrying out the engagement types relevant to the primary work domain of the member body, as well as the limitations of those techniques.

89. At the prequalification stage, the skill level requirements in this area would be based around the member body's principal orientations. For example, if the orientation were towards public accounting, the skill level requirements would focus primarily, although not exclusively, on the IT concepts involved in a financial statement-oriented attest audit. If the orientation were towards management accounting, less emphasis would be given to such topics and more emphasis would be given to the IT concepts involved in, for example, evaluating effectiveness and efficiency of information systems and their compliance with relevant policies, statutes and regulations.

90. Since evaluation procedures in an IT context may require the use of computer-assisted tools and techniques, all aspiring candidates working in an evaluative capacity must have an understanding of the types of computer-assisted tools and techniques available, their strengths and limitations and their design, execution and control requirements.

Practical Content

91. Practical IT skills in connection with the accountant's role as evaluator would depend on the evaluation objective. For example, in a public accounting context the skill level requirements would focus primarily on the IT skills involved in a financial statement-oriented attest audit such as:

- the ability to obtain and document an understanding of the flow of transactions and elements of the control structure relevant to the audit;

- the ability to test and evaluate relevant information systems controls over financial reporting processes and asset safeguarding; and

- the ability to test computer-based records to establish their accuracy and to substantiate financial representations.

92. In a management accounting context less emphasis would be given to such requirements and more emphasis would be given to IT skills such as:

- the ability to evaluate effectiveness and efficiency of information systems; and

- the ability to assess the degree to which an information system meets the needs of users and serves the objectives of the entity.

93. All professional accountants involved in an evaluative role at the prequalification stage must have the ability, with limited supervision, to plan, execute and communicate the results of an evaluation approach tailored to the specific types of evaluations relevant to their work domain in the context of specific circumstances that involve information systems.

94. All professional accountants involved in an evaluative role at the prequalification stage must also have the ability to plan, execute and communicate the results of applying at least the following computer-assisted auditing techniques:

- audit software

- test data

95. Since evaluation skills are exercised in an interactive context, interpersonal and communication skills are essential ingredients of the education program aimed at supporting a professional accountant's role as evaluator.

96. At the prequalification stage, only general familiarity would be required in connection with the topics listed under the column headed "Key sub-topics" listed in Appendix 6 to this Guideline.

97. It is estimated that, in addition to the general education requirements and the user-oriented requirements, the equivalent of one course, as described in paragraph 46, would be required to enable an aspiring accountant to acquire the knowledge and skills outlined in paragraphs 87-96.

POSTQUALIFICATION IT KNOWLEDGE AND SKILL REQUIREMENTS

Introduction

98. This part of the Guideline addresses postqualification IT knowledge and skill requirements. In general, this part of the Guideline focuses on higher levels of knowledge and addresses more specialized skill sets.

99. In the postqualification curriculum, accountants may choose to continue working in the same domain as prior to qualification, to change to another area or to focus on some more specialized aspect of a more general role. For example, a management accountant who initially qualifies as an accountant in the public sector domain may subsequently choose to work in industry. Similarly, an individual who initially qualifies as a public accountant may eventually choose to work primarily in a management advisory capacity in connection with a specific industry or in connection with a specific hardware or software platform.

100. Postqualification education requirements related to IT are oriented to ensuring that standards of competence and service quality are maintained by professional accountants in their chosen field of IT-related activity after qualification.

Continuing Professional Education

101. Continuing professional education (CPE) is necessary to maintain professional competence in the rapidly changing IT field. CPE can include self-study, teaching, lecturing and presentations, publication of articles, monographs and books, participation in workshops, seminars, conferences, professional meetings and similar activities, and formal courses provided by colleges, universities, professional associations, and software and hardware vendors.

102. Because the IT field is subject to continuing change, all professional accountants must maintain their professional competence in connection with IT subsequent to qualification through appropriate CPE as required by their particular IT-related activities. Alternatives that could be considered range from voluntary CPE to monitored voluntary CPE to mandatory CPE activities. IFAC recommends that member bodies work towards developing mechanisms for recording and monitoring the CPE activities of their members.

103. After qualification, all professional accountants must, at a minimum, maintain their knowledge and skill levels as users of IT in their particular work domain. In addition, if their area of activity involves management, design or evaluation of information systems, they must maintain the knowledge and skill levels identified for these roles in this section of the Guideline.

104. Professional accountants' areas of activity may be more specialized than these three broad roles. IFAC recommends that, where appropriate, member bodies work towards developing IT-related CPE requirements for such other work domains related to IT to ensure that a minimum level of service quality is maintained.

Specialization

105. After qualification, some professional accountants will choose to focus their involvement with IT by specializing. Examples of specialist areas which are not themselves IT fields, but are fields in which the use of IT may be significant, include treasury and finance, financial planning services, taxation, insolvency and reconstruction, and small business advisory services. Examples of specialist areas which are IT fields are business system development and integration, information system privacy and security, and various areas of industry specialization such as financial institution information systems, health care information systems, and so on.

106. Member bodies may wish to recognize the qualifications of members who have achieved specialist status in a recognized domain of IT activity by granting them specialist designations or other appropriate recognition.

107. Specialist status would normally be achieved through an appropriate combination of prescribed theoretical education, practical skills development, and specific experience in a specialized work domain. Supervised practical experience of a reasonable duration in a given area and, in some cases, tests of professional competence at the specialist level, should be required to qualify the accountant as a specialist.

108. The following sections discuss postqualification knowledge and skill level requirements for each of the four roles identified earlier.

The USER Role

109. Appendix 3 to this Guideline addresses the topics relevant to this role. At the postqualification stage, professional accountants as users of IT will likely focus their use of IT by specializing in the use of particular information technologies that are most appropriate to their work domain.

Theoretical Content

110. At the postqualification stage, professional accountants as users of IT must have a sound conceptual knowledge of the information technologies that are most appropriate to their work domain. For example, management accountants must have a reasonable knowledge of the major types of business systems in use, their inherent risks, and effective internal control practices. Professional accountants working in the tax advisory services domain must have a reasonable knowledge of the main personal and corporate tax preparation packages, their strengths and weaknesses, electronic filing systems, tax planning software and tax research databases. Auditors must have a reasonable knowledge of the main computer-assisted auditing techniques, their strengths, requirements and limitations.

Practical Content

111. At the postqualification stage, professional accountants as users of IT must have practical skills in the use of relevant information technologies. For example, all professional accountants should be able to utilize Internet tools for professional research and communication. Professional accountants serving in an audit role should be able to use at least one major computer-assisted auditing package, a work paper generation package, an on-line or local database system or professional research tool and relevant time management technologies such as time keeping and billing systems. Professional accountants working in the tax advisory services domain should have a working knowledge of at least one personal and one corporate tax preparation package and, where feasible, have practical training in the use of an electronic filing system, tax planning software and a tax research database.

The MANAGER Role

112. At the postqualification stage, professional accountants as managers of information systems will be involved in the specific information technologies that are used in their work domain. Nevertheless, there are general

knowledge and skill requirements that are common to all accountants employed as managers of information systems. Appendix 4 to this Guideline addresses the topics relevant to this role.

113.   At the postqualification stage, the level of knowledge and skill requirements would include mastery of the topics identified in Appendix 4 under the column headed "Main topic coverage" and the topics listed under the column headed "Key sub-topics."

Theoretical Content

114.   At the postqualification stage, professional accountants serving as managers of information systems must have a sound understanding of the business functions that information systems can fulfill and the related managerial processes of directing, leading, controlling and communicating in an IT context. The professional accountant must therefore have a fairly detailed understanding of information system organizations best suited to different entities, approaches to IT staffing, budgeting, personnel development and performance evaluation, computer system operations procedures and controls, including environment controls, security, backup and recovery procedures, project management techniques and controls applicable to information systems projects.

115.   The level of knowledge required is that necessary to effectively apply the practical skills required to manage in an information system context.

Practical Content

116.   At the postqualification stage, professional accountants serving as managers of information systems must be able to plan and co-ordinate, organize and staff, direct and lead, and monitor and control. These skills include communication skills and interpersonal skills required to support the manager's interactions with top management, users, steering committees, and suppliers of information system services, both internal employees and external contractors. In contrast with general communication and interpersonal skill requirements, these skills must be developed in an IT context.

117.   The skill level requirements are the ability to manage information systems professionally, adhering to sound business practices and applicable statutes, standards and guidelines.

The DESIGNER Role

118.   At the postqualification stage, professional accountants as designers of information systems will be involved in a variety of specific information technologies. Nevertheless, there are general knowledge and skill requirements that are common to all accountants employed as designers of business systems. Appendix 5 to this Guideline addresses the topics relevant to this role.

119.   At the postqualification stage, the level of knowledge and skill requirements would include mastery of the topics identified in Appendix 5 under the

column headed "Main topic coverage" and the topics listed under the column headed "Key sub-topics."

Theoretical Content

120. At the postqualification level, professional accountants serving in a design capacity must know about alternative system design approaches and techniques, their strengths and weaknesses, and their suitability in a specific context. Also, professional accountants serving in this domain must have a broad familiarity with the major system architectures in use and related hardware and software systems, their strengths and weaknesses, and effective management and internal control practices. In addition, professional accountants working in this domain must have detailed knowledge of relevant codified standards, guidelines and preferred system development methods.

121. The knowledge level requirements at this stage are linked to the practical skill requirements stated as skills sufficient to enable the accountant to apply, or advise on the application of, appropriate techniques in the development of specific business systems.

Practical Content

122. At the postqualification stage, professional accountants serving in a design capacity must have significant practical exposure to some of the important techniques that are used in key phases of system design, such as preparation of a feasibility study, information requirements elicitation and documentation techniques, data file design and documentation techniques, and document, screen and report design techniques.

123. The skill level requirements at this stage are the ability to apply, or advise on the application of, appropriate system techniques, particularly internal controls, in the development of specific business systems without supervision.

The EVALUATOR Role

124. At the postqualification stage, professional accountants as evaluators of IT will be involved in the specific evaluations conducted in their work domain. Nevertheless, there are general knowledge and skill requirements that are common to all accountants employed as evaluators of information systems. Appendix 6 to this Guideline addresses the topics relevant to this role.

125. At the postqualification stage, the level of knowledge and skill requirements would include mastery of the topics identified in the Appendix 6 under the column headed "Main topic coverage" and the topics listed under the column headed "Key sub-topics."

Theoretical Content

126. At the postqualification stage, in their evaluator role, professional accountants must be able to distinguish between information systems evaluation issues and approaches that are appropriate for addressing specific

evaluation purposes relevant in their work domain. In this regard, a professional accountant must have detailed knowledge of the steps involved in applying a particular evaluation approach in an IT context, relevant standards and practices governing the conduct of a particular evaluation approach and the potential contribution that a particular evaluation could make in a specific context.

127. The knowledge level requirements in this area are the degree of knowledge that is required to work effectively in this domain.

Practical Content

128. At the postqualification stage, the professional accountant must be able to tailor standard evaluation approaches to specific contexts and to offer practical recommendations for information system improvement where appropriate. In addition, the accountant must be able to apply relevant IT tools and techniques when conducting the evaluation process.

129. The skill level requirements in this area are that the accountant have the ability to plan, execute and communicate the results of an evaluation approach in an IT context without supervision, while meeting relevant professional standards governing the particular evaluation objective.

Core IT Knowledge and Skill Areas for

Professional Accountants by Role

This section contains the following appendices:

General Information Technology Education Requirements-
Information Technology Concepts for Business Systems 1

General Information Technology Education Requirements-
Internal Control in Computer Based Systems 2

The Professional Accountant as a User of Information
Technology 3

The Professional Accountant as a Manager of Information
Systems 4

The Professional Accountant as a Designer of Business
Systems 5

The Professional Accountant as an Evaluator of Information
Systems 6

These appendices should be read in conjunction with the Guideline.

They define broad areas of knowledge and skills that should be covered in the IT curriculum of professional accountants, organized by role.

General IT Education Requirements at the pre-qualification level address the following five major content areas:

- Information technology concepts for business systems

- Internal control in computer-based systems

- Management of IT adoption, implementation and use

- Development standards and practices for business systems

- Evaluation of computer-based business systems

The General IT Education Requirements of this guideline specify that prior to qualification all professional accountants must have at least a general level of knowledge of each of the content areas identified above. For greater clarity, this appendix lists the key topics within these content areas under three columns headed

"**Broad knowledge/skill area**," "**Main topic coverage**" and "**Key sub-topics**."

A general level of knowledge requires that professional accountants understand the meaning of the topics listed under the column headed "**Main topic coverage**" and their importance in the context of business systems. The topics listed under the column headed "**Key sub-topics**" are provided to clarify the coverage expected for each topic; however, detailed knowledge of every sub-topic listed is not required as part of the General IT Education Requirements.

In addition to the general level of knowledge required as part of the General IT Education Requirements, this guideline requires that, prior to qualification, all professional accountants acquire knowledge and skills associated with their role as users of IT and knowledge and skills associated with at least one of the roles of designer, manager and evaluator, depending on their anticipated work domain upon qualification. This Appendix contains specific sections dealing with each of these roles. The required depth of understanding of the topics listed in these sections goes beyond general knowledge and comprehension of the topics listed under the column headed "**Main topic coverage**" and requires an ability to apply the knowledge represented by the associated "**key sub-topics**" in an appropriate client or employer setting with limited supervision.

At the post-qualification stage, this guideline requires that professional accountants who practice in a specialized domain have mastery of the topics required by their specialized practice in the role of user, designer, manager or evaluator. Thus, all professional accountants would be expected to have detailed understanding of the listed knowledge and skill areas, topics and sub-topics associated with the role represented by their area of practice or employment, the ability to apply the relevant skills in a particular domain without any supervision and the ability to supervise others in the performance of key role-related tasks.

GENERAL INFORMATION TECHNOLOGY EDUCATION REQUIREMENTS

Information Technology Concepts for Business Systems

Broad knowledge/skill area	Main topic coverage	Key sub-topics
General systems concepts	Nature and types of systems	General systems theory, system objectives Open/closed systems, well/ill structured, formal/ informal, etc.
	System architectures	Sub-systems, networks, distributed systems, mobile Hardware, system software, application software systems, etc. Data organization and access methods Networks and electronic data transfer
	Control and feedback in systems	Objectives, measures, monitoring, feedback and follow-up
	Nature and types of information	Routine, exception, ad hoc, predictive Transaction documents, screens, reports, messages, etc.
	Attributes of information	Timeliness, currency, frequency, accuracy, level of aggregation, etc. Decision value
	Role of information within business	Monitoring, problem finding, action, decision support, etc. Reporting concepts and systems Transaction processing system (TPS) Management information system (MIS) Decision support system (DSS)

GENERAL INFORMATION TECHNOLOGY EDUCATION REQUIREMENTS

Information Technology Concepts for Business Systems

Broad knowledge/skill area	Main topic coverage	Key sub-topics
General systems concepts (cont'd)	Role of information within business	Executive information system (EIS) Expert system (ES), neural network (NN)
Management use of information	Decision theory Human information processing Transaction processing in typical business applications	Process transactions, maintain master files, produce reports, process inquiries, support planning and control, etc.
	Communication of information Financial analysis	
Hardware	Components of a computer configuration	Micro/workstation/mini/mainframe/supercomputer hardware designs Stand alone or multi-user/network
	Processing units	Central processing unit (CPU), server, main memory, etc. Buslines, cables, integrated circuit cards, micro-code, registers, etc.
	Input/output devices, processing speeds, etc.	Keyboard, mouse, text recognition, voice recognition, smart card, pen, display, tape, disk, scanner, printer, etc. Control units, buffers, channels, etc.

GENERAL INFORMATION TECHNOLOGY EDUCATION REQUIREMENTS

Information Technology Concepts for Business Systems

Broad knowledge/skill area	Main topic coverage	Key sub-topics
Hardware (cont'd)	Physical storage devices	Data representation by computer, data compression Tape, disk, compact disk read only memory (CD-ROM), write once read many (WORM), computer output microfilm (COM)
	Communication devices	Modem, transmission line, carrier, etc.
System software	Software configuration	Micro/workstation/mini/mainframe/supercomputer software designs Open/proprietary systems
	Operating systems	Graphical user interfaces Network, client/server, etc.
	Communications systems	Terminal monitor, etc.
	Security software	Access control software Anti-virus software
	Utility software	Text editor, directory manager, file backup/recovery, file compression, etc. Performance monitoring software, scheduling software, etc.
	Programming languages/compilers	Language evaluation and selection approaches Machine code/assembly/procedural/4th generation languages

GENERAL INFORMATION TECHNOLOGY EDUCATION REQUIREMENTS

Information Technology Concepts for Business Systems

Broad knowledge/skill area	Main topic coverage	Key sub-topics
System software (cont'd)	Programming languages/compilers (cont'd)	Object-oriented languages, multimedia authoring systems, etc.
	Programming aids, interactive programming software	Program generators/computer assisted software engineering (CASE) Programmer workbench tools Methods of program design and development Testing and documentation
	Library management systems	Version control, migration, etc.
	Data management systems	Tape/disk management systems Hardcopy/microfiche/optical imaging On-line, archival Report generators and data retrieval software
Application software	Application software strategy	Competitive advantage Piecemeal vs. organization-wide development/ integration of systems Package vs. custom software Distributed vs. centralized processing End user computing Internet/intranet/extranet applications

GENERAL INFORMATION TECHNOLOGY EDUCATION REQUIREMENTS

Information Technology Concepts for Business Systems

Broad knowledge/skill area	Main topic coverage	Key sub-topics
Data organization and access methods	Data structures and file organization	Data coding File/record design
	Access methods and file maintenance	Sequential access Direct access (random access) Indexed sequential access Relational
	Types of data files	Master/transactions/tables Array, list, stack, queue, tree, index
	Data base management systems	Data storage, access, and sharing Design principles–characters/fields/records Data base administration Conceptual data modelling Defining/documenting data base requirements File layout/schema/data dictionary Model data bases, distributed systems
	Document management	Capture, index, store, retrieve, display/print Computer output microfilm (COM), microfiche, optical imaging systems

GENERAL INFORMATION TECHNOLOGY EDUCATION REQUIREMENTS

Information Technology Concepts for Business Systems

Broad knowledge/skill area	Main topic coverage	Key sub-topics
Networks and electronic data transfer	Network components, configurations and designs	Local area networks/micro to mainframe links/wide area networks/distributed processing networks/mobile systems Data transmission options, carrier services, etc.
	Internet/intranet/extranet applications	Electronic commerce, knowledge management
	Data communication and transmission devices/software	Modem, switch, concentrator, bridge, router, terminal monitor, etc.
	Message and document communication	Electronic data interchange (EDI), point of sale (POS), electronic funds transfer system (EFTS), e-mail, etc.
	Operations, management and control	
Transaction processing in typical business and accounting applications	General application processing phases	Data entry Edit Master file update Reporting, accounting, control, management Query, audit trail, ad hoc reports
	Processing modes	Batch-oriented processing Transaction-oriented processing On-line processing

GENERAL INFORMATION TECHNOLOGY EDUCATION REQUIREMENTS

Information Technology Concepts for Business Systems

Broad knowledge/skill area	Main topic coverage	Key sub-topics
Transaction processing in typical business and accounting applications (cont'd)	Processing modes (cont'd)	Real-time processing Distributed processing Multi-programming, multi-tasking and multi-processing
	Revenue/receivables/receipts	Business documents, accounting records, data bases, control/management reports
	Purchases/payables/payments	Business documents, accounting records, data bases, control/management reports
	Inventories/cost of sales	Business documents, accounting records, data bases, control/management reports
	Materials requirements planning and control/costing	Business documents, accounting records, data bases, control/management reports
	Production planning & scheduling; tracking, monitoring & control; quality management; computer integrated manufacturing (CIM)/computer assisted design (CAD)/computer-assisted manufacturing (CAM)	Business documents, accounting records, data bases, control/management reports
	Payroll and personnel	Business documents, accounting records, data bases, control/management reports

GENERAL INFORMATION TECHNOLOGY EDUCATION REQUIREMENTS

Information Technology Concepts for Business Systems

Broad knowledge/skill area	Main topic coverage	Key sub-topics
Transaction processing in typical business and accounting applications (cont'd)	Fixed assets Treasury/ Administration	Business documents, accounting records, data bases, control/management reports
	General ledger/budgeting/ information systems	Business documents, accounting records, data bases, control/management reports

GENERAL INFORMATION TECHNOLOGY EDUCATION REQUIREMENTS

Internal Control in Computer-Based Systems

Broad knowledge/skill area	Main topic coverage	Key sub-topics
Control objectives	Risks and exposures in computer-based information systems	Fraud, error, abuse, excessive cost, competitive disadvantage, statutory sanctions, business interruption, social costs, etc.
	The effect of the computer on processing controls	Behavioral considerations Cost/benefit
	Effect of IT audit on organization, controls	
	Responsibility for control	Management, users, IT personnel, auditors
	Effectiveness and efficiency of operations	
	Reliability of financial reporting	Prevention/detection of fraud, error and illegal acts
	Compliance with applicable laws and regulations	
	Cost effectiveness of control procedures	
Control framework	Layers of control	Organizational, facility management, access control, environment, operations, application Physical, logical; hardware, software
Control environment	Management philosophy and operating style	
	Plan/structure of organization	Segregation of incompatible functions

GENERAL INFORMATION TECHNOLOGY EDUCATION REQUIREMENTS

Internal Control in Computer-Based Systems

Broad knowledge/skill area	Main topic coverage	Key sub-topics
Control environment (cont'd)	Methods to communicate the assignment of authority and responsibility	
	Management control methods	
	Systems development methodology	
	Controls over system selection, acquisition/development	Standards and controls applicable to IS development projects
		Developed/acquired systems
		Structured analysis and design
	Controls over system implementation	Acceptance testing methodologies
		System conversion methodologies
	Control over system and program changes	Authorization controls
		Documentation standards and controls
		Implementation controls
		Custody
		Emergency change controls
	Personnel management methods	Testing and quality control
	External controls	Copyright, warranty, etc.

GENERAL INFORMATION TECHNOLOGY EDUCATION REQUIREMENTS

Internal Control in Computer-Based Systems

Broad knowledge/skill area	Main topic coverage	Key sub-topics
Risk Assessment	Risk exposures Probability of loss	Fraud, error, vandalism, excessive costs, competitive disadvantage, business interruption, social costs, statutory sanctions, etc.
	Consequences Preventive/detective/corrective strategies	Monetary, non-monetary
Control activities	Accounting system	Identification and recording of all valid transactions Proper/timely classification of transactions Appropriate measurement/valuation Appropriate timing/cut-off Appropriate presentation
	Control procedures	Authorization Separation of incompatible functions (organizational design, user identification, data classification, user/data authorization matrix, user authentication) Adequate documents and records Asset safeguards; limitation of access to assets
	Control design	Independent checks on performance; verification of accounting records, comparison of accounting records with assets Effect of general controls Preventive controls

GENERAL INFORMATION TECHNOLOGY EDUCATION REQUIREMENTS

Internal Control in Computer-Based Systems

Broad knowledge/skill area	Main topic coverage	Key sub-topics
Control activities (cont'd)	Control design (cont'd)	Detective controls Computer-dependent controls (edit, validation, etc.) User controls (control balancing, manual follow-up, etc.) Audit trails Error identification/investigation/correction/tracking
	Control over data integrity, privacy and security	Classification of information Access management controls Physical design and access controls Logical access controls (user authorization matrix) Network security (encryption, firewalls) Program security techniques Data security techniques Monitoring and surveillance techniques
	Continuity of processing/ disaster recovery planning and control	Threat and risk management Software and data backup techniques (problems of on-line systems, etc.) Alternate processing facility arrangements Disaster recovery procedural plan, testing, documentation

GENERAL INFORMATION TECHNOLOGY EDUCATION REQUIREMENTS

Internal Control in Computer-Based Systems

Broad knowledge/skill area	Main topic coverage	Key sub-topics
Control activities (cont'd)	IS processing/operations	Integration with departmental plans; Insurance Planning and scheduling Performance monitoring Control over productivity and service quality Web site mirroring Library management Input/output distribution and control Security and backup and recovery
Monitoring of control compliance	Roles of management users, internal auditors, external auditors	

GENERAL INFORMATION TECHNOLOGY EDUCATION REQUIREMENTS

Management of IT adoption, implementation and use
See Appendix 4 "The Professional Accountant as a Manager of Information Systems."
As part of the General Education component, the topics under the column headed "Main topic coverage" would be covered at a general level.

Development standards and practices for business systems
See Appendix 5 entitled "The Professional Accountant as a Designer of Business Systems."
As part of the General Education component, the topics under the column headed "Main topic coverage" would be covered at a general level.

Evaluation of computer-based business systems
See Appendix 6 entitled "The Professional Accountant as an Evaluator of Information Systems."
As part of the General Education component, the topics under the column headed "Main topic coverage" would be covered at a general level.

THE PROFESSIONAL ACCOUNTANT AS A USER OF INFORMATION TECHNOLOGY

Broad knowledge/skill area	Main topic coverage	Key sub-topics
Experience with business and accounting applications	Key IT acquisition decisions and approaches to them	Defining needs and costs Identifying alternatives Deciding whether to acquire/develop/outsource Selecting appropriate hardware and software
	Assessing IS	System testing System operation System maintenance
	Organizing system resources	Managing hardware, software, data, assistants, supplies, etc.
	Control and safeguarding of IS	Errors in use Theft of hardware, software, supplies Unauthorized use, vandalism Software piracy Virus attacks System failure
	Electronic commerce	Risk, security issues and techniques
Software	Operating systems System architectures	DOS, Windows, etc. Single user, local area network, wide area network, etc.
	Basic accounting packages	
	Small business systems	Industrial automation/CIM/CAD/CAM Office automation products

THE PROFESSIONAL ACCOUNTANT AS A USER OF INFORMATION TECHNOLOGY

Broad knowledge/skill area	Main topic coverage	Key sub-topics
Software (cont'd)	Financial spreadsheets	Design, documentation, operation, risks, control
	Word processing	Operation
	E-mail software	Operation, risks, control
	Web browser	Operation
	Business graphics and presentation software	Practices, misleading graphs, operation, etc.
	Data Base (on-line, local, professional research tool)	Data base design Operation Report generators Retrieval software DB query language (4GL)
	Utility programs	Text editor Directory manager File backup/recovery File compression software
	Access control software	User profile, menu, password, transaction logging, etc.
	Anti-virus software	Types of viruses, etc.

THE PROFESSIONAL ACCOUNTANT AS A USER OF INFORMATION TECHNOLOGY

Broad knowledge/skill area	Main topic coverage	Key sub-topics
Software (cont'd)	Communications software	E-mail, file transfer, micro/server link, etc. Internet, World Wide Web, etc.
	Statistical analysis, forecasting models	Statistical analysis products, uses, etc.
	Tax preparation	Personal Corporate
	Audit software	Data extraction/analysis, work paper generator, etc.
	Decision support and expert systems	Features, strengths, weaknesses, etc.

THE PROFESSIONAL ACCOUNTANT AS A MANAGER OF INFORMATION SYSTEMS

Broad knowledge/skill area	Main topic coverage	Key sub-topics
Strategic considerations in IT development	Planning of information systems based on business success factors/criteria Components of long range plans Alignment/integration with business objectives and success factors	Measuring IS effectiveness and productivity Costs/benefits (quantitative and qualitative, impact on management, jobs and office procedures) Facilitating business process re-engineering Technology assessment and capacity planning Allocation of resources/prioritization Management of technology diffusion, including end-user computing
	Participation in strategic planning (membership on steering committee)	Assessment of IT function, quality assurance processes, continuous improvement
Administrative issues	Job functions/Organization/ Reporting relationships of the IT department	IT manager Business analyst Systems analyst Programmers Operations manager and staff Data base administrator/data administrator Network controller Librarian Webmaster, web designer Quality assurance
Administrative issues (cont'd)	Recruiting/developing IS human resources	Approaches to staffing, personnel development and performance evaluation

THE PROFESSIONAL ACCOUNTANT AS A MANAGER OF INFORMATION SYSTEMS

Broad knowledge/skill area	Main topic coverage	Key sub-topics
Financial control over IT	IT budgeting and cost control	Capital budgeting Accounting for system costs Systems for tracking costs Expense monitoring
Security and backup and recovery	Access, availability and continuity	Access control (physical, logical/electronic) Backup recovery Disaster planning
Operational issues	Developing operational priorities	Human factors Impact on management, jobs and office procedures
	Management of computer operations	Planning and scheduling Performance monitoring Control over productivity and service quality Developing/maintaining responsive IT infrastructure Information architecture Communication networks Facilities, equipment management and safeguarding Library management Input/output distribution and control

THE PROFESSIONAL ACCOUNTANT AS A MANAGER OF INFORMATION SYSTEMS

Broad knowledge/skill area	Main topic coverage	Key sub-topics
Operational issues (cont'd)	Management of inter-organizational computing	EDI Outsourced services Collaborative computing systems Distributed systems In-house/bureau/outsourcing
Management of system acquisition, development and implementation	Development acquisition alternatives Standards and controls applicable to IS development projects	System development project management techniques Maintaining consistency and compatibility of hardware, software, networks, data architectures and types, integration of new and existing applications Managing expectations Determining skill requirements and staffing Requests for proposals Evaluation and selection Reporting and presentation techniques Behavioral and technical management
Management of system maintenance and change	Standards and controls applicable to IS maintenance activities	Version management/legacy applications Migration Custody Authorization Emergency change controls

THE PROFESSIONAL ACCOUNTANT AS A MANAGER OF INFORMATION SYSTEMS

Broad knowledge/skill area	Main topic coverage	Key sub-topics
Management of system maintenance and change (cont'd)	Standards and controls applicable to IS maintenance activities (cont'd)	Testing and quality control Copyright, warranty, etc.
Management of end-user computing	Role of information centres	Security Support for user-developed systems Advice

678

THE PROFESSIONAL ACCOUNTANT AS A DESIGNER OF BUSINESS SYSTEMS

Broad knowledge/skill area	Main topic coverage	Key sub-topics
Role of information in organization design and behavior	Data bases and data base management systems	Data organization, acquisition, storage, access, sharing, and control Implications of centralized, distributed, client/server, network
	System development life cycle (SDLC)	Project management/planning/control Documentation requirements
	Risks: economic, technical, operational, behavioral	Main risks and reasons for failure of computer projects
	Controls	Effect of new development techniques and management theories on formal systems development life cycle
System analysis and design techniques	Information requirements elicitation, documentation, system design	Data flow diagrams Entity-relationship model, etc. Decision tables and decision trees Prototyping Computer aided software engineering (CASE) tools object methods, etc. Design of data bases/files/records/forms/screen layouts

THE PROFESSIONAL ACCOUNTANT AS A DESIGNER OF BUSINESS SYSTEMS

Broad knowledge/skill area	Main topic coverage	Key sub-topics
System acquisition/development life cycle phases, tasks and practices and maintaining control over system development processes	Investigation and feasibility study	Analysis of existing or IT systems Scope of proposed system and information needs Nature and size of business Cost/benefit analysis Statement of application requirements
	Requirements analysis and initial design	Volumes and system sizing Incorporating controls within systems
	Detailed design specification/documentation	Screen and report design Data base/file design Flowcharting hardware and software requirements Statement of technical requirements
	Hardware evaluation and acquisition	Selection and implementation of computers and related hardware components
	Software evaluation and acquisition/development	Selection of software packages, programming languages/compilers Programming aids Structured, event driven, object-oriented approaches System and data base integration

THE PROFESSIONAL ACCOUNTANT AS A DESIGNER OF BUSINESS SYSTEMS

Broad knowledge/skill area	Main topic coverage	Key sub-topics
System acquisition/ development life cycle phases, tasks and practices and maintaining control over system development processes (cont'd)	Selection of Internet service provider	Selection of web hosting, electronic commerce sites, etc.
	Hardware contracts and software licenses	Key issues
	System installation/ implementation	Planning, scheduling, training, etc.
	Testing (system verification)	Role of specifications; test design, execution, control, etc.
	User procedures and training	Documentation, etc.
	Design of user/operator control procedures	Documentation, etc.
	Testing (system validation)	User Involvement
		Audit trail
		Testing transaction flows
		Testing computerized controls
		Benchmarking
		Test data

THE PROFESSIONAL ACCOUNTANT AS A DESIGNER OF BUSINESS SYSTEMS

Broad knowledge/skill area	Main topic coverage	Key sub-topics
System acquisition/ development life cycle phases, tasks and practices and maintaining control over system development processes (cont'd)	System conversion and start-up	Different methods of changeover Pilot running and going live File transfer/conversion/creation
	Post-implementation review	Achievements and failures Assessment of benefits/costs Impact on management and staff
	Maintenance of hardware and software	Maintaining control over system changes
	Systems documentation and operations manuals	

THE PROFESSIONAL ACCOUNTANT AS AN EVALUATOR OF INFORMATION SYSTEMS

Broad knowledge/skill area	Main topic coverage	Key sub-topics
Legal, ethical, auditing and information system control standards	Legal and ethical requirements Auditing standards relevant to IT	Privacy, copyright issues
	Computer control guidelines and standards	Effect of the computer on controls Effect of audit on organization Behavioral and cost considerations
Evaluation objectives	Efficiency/effectiveness/ economy of IT use Compliance with policies, statutes and regulations Evaluation of internal control in computer-based systems Fairness of financial statement representations and the accuracy and completeness of accounting records	Issues and approaches, evaluation phases and tasks (see below)
Evaluation methods and techniques	Planning, scheduling and staffing Obtaining an understanding of systems in business context Documenting systems and elements of control structure	
Evaluation methods and techniques (cont'd)	Tests of features, controls, transactions and balances	

THE PROFESSIONAL ACCOUNTANT AS AN EVALUATOR OF INFORMATION SYSTEMS

Broad knowledge/skill area	Main topic coverage	Key sub-topics
	Supervision, review and quality assurance	
Communicating results of evaluations	Types of reports, levels of assurance	
	Communication skills	Effective report writing Oral communications
Following up	Frequency, timing, reporting	
Specific types of evaluations	System acquisition and development	Evaluation of acquisition/development standards and methods Tests of compliance of development methods with standards Evaluation of acquisition/development controls Evaluation of system development technology (e.g., CASE)
	System implementation	Acceptance testing methodologies System conversion methodologies Post-implementation review
Specific types of evaluations (cont'd)	System maintenance and program changes	Evaluation of system maintenance and program change standards Tests of system maintenance and program change controls Tests of production library security and controls

THE PROFESSIONAL ACCOUNTANT AS AN EVALUATOR OF INFORMATION SYSTEMS

Broad knowledge/skill area	Main topic coverage	Key sub-topics
Specific types of evaluations (cont'd)	IT asset safeguarding	Evaluation of system maintenance and program change controls
		Evaluation of facilities management and IT asset safeguarding
	Data integrity, privacy and security	Understanding of data protection legislation
		Consideration of personnel issues and confidentiality
		Evaluation of security standards and procedures
		Evaluation of security technologies, physical and logical access controls
		Tests of compliance with security standards and policies and effectiveness of controls
		Tests of effectiveness of controls
	Continuity of processing/disaster recovery planning	Evaluation of threat and risk management methods
		Evaluation of software and data backup techniques
		Evaluation of alternate processing facility arrangements
		Evaluation of disaster recovery procedural plan, testing, documentation
	Continuity of processing/disaster recovery planning (cont'd)	Evaluation of integration of IS plans with user department plans
		Tests of compliance of recovery procedures with standards
		Tests of effectiveness of recovery procedures

THE PROFESSIONAL ACCOUNTANT AS AN EVALUATOR OF INFORMATION SYSTEMS

Broad knowledge/skill area	Main topic coverage	Key sub-topics
	System processing operations/activities	Evaluation of operational activities
		Evaluation of performance monitoring methods
		Evaluation of controls over productivity and service quality
		Evaluation of technologies used to automate IS operations
		Tests of compliance with operational policies
		Tests of effectiveness of controls
		Tests of performance achievements
	Application processing	Identification of transaction flows
		Evaluation of strengths and weaknesses
		Tests of controls
		Integration of evaluation of application controls and general controls
Computer-assisted audit techniques (CAATs)	Approaches	Auditing around the computer
		Auditing through the computer
		Auditing with the computer
Computer-assisted audit techniques (CAATs) (cont'd)	Professional standards	
	Feasibility considerations	Effort and time required
		Availability of data files
		Availability of processing facilities, hardware and software
		Availability of qualified personnel
		Economic considerations

THE PROFESSIONAL ACCOUNTANT AS AN EVALUATOR OF INFORMATION SYSTEMS

Broad knowledge/skill area	Main topic coverage	Key sub-topics
	Categories of CAATs	System analysis and documentation (e.g., flowcharting packages, review of program logic, etc.)
		System/program testing (e.g., test data, integrated test facility, parallel simulation, etc.)
		Data integrity testing (e.g., generalized audit software, utilities, custom programs, sampling routines, etc.)
		Problem solving aids (e.g., spreadsheet, database, on-line data bases, etc.)
		Administrative aids (e.g., wordprocessing, audit program generations, work paper generators, etc.)
	Definition and design	Definition of objectives
		Selection of techniques
		Design of input, processing and output requirement
		Testing
		Review
	Execution and control	Selection and arrangement of facilities and resources
Computer-assisted audit techniques (CAATs) (cont'd)	Execution and control (cont'd)	Preparation of specifications
		Desk checking and testing
		Execution
		Documentation
		Control

687

SUMMARY OF DISCUSSION PAPERS AND STUDIES

The Committee has issued the following discussion papers, and studies as summarized below.

Discussion Paper
Specialization in the Accounting Profession
Issued September 1992

The complex business environment of the 1990's makes many new demands on the professional accountant and results in a significant expansion in the body of knowledge required by professional accountants. Users expect a breadth of competence of the profession which some believe can only be satisfied through some form of specialization.

The purpose of the paper is to encourage discussion within and among member bodies and IFAC. The paper outlines some trends and forces which are operating to lead the profession towards specialization; it suggests possible approaches to the question, and discusses some of the advantages and disadvantages associated with formal specialization.

Discussion Paper
Minimum Skill Levels in Information Technology for Professional Accountants
Issued November 1993

Rapid changes taking place in information technology (IT) have impacted on both the work environment, and the work itself, of the professional accountant. This in turn requires that changes be made in the training and education process. This discussion paper provides guidance to accounting educators by defining in some detail the skills to be imparted. The paper lists the various topics to be covered and provides guidance as to the emphasis to be attached to each of these. This is done by classifying major subtopics according to both the desired knowledge level, e.g., "thorough and detailed", or "general familiarity" - and the deemed importance of the topic to the professional accountant, and hence the emphasis to be placed on the topic in the evaluation process.

The paper will also be of value to professional accountants who wish to ensure that their IT skill levels remain current. Topics covered include:

- concepts in, and elements of, computerized systems;

- system development, acquisition, implementation and maintenance;

- information system control concepts;

- auditing and information system control techniques;

- practical experience of using microcomputers; and

- current developments and trends.

Discussion Paper
2000 AND BEYOND A Strategic Framework for Prequalification Education
for the Accountancy Profession in the Year 2000 and Beyond
Issued June 1994

The constantly changing political, social and economic environment faced today, and the uncertainties of the future, raises the need to critically examine the education process, and to implement changes in both professional and academic accounting curricula.

The objective of this discussion paper is to provide guidance to member bodies and accounting educators on the design of their education programs. While the emphasis of the paper is on the required education process, there is throughout reference to the need to use a strategic planning model which capitalizes on the internal strengths and external opportunities.

The first part of the paper addresses the skills and knowledge requirements of accountants in the year 2000 and beyond. The frequently used approach of including more and more technical material in order to cope with the ever increasing complexities of the general business environment is rejected in favor of an approach which emphasizes learning to learn and which develops a base on which life-long learning habits can be built. Learning to learn involves developing skills, knowledge and professional orientation that help candidates learn more effectively and to use these effective learning strategies to continue to learn throughout their lifetime as new knowledge and skills are required. The required knowledge and skills, and approaches to incorporating them into the curriculum, are outlined in an Appendix to the discussion paper.

The second part of the paper discusses the various approaches to acquiring an accounting designation. Because of the trend to greater involvement of full-time educational institutions in the professional education process the paper suggests ways in which the profession needs to take a leadership role in their relationships with these institutions.

Discussion Paper
INTEGRATING INFORMATION TECHNOLOGY ACROSS THE
ACCOUNTING CURRICULUM: The Experience of the Certified General
Accountants' Association of Canada
Issued December 1995

This paper describes the process by which the Certified General Accountants' Association of Canada (CGA) with its affiliated regional associations has integrated information technology (IT) across a six-level program of professional accounting education.

The paper suggests that the central question about IT-integration for a professional accounting body (and by those who deliver its education program) is: *What is the best way to integrate IT into the professional accounting curriculum so that newly certified accountants are ready to use the tools of computer technology in their professional work?*

A brief introduction indicates why the association was well positioned to integrate IT into its curriculum as early as the 1980s. The association numbered over 30,000 certified members and students; it had full control over its own program of professional studies; it had close links with course authors and examiners in many Canadian universities; and it had built up some thirty years' experience in the design, development, and delivery of university-level professional courses. In the area of information technology, the education program had included a principles course in Information and Computer Systems since 1970, and an Advanced Systems course since 1982.

In 1984, a CGA task force conducted a major curriculum review, consulting extensively with the academic, business, and professional communities across Canada. The task force also reviewed education and credentialing developments in the USA, United Kingdom, and Australia. A report entitled *Knowledge Requirements of a Professional Accountant in the 1990s* led to a revised program of studies. Each course was updated to bring it in line with the latest developments in that field, in accounting standards, and — particularly — in information technology. CGA program development staff, professional accountants, and academics from some thirty universities across Canada rewrote and reviewed some twenty courses and tutorials. The new courses were implemented at all program levels in 1991.

The main part of this paper describes the route by which CGA brought the integration of information technology to reality. Sections of the paper address the practical aspects of alternative ways of providing access to computers; the yearly review of assumptions about technology and the end-users; the standardization of course software; principles and practices of course design; the team approach to course writing and development; the design of hands-on computer examples, illustrations, assignments, and examinations; and the methods of evaluating IT-integrated courses.

The final sections of the paper revisit the assumptions made in 1984 at the outset of the integration project, assess the critical success factors, and look at some of the emerging issues identified in 1995 in CGA's *Initiative 21* strategic plan for accounting education in the next decade.

Discussion Paper
IMPLEMENTING INTERNATIONAL EDUCATION GUIDELINE 11:
Strategies of the American Institute of Certified Public Accountants
Issued November 1996

International Education Guideline 11 (IEG 11), *Information Technology in the Accounting Curriculum* highlights trends, challenges, and opportunities derived from the increasing importance of Information Technology (IT) to professional accountants. IT has grown so extensively that it is now a discipline which is intimately interconnected with accounting, yet the speed of its development has far outstripped the preparedness of the various domains to adequately address it.

This paper was prepared to remedy that situation. It was developed by a Task Force of the American Institute of Public Accountants (AICPA) to address implementation and implications of IEG 11 for various constituency groups in the United States. In particular, the document is intended for accounting educators, public accountants,

accountants in industry and government, regulators, and individuals involved in continuing professional education and professional evaluation of accountants.

Although the paper was prepared for a US audience, and its environment of high technology, the Education Committee believed that much of the document is universally applicable.

For example, all students should study IT from the perspective of its usefulness, application and impact, and all educators should be encouraged to integrate the study of technology with the study of accounting. This will require the making of an action plan by the educators, wherever they may be, which can usefully be based on the one described in the paper.

Similarly, organizations can learn much from the section on training in the work environment, with its discussion of the three year plan and budget, or the action plan to incorporate IT training in the continuing professional education (CPE) programs of professional accountancy organizations.

It was for this reason that the paper was issued, with permission of the AICPA, as an IFAC document.

Discussion Paper
Competence-Based Approaches to the Professional Preparation of Accountants
Issued June 1998

This Study discusses the challenge posed to member bodies by new approaches to the definition and assessment of competence and, in particular, their proposed application to the development of future professional accountants. It is accepted that professional qualifications should indicate that newly qualified accountants have achieved the standard of performance expected by employers and the general public in all the specified areas. Competence-based approaches offer a systematic and effective way of achieving this aim. However, their development and implementation will require close co-operation between member associations, higher education, and employers.

The discussion covers likely problems and benefits that will need to be addressed by developers of competence-based approaches in order to indicate how a member body could prepare the ground for internal discussion and/or decision making. It also suggests how interested parties could usefully adopt a stage-by-stage procedure for developing their policy on competence. This process can be designed so that early stages confer benefits in their own right even if no further stages are being commissioned. It gives time for learning from experience and allows adjustments to be made at each stage. There is both merit and danger in adopting competence-based approaches. Careful preparation is needed, problems have to be anticipated, and the approach has to be adapted to the local context. But if the process is too rushed or the documentation is too lengthy or too complex, the search for improved professional preparation can be compromised.

Discussion Paper
Practical Experience
Issued August 1998

The discussion paper expands on the practical experience requirements spelled out in International Education Guideline 9 which recommends an appropriate period of practical experience be a component of the prequalification program. It describes what the committee considers "good practice" and recommends steps for member bodies to take to ensure the experience gained is acceptable, including:

- Establishing a system for monitoring and reporting on the experience actually obtained by the student.

- Providing detailed written guidance through manuals for employers and students.

- Assessing and approving the work experience environment before students commence work.

- Post-employment assessment of the work experience based on feedback from students with appropriate employer support, when they apply to join national accounting bodies.

Study 1
An Advisory on Examination Administration
Issued March 1998

This study identifies the major administrative issues that need to be considered by organizations administering examinations, whenever they are given, and in many cases describes in a general way how various contributors handle these issues.

Various approaches are used by IFAC member bodies to examine and evaluate candidates for entry into the profession. Some rely on one comprehensive examination at the end of the pre-accreditation process, while others make assessments at various stages in the process. It is beyond the scope of this Study to address the relative merits of these approaches, and it should be recognized that the approach taken by an organization will necessarily affect at least some of the specific administrative policies and procedures adopted by that organization.

Although some of the specific procedures described in this Study may apply more to larger organizations than to smaller ones, every organization needs to adopt suitable procedures that address the issues identified therein. Those procedures will vary substantially because of differences in matters such as the approach taken to examinations (see above), the number of candidates to be examined, the size of the geographic area from which candidates come, the nature and extent of governmental regulation, the availability of examination authors within the country, the electronic data processing tools and staff available to the organization, and the language used in accountancy texts and standards, among others. Thus, this Study cannot and does not propose specific procedures for adoption by an organization. However, any organization desiring further assistance in developing its own procedures should advise IFAC's Education Committee of its needs. The Committee will try to provide any such additional assistance after consultation with IFAC member bodies that are familiar with the examination process and that have experienced similar situations.

This Study does not address the complex issues surrounding computerized examinations.

Study 2
An Advisory on Education and Training of
Technical Accounting Staff
Issued July 1999

This Study replaces the IFAC Guideline on the Education and Training of accounting technicians was first published in October 1987 (IEG7) in order to allow organizations maximum flexibility when considering the education and training of technical accounting staff.

The term "technical accounting staff" refers to staff, engaged in technical accounting work, which are directed by, and support professional accountants and includes staff customarily known as "accounting technicians". Such technical accounting staff does not include trainees who are in the process of qualifying as professional accountants.

The purpose of this study is to:

- describe the various roles undertaken by technical accounting staff;

- provide guidance to bodies wishing to organize education and training schemes for technical accounting staff; and

- provide evidence of best practice for the development of technical accounting staff.

The provision of competent technical accounting staff is relevant to developed and developing countries although the particular needs of countries will be different depending on the size of the population, the developmental stage of the accountancy profession and other local circumstances.

This study provides a structure for the training and education of technical accounting staff which is applicable to all, but which is flexible and can be adapted to meet different training requirements. Although detailed training schemes are included in the Appendices, they are not intended to be prescriptive.

FINANCIAL AND MANAGEMENT ACCOUNTING

CONTENTS OF THIS SECTION

		Page
Preface to Pronouncements on Management Accounting Issued by the International Federation of Accountants		697
Practice Statements:		
1.	Management Accounting Concepts	704
2.	The Capital Expenditure Decision	723
3.	Currency Exposure and Risk Management	743
4.	Management Control of Projects	783
5.	Managing Quality Improvements	799
6.	Post Completion Review	838
7.	Strategic Planning for Information Resource Management	870
Summary of Studies:*		
1.	Control of Computer Applications	917
3.	Revised – An Introduction to Strategic Financial Management	917
4.	Reporting Treasury Performance – A Framework for the Treasury Practitioner	918
5.	The Role of Management Accounting in the Emerging Team Approach to Work	919
6.	Environmental Management in Organizations – The Role of the Management Accountant	920
7.	The Measurement and Management of Intellectual Capital: An Introduction	920

8. Codifying Power and Control: Ethical Codes in Action 921

9. Enhancing Shareholder Wealth by Better Managing
   Business Risk 922

10. Target Costing for Effective Cost Management 923

Other Publications:
Annual Theme Booklets 923
Article Award for Distinguished Contribution to
   Management Accounting.. 924
Financial Management Fundamentals 924

* Study 2 has been superseded by Practice Statement 3.

For additional information on the Financial and Management Accounting Committee, recent development, and/or to obtain outstanding exposure drafts, visit the Committee's page at http://www.ifac.org/Committees/FMAC.

July 1999

Preface to Pronouncements on Management Accounting Issued by the International Federation of Accountants

This Preface to Pronouncements on Management Accounting is issued to facilitate understanding of the objectives and operating procedures of the Financial and Management Accounting Committee and the scope and authority of pronouncements issued by the Committee.

CONTENTS

Paragraphs

Part I

Introduction to the Financial and Management Accounting
Committee of the International Federation of Accountants 1-6

    The Financial and Management Accounting Committee 2-6

Part II

Explanatory Foreword to Pronouncements Issued by the
Financial and Management Accounting Committee of IFAC................ 1-10

    Working Procedures – International Management
    Accounting Practice Statements 5-6

    Working Procedures – Studies 7-9

    Working Procedures – Other Publications 10

    Language 11

PART I

INTRODUCTION TO THE FINANCIAL AND MANAGEMENT ACCOUNTING COMMITTEE OF THE INTERNATIONAL FEDERATION OF ACCOUNTANTS

1. The mission of the International Federation of Accountants (IFAC) as set out in paragraph 2 of its Constitution is "the worldwide development and enhancement of an accountancy profession able to provide services of consistently high quality in the public interest."

The Financial and Management Accounting Committee

2. The Financial and Management Accounting Committee (FMAC) is a standing committee of the Council of IFAC. Its mission is:

    *   To support IFAC member bodies in the global development and promotion of the financial and management accounting aspect of the profession.

    The vision of the Committee is:

    *   To lead the profession to recognize that the scope of management accounting has expanded to the extent that it has become an essential component of contemporary management processes for the achievement of strategic intent.

    The general objectives of the Committee are:

    *   To achieve increased recognition of the professional capabilities of management accountants.

    *   To provide a source of comment and suggestions from a management accounting point of view on issues that fall within the terms of reference of other committees of IFAC.

    *   To encourage management accounting research, by member bodies and others, into matters of importance and assist in disseminating the results internationally.

    *   To select and disseminate information on best practices in management accounting.

    *   To identify the future directions of management accounting practice, and communicate the implications of this to the profession at large.

    *   To influence and assist IFAC member bodies in developing and promoting the financial and managerial aspects of the profession.

3. FMAC has also been given the specific responsibility to issue, on behalf of the Council of IFAC, pronouncements on management accounting in the form of "practice statements," "studies" and other publications.

4. The members of FMAC are those nominated by the member bodies in the countries selected by the Council of IFAC to serve on FMAC. The representative designated by a member body or bodies to serve on FMAC must be a member of one such body.

5. To obtain a broad spectrum of views, it is contemplated that, whenever appropriate, subcommittees of FMAC will include representatives from countries which are not members of FMAC.

6. For additional information on the FMAC, visit the Committee's web site at http://www.ifac.org/Committees/FMAC.

PART II

EXPLANATORY FOREWORD TO PRONOUNCEMENTS ISSUED BY THE FINANCIAL AND MANAGEMENT ACCOUNTING COMMITTEE OF IFAC

1. Pronouncements on management accounting cover the application of technologies and accounting principles as they relate to the management and control of organizations in both the private and the public sectors. They are aimed at promoting practices and techniques in the field of work, but do not override the local statements referred to in paragraph 2 below.

2. FMAC adopts and/or builds upon the work of professional accounting bodies of various countries.

3. Pronouncements issued by FMAC give attention to the broad array of work conducted and structures adopted by an organization to manage progress and of the contribution thereto of the accountant. Statements may be issued in the following fields:

External Reporting: the design and operation of information and reporting systems directed to external parties. Such systems include financial and non-financial information and involve accountability for environmental as well as for fiscal matters.

Internal Control: the establishment and separate evaluation of, and reporting on, financial and managerial control, processes and systems.

Management Control: the efficient and effective use of limited resources.

This involves supporting the processes, methodologies, and techniques through which management, by working with and through others, determines and achieves organizational objectives in a changing environment.

Included in this category is work related to strategic planning, organizational structure and design, operational accountability and control and the tools and practices that provide for the effective alignment of activity to strategy and objectives.

<table>
<tr><td>Taxation
Management:</td><td>the design and operation of systems that assure compliance with prevailing law and regulations and, minimizing tax expenditures while achieving strategies and objectives of the enterprise.</td></tr>
<tr><td>Treasury
Management:</td><td>the organization and control of activity related to the sourcing and management of funds and of the management of financial risk.</td></tr>
</table>

4. In producing pronouncements to guide practice in its sphere of responsibility, FMAC will seek to amplify and supplement work that is undertaken by IFAC member bodies to:

- develop research findings or emerging practices within organizations into operation principles and procedures for practical use;

- specify relevant information, including operating procedures, for problem areas or issues, to assist in arriving at an appropriate decision in given circumstances; and

- offer guidance on "good" or "best" practice, based on accumulated practical experience and distilled wisdom.

The pronouncements issued by FMAC may cover any of the types of work described in paragraph 3. Three types of pronouncements are produced, differentiated as follows:

International Management Accounting Practice Statements

These address basic issues about matters in the work area. They seek to represent widespread accepted practice based on a careful study of options across many sites and circumstances. They reflect accumulated practical experience and distilled wisdom, and seek to provide guidance on "good" or "best" practice.

Studies

These are intended to contribute to the growth or accessibility of knowledge about matters in the work area. They draw from the following range of activities, or their synthesis: literature searches, questionnaire surveys, interviews, experiments, field or case studies, or critical analysis. They are expected to provide new information or fresh insights, in accessible formats for practitioners.

Other Publications

Other publications are intended to provide information that contributes to the body of management accounting knowledge and also serve such objective of the FMAC as to disseminate, on an international basis, documents that do an excellent job in assisting managers in the field of financial and management accounting.

Working Procedures: International Management Accounting Practice Statements

5.   The working procedure of FMAC related to the issuance of International Management Accounting Practice Statements is to select subjects for detailed study and then form a subcommittee which has the initial responsibility for the preparation and drafting of the statement. The subcommittee studies background information in the form of statements, recommendations, studies or standards issued by member bodies, regional organizations, or other bodies, and as a result, an exposure draft is prepared for consideration by FMAC. If approved by at least three-quarters of the total voting rights of FMAC, the exposure draft is widely distributed for comment to member bodies of IFAC, to the FMAC network of senior financial and management accounting executives (FMAC/Network), and to appropriate international agencies. Adequate time is allowed for each exposure draft to be considered by the persons and organizations to whom it is sent for comment.

6.   The comments and suggestions received as a result of this exposure are then considered by the subcommittee and the exposure draft is revised as appropriate. Provided that the revised draft is approved by at least three-quarters of the total voting rights of FMAC, it is issued as a definitive statement on International Management Accounting Practice Statements.

Working Procedures: Studies

7.   The initial steps in the preparation of a study is similar to that detailed for the statements on International Management Accounting Practice Statements in paragraph 6. Namely, FMAC is to select subjects for detailed study, develop an outline for the project and then form a subcommittee. FMAC delegates to the subcommittee the responsibility for the preparation of the study. The subcommittee reviews the material submitted by the author(s) in light of studies or standards issued by member bodies, regional organizations, other bodies and what is, in their view, good management accounting. Suggested modifications or revisions to the manuscript are then passed on to the author(s) for consideration and, where appropriate, are incorporated into the manuscript.

8.   The revised manuscript, if approved by the subcommittee, is then submitted to FMAC and if approved by at least three-quarters of the total voting rights of FMAC, the study is published and released.

9.   For the purpose of voting referred to in paragraphs 5, 6 and 8 above, each country represented on FMAC has one vote.

Working Procedures: Other Publications

10.   Other publications are issued as determined by the FMAC, if approved by at least three-quarters of the total voting rights of FMAC.

Language

11.   The approved text of an exposure draft or statement is that published by FMAC in the English language. Member bodies of IFAC are authorized after

obtaining IFAC approval to prepare translations of exposure drafts and statements, at their own cost, to be issued in the language of their own countries as appropriate. These translations should indicate the name of the accountancy body that prepared the translation and that it is a translation of the approved text.

1

First Issued February 1989
Revised March 1998

Management Accounting Concepts

CONTENTS

	Paragraphs
Introduction	1-6
Evolution and Change in Management Accounting	7-20
Management Accounting and the Management Process	21-36
The Conceptual Framework	37-72
Function Related Concepts	41-48
Resource Productivity Focus	42
Value Orientation	43-45
Business Process Orientation	46
Team Orientation	47-48
Outcome Utility Related Concepts	49-52
Accountability	50
Performance Criteria	51
Benchmarking Performance	52
Process and Technology Related Concepts	53-61
Equation of Resource Use and Value Generation	54-57
Management Process Interfaces	58
Technology Development and Evaluation	59-61

Function Capability Related Concepts.. 61-72

    Core Competences... 63-65

    Continuous Improvement.. 66

    Creating Opportunities... 67-69

    Critical Consciousness 70-72

Using the Conceptual Framework.. 73-77

Conclusion 78-79

Appendix

INTRODUCTION

1. This statement describes that field of organizational activity known as management accounting. It is an activity that is interwoven in the management processes of all organizations. The purposes, tasks and parameters of management accounting are described, and are elaborated in terms of a conceptual framework.

2. The statement recognizes that

   - different labels, in different languages, are used to refer to management accounting around the world;

   - this field of activity is approached and organized differently in different countries, cultures and organizations; and

   - the body of thought and practice encompassed by management accounting has changed and evolved, and will continue to do so.

3. The statement has two main elements.

   - First, management accounting is described by reference to leading edge practice internationally.

   - Second, a conceptual framework elaborates the description and serves both as a set of assumptions for reasoning about appropriate directions for practice, and as a set of criteria for evaluating good practice.

4. Together the description and conceptual framework provide a benchmark of best practice in management accounting, and can serve as a resource in developing practice in this direction.

5. The statement can be used to answer the following critical questions:

   - How should management accounting practice be developed?

   - How should the usefulness of management accounting practice be tested?

   - How should management accounting work technologies be developed?

   - How should the usefulness of management accounting work technologies be tested?

6. By describing the motivation and fundamental qualities involved in modern management accounting, the statement should contribute both to understanding and improving practice worldwide.

EVOLUTION AND CHANGE IN MANAGEMENT ACCOUNTING

7. The field of organizational activity encompassed by *management accounting* has developed through four recognizable stages.

   - **Stage 1** — Prior to 1950, the focus was on cost determination and financial control, through the use of budgeting and cost accounting technologies;

- **Stage 2** — By 1965, the focus had shifted to the provision of information for management planning and control, through the use of such technologies as decision analysis and responsibility accounting;

- **Stage 3** — By 1985, attention was focused on the reduction of waste in resources used in business processes, through the use of process analysis and cost management technologies;

- **Stage 4** — By 1995, attention had shifted to the generation or creation of value through the effective use of resources, through the use of technologies which examine the drivers of customer value, shareholder value, and organizational innovation.

8. While these four stages are recognizable, the process of change from one to another has been evolutionary.

9. Each stage of evolution represents adaptation to a new set of conditions facing organizations, by the absorption, reshaping, and addition to the focus and technologies used previously. Each stage is a combination of the old and the new, with the old reshaped to fit with the new in addressing a new set of conditions in the management environment.

10. The following diagram illustrates the four evolutionary stages of management accounting:

Evolution of Management Accounting

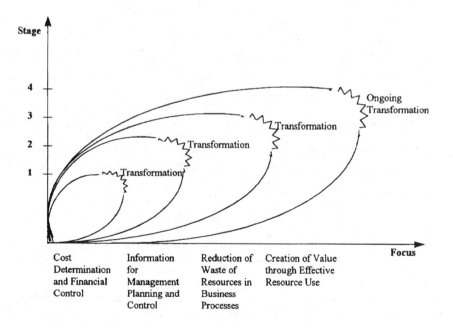

11. There is little doubt that management accounting will continue to evolve in the future.

12. In this context, the use of the label *management accounting* is problematic, for three reasons.

    • In many countries around the world the label has never been used to refer to the organizational activities in focus in any of the stages; instead unique language and culture specific labels have been used.

    • In some countries, the label has been used to refer to one or more of the four stages.

    • In other countries (English speaking mainly) the label has been used to encompass the processes in focus in all four stages.

13. Thus, for many the label may be meaningless, and for others the meaning may be unclear.

14. The label *management accounting* is used in this statement with an appreciation of these difficulties, and with an acknowledgement that it may be replaced by other labels in the future.

15. *Management accounting* here refers to the outcome of the process of evolution over the four stages.

16. While this statement of Management Accounting Concepts describes management accounting as it has evolved at Stage 4, the statement which it replaces described management accounting as it had evolved at the juncture of Stages 2 and 3 — when the focus was on the provision of information for management planning and control. For illustrative purposes, extracts from the previous Statement of Management Accounting Concepts are attached as an Appendix.

17. A critical difference in the shift between Stage 2 and Stages 3 and 4 is the change in focus *away from information provision* and *towards resource management*, in the forms of waste reduction (Stage 3) and value generation or creation (Stage 4). The focus on information provision (Stage 2) is not lost, but is refigured in Stages 3 and 4. In Stages 3 and 4, information is seen as an organizational resource, along with other organizational resources; the focus now, however, is on reducing the loss or waste of this resource (in both financial and real terms) and on conserving or leveraging its use in value generation or creation.

18. Like other resources, information (alone or in combination with other resources) may have present strategic significance or may be a core competency used to create new organizational futures. In any case, it is brought within the ambit of organizational activities designed to manage resources strategically (management accounting at its current evolutionary stage).

19. A second critical difference is the way in which management accounting as a field of activity is positioned within organizations.

    • In Stage 1, it was seen as a *technical* activity necessary for the pursuit of organizational objectives.

- By Stage 2, it seen as a *management* activity, but in a *staff* role; it involved *staff* (management) support to *line* management through the provision of information for planning and control purposes.

- In Stages 3 and 4, it is seen as an *integral part of the management process*, as *real time* information becomes available to management directly and as the distinction between *staff* and *line* management becomes progressively blurred. *The focusing of the use of resources (including information) to create value is an integral part of the management process in organizations.*

20. Management accounting (at its current evolutionary stage) addresses the needs of organizations operating in dynamic and competitive *contexts*. In these contexts, organizations currently are

- flattening their hierarchical structures, whilst progressively empowering front-line employees — in order to increase their agility as well as employee commitment;

- removing functional specialization (through the use of cross-functional teams, as well as the elimination of traditional specializations), to more clearly focus on the business processes which support strategic product/service portfolios;

- removing divisions between themselves and suppliers and customers (for example, by alliances or partnerships), in order to more firmly locate their business processes in relevant value chains;

- undertaking experiments in seeking to understand their *core competences* and their identity within relevant value chains, by progressively becoming more *virtual* as they respond to rapidly shifting product/service life cycles in the face of global competition;

- simultaneously integrating their information systems and highlighting the availability of localized information in *real time* at points of need;

- removing reliance on *remote* forms of financial control, by creating real time localized control based on non-financial Performance Indicators;

- treating ambiguity and paradox as realities to work with and through, rather than as impediments to be removed by continuing investments in information and rationality; and

- pursuing cultural integration through a focus on understood and accepted visions, rather than accepting the forms of cultural separation associated with traditional forms of employment or professional specialization.

MANAGEMENT ACCOUNTING AND THE MANAGEMENT PROCESS

21. The purpose of management has been described as making people capable of joint performance through common goals, common values, the right structure, and providing the training and development they need to perform and to respond to change. The central purpose, then, of the management process is to secure, as it faces change, the vitality and endurance of an organization through the ongoing co-ordination of activities, efforts and resources. Thus, the management process includes

709

- establishing organizational directions in terms of objectives and strategies;
- aligning organizational structures, processes and systems to support established directions;
- securing the commitment at a requisite level of those contributing essential skills and effort; and
- instituting controls that will guide an organization's progress towards the realization of its strategies and objectives.

22. The level of contextual change faced by organizations, however, requires that management is involved in an ongoing *redirection* of objectives and strategies, and thus in ongoing *change* of structures, patterns of commitment, and controls.

23. The pursuit and realization of organizational objectives and strategies requires the mobilization or development of requisite capabilities through the effective deployment of resources. Resources are deployed in structures, controls, and securing commitments to create the capabilities necessary for organizational success. Without effective resource deployments, requisite capabilities are unlikely to be developed; and resources are likely to be wasted in ineffective structures, controls, and commitments. Moreover, as requisite organizational capabilities are redefined through ongoing organizational redirection, it is likely that resource deployments will need to alter. Resourcing thus is an integral part of the management process.

24. The management of resourcing and resource use is integral to both strategy realization and organizational change; effective resource deployments are necessary to support organizational objectives and strategies, and ongoing organizational change is likely to require ongoing redeployments of resources. Indeed the success of management in securing the vitality and endurance of an organization is likely to be dependent on the effectiveness with which it deploys and redeploys resources.

25. The management process may be partitioned in various ways. In this statement it is divided into component parts that focus respectively on

- organizational direction setting;
- organizational structuring;
- organizational resource use;
- organizational commitment;
- organizational change; and
- organizational control.

26. While these components of the management process are isolated analytically, it is emphasized that they are intertwined in practice. Thus, each component part will be in interaction with the others, as organizational survival or success is pursued.

27. Distinctive *technologies* — modes of thought and practice used in the processes involved in a field of activity, are associated with each part of the management process.

28. In this statement management accounting refers to that part of the management process which is focused on organizational resource use. Thus, it refers to managerial processes and technologies that are focused on adding value to organizations by attaining the effective use of resources, in dynamic and competitive contexts.

29. Management accounting, as an integral part of the management process, distinctly adds value by continuously probing whether resources are used effectively by organizations — in creating value for shareholders, customers or other stakeholders.

30. Distinctive modes of thought and practice, referred to as *technologies*, are used in management accounting.

31. In this regard, *resources* include not only those in financial form, but also all other resources created and used by organizations as a result of financial expenditures. Thus, work processes and systems, trained personnel, innovative capacities, morale, flexible cultures, and even committed customers may be included as *resources* — along with special configurations of resources that may be identified as strategic capabilities, core competences or intellectual capital.

32. Management accounting refers to that part of the management process focused on the effective use of resources in

   • establishing *strategy* mixes that support organizational objectives;

   • developing and maintaining the organizational *capabilities* necessary for strategy realization; and

   • negotiating the strategy and capability *change* necessary to secure ongoing organizational success and survival.

33. Information and knowledge are likely to be resources that are central to an organization's success and survival in an increasingly competitive and fast changing world. Thus, emphasis is likely to be given within the management accounting process to the effective use of these resources in supporting strategic positioning and developing the capabilities necessary for organizational success and survival.

34. Management accounting is only one part of the management process of organizations. It provides a focus and distinctive perspective on one key dimension of organizational activity — resourcing and resource use. It stands beside other parts of the management process which focus respectively on other key dimensions of organizational activity — direction setting, structuring securing commitment, control, and change. However, it is interwoven with other parts of the management process, by being associated with

   • organizational direction setting, *from a resource perspective*, through involvement in

      – objective setting;

      – strategy formulation and implementation;

      – project appraisal and implementation;

- business planning;
- resource deployment;
- decision support.

- organizational structuring, *from a resource perspective*, through involvement in
  - designing organizational and business processes to support strategies;
  - designing systems to support processes;
  - aligning capabilities with processes and systems;
  - decision making about the outsourcing or insourcing of processes, capabilities and systems;
  - assigning responsibilities for processes, systems and capabilities;
  - deploying resources to processes, systems and capabilities.

- organizational commitment, *from a resource perspective*, through involvement in
  - establishing the vision of an organization, and its core values;
  - establishing the organization's core capabilities and competences;
  - building understanding of key organizational success factors and capabilities;
  - building motivation and trust across all organizational participants;
  - establishing and implementing mechanisms for the sharing of gains and success;
  - providing feedback on individual, team and organizational development.

- organizational change, *from a resource perspective*, through involvement in
  - focusing change on strategy realization;
  - establishing change targets and goals;
  - embedding change in organizational and business processes;
  - re-engineering or continuous improvement initiatives;
  - providing information or feedback related to change initiatives;
  - monitoring the outcomes of change initiatives.

- organizational control, *from a resource perspective*, through involvement in
  - profiling the risk exposures associated with organizational strategies and business processes;
  - establishing and managing control parameters related to risk exposures;
  - establishing Performance Criteria and Measures related to an organizations strategic success, and financial and operational processes;

- designing and operating information systems supporting an organization's operations, performance measures, controls and accountabilities;
- instituting accountabilities related to risk management, and operational and strategic performance.

35. While the term *function* can be used to refer to characteristic and distinctive parts of an organization (e.g., departments, divisions) or to the assignment of activities or responsibilities to individuals, it is *not* used in this way in this statement. It is used here to refer to characteristic and distinctive parts of the *management process*. Thus, that part of the management process concerned with effective resource use over time can be referred to as the *management accounting function*.

36. Distinctive management functions, however, also need to be brought under management oversight and direction, to ensure that they add value to an organization through their distinctive focus and purpose. Management accounting is no exception.

- The management of the management accounting function is likely to involve
  - establishing objectives and strategies for the function;
  - structuring the work of the function;
  - building the capability of the function;
  - resourcing the function appropriately;
  - responding creatively to, or proactively addressing new challenges bearing on the work of the function;
  - assessing the ongoing efficiency and effectiveness of the function.

THE CONCEPTUAL FRAMEWORK

37. The description of management accounting developed in this statement can be elaborated through a set of concepts categorized in terms of

- the distinctive *function* of management accounting within the management process in organizations;
- the way in which the *utility* of the outcomes of the management accounting process can be tested;
- *criteria* which can be used to assess the value of the processes and work technologies used in management accounting; and
- *capabilities* necessarily associated with the effectiveness of the management accounting function overall.

38. Each category of concepts articulates with the others as a conceptual framework for management accounting. The conceptual framework can be illustrated as follows:

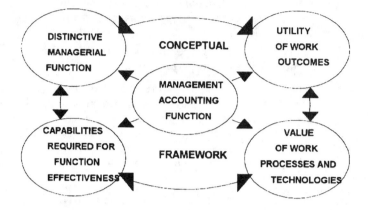

39. The conceptual framework can be used to describe *best practice* in management accounting because it focuses attention on

- the capabilities required for effective performance of the distinctive work of the function;

- assessments of the organizational value of the work outcomes of the function; and

- the usefulness of the function's work processes and technologies in securing such outcomes.

40. Within each category of the conceptual framework, the following specific concepts can be developed in further elaboration.

Function Related Concepts

41. These concepts describe the function in terms of its resource productivity focus, value orientation, business process orientation and team orientation.

Resource Productivity Focus

42. The management accounting process is focused on the efficient and effective use of resources in organizations. Attention is focused on the transformation of resources in and out of financial forms, and on attendant patterns of waste (resource loss) and value generation (effective use of resources). Resources in monetary and physical forms are scrutinized, along with resources consumed by organizational structures, systems, procedures, processes and human resources practices.

Value Orientation

43. The effectiveness of resource use is judged in terms of the value generated in both product/service markets (for customers) and capital markets (for shareholders), while satisfying the requirements of other key organizational stakeholders (including suppliers, staff, financiers, and the community at large).

44. Resource use is judged effective if it optimizes value generation over the long run, with due regard to the externalities associated with an organization's activities.

45. Waste (resource loss, idle resources), unfocused use or consumption of resources, and inattention to environmental or social concerns are likely to be judged ineffective.

Business Process Orientation

46. Management accounting work is centered on the core and enabling business processes of an organization, involving customers, suppliers and other stakeholders. Thus, it is concerned with

    - inter-relationships between organizational processes and inter-organizational value chains;
    - interfaces between organizational processes and work technologies, structures, systems and cultures;
    - the alignment between organizational processes and product/service strategies; and
    - the way in which resources are deployed, used and consumed by organizational processes in generating value over time.

Team Orientation

47. The management accounting process is deployed within, and conducted through the various types of teams established to undertake the work of organizations.

48. Teams may have a strategic, managerial or operational focus; they may have a task, activity, process or cross-functional orientation; and they may be given various forms of empowerment and developmental expectation.

Outcome Utility Related Concepts

49. These concepts address the utility of the work outcomes of the management accounting function, and how it might be assessed in terms of accountability, performance criteria, and benchmarked performance.

Accountability

50. The outcomes of the management accounting process are assessed in terms of the value they add to an organization, judged from the perspective of users of the outcomes. Thus, the accountability of the management accounting function is outwardly directed, to organizational participants served by the function.

Performance Criteria

51. The value to be added by management accounting work to an organization can be expressed in terms of staged performance objectives, negotiated and agreed to within an organization.

Benchmarking Performance

52. The performance objectives used to express management accounting accountabilities within an organization should reflect the outcomes of benchmarking management accounting work across organizations.

Process and Technology Related Concepts

53. Management accounting processes interface with other management processes and are informed by a distinctive mode of thinking, which can be used also to assess or guide the development of the work technologies used in management accounting.

Equation of Resource Use and Value Generation

54. The management accounting process draws on a distinctive mode of thinking, focused on the equation of resource use and value generation over time.

55. Ideally, resource use is measured by opportunity cost, or approximations thereto.

56. Value generation is measured from the perspectives of customers or shareholders, and their respective utility functions - after due consideration of the interests of other stakeholders and any external impacts on society generally as a result of an organization's operations.

57. Exploration of relationships over time involves an active consideration of interactions between short-run and long-run effects.

Management Process Interfaces

58. Management accounting adds a resource perspective to other management processes concerned with organizational direction-setting, structuring, change and control. These points of interface are themselves likely to require management, to ensure that organizational value is created as a result.

Technology Development and Evaluation

59. The work technologies used in the management accounting process also can be evaluated in terms of the equation between resource use and value generation.

60. The value generated by a work technology used in the management accounting process should more than compensate for the resources it uses or consumes.

61. Deficiencies in existing work technologies assessed relative to this criterion, should prompt the development of new or revised work technologies. In turn, such development can be guided by the equation between value generation and resource use.

Function Capability Related Concepts

62. The capabilities required for effective performance by the management accounting function within the management process of organizations are centered on the core competences seen as necessary, on a culture that embodies continuous improvement and opportunity creation, and on a capacity for critical self-consciousness about the function's effectiveness.

Core Competences

63. The work of the management accounting function should be organized around, and pursued though an identified set of core competences which reflect best practice and which are sufficient to secure effective outcomes.

64. These core competences may consist of the expertise of staff involved, the interactive work processes used, the types of systems support available, the technologies utilized in work processes, the legitimacy and respect accorded to the work of the function, the quality of management of the function, and other relevant factors.

65. The identification of a requisite set of core competences will be guided by an understanding of what needs to be achieved by the function in terms of outcome effectiveness, and by the core competences possessed by representative 'best practice' management accounting functions.

Continuous Improvement

66. A management accounting function should embody a culture of continuous improvement. This culture will be represented at any time by a range of initiatives designed to improve the work of the function, through the enhancement of its competences and the ways in which these are mobilized and used.

Creating Opportunities

67. A management accounting function should embody a culture of proactivity, in seeking out and finding opportunities for value creation within organizations.

68. This culture will be represented by creative responses to externally generated challenges, by the anticipation and identification of needs, by a readiness to capitalize on possible or emerging opportunities, and by the creation of opportunities for value generation, which might not be realized otherwise.

69. This cultural attribute should be seen as a core competence of the function.

Critical Consciousness

70. The work of the management accounting function, including improvements to it, should be subjected to a continuous evaluation in terms of efficiency and effectiveness.

71. Both the work processes and the outcomes of the work of the function should receive a critical assessment in terms of the value they generate relative to the resources used, over time.

72. The specific concepts described form part of the conceptual framework of management accounting, as illustrated on the following page.

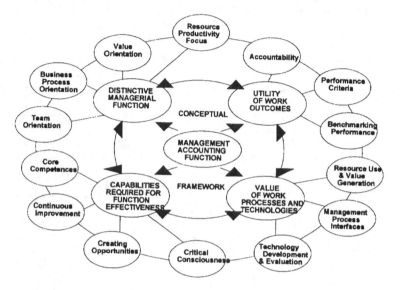

USING THE CONCEPTUAL FRAMEWORK

73. The conceptual framework elaborates the description of management accounting, by reference to best practice internationally. Thus, it can serve also as a guide for the evaluation or development of management accounting practice in particular organizational applications. Consider how the answers to the following questions can be derived directly from the conceptual framework.

74. How should management accounting practice be developed?

- So that it focuses on the effective use of organizational resources (Resource Productivity Focus), where effectiveness is judged in terms of the value generated for key organizational stakeholders (Value Orientation).

- So that it is centered on the key business processes of the organization (Business Process Orientation).

- So that it is integrated with the work of other specialist functions, as part of the management team of the organization (Team Orientation).

- So that it draws from a commonly understood set of core competences relating to the work of the function (Core Competences).

- So that it is driven by continuous improvement initiatives related to the work of the function (Continuous Improvement).

718

- So that it proactively seeks opportunities for value creation within organizations (Creating Opportunities).

- So that it is continuously reviewed in terms of the value it generates relative to the resources it consumes (Critical Consciousness).

75. How should the usefulness of management accounting practice be tested?

- In terms of its embodiment of a culture of proactivity in finding opportunities for value creation within organizations (Creating Opportunities).

- In terms of the value it adds to the organization, from the perspectives of other organizational participants (Accountability).

- Where such accountability is expressed in terms of staged performance objectives, negotiated and agreed to within the organization (Performance Criteria).

- Where the performance objectives are reflective of externally referenced competent practice (Core Competences), and performance outcomes are benchmarked across organizations (Benchmarking Performance).

76. How should the usefulness of management accounting work technologies be tested?

- In terms of the value they create in adding a resource perspective to other management processes (Management Process Interfaces).

- Through an ongoing critical assessment in terms of efficiency and effectiveness (Critical Consciousness).

- Which is focused on the resources they consume relative to the value they generate over time, in the full range of organizational involvements of the management accounting process (Technology Development and Evaluation).

77. How should management accounting work technologies be developed?

- By constant reference to the distinctive mode of thinking used in management accounting work, centered on an equation of resource use and value generation over time (Equation of Resource Use and Value Generation).

- By reference to the value added by a resource perspective to other management processes (Management Process Interfaces).

- Through processes of continuous improvement built into the culture of the management accounting function (Continuous Improvement).

- And by reference to the set of core competences deemed necessary for the effective performance of management accounting work (Core Competences).

CONCLUSION

78. This statement is designed to be used and useful; it is to be judged by its practical value in various domains. It can be used by

- *managers* in organizations for understanding, evaluating and developing that distinctive area of their work concerned with the effective use of resources;

- *professional accountants in management* in focusing, benchmarking and developing their contributions to management accounting processes in organizations;

- *educators* in refocusing and consolidating their efforts on a rapidly evolving area of practice, where capacities to both understand and contribute to change are important outcomes of learning processes;

- *professional associations and others* in reformulating and consolidating the work technologies to be associated with management accounting now and in the future.

79. It can be used also as an international point of reference for understanding different institutional and cultural approaches taken to management accounting work around the world.

Appendix

The statement of Management Accounting Concepts issued in February 1989, clearly identified management accounting as an integral part of the management process, which provided *information* for management planning and control. Accordingly, its framework of concepts focused on *the qualities that should be possessed by such information*, "as the foundation on which management accounting practices and techniques are developed and their usefulness tested".

The following *extracts* are illustrative.

****

Management Accounting

3. Management accounting may be defined as the process of identification, measurement, accumulation, analysis, preparation, interpretation, and communication of information (both financial and operating) used by management to plan, evaluate, and control within an organization and to assure use of and accountability for its resources.

4. Management accounting, therefore, is an integral part of the management process. It provides information essential for

    *   controlling the current activities of an organization;
    *   planning its future strategies, tactics and operations;
    *   optimizing the use of its resources;
    *   measuring and evaluating performance;
    *   reducing subjectivity in the decision making process; and
    *   improving internal and external communication.

The Concepts

Accountability

7. Management accounting presents information measuring the achievement of the objectives of an organization and appraising the conduct of its internal affairs in that process. In order that further action can be taken, based on this information, it is necessary at all times to identify the responsibilities and key result areas of the individuals within the organization.

Controllability

8. Management accounting identifies the elements of activities which management can or cannot influence, and seeks to assess risk and sensitivity factors. This facilitates the proper monitoring, analysis, comparison and interpretation of information which can be used constructively in the control, evaluation and corrective functions of management.

Reliability

9. Management accounting information must be of such quality that confidence can be placed in it. Its reliability to the user is dependent on its source, integrity and comprehensiveness.

Interdependency

10. Management accounting, in recognition of the increasing complexity of business, must access both external and internal information sources from interactive functions such as marketing, production, personnel, procurement, finance, etc. This assists in ensuring that the information is adequately balanced.

Relevancy

11. Management accounting must ensure that flexibility is maintained in assembling and interpreting information. This facilitates the exploration and presentation, in a clear, understandable and timely manner, of as many alternatives as are necessary for impartial and confident decisions to be taken. The process is essentially forward looking and dynamic. Therefore, the information must satisfy the criteria of being applicable and appropriate.

2

October 1989

The Capital Expenditure Decision

MANAGEMENT ACCOUNTING

CONTENTS

	Paragraphs
INTRODUCTION	1-4
SECTION 1 — QUANTITATIVE ESTIMATES	5-44
Fixed Investment Estimates	8-11
Working Capital Estimates	12
The Planning Horizon-Economic Life	13-18
Physical Life	14
Technological Life	15
Product-Market Life	16-18
Market Estimates	19-28
Market Study	20-25
Competitive Factors	26
Price Estimation	27
The Organization's Position in the Market	28
Operating Cost Estimates	29-38
Labor — Associated Payments, etc.	30
Labor — Savings from Reducing Time Required of Individuals	31-32
Efficiency Improvement	33
Services	34
Maintenance	35
Depreciation	36
Property-Related Costs	37
Plant Administration, Service Departments, etc.	38

Estimating Terminal Values (Salvage, Trade-in or Disposal
  Values) 39
Estimating the Effects of Inflation 40-42
Risk Analysis 43-44

SECTION 2 — DECISION MODELS 45-58
Evaluation Techniques 45-49
Ranking of Capital Expenditure Projects 50-52
Selection of the Required Rate of Return 53-54
Non-Quantitative Evaluation Considerations 55
Government and Nonprofit Organizations 56-58

SECTION 3 — ADMINISTRATION OF THE CAPITAL
  EXPENDITURE DECISION 59-84
Policy Manual 60-62
Preliminary Project Review 63-64
The Appropriation Request 65-70
Appropriation Request Documentation 71-83
Review and Approvals 83
Benefits of Documentation 84

EXHIBIT 1 - THE APPROPRIATION REQUEST (Cover Page)

Introduction

1. Capital expenditures are defined as investments to acquire fixed or long lived assets from which a stream of benefits is expected. Such expenditures represent an organization's commitment to produce and sell future products and engage in other activities. Capital expenditure decisions, therefore, form a foundation for the future profitability of a company.

2. Capital expenditure activities are made up of two distinct processes: (a) making the decision and (b) implementing it, which may include performing a post-appraisal. This Practice deals only with the first process.

3. The following material prescribes procedures to follow in making the capital expenditure decision. For purposes of presentation, it is broken up into three sections. Section 1 discusses the development of quantitative estimates. Section 2 represents the decision models. Section 3 describes the administration of the capital expenditure decision process.

4. The capital expenditure decision is derived from and is closely associated with strategic planning which is an effort by an organization to define its mission and goals and the policies and strategies it will follow to attain them.

Section 1 — Quantitative Estimates

5. Reliable estimates and forecasts are vital to the capital investment decision. A sophisticated process of analyzing financial information and managing the decision related to a project is of little value if a casual approach is taken to development of these estimates. The foundations for good capital planning are reliable forecasts of marketing opportunities, competitive technology, likely actions by competitors and governments, sales volumes, selling prices, operating costs, changes in working capital, taxes payable and capital costs of equipment. Effective management of capital expenditure decisions, therefore, requires that controls be designed and operated to ensure that projections are realistic at the time decisions are made.

6. The estimate of the costs and benefits of a capital project should show the difference that results from making the investment. The important information is the change in cash flows as a result of undertaking the project, i.e., the differential principle.

7. The degree of precision necessary for the estimates related to the capital expenditure decision depends on:

   a) the stage of evaluation of the project (i.e., in early stages less precision is needed),

   b) the sensitivity of the project's economics to the level of accuracy and timing of each of the elements within the estimates, and

   c) the similarity of the project to others already undertaken.

Fixed Investment Estimates

8. Fixed investments consist of all the costs necessary to bring the project to full operation. These include the equipment costs, installation, training, commissioning, initial spoilage, spare parts inventory, etc. The capital investment in a project can usually be estimated with greater precision than the other factors required for the capital expenditure decision, primarily because capital investments occur in the near future whereas operating costs and revenues are incurred over the life of the project.

9. The simplest means of estimating capital costs is to adjust the known investment of a project of similar nature. The most complex means of estimation requires a detailed project plan from which the costs of individual items and other costs are developed. In between, various yardsticks may provide adequate approximations of investment required. For example, the cost of a building may be approximated by the estimated cost per square foot to construct the building times the estimated square footage of the building.

10. In lieu of firm bids from manufacturers and suppliers, quick estimates can often be obtained without involving a great deal of their time as published information is often available.

11. If the project will result in the replacement of existing equipment, the net cash inflows or outflows from the removal and disposal of that equipment, including the tax implications, should be taken into account.

Working Capital Estimates

12. The analysis includes estimates of all investments required for a project. The project may require increases (or decreases) in cash, accounts receivable, accounts payable, or inventory. These changes in working capital should be included in the calculation as should the changes to these at the end of the economic life of the project.

The Planning Horizon — Economic Life

13. It is often difficult to estimate the life of a project (i.e., its planning horizon). The criterion is the continued ability to generate satisfactory cash flows or other intangible benefits. The economic life of a project is the lesser of its physical life, technological life or product-market life.

Physical Life

14. Physical life represents the time taken for an asset to become physically worn out so that it can no longer be efficiently maintained and must be replaced. However, equipment will often be disposed of before its physical life has expired.

Technological Life

15. Technological life is the period of time that elapses before an even newer machine or process becomes available which would make the proposed machine or process obsolete. Improvements will almost certainly be made

sometime in all machines or processes now in existence, but questions of which machines or processes will be improved, and how soon they will be on the market are most difficult to answer. To ignore a process' or machine's technological life is to imply that the technological life is the same as the physical life.

Product — Market Life

16. Although a machine may be in excellent physical condition, and although there may be no better machine on the market, its economic life has ended for the organization as soon as it ceases to market the product. The product-market life of the machine may end because the particular operation performed by the machine is made unnecessary by a change in style or because the market for the product itself has disappeared.

17. The projected economic life of the return on investment is particularly important if the project lasts for a relatively short period, say ten years or less, and is less important for longer projects. It is therefore particularly important that special consideration be given to estimates of economic life if there is a high probability that the economic life may be short.

18. Because of the inherent uncertainties of making estimates in distant years, especially estimates related to sales volumes, some organizations set an arbitrary limit on the planning horizon to be used in the analysis. This planning horizon can be shorter than the estimated economic life of the project; in some organizations, it is ten years. In some organizations, cash flows beyond this planning horizon are disregarded in the interest of conservatism or if not significant to the project. Other organizations apply an arbitrary estimate of value for the benefits beyond the planning horizon.

Market Estimates

19. Some methods of developing market estimates are discussed in the following paragraphs.

Market Study

20. A market study forecasts sales revenue through the life of a project. It should describe fully all aspects of the company's position in the market and estimate the degree of marketing risk associated with the venture. It provides information on demand, supply and price trends in the overall market, and specific forecasts of market share, sales volume, net returns and selling costs, as well as what competitors are or may be doing in the market place.

21. Usually, this forecast proceeds from stated assumptions regarding the economic environment and general business conditions, to estimates of total market, subdivided by end-use, region, and major customer, and then concludes with estimates of specific sales potential available within that market.

22. When developing sales forecasts, consideration should be given to the possible obsolescence of products or services. Such items have a life of only a few years, so that organizations must compete, not necessarily on the basis

of being the low-cost producer, but by being product innovators. The demand forecast must, therefore, consider: frequent introduction of new products, timely delivery, and flexibility in the production process to adapt to customer preferences. Such considerations must also be factors in the selection process for capital equipment.

23. Significant relationships between an organization's sales and economic indicators for the market as a whole, or other industry statistics, may be determined by using correlation analysis.

24. An alternative way of projecting sales is to use internal sources of data, such as information supplied through salesmen's call reports, supplementary information developed through interviews of market researchers, credit statistics, and general knowledge of the customer and his or her competitive situation.

25. Either method may produce a set of possible outcomes to which a probability figure could be developed. The appropriate figure to use is a weighted average[1] of the possible outcomes. It is known as the expected value. However, in many projects such a probability distribution is either not feasible or not worthwhile.

Competitive Factors

26. The demand forecast should indicate the competitors and their market share. The productive capacity in existence and potentially available would then be assessed in relation to the forecasted demand to show the volume and timing of expansion needs. Competitors' expansion possibilities and economics should also be considered along with their product and technology life cycles.

Price Estimation

27. The estimation of price trends is frequently the most difficult area of market forecasting. However, analysis of the supply/demand balance and estimation of competitors' economics can provide a guide. The elasticity of demand in relation to the price may also be considered. A careful study of the product life cycle is often needed since, in the early development stages of a new product, the price is often high; it falls as demand levels off at maturity, and then declines further as new substitutes appear on the market.

The Organization's Position in the Market

28. The analyses of supply, demand and price are consolidated into specific forecasts of market share, sales volume and annual cash inflow through the project's expected life. In addition, it is important to state the major assumptions, the reliability of the market data and, if worthwhile, attach confidence limits to the forecasts. By doing so, the degree of marketing risk

---

[1] The weighted average is found by multiplying each outcome by its probability, calculating the total and then determining the average.

associated with the project is conveyed, and the sensitivity of the project to inaccuracies in the marketing appraisal can be evaluated.

Operating Cost Estimates

29. When estimating operating costs for capital expenditures, the following should be kept in mind:

   a) Only cash costs after the payment of tax on income[2] are relevant; non-cash expenses such as depreciation are excluded except to the extent they affect taxable income.

   b) Only future costs are relevant. Historical costs may be useful in terms of providing a basis for prediction, but they do not represent what future costs will be.

   c) Only differential costs are relevant. This means that only the difference in cash operating costs between implementing or not implementing a proposal need be considered.

Labor — Associated Payments, etc.

30. Labor costs should include, in addition to the direct wage rate, overtime and all associated payments and benefits.

Labor — Savings from Reducing Time Required of Individuals

31. Labor savings often result from the saving of part of several individuals' time.

32. Over the long run, it would normally be expected that the time set free for these individuals could be productively utilized elsewhere or that the aggregate saving in time will cause reduction in the number of employees.

Efficiency Improvement

33. Cost reduction projects often include improvements in efficiency which either reduce material consumption or increase output. The additional output should be valued at the probable profit which can be realized.

Services

34. The differential cost of services, (e.g., utilities, transport, computer services) often present problems. An investment proposal may result in the consumption of fewer services due to efficiency improvements. In such a case, the effect on a project's differential cost depends upon what can be done with the unused service. If any cash costs associated with keeping the service at the level prior to the investment can be eliminated, then the amount

---

[2] Taxes on income can have a significant influence on the decision as they impact on the amount and timing of cash inflows or outflows. Variations in tax laws throughout the world prevent discussion of this topic in this practice. However, the reader should be aware of its significance and adjust calculations accordingly.

involved can be treated as a cash cost saving (negative cost). If the freed-up service can be used elsewhere and would have to be bought for this other use, then the amount saved by not having to buy for this other purpose would be a cost saving of the investment. If the freed-up service cannot be used elsewhere and must still be paid for, then there would be no incremental cost saving for the investment (the cost would continue whether or not the investment was made).

Maintenance

35. Maintenance costs should normally be the cost expected to be incurred in each year of the life of a project. Sometimes the use of an average may be justified. An average will sometimes be a greater amount than the maintenance cost in the initial years. Provision should also be made, as appropriate, for periodic overhauls. Estimates should also be made of the incremental costs for maintenance material and operating supplies.

Depreciation

36. No amount for depreciation should be included in calculating the cash flow since this is an allocation of the investment cost required to match expenses against revenues over the life of the investment. It does not require a cash outflow each year. In capital budgeting, the cost of the investment is taken into account when cash outlays or their equivalent take place. If depreciation were counted in determining cash flows, the investment cost would be inappropriately double counted. However, in the determination of taxes on income allowances for depreciation should be considered.

Property-Related Costs

37. Certain insurances and taxes are related to investment costs and should be estimated accordingly.

Plant Administration, Service Departments, etc.

38. If an organization is expanding, plant administration and service departments also expand, but such expansion may not be directly attributed to individual capital investment projects. Nevertheless some allowance for the cost of expansion is needed. It is suggested that general ratios may be applicable to most appropriations being prepared at a time. Periodic revision of these ratios is necessary.

Estimating Terminal Values (Salvage, Trade-in or Disposal Values)

39. The terminal value of a capital asset at the end of its useful life should include disposal values less the dismantling and/or site restoration costs plus the release of any associated working capital.

Estimating the Effects of Inflation

40. The effect of inflation on a capital project is to reduce the purchasing power of net cash flows over time.

41.	Several techniques for recognizing the effect of inflation are used in practice. They include:

a)	use of a discount rate that is high enough to incorporate inflation,

b)	adjusting all cash flows by a single percentage that allows for inflation, or

c)	adjusting individual cash flows by rates that include the effect of inflation on each of them.

42.	The first technique is perhaps the most common. Care must be taken to insure that the effect of inflation is not double counted, which can happen if two of the above methods are used together.

Risk Analysis

43.	Risk exists in capital budgeting when more than one outcome may occur. A quantitative evaluation of a capital expenditure proposal requires that several predictions be made, often far into the future. As a general rule, the risk associated with achieving an expected cash inflow or outflow in a given year increases as one moves further into the future as there are more factors in the long term which cannot be foreseen but which will affect cash flows.

44.	Most organizations do not make a specific allowance for risk. Some, however, provide the following information:

a)	the range of accuracy for the estimate stated as a plus or minus percentage,

b)	the expected value of the estimate based on a weighted average of all possible outcomes, and

c)	the effect on the appraisal results using the widest range of error. Of particular interest is the amount by which a key variable can be varied before the project fails to meet its decision criterion, all other things being held constant.

Section 2 — Decision Models

Evaluation Techniques

45.	Several techniques are available to arrive at a financial decision regarding a capital expenditure project. These include:

a)	the net present value method. This method discounts all cash flows to the present using a predetermined minimum acceptable rate of return as the discount rate. If the net present value is positive, the financial return on the project is greater than this minimum acceptable rate and indicates the project is economically acceptable. If the net present value is negative, the project is not acceptable on economic grounds.

b)	the internal rate of return method. The internal rate of return is defined as the discount rate that makes the net present value of a project equal to zero. It is the highest rate of interest that a company could incur to obtain funds without losing money on the project.

c) the equivalent annual cost method. When considering alternative proposals, it may be that only costs are involved. In such situations, a choice of alternatives can be made by determining which has the lowest equivalent annual cost. Under this method, capital expenditures are converted to their "equivalent annual cost" and added to the annual "operating" costs. Equivalent annual cost is the annual amount that would repay the capital over the life of the project at a specified discount rate. It is similar to an annual, level repayment schedule for a mortgage. The alternative with the lowest total cost would be the most attractive (ignoring intangibles).

d) the payback method. This method estimates the time taken to recover the original investment outlay. The estimated net cash flows from a proposal for each year are added until they total the original investment. The time required to recoup the investment is called the payback period. Projects with a shorter payback period are preferred to those with longer periods.

e) the discounted payback method. The discounted payback period is the number of years for which cash inflows are required to (a) recover the amount of the investment and also (b) earn the required rate of return on the investment during that period. In this method, each year's cash inflow is discounted at the required rate of return, and these present values are cumulated by year until, their sum equals, the amount invested. Projects with a shorter discounted payback period are preferable to those with longer periods.

f) the accounting rate of return method. The accounting rate of return is a measure of the average annual income after tax over the life of a project divided by the initial investment or the average investment required to generate the income. It is important to note that this method assesses net income and not cash flows which are used in the other methods.

46. The internal rate of return, discounted payback, net present value and equivalent annual cost methods use discounted cash flows (DCF). The DCF concept considers the time value of money in making investment decisions, whereas the other methods do not.

47. The payback method (or discounted payback method) is useful where:

a) preliminary screening of many proposals is necessary;

b) a weak cash position has an important bearing on the selection of projects;

c) the proposed project is extremely risky; or

d) projects, such as routine replacement projects, have similar economic lives.

48. When the payback method is used, the required payback period should be consistent with that developed by applying the required rate of return on projects with similar characteristics.

49. The accounting rate of return method is useful when management is especially concerned with the effect of a large capital investment on reported financial results.

Ranking of Capital Expenditure Projects

50. Many organizations have several proposed capital projects which are economically acceptable, but they have only limited financial resources. Thus the entity must rank the projects and select those that promise the higher returns.

51. At any given time, management is likely to be considering several projects at various stages of refinement. At each stage in the evaluation process, proposals are assessed and accepted into the next stage, referred back to the sponsor for further work or rejected. A ranking procedure should be used at each stage. Ranking projects on the basis of quantitative criteria may be established by specifying a minimum desired rate of return on a project. This minimum rate is called the required rate of return (also the discount rate or the hurdle rate). This rate is used to calculate the net present value of each project and to rank them accordingly.

52. The internal rate of return and net present value methods are also used to resolve the capital rationing problem. If the internal rate of return method is used, the higher the rate of return, the better the project. If the net present value is used, it is necessary to first divide the present value of the cash inflows by the amount of the investment. The higher the resulting number, called the profitability index, the better the project.

Selection of the Required Rate of Return

53. In selecting the required rate of return to evaluate capital expenditure proposals, two approaches are widely used: calculating a cost of capital, or use of a number generally accepted by the industry.

54. In theory, the required rate of return on a project of average risk should be at least as high as the organization's cost of capital.

Non-Quantitative Evaluation Considerations

55. Qualitative or policy considerations may override quantitative criteria in the ranking or acceptance of projects. Some examples of qualitative considerations are:

a) relationship to business strategy;

b) product line or location and its significance to the enterprise;

c) timing of fund flows from the project versus the timing of fund flows required;

d) management, technical engineering and marketing capacities or constraints; and

e) balance desired in spending by product classification.

Projects may be worthy of approval on such non-financial grounds as protection of company property, employee health and welfare or to comply with government regulations in such areas as pollution.

Government and Nonprofit Organizations

56.   The capital expenditure process for government and nonprofit organizations is conceptually similar to that in for profit organizations, and although the method of estimating costs and benefits is also similar, there are important differences in measuring benefits.

57.   If feasible, government and nonprofit organizations attempt to measure both financial and social benefits. Social benefits can be difficult to quantify but include:

- direct benefits that accrue to the taxpayer or member, and
- indirect benefits that accrue to individuals or groups that may or may not be taxpayers or members.

58.   The required rate of return on government or nonprofit funds is the return on alternative uses of these funds. The methods used to evaluate capital expenditure proposals are the same as the ones described above.

Section 3 — Administration of the Capital Expenditure Decision

59.   Figure 1 depicts, in general terms, the process which an organization may use in making the capital expenditure decision.[3] This Practice describes only the decision making process (i.e., up to the "final approval" decision).

---

[3] For the capital expenditure decision, it is important that the project be comprehensively and fully defined. This is intended to prevent avoidance of approval limits or making relatively low initial investments which require larger follow-up investments for which no yes/no decision can be made at that time.

Figure 1

The Capital Expenditure Decision[4]

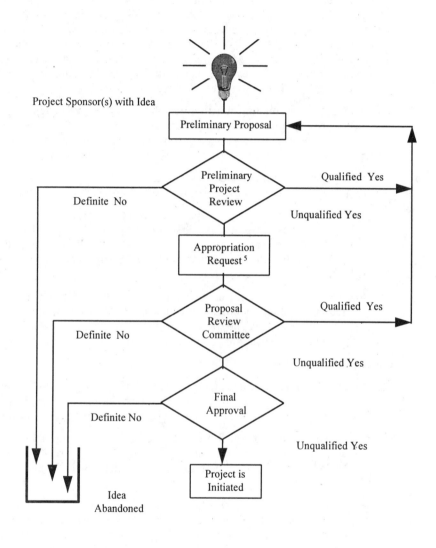

Project Sponsor(s) with Idea

Preliminary Proposal

Preliminary Project Review

Qualified Yes

Definite No

Unqualified Yes

Appropriation Request[5]

Proposal Review Committee

Qualified Yes

Definite No

Unqualified Yes

Final Approval

Definite No

Unqualified Yes

Project is Initiated

Idea Abandoned

---

[4] Smaller or routine capital expenditure projects may not require such a formal approach.
[5] In some systems this document is labelled "Project Proposal."

Policy Manual

60. Each proposed capital expenditure competes for, and should justify its share of, the limited resources available. Formal procedures and rules should be established to assure that all proposals are reviewed fairly and consistently. Managers and supervisors who make proposals need to know what the organization expects the proposals to contain, and on what basis their proposed projects will be judged. Those managers who have the authority to approve specific projects need to exercise that responsibility in the context of an overall organizational capital expenditure policy [as approved by the Board of Directors or senior managers where appropriate].

61. The management accounting function, which has the task of developing the internal controls in an enterprise, also has the responsibility for coordinating the input of the various functional groups and obtaining approval of this policy manual.

62. The policy manual should include specifications for:

a) **an annually updated forecast of capital expenditures.** This project by project forecast should cover a period of three to five years and should include: previous expenditures for approved projects, expenditures for the current budget year, a forecast of the capital expenditures required for the following two to four years, and the supply (both internal and external) of funds in the ensuring year.

b) **the appropriation steps.** These should be sufficiently detailed to ensure that the proposal and approval procedures are identified in a consistent and orderly manner. The procedure for a revision to a previously approved capital expenditure application should also be specified.

c) **the appraisal method(s) to be used to evaluate proposals.**

d) **the minimum acceptable rate(s) of return on projects of various risk.** Normally, this provides guidelines rather than an absolute requirement, because not all projects are evaluated solely in terms of financial benefits.

e) **the limits of authority.** Here the specification of the appropriate managers attesting to the desirability of the project in relation to the responsibility of these managers should be required as the basis for their accountability.

f) **the control of capital expenditures.** The manual should indicate who is responsible for controlling capital expenditures once the project is approved and authorizing capital expenditures against authorized amounts.

g) **the procedure to be followed when accepted projects will be subject to an actual performance review after implementation.** As a minimum, the policy manual should specify the expenditure limit above which a review will be required; the time it will commence after completion of the project; and by whom it will be undertaken.

Preliminary Project Review

63. The first formal step in the capital expenditure decision is a preliminary project review. This assessment is often needed:

   a) to give early consideration of and guidance to a project which could result in an appropriation request and to provide an early screen for ideas not worthy of pursuit,

   b) to minimize the lead time to implement a promising project, and

   c) to coordinate activities associated with a project.

64. An appropriate project sponsor should be identified who should ensure that all required documentation contains the information needed to reach a decision on the preliminary proposal. The organization's policy regarding the preparation of estimates for capital expenditure proposals should encourage managers to seek out and use the expertise of others who can help in the derivation of cash flows.

The Appropriation Request

65. Of all the documentation required in the capital expenditure decision, the appropriation request is the most important since it is from this document that a decision is to be made. It is the request for authorization to spend money.

66. The appropriation request is also used to provide information as to the expected timing and amount of cash inflows and out-flows.

67. Management accounting personnel are usually responsible for coordinating and compiling information with the aim of prompt completion and issue of the appropriation request. Marketing, technical, production and engineering staff, and others may make a considerable contribution. While sponsors of projects must take ultimate responsibility for preparation of the appropriation request, the responsibility for development of the report on their behalf should be defined. The management accountant, as an objective member of management is well placed to fill this role.

68. Decisions on major appropriations are taken at senior management levels, and by the Board of Directors, as they have far-reaching implications on the future profitability of the company. These persons who are involved in the final decision cannot be expected to have an intimate knowledge of all aspects of a project. Consequently, they rely heavily on the facts, estimates, and appraisal contained in an appropriation request.

69. Appropriation requests should be prepared for all capital expenditures above a minimum amount and should also be required for major expense items such as non-routine repairs.

70. In addition, appropriation requests are required for supplemental funding when original estimates have been exceeded, and for retirement requests for assets no longer required.

Appropriation Request Documentation

71. The information included in an appropriation request should be designed to show:

    a) the purpose, by a brief description of the project;

    b) the timing and amount of the operating cash flows expected;

    c) the timing and amount of the investment required and expected net salvage value, if any, at the end of its useful life and the degree of accuracy of the estimates;

    d) the major assumptions that bear on the accuracy of the cash flow estimates;

    e) the economic desirability of the project, and the sensitivity of the discounted cash flow rate of return after tax to changes in the basic data;

    f) a review, if appropriate, of the alternatives to the project and the impact on the economics of the project;

    g) implications of not proceeding with the project;

    h) the financing method or availability of internally generated funds to underwrite the project; and

    i) the actions recommended.

72. The appropriation request would give a concise, readable picture of the whole project. It would indicate why the project was proposed, why it should be carried out at the present time, and why it should be done in the way proposed. It should also show linkages to the strategy, goals and objectives of the enterprise and to any concurrent projects or programs which bear on the project.

    Examples of reasons for capital expenditures are:

    • expansion,
    • maintenance of the current level of activity,
    • cost reduction and/or quality achievement,
    • replacement,
    • modernization,
    • research and development,
    • protection of property,
    • to meet legal requirements, and
    • safety and health.

    The classification would be tailored to each organization's needs. The first five examples lend themselves to a DCF analysis while expenditures for the last four are often assessed on more qualitative grounds.

73. There is generally more than one method of carrying out a project, and alternatives should be examined to assess the effect of differences in cash flows, investment costs and other factors. The report should show that the best alternative has been selected. Also the carrying out of the project under

review may preempt the carrying out of another project and this should be clearly stated.

74. The report should be logically arranged so that facts lead to conclusions and arguments are progressively developed. Evidence should be given of the adequacy and completeness of the facts and the degree of accuracy of the estimates.

75. The appropriation request should include a market report when a) a change in quantity or quality of product is involved, b) an investment is required to maintain the existing quantity or quality of a product, or c) there is a change in the market for an existing product. The content of this report is described in paragraphs 19 to 28.

76. The appropriation request should include an engineering and production report for projects involving installation of plant facilities. It should contain all data necessary for assessment of the physical nature of the undertaking, the investment involved and the yields, efficiency and cost of the output from the new facilities. Capacity to be installed by the project under review should be shown. Where an addition to existing capacity results, the total installed capacity before and after the expenditure should be indicated. A reader should be able to accurately assess the extent of any technological risk associated with any new equipment involved in the project.

77. When appropriate, a research and development report should accompany the appropriation request. It should present a concise summary of the status of the organization's knowledge and define the uncertainties with regard to technology related to product or processes involved in the project.

78. Where new appropriations free existing assets, a retirement request should accompany and form part of the appropriation request.

79. Retirement requests should clearly indicate if the asset is to be sold or retained for future use. If retained, a justification is required for retention compared to disposing of the asset for cash. Sound financial management requires that assets no longer required be sold and the cash obtained used to earn a return elsewhere in the organization.

80. A retirement request should state why the assets were no longer required, and should indicate their original cost, age, dismantling costs and expected salvage value. This would guide the decision maker on the reasonableness of the value to be obtained on disposal.

81. The value on disposal also presents problems in determining the levels of authority for approval. Practice seems to favor use of original cost for determining the level of approval.

82. Exhibit 1 is an example of a cover page of an appropriation request.

Review and Approvals

83. Certifying signatures are used to assist the ultimate decision maker in determining whether to approve the expenditure. Certification may be partial or complete; a partial certification contains any qualification on the project's desirability. For example, the engineering department certifies that the

proposal will meet the organization's engineering standards, and that the capital cost estimate is accurate. The production manager similarly certifies the physical production data, capacities, yields, efficiencies and production costs. The sales manager certifies the market data, sales volume and selling prices. Signatures of controllers, treasurers, general managers and presidents certify their opinion as to the total financial and overall desirability of the proposed expenditure.

Benefits of Documentation

84. Formal procedures for initiating, preparing, reviewing and approving appropriation requests have several advantages:

   a) Standard terminology, estimating techniques and methods of appraisal enhance the comparability of appropriations originating in different parts of the organization.

   b) The requirement that certain facts appear in support of each type of appropriation, that the reasons for the appropriation are set forth in a report and that the report is to be reviewed by the principal managers of an organization, all tend to promote increased objectivity.

   c) Encourage decisions to be made in the same manner throughout the organization and that authorities for approving expenditures can be delegated with greater confidence.

   d) Standardization of appraisals enables senior management to concentrate on the strategic and intangible aspects of major expenditures as it is these aspects which often have the greatest impact on the long-term future of the organization.

Exhibit 1

The Appropriation Request (Cover Page)

Title, Objective and Description of Project:	Number: Review # Department: Location:
Amount included in — Expense $ — Capital $ Budget for this project $	Date: Expected Start-up Date: Date of Completion:

OBJECTIVE AND SUMMARY OF SUPPORTING DATA:

APPRAISAL INDICATORS:	**INVESTMENT ($'000)**
D.C.F. (after tax) Rate of Return (%) NPV ($) Equivalent annual costs ($)	Pre-construction . . . .$
	Initial cost — bldgs. . . . . . . — equip. . . . . . .
Payback in years (after tax)	Working capital . . . . Additional Manpower. . . . .
Capacity Utilization Assumed	Impact on Overall Costs . . . Future Obligations . . . .
Economic Life of Project (years)	**TOTAL** . . . . $
	_____ (Authorized Signature)

Exhibit 1

The Appropriation Request (Cover Page)

CASH FLOW PROFILE

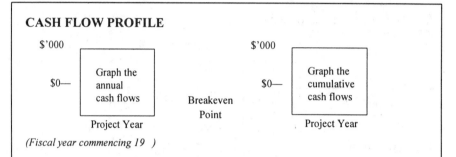

$'000 $'000

$0— | Graph the annual cash flows | $0— | Graph the cumulative cash flows |

              Breakeven
                Point

Project Year   Project Year

(Fiscal year commencing 19)

SENSITIVITY ANALYSIS   **Comments**

Variable	Estimate	Estimate Range	NPV Effect $M
Fixed capital	$M		
Working capital	$M		
Sales price —	$/kg		
—			
Sales volume —			
—			
—			
Processing costs	$M		
Raw material cost	$/kg		
Project life	Yrs.		

REVIEW AND APPROVALS

TITLE	SIGNATURE	DATE	ACTION (RECOMMEND, REVIEW, APPROVE)

3

February 1996

Currency Exposure and Risk Management

CONTENTS

	Paragraphs
PREFACE	
BACKGROUND	1-23
Currency Markets	1-3
International Trade	4-6
Exchange Rates	7-16
Business Implications	17-23
EXPOSURE	24-42
Definition	24
Types of Exposure	25-30
Translation Exposure	25-26
Transaction Exposure	27-28
Economic Exposure	29-30
Identification of Exposure	31-42
RISK	43-60
Definition	43-45
Assessment of Risk	46-60
Forecasting	47
Assumptions	48-53
Measurement	54-60

MANAGEMENT OF EXPOSURE AND RISK...................... 61-103
Introduction 61-62
Corporate Philosophy and Policy.................................... 63
Management Objectives.. 64-65
Organization and Responsibility.................................... 66-75
Tactics and Techniques 76-103
Forecasting.. 76-80
Management Techniques.. 81-103

ACCOUNTING, TAXATION AND FISCAL CONTROLS 104-113
Accounting Standards and Practices 104-107
Taxation Considerations 108-110
Foreign Exchange Controls 111-113

CONCLUSION... 114 -115

APPENDIX 1 — Translation Accounting Conventions
APPENDIX 2 — Example of an Organizational Flow Chart
                   Which Would Support an Active Exposure
                   Management Program
APPENDIX 3 — Example of a Translation Exposure Report
APPENDIX 4 — Example of a Transactional Cash Flow Report
APPENDIX 5 — Example of an Economic Exposure Cash Flow Forecast

GLOSSARY OF TERMS

This International Management Accounting Practice Statement has been prepared in order to summarize for the benefit of senior management and, in particular, financial and accounting managers, those matters concerning the management of foreign currency exposures and the risks associated with changes in the rates of exchange between currencies. It is intended to serve as a framework for those who are required to determine overall policy in this regard as well as for those who are expected to manage such exposures and risks.

While some background and causative influences are discussed, no attempt is made to analyze the economic theory behind exchange rate fluctuations. Rather, it is accepted that such fluctuations are an integral part of the present international financial environment and the objective of the paper is to provide managers with a more systematic approach to the issues involved.

It would not be possible in a statement of this length to deal exhaustively with the subject. However, the main concepts are highlighted and the general principles discussed.

BACKGROUND

Currency Markets

1. Since the beginning of the seventies there has been extreme movement and instability in international currency markets, bringing about violent fluctuations in currency relationships. Differences in the economic performances of countries, as well as in their political, monetary and fiscal policies, have aggravated this situation. Attempts to impose a fixed exchange rate system, first in relation to gold and later in terms of the U.S. dollar, were dropped in favour of a free float by all the major currencies in the early seventies.

2. A number of secondary monetary systems have evolved out of the attempts to introduce some stability. Many smaller countries have sought to tie the value of their currencies to that of a major currency or basket of currencies. A series of currency blocks has emerged. Within each block, the currencies involved float in a narrow band, while the main blocks themselves float relative to each other, significantly influenced by the dominant currency in each block (i.e., the exchange rate mechanism of the European Monetary System).

3. Despite these developments, volatility of exchange rates has been the rule rather than the exception. They remain highly sensitive to national and international economic and political conditions and expected changes. Uncertainty has also spawned increased speculative activity in the currency markets themselves.

International Trade

4. World output continues to expand and the increasing liberalization of international trade and financing has dramatically increased cross-border flows of goods, services and investments. While this has greatly assisted economic integration and growth, it has brought about widely fluctuating fortunes in the countries involved.

5. Large multinational enterprises have become more and more prevalent as the needs to grow, diversify, spread risk and extend markets have led to the expansion of activities into foreign countries. Business enterprises in the present day have ready access to most foreign markets and can exercise a wide geographical choice in the procurement and distribution of products and services. Foreign financing (especially with increased focus on cross-border risks), investing and, sometimes, disinvesting occur on an ever increasing scale. These activities inevitably exert a high degree of influence on the economic performance of countries and the strength of their currencies.

6. Changes in the availability and price of key *commodities,* e.g., food and mineral resources have precipitated financial crises in many countries and subjected their exchange rates to a high degree of vulnerability.

Exchange Rates

7. Variations in the relative purchasing powers of currencies may result in sharp and often severe exchange rate corrections. The purchasing power parity theory suggests that, over time, the cost of a *common set* of goods in one country should equal the cost of those same goods in another, when translated at the ruling rate of exchange. Disparities in relative purchasing powers are created where:

   * the domestic price of goods remains stable over a period of time but the exchange rate alters significantly. The result is that a country with a declining exchange rate is able to offer its goods on the international market at a lower price than that of another country whose currency is appreciating; or

   * there is no change in the exchange rate between the two countries but a high level of inflation in one country has the effect of increasing its domestic price of goods as against another country's domestic price.

8. Disparities can also occur because of:

   * capital flows

   * transport and associated costs

   * only certain goods being traded

   * quotas, import surcharges, tariffs or other government constraints

9. Real interest rate differentials play an important part in determining the rate of a currency. As domestic interest rates are raised or lowered, the investment of funds in one currency is made more or less attractive than in another, and this may result in the movement of short- and long-term funds between countries. Any significant net movement of funds into a country will usually

improve its exchange rate while weakening the currency of the country from which the funds have come.

10. However, the establishment of the Group of Seven (G-7) by the seven major industrialized nations, *in part* to facilitate coordinated movements of interest rates, is an important initiative in seeking to keep real interest rate differentials reasonably static in the long term.

11. The extent to which countries enforce or relax foreign exchange controls will affect the international flow of funds in and out of the countries concerned and influence their relative exchange values.

12. The net result of all current transactions a country has with all other countries is reflected in its balance of payments, as either a surplus or a deficit. Where a country has to consistently draw on its reserves to rectify any deficit in its balance of payments, its currency will weaken. The converse applies when surpluses are generated.

13. Different economic and political conditions among countries as well as their contrasting economic policies cause realignments in relative exchange values. It becomes important, therefore, to identify the dominant influences as well as the other exacerbating or alleviating factors. Perceptions, more than actualities, are often key determinants in the pricing of a country's currency.

14. Because of the scale of financial, interbank (or secondary), speculative and interventionist transactions, the proportion of foreign exchange dealings that relate directly to payment of goods and services is *normally* relatively small and the volatility in the foreign exchange markets is increased. The role played by currency speculators, particularly, should not be underestimated, as it exerts significant influence on the market. In addition, foreign investment in equities/stock, property and bond markets can play an important role in influencing a currency market.

15. Central bank intervention can create pre-determined trading ranges for specific currencies. Although isolated intervention may not have a material effect, concerted intervention by a group of central banks can force market participants to honor these price levels for a limited length of time. The market will attack these ranges only when there is a perception that fundamentals have changed sufficiently to warrant policy changes by the countries concerned.

16. The short-dated forward foreign exchange market, which is driven primarily by trade flows and short-term capital movements, either genuine or speculative, is used extensively by central banks as a mechanism for intervention to influence market conditions or exchange rate movements. The forward market is closely allied to short-term money markets in the relevant currencies and the process of arbitrage forces the forward rates on currencies to reflect the interest rate differentials between the respective currencies.

Business Implications

17. An enterprise faces the risk that fluctuations in the exchange rate between the domestic and the foreign currencies involved will affect the cash flows of the

enterprise, its profitability and even its solvency. The more currencies involved and the longer the time period before settlement, the more complex is the management of the risk and the greater the implications of its mismanagement. Normally the more the proportion of foreign currency exposure relative to the domestic currency, the larger is the actual risk.

18.	Exchange rate movements focus attention on cash flows and on those assets and liabilities, revenues and expenses of an enterprise which are *denominated* in foreign currencies, and create the possibility of foreign exchange gains and losses. What could otherwise be a profitable economic transaction or investment may be rendered unprofitable on realization because of exchange rate fluctuations. Conversely, movements in the opposite way may render potentially unprofitable transactions profitable. The performance measurement of certain *divisions* and products can be significantly affected by exchange rate movements as can also their competitiveness against locally available foreign products.

19.	There is a close relationship, even at times a mutual *interdependence,* between currency rates and interest rates. Both need to be considered when loan arrangements in foreign currencies are contemplated.

20.	The trend towards expanded accounting disclosure requirements has *accompanied* increased visibility of foreign exchange matters and the related accounting practice rules have more properly circumscribed the methods of accounting for them. This is especially applicable to disclosure of speculative positions and to unrealized profits and losses.

21.	Greater central bank restrictions and controls may severely limit an enterprise's freedom of action and, therefore, these warrant close monitoring.

22.	An increasing number of fiscal authorities are devoting more attention to their rules and practices regarding the tax treatment of exchange gains or losses incurred by an enterprise. The implications of this cannot be ignored in assessing the desirability or otherwise of any contemplated foreign currency action.

23.	The management of foreign currency exposure and risk by senior management, especially the financial executives, but also the marketing, sales and purchasing executives, is an important area of responsibility in many enterprises. It is an aspect of management that enterprises can no longer afford to ignore as there are risks which must be addressed and opportunities which could be exploited.

EXPOSURE

Definition

24.	Foreign currency exposure is the extent to which the future cash flows *of an enterprise,* arising from *domestic* and foreign currency denominated transactions *involving* assets and liabilities, *and generating* revenues and expenses are susceptible to variations in foreign currency exchange rates. It involves the identification of existing and/or *potential* currency relationships which arise from the activities of an enterprise, *including hedging and other risk management activities.*

Types of Exposure

Translation Exposure

25. *Translation exposure* is also referred to as accounting exposure or balance sheet exposure. The restatement of foreign currency financial statements in terms of a reporting currency is termed translation. The exposure arises from the periodic need to report consolidated worldwide operations of a group in one reporting currency and to give some indication of the *financial position* of that group at those times in that currency.

26. *Translation exposure* is measured at the time of translating foreign financial statements for reporting purposes and indicates or exposes the possibility that the foreign currency denominated financial statement elements can change and give rise to further translation gains or losses, depending on the movement that takes place in the currencies concerned after the reporting date. Such translation gains and losses may well reverse in future accounting periods but do not, in themselves, represent realized cash flows unless, *and* until, the assets and liabilities are settled or liquidated in whole or in part. This type of exposure does not, therefore, require management action unless there are particular covenants, e.g., regarding gearing profiles in a loan agreement, that may be breached by the translated domestic currency position, or if management believes that translation gains or losses will materially affect the value of the business. *International Accounting Standards set out best practice.*

Transaction Exposure

27. This is also referred to as conversion exposure or cash flow exposure. It concerns the actual cash flows involved in setting transactions denominated in a foreign currency. These could include, for example:

- sales receipts
- payments for goods and services
- receipt and/or payment of dividends
- servicing loan arrangements as regards interest and capital

28. The existence of an exposure alerts one to the fact that any change in currency rates, between the time the transaction is initiated and the time it is settled, will most likely alter the originally perceived financial result of the transaction. It is, for example, important to commence monitoring the exposure from the time a foreign currency commitment becomes a possibility, not merely when an order is initiated or when delivery takes place. The financial or conversion gain or loss is the difference between the actual cash flow in the domestic currency and the cash flow as calculated at the time the transaction was initiated, i.e., the date when the transaction clearly transferred the risks and rewards of ownership. Where financing of a

transaction takes place, such as a loan obligation, there are also gains/losses which may result.

Economic Exposure

29. *Economic exposure* or operational exposure moves outside of the accounting context and has to do with the strategic evaluation of foreign transactions and relationships. It concerns the implications of any changes in future cash flows which may arise on particular transactions of an enterprise because of changes in exchange rates, or on its operating position within its chosen markets. Its determination requires an understanding of the structure of the markets in which an enterprise and its competitors obtain capital, labour, materials, services and customers. Identification of this exposure focuses attention on that component of an enterprise's value that is dependent on or vulnerable to future exchange rate movements. This has bearing on a corporation's commitment, competitiveness and viability in its involvement in both foreign and domestic markets. Thus, economic exposure refers to the possibility that the value of the enterprise, defined as the net present value of future after tax cash flows, will change when exchange rates change.

30. *Economic exposure* will almost certainly be many times more significant than either transaction or translation exposure for the long term well-being of the enterprise. By its very nature, it is subjective and variable, due *in part* to the need to estimate future cash flows in foreign currencies. The enterprise needs to plan its strategy, and to make operational decisions in the best way possible, to optimize its position in anticipation of changes in economic conditions.

Identification of Exposure

31. The three types of exposure mentioned earlier require to be identified, classified and collated in terms of the foreign currencies involved and their related time frame. This is crucial for management reporting within an enterprise. At no time should the enterprise lose sight of the overall position in the process of managing any one particular type of exposure.

32. The detail to be assembled, and the frequency at which it is done, should be directly related to the size and significance of the exposures in relation to the enterprise as a whole, or to any particular sub-activity or area of operation.

33. In essence, the overall position must first be determined by way of a set of exposure reports, containing information on each form of currency exposure to which the corporation is subject. In the case of translation and transaction exposure, the normal format for such statements (see Appendices 3 and 4 to this Statement respectively for examples) is to distinguish the local currency items which together constitute the final translated numbers. The format can be adapted to show changes from the date a transaction is first initiated to the date on which it will be concluded - the selection of the time period of measurement is totally flexible.

34. The balance sheet should address the closing (future) position on two bases:

- assuming no change in the actual opening (present) exchange translation rates

- applying forecasted closing rates available from the currency markets

35. From this it is possible to make an assessment of the size of the net translation exposure as well as of the possible impact which any expected exchange fluctuations would have on that position.

36. As regards the income statement, where the currencies concerned are relatively stable, it is usually adequate to utilize the average exchange rates expected over the period unless there are significant seasonal or volume imbalances. *International Accounting Standards should be followed.* Again, the nature and quantum of the exchange sensitive items can be determined.

37. *IAS 21 and national equivalents specify the accounting and external reporting methods for exchange rate effects* (see Appendix 1 to this Statement for details). *Within those standards,* consistent and informative treatment is the key to any determination being made.

38. From the foregoing information, a transactional cash flow report can be extracted (see Appendix 4 to this Statement for an example). This deals only with foreign currency receipts and payments, separates the currencies involved and identifies the applicable settlement or maturity dates.

39. A weekly/monthly/quarterly position can thus be established detailing the expected exposures to be managed, as well as any unmatched surplus or deficit positions which may require to be hedged. Where applicable, cash outflows can be matched and offset against cash inflows. An important input to this exercise will be the extent to which the maturity dates of the cash flows can be varied.

40. The net of the aforementioned outflows and inflows gives the net transaction exposure for each time period.

41. However, first consideration must be given to identifying economic exposure whose management will normally fundamentally influence the shape of future transaction and translation exposure. This is a far more sophisticated exercise which calls for detailed short and longer term analyses of optional foreign investment, borrowing and transaction decisions using simulation or modelling techniques, and/or conducting regular sensitivity analyses. Factors that would be considered include the extent to which commitments have already been made, the actions and market positions of major competitors, the flexibility to vary pricing in the market places concerned, and whether acquisitions and operations in foreign countries can be effectively financed in the currency of the country concerned. The examination of the implications of this exposure should be undertaken prior to the commitment and be subjected to regular review thereafter.

42. To the extent that it is quantifiable, economic exposure can be identified in a similar manner to transaction exposure, by focusing on the cash flows involved. The time horizon will, however, be much less specific for economic exposure and will depend on the particular circumstances of the

751

enterprise and the degree of detail and expertise available. It may help to look at how economic exposure has affected the business in the past as a starting point for assessing how it may do so in the future.

RISK

Definition

43. Foreign currency risk is the net potential gain or loss which can arise from exchange rate changes to the foreign currency exposures of an enterprise. It is a subjective concept and concerns anticipated or forecasted rate fluctuations together with the assessment of the vulnerability of an enterprise to such fluctuations. The element of uncertainty gives rise to the risk and creates an opportunity for profitable action.

44. Currency risk may be usefully classified as recurring or nonrecurring. Recurring risks may arise from the financial structure of the enterprise and are directly attributable to the exchange rate movements arising from an enterprise's currency composition. Or they may result from the enterprise's specific line of business and hence are related to an enterprise's operating activities. Nonrecurring risks result from one-off transactions and relate to transaction exposure.

45. The solutions to currency risk differ depending on whether the risk is nonrecurring or ongoing. Short-term strategies are more appropriate for nonrecurring risks, whereas ongoing risks should be dealt with using long-term strategies. An analysis of the frequency of the risk determines the appropriate method of managing that risk.

Assessment of Risk

46. The process of assessing risk is an ongoing, dynamic activity extending from the time an initial forecast is made (when the risk concerns the potential for fluctuations between the contract rate and the market rate) right up to the eventual conclusion (when the risk relates to the settlement of the transaction and the resultant variation from that originally contemplated). The existence of a net transaction or translation exposure or the contemplation of a possible net economic exposure requires the use of suitable and practical techniques to measure and evaluate the risks involved.

Forecasting

47. The environment for the assessment of exchange rates is a constantly changing one and the available sources of information vary considerably in their reliability and sophistication. Nevertheless, from such governmental and monetary authority statistics as are available, as well as from the worldwide exchange markets themselves, it is necessary to obtain the appropriate external inputs to facilitate the requirement for any internal prediction (see also paragraphs 76-80). Within each enterprise the availability of expertise will vary and this must also be recognized in any risk assessment. In some enterprises, the view adopted may be that future exchange rates cannot be

forecasted. If this is the case, forward rates reflect the market's best expectations, and these rates should be used.

Assumptions

48. It is essential to determine and record each and every assumption used in the measurement and forecasting processes and its source, in order to be quite clear as to the starting point and to be in a position to monitor, investigate, explain and quantify each and every subsequent deviation or variance that occurs.

49. The regulations, restrictions and constraints imposed by legislation or other regulatory bodies must be identified and their likely impact and evolution has to be anticipated, both as regards the situation:

- nationally
- internationally, by currency or country involved

50. The course and pattern of economic events has a crucial bearing on exchange rate trends and movements. Predictions *may be* required in the areas of:

- economic growth
- interest rates
- movement in money aggregates and reserves
- central bank actions
- governmental actions
- political perceptions
- inflations rates
- taxation rates

This applies again:

- nationally
- internationally, by country involved, as well as globally in certain instances

51. Risk is dependent on the possible degree of exchange rate fluctuations in the currencies involved. The expectations of such fluctuations in the currency markets themselves are reflected in *changes in* the premium or discount between the spot and forward exchange rates for any currency. Where the enterprise has a choice as regards the currency in which a transaction may be settled or initiated, these options should also be considered. Then, for each currency, dependent on the materiality of the currency exposure, the enterprise should forecast its expected or likely exchange rate movements:

- on a month by month basis *or as otherwise required for the cash-management cycle* for transaction exposures
- on a semi-annual or annual basis for translation exposures
- over time periods which are consistent with the particular circumstances of the enterprise for economic exposures

52. Risk analysis is concerned with the future and with predictions of exchange rates. This, by definition, involves uncertainty and it is crucial to examine many alternative scenarios and possible trade-offs for any assumptions made. It is normally advisable to assess the future on the basis of:

- optimistic assumptions
- pessimistic assumptions, or
- *most likely assumptions*

with probability ratings applied to each basis.

53. The degree of sophistication used in dealing with the variable factors will depend on the scale of the operations concerned, the significance of the risks involved, the resources available to the enterprise and the cost/benefit thereof.

Measurement

54. When attempting to measure risk, the enterprise should first look at the most likely time frame and resulting exposure position. This time frame may be *specific or variable*:

- *specific,* where the period of exposure is capable of precise identification and is not at the discretion of the enterprise
- *variable,* where the period of exposure extends over a long period of time or the dates of settlement are, to some extent at least, at the discretion of the enterprise

55. The timing of cash flows, and, therefore, the different time value of transactions, must always be clearly identified. Moving certain settlement dates could reduce the net exposure.

56. In its simplest form, the formula for calculating possible foreign exchange gains and losses is stated as: the amount of net foreign currency exposure multiplied by the expected percentage change in the exchange rate.

57. In measuring risk, the various currencies must be examined separately, and not merely aggregated. However, interrelationships between currencies must be considered in evaluating the overall risk of the enterprise. Where currency blocks have been established in which currencies move in tandem, it may be possible to offset a potential loss in one currency against a potential gain in another.

58. The measurement of risk should include a determination of the cost (actual or estimated) to close any mismatched positions in the forward market.

59. Since risks arise from many different sources and most enterprises operate within the constraints of scarce resources, it is necessary to determine the importance of the various risks being faced, to rank them as regards their impact on the enterprise and to identify the tolerance of the enterprise to any range of exchange rate movements.

60. Total exchange risk can, finally, be expressed in aggregation together with supporting sensitivity analyses and probability ratings.

MANAGEMENT OF EXPOSURE AND RISK

Introduction

61. The approach of an enterprise to the management of foreign currency exposure and risk is ultimately based on the costs and benefits of alternative strategies. Some enterprises may adopt a comprehensive system of risk management, particularly where the extent of exposure is large, or where management has a defensive attitude to risk. On the other hand, the costs of a comprehensive risk management strategy may outweigh the benefits where the extent of exposure is small, or where management chooses to adopt a speculative approach to exchange rate movements.

62. Whatever approach is adopted, it is absolutely necessary that the basic philosophy, policies, objectives and organization structure of the enterprise concerning the management of foreign currency exposure and risk are set at the highest level, formally recorded and communicated, as well as regularly reviewed and modified.

Corporate Philosophy and Policy

63. The fundamental questions to be considered include:

- What is the relationship between the policies and the philosophy of the enterprise generally and those specific to currency exposure?
- Is the enterprise able and willing to forecast exchange rates?
- How extensive is the enterprise's exchange risk?
- What is an acceptable level of foreign exchange risk?
- What is the enterprise's capacity to absorb foreign exchange losses?
- Is exposure to an exchange risk to be accepted without further management?
- Are exchange losses to be minimized, or are exchange gains to be maximized or a combination of both?
- Is the extent of any foreign exchange risk to be set or fixed at the outset of a transaction or left partly or wholly open for subsequent management?
- What are major competitors doing regarding the impact of currency fluctuations on their prices and costs and what opportunities or threats do these actions pose?
- Are the short-term effects crucial, or is it the longer-term position that is important, or are both to be given due consideration?
- Is a flexible stance to be adopted, changing as circumstances demand or are there certain "non negotiables"?
- Is currency dealing to be actively engaged in, or is management merely to be reactive to existing exposures?
- Is there any latitude to move off full cover to partial cover and how much open risk can be accepted?

- Are speculative currency transactions permitted and within what limits?
- What degree of responsibility and authority is to be delegated through the organization structure?
- Does this require an ongoing structured (proactive) or an ad hoc (reactive) but formalized approach?
- How comprehensive is the market information system?
- Are there any particular taxation implications?

Management Objectives

64. Management of foreign currency exposure and risk must always distinguish between realized and unrealized currency gains and losses and be concerned with the response required to achieve the enterprise's overall policy objectives as it concerns the following aspects:

- the maintenance of the reporting enterprise's book value of global investments in terms of accounting communication in the reporting currency. This is synonymous with managing translation exposure.
- the maintenance of exchange values on contractual receipts and payments which are denominated in foreign currencies. This is synonymous with managing transaction exposure.
- the maintenance of future foreign currency cash flows in terms of the reporting currency. This is synonymous with managing economic exposure.

65. In determining management's response, the following need to be addressed:

- The exposure management process should be proactive and should, as far as practicable, commence before the exposure is generated.
- The resources to be committed and the money which can be spent to protect a new exposure position should be explicitly agreed.
- A defensive approach should be adopted if the risk is to be minimized or eliminated.
- An active or aggressive approach should be adopted if the exposure is seen as an opportunity for gain.
- Appropriate risk/buffer ratios should be set and regularly reviewed.
- Performance measurements should be agreed at the outset.
- Disciplines, limits and constraints should be clearly defined (these require to be addressed in total terms as well as in detail by transaction, currency, dealer, etc.).
- Internal control procedures should be established to ensure adherence to the agreed policies and to minimize the dangers of fraud and unauthorized dealing or position taking.
- Regular feedback should take place between the exposure managers and, where different, the line operating managers in order to facilitate better decision making at the outset of a transaction or investment.

Organization and Responsibility

66. No single organization structure and exposure management system is appropriate to all enterprises because of their differing operating styles, management philosophies, skills, business environments, sizes and available expertise and resource. There are, however, four criteria which must be present in an effective exchange management organization structure:

- an accurate and timely flow of information;

- a centrally coordinated information system for all inputs, directives, actions and evaluations;

- full interaction between all departments and individuals participating in the management of currency exposure in the enterprise; and

- clearly defined functions, duties and levels of delegated authority and responsibility.

67. Consideration must also be given to the alternatives of:

- a centralized management approach

- a decentralized management approach

68. Since exchange exposure can result from one or a combination of financing, marketing or production decisions, there is a great potential for conflict and information flow constraints. As a result, the questions of responsibility, consultation and control assume added importance.

69. In order to minimize conflict, it is necessary to take an overall or global viewpoint and to ensure that there is close coordination between central or corporate finance management and line management or the operating side of the business. There is always potential for conflict between the management of the reporting enterprise and the management of its foreign operations, which should be avoided through speedy and comprehensive communications.

70. Appendix 2 to this Statement gives an example of a possible organizational flow chart to support an active exposure management program. It should be emphasized that this is an illustration and should be varied in order to meet the needs of a particular enterprise. Depending on the size of the enterprise and its cost constraints, certain functions may require to be allocated to external professionals.

71. The *size* of the activity *will likely influence* the extent to which decision making can be delegated. The key components of the illustration are as follows:

72. Board of directors:

- determines its fundamental philosophy towards foreign exchange risks;

- details the objectives for and constraints applicable to the risk management program;

- defines where the organizational responsibility for the program will be;

- ensures that the program is reviewed or confirmed at least annually;

- makes provisions on permissible or non-permissible tactics and techniques;
- approves the overall reporting framework; and
- reviews appropriate reports as to risk and its management.

73. Corporate currency committee:

- consists of selected members of the corporate finance department (and the treasury if there is one), such as the chief financial officer (chairman), the treasurer and exposure manager, the senior management accountant, a senior manager responsible for strategy/corporate planning, together with line operating executives in the fields of purchasing (importing) and selling/marketing (exporting) as appropriate.

Many corporations do not have a dedicated treasury, so the existence of one should not be assumed. The senior management accountant should be on the committee as currency issues are vital to costing, pricing, budgeting, investment appraisal, etc. The subject is also of major strategic concern, so a senior *manager* or strategist should be on the committee.

- considers all the available input in order to indicate the broad strategy to be adopted in managing exposure; and
- *may, in some organizations, have a remit which includes operational matters such as agreeing procedures, issuing guidance and periodically reviewing the currency management activity.*

74. Corporate finance (treasury) and/or accounting departments (as appropriate):

- establish proper channels of communication between all involved persons, and/or departments, in order to ensure that the corporate currency committee receives the correct information on which to base its decisions and that such decisions are communicated to the correct individuals for implementation;
- develop such external relationships as will improve access to pertinent information and facilitate the implementation of any action required;
- define the accounting policies to be used in recording and reporting the results of foreign currency transactions, within the constraints of applicable legislation and accounting standards;
- formulate *and maintain* the necessary information systems and the supporting analytical and operating control procedures;
- ensure it is equipped with appropriate processing hardware and software to support the information needs;
- collect and analyze data for submission to the corporate currency committee *and provide appropriate reports to the exposure manager;*
- act on the advice and directives of the corporate currency committee;
- issue the detailed day to day tactics and techniques to the exposure manager;
- provide guidelines which ensure vigorous separation of speculative from nonspeculative action and which cater for divergent risk profiles;

- set levels of authority and responsibility for dealing in currencies; and

- define and set stoploss limits and risk/buffer ratios.

75. Exposure manager:

- carries out the day to day transactions in accordance with the instructions and authorizations received from the corporate finance, treasury and/or accounting department (as appropriate);

- obtains frequent and regular market information from external banking sources; and

- *provides* corporate transactional information *to the information system.*

Tactics and Techniques

Forecasting

76. A program of active exposure management needs to have access to a considerable amount of data which requires analysis and assessment leading to recommendations for direction and action. Formal forecasts should, therefore, be prepared at least semi-annually and reviewed at least monthly, having due regard to the volatility of currency markets. Predictions are to be made not only of future rates, but also their likely movement, *volatility* and trends.

77. There are five main sources of input which assist in the forecasting process:

- the highly efficient currency markets themselves and the forward rates prevailing in these markets;

- ongoing daily contact with foreign currency dealers;

- economic and financial information from public or proprietary sources;

- external currency forecasting specialists, notably the international divisions of major banking groups; and

- journals and newsletters which concentrate on analyzing currency movements and predicting trends.

78. Depending on the resources available, some or all of these sources should be used. They, in turn, would rely on one or all of the following forecasting techniques, each having a role to play in arriving at a recommendation:

- time-series and other statistical or econometric analyses;

- opinion gathering and judgment; and

- alternative scenario and sensitivity analysis.

79. Without any forecasting activity, the scope of the exposure management function becomes unduly curtailed to little more *than* the use of simple hedging techniques or the implementation of a straightforward formal cover or uncover policy.

80. The purpose of any forecasting activity is to identify the possible/probable exchange rate fluctuation *and at the same time* to determine:

- What is acceptable as a range of variation in exposure?
- What risk exceeds the tolerance capacity or buffer limits of the enterprise?

but, at all times, there must be the realistic acceptance that forecasts do not provide certainty, but, at best, a reasoned prospect.

Management Techniques

81. Where relevant, the various techniques for managing currency exposure (which are only briefly identified in the following paragraphs) are used, subject to the approval of any exchange control authority, and subject to the availability of the particular technique in the market place. The extent to which the techniques can be employed is also dependent on their commercial practicality in particular situations, as well as on the enterprise's size and negotiating strength. Only brief definitions are given of the general and specific techniques more commonly in use, without attempting, in the space limitation of this Statement, to discuss them in any detail or their respective merits. They are included merely as useful examples.

82. Where many companies operate within an overall group of companies, whether they be subsidiaries or associates, the opportunities to apply balancing techniques between companies should always be explored at group level.

83. **Netting** — This process offsets intra-group transactions (between parent and subsidiary, or subsidiary and fellow subsidiary) in order to reduce transfer values and only reflect and account for the net balance.

84. Typically, a group of companies would modify settlement dates to select a single date for settling the net amount. Each subsidiary still retains the same currency risk, but a netting system, which offsets and manages exposures centrally, enables cover to be limited to net currency positions.

85. **Substitution** — Changing the source of raw materials, finished products, and/or markets operated in, as a reaction to, or in anticipation of, changes in currency relationships.

86. **Matching** — The action within an enterprise whereby receipts and payments or loans and investments in the same or correlated currencies are specifically matched so that only the net exposure difference on each transaction date or reporting date needs to be addressed.

87. **Leading and lagging** — A mechanism whereby a company accelerates (leads) or delays (lags) payments or receipts in anticipation of exchange rate movements. This requires an appraisal of both the exchange rates and the interest rates of both countries, since the interest earned on a local currency investment may compensate for any depreciation in that currency.

88. **Pricing policy** — This technique requires a choice to be made in advance of the currency in which the transaction is to be designated and subsequently settled, or regularly adapting and amending prices to take account of altered

exchange rates or even incorporating price adjustment/escalation clauses into the terms of the contract, whereby the currency risk is transferred away. It assumes the cooperation of the outside party (supplier or customer). For example, if customers agree, an enterprise can effect all its foreign invoicing in its local currency and thereby reduce its exposed receivables.

89. **Asset/liability management** — The process whereby equal and opposite deposits or borrowings are created in a particular currency to match payments or receipts, or liabilities and assets or, alternatively, where foreign and domestic banks accounts are denominated in appropriate currencies through which settlements can be effected. This technique may be used in the Euro currency markets or in the local market where the exposure exists. An appraisal of the exchange rates and interest rates of both countries is necessary.

90. **Hedging** — This is the general term used for the process of protecting the accountable value of foreign currency monetary assets and liabilities by anticipating future exchange rate movements. Exposure to unrealized foreign exchange (translation) losses can be reduced to nil, or to a defined or budgeted amount, by entering into forward exchange contracts or using other hedging instruments, taking due consideration of the cost/benefit relationships. It can be also achieved by "natural" hedging, for instance, whereby foreign assets are financed by foreign borrowings, both in the same currency.

91. **Forward exchange contracts** — The "classic" exposure management technique is the purchase or sale (i.e. covering) of a company's future currency commitments in the forward markets which exist in all major industrial countries. This technique is normally used for the protection of transaction exposure with a time frame of up to twelve months. It is, however, possible in some currencies to obtain longer periods of cover or to roll over cover arrangements. By using a forward exchange contract, the counterparties agree to exchange two currencies at a rate which is fixed at the time the contract is made (the forward rate), on a specified value date which is more than two business days in the future.

92. The forward rate is either higher (premium) or lower (discount) than the spot rate and the price (premium or discount) may be influenced by a number of factors, including:

- forecast inflation differentials
- interest rates in the relevant countries
- expectations of spot rate movements
- supply and demand

93. In practice, however, the forward rate is determined principally by computing the interest rate differentials between the relevant currencies.

94. **Forward/forward or forward swap** — Often the precise date for the settlement of a transaction is not known. The original forward contract, in such cases where it does not coincide with the final transaction date, needs therefore to be extended (or in some cases brought back) to the now known

settlement date. This is done by the simultaneous purchase and sale of a currency for different maturity dates, effectively cancelling the original contract and reinstating it to the new forward date.

95. A forward/forward is a swap whereby the foreign currency is bought (or sold) for one future date (say one month later) and sold (or bought) back for another future date (say three months later).

96. A forward swap (or spot against forward spot) is where a currency is bought (or sold) for the spot value date and simultaneously sold (or bought) back for a future value date. It is sometimes referred to as a currency swap.

97. **Rolling cover** — Where there exists a continuous stream of a large number of relatively low value transactions, it is more cost effective to take out one single large forward contract. This contract is renewed or "rolled forward" on maturity and the individual transactions can be accumulated on a currency advance account rather than settled on a spot basis.

98. **Currency option** — This allows the buyer the right, but not the obligation to purchase (or sell) currency at an agreed price on the expiry date (European) or within a specified option period (American). For this right, the buyer pays the seller a non-refundable premium. Normally options and futures, singly or in combination, are used as a stoploss mechanism or can be traded in and out, up to the date they expire.

99. **Currency futures contract** — Such a contract gives rise to an obligation to purchase (or sell) a standard amount of a currency at a specified price on a future standard date through an organized exchange. The buyer or seller of a futures contract is required to lodge an initial deposit (margin) with the clearing house of the exchange and this must be left in place for as long as the position is held. In addition, variation margin is received from, or paid to, the clearing house as the position held generates profits or losses through movements in market prices. Futures contracts are tradeable up to expiry date and may be used in place of forward exchange contracts.

100. **Cross-currency swaps** — The technique whereby two parties with either existing or anticipated liabilities (or assets) in different currencies agree, usually via an intermediary, to exchange (swap) their liabilities (assets) so that the first party would be servicing (receiving the cash flows from) the liability (asset) of the other party and vice versa. Cross-currency swaps may take various forms, but the conventional structures include fixed-to-fixed, floating-to-fixed and floating-to-floating interest rate swaps. By executing a cross-currency swap, a borrower may thereby alter or eliminate the exchange risk for the remaining life of the liability (asset).

101. **Risk transfer (Risk guarantee) arrangement** — To encourage exports, government agencies offer insurance in the form of accepting the currency risk inherent in receivables denominated in foreign currencies. Typically, the exporter will, for a small premium, transfer the risk of all subsequent movements in the exchange rate relative to the specific transaction.

102. **Barter trade** — Cross-border barter transactions can be a direct response to exchange rate uncertainties in that they eliminate any form of exposure by virtue of matching, in advance, corresponding financial assets/liabilities

created by the underlying movement of goods or services between two countries and arranging for them to be settled by the originators of the transactions in their country of origin.

103.   **General** — The foregoing techniques are among the most widely used but consideration should also be given to other techniques including any of the new sophisticated variations constantly being developed. It is important to consider the impact of using these techniques singly or in combination. The techniques used must relate to the nature of the combined exposures the enterprise faces. The overall question to ask is, "Do the techniques employed *adequately and appropriately* address the exposures faced by the enterprise?"

ACCOUNTING, TAXATION AND FISCAL CONTROLS

Accounting Standards and Practices

104.   The accounting treatment of foreign currency transactions and operations and the resulting exchange differences have been dealt with in International Accounting Standard 21 issued by the International Accounting Standards Committee.

105.   This standard sets forth proper methods of accounting for transactions in foreign currencies in the financial statements of an enterprise and for the translation of the financial statements of foreign operations into a single reporting currency for the purpose of including them in the consolidated financial statements of the reporting enterprise. Accordingly, it warrants close study and consideration.

106.   Considerable progress has been made in harmonizing the different provisions in the various national accounting standards in *International Accounting Standards (see IAS 21 and the forthcoming IAS 32 on financial instruments).* However, as regards the accounting treatment of foreign currency transactions and operations and the resulting exchange differences, some significant points of difference still remain:

- whether the income statement should be converted at the closing rate or the average rate;
- what treatment is appropriate for translating currencies in highly inflationary economies;
- the treatment of equity investments especially when financed by borrowings;
- in what circumstances the temporal method or the current rate method of translation is appropriate;
- the treatment of foreign exchange reserves on the disposal of an investment which has already given rise to such reserves;
- the treatment of forward exchange contracts;
- the treatment of exchange differences arising from the effect of currency fluctuations on long-term loans;
- the treatment of deferred taxation balances;

- the merits of dealing with highly uncertain and unstable country situations on a cash received basis only and without recognizing any ongoing value;
- the treatment of speculative transactions;
- the treatment of hedge instruments; and
- the treatment of gains and losses on hedge transactions, general or specific.

107.   Consequently, a diversity of practices still exists around the world. It is, in fact, not possible to generalize about the prevailing practices in the various countries. It is, therefore, imperative for the purposes of reporting on foreign currency transactions, translations and gains and losses, that the applicable standards or practices are clearly and explicitly identified and the relevant accounting policies noted in the annual financial statements. It would be appropriate to comply with the International Accounting Standards *as well as with the applicable national standards, except where national and international standards require materially different measures.*

Taxation Considerations

108.   Gains or losses on foreign currency transactions receive widely different tax treatment from one country to another. This diversity in itself presents opportunities for an enterprise to optimize the after-tax cost of its multinational dealings. It is possible, therefore, to institute parallel tax strategies which would operate alongside the foreign currency management activity. Benefit can then be obtained in a planned and proper manner from the lack of symmetry in the tax laws of various countries.

109.   The essential questions to be addressed when dealing with taxation authorities are generally:

- the need to disclose material effects;
- the source of the gain or loss, either actual or deemed;
- whether the translation giving rise to the gain or loss is of a capital or revenue nature;
- the inclusion of the gain or loss as forming part of the underlying transaction or the separation of the gain or loss for special treatment; and
- the extent to which the gain or loss is considered realized.

110.   It must be remembered, however, that the rates of taxation vary between countries and, sometimes, between categories of taxation within a particular country. Also, the pace of change in the various tax regulations adds further complication and risk.

Foreign Exchange Controls

111.   Ultimately, the value of a currency depends on its supply and demand equation. A free market will always find an equilibrium value which balances out the forces of supply and demand. However, dramatic fluctuations in this value can be regarded as particularly harmful to national interests. Governments, often unwillingly, are forced to intervene, in one form or

another, in attempts to alter the free market value and to influence the exchange rate of their currency.

112. It is comparatively rare to find simple and concise exchange control regulations outside of the major developed Western nations and, accordingly, an enterprise has to be equipped with expert knowledge of the complexities of the rules applied in the countries with which it is involved, as well as to be sure that it receives speedy communication regarding any changes.

113. Again, within these complexities, foreign currency management can seek to obtain advantage by directing transactions into currencies or countries where the exchange control regulations are more favourable.

CONCLUSION

114. As referred to in the Preface, this Statement of recommended practice is intended to provide a basic framework to senior management. The specific practices are, however, continuously evolving and, accordingly, further reading and interface with experts in the field of foreign exchange dealings are absolutely essential.

115. In the final analysis, foreign currency risk management seeks to identify and manage risk, not create risk. This can only be tackled with commitment from the chief executive of an enterprise downwards and with appropriate professionalism.

MANAGEMENT ACCOUNTING

Translation Accounting Conventions

The principal alternative methods of translating foreign currency financial statements to domestic financial statements are briefly explained below. Each of these methods will produce a different reported amount of gain or loss.

The Current, Closing Rate or Net Investment Method

The Current Rate Method translates all assets, liabilities, revenues and expenses at the current rate of exchange. Under this method, a devaluation of the foreign currency results in a translation loss; a revaluation results in a translation gain. The occurrence of the translation gain (or loss) is recognized in the period in which the exchange rate changes, usually through reserves.

The rationale for this method is the maintenance of the operating relationships and income statement ratios intact throughout the translation process. However, this method often leads to substantial variations in valuations that may reverse over time. The methods which follow are, therefore, derivatives which seek to address the substantial variations regarded by many people as inconsistent with the going concern concept.

The Temporal Method

Using this method, fixed assets, long-term investments, inventories and short-term investments valued at cost, are translated at the historical rates prevailing when the assets were acquired. All monetary assets and liabilities are translated at foreign exchange rates ruling at the current reporting date. Revenues and expenses are translated at rates ruling at the time of their occurrence.

The rationale for this method is that the translation is treated simply as a measurement conversion process and that, as opposed to transactional items, this process should not change the characteristics of the items being measured. The amount of an item is determined at a given point in time by the foreign exchange rate for the currencies at that time. If the historical rate is used, the temporal characteristics of the item being measured can be retained.

This method is regarded as flawed by some in that it fails to address fluctuations arising from long-term liabilities which may be linked to long-term assets. The translation at current rates of inventories and short-term investments valued at net realizable value is inconsistent with the monetary characteristics of the assets. However, this method is considered suitable for self-sustaining foreign operations.

The Current/Non-current Method

This method translates the current assets and current liabilities of the foreign operation at the current exchange rate. The non-current assets and non-current liabilities of the foreign operation are translated at the foreign exchange rates that were in effect when the assets and liabilities were acquired or incurred in the foreign operation's records. Revenue and expense items relating to current assets and liabilities are translated using the average exchange rate computed for the time period being reported. Other items (for example, depreciation) are translated at the rate that corresponds to the particular non-current asset or liability on the balance sheet. If the foreign operation is in a positive net working capital position, the parent will incur a translation gain from a foreign currency revaluation and a loss from a devaluation. Contrary effects occur if the foreign operation is in a negative working capital position.

The rationale for this method is to recognize the time frame of assets and liabilities rather than their monetary characteristics. However, this method can lead to problems when long-term assets and/or liabilities are liquidated or settled.

The Monetary/Non-Monetary Method

Monetary assets and liabilities are translated at the current rate, while non-monetary assets and liabilities are translated at the rate ruling at the time they were acquired or incurred. There are two variants of these procedures.

In the first method, for inventories that are valued at cost, the historical rate is used, and for other current items carried at net realizable value, the current rate is used. The rationale for this approach is to focus on the monetary/non-monetary characteristics of the assets and differs from the temporal method only in that inventory is always converted at the historical rate, while investments are always converted at the current rate.

The second variant translates all assets and liabilities using the monetary/non-monetary approach, except long-term debt, which is translated at the historical exchange rate. Revenue and expense items relating to non-monetary assets or liabilities are translated at the same rates as the corresponding balance sheet items. A positive net monetary position results in a gain in a revaluation and a loss in a devaluation. The opposite occurs with a negative net monetary position. The rationale for this approach is to recognize the linkage that can exist between long-term assets and long-term liabilities. It seeks to eliminate distortions arising in such circumstances by using varying exchange rates for such items.

The Combination Method

This method simply translates all revenue and expense items at the average exchange rate computed for the time period being reported and all balance sheet items at the closing rate ruling at the end of that time period.

Neither the time frame differences of assets or liabilities nor their different monetary characteristics are recognized under this method. Nevertheless, wide support exists for the "broad bush" effect of this method and for its very simplicity.

Example of an Organizational Flowchart Which Would Support an Active Exposure Management Program

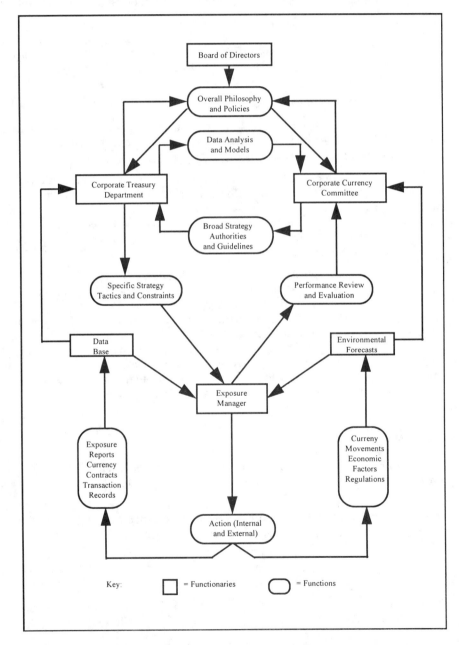

Example of a Translation Exposure Report

Appendices 3A and 3B are formats for estimating income statement and balance sheet translation exposure respectively. A separate statement would need to be produced for each foreign subsidiary and a consolidated statement for foreign subsidiaries as a whole. Totals for Income Statement and Balance Sheet items are entered in the first column in local currency. The figures in the first column are multiplied by the budgeted conversion rate entered in column two and the resulting sum, the budgeted parent currency amount, is entered in column three. The forecast end of period or average rates are entered in column four. These are then multiplied by the local currency amount in column one to produce a forecast parent currency amount. The difference between the budgeted parent currency amounts and the forecast parent currency amount is the variance in total exposure from budget. The net income in the total exposure column is the net exposed position. The net uncovered position is the net exposed position less the amount covered.

Exposure Report Example
Format for an Income Statement Exposure Forecast
Items Translated at Current or Average Exchange Rate

Income Statement Category	Local Currency (Amount)	Budgeted Conversion Rate	Budgeted Parent Currency Amount	Forecast End Period/Average Conversion Rate	Forecast Parent Currency Amount	Total Exposure
	1	2	1 x 2 = 3	4	1 x 4 = 5	3 – 5
Revenues (By Category)						
Less Cost of Sales (By Category)						
Gross Profit		–		–		
Less Expenses (by Category)						
Expenses Before Interest and Tax		–		–		
Interest Earnings Before Tax						
Net Income		–		–		

Net Exposed Position

Net Covered Position

Net Uncovered Position

Exposure Report Example
Format for a Balance Sheet Exposure Forecast
Items Translated at Current or Historic Exchange Rate

Balance Sheet Account	Local Currency (Amount)	Budgeted Conversion Rate	Budgeted Parent Currency Amount	Forecast End Period/Historic Conversion Rate	Forecast Parent Currency Amount	Total Exposure
	1	2	1 x 2 = 3	4	1 x 4 = 5	3 – 5
Current Assets (By Category)						
Fixed Assets (By Category)						
Total Assets		–		–		
Current Liabilities (By Category)						
Long-Term Liabilities (By Category)						
Total Liabilities Share Holder Funding (By Category)						
Total Equity						
Total Liabilities and Equity		–		–		

Net Exposed Assets/ Liabilities

Net Covered Assets/ Liabilities

Uncovered Net Position

Example of a Transactional Cash Flow Report

Appendix 4 is for calculating transaction exposure. A separate statement would need to be produced for each foreign subsidiary and also for the parent company and a consolidated statement would have to be produced for the group as a whole. Using the agreed dates for payment of already contracted transactions, foreign currency denominated receipts and payments for transactions already entered into are listed currency by currency in the rows marked receipts and payments. Contracted for payments are then deducted from contracted for receipts for each currency to give contracted for net receipts for each currency. The amount of forward cover for each currency, either foreign currency purchased or sold at current rates is then entered in the forward cover rows. The amount of net forward cover for each currency is calculated by deducting from the forward cover receipts the forward cover payments. The unmatched surplus/deficit for each currency is the net receipts or payments for a currency less the net forward cover for that currency. The total column sums the position for the total number of weeks, months, quarters, etc., analyzed.

Example of a Transactional Cash Flow Report
Transactional Cash Flow Exposure Forecast

	WEEKS, MONTHS OR QUARTERS (Detail in separate columns)	TOTAL
RECEIPTS (By Currency)		
PAYMENTS (By Currency)		
NET RECEIPTS/(PAYMENTS) (By Currency)		
FORWARD COVER – Receipts (By Currency) – Payments (By Currency)		
NET FORWARD COVER (By Currency)		
UNMATCHED SURPLUS/DEFICIT (By Currency)		

MANAGEMENT
ACCOUNTING

Example of an Economic Exposure
Cash Flow Forecast

Although transaction and translation exposure can be formatted relatively straightforwardly on a single document, economic exposure is best analyzed using a spreadsheet. This can be done by setting out the impact which a range of possible exchange rates are calculated to have on the expected pattern of future cash flows of a business when these are estimated using expected future exchange rates. (Exchange rates relevant to the business are the exchange rates of markets in which the business, its suppliers, its customers and its competitors operate).

The exercise carried out is one which summarizes the cash flow impact on **different** aspects of the operations of a business which result when different exchange rates scenarios are used. The exercise will need to be repeated for different possible exchange rate scenarios as a series of "what ifs". Since a number of currencies may be relevant and the rate of exchange between different currencies can vary continuously into the future, only a manageable number of likely scenarios can sensibly be analyzed.

The analysis is conducted by listing the changes in cash flow expected as a result of the impact on the different aspects of the business listed, of the exchange rate scenario predicated on the current exchange rate or exchange rate scenario budgeted, if different from the current exchange rate.

Economic Exposure Report Example
Economic Exposure Cash Flow Forecast

Impact of the following **potential events** on forecast cash flow at expected exchange rates if exchange rates change:	MONTHS/QUARTERS/YEARS (details in separate columns) Increase in cash inflow and reduction in outflow (+) Reduction in cash inflow and increase in outflow (−)
Price changes of important inputs: 1) priced in local currency 2) priced in foreign currency	
Indirect impact due to currency exposure of those in the supply chain of direct suppliers.	
Impact on long-term contracts with present price structures.	
Impact on pre-contractual foreign currency quotation and price lists.	
Change in customer demand due to currency induced price changes.	
Change in margin on sales priced in foreign currency.	
Market share lost to or gained from competitors with different currency exposure in sales and/or costs.	
Indirect impact due to currency exposure of those further down the supply chain who are supplied by direct customers.	
Total change in cash flow per period:	

Source: British Corporate Currency Exposure and Foreign Exchange Risk Management, D. J. Edelshain, PhD Thesis, London Business School

Glossary Of Terms

American Option	An option, wherever written, which may be exercised on any business day within the option period.
Arbitrage	Arbitrage is that activity which attempts to take advantage of temporary rate discrepancies between different foreign exchange markets. Arbitrageurs buy in the low cost market and sell in the high cost, thereby forcing spot and forward rates in the different markets towards a common price.
At-the-money	An option with an exercise price equal to or near the current spot price.
Band	Maximum permitted range of fluctuation of a given currency against a reference currency according to the existing international agreement.
Bid or Bid Rate	The rate of exchange at which a foreign exchange dealer will buy a currency.
Bilateral Netting	The process whereby two affiliated companies regularly offset their receipts and payments with each other, so that a single net intercompany receipt or payment is made between the two in each period. (This can also be extended to a multilateral process).
Blocked Account	The bank account of a non-resident of a country, where the amount of currency in the account cannot be transferred to another country or currency without special permission.
Broken Date, Odd Date	Interbank dealing is usually for fixed periods of 1, 2, 3, 6 or 12 months as standard periods. Any other value date (such as 4 months 6 days) is a broken or odd date. Broken date quotes interpolate between available fixed date prices.
Broker	An intermediary who arranges the buying or selling of currencies between third parties, usually banks. He does not buy or sell currency on his own account.
Brokerage	Commission charged by a broker for his services.
Business Day	Any day on which a foreign exchange contract can be settled, i.e., the banks at both ends of the deal must be open for business that day.
Buyer's Option	The owner of a buyer's option can take delivery of the currency contract at any time between the dates specified in the option.

Buyer's Rate	The rate at which the bank buys the quoted currency.
Cable	The spot exchange rate between the U.S. dollar and sterling.
Call Option	Confers on the holder the right to buy a specified currency.
Closing Exchange Rate	The exchange rate prevailing at a financial reporting date.
Confirmation	This is the written document confirming the verbal foreign exchange contract agreed by telephone between dealer and dealer or dealer and client.
Convertible Currency	A currency having a reasonably adequate international market through which it may be readily converted into any other currency.
Counterparty	A principal in a foreign exchange deal.
Countervalue	The equivalent currency obtained. For example, in a foreign exchange deal, if a principal buys DM500,000 against dollars at a rate of say 1.80, the countervalue would be $277,777.78
Covered Interest Arbitrage	This refers to borrowing in one currency, converting the proceeds into another currency in which it is invested and simultaneously selling this other currency forward against the initial currency. Covered interest arbitrage takes advantage of — and in practice quickly eliminates — any temporary discrepancies between the forward rate and the interest rate differential of the two currencies.
Covering	Protecting the value of the future proceeds of any international transaction, usually by buying or selling the proceeds in the forward market.
Cross Rate	The rate of exchange between two foreign currencies. For example, when a dealer in New York buys (or sells) Italian lira for French francs, he uses a cross rate.
Deal	A single transaction in foreign exchange. A customer calling his bank and effecting forward cover for a series of four payments due under a commercial contract, will do four "deals", one for each date.
Dealer	Specialist in a bank, financial institution or enterprise who is authorized to effect exchange transactions. The dealer usually attempts to keep his book in balance but may be allowed to take up a position in his own right.

Deposit Margin	A deposit made to the clearing house on establishing a futures or options position. This can either be an initial margin (a fixed amount per contract, deposited when a position is opened) or a variation margin (being the daily calculation of the unrealized profit or loss on the contract).
Depth of Market	Extent to which transactions may easily be placed in the market without causing disturbances to the rate.
ECU	European Currency Unit.
Eurocurrency	Currency held by non-residents and placed on deposit with banks outside the country of the currency; e.g., U.S. dollars owned by a Middle East country and deposited in London.
Eurodollars	U.S. dollars deposited outside the United States being held by one who is not a resident of the United States. These are mostly deposited in Western Europe.
European Option	An option, wherever written, which can only be exercised on the expiry date.
Exchange Control	Country regulations restricting or forbidding certain types of foreign currency transactions by nationals.
Exchange Contract	A contract to exchange one foreign currency for a given amount of another on a given date.
Exercise (or Strike) Price	The agreed price at which a currency can be bought or sold under an option contract.
Exotic Currencies, Exotics	Currencies not having a developed and international market, and which are, therefore, infrequently traded.
Fixed Dates	Forward dates for which market prices are readily available (usually in whole months).
Fixed Exchange Rate	The monetary authority of a country agrees to keep the value of its currency within a given percentage of the fixed value of certain other currencies.
Fixed Rate Currency	Currency having a fixed rate of exchange within narrow limits versus another reference currency, usually the dollar, sterling or the French franc.
Floating Exchange Rate	The exchange rate of a currency is allowed to find its own level depending on the supply of and demand for the currency.
Floating Rate Currency	Currency having its exchange rate determined by market forces including central bank intervention, but having no limits to its fluctuation relative to any reference currency.

Foreign Exchange Deal	A contract to exchange one currency for another at an agreed price for settlement on an agreed date.
Forex	Foreign exchange.
Forward Book	The net position arising from all forward transactions in a given currency.
Forward Contract	A contract to exchange a given amount of one currency for another at some future date (usually at one, three or six months ahead).
Forward/Forward Deal	Simultaneous purchase and sale of one currency for different forward value dates or simultaneous deposit and loan of one currency for different maturity dates, which effectively provides a deposit to commence on a future date.
Forward/Forward Swap	A pair of forward exchange deals involving forward (or Forward Swap) purchase and a forward sale of a currency, simultaneously entered into, but of different maturities.
Forward Margin	The difference between the forward rate and the spot rate of a currency. The forward margin is either at a discount or a premium to the spot rate.
Forward Market	The future market in foreign exchange.
Forward Premium	The excess of the forward rate over the spot rate.
Full Cover	An exposure is fully covered if the value of the future proceeds of any international transaction is fully protected against exchange rate fluctuations.
Group of Seven (G-7)	An informal group established in 1985, consisting of finance ministers from the United States of America, Japan, Germany, the United Kingdom, France, Italy and Canada. The main intentions of the group are to stabilize exchange rates and interest differentials and to reduce distortions in trade balances by ensuring that policy decisions and actions are coordinated.
Hedge	Action taken by a company to reduce or eliminate a currency exposure.
Hedging	The protection of the accounting value of foreign currency assets and liabilities against unrealized foreign exchange (translation) losses.
IMM	International Money Market.
In-the-money	An option which has a more favourable rate for the holder of the option than the current spot price.

MANAGEMENT ACCOUNTING

Indirect Quote	A quotation in which the local currency is the base currency.
Intervention	Action taken by a central bank to influence the rate of exchange of its currency in the market.
LIFFE	London International Financial Futures Exchange.
Leading and Lagging	The adjustment of credit terms, "leading" meaning a prepayment of an obligation and "lagging" a delayed payment. The converse applies to receipts.
LIBOR	London Interbank Offered Rate. The rate at which principal London banks offer to lend currency (especially dollars) to one another at a given instant. Often used as a base rate for fixing interest rate on bank loans: i.e., "Interest to be fixed at 1 1/4% per annum over LIBOR".
"Long" Exposure	A net asset, net revenue and/or net cash inflow position in a currency. If the currency appreciates, a foreign exchange gain is generated. If it depreciates, a loss is incurred. The opposite is true of a "short" position.
Mandate	Formal authority from a customer to its banker specifying what shall constitute proper instruction for the bank to act on the customer's behalf.
Matching (or "Natural" Matching)	A process whereby an enterprise matches its long positions in a given currency (assets, revenues or cash inflow) with its offsetting short positions in that currency (liabilities, expenses or cash outflows). The remaining unmatched position is the net exposure in the currency.
Maturity (or Settlement) Date	The date on which a foreign exchange contract is due to be settled.
Middle Price	An average of the buying and the selling price for a given currency.
Netting	Practice of dealing only for net amounts in a currency where an enterprise has a two way cash flow. For example, if an enterprise has an inflow of $5 million and an outflow of $2 million in a given period, the enterprise could "net" and deal only for $3 million.
Odd Date	Most contracts on the forward market are settled one, three or six months ahead. Dates outside these standard periods are called "odd" dates.
Offer Rate	The rate of exchange at which a foreign exchange dealer will sell a currency.
Open (or Net Position)	The difference between the long and short positions in a given currency.

Optional Date Forward Contract (or Forward Option Contract)	A forward exchange contract where the rate is fixed but the maturity is left for the enterprise to decide subsequently, within a specified range of dates.
Out-of-the-money	An option which has a less favourable rate for the holder of the option than the current spot price.
"Parallel" Matching	A long (or short) position in one currency is matched against a short (or long) position in a different currency, since movements in the two currencies are expected to run closely parallel.
Parent Country	The country in which the parent enterprise is located.
Parent (or Home) Currency	The currency of the parent enterprise.
Parity	The official rate of exchange between two currencies.
Partial Cover	An exposure is partially covered if the value of future proceeds of any international transaction is only partially protected against exchange rate fluctuations, leaving some degree of the exposure still uncovered.
Pip	Usually the most junior digit in a currency quotation: e.g., (£)1 = \$2.10364. The fifth place after the decimal point is "4 pips".
Point	The second most junior digit in currency quotations (e.g., (£)1 = \$2.10364, when the fourth place after the decimal point is "6 points").
Premium	Difference between spot price and the price for forward settlement. Forward price equals the spot price less the premium.
Put Option	Confers on the holder the right to sell a specified currency.
Rollover	The extension of a maturing forward contract or the extension of a maturing loan: i.e., a new interest determination date. Medium term Euro-currency loans are often arranged "for a period of five years with a rollover every six months".
Selling Rate	The rate at which the bank sells the quoted currency.
Settlement	Payment of funds on the maturity of a foreign exchange contract.
"Short" Position	An oversold position where the liabilities in the currency exceed the assets in that same currency.
"Spot Forward" Swaps	The simultaneous spot purchase or sale of a currency and an offsetting sale or purchase of the same currency in the forward market.

Spot Deal	A deal for currency for delivery two business days from today.
Spot Market	The currency market for "immediate" delivery. Delivery is usually two working days after transaction date, though in some markets spot transactions may be executed for next day value.
Spot Next	A deal from the spot date until the next day, either as a deposit or a swap.
Spot Rate	The current rate of exchange quoted between two currencies. The spot rate is usually quoted as a bid rate and an offer rate.
Spot Transaction	A purchase or sale of foreign currency for "immediate" delivery.
Spread	The difference between the buying and selling rate for a currency.
Stoploss Mechanism	A mechanism whereby orders are placed in the market to purchase or sell a particular amount of a currency if a specified price level is reached, which may be either above or below the price that prevailed when the order was given. This provides protection against the degree of adverse fluctuation that may occur in a currency.
Swap Deal	A simultaneous spot sale and a forward purchase, or a simultaneous spot purchase and a forward sale.
Thin Market	A low turnover market, where an attempt to do a substantial transaction will result in a definite movement in the market rate. Spreads are wide in a thin market as dealers are apprehensive as to the rate at which they will be able to lay off any deal done.
Tom Next	Short for "from tomorrow to the next day". A deal from the next business day until the one after, either as a deposit or a swap. Note that on Friday "tom next" is from Monday to Tuesday
Transaction Date	In the foreign exchange market, the date on which a foreign exchange contract is agreed.
Value Date (or For Value)	The date agreed for settlement of an exchange transaction.

4

October 1991

Management Control of Projects

MANAGEMENT
ACCOUNTING

CONTENTS

	Paragraphs
INTRODUCTION	1
SECTION 1 — NATURE OF PROJECTS	2-5
SECTION 2 — THE CONTROL ENVIRONMENT	6-25
Project Organization Structure	6-7
Evolution of Organization Structure	8
Contractual Relationships	9-10
Fixed-Price Contracts	11-12
Cost-Reimbursement Contracts	13
Analysis of Fixed-Price Contracts and Cost-Reimbursement Contracts	14-19
Information Structure	20
Work Packages	21-23
Indirect Cost Accounts	24-25
SECTION 3 — PROJECT PLANNING	26-32
Nature of the Project Plan	29-30
Preparing the Control Budget	31-32
SECTION 4 — PROJECT EXECUTION	33-53
Nature of Reports	36-37
Quantity of Reports	38
Incomplete Work Packages	39

Summarizing Progress 40

Use of Reports 41-44

Trouble Reports 41

Progress Reports 42-44

Cost to Complete 45-46

Informal Sources of Information 47-48

Revisions 49-52

Project Auditing 53

SECTION 5 — PROJECT EVALUATION 54-60

Evaluation of Project Control 55-60

SECTION 6 — IMPLEMENTATION 61-62

Introduction

1. This Statement describes the management control of projects, as contrasted with the management control of ongoing operations. As used here, a project is a set of activities intended to accomplish a specified end result of sufficient importance to be of interest to management. Projects include construction projects, production of a sizable unique product (such as a turbine), rearranging a plant, developing and marketing a new product, consulting engagements, audits, acquisitions and divestments, litigation, financial restructuring, research & development work, development and installation of information systems, and many others.

Section 1 — Nature of Projects

2. Project control begins when management has approved the general nature of what is to be done and has authorized the approximate amount of resources that are to be spent in doing this work. The project ends when its objective has been accomplished or if it has been abandoned. An important difference between a project and ongoing operations is that a project team usually is disbanded when the product is produced, whereas in ongoing operations, the organization tends to operate indefinitely. The construction of a building and the renovation of a building are projects; the routine maintenance of the building is not. The production of a motion picture is a project; the production of a daily television program is an ongoing operation.

3. The completion of a project may lead to an ongoing operation, as in the case of a successful development project. The transition from the project organization to the operating organization involves complex management control issues.

4. Projects vary greatly. At one extreme, a project may involve one or a few persons working for a few days or weeks, performing work similar to that done many times previously, as on an annual financial audit that is conducted by a public accounting firm. At the other extreme, a project may involve thousands of people working for several years, performing work unlike anything ever done before, as was the case with the project to land the first men on the moon. This Statement is limited to projects that involve enough people so that a formal project organization is necessary and enough resources so that a formal management control system is necessary.

5. The function of the management accountant is fundamental to the management control of projects. It is to provide timely and reliable information and assistance to management as a basis for planning and controlling decisions by:

    a) developing, installing, and operating the systems used to collect and report this information;

    b) ensuring that this information conforms to the rules prescribed in these systems; and

c) assisting management in using this information in planning and controlling the project.

Section 2 — The Control Environment

Project Organization Structure

6. A project organization is a temporary organization. A team is assembled for conducting the project, and the team is disbanded when the project has been completed. Team members may be employees of the organization that authorized the project (the sponsoring organization), they may be hired for the purpose, or some or all of them may be engaged under a contract with an outside organization. The sponsor may be a single organization, or the project may be a joint venture sponsored by several organizations.

7. If the project is conducted entirely, or partly, by an outside contractor, the sponsoring organization should ensure that there is a proper management system in place to deal with tenders and that the best tender is accepted. The sponsoring organization should designate someone to act as liaison with the project, and that person should quickly establish satisfactory working arrangements with the contractor's personnel. These arrangements are influenced by the terms of the contract, as will be discussed below. If the project is conducted by the sponsoring organization, some of the work may be assigned to support units within the organization, and similar relationships should be established with them. For example, a central drafting unit in an architectural firm may do drafting for all projects, and management control problems of such arrangements are similar to those involved in contracting with an outside drafting organization.

Evolution of Organization Structure

8. Different types of management personnel and management methods may be required as the project evolves.

   a) The planning phase emphasizes the skills of architects, engineers, and management accountants.

   b) The execution of the project will often require the input of production managers and trouble-shooters.

   c) As the project matures, the principal test will be to obtain approval of the sponsor; marketing skills will often predominate (especially in consulting projects).

The management accountant should be able to make a significant contribution throughout the planning, execution, and commissioning of a project.

Contractual Relationships

9. If the project is conducted by an outside contractor, an additional level of project control is created; in addition to the control exercised by the

786

contractor who does the work, the sponsoring organization has its own control responsibilities. The contractor may bring its control system to the project, and this system may need to be adapted to provide the information that the sponsor needs; it is essential that a consistent set of data be used by the sponsor and the contractor. The sponsor reserves the right to revise the scope or schedule of the project under certain circumstances, and may put pressure on the contractor to improve performance. The sponsor's management control system, therefore, should identify the need for changes in the project, document the specifics of changes that have been agreed to, and facilitate the implementation of these changes. (This does not mean that there should be two separate systems; a summary of information collected by the contractor becomes a part of the sponsor's system).

10. The form of the contractual arrangement has an important impact on management control. Contracts are of two general types: fixed-price and cost-reimbursement, with many variations within each type.

Fixed-Price Contracts

11. In a fixed-price contract, the contractor agrees to complete the specified work by a specified date at a specified price. Usually, there are penalties if the work is not completed to specifications or if the scheduled date is not met. It would appear, therefore, that the contractor assumes all the risks and, consequently, has all the responsibility for management control; however, this is by no means the case. If the sponsor decides to change the scope of the project or if the contractor encounters conditions not contemplated by the contractual agreement, a change order (also known as a "variation order" or "contract modification") is issued. The parties must agree on the scope, schedule and cost implications of each change order. To the extent that change orders involve increased costs, these costs are borne by the sponsor. On some complex fixed-price projects, there are thousands of these change orders. In these circumstances, the final price of the work is in fact not fixed in advance. Thus, the sponsor ultimately is responsible for the project.

12. In a fixed-priced contract, the sponsor is responsible for auditing the quality and quantity of the work to ensure that it is done as specified. This may be as comprehensive a task as auditing the cost of work under a cost-reimbursement contract.

Cost-Reimbursement Contracts

13. In a cost-reimbursement contract, the sponsor agrees to pay reasonable costs plus a profit; therefore the sponsor has considerable responsibility for the control of costs. In these circumstances, the sponsor needs a management control system and associated control personnel used by a contractor with a fixed-price contract. A cost-reimbursement contract is appropriate when the scope, schedule, and cost of the project cannot be reliably estimated in advance.

Analysis of Fixed-Price Contracts and Cost-Reimbursement Contracts

14. The price for a fixed-price contract is bid by, or at least proposed by, the contractor. In arriving at this price, a competent contractor includes, *in addition to a profit component*, an allowance for contingencies; the size of this allowance varies with the degree of uncertainty. Thus, for a project with considerable uncertainty and a correspondingly large contingency allowance, the sponsor may end up paying more under a fixed-price contract than under a cost-reimbursement contract in which there is no such contingency allowance. This extra payment is the contractor's reward for the assumption of risk.

15. Fixed-price contracts are appropriate when the scope of the project can be closely specified in advance and when uncertainties are low. In these circumstances, the contractor cannot significantly increase the price by negotiating change orders and is therefore motivated to control costs. If the contractor signs a contract that does not include adequate provisions for adjustments caused by changes in scope or by uncontrollable uncertainties, it will resist the sponsor's requests to make desirable changes and in the extreme case may be unwilling to complete the project. If the contractor "walks away from the project," no one gains; the sponsor doesn't get the product, the contractor doesn't get paid, and both parties may incur legal costs.

16. In a cost-reimbursement contract, the profit component, or fee, usually should be a fixed monetary amount; if it is a percentage of costs, the contractor is motivated to make the costs high and thereby increase its profit. However, the fixed fee is normally adjusted if the scope or schedule of the project is significantly changed. Moreover, many cost-reimbursement contracts have a "not to exceed" upper limit, and this too may be adjusted.

17. There are many variations within these two general types of contracts. For example, in an incentive contract, completion dates and/or cost targets are defined in advance, and the contractor is rewarded for completing the project earlier than the target date or for incurring less than the target cost. This reward is in the form of a completion bonus that is set at an amount per unit of time saved, and/or a cost bonus that is set as a percentage of the costs saved. Such a contract would appear to overcome the inherent weakness of a cost-reimbursement contract, which has no such rewards. However, if the targets are unrealistic, the incentive may be nonexistent. Thus, an incentive contract is a middle ground; it is appropriate when moderately reliable estimates of completion and cost can be made.

18. Different contract types may be used for different activities on the project. For example, direct costs may be reimbursed under a cost-reimbursement contract because of the high degree of uncertainty, while the contractor's overhead costs may be covered by a fixed-price contract, either for the total project or for each month. A fixed-price contract for overhead motivates the contractor to control these costs; avoids the necessity of checking on the reasonableness of individual salary rates, fringe benefits, bonuses, and other amenities; reduces the contractor's tendency to load the overhead payroll with less qualified personnel, and encourages the contractor to complete the

work as soon as possible so that supervisory personnel will be freed for other projects. However, such a contract may also motivate the contractor to skimp on supervisory personnel, a good control system, and other resources that help get the project completed in the most efficient manner.

19. If unit costs can be estimated reasonably well, but the quantity of work is uncertain, the contract may be for a fixed price per unit applied to the actual number of units provided. An example is an extractive contract with payment made at a specified price per unit of output.

Information Structure

20. In a project control system, information is structured by the elements of the project. For the project as a whole and for each of its elements, information is collected in three categories:

a)   its scope, or specifications for the end product;

b)   its schedule, or the time required; and

c)   its cost.

Work Packages

21. The smallest units of the project with which these elements are associated are called work packages, and the way in which these work packages are aggregated is called the work breakdown structure.

22. A work package is a measurable increment of work, usually of fairly short duration (a month or so). It should have an identifiable starting point and completion point so that there is an unambiguous way of knowing when a work package has been completed. The completion point is called a milestone. Each work package should be the responsibility of a single manager.

23. If the project has similar work packages (e.g., a work package for the electrical work on each floor of an office building), each should be defined in the same way, so that information about one work package can be compared with similar ones. If an industry has developed cost or time standards for the performance of certain types of work packages (as is the case in many branches of the construction industry), or if the project organization has developed such standards on the basis of prior work, definitions used in these standards should be followed so that the actual cost for a work package can be compared with these standards costs.

Indirect Cost Accounts

24. In addition to work packages for direct project work, cost accounts are established for overhead and support activities. Unlike the work packages, these activities have no defined output. Their costs are usually stated per unit of time, such as a month, just as the overhead costs of ongoing responsibility centers are stated.

25. The chart of accounts and the rules for charging costs to projects are also developed in advance. During their development several questions need to be considered:

- Which cost items will be charged directly to work packages?

- How, if at all, will indirect costs be allocated to work packages?

- What will be the lowest level of monetary cost aggregation? (Small work packages might be monitored in terms of person days, rather than money, for example.)

- Should committed costs be collected, in addition to actual costs? (For many types of projects, this is highly desirable.)

- How will off-site overheads and the cost of equipment be treated?

Section 3 — Project Planning

26. In the planning phase, the project team takes as a starting point the rough estimates that were used as the basis for the decision to undertake the project. It refines these estimates into detailed specifications for the product, detailed schedules, and a cost budget. It also develops a management control system, underlying task control systems (or adapts these from systems used previously), an asset control system, and an organization chart. The boxes on this organization chart gradually are filled with the names of personnel who are to manage the work, and who report to the one person who has final responsibility and authority for the entire project. An asset control system is required to exercise proper control over the acquisition, operation, and eventual disposal of major items of plant and equipment used for the project and disposed of when used. Disposal proceeds may be a significant contributor to cash flow and overall profitability.

27. On a project of even moderate complexity, there is a "plan for planning," that is, a description of each planning task, who is responsible for it, when it should be completed, and the interrelationships among tasks. The planning process is itself a sub-project within the overall project. There is also a control system to ensure that the planning activities are properly carried out.

28. If during the project it turns out that the work breakdown structure or the accounting system does not provide a useful way of reporting what is happening on the project, the structure must be revised. This may require re-analyzing much information, both information already collected and information describing future plans. Revising the information structure in midstream is a difficult, time consuming, frustrating task. In order to avoid this work, the project planners should give considerable attention to designing and installing a sound management control system before the project starts.

Nature of the Project Plan

29. The final plan consists of three related parts: scope, schedule, and costs.

a) *scope*. This states the specifications of each work package and the name of the person or organization unit responsible. If the project is one in which specifications are nebulous, as is the case with many consulting and research & development projects, this statement is necessarily brief and general.

b) *schedule*. This states the estimated time required to complete each work package and the interrelationship between work packages (i.e., which work package(s) must be completed before another can be started). The set of these relationships is called a network. The schedule may be stated as a PERT (Program Evaluation and Review Technique), Line of Balance, or Critical Path Method chart.

c) *costs*. Costs are stated in the project budget, usually called the control budget. Unless work packages are quite large, monetary costs are shown only for aggregates of several work packages, rather than for individual work packages. Resources planned to be used for individual work packages are stated as nonmonetary amounts, such as person-days or cubic meters of concrete.

30. In order to compare actual performance to the plan, the scope, schedule, and cost dimensions must be carefully related to one another. The work package device is the basis for maintaining this relationship. The estimated time required and the estimated cost of each work package are established for the scope specified in each work package. Both actual time and actual cost are measured in relation to the work accomplished on the work package (i.e., its scope).

Preparing the Control Budget

31. The control budget is prepared close to the inception of the work, allowing just enough time for approval by decision makers prior to the commitment of costs. It supersedes the preliminary cost estimate that was prepared in an earlier planning phase. For a lengthy project, the initial control budget may be prepared in detail only for the first phase of the project, with fairly rough cost estimates for later phases; detailed budgets for later phases are deferred until just prior to the beginning of work on these phases. Delaying preparation of the control budget until just prior to the start of work ensures that the control budget incorporates current information about scope and schedule, the results of cost analyses, and current data about wage rates, material prices, and other variables. It also avoids creating budgets based on what may turn out to be obsolete information.

32. The control budget is an important link between planning and control of performance. It represents both the sponsor's expectations as to what the project will cost and also the project manager's commitment to carry out the project at that cost. If, as the project proceeds, it appears that there will be a significant budget overrun, the project may no longer be economically justified. In these circumstances the sponsor may re-examine the scope and the schedule, and perhaps modify them.

This re-examination is necessary even for fixed-price projects; large cost overruns may indicate a need to renegotiate the price.

Section 4 — Project Execution

33. At the end of the planning process, there exists for most projects a specification of work packages, a schedule, and a budget; the manager who is responsible for each work package is identified. The schedule shows the estimated time for each activity, and the budget shows estimated costs of each principal part of the project. The cost information is often stated in a financial model. If resources to be used in detailed work packages are expressed in nonmonetary terms, such as the number of person-days required, the control budget states monetary costs only for a sizable aggregation of individual work packages. In the control process, data on actual cost, actual time, and actual accomplishment (in terms of both quantity and quality) are compared with these estimates. The comparison may be made either when a designated milestone in the project is reached, or it may be made at specified time intervals, such as weekly or monthly.

34. The sponsor and the project manager are basically concerned with these questions:

    a) Is the project going to be finished by the scheduled completion date?

    b) Is the completed work going to meet the stated specifications?

    c) Is the work going to be done within the estimated cost?

    If at any time during the course of the project the answer to one of these questions is "no," the sponsor and the project manager need to know the reasons and what can be done to correct the situation.

35. These three questions are not considered separately from one another, for it is sometimes desirable to make trade-offs between time, quality, and cost, using the financial model and other available information. For example, overtime might be authorized in order to assure completion on time, but this would add to costs; or some of the specifications might be relaxed in order to reduce costs.

Nature of Reports

36. Managers need three somewhat different types of information which may be described as trouble reports, progress reports, and financial reports.

    a) *trouble reports.* These report both on trouble that has already happened (such as a delay resulting from any of a number of possible causes) and also on anticipated future trouble. Critical problems are flagged. It is essential that these reports get to the appropriate manager quickly so that corrective action can be initiated; they often are transmitted by face-to-face conversation or by telephone. Precision is sacrificed in the interest of speed; rough numbers are often used — person-hours rather than labor costs, or numbers of bricks rather than material cost. If the matter reported on is significant, the oral report is later confirmed by a written document so that a record is maintained.

    b) *progress reports.* Progress reports compare actual schedule and costs with planned schedule and costs for the work done, and contain similar comparisons for overhead activities not directly related to the work. Variances associated with price, schedule delays, and similar factors may be identified and measured quantitatively, using techniques for variance analysis that are similar to those used in the analysis of ongoing operations. Expected differences between planned and actual scope, schedule, and cost for the whole project are included in these reports.

c) *financial reports.* Financial reports of project costs must be accurately prepared if there is a cost-reimbursement contract because they are the basis for any contractual progress payments; usually they are necessary even for a fixed-price contract because they are the basis for financial accounting entries. The time required to produce accurate, validated reports for such purposes diminishes the value of financial reports for management control purposes. Less precise information that is available quickly, such as the reports described in a) and b) above, is more important to project management.

37. Much of the information in management reports comes from detailed records collected in task control systems. These include such things as work schedules, time sheets, inventory records, purchase orders, requisitions, and equipment records. When designing these task control systems, their use as a source of management control information is one consideration.

Quantity of Reports

38. In order to make certain that all needs for information are satisfied, management accountants sometimes create more than the optimum number of reports. An unnecessary report, or extraneous information in a report, incurs extra costs in assembling and transmitting the information. More importantly, users may spend unnecessary time reading the report, or they may overlook important information that is buried in the mass of details. In the course of the project, therefore, a review of the set of reports is often desirable, and this may lead to the elimination of some reports and the simplification of others.

Incomplete Work Packages

39. Some work packages will be only partially completed at the reporting date, and the percentage of completion of each such work package must be estimated as a basis for comparing actual time with scheduled time and actual costs with budgeted costs. If accomplishment is measured in physical terms, such as cubic meters of concrete poured, the percentage of completion for a given work package can be easily measured. If no quantitative measure is available, as in the case of many research & development and consulting projects, the percentage of completion is subjective. Some organizations compare actual labor hours with budgeted labor hours as a basis for estimating completion, but this assumes that the actual labor effort accomplished all that was planned, which may not have been the case. Narrative reports of progress may be of some help, but these often are difficult to interpret. If the percentage of completion is not determinable from

quantitative data, the manager necessarily relies on personal observation, meetings, and other informal sources as a basis for judging progress.

Summarizing Progress

40. In addition to determining the percentage of completion of individual work packages, a summary of progress on the whole project is also useful. Progress payments often are made when specified completion points are reached. The employment of a "third party" expert for an opinion in this regard may be advisable if such skills are not otherwise available to the sponsor. The system usually contains some method of aggregating individual work packages, so as to develop an overall measure of accomplishment to date. A simple approach is to use the ratio of actual person-hours for work packages completed to date to total person-hours for the project, but this is reliable only if the project is labor intensive. A weighting based on the planned cost of each work package may be more informative, subject to the limitation that the system may not include costs at the level of individual work packages.

Use of Reports

Trouble Reports

41. Managers spend much time dealing with reports of trouble. A large project has many such reports, and one of the manager's tasks is to decide which ones have the highest priority. In the limited number of hours in a day, the project manager cannot possibly deal with all the situations that have caused, or may cause, the project to proceed less than smoothly. The manager, therefore, has to decide which problems will get his or her personal attention, which will be delegated to someone else, and which will be disregarded on the premise that operating personnel will take the necessary corrective action.

Progress Reports

42. Not only do managers limit the number of trouble spots to which they give personal attention, but they also are careful not to spend so much time solving immediate problems that no time remains for careful analysis of the progress reports. Such an analysis may reveal potential problems that are not apparent in the reports of current trouble, and the manager needs to identify these problems and plan how they are to be solved. The temptation is to spend too much time on current problems and not enough time identifying problems that are not yet apparent. Some managers deliberately set aside a block of time to reflect on what lies ahead.

43. The approach to analyzing progress reports is the familiar one of "management by exception." If progress in a particular area is satisfactory, no attention needs to be paid to that area (except to congratulate the persons responsible). Attention is focused on those areas in which progress is, or may become, unsatisfactory.

44. The analyses of reports that show actual cost compared to budget, and actual time compared to the schedule, are relatively straightforward. In interpreting the time reports, the usual presumption is that if a work package is completed

in less than the estimated time, the responsible supervisor is to be congratulated, but if more than the estimated time has been spent, questions are raised. The interpretation of the cost reports is somewhat different, for the possibility exists that if actual costs are less than budget, quality may have suffered. For this reason, unless there is some independent way of estimating what costs should have been, good cost performance is often interpreted as meaning being on budget, neither higher nor lower.

Cost to Complete

45. Some organizations compare actual costs to date with budgeted costs for the work accomplished to date. Others report the current estimate of total costs for the entire project, compared with the budgeted cost for the entire project. The current estimate is obtained by taking the actual cost to date and adding an estimate of the costs required to complete the project. The latter type of report is extremely important; it shows how the project is expected to come out, provided that the estimated cost to complete is properly calculated.

46. Experience to date in over running or under running estimated costs for work undertaken should be reflected in the estimates of the costs yet to be incurred. If overruns to date are caused by factors that are likely to persist in the future, such as unanticipated inflation, the current estimates of future costs probably should be higher than the amounts estimated originally.

Informal Sources of Information

47. Because written reports are visible, the description of a management control system tends to focus on them. In practice, the documents are usually less important than information that the project manager gathers from talking with people who actually do the work, with members of his or her staff, from regularly scheduled or ad hoc meetings, from informal memoranda, and from personal inspection of how the work is going. From these sources, the manager learns of potential problems and of circumstances that may cause actual progress to deviate from the plan. This information also helps the manager to understand the significance of the formal reports because these reports may not disclose important circumstances that affected actual performance.

48. In many cases a problem may be uncovered and corrective action taken before a formal report is prepared, and the formal report does no more than confirm facts that the manager has already learned from informal sources. This is an illustration of the principle that the formal reports should contain no surprises. Nevertheless, formal reports are necessary. They document the information that the manager has learned informally, and this documentation is important if questions about the project are raised subsequently, especially if there are legal issues. Also, subordinate managers who read the formal reports may discover that the reports are not an accurate statement of what has happened, and the managers may take steps to correct the misunderstanding.

Revisions

49. If a project is complex, or if it is lengthy, there is a good chance that the plan will not be adhered to in one or more of its three aspects; scope, schedule, or cost. A common occurrence is the discovery that there is likely to be a budget overrun; that is, actual costs will exceed budgeted costs. If this happens, the sponsor might decide to accept the overrun and proceed with the project as originally planned; to cut back on the scope of the project with the aim of producing an end product that is within the original cost limitations; or to replace the project manager if the sponsor concludes that the budget overrun was unwarranted. Changes in scope or schedule may also be made. Whatever the decision, it usually leads to a revised plan. In some cases, the sponsor may judge that the current estimate of benefits is lower than the current estimate of "cost to complete" and, therefore, decide to terminate the project.

50. If the plan is revised, the following question arises: Is it better to monitor future progress against the revised plan or against the original plan? The revised plan is presumably a better indication of the performance that is currently expected, but the danger exists that a persuasive project manager can negotiate unwarranted increases in budgeted costs or that the revised plan will incorporate, and thus hide, inefficiencies that have accumulated to date. In either case, the revised plan may be a rubber baseline; that is, instead of providing a firm benchmark against which progress is measured, it may be stretched to cover up inefficiencies.

51. The possibility of a rubber baseline can be minimized by taking a hardheaded attitude toward proposed plan revisions. Nevertheless, there is a tendency to overlook the fact that a revised plan, by definition, does not show what was expected when the project was initiated. On the other hand, if performance continues to be monitored by comparing it with the original plan, the comparison may not be taken seriously because the original plan is known to be obsolete.

52. A possible solution to this problem is to compare actual cost with both the original plan and the revised plan. Such a summary report starts with the original budget, and in the first section sets forth the revisions that have been authorized to date and the reasons for making them. Another section shows the current cost estimate and the factors that caused the variance between the revised budget and the current estimate of costs.

Project Auditing

53. In many projects, the audit of quality must take place as the work is being done; if it is delayed, defective work on individual components may be hidden; it is covered up by subsequent work. (For example, the quality of electrical work on a construction project cannot be checked after walls and ceilings have been finished.) In some projects, audits of costs and quality are also done as the work progresses; in others, cost and quality audits are not made until the project has been completed. In general, auditing as the work progresses is preferable, for it may uncover potential errors that can be corrected before they become serious. However, project auditors should not

absorb an undue amount of the time of those who are responsible for doing the work.

Section 5 — Project Evaluation

54. The evaluation of projects has two separate aspects:

    a) an evaluation of performance in executing the project, and

    b) an evaluation of the results obtained from the project.

    The former is carried out shortly after the project has been completed; the latter may not be feasible until several years thereafter. During a long project, re-evaluation of anticipated results may occur in order to determine if the project is worth continuing.

Evaluation of Project Control

55. The evaluation of performance in executing the project has two aspects:

    a) an evaluation of project management, and

    b) an evaluation of the process of managing the project.

    The purpose of the former is to assist in decisions regarding project managers, including rewards, promotion, constructive criticism, or reassignment. The purpose of the latter is to discover better ways of conducting future projects. In many cases these evaluations are informal. If the results of the project were unsatisfactory and if the project was important, a formal evaluation is worthwhile. Also, formal evaluation of a highly successful project or of an important unsatisfactory project may identify techniques that will improve performance on future projects.

56. Because work on a project tends to be less standardized and less susceptible to measurement than work in a factory, evaluation of a project is more subjective than evaluation of production activities. It resembles the evaluation of marketing activities in that appraisal of performance requires that the effect of external factors on performance be taken into account.

57. In looking back at how well the work on the project was managed, the natural temptation is to rely on information that was not available at the time. With hindsight, one can usually discover instances in which the "right" decision was not made. However, the decision made at the time may have been entirely reasonable: the manager may not have had all the information at that time; or the manager may not have addressed a particular problem because other problems had a higher priority; or the manager may have based the decision on personality considerations, trade-offs, or other factors that are not recorded in written reports.

58. Nevertheless, some positive indications of poor management may be identified. Diversion of funds or other assets to the personal use of the project manager is an obvious example. If there were major specification changes or cost overruns, these changes should have been authorized, and cash flows should have been recalculated so as to determine whether the return on the

project was still acceptable. Still another example of poor management is a manager's failure to tighten a control system that permits others to steal, but this is more difficult to judge because overly tight controls may impede progress on the project. Evidence that the manager regards cost control as much less important than an excellent finished product completed on schedule, is another indication of poor management, but it is not conclusive. The sponsor may overlook budget overruns if the product is outstanding, as often happens for motion picture projects.

59. The evaluation of the process may indicate that reviews conducted during the project were inadequate, or that timely action was not taken on the basis of these reviews. For example, the review may indicate that on the basis of information available at the time, the project should have been redirected or even discontinued, but this was not done. This may suggest that more frequent or more thorough analyses of progress should have been made; consequently, requirements for such reviews on future projects should be modified.

60. The evaluation may also lead to changes in rules or procedure. It may identify some rules that unnecessarily impeded efficient conduct of the project. Conversely, it may uncover inadequate controls. As part of the evaluation, suggestions for improving the process should be solicited from project personnel.

Section 6 — Implementation

61. Some projects lead to ongoing operations. For example, a development project may lead to a promising new product. Although the skills needed to produce and market a new product may be different from the skills possessed by the project team, team members often have information and insights that are valuable to the managers who are responsible for turning the project results into successful operations. If the project team disbands too quickly, the new managers may not be able to take advantage of this knowledge. On the other hand, project team members usually are anxious to go on to something new once their report has been finished and sold. Thus, the transition from the project to an ongoing operation may be difficult.

62. The schedule should include work packages that define end-of-project hand-over tasks such as writing manuals; liaising with, and training the staff of, operations management; and post-completion consultation or monitoring.

5

March 1993

Managing Quality Improvements[1]

CONTENTS

	Paragraphs
RATIONALE	1-8
SCOPE	9-12
DEFINING QUALITY	13-18
TOTAL QUALITY MANAGEMENT	19-28
THE ROLE OF MANAGEMENT ACCOUNTING	29-38
TQM IMPLEMENTATION GUIDELINES	39-55
MANAGEMENT PROCESSES, TOOLS AND MEASURES	56-80
TQM IMPLEMENTATION EXAMPLE	81-89
COST OF QUALITY	90-106
COST OF QUALITY IN SERVICE INDUSTRIES	107-111
QUALITY COST RELATIONSHIPS	112-116
MANAGEMENT ACCOUNTING CHALLENGES	117-127
SUMMARY AND CONCLUSIONS	128-134

[1]ACKNOWLEDGEMENT: The Financial and Management Accounting Committee is indebted to The Society of Management Accountants of Canada for allowing it to reproduce the Society's Management Accounting Guideline 14, "Managing Quality Improvements" as an International Management Accounting Practice Statement.

	Following Paragraph
EXHIBIT 1—QUALITY LEVER	5
EXHIBIT 2—TOTAL QUALITY MANAGEMENT	23
EXHIBIT 3—TQM FOR A MANUFACTURING COMPANY	28
EXHIBIT 4—POLICY DEPLOYMENT	61
EXHIBIT 5—QUALITY EDUCATION MATRIX	73
EXHIBIT 6—OPTIMAL QUALITY COST	116
EXHIBIT 7—COST OF QUALITY PROPORTIONS	116
EXHIBIT 8—QUALITY COST PROCESS SUMMARY	131
EXHIBIT 9—COST OF QUALITY REPORT	
EXHIBIT 10—COST OF QUALITY GRAPH	
EXHIBIT 11—REWORK AND REJECT COSTS BY PRODUCT ANALYSIS	
APPENDIX 1—CASE STUDY	
APPENDIX 2—STATISTICAL TOOLS AND PROCESSES MEASURES	
APPENDIX 3—ADDITIONAL QUALITY MEASURES	

RATIONALE

1. The world economy has changed. Enterprises in many countries now have the ability to compete globally. In many sectors, supply exceeds demand. Consumers faced with greater choices have become more cost- and value-conscious, and are turning to alternative sources for products and services. Consumers are also demanding improved quality. A customer lost because of a quality problem may never return but, more importantly, may take other customers with him or her.

2. In the economic marketplace, every enterprise is required to define its chosen battlefield and competitive weapons. Today, quality, cost, innovation and response times to customers are the competitive weapons of choice for the successful enterprise.

3. In the 1970s and '80s, traditionally managed businesses that competed with those that mastered total quality management lost markets that they previously dominated. The successful companies proved that a better quality product or service, produced and delivered in a timely manner, can be less, not more, expensive for the producer.

4. Quality, cost and time frequently seem to conflict with one another, necessitating trade-offs. These conflicts exist because traditional cost accounting practices do not always consider the hidden costs of (poor) quality. For example, an executive in the computer industry once observed, "If you catch a faulty two cent resistor before you use it and throw it away, you lose two cents." However, if you don't find it until it has been soldered into a subassembly, it may cost $ 10 to repair the part. And if you don't catch it until it is in the computer, the expense may be well in excess of the manufacturing costs.

5. This is illustrated by the Quality Lever for a manufacturing company (see Exhibit 1).

6. Traditional accounting practices measure product costs at the end of the manufacturing process. This process identifies and captures a limited amount of savings by focusing on scrap, rework, testing, etc. But if the quality cost opportunities were identified in the inspection stage before the manufacturing process was finalized, the savings would be greater.

7. Similarly, the savings would be even greater if quality and cost opportunities were identified in the product design phase.

8. Unfortunately, the "fire fighting" mode of problem solving at the production stage frequently occurs. Enterprises tend to focus on solving instead of preventing problems. While they may not have consciously decided to do this, enterprises fall into a pattern of behavior that favors the "find and fix" approach. Hence, there is a need for a disciplined quality management that will redirect all efforts to improving quality in all stages, from the concept of the product or service through to its delivery to the customer.

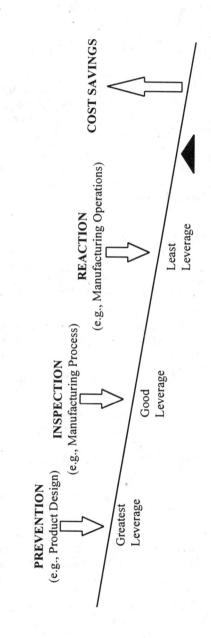

Exhibit 1

QUALITY LEVER

9. This Statement provides practical operating principles and recommended approaches for implementing Total Quality Management (TQM). It is addressed to management accountants so they can fully employ their unique skills in the quality management process. It is designed to:

   - help make the management accountant a key contributor to the achievement of quality through the use of Cost of Quality, statistical measures, and other quality management tools and processes.

   - help in implementing the initial process of a TQM system and the ongoing continuous improvements in the enterprise.

10. This Statement assumes an organization where the decision to implement a TQM process has already been made.

11. This Statement is, of necessity, both descriptive and prescriptive. The descriptive parts shape a vision of the future, build commitment for the change, and define quality concepts and techniques. The prescriptive part addresses how to lead, plan, and implement TQM.

12. The concepts, techniques, and the case study included in the guideline are all structured to be applicable to:

   - businesses that produce a product or a service;

   - all levels of an enterprise, from the CEO down;

   - all functions in an enterprise; and

   - enterprises in all business sectors.

DEFINING QUALITY

13. Quality, like excellence, is a concept that is easy to visualize but exasperatingly difficult to define. It remains a source of confusion to managers. Quality improvement is unlikely in such settings. Even when quality has been precisely defined, it has been focused narrowly on the factory floor or has relied primarily on traditional methods of quality control. Little attention has been paid to the underlying sources of superior quality, such as contribution of product design, vendor management and selection, production and workforce management.

14. Quality remains a difficult concept because it has undergone a significant evolution since the 1950s. Quality methods have expanded in ever-widening circles, each incorporating the elements of the preceding method.

15. During the evolution of quality, five principal approaches to defining quality have been tried. These are:

   - *Transcendent:*   Neither mind nor matter.
                          I know it when I see it.

- *Product-based:*
    Quality of product ingredient or attributes, such as performance, features, reliability, durability, serviceability and aesthetics.

- *User-based:*
    Ability to satisfy wants.

- *Manufacturing-based:*
    Conformance to specification.

- *Value-based:*
    Quality at an acceptable price.

16. These differing approaches coexist because of the competing views of quality held by members of the marketing, engineering and manufacturing departments. Despite the potential for conflict, an enterprise can benefit from such multiple perspectives. Reliance on a single definition can cause problems. For example, a company may discover that its product does not meet customer requirements, even though it conforms to all the specifications. Conversely, the customer satisfaction rating may be very high, but at a high cost of rejects, scraps, rework, and warranty costs.

17. In both cases, managers thought that they were producing high-quality products. And they were, but according to only one of the approaches to quality described above. Because each approach has a blind spot, TQM encourages multiple perspectives on quality, actively shifting the measures of products more from design to quality.

18. The TQM concept is the most comprehensive quality concept to date. It is no longer an isolated, independent function dominated by technical experts. It has entered the corporate mainstream, becoming an activity as worthy of attention as marketing or production.

TOTAL QUALITY MANAGEMENT

19. TQM, as discussed in this Statement, integrates the contributions of major quality masters such as Deming, Juran, Taguchi, Ishikawa and Crosby.

20. The TQM approach starts with identifying the customers and their requirements.

21. Every function, and every individual within a function, has a set of customers. Each of these customers has a set of spoken and/or latent needs or requirements.

22. The focus on the customer-supplier relationship is crucial to any attempt to improve quality. This recognizes that everyone in a process is at some stage a customer or supplier of someone else, either inside or outside the organization.

23. At an enterprise level, TQM starts with the external customer requirements, identifies the internal customer-supplier relationship and requirements, and continues with the external suppliers. In a chain of operations to produce a product or service, there are many internal customer-supplier links. The ultimate, external customer is better served if each internal customer is also served to the fullest-in terms of timeliness, completeness, and accuracy (See Exhibit 2).

Exhibit 2

Total Quality Management

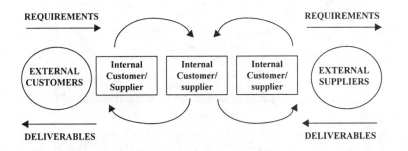

24. Understanding and meeting these customer requirements completely is the premise of TQM. See Exhibit 3 for an example using a manufacturing company.

25. The implementation of TQM requires care because the various customer requirements are not always translated properly. The traditional structure of large organizations and the complexity of the product/service delivery processes often stand in the way.

26. For example, most companies are organized, out of necessity, along vertical reporting hierarchies. But the delivery of a product or a service requires a great deal of cooperation among horizontal linkages.

27. The horizontal linkages in large organizations tend to be weak and lead to differences in interpretation and conflicting priorities. If the product development cycles are long, several key players may also change or be promoted before completion of the output.

28. Because of these complexities, TQM needs to be formally articulated and understood across all horizontal and vertical linkages. Ford utilized this concept to develop the Ford Taurus and Mercury Sable. To bring these cars to market, a cross-function "Team Taurus" was organized to strengthen internal linkages and to ensure that quality was designed into the new cars at every stage.

Exhibit 3

TQM FOR A MANUFACTURING COMPANY

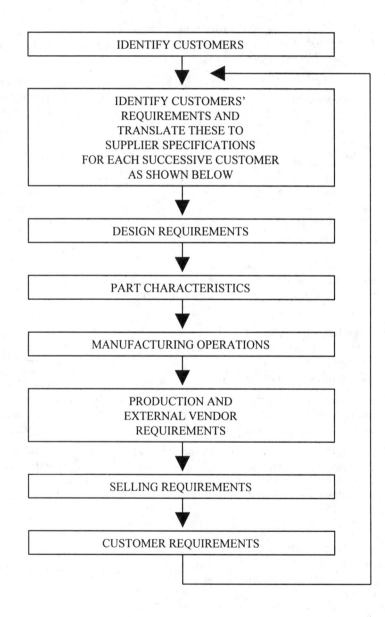

THE ROLE OF MANAGEMENT ACCOUNTING

29. Traditionally, the management of quality has been seen as the exclusive domain of the quality management staff, manufacturing and production engineering department personnel, and product design and engineering department personnel.

30. On the other hand, the modern concept of TQM is seen as a company-wide function and need that requires many new players.

31. Most existing quality information gathering, measurement and reporting systems have been developed and operated by non-accountants. The problem with these systems is that quality data are seldom accumulated and reported in a manner that emphasizes quality costs and clearly indicates the impact of quality on financial performance. Instead, these cost/benefit relationships are buried in a variety of product cost, marketing, engineering, and service department accounts.

32. Since management accountants are trained in analyzing, measuring, and reporting information focused on user needs, their expertise can be of assistance in the design and operation of comprehensive quality information gathering, measurement, and reporting systems.

33. To leverage this advantage, management accountants should integrate quality cost systems into the existing management reporting and measurement systems. With full knowledge of cost concepts and allocation procedures, they can measure and report quality costs in a manner that will contribute to the solution of quality problems. (The case study in Appendix 1 to this Statement highlights this further.)

34. These efforts will enhance the role and responsibility of the management accountant in the enterprise. He or she can highlight the fact that poor quality can be a significant cost driver. The absence of good materials, trained labor, well-maintained equipment, and well-conceived management processes can dramatically increase quality costs. These include scrap, rework, excess inventories, process and equipment breakdowns, field service, and product warranty claims.

35. As an example, the material management function in some organizations is evaluated on a purchase price variance from standard cost. This encourages the acquisition of materials on a price basis alone rather than on the merits of design quality and price. If low-cost materials do not possess the right quality, this accounting process results in high manufacturing costs. Such costs include scrap, rework, schedule disruptions, etc., all downstream functions for which the material management function is not accountable. If not managed, the downstream costs of this lack of quality could exceed the price savings achieved.

36. The management accountant should be totally involved in all activities of the enterprise. The following activities illustrate the role of the involved management accountant.

- ensure that he or she is well represented on the main quality control committees and employee involvement teams;

- ensure that the company knows the competitive benchmarks, competitive gaps, customer retention rate, and the Cost of Quality;

- help identify areas of greatest quality opportunities;

- create a system of quality measures to monitor ongoing progress against quality goals. The existing reporting systems may need extensive reworking;

- ensure that accounting is involved intimately in vendor rating decisions;

- ensure that he or she takes part in selection procedures for new manufacturing equipment by attending outside trials and viewings;

- discuss quality control effectiveness and the value of training courses for quality control personnel and operators with the human resources department; and

- continually review scrap and recovery costs and the basis of their evaluation.

37. In service industries, some adjustment from the management accountant's role may be required if:

- services are delivered away from headquarters, at customer premises, and in direct interface with customers; and

- operating personnel (i.e., repair technicians) are away from headquarters.

38. The management accountant should be informed and willing to be an active participant in the TQM process. The management accountant's training and field of expertise will be of value in this process but the achievement of quality goals will not be driven, only aided by the application of such expertise.

TQM IMPLEMENTATION GUIDELINES

39. The overriding lesson to be learned from the evolution of quality in Japan is that there are no easy answers. TQM cannot be reduced to a cookbook. Many early converts to the quality approach implemented quality circles, work teams, and other faddish techniques that merely copied the Japanese style while missing its substance. Each enterprise that has implemented TQM has developed its own implementation plans. TQM does not occur overnight; there are no shortcuts. It took the Japanese more than 15 years to approach and then surpass the quality levels of the West.

40. In general, the movement within an enterprise from traditional management to TQM will take between three to five years and will be difficult as well as time consuming. Many specific projects along the way, however, can yield high returns quickly.

41. While there is no one perfect implementation prescription for TQM, the following phases have been used by the winners of the U.S. Malcolm Baldrige awards for effectively managing quality.

Year 1

- Create CEO/Quality council and staff
- Conduct executive quality training programs
- Conduct quality audit
- Prepare gap analysis
- Develop strategic quality improvement plans.

Year 2

- Conduct employee communication and training programs
- Establish quality teams
- Create measurement system and set goals.

Year 3

- Revise compensation/appraisal/recognition systems
- Launch external initiatives with vendors
- Review and revise.

Create CEO/Quality Council and Staff

42. Most companies seeking to implement TQM have found the transition impossible to achieve without the direct involvement of the most senior managers, including the chief executive/president. Leadership for such a change cannot be delegated. It requires active, unwavering leadership from the CEO. If it means no more than a few speeches and a lapel pin, quality will not work. CEOs must lead this change. Most TQM companies establish an executive-level quality council to oversee the change process, chaired by the CEO or president and composed of the top management team. The council develops quality mission and vision statements, the company's long-range quality strategy, and company-wide quality goals. To support the council, some TQM companies develop a small quality staff to coordinate and track the quality improvement process, provide technical guidance and oversight to improvement teams, develop the content of quality training, and assist professional trainers. Other TQM companies look to major segments of the total organization to manage this activity and provide the required information to the corporate offices.

Conduct Executive Quality Training Programs

43. Most TQM companies invest considerable time and effort raising senior management's awareness of the need for a systematic focus on quality improvement, creating a common knowledge base concerning total quality, establishing reasonable expectations, and avoiding misunderstandings and miscommunications as the change effort progresses.

Conduct Quality Audit

44. The quality audit assesses the effectiveness of efforts to provide background information to support the development of a long-term strategic quality improvement plan. It may include an analysis of the quality improvement initiatives and quality performance levels of "best-in-class" competitors to identify the company's strengths and weaknesses versus the competition. It should also identify improvement opportunities that are likely to provide the greatest return to the company in both the short and long term.

Prepare Gap Analysis

45. A gap analysis against the "best-in-class" competitors tells a company what it lacks to move from one point to the other or to "leap-frog" the competition to become the new industry leader. It identifies strengths, weaknesses, and target areas for improvement, which are then fed back to managers and employees. The purpose of the gap analysis is to provide a common objective data base from which a strategic quality improvement plan can be developed.

Develop Strategic Quality Improvement Plans

46. Next, the quality council sets priorities for quality improvement by developing a one-year short-term strategic quality plan and a five-year long-range plan based on the gap analysis and target criteria. Successful TQM plans need to have the support and participation of every group in the company including unions, where they exist.

Conduct Employee Communication and Training Programs

47. Training is used both to communicate management's commitment to total quality and to provide employees with significantly enhanced skills in data analysis and problem solving. Training should be done from the top down: managers who actively participate in staff training reinforce the importance the company attaches to quality improvement.

Establish Quality Teams

48. Most successful TQM companies use a wide variety of employee and management teams. In addition to work-unit and self-managed teams, companies have devised quality management boards to oversee the continuous improvement effort for their line of business and quality task forces. These are temporary teams that address cross-functional quality teams.

49. TQM coordinators should serve as monitors for quality teams. But if the workforce has been provided with proper TQM training, then the teams should be able to structure themselves and handle problems on their own.

50. Unique quality teams, including representatives from the areas involved and a chairperson from an unrelated area, should be assembled to handle specific problems. Involving people from unrelated areas gives everyone a chance to share their experiences on how the TQM process has worked elsewhere.

51. A target should be established at the outset of the company's TQM process as to the number of quality teams and issues that will be dealt with at any one point in time. This will ensure that resources are not being spread too thin and that issues are being resolved before new topics are added to the process.

Create Measurement System and Set Goals

52. Crucial to the success of TQM implementation is the ability of quality teams to develop a better understanding of their internal and external customer needs and expectations, and to develop measures that truly reflect these expectations. Frequently, TQM companies find that traditional measures are not only inadequate, but misleading, and must be overhauled or discarded. They adopt high goals that call for improvements by tenfold or more over the span of a few years. They also measure their performance against not just the "best-in-class" among their competitors but the "best-in-class" for a function or business process.

Revise Compensation, Appraisal and Recognition Systems

53. As TQM companies revise their measurement systems, they also revise their compensation, appraisal, and recognition systems to reflect the emphasis on quality.

Launch External Initiatives with Vendors

54. It is important that quality management be extended beyond the firm. Some of the most significant benefits of a quality program come about when the concept is also adopted by the firm's suppliers. In general, TQM efforts should become part of the entire business system that extends from raw materials to the final customer.

Review and Revise

55. Quality progress is constantly reviewed by quality teams and the entire quality improvement effort should be reassessed at least annually. There is no finish line in the race for quality.

MANAGEMENT PROCESSES, TOOLS AND MEASURES

56. Implementing quality is not easy. It requires active, unwavering leadership, firm goals, and time from the CEO. Many quality initiatives fail because top management often has other priorities. If all an enterprise has is symbolism, nothing happens.

57. All enterprises have general access to the same equipment, technology, financing, and people. The real difference lies in how these resources are developed and deployed. In addition to the general implementation guidelines described earlier, the following management processes, tools and measures need to be adopted by an enterprise embarking on the road to quality:

- Policy Deployment
- Quality Function Deployment
- Kaizen
- Employee Involvement
- Suppliers' Management
- Competitive Benchmarking
- Quality Training
- Reward and Recognition
- Customer Retention
- Statistical Methods.

Policy Deployment

58. Policy Deployment is a system for planning corporate objectives and the related means for meeting them. The Japanese quality commentators describe it as the key to the TQM system. This reflects its primary characteristic: that of providing a measurable link between a company's strategic vision and plans, and the detailed means by which each level within the company will move toward achieving its related objectives. Policy Deployment is thus the method that TQM companies use to ensure goal congruence throughout the organization.

59. Policy Deployment evolved as the linking or umbrella TQM system in Japan over the last decade. It followed years of quality effort that had already resulted in a process-centered business environment where the use of the Plan-Do-Check-Act cycle and statistical performance measurement was common at all levels. The Plan-Do-Check-Act process is:

- Plan for improvements
- Search for problems
- Search for causes
- Attempt corrective action
- Verify if it succeeded
- If successful, incorporate into the process
- Continue the cycle.

60. As a result, when Japanese companies refined their strategic planning processes to improve their long-term competitive advantage, they had the considerable advantage of already knowing their business process capability. They were already able to "manage by fact" on a day-today basis. As a result, Policy Deployment offered Japanese companies two major business benefits. The first was a method of developing strategic plans that were not only customer-centered, but incorporated detailed means and related measures for implementing the plans over the plan period. The second was a method of focusing each organizational level on common, vital business objectives and testing the capability of the business entities to achieve the required performance.

61. Policy Deployment is deliberate, time consuming and, at times, difficult. It requires organizational discipline to be sustained in the face of day-today pressures. However, there is a greatly improved chance for TQM by using Policy Deployment (see Exhibit 4).

Exhibit 4

Policy Deployment

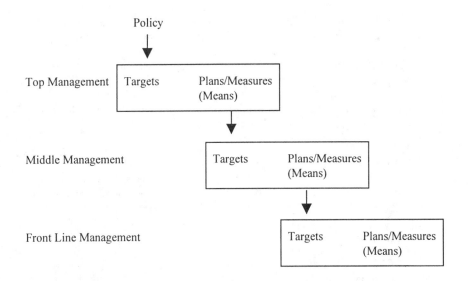

Quality Function Deployment (QFD)

62. QFD is a means of ensuring that customer requirements are accurately translated into relevant design requirements throughout each stage of the product development process. This means that the ends and means are linked at each stage. The process, like Policy Deployment, is simple but very detailed and disciplined. The rewards of QFD are well worth the extra up-front effort in planning. Toyota reports that, with QFD, its design cycle was reduced by one-third and the customer requirements were better reflected in the end product.

Kaizen

63. This is a Japanese term for Continuous Improvement in all aspects of a company's operations at every level. The process is often thought of as a staircase of improvement. As you move from step to step, you follow an improvement, maintain the improvement, follow an improvement, maintain an improvement, etc. Each step is a small upward movement (the vertical part of the step). While the steps are small, the staircase continues to move you upwards.

Employee Involvement (EI)

64. There is little chance that a firm's customers will be excited about its products and services if its workers are not. EI results in excited and committed workers. EI is more than simply organizing a few quality control circles or worker teams. Teams are only part of the picture. The creative energies of all employees must be used for problem solving and continuous improvement. This means that employees must be trained in new skills and encouraged to apply them on the job. Eventually, the number of ideas generated and the percentage of these ideas implemented become important measures of both individual and team performance.

65. As the EI process is absorbed, many of the roles, responsibilities, and activities of departments and individuals begin to overlap. The organization will de-layer and decompress. Responsibility for judgments, decisions, and problem resolutions will shift downward to those closest to the point of activity.

Suppliers' Management

66. A supplier is an extension of a company's own process. An enterprise's ability to serve its customers and to create a perception of value depends on the suppliers' ability to serve the enterprise's needs. Building a quality supplier base requires:

    • reducing the supplier base to reduce variation and to increase supplier commitment and the efficient use of a buyer's resources;

- selecting suppliers not only on price but on their capability to improve quality, cost, delivery, flexibility, and their willingness to become world class;

- forming new and long-term relationships with suppliers as working partners; and

- specifying precise customer and supplier expectations and agreeing to their consistent delivery.

Competitive Benchmarking (CB)

67. Most organizations do not really know who or what is best in their industry. Consequently, most quality improvement targets are set internally based upon past performance. This results in conservative estimates of further expected improvements. CB is the creative tool that enables enterprises to break free of these self-imposed limits and focus on the competitors and how to exceed their performance.

68. CB is the continuous process of measuring an enterprise's products, services, and practices against its toughest competitors. Benchmarks should include a measure of the results as well as an analysis and the appropriate measures of the process used to achieve those results. Common benchmarks used are: cost, staffing, yield, cycle time, on-time, inventory level, and rework.

69. Of all the benchmarks, the most important may be customer satisfaction. Quality is only as good as the customer says it is, not what the numbers on the quality control chart show. In fact, customer satisfaction shows up as the most important criterion of the U.S. Malcolm Baldrige Quality Award.

70. CB emerged as a management tool with Xerox in 1979. Several other corporations such as IBM, General Motors and Motorola-all Malcolm Baldrige Quality Award winners in the United States-have since adopted it. It helps facilitate a culture that values continuous improvement, increases sensitivity to changes in the external environment, and prioritizes the areas to be worked on first.

71. To make CB easier, several best practices data bases are being developed. One of these is the Ernst & Young and the American Quality Foundation data base. This is based upon a study of 500 companies in the automotive, banking, computer, and health care industries in four countries.

Quality Training

72. An important development tool is quality training. All employees must be familiar with the tools for preventing, detecting, and eliminating non-quality.

73. The education process needs to be customized for the various audiences: executives, middle managers, supervisors, and workers. A suggested quality education matrix for these target audiences is provided in Exhibit 5.

Exhibit 5

Quality Education Matrix

	Executives	Middle Managers	Super-visors	Workers
Quality improvement overview	X	X	X	X
Employee involvement	X	X	X	X
Leadership/facilitator workshop	X	X	X	
Team building	X	X	X	X
Creative thinking	X	X	X	X
Problem solving — basic	X	X	X	X
Problem solving — advanced	X	X	X	X
Statistical Process Control			X	X
Problem solving — train the trainer	X	X	X	
Design of experiments		X	X	X
Total quality control audit	X	X		
Competitive benchmarking	X	X		
Statistical thinking (how to understand variability and the correct approach to reducing it)	X	X	X	X
Quality function deployment	X	X	X	
Total productive maintenance	X	X	X	X
General business perspective			X	X
Parameter design using Taguchi methods		X		
Policy deployment	X	X	X	

Reward & Recognition

74. Reward and Recognition are the best means of illustrating the emphasis on TQM. Recognition can range from public acknowledgment of team accomplishments to rewards such as mugs, jackets, or monetary bonuses. Rewards should be group-oriented rather than individual. For example, "TQM DAY" would involve all employees and would be used to mark a major milestone in the company's effort to attain Total Quality. "TQM Improvement Team of the Week" would honor a group effort.

75. A Reward and Recognition structure based upon quality measures can be a very powerful stimulus to promote TQM in a company.

Customer Retention

76. Progressive service companies use an integrated measure of service quality (i.e., customer retention). This is the yardstick that all service companies need to measure their quality. In most industries, boosting customer retention can have the same effect on profits as cutting costs by 10%. Loyal customers spend more, refer new clients, and are less costly to do business with.

77. Organizations must make it easy for customers to respond to both what is right and what is wrong. The response must address issues key to the quality of product or service delivery.

78. Some customers will complain that the company's product or service does not meet their expectations. But many find it too easy to simply go somewhere else the next time. It is these customers that the firm must address.

79. As well, customers rarely make the effort to say "yes, you gave me exactly what I wanted." This is fair; they should not have to. But the feedback system should actively pursue this information so that the organization knows it is proceeding in the right direction.

Statistical Methods

80. Organizations should have the ability to apply statistical concepts and methods if they intend to implement quality improvement programs. Useful statistical concepts for implementing TQM are described in Appendix 2 to this Statement.

TQM IMPLEMENTATION EXAMPLE

81. In a manufacturing setting, the following is a summary of the approach used by Motorola, a winner of the U.S. Malcolm Baldrige Quality Award, to implement TQM. This approach is similar to the eleven-point TQM implementation process discussed earlier.

82. The Company was a successful multinational in the 1960s and 1970s. It had such a stranglehold on the market that it hardly paid attention when Japanese competitors first entered the marketplace in the late 1970s. It had grown up to

be a bureaucratic company in which one function battled another and operating people constantly bickered with corporate staff. Disputes over issues as minor as the color scheme of products had to be resolved by the CEO. The result was painfully slow product development, high manufacturing costs, and unhappy customers.

83. The Japanese exploited this weakness with aggressive pricing and proceeded to gain a sizable market share. By the early 1980s, the company recognized that it had to evolve rapidly into a world-class organization if it was to survive.

84. The company began by assessing its corporate strengths and weaknesses as well as those of its competitors. An important management step was taken in the early '80s when the company initiated a format benchmarking process to identify the successful practices of top competitors.

85. The competitive benchmarking revealed that, to compete successfully, the company had to be driven by its customers and competitors. It instituted several changes in organizational structure, product development processes, and supplier relations. It also set out on a quest for quality.

86. The quality practices and results were studied at leading-edge U.S. and Japanese corporations. The study convinced management that the effort had to appear more lasting and convincing than mere symbolism. A high-level quality council, staffed by senior executives, was created for a period of a year to study the quality gap, competitive practices, and to recommend company-specific quality vision, goals, and action plans.

87. The quality council recommended the following:

- TQM needs to be a strategic imperative.
- TQM means meeting market and customer requirements.
- The quality responsibility lies with everyone, with top management exercising strong leadership.
- The quality journey would take approximately three years. The implementation steps included: extensive training, re-engineering of work processes, employee involvement, quality audits, gap analysis, quality teams, measurement systems, and reward structure. Some of these were to be extended to the vendors as well.
- To support the three-year implementation process, a small quality staff needed to be established. It would coordinate and track the quality improvement process, provide technical guidance and oversee the improvement teams, develop the content of quality training, and assist professional trainers.

88. These recommendations were accepted. Over the following two years, the company invested considerably in quality training-particularly in Employee Involvement, Team Building, Problem Solving, Design of Experiments, Statistical Analysis, Quality Function Deployment, and Policy Deployment. The training began with the CEO and his staff and cascaded in groups across the company and its suppliers.

89. The above training and accompanying work process changes began to transform the company. Within three years the quality and cost competitive gaps were reduced by more than 50%. Encouraged by this progress, the company set an even more aggressive goal-to apply for and win the U.S. National Quality Award in the following three years. This required further intensive TQM efforts. At the end of the period, the company had increased its customer satisfaction index by 50%, reduced costs by an additional 20%, improved product quality, as measured by the customers, by 50%, and had begun to win back market share from competitors. These results, and the quality journey that had made them possible, were recognized by the U.S. Department of Commerce which awarded the company the National Quality Award.

COST OF QUALITY

90. Converting the language of quality into something that management is familiar with, such as dollars, gives everyone a common language and also facilitates measuring, tracking and analyzing. Dr. Juran first proposed the concept in the Quality Control Handbook published in 1951 and it has been greatly refined since.

91. The Cost of Quality is a measure of what an organization is spending for its overall quality. It can be viewed as the difference between the actual cost of making and selling products and services and the cost if there were no failures of the products and services during manufacture or use.

92. Unfortunately, the term "Cost of Quality" can leave a negative impression that reflects the thinking of the 1960s when it was believed that better quality products cost more to produce. But Cost of Quality can provide a very useful tool to change the way the enterprise thinks about errors.

93. Examples include:

- getting management attention by taking quality out of the abstract and into dollar terms, thereby competing with other cost and scheduling priorities;

- changing the way employees think about errors;

- identifying and prioritizing areas for corrective actions;

- measuring the effect of corrective actions and changes; and

- providing new emphasis on doing the job right the first time, every time.

94. The Cost of Quality has two basic components:

A) Cost of conformance, i.e.,

cost of prevention
cost of appraisal

B) Cost of non-conformance or failures, i.e.,

cost of internal failure
cost of external failure or lost opportunity.

Leading companies supplement these Cost of Quality measures with other non-financial measures depending upon the nature of the enterprise. Examples of additional quality measures are illustrated in Appendix 3 to this Statement.

95. Most enterprises accept that poor quality is costing them a great deal of money, but they are shocked when they find out how much. In the 1980s, the cost of poor quality was estimated to be 10 to 20% of sales dollars or two to four times the profit for an average company.

Cost of Prevention

96. The cost of prevention is the cost to ensure that customer requirements are met. It is associated with maintaining quality systems, such as quality control systems. These are incurred prior to or during production to prevent defective units of output.

97. This is a necessary cost for error prevention. By far the best way an enterprise can spend its Cost of Quality dollars is to invest in preventive actions. Unfortunately, many companies have neglected this valuable investment because of difficulties in identifying the downstream returns.

98. Examples of preventive actions include:

- quality planning
- quality engineering
- training to improve quality
- maintenance and calibration of production and inspection of equipment
- supplier assurance.

Cost of Appraisal

99. The cost of appraisal is the cost to ensure the work processes are producing outputs that meet customer needs or requirements, such as the inspection of raw materials. Here the term refers to both internal and external customers. These are incurred after production, but before sales, to identify defective items.

100. Examples include:

- quality data acquisition and analysis
- quality measurement criteria
- quality audits
- laboratory acceptance testing
- field evaluation and testing
- inspection and testing
- raw materials testing
- in-process testing
- review of test and inspection data.

101. Unlike preventive actions, appraisal actions do not reduce the number of errors; they only detect a higher percentage of errors in output before it is delivered to the customer.

Cost of Internal Failure

102. These are costs of not meeting customer requirements, such as the cost of having to do work again (rework). These are easy to identify because many accounting systems already track them. They are incurred to fix or dispose of the defective items before they are sold.

103. Unlike the cost of prevention and appraisal, these costs are not value added and never necessary.

104. Examples include:

- scrap
- rework or repair
- trouble shooting
- re-inspect and re-test.

Cost of External Failure or Lost Opportunity

105. These costs represent the lost profits associated with not meeting external customer needs or requirements. If the external customers become dissatisfied with an enterprise's offerings, they are likely to return the product, not buy from the firm again and, more importantly, tell other potential customers about their experience. The cost of a lost opportunity, therefore, includes lost profits from order cancellations and market share loss.

106. Examples include:

- customer service faults
- products or services rejected and returned
- products or services recalled for modification
- repairs and replacements or added service provided under warranty
- admitted repairs beyond warranty
- product liability
- customer losses due to poor quality.

COST OF QUALITY IN SERVICE INDUSTRIES

107. Costing quality in service industries is similar to costing quality in manufacturing. External failures, however, are a more important quality cost in service industries. Errors in service are not amenable to rework. In manufacturing industries, customers can call and demand warranty repairs on a faulty product. In the service industry, it does not always work that way. The service failure can result in the company's losing the customer-even without knowing it.

108. For example, an airline that is either tardy or has poor in-flight service may not win the loyalty of frequent business travelers and thereby will lose market share.

109. Management accountants should be aware that a service company's profit has more to do with customer defections than with unit costs, economy of scale, and other factors traditionally tracked by cost accounting. For example, in some industries, companies can boost profits by 50% just by retaining 10% more of their customers.

110. The cost of lost opportunity in a service industry, therefore, needs to be strengthened to include the probability of market damage done by poor service.

111. Another major difference between service industries and manufacturing is that labor costs take up a far greater proportion of operating costs. This can lead to several challenges. For example, time cannot be reworked or reclaimed. In a manufacturing organization, raw material can be reclaimed. But when the material is people's time it cannot. This means that, by looking at the percentage of time spent on various activities, Cost of Quality data may equate a reduction in failure costs with job losses, and cooperation may diminish.

QUALITY COST RELATIONSHIPS

112. Since prevention and appraisal costs are a function of managerial discretion, they are referred to as voluntary costs. Management makes direct decisions about the current funds to be budgeted for these voluntary costs. In contrast, investments to manage non-conformance or failure costs may not be directly controllable by management. For example, the cost of customer dissatisfaction, while not easily measurable, may trigger a cost for management to contain.

113. Even though non-conformance costs may not be directly controllable, they are definitely related to voluntary costs. When additional resources are allocated for prevention and appraisal activities, quality improves and non-conformance costs tend to decline. Conversely, when quality conformance efforts are reduced across the supplier, manufacturer and distribution chain, non-conformance costs increase. Accordingly, voluntary costs and failure costs move in the opposite direction.

114. Therefore, the minimum amount of total quality cost is located at the point where the marginal voluntary expenditures are equal to the marginal savings on non-conformance costs (see Exhibit 6).

115. From Exhibit 6, it is clear that the minimum total quality cost per unit is located at a level of quality assurance that is less than 100%. At very low levels of assurance, significant internal and external failure costs outweigh any cost savings that could be attained by avoiding voluntary costs. In contrast, extremely high levels of quality assurance result in voluntary cost expenditures that cannot be offset by non-conformance cost savings.

Exhibit 6

Optional Quality Cost

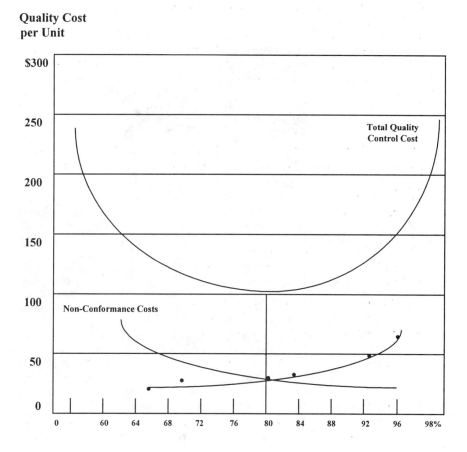

116. For an organization not steeped in TQM, the costs of internal failures and lost opportunities will comprise the biggest part of the total Cost of Quality. As these non-conformance costs are identified and managed, the relative balance between conformance and non-conformance costs shifts. In a steady state, both the conformance and non-conformance costs decline, though as a percentage of total Cost of Quality, the conformance costs increase as shown in Exhibit 7.

Exhibit 7

Cost Of Quality Proportions

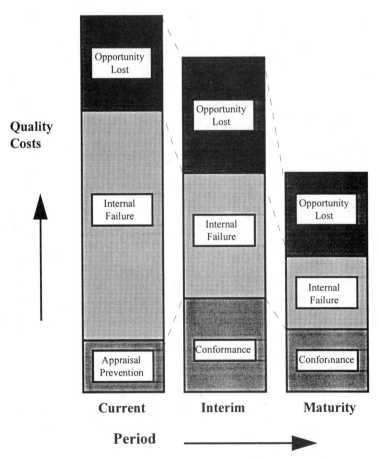

MANAGEMENT ACCOUNTING CHALLENGES

117. Management accountants require a clear understanding of TQM methodology. They should also be able to create a system of quality information measurement and to evaluate exactly what is required by each organizational unit and by the total enterprise.

118. The management accountant may need to extensively rewrite existing product costing and reporting systems. The costs associated with lost opportunities or loss of market prominence as quality falls below customer expectations may require more subjective reasoning than normal. These costs may have to be subjectively estimated before managers have an idea of their total quality costs.

119. Most accounting systems don't reflect all the specific quality cost categories that are required for quality management purposes. The management accountant, therefore, must:

- determine which accounts contain valid information for TQM,

- reorganize and restructure the existing accounting system to provide accurate quality cost data; and

- revise the chart of accounts to reflect each quality cost category.

120. Another shortcoming of most accounting systems is their failure to associate costs with activities. The systems do not provide individual managers and employees with the information they require to make improvements. Therefore, quality teams will not have the information necessary to focus on the most important quality problems.

121. The management accountant needs to relate quality costs to activities to help quality improvement teams focus their efforts appropriately in order to assure the success of the TQM effort.

122. The solution lies in applying techniques from activity-based costing to TQM. Activity-based costing yields improved information because of its use of an extensive cost driver identification process to relate activities to products or services.

123. Cost drivers (such as the number of different parts used or the effort expended by a product) reflect the consumption activities of a product or service. Examples of activities include:

- Tapping threads in a hole in a metal part

- Issuing a purchase order.

Cost drivers allow quality teams to pinpoint activities which are the result of not doing things the right way.

124. Since no standard format has been developed for Cost of Quality reporting, the types of items included vary within and among companies. For example, some Cost of Quality reports include overhead related to internal failure costs while others do not. These differences make it difficult to compare the performance of organizational units. If managers are to be evaluated on the

quality cost performance of their units, the management accountant should ensure that the Cost of Quality reports are standardized.

125. In addition to these challenges, the management accountant must recognize that the quality cost performance measures will vary widely depending upon the organization. Nevertheless, he or she should ensure that the measurement and reporting process meets the following criteria:

- directly relates to the requirements of the internal customer using these measures and reports;
- uses Cost of Quality measures as well as other non-financial measures,
- uses measures that vary between locations depending upon quality and business challenges;
- uses measures that change over time as the needs change;
- is simple and easy to use, implement and monitor;
- provides fast feedback to users and managers;
- is intended to foster improvement rather than just to monitor; and
- motivates people to achieve quality gains.

126. Management accountants will need to be aware that, although Cost of Quality data can be an attention-getter for senior management, precision measurement may be redundant. Arguments can arise over the correct classification of costs. If the Cost of Quality runs as high as 20% of revenue, greater precision in calculating cost seems to be of little value and perhaps very expensive to achieve. Therefore, techniques such as periodic audits of Cost of Quality may suffice if the accounting system changes prescribed earlier are prohibitively expensive. The primary benefits of the Cost of Quality are its initial shock value and its function as a means to measure improvement over time.

127. Based upon these challenges, a proposed summary of the quality cost process is described in Exhibit 8.

SUMMARY AND CONCLUSIONS

128. Examining the Cost of Quality allows the enterprise to identify, prioritize and monitor quality improvements. Other measures and processes (such as statistical analysis, Quality Function Deployment, Policy Deployment, quality circles and benchmarking) will also be required.

129. The leadership for a company-wide quality transition has to start at the top. It cannot be delegated. The companies that have successfully moved to the quality paradigm established an executive-level quality council to oversee and propel the change process. The council must be chaired by the CEO or the president and composed of the top management team.

130. The management accountant has the skills required to be a valuable contributor to the executive quality council, advising on quality opportunity areas and the measures and reports required to monitor progress.

Exhibit 8

Quality Cost Process Summary

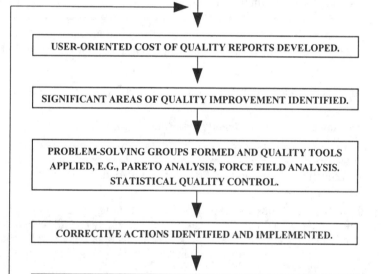

CEO/QUALITY COUNCIL BECOME THE NUMBER ONE QUALITY IMPLEMENTORS.

THE CEO IS A MAJOR PLAYER IN THE PROCESS OF IDENTIFICATION OF COST OF QUALITY, QUALITY CONTROL, CONTROLLER'S OFFICE ESTABLISHES COST OF QUALITY ACCOUNTS, SOURCE DOCUMENTS, E.G., TIME SHEETS AND LABOR ACCOUNTS, MAY NEED TO BE RESTRUCTURED TO IDENTIFY QUALITY COST CATEGORIES.

USER-ORIENTED COST OF QUALITY REPORTS DEVELOPED.

SIGNIFICANT AREAS OF QUALITY IMPROVEMENT IDENTIFIED.

PROBLEM-SOLVING GROUPS FORMED AND QUALITY TOOLS APPLIED, E.G., PARETO ANALYSIS, FORCE FIELD ANALYSIS. STATISTICAL QUALITY CONTROL.

CORRECTIVE ACTIONS IDENTIFIED AND IMPLEMENTED.

QUALITY BECOMES A FUNDAMENTAL WAY OF MANAGING THE COMPANY.

131. The journey on this quality path is difficult. It can take several years to make significant progress. Several behavioral factors common to large organizations can become inhibitors. For example, some functions may be identified as contributing to the Cost of Quality. The managers of these functions may not cooperate. There may also be debates about what should be considered as opportunities for managing the Cost of Quality. Finally, change at one step of the production process may cause unexpected or hidden changes in subsequent processes.

132. A company that has successfully implemented TQM can expect improved market share or profits or both. Cost reductions of 5 to 10%, out of a potential 20% of sales, are not uncommon.

133. Companies near the end of their transition to TQM appear very different from when they started. The differences show up, for example, in the following areas:

- the organizational structure becomes more efficient and flexible. Internal communication improves as some non-value-added or "find and fix" functions are reduced;
- internal measures of performance are replaced or supplemented by customer-oriented quality measures. Several new financial and non-financial measures (such as customer satisfaction) are added;
- all employees in all departments are introduced to the basic tools and philosophy of TQM. Decision making becomes more broadly distributed;
- there are many cross-functional improvement efforts;
- suppliers become heavily involved and "buy in" to programs related to the quality quest;
- key products/services and markets are reorganized;
- several management processes are institutionalized, such as benchmarking, continuous improvement, elimination of waste, prevention not detection, JIT, reduction of variation, statistical thinking, and consistent management practices.

134. While many companies can expect a successful transition, others will falter or achieve only partial benefits. They fail because they do not recognize that the total journey can take several years. Over this time there can be changes in the key players or competing management priorities. This Statement is designed to alleviate some of these pitfalls.

Case Study

It is impossible to provide a general model of quality costing for all companies.

Since a standard format for Cost of Quality reporting has yet to be developed, management accountants may not be aware of the analytical methodologies. Various types of analysis, reports and graphs can be developed once the data has been gathered, surveyed by questionnaires, or estimated by knowledgeable personnel. A case study in a manufacturing environment is described below to highlight the analytical methodologies used to identify the areas for quality improvement.

Manufacturing Example

Manufacturing company X operates in a highly competitive environment and has been experiencing increasing cost and quality pressures from new Japanese entrants. By Year 1, the external failure costs as measured by warranty claims, customer dissatisfaction, and share loss had increased to 60% of the total Cost of Quality.

Realizing this, the company instituted a corporate-wide quality program, using a three-year TQM process, to win customers back. This required considerable investments in voluntary prevention and appraisal costs.

In the first year, the company increased the voluntary prevention and appraisal costs by approximately 50%. In the second year, the investment began to pay dividends.

The management accountant gathered and summarized the quality costs in the following Cost of Quality report. The purpose of the report was to communicate to management the magnitude of the Cost of Quality and provide a baseline for measuring the impact of future improvement activities (see Exhibit 9).

Exhibit 9

Cost of Quality Report

	Year 2	Year 1	% Change
PREVENTION COSTS			
Training	$ 90,000	$ 50,000	+80
Processes/Procedures	50,000	35,000	+42
Quality Planning	86,000	65,000	+32
Other Quality Improvement Efforts	60,000	45,000	+33
Data Analysis	40,000	30,000	+33
Total	**$ 326,000**	**$ 225,000**	**+45**
APPRAISAL COSTS			
Testing	140,000	90,000	+55
Performance Measurement	75,000	50,000	+50
Supplier Monitoring	65,000	40,000	+62
Customer Surveys	30,000	20,000	+50
Total	**$ 310,000**	**$ 200,000**	**+55**
INTERNAL FAILURE COSTS			
Rework and Reject	55,000	100,000	−45
Reinspection and Testing	35,000	40,000	−13
Equipment Failure	30,000	35,000	−14
Other Failures	20,000	30,000	−33
Total	**$ 140,000**	**$ 205,000**	**−31**
EXTERNAL FAILURE COSTS			
Warranty	70,000	200,000	−65
Cost of Warranty	100,000	120,000	−16
Customer Losses (estimated)	600,000	1,140,000	−47
Total	**$ 770,000**	**$1,460,000**	**−47**
TOTAL QUALITY COSTS	**$1,546,000**	**$2,090,000**	**−26**

The report indicated that prevention and appraisal investments had begun to pay off in Year 2. The internal failure, external failure, and total costs had all decreased.

	Increase/Decrease
• Prevention Costs	+45%
• Appraisal Costs	+55%
• Internal Failure Costs	–31%
• External Failure Costs	–47%
• Total Quality Costs	–26%

A decrease in the warranty costs resulted from a decrease in defective products delivered to customers. The market share, however, did not yet show a gain. This can be expected when a company first begins to emphasize quality. It takes time for quality to work its way through to the market share. Increased quality should show up later as the customers experience it and the company re-establishes itself.

Year 1 and 2 quality costs were further summarized (see Exhibit 10). This graph showed the magnitude of the quality costs and compared the current period's costs with the prior year's. As TQM is fully implemented by company X, total quality costs will decline. Prevention and appraisal costs, however, will increase in proportion.

Exhibit 10

Cost of Quality Graph

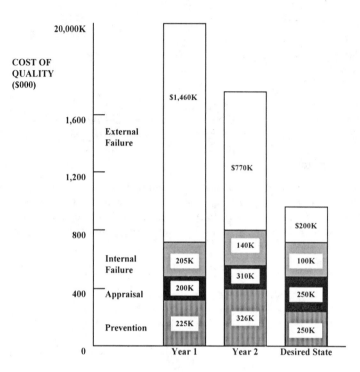

The quality cost data provided by the management accountant pointed to the areas that needed quality improvement. The problem areas were addressed through quality circles and problem solving groups. Several times, further analysis of the data through statistical analysis techniques was necessary.

Rework and reject was the biggest line item in the internal failure costs. The company found it necessary to break it down by product. One of the most powerful analytical tools is Pareto Analysis. This technique was used to identify the products requiring further root cause analysis. Exhibit 11 showed that three product lines out of fourteen accounted for 70% of the total scrap.

Further root cause analysis explained that the parts on these three product lines were scrapped because of the overall sub-system tolerance requirements. With this information, management investigated the reasons for the low part tolerance parameters and formulated a plan to correct the situation.

Exhibit 11

Rework and Reject Costs by Product Analysis

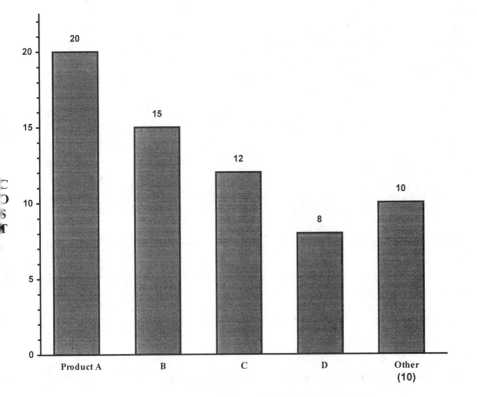

PRODUCT LINES

Statistical Tools and Processes Measures

Traditional accounting systems do not provide sufficient information to personnel responsible for observing the production process, charting quality performance, or identifying special causes of variation.

Management accountants need to understand the use of statistical tools and processes measures so that they can actively participate in and contribute to the TQM process. A sample listing is presented below.

Closed loop

In a closed loop process, feedback provides information about the process output. When this information shows the need for correction, the process output is corrected automatically. A closed loop can be effective in reducing variability and centering a process if the process feedback is correctly analyzed and if process adjustments are appropriate.

Error

The result of failing to correctly perform an action. Errors result in non-conforming outputs if left uncorrected.

Error Reduction

The reduction of errors, measured in terms of error rate. Improvement efforts should be directed to reducing errors rather than correcting non-conforming outputs.

Non-random Variations

A term referring to variation in a process output, sometimes used in analyzing control charts. This variation is the result of "special" causes and can often be improved by the employees (supported by their managers) who use the process being measured. Usually these variations show up on control charts as points outside the control limits, or as trends, shifts or periodic changes.

Process Capability Measurement

A measurement to determine if a process can produce output that is both centered on the target and well within the specifications limits. A process is "capable" if it fully conforms to customer requirements; meets predetermined levels of centering on the target value and variability within the specifications limits; and is in control.

Process Quality Assurance

A system that verifies that the process is being followed, that the enablers for the process are in place, and that the process is consistently capable of achieving specified outputs.

Random Variation

A term referring to inevitable variation in a process output, sometimes used in analyzing control charts. Random variation is usually the result of "common" causes that can often be improved only by management (in contrast to "special" causes that the employee using the process may often address). While the causes may appear to have a small effect, a single cause may substantially influence the size of the variation.

Six Sigma Quality

Sigma is a measure of variation in a product or process. It is a symbol for a statistical parameter known as standard deviation. In a typical process, X represents the process average and sigma its standard deviation. Generally, the process width is defined as $X \pm 3$ sigma. If the specification width was the same, the process used to be considered in control. But in real terms, such a process would have a defect rate of 0.27 percent or 2,700 defects per million units. If, however, the process width is halved and the specification width remained the same, the latter's boundaries would be at $X \pm 6$ sigma. In such a case, the defect rate would be only 2 defects per million units. And even if the process average shifted by 1.5 sigma to one side, the defect rate would only be 3.4 defects per million units. This is the statistical meaning of ± 6 sigma.

In product terms, Motorola's goal is for every important parameter to be designed, built, and brought to ± 6 sigma; that is, the process width would be no more than half the specification width. In administrative terms, ± 6 sigma is simply perfection; that is, having a defect rate of no more than 3.4 errors per one million opportunities for error. Motorola is dedicated to achieving this state of perfection by 1992.

Standardization

This ensures the consistent use of a process or procedure across all applicable areas. After a process improvement has been tested and verified, the improved process must be standardized to maintain the benefit across the corporation.

Statistical Process Control (SPC)

The application of statistical techniques for measuring and analyzing the variation in processes.

Statistical Quality Control (SQC)

The application of statistical techniques for measuring and improving the quality of processes. SQC includes SPC, diagnostic tools, sampling plans, and other statistical techniques.

Statistical Tools

Graphical and/or numerical methods that assist in the analysis of a process or population of events. Often the tools use a sampling of the population to make a judgment and decision about the entire population.

Listed below are the seven most commonly used statistical tools for analytical problem solving.

1. Check Sheets
2. Cause and Effect Diagrams
3. Histograms
4. Pareto Diagrams
5. Control Charts
6. Scatter Diagrams
7. Graphs.

Stratification

The process of classifying data into two or more sub-groups based on categories or characteristics. This is a powerful and frequently used tool. When the data are stratified according to the variables, which are thought to cause variation, the causes of variation can be detected more easily.

10X Improvement

(Also known as "tenfold reduction.") 10X Improvement means reducing the process's error or non-conforming output rate to 10% of its existing rate. Improvement is measured by examining ongoing quality in terms of error and non-conforming output rates.

Variability

The inevitable changes in the measured values of a process output. Changes are due to random causes (natural or common causes) or non-random causes (special causes). Variability can be measured. It describes the spread of the measured output values around the average. Sigma (standard deviation) is an often used numerical measure of variability. Variation can be visually represented through the use of graphical techniques.

Variability Reduction

The process of reducing the spread of values of a process output. To reduce variability, you separate the random from the non-random variation before you develop corrective action plans. You then use different corrective actions for the random and non-random causes.

Additional Quality Measures

Cost of Quality by itself cannot resolve quality problems. It is only designed to help management understand the magnitude of the problem, identify opportunities, and measure progress. It must be accompanied by an effective improvement process to reduce the errors in an enterprise. An enterprise should supplement the Cost of Quality measures with additional measures to maintain focus on unique quality elements. The management accountant must achieve a working knowledge of these measures to help quantify the Cost of Quality.

Some of these measures are common to most organizations. Others may be unique to the nature of an enterprise, i.e., industry, competition, current and desired state of quality, etc.

An exhaustive list of quality measures for manufacturing and service industries is impossible to create. Many of these measures have to be developed specifically for the industry, company or quality need. A sample listing is presented below.

- Installation failures

- Scrap and rework

- Reinspection and retest

- Redesign and engineering changes

- Soft toolings

- Abandoned programs

- Billing errors

- Bad debts

- Premium shipping costs

- Supplier cancellation costs

- Overdue accounts receivable

- Off-spec/waivers

- Excess inventory

6

April 1994

Post Completion Review

CONTENTS

Paragraphs

EXECUTIVE SUMMARY

INTRODUCTION 1-3

SECTION 1—SCOPE AND PURPOSE OF POST
    COMPLETION REVIEWS 4-15

SECTION 2—THE POST COMPLETION REVIEW
    DECISION 16-33
The Benefits of a Post Completion Review 17-20
Choice of the Projects to Review 21-30
Significant Projects 23
Nature of the Objectives of the Project 24-26
Nature of the Project 27-30
Allocation of Post Completion Review Costs 31-33

SECTION 3—THE POST COMPLETION REVIEW
    COMMITTEE 34-42
Key Conditions for a Successful Committee 37
Composition of the Post Completion Review Committee 38-42

SECTION 4—THE METHODOLOGY OF POST
    COMPLETION REVIEW 43-53
When Must the Review Be Carried Out? 43-45

Steps in the Implementation of a Post Completion Review 46-50

Post Completion Reviews Are Positive and Constructive 51-53

APPENDIX 1—FACTORS RELATED TO DOCUMENTATION
  SUPPORTING A POST COMPLETION REVIEW

APPENDIX 2—EXAMPLE OF A POST COMPLETION REVIEW
  CHECKLIST

APPENDIX 3—A CASE ILLUSTRATION (ACME Corporation)

ATTACHMENT 1—P & L ESTIMATE 1991-1995

ATTACHMENT 2—CASH FLOW ANALYSIS 1991-1995

EXECUTIVE SUMMARY

Scope

Post completion reviews are about learning in organizations.

A post completion review is a process aimed at assessing, *ex post*, the efficiency and effectiveness of a capital budgeting decision and of the management of its implementation. It is based on a comparison between planned and actual actions, costs and resource usage, results and benefits. It encompasses the review of all assumptions about markets, technology, personnel, environment, competition, cost of capital, etc. that were made during the decision-making period. It focuses both on the prior assumptions and on the actual outcome. It is one of the ongoing continuous processes through which the organization learns and improves.

A post completion review asks the questions: Why? and How? For instance, why has the project been successful? Why has the project been unsuccessful? Why have problems arisen during the decision and implementation process? Why have no problems been encountered? How did we really do this? How did our suppliers get the information? How did we communicate with the "customer"? How can we ensure that the lessons learned in this project are not forgotten in the future?

The post completion review process is based on an integrated and systematic program of data accumulation and analysis that is defined prior to the implementation of the decision.

Purpose

The purpose of a post completion review is threefold:

1) To support continuous improvement in the capital investment and implementation process. This process is oriented towards the future.

2) To allow for the identification and implementation of corrective actions on the project under review or in similar projects. This is an opportunity to review not only the current cash flows of a project at the date of review, but also to review the updated future cash flows of that project.

3) To allow for the review of current procedures and the design of better ones to improve future decisions, to guarantee better implementation and better conformance.

The term "project" refers to all investments (resource allocation) of significant size decided and implemented by an enterprise in order to shape its future. All projects are considered to be the result of a capital budgeting decision. In this document the term project covers investments in tangible or intangible assets such as acquisitions of existing business entities, information systems technology, new machinery, plant facilities or equipment, process or product development as well as investments in identifiable research programs or investments in developing a market share in a current or new market or transfers of production to a different site. Projects in such difficult-to-evaluate projects as human resource development, marketing or basic research could be included in this list, and they should be when factual measures of outcome can be identified.

Types of Post Completion Reviews

A project comprises three distinct time phases that may overlap:

a) The assessment phase is the period during which the capital decision is prepared and made (this aspect is covered in the International Management Accounting Practice Statement n°2, *The Capital Expenditure Decision*).

b) The investment phase defines the period during which the resources are invested (this aspect is covered in the International Management Accounting Practice Statement n°4, *Management Control of Projects*).

c) The outcome period defines the period of time during which the benefits are derived from the original investment. If the project was assessed using a form of breakeven analysis (such as discounted cash flow or internal rate of return), the breakeven period would be considered to be the outcome period.

Generally, the post completion review is carried out during the outcome period; however, a post completion review may be carried out immediately at the end of the investment period to review the implementation process. For projects of long duration, for which the investment period and the outcome period may overlap significantly, an interim review is possible and recommended.

Steps to a Post Completion Review

A post completion review involves:

• Reviewing all the assumptions that were formulated during the assessment period, and the process that led to their formulation; special attention should be given to the process that led to the definition of the cost of capital used in the decision process;

• Comparing the actual resources consumed by the project with the forecasts made at the assessment period;

• Comparing the actual outcome or performance of the project with the forecasts made at the assessment stage;

• Reviewing the procedures used to obtain an effective and efficient project control process; and,

• Reviewing conformance with company policy, particularly in respect of the proper authorization levels.

A successful post completion review requires the development of a data gathering process that will be operational from the first moment of the initial capital budgeting analysis. This systematic collection of detailed information about the reasoning behind decisions is critical to the success of the post completion review and thus to the learning within the organization.

Composition of the Post Completion Review Team

The carrying out and the exploitation of the post completion review is a management function. It requires the support of the financial function. It is a team effort.

The post completion review should be carried out by a committee composed of persons who are experienced in the firm's capital expenditure control system and sufficiently familiar with the processes used in assessing technical, financial and marketing aspects of both the implementation of the project and of its outcome. Since the scope of a post completion review extends beyond financial information, the accountant, the internal controller, the management controller or the financial officer serving on a post completion review committee should do so as a manager first, not just as an accountant. The size of the committee is a function of the size of the firm and of the relative size of the project.

The Post Completion Review Is a Positive and Constructive Tool

The post completion review is a positive and forward looking tool. The carrying out of such a review can lead to the identification of individuals who may appear to be responsible for deviations from forecast. The post completion review team should always aim to determine why and how deviations occurred, not who can be blamed for them. Once the original cause has been determined, a key step has been taken toward choosing the appropriate action for the future. The emphasis is to be placed on collecting factual and quantifiable data and information, not on second guessing the decision makers who made decisions during the various phases of the project.

The post completion review is not geared to apportioning blame; it is geared at understanding and at generating continuous progress. It is a major component of the strategic development of the firm. The decision to carry out post completion reviews is the expression of a managerial philosophy consistent with the concept of the learning organization.

INTRODUCTION

1. This Statement describes the process and benefits of reviewing capital investments after their implementation. It is distinct from and completes both the capital budgeting decision, covered in International Management Accounting Practice Statement n°2, *The Capital Expenditure Decision*, and project management covered in International Management Accounting Practice Statement n°4, *Management Control of Projects*.

2. The term "post completion review" is equivalent to other terms used in the literature such as post completion audit, post completion appraisal, investment post audit, post appraisal of investment decisions, post project appraisal. All these terms are generally equivalent and differ only in nuances.

3. Although this Statement can be seen to be aimed at large organizations, its message is pertinent to firms of all sizes. The procedures described below must be adapted, in keeping with the spirit of the text, to fit the needs and resources of each firm.

SECTION I—SCOPE AND PURPOSE OF POST COMPLETION REVIEWS

4. The main purpose of a post completion review is to contribute to the learning of the organization. It is one of the procedures and practices that help create the "learning organization." It is a managerial philosophy anchored in rigorous policies and procedures. The post completion review of project decisions is one of the components of the management practice of systematically monitoring and providing feedback on the performance of past actions in planning or implementation.

5. A post completion review is a process aimed at assessing, *ex post*[1], the efficiency and effectiveness of a capital budgeting decision and of the management of its implementation. It is based on a comparison between planned and actual actions, costs and resource usage, results and benefits. It encompasses the review of all assumptions about markets, technology, personnel, environment, competition, cost of capital, etc. that were made during the decision-making period. It focuses both on the prior assumptions (and their development process) and on the actual outcome (and its measurement).

6. The post completion review process is based on an integrated and systematic program that is defined prior to the performance of the review.

7. A post completion review asks the questions: Why? and How? For instance, why has the project been successful? Why has the project been unsuccessful? Why have problems arisen during the decision and implementation process? Why have no problems been encountered? How did we implement this or that decision? How can we ensure that the lessons learned in this project are not forgotten in the future?

---

[1] The term *ex post* is used here and later in the text with the meaning of "after the event."

8. The purpose of a post completion review is threefold:

    1) To support continuous improvement in the capital investment and implementation process. This process is oriented towards the future. It is a continuous process built on discrete elements.

    2) To allow for the identification and implementation of corrective actions for the project under review or in similar projects. This is an opportunity to review not only the current cash flows of a project at the date of review, but also to review the updated future cash flows of that project.

    3) To allow for the review of current procedures and the design of better ones to improve future decisions, to guarantee better implementation and better conformance.

9. The post completion review includes an evaluation of: (a) the quality of procedures for assessing the potential costs and benefits of a project; (b) the quality of the decision-implementation process; (c) the quality of the forecasts of the benefits and costs; and (d) whether or not the expectations about the future and the issues having potential influence over the project were subsequently confirmed and if not, establish the reasons for the deviation observed.

10. The term "project" refers to all investments (resource allocation) of significant size decided upon and implemented by an enterprise. All projects are considered to be the result of a capital budgeting decision. In this document the term project covers investments in tangible or intangible assets such as acquisitions of existing business entities, information systems technology, new machinery, plant facilities or equipment, as well as investments in identifiable research and development programs or investments in developing a market share in a current or new market or transfers of production to a different site. Conceptually, investments in difficult-to-evaluate projects such as human resource development, marketing or basic research should be included whenever objective measures of outcome can be established.

11. A project comprises three distinct time phases that may overlap:

    a) The assessment phase is the period during which information to enable the capital decision is assembled and the decision is made.

    b) The investment phase defines the period during which the resources are invested.

    c) The outcome period defines the period of time during which the benefits are derived from the original investment.

12. Generally, the post completion review is carried out during the outcome period; however, a post completion review may be carried out immediately at the end of the investment period to review the implementation process. For projects of long duration, for which the investment period and the outcome period may overlap significantly, an interim review is possible and recommended.

13. A post completion review involves:

- reviewing all the qualitative and quantitative reasons for the selection of the project;

- reviewing all the assumptions that were formulated during the assessment stage, and the process that led to their formulation;

- reviewing the assumption as regards cost of capital or discount factor applied in the decision process. An independent review and setting of the discount factor is recommended that is undertaken on a regular basis and within one year of the time of assessment of a significant investment project;

- comparing the actual resources consumed by the project with the forecasts made at the assessment stage and determining the contributing reasons for the deviation noted;

- comparing the actual outcome or performance of the project with the forecasts made at the assessment stage and determining the contributing reasons for the deviation noted;

- reviewing the procedures used to obtain an effective and efficient project control process; and,

- reviewing conformance with company policy, particularly with respect to authorization levels.

14. A prerequisite for a successful post completion review is that various formal capital expenditure policies and procedures exist, such as:

- documentation of the levels of approval for capital appropriations;

- documentation of the investment analysis process and reporting specifications;

- documentation of the investment decision criteria;

- an approval process for expenditure overruns;

- a policy specifying how and when post completion reviews will be performed;

- documentation of the issues intended to be addressed by the investment and the other choices considered;

- procedures for accounting and control of capital projects.

15. In some organizations the value of performing post completion reviews lies in the realization that a formal, clear set of capital expenditure policies and procedures have not been developed.

SECTION 2—THE POST COMPLETION REVIEW DECISION

16. The decision to carry out a post completion review is normally made before the project is engaged. Unless an appropriate information system already exists, one must be set up from the beginning to assure that the information needed for a proper review is available as the project progresses.

The Benefits of a Post Completion Review

17. Most enterprises can benefit from a formal system of post completion reviews. The degree of formality and of complexity of the system is a function of the size of the organization. Generally, post completion reviews are performed on types of projects or parts of projects that are likely to be repeated in the future. However, much can be learned from the review of unique projects.

18. Post completion reviews should be a normal part of management. A review should be carried-out regularly on all significant capital investment projects and on all decisions affecting the strategy or the future of the business. Even organizations which do not undertake new projects on a regular basis benefit from carrying-out a post completion review as they gain a valuable understanding of their decision making process.

19. The post completion review is an organizational learning process.

20. Specific benefits of a review include:

- Reinforcement of the link between the past and the future in the mode of thinking of managers. The actual implementation of the project is a sunk cost at the date of review. The decisions, based on an analysis of the past, will focus on the remaining future outcome of the project and on future projects.

- Allowing an assessment of the quality of forecasts and of the forecasting process of decision parameters. The review requires that the decision process be carried out in an explicit manner following, for example, the *Capital Budgeting Decision* International Management Accounting Practice Statement n°2. The post completion review compares the actual results achieved with the environmental, social, labor, market, technical, financial, cost and cash forecasts and schedules upon which the original decision was made. The analysis of the identified deviations will improve the understanding of the underlying causal model and thus will improve current and future decision making.

- Ensuring that capital expenditure procedures are understood and followed.

- Reviewing the appropriateness of the sensitivity analysis of the key variables in the capital budgeting decision process and specifically of the contingency reserves and allowances.

- Improving the management control of projects. The post completion review focuses on the reasons for the existence of problems and guides managers to correct the cause of the problems for other projects.

- Serving as a basis for the identification of the need for and the implementation of corrective actions. The post completion review may accelerate the decision to interrupt or significantly re-orient a project through the timely identification of (a) unforecasted and unalterable deviations in specifications or (b) environmental changes which are detrimental to the remaining future outcome of the project.

- Identifying the causes of significant deviations. The post completion review provides explanations for the over/under performance of a given project in terms of internal and external factors. The reasons provided may help to achieve more successful or positive results in the implementation of future projects.

Choice of the Projects to Review

21. Post completion reviews are expensive both in terms of the cost of the information system that is required to support the reviews as well as the cost of carrying out the review itself. However, the benefits of an improved decision-making process, that can be expected to result, will apply to all future decision-making and may be substantial in value to the enterprise.

22. Care should be given to the choice of the projects that will be reviewed. The criteria used in the cost benefit decision to implement or reject the completion review are specific to each firm and may differ depending on the importance, the purpose and the nature of the project. Three categories of criteria are:

- significant projects;
- nature of the objectives of the project;
- nature of the project.

Significant Projects

23. An organization can chose to define a project as significant on the basis of any or all of the following criteria:

- strategic scope—any project that significantly affects the strategic direction of the enterprise;
- financial scope of the project compared to the size of the enterprise—in this respect, each firm should establish a threshold, an amount beyond which the post completion review will automatically be performed;
- approximate duration of the project—beyond a certain time horizon the cash flow from the project may be deemed uncertain because of potential changes in environmental conditions. It will therefore be interesting to know whether such changes have been correctly identified and whether management's response has been adequate;
- the risks involved in the project—risk of failure, risk of liability, risk of take-over, increased business risk due to entering a new field, a new market or a new product, political risk, etc.; and
- the requirement to use new techniques of forecasting or planning for the project decision, or the requirement of estimation and forecasting of new domains (such as societal issues) never before considered by the firm.

Nature of the Objectives of the Project

24. The very nature of the objectives of a project may be sufficient to justify a post completion review. Innovative and/or strategic projects should be reviewed systematically, regardless of the amounts involved.

25. Projects which are neither significant, nor especially exemplary in terms of the nature of their objective often constitute a large part of the capital budgeting activities of a firm. Such "small" projects may be reviewed on a statistical basis so as to ensure organizational learning.

26. Projects concerning solely the routine and recurring business of the enterprise should be reviewed only if another of the criteria listed above and below applies.

Nature of the Project

27. *Recurring/Non-recurring projects.* Some projects, or some parts of projects, are likely to be of a recurring nature. A post completion review represents a key source of information for the decision and control of similar projects in the future. On the other hand, projects not likely to recur normally can be rejected if they add nothing useful to the organization's collective memory. However, even in such cases, the post completion review process can allow the managers an opportunity to better understand their current way of managing and thus help clarify objectives and aspirations.

28. *Exemplary projects.* Successful, failed or rejected projects. Such projects can, by definition, only be known after the fact. We assume here that the organization had adopted the philosophy that *all* projects can potentially be submitted to a review and is organized accordingly. The question is thus only to choose, *ex post*, which project(s) to review.

    - From a continuous improvement point of view projects which have achieved outstanding results should be singled out for review. Their post completion review may identify some of the reasons for success such as a favorable environment or some aspects of the decision and implementation process.

    - A post completion review should also be undertaken when all or parts of the project have not been performed as expected: for example, when operational problems arise (especially if these are due to the delegation system) or when a significant rise in costs has been identified or when underlying parameters have shifted significantly, even though their effect on costs and benefits might only take place in the distant future.

    - Some of the rejected projects should be revisited on the basis of *ex post* information so as to confirm that the *ex ante*[2] analysis that led to their rejection had been performed accurately and properly. Much organizational learning can take place from the analysis of such rejected projects, once what used to be the future is now the present or the past.

29. *Projects most likely to provide learning.* A cost/benefit analysis should be used in deciding whether or not a post completion review should be performed. Since a post completion review is costly, it should only be undertaken when its benefits are expected to outweigh the costs. However, the benefits of learning and of continuous improvement are often difficult to evaluate while the costs attached to carrying out the review are often quite

---

[2] The term *ex ante* is used here and later in the text with the meaning of "before the event."

clear and visible. A business, whether large or small, always benefits from a post completion review and the carrying out of such reviews is a matter of principle. The frequency and scope of the review will be determined by management.

30. *Projects containing recurring steps.* A project may be unique, but some of its components may be of a recurring nature or exist in other contexts. The post completion review might allow the creation of a body of knowledge about the business process of these steps leading to some relative standardization and thus cost savings.

Allocation of Post Completion Review Costs

31. In some instances the costs of a post completion review may represent a significant percentage of the costs of the investment in projects. In any case, the benefits derived from carrying out a post completion review far outweigh these costs and add long term value to the organization. The major cost of a review process lies in the design and operation of the information system that will support the review. The design of the information system is critical as it will condition the availability of factual information and thus the possibility of carrying out the post completion review.

32. Post completion review costs are strategic costs incurred for the benefit of the whole enterprise and should not be attached to any specific project.

33. Although it might be tempting, in a spirit of traceability to attach the cost of carrying-out post completion reviews to those projects reviewed, it must be borne in mind that the beneficiaries of the reviews and thus of these costs are essentially future projects. The fact that a sample of projects is specifically chosen for review for the purpose of learning emphasizes the lack of logic in allocating the cost of the reviews to such projects.

SECTION 3—THE POST COMPLETION REVIEW COMMITTEE

34. The post completion review is a management function. It requires the support of the financial function.

35. The post completion review should be carried out by a committee composed of persons who are experienced in or familiar with the firm's capital expenditure control system and sufficiently knowledgeable of the processes used in assessing technical, financial and marketing aspects of both the implementation of the project and of its outcome. Since the scope of a post completion review extends beyond financial information, the accountant, internal auditor or financial officer serving on a post completion review committee should do so as a manager first, not just as an accountant.

36. In small organizations or for small projects, the post completion review can be carried out by one individual. Such an individual, most likely a senior manager, should not have been significantly involved in the project choice or implementation.

Key Conditions for a Successful Committee

37. A successful post completion review requires that:

   - some of the persons who have been involved in the decision and implementation processes will participate in the committee work for their own as well as for organizational learning;

   - the post completion review committee includes independent analysts and managers;

   - the members of the committee, or at least its senior members, have the appropriate level of authority to have access to the required information. The post completion review committee is not necessarily a permanent committee. Its composition may vary with each project so as to gain the most from the learning experience;

   - management supports the committee and provides it with the required resources;

   - individual responsibilities of the committee members are clearly specified. In some cases designing a procedures manual will be useful;

   - committee members must understand the enterprise's strategy, operations, context and environment;

   - committee members must be provided with the opportunity to communicate and cooperate with the personnel in all functions and departments. They may also be authorized to seek assistance from consultants or outside agencies; and

   - the experience of previous post completion reviews must be made available to the committee.

Composition of the Post Completion Review Committee

38. Supervision of the post completion review committee should, in principle, be assigned to a senior manager. The actual composition of the committee will be a function of many circumstantial variables specific to each firm. The next few paragraphs provide some guiding principles for the selection of the committee members.

39. Even though non-financial parameters will be reviewed, the synthesis of all that information is financial. The management accountant or financial officer on the committee, thus, plays an important role in structuring the findings of the committee.

40. In certain situations where the review of the technical or marketing aspects of the project is particularly difficult or critical, the lead role will best be filled by someone with the necessary skills and experience. In this case the management accountant or management controller will work closely with the lead person.

41. In all cases the management accountant will have a leading role in the review of the actions taken to insure adherence to the company policies and procedures. The internal audit department should be represented on the committee to ensure that it meets internal auditing standards. Accountants

and auditors should not represent the core of the committee. The Chief Internal Auditor should always be represented on the committee or be kept informed of its progress to eliminate the need for subsequent audits that might duplicate the post completion review. The presence of operational executives on the committee is crucial to ensure that the findings of the committee are credible to all on the senior management team.

42. The success of a post completion review rests on complete and adequate records. For this reason the committee is appointed before the project is undertaken, and one person, generally a management accountant or management controller, should be made responsible for designing and supervising the operation of the information system required to supply information to the post completion review file. An illustration of a post completion documentation program is provided in Appendix 1 to this Statement.

SECTION 4—THE METHODOLOGY OF POST COMPLETION REVIEW

When Must the Review Be Carried Out?

43. The financial impact of capital expenditure of an enterprise is generally felt over several years. It is first a cash outflow (the investment phase of the project) and later becomes, after completion, a series of cash outflows and cash inflows (the outcome phase). Thus there are two types of post completion reviews:

- An "investment" post completion review or "post investment" review takes place immediately after the completion of the investment. Its purpose is to focus (1) on how the project was carried out, (2) on a comparison between forecasted and actual expenditures, and (3) on a comparison between forecasted and actual nominal project capabilities.

- An "outcome" post-completion review can take place at any time during the life of the outcome of the project. Its purpose is to focus on a comparison between the forecasted and actual outcomes, between the assumptions and the actuals.

44. The date of the "outcome" post completion review is set at the beginning of the project. It is defined as the date at which the project is expected to have reached a steady state of outcome.

45. Multiple post completion reviews on a single project may be justified only where the assessment stage has established that the project's economic performance is liable to change considerably over time or where the project's estimated useful life is critically important.

Steps in the Implementation of a Post Completion Review

46. The post completion review is strategic in scope and orientation since it should emphasize lessons for the future. Giving too much attention to near-term financial aspects may distort the objective of the post completion review.

47. A post completion review should provide an overview of the way in which the capital expenditure decision-making process can be improved. It should provide an opportunity for management to assess their understanding of the impact of various key variables on decision making and on implementation.

48. There are three components of the post completion review, whether it is a post investment review or an outcome review:

- the decision review (dealing with the assessment process);

- the planning and budgeting assumptions and process review; and

- the performance review (dealing with the implementation and above all, with the outcome).

49. The review should ensure that the stated objectives are achieved (effectiveness criterion) and that resources were judiciously employed (efficiency criterion). The post completion review should indicate whether the results achieved are consistent with those which were expected. If not, the reasons for any variances should be analyzed. An example of a post completion review check list is given as Appendix 2 to this Statement.

50. An explanation is also expected when actual results are consistent with the forecasts. Post completion reviews do not only apply to projects in which something has gone wrong. They also cover highly successful projects or aspects thereof.

Post Completion Reviews Are Positive and Constructive

51. Although the post completion review is essentially a positive and constructive tool aimed at enhancing learning, its process can lead to the identification of individuals responsible for deviations from forecast. The post completion review team should always focus its attention on why and how deviations occurred, not on who can be blamed for them. Once the original cause has been determined, a key step has been taken toward solving the problem. The emphasis is to be placed on collecting factual and quantifiable data and information, not on second guessing the decision makers involved in the various phases of the project.

52. The post completion review is geared at understanding and at generating continuous progress.

53. An illustrative example of a post completion review is provided as Appendix 3 to this Statement.

FACTORS RELATED TO DOCUMENTATION
SUPPORTING A POST COMPLETION REVIEW

A program must be put in place as soon as the project is conceived in order to collect information even though the final assessment may be carried out only at the end of the project.

All key decisions must be documented. Decision reports must be prepared in a coherent format in order to be useful to the post completion review. Decisions about the funding of the project are independent of the decision process regarding its economic or strategic interest. The post completion review may include a review of the actual implementation of the funding process but such review should be kept separate from that of operational implementation and of strategic decision making.

All parameters likely to influence the project should be identified at each step of the decision process. They should be updated throughout the life of the project both in terms of their value and state. The original and the updated values and state of all parameters are collected in the post completion review file.

All project management reports describing how the different phases were carried out are to be retained in the project post completion review file.

The post completion review team must specifically address the question of the adequacy of the data gathering process and procedures: content, timing, quality, scope, etc.

Information Contained in the Post Completion Review File

Decision Phase

- The proposal file.

- The approval decision.

- The funding information.

Planning Phase

- A statement of the scope and purpose of the project.

- A statement of the original subdivision of the project into a given number of activities and the criteria used to determine this subdivision. Responsibility for implementation and resource requirements should also be included.

- An estimate of the time required to carry out each activity and the method used to determine this estimate.

- The timing of the various activities and the reasons why this timing method was chosen over alternative solutions.

- The time interval between each pair of activities.

- The critical path determined.

- The documentation related to the activities selected for subcontracting.

Operations Control

- The detailed flow of the assessment and reporting system used for actual and acquired values.

- Information related to purchase orders.

- The qualifications, training and experience of all staff involved.

- The dates when values were determined, possibly updated and reported.

- The position of the individuals responsible for determining the values and those for whom the values were prepared.

- The procedures used to verify and monitor data capture.

- The list of source documents, i.e., those used to make calculations and those to be found only in the field (on the construction site, for example).

- The means used to inform potential subcontractors of assessment techniques.

- Procedures relating to direct materials (supply, receiving, storage, delivery to site).

- Standard procedures for accounts payable (receiving invoices, checking quantities and prices, approvals).

- Time sheets (establishing origin, checking and remitting).

- Information on the progress of activity groups.

- Changes in authorization procedures and the scope of any such changes.

- Distribution of budgeted hours per activity.

- Facts related to errors which were detected too late.

- A list of staff members originating corrective action.

- For each alternative contemplated regarding possible ways of realization of the project, a list of the variables and parameters involved.

- The range of tools and actions available to act upon the variables to be corrected.

- Inclusion of all published background information, reports (market, technology, fiscal, legal, social, financial, etc.) with a view to determining how relevant they are.

- Supplemental information concerning the assessment techniques used in each report when these were not clearly identified.

- Cost, completion and financial management reports indicating the original plan in addition to the progress of the project in relation to the various forecasts.

- Description of frequency of reporting and origin of reports.

- Executive summary for the decision makers.

How to Report

A post completion review report should clearly indicate what was expected, when the project was initiated, and what actually occurred. It provides a summary of the lessons drawn from the decision, planning and performance audits and also examines the project's operations in relation to the overall strategy of the firm. The report's major objective is to identify lessons for the future.

After reviewing the post completion review report, management should be aware of the following:

- whether options have been considered in accordance with each stage of the project;

- whether the sensitivity of the various options to alternative environmental assumptions has been tested;

- whether problems have been encountered with a major section or with individual data;

- whether the project was implemented in accordance with original or revised plans;

- whether the project has delivered the benefits expected originally or subsequently; and

- the extent to which the success or failure of the project was due to the internal management and/or planning of the project and/or to environmental changes.

The results of individual post completion reviews will be submitted to the management group responsible for the project. In addition, post completion review reports should be presented to senior management at regular intervals. In many cases this review function will be the responsibility of a management committee which may be also responsible for the review of project proposals. Combining project review considerations with new project proposals should foster a direct link with the lessons drawn from past experience.

MANAGEMENT ACCOUNTING

EXAMPLE OF A POST COMPLETION REVIEW CHECK LIST

This example is geared to a relatively large organization. A smaller organization would have to adapt this list to fit its needs and resources while keeping the spirit of the original.

Questions Related to Decision-Making:

- How was the project selected?

- Who conducted the assessment?

- How were the data selected for this assessment?

- Was a risk analysis carried out that outlined the range of possible outcomes? If yes, how and why?

- What information was analyzed in arriving at the decision? Could the decision have been different if more information had been provided for the assessment?

- Has the project's strategic role within the company been clearly and formally presented?

- If there was no overall strategy at the time of the assessment, was a strategy worked out subsequently and, if yes, was the project consistent with it?

- Were the anticipated strategic benefits achieved, exceeded or not achieved? What are the major factors contributing to the actual results?

- Do the procedures provide the assessment system with the requisite level of information to pass judgment on project proposals?

- Is such a level of detail required for all capital expenditures?

Questions on Planning and Budgeting:

Planning:

- Was the purpose of the project clearly identified?

- Were responsibilities for planning clearly established?

- Was a cost accounting and classification system designed appropriate to the project's methods for budgeting, assessing, analyzing and reporting costs?

- Was an implementation plan established for specific activities with predetermined resource constraints?

- Were contingency plans identified?

Budgeting:

- Have the most effective budgeting methods been used on the basis of available information?
- Was information on unit resource costs taken from reliable sources?
- Were forecasted inflation rates based on realistic assumptions?
- Were the reserves for contingencies determined after careful consideration?
- Were changes in scope correctly treated and approved?
- Was information on actual expenditure available on a timely basis?
- Was a performance review system put in place for internal services, operations and equipment?
- Were progress reports available on a timely basis?

Questions Related to Performance and Outcome:

Analysis:

- Was the project used for the purpose specified and are the objectives being met?
- Have significant variances always been analyzed according to the same criteria? Given the available information, have the reasons for cost and scheduling variances always been analyzed and interpreted and have these reasons led to actions?
- Has data analysis been done early enough to contribute to the formulation of a corrective action plan?

Control:

- Have major changes to the implementation strategy been based on a careful review of options?
- Have the individuals in charge taken prompt control measures?
- Have the funds allocated to the project been administered so as to minimize the cost of funding?
- Did cost and completion date estimates fully take into account performance variances and the consequences of corrective actions?

Information:

- Were appropriate information parameters used (contents, presentation, scope, level of detail and frequency of reports)?
- Were reports submitted on time and was information presented consistently from period to period?
- Did the reports submitted to senior executives present, concisely and precisely, information in compliance with cost and performance estimates?
- Did the reports help the individuals in charge to make their decisions?

A CASE ILLUSTRATION

The ACME Corporation case example is provided only as an illustration and should not be considered to be either a "perfect" case nor an exhaustive case. It is a real case in which the data have been disguised and simplified to guide the user in understanding how to implement Post Completion Review Techniques.

The post completion report is composed of the following documents:

- Excerpts from the Corporate Financial Manual
- Post Completion Executive Summary (October 1992)
- Post Completion Review (October 1992)
    - Summary Evaluation.
    - Background.
    - Project Description.
    - Actual Results.
    - Actual Financial Benefits.
    - Project Evaluation.
    - Conclusion.
    - Attachment 1: P & L estimate 1991-1995
    - Attachment 2: Cash Flow Analysis 1991-1995
- Audit Report (November 6, 1992)

ACME Corporation
Excerpts from the Finance Manual
Post Completion Review Section

PURPOSE

To establish a standard method to compare the actual costs, results and benefits of selected capital projects with the stated targets contained in the final approved Appropriation Request. The tracking of post-completion evaluations will serve to improve the planning, evaluation and implementation of future capital projects.

APPLICATION

Applies to ACME Corporation, its divisions and all subsidiaries.

POLICY

1. Projects[3] over FF 10 million total cost will be subject to post-completion review by the Capital Projects Review Committee (CPR). Projects below this

---

[3]Acquisitions whose primary purpose was to acquire facilities in lieu of constructing our own and market development projects are, for the purposes of this policy, included within the definition of capital projects.

level may be selected for review at the Committee's discretion. The Committee may waive the post-completion review requirement on any project.

2. For projects of less than FF 1 million, the sponsoring unit may establish its own criteria for internal post-completion reviews.

3. The time-frame for post completion reviews will be established in accordance with the time schedule contained in the final approved Appropriation Request or A-R (excluding supplemental requests) as follows:

A. For projects supported by financial payback, the post-completion review will be performed within the calendar year following the attainment of either:

- the midpoint of the expected payback period, or
- the completion of two years of operation; *whichever comes first.*

B. For projects not so supported, the post-completion review will be performed within the calendar year following the completion of one and a half years of operation.

RESPONSIBILITIES

Divisions

Annually, by September 30, Divisions will prepare a list of projects scheduled for post-completion review during the forthcoming year and submit to the Director, ACME Capital Planning and Economic Analysis.

ACME Capital Planning and Economic Analysis Unit

Will prepare a consolidated listing of projects scheduled for post-completion review during the forthcoming year and arrange for CPR's review in October.

Subsequent to this review, will notify the affected units of the annual requirements and establish an appropriate time schedule for submission of post-completion reviews.

Division

Will prepare the required post-completion reviews including an operational review addressing significant financial as well as physical, technical, and market-parameter variances from anticipated targets and actions taken to alter or change existing conditions. Upon obtaining required divisional approvals, i.e., Chief Financial Officer and Division Chief Executive Officer, will forward approved post-completion reviews to ACME Capital Planning and Economic Analysis per the established time schedule.

ACME Capital Planning and Economic Analysis

Will coordinate the distribution of reviews for evaluation by CPR.

Will notify the appropriate division after CPR review if additional analysis or comments are required on any presented project.

PREPARATION OF FORMS

Post-Completion Review Form

Use form n° 0278-93, CAPITAL PROJECT POST-COMPLETION REVIEW (Summary Evaluation) to present comparison of projected versus actual/estimated project costs/objectives/benefits. (See below for instructions.)

Additional information may, at the discretion of division management, be presented in a format which best displays the data for a particular business or operation.

For projects supported by financial payback, form n° 2371-93, FINANCIAL EVALUATION, is to be used to supply a detailed financial evaluation indicating actual project costs and operating results, to date, as well as updated operating projections for future time periods.

INSTRUCTION for:
CAPITAL PROJECT POST COMPLETION REVIEW FORM n° 0278-93

This form is used to present the summary comparative financial, technical and market data for the Post-Completion Review (abbreviated PCR) of major capital projects. Where applicable, all financial data should be obtained from form n° 2371-93 (Financial Evaluation) as contained in the various Appropriation Requests and/or the Post-Completion Review work-up.

On projects which were not justified on financial grounds, such as anti-pollution investments, capacity maintenance investment or discretionary investments, only the capital expenditures are to be shown under *Project Data*, with appropriate commentary on the realization of the project's objectives included under the *Project Analysis/Recommended Corrective Action: Synopsis* section.

Project Data:

- Presents a summary comparison between the final approved Appropriation Request and the actual/projected operating results.

- Capital Expenditures. Total cost of investments in fixed assets. Coincides with the final approved Appropriation Request.

- Average Working Capital. The average of year-end working capital requirements through the period covered by the analysis.

- Market and operating technical data: by quarter or by month, whichever is appropriate to show operating efficiency and market penetration compared to competitors.

- Other. The total of other investment components not included above.

Project Analysis/Recommended Corrective Action: Synopsis. All commentaries should be brief and in synopsis form. Include a description of the project and review its current status versus the final Appropriation Request data. Comment on significant factors which have affected either the investment cost, profits, market share or volume, or other objectives of the project since it was authorized, e.g., altered start-up costs, change in anticipated yields, different labor or material costs, change in regulations, etc. Discuss any recommended corrective actions that could be taken to counter unfavorable aspects of the project's performance.

The post-completion review should be geared toward the operational factors relating to the project. Emphasis should be placed on actual project achievements versus the project purpose as stated in the original Appropriation Request, with explanations describing the differences.

ACME Corporation
Widget Division
Post Completion Review of Widget-K Transfer from
Orleans Plant to Bari Plant

Executive Summary (October 1992)

Original Approval

- The original appropriation request (approved 3/91) funded the transfer of filling and packaging equipment for Widget-K 15 unit packages and 30 unit packages from Orleans to Bari.

- Capital required (FF 12 million) included compounding equipment, storage tanks and required ancillary equipment as well as necessary building modifications and construction of a storage shed for staging production components.

- It was anticipated that the transfer of Widget-K 15 and 30 would result in an estimated FF 10 million annual tax savings to the Corporation due to the favorable situation of the Mezzogiorno with regards to tax exemption and EEC subsidies and provide an IRR of 81 %, with payback in 1.2 years.

Actual/Estimated Results

- The primary objective of the project was met, i.e., the transfer of production of Widget-K from Orleans to Bari, which began 10/91.

- The transfer will result in average annual tax benefits of FF 10 million with an 89% IRR. Payback was generated in 1.3 years.

- This project also enabled Bari to manufacture Mombat-S Widgets and paved the way for the transfer of the manufacturing of Schtrumpf-Z-Widget in 1993 with a lower amount of capital investment.

Financial Overview (in FF 000)

Comparison of Original Appropriation Request (A-R) vs. Post Completion Review (PCR)

	Estimate Per Appropriation Request	Actual Per Post Completion Review
Capital Requirement	FF 12,000 (see below for details)	FF 11,295 (see below for details)
Avg. Annual Tax Svgs.(Approx.)	10,000	10,000
IRR	81%	89%
Payback	1.2 yrs	1.3 yrs
Tax Basis	50/50 split	50/50 split
Tax Savings Rate (35%-20%)	15%	15%

Comparison of Fixed Assets Requirements (in FF 000)

	Estimate per Appropriation Request	Actual per Post Completion Review	Difference
Land improvement	—	90	(90)
Building	1,060	1,440	(380)
Building improvements	1,235	1,160	75
Building machines and equipment	1,025	910	115
Machines and equipment	5,795	5,650	145
Computer equipment	—	50	(50)
Design and engineering	725	500	225
Other costs	—	380	(380)
Freight	60	240	(180)
Start-up costs	500	875	(375)
Contingency reserve	1,600	—	1,600
Total	12,000	11,295	705

ACME Corporation
Widget Division

Post Completion Review of Widget-K Transfer from Orleans Plant to Bari Plant

Summary evaluation (dated: October 1992)

Approved by:

VP Manufacturing: Rodolfo Impemba

Manager Technical Operations: Arthur Roig

Widget Division Manager: Isabella Guglielmini

Widget Division Controller: François Berrichon

Chief Financial Officer, Machine Division, Wilfried Drücker

Project Data (in FF 000)		
	Final Appropriation Request	Post Completion Review
Capital Expenditure	12,000	11,295
Average Working Capital	—	—
Other	—	—
TOTAL INVESTMENT	12,000	11,295
Return on investment/Internal rate of return	81%	89%
Payback period	1.2 years	1.3 years
Date of acceptance	09/91	12/91

In 1989, an evaluation concluded that the transfer of Widget-K 15 and 30 unit production from Orleans to Bari would result in an estimated FF 10 million in tax savings to the corporation due to the different tax rates between France and the Mezzogiorno of Italy. Additionally, production cost would be reduced by approximately FF 500,000 per year due to lower staffing and pay rates in Bari. However, it was anticipated that the labor savings would be offset by additional freight costs to ship the product from Bari and the need to lease additional warehouse space in Bari.

The primary objective of this project was to transfer the existing stuffing and packaging equipment from Orleans to Bari, purchase and install machining and required ancillary equipment, make the necessary building modifications and construction to the existing space in the Bari ACME Italia industrial building and build a storage shed for storing production components.

The major objective of the project was met and production began in October 1990. The total cost of this project to date is FF 11.295 million, FF 705,000 less than initially projected. The actual return on the investment is to date 89% and higher than originally anticipated due primarily to higher tax savings resulting from increased sales volumes.

WIDGET-K TRANSFER TO BARI

BACKGROUND

In 1989, an evaluation concluded that the transfer of Widget-K 15 and 30 which was being produced in France at the Orleans plant could be transferred to the Bari, Italy site for FF 12 million in capital cost and result in an estimated FF 10 million in annual tax savings to the Corporation.

The existing stuffing and packaging equipment would be transferred from Orleans to Bari and the necessary machining and ancillary equipment would be purchased and installed in the existing space within the Bari ACME Italia industrial building. Additionally, a storage shed would be constructed on the site for staging production components.

In addition to the subsidies and tax savings, production of Widget K 15 and 30 in Bari was expected to provide approximately FF 500,000 annually in labor savings due to lower pay rates and staffing requirements in Bari versus Orleans. As a result of the transfer, 19 positions were to be eliminated in Orleans with personnel reassigned and absorbed into other positions created by new products and increased volume, thus generating a net headcount gain of 19 persons in the French operations. The project anticipated that 15-17 additional personnel would be required in Bari to meet the increased workload.

PROJECT DESCRIPTION

The initial project, as proposed, required a capital investment of FF 12 million to:

- Transfer the existing Widget-K packaging and stuffing line from Orleans to Bari.

- Purchase the necessary machining and ancillary equipment.

- Make building modifications and additions needed to install the equipment in the existing space within the Bari ACME Italia industrial building and build a storage shed for staging of components.

(The construction of the storage shed was not identified in the original A-R but was included in the presentation to the CPR.)

Production of Widget-K 15 and 30 unit packages in Bari was expected to provide an estimated FF 10 million annually in subsidies and tax savings to the Corporation. Additionally, the reduction in product cost from labor savings, estimated at FF 500,000 per year would be offset by additional freight costs incurred to ship the finished product from southern Italy to the northern European market. The project also anticipated that Bari would need to lease additional warehouse space for storage of finished products.

Funding for the project was provided through one appropriation request approved for FF 12 million in February 1990, with start up projected for September 1990.

ACTUAL RESULTS

The major goal of this project was met and production of Widget-K 15 and 30 unit packages began in October 1990.

The total capital spending to complete the project was FF 11.295 million including FF 875,000 in start-up costs.

During the project, a computerized statistical process control program costing FF 50,000 was implemented to improve productivity and product quality on the Widget-K line and was included in the total project cost. Although this was not specifically identified in the A-R, it was part of the project and a scope change was not required.

Overall, the total project cost was favorable by FF 705,000. However, problems were incurred in the initial start-up which resulted in additional spending of FF 375,000 for temporary help and overtime. Also, because Widget-K production required a second shift, an additional parking area costing FF 90,000 was constructed to accommodate the overflow during the shift change which was not anticipated in the original A-R. Other modifications to build a loading area and install partitions to segregate the production lines for Health and Environment Regulation compliance, were not originally anticipated and resulted in an overrun of FF 305,000 for building and for building improvements. Reductions in the cost of the building air conditioning machinery and equipment (due to the possibility of inexpensive sourcing in Greece as opposed to sourcing in Germany in the original A-R and due to the more favorable rate of exchange drachma to lira versus deutsche mark to lira), and design fees more than offset the unanticipated additional spending.

The actual staff additions, and the equipment transfer occurred as planned.

ACTUAL FINANCIAL BENEFITS

The actual sell through for 1991 from products manufactured at Bari was lower than originally anticipated, resulting from a higher than expected inventory build-up in Orleans prior to the transfer. However, the estimated 1992-1995 sales are higher than anticipated due to a stronger market position.

Labor savings which were anticipated as a result of lower staffing requirements and pay rates did not materialize in 1991 and in the first half of 1992 due to start-up problems. They are, however, anticipated for 1992-1995. Conversely, the incremental/additional freight expenses as originally anticipated did not result due to a later decision to ship directly from Bari to the expedition center in Brussels. Although additional warehouse space was leased, this was due to increased in-line volumes and not driven by Widget-K. Therefore, no additional expense was incurred for this project.

Tax savings are calculated at 15% of the Profit Contribution, based on the difference between French rates and the effective Southern Italy rate based on a 50/50 profit split.

Due to the increase in projected sales and lower capital investment, the actual financial return of this project is 89%. A comparison of the current estimate to the final appropriation request is summarized below:

Summary of Comparison of Final Appropriation Request and Current Estimate (in FF 000)		
	Original Appropriation Request	Actual (per PCR)
Capital Expenditures	FF 12,000	FF 11,295
Average Annual Savings After Tax	FF 7,000	FF 8,845
Internal Rate of Return	81%	89%
Payback	1.2 years	1.3 years

An analysis of the estimated tax savings and cash flow is provided in Attachments 1 and 2.

PROJECT EVALUATION

The experiences from this project are well documented and as a result, the following recommendations can be made:

• Future projects should clearly state items and allocations of shared assets.

• Final document presented to CPR should be reviewed by the sponsoring unit in order to assure detailed data is referenced in final write-up.

• Financial assumptions should be documented separately and kept by the finance representative in order to facilitate future reference to these when revisiting the project for post completion purposes.

CONCLUSION

In addition to the significant tax savings realized from the transfer of Widget-K production to Southern Italy, this project has also operationally enabled Bari to manufacture Mombat-S Widgets and paved the way for the transfer of Schtrumpf-Z Widgets in 1993 with a lower amount of capital investment. The Widget-K transfer in itself was successful from both the financial and operational benefits.

P & L ESTIMATE 1991-1995

Widget-K transfer to Bari
Post Completion Review

P & L Estimate (in FF 000) Widget-K Line Plant Transfer Project				
	Actual 1991	Estimate 1992	Forecast 1993	Forecast 1994	Forecast 1995
Sales	159,465	217,775	224,000	233,000	237,000
Cost of sales	16,580	25,750	25,850	26,975	27,410
Gross margin	142,885	192,025	198,150	206,025	209,590
Promotion	31,255	42,685	43,905	45,670	46,450
Sales force	11,960	16,335	16,800	17,475	17,775
Marketing administration	7,975	10,890	11,200	11,650	11,850
Discounts and freight	6,380	8,710	8,960	9,320	9,480
General and administrative	7,975	10,890	11,200	11,650	11,850
Product margin	77,340	102,515	106,085	110,260	112,185
Research allowance	24,720	33,755	34,720	36,115	36,735
Profit before tax	52,620	68,760	71,365	74,145	75,450
Tax savings to Corp. at 15% due to transfer	7,893	10,314	10,705	11,122	11,318

Assumptions:

1) Sales are based on actuals for 1991 and on projected sales and costs for 1992 to 1995, based on the Widget Division Operational Plan.

2) Cost of Sales for 1991 based on actual sell through per tax audit and 1992 to 1995 based on Operational Plan based on the forecasted evolution of the sales mix.

3) Other expenses estimated on the basis of a percentage of sales as follows: Promotion: 19.6%; Sales Force: 7.5%; Discounts and Freight: 4%; Marketing and General and Administrative Expenses: 5% each; and, Research allowance at 15.5%.

4) Actual and estimated tax savings based on the difference between the French rate of 35% and the effective southern Italy rate of 20% and based on a transfer price allowing a 50/50 split of profit between France and Italy.

CASH FLOW ANALYSIS 1991-1995

Widget-K transfer to Bari
Post Completion Review

Incremental Cash Flow Analysis (in FF 000)
Widget-K Line Plant Transfer Project

	Actual 1990	Actual 1991	Estimate 1992	Forecast 1993	Forecast 1994	Forecast 1995
Labor savings		0	0	500	500	500
Start-up cost	−875					
Incremental depreciation		−575	−695	−695	−695	−695
Asset write-off						−7,065
Pre-tax operating impact	−875	−575	−695	−195	−195	−7,260
Taxes @ 20%	−175	−115	−139	−39	−39	−1,452
After tax operating impact	−700	−460	−556	−156	−156	−5,808
French tax savings	0	7,895	10,315	10,705	11,120	11,320
Depreciation add-back		575	695	695	695	695
Write-off add-back						7,065
Capital investment	−8,655	−1,765				
Cash flow	−9,355	6,245	10,454	11,244	11,659	13,272
Internal rate of return: 89.1%						
Payback: 1.3 years						

Notes:

1) Labor savings did not materialize as originally anticipated for 1991 and 1992 and are as expected, per revised action plan for 1993-1995.

2) Additional freight cost as anticipated did not occur based on later decision to ship directly from Bari to Brussels.

3) Depreciation allowance is based on straight line over a 15 year life.

4) Additional warehouse rental expense not incurred as anticipated.

Audit Report n° 92-159

Post Completion Review of Widget-K Transfer from Orleans Plant to Bari Plant

[Memo-dated November 6, 1992]

An audit of the attached Capital Project Post-Completion Review Report relating to the Appropriation Request to transfer manufacturing operations of Widget-K from Orleans, France, to Bari, Italy, was performed by Corporate Internal Audits.

The project was designated by the Capital Projects Review Committee for a Post-Completion Review and requested that Corporate Audits review the report prior to its submission to the Committee.

Corporate Audits did not participate in the preparation of the Post-Completion Report and the supporting financial data.

Our review included the following:

- Determining that the Post-Completion Review Report was completed in accordance with ACME Corporation Finance Policy: "Capital Investment Guidelines-Post-Completion Reviews."

- Verifying that the financial information included in the Post-Completion Review Report agreed with the information stated in the Appropriation Request.

- Verifying that the total project cost was in agreement with the underlying accounting records.

- Reviewing the explanations included in the Project Analysis for reasonableness.

- Testing the mathematical accuracy of the data provided.

- Verifying that the Post-Completion Review Report relating to the Appropriation Request to transfer the manufacturing operations of Widget-K from France to Southern Italy was properly completed in accordance with ACME Corporation Finance Policy: "Capital Investment Guidelines—Post-Completion Reviews." The project cost data is reasonably stated and is in agreement with the underlying records.

Signed: Aloysius Van Der Beck

MANAGEMENT ACCOUNTING

7

February 1996

Strategic Planning for
Information Resource Management[*]

CONTENTS

	Paragraphs
RATIONALE	
SCOPE	1-5
TOWARD KNOWLEDGE-BASED BUSINESS.	6-16
A New Role for Information Technology	9-10
The Force of Packaged Software	11
Importance of Technology Flexibility	12
Emergence of New Work Systems.	13-16
THE ROLE OF IRM.	17-22
OBJECTIVES OF IRM	23-26
DEVELOPING THE IRM STRATEGIC PLAN	27-72
Determine Strategic Information Resource Requirements	35-40
Baseline Existing Environment	41-46
Define the Information Resource Environment.	47-72
Develop Information Models	49-51

[*] ACKNOWLEDGMENT: The Financial and Management Accounting Committee is indebted to The Society of Management Accountants of Canada for allowing it to reproduce the Society's Management Accounting Guideline 9, "Strategic Planning for Information Resource Management", as a an International Management Accounting Practice Statement.

Develop Target Architectures.. 52-70
Maintaining the Target Architecture 71-72

PREPARE THE IRM IMPLEMENTATION PLAN 73-91
Project Selection Mechanism 74-86
Scoring Criteria 77-80
The Scoring Process... 81-87
Selection Process 88-91

IMPLEMENTING THE STRATEGIC PLAN 92-95
MEASURING SUCCESS — POST-IMPLEMENTATION
    REVIEW 96-100
Strategic Review 96-98
Tactical Review 99-100

IRM POLICIES, STANDARDS AND PROCEDURES 101-103

IRM ROLES AND RESPONSIBILITIES 104-119
Chief Information Officer 105-107
Information Systems Steering Committee 108-111
User Department Management 112-115
Management Accountants 116-117
Internal Auditors 118
Information Systems Specialists 119

APPENDIX — MODELING TECHNIQUES

GLOSSARY

RATIONALE

Public and private sector organizations alike are reshaping and streamlining their business processes, placing increased emphasis on the customer. Success in this initiative depends on understanding the customer base, its preferences, its behaviors and its needs, as well as the company's ability to respond. In this situation, most organizations have an abundance of information upon which to draw. Unfortunately, if the infrastructure does not provide for the effective creation, use, management, access and delivery of relevant data, the organization will be totally frustrated in its efforts to capitalize on its base of information.

Fragmented automation efforts, unilateral commitment to mainframe-based applications, incompatible proprietary hardware platforms, disparate software, and inaccessible data do not satisfy the need for information systems to be an essential, indispensable and strategic component of service delivery and no longer satisfy the business and service goals of many organizations. A revised approach to planning that recognizes the relationship between business planning and technical infrastructure is needed.

It is critical that this approach address the requirement for:

- satisfying customer needs;

- responding to changing organizational structures;

- taking advantage of open system concepts;

- adhering to industry standards;

- providing distributed, coordinated and accessible hardware, software and data resources;

- supporting redesigned processes;

- responding to changing requirements;

- being easy to use; and

- recognizing the significance of data as a corporate resource.

From a purely technological perspective, most information systems organizations recognize that data need to be managed, but relatively few organizations recognize that the knowledge housed in the organization's databases can provide the means to rapidly propel the organization forward, moving ahead of its competitors in the process. The first organization in an industry to recognize and exploit the value of a particular piece of information, often something that is available to all industry members, gains a competitive advantage.

Information Resource Management (IRM) takes a broad view of the enterprise and does not focus too narrowly on the requirements of a particular group or department.

An effective strategic IRM plan describes an organization's information requirements and strategies for satisfying them and can yield the following benefits:

- development of systems that are targeted to support strategic and operational objectives;

- increased integration of technologies, which improves the sharing of information across the organization and makes it easier to obtain information for changing decision-making needs;

- identification and adoption of appropriate information technology standards, minimizing dependence on specific suppliers of hardware or software;

- identification of opportunities to improve the relevance and adequacy of information provided and activities performed;

- a technological infrastructure that will support the strategic business plan;

- minimization of duplicate, and possibly inconsistent, data and processing capabilities within the organization's portfolio of information systems;

- prioritization of projects to be implemented; and

- greater cost-justification of system development and maintenance activities.

Information is an invaluable asset — IRM assists an organization in its efforts to move beyond data management to the strategically beneficial ability to leverage its information. This guideline is designed to provide the necessary background for an organization to proceed with planning and implementing a cohesive approach to capitalizing on its information assets.

SCOPE

1. The foundation for the IRM strategic planning process is the organization's business strategy, its statement of business goals and objectives and challenges. For the purposes of this Statement, it is assumed that the organization has:

   - defined what business(es) it wants to be in
   - identified its core business processes
   - identified and analyzed the factors critical to its future success
   - defined its markets
   - studied its industry and competitors
   - identified its strengths and weaknesses

2. The principles described in this Statement are broad-based, but sound: statements of preferred direction, goals and concepts for guiding the development and use of computers, telecommunications equipment and software in support of an IRM environment. Circumstances may indicate that

an organization should pursue a specific direction, e.g., buy vs build software or outsource the information systems function. In these instances, the approach outlined in this Statement will provide a systems approach and an appropriate framework for the decision-making process.

3. The principles are subject to modification according to the size and type of business and as technology evolves and business requirements change. Adoption of these principles will have a profound impact on the management of technology, the structure and configuration of technical facilities, and the delivery of responsive, value-added services to clients and customers.

4. Using the strategic business plan of the organization as a starting point, this Statement outlines the process for creating an IRM plan. The IRM plan will be of help in the design and implementation of the information systems necessary to support the business plan.

5. This Statement provides a discussion of the objectives of IRM, the core concepts involved and the functions and responsibilities associated with IRM. It describes the stages of the IRM planning process:

- translating the strategic business plan into strategic information requirements;

- constructing business models based on identified strategic information requirements;

- constructing target architectures from the business models;

- creating a strategic implementation plan that specifies how the target architectures are to be implemented; and

- conducting a post-implementation review to ensure that IRM is achieving its intended objectives.

TOWARD KNOWLEDGE-BASED BUSINESS

6. According to Vita Cassesse, Vice President of Systems and Market Research for the U.S. Pharmaceuticals Group of New York-based Pfizer Inc.: "Technology is just one small component of the continuum. ...You can't effectively manage the information unless you know how it needs to be — and why it needs to be — communicated."[1] Equally important is the need to recognize that information technology cannot, by itself, transform data into knowledge. Thomas H. Davenport, Director of the Information Systems Management Program at the University of Texas in Austin, says: "Nobody can say they're not interested in how to make effective use of information ...You can't become a successful executive unless you've mastered that to some degree."[2]

7. There is no one in any information technology-related function, business or organization that does not think about information as an asset in today's knowledge-based business environment. The question of whether you are in a

---

[1] Dragoon, Alice. Knowledge Management — Rx for Success. *CIO* (July 1995), 48-56.

[2] Buchanan, Leigh. The CIO Role — The Medium and the Message. *CIO* (July 1995), 68-76.

technology business or an information business is irrelevant: the real issue is how to assemble a technology infrastructure through which the best and most appropriate content (i.e., information) for your organization's needs can flow. This is a major challenge when the volatile business environment of today is coupled with the dynamics of the contemporary technology environment.

8. There are many events currently underway that could have a profound effect on how an organization should deal with the coming together of business and technology. In many instances, these events are external and uncontrollable. Nevertheless, it will remain the responsibility of each organization to incorporate these unplanned (and often unsolicited) occurrences into their everyday business activities. In order to provide the insight necessary to keep the advice provided in this guideline in the proper perspective, a few such significant shifts are discussed in the following paragraphs.

A New Role for Information Technology

9. There are some fundamental shifts now occurring in the application of computers in business, each affecting a different level of business opportunity. Information technology supports the implementation and maintenance of a high performance team structure, allowing the organization to function as integrated businesses despite high business unit autonomy, and to reach out and develop new relationships with external organizations — to become an extended enterprise.

10. The virtual corporation, i.e., a radical approach to organizational transformation that results in a flexible, responsive and effective entity designed to satisfy the demands of a volatile marketplace, would not have been possible without today's sophisticated information technology. "Unlike yesterday's producers, the virtual corporation can use technology to overcome the barriers imposed by time and distance. ...By the end of this century, the computing environment will be essentially unrestricted, and technology will be sufficiently portable that it will become part of a person's daily work apparel. ...Today, even basic technology is more than a tool; it is an ubiquitous member of the work team, undertaking tasks that are routine and mundane and gathering information about the process, about the end product or service and about the eventual customer. Over time, consistent exploitation of this information can provide an organization with a competitive advantage, assuming that it is able and willing to take action."[3]

The Force of Packaged Software

11. Today many software packages are designed specifically for particular applications and for specific vertical industries and are hardware independent, i.e., they can be installed on many different computing platforms and on multiple sizes of computing equipment. Consequently, in many cases it is much more cost effective to acquire such "off the shelf"

---

[3] The Society of Management Accountants of Canada. *Virtual Corporations — How Real?* (Hamilton, ON: The Society of Management Accountants of Canada, 1993), 27.

software than it is to design and develop code from scratch. The best approach in this situation is to aggressively pursue documentation of requirements before proceeding with the selection of a package. Otherwise, it becomes all too easy to select the application software with the most features, regardless of whether or not it matches the organization's processing requirements or can accommodate its information needs. While packaged software can, in most cases, be adapted to suit specific needs, if the required modifications are extensive, little of the original code will remain, resulting in a unique, and often costly, installation that is difficult to maintain. Nevertheless, "buy vs build" is the direction taken by many organizations when new software applications are needed.

Importance of Technology Flexibility

12. There are three distinct, but related, technology developments that are key to flexibility and adaptability:

- *Open systems* are based on standards that are vendor independent and commonly available. Because of the opportunity for migration to newer, updated technologies based on the organization's own requirements and timetable, adherence to open systems policies results in reduced information technology-related costs and provides value added benefits such as reduced risk of vendor dependence, architectural flexibility, improved interoperability amongst applications, easier migration to newer, innovative technologies and a much better choice of packaged software.

- *"Client/server systems* are built from readily available, standardized components that can be expanded as needed and distributed as most appropriate to the needs of the organization."[4]

- *"Object-oriented systems* are built on a similar extensible model — function specific objects are used to build the desired system. Alterations to a system, to accommodate changing business requirements or to incorporate improvements, can easily be made."[5]

Emergence of New Work Systems

13. The rate of organizational change is almost overwhelming — on a daily basis we face new ways of doing things, new tools to use, new things to be done and different people to do them with. New business themes, each of which demands a new information technology paradigm, are emerging in today's strategic plans as firms re-engineer themselves for the environment, for example:

- productivity of knowledge and service workers

- quality

- responsiveness

---

[4] Duffy, Jan and Ken Matheson. The Need for Flexible Technologies. *CMA Magazine* (October 1994), 9-12.

[5] ibid

- globalization
- outsourcing
- partnering
- social and environmental responsibility

14. Organizations are taking tough actions and making difficult decisions and irreversible changes. Incremental continuous change is part of total quality management programs; periodic radical change is part of business process re-engineering; reduced workforces are part of downsizing; the shift from personal to work group computing is part of the movement toward the work-team approach to employee empowerment. There is no question that survival will be difficult without a major overhaul of organizational structures, job content, human resource policies and practices and, of course, the provision of a technological infrastructure that provides access to information — the key ingredient of contemporary business.

15. New work systems take advantage of a synergistic relationship among people, process and technology. New technology and new work systems must change the nature of jobs if they are to achieve the objective of improved productivity. The corporate culture, whatever its philosophy, will in turn be affected as the flow of work and employee responsibilities change. Management must assess and respond to employees' reactions to this new environment.

16. As well as expecting technology to be intuitively obvious to use, we must focus on developing employees who can intuitively deploy technology to full advantage. At issue is what we can reasonably expect of workers. In order to develop the necessary level of "know-how" people will need to be exposed to learning situations. Technical resources cannot typically provide the type of coaching and facilitation we now find ourselves needing. It is extremely important for human resource professionals to be partners in these development programs.

THE ROLE OF IRM

17. In the past, information was considered only as an internal resource, but, today, an organization's data may be part of a national or international knowledge base. For example, many health-care reform scenarios are expected to call for a national network of local health information systems that speak a common language.[6]

18. An organization's strategic plan describes how it will advance into the future. The IRM strategic plan should focus on how information and technology will support the goals and objectives outlined in the corporate strategy. IRM strategies must be creative and flexible to address current needs and potentially expanded future needs. There is a need for the organization's IRM

---

[6] Health Care Financing Administration's Strategic IRM Plan (FY 1996-2000). This is the primary Federal Agency responsible for administering the Medicare program in the United States.

plan to mirror corporate strategy, e.g., if the enterprise's strategy emphasizes customer service then the IRM plan must also.

19.   IRM is an approach to strategic information systems planning that emphasizes the importance of information as a corporate resource. It focuses on designing, implementing and maintaining a balanced, enterprise-wide system of information, processes and technology. In the IRM environment, technology is viewed as a means to assist the business to do things better, faster and cheaper — not as an end in itself.[7]

20.   It is not unusual for an organization to have a customer information system to manage its customer list, a general ledger accounting system to manage its financial portfolio, personnel and payroll systems to manage its employee information, and inventory control systems to manage its investment in raw materials. All of these house facts about the organization, its customers' buying patterns, its suppliers' pricing fluctuations, currency shifts, etc., information that could be used to advantage. IRM is the term used to describe the function that manages, organizes and coordinates the data resources so that it best supports enterprise activities.[8] In this context, information systems are considered to be the backbone of a valuable data resource, providing the means to successfully deliver these activities.

21.   An information system is a set of interacting components, e.g., computers, data, human resources, telecommunications, etc., with multiple interactions and relationships among them. Effective information management systems are the product of a carefully constructed IRM environment.

22.   It is often difficult to tell where an information system ends and where its environment begins. Indeed, for the remainder of the 1990s, it is likely that the environment within which IRM is being planned, designed and developed will have many complex and conflicting priorities — business process re-engineering, total quality management, downsizing, mergers, acquisitions and economic volatility. This fact only serves to increase the need for a systems approach to change, one that will provide a stable framework in which change can occur. IRM provides the principles, parameters and standards that define the environment within which information technology will be deployed and information systems developed.

OBJECTIVES OF IRM

23.   The fundamental objective of IRM is to ensure that an organization's information systems support its strategic direction and business plans and enhance the quality, applicability, accessibility and value of the information resources of the enterprise. Its success in an organization is dependent on the acceptance of four fundamental principles:

---

[7] Custer, Jeffrey A.   The Role of IRM in a Client/Server Environment.   *Data Base Newsletter* (March/April 1995).

[8] van den Hoven, John.   Data Base Management, IRM: An Enterprise View of Data.   *Information Systems Management* (Summer 1995), 69-72.

- Data are valuable resources that require proper management.

- Most data are highly shareable.

- The ability to share and use data more effectively is a critical success factor for most businesses.

- Information systems should incorporate a broad view of the enterprise.

24. An effective IRM program provides for continuously scanning the environment for opportunities that could drive the direction of an organization's business. Information technology planners must have a strategic view on how information systems can increase the opportunities available to an organization and also how to extend traditional business boundaries to include information resource links with customers and suppliers.

25. David Norton points out in "Stage by Stage"[9] that "Traditional boundaries are meaningless. In the organizations of the future, the basic components will be the same but the boundaries of the system will differ as will the relationships of the internal parts." He continues, citing specific examples "...in each case, a strategic advantage was gained by redefining the traditional boundaries of the business. American Airlines and American Hospital Supply extended their franchises to include the customers (or their intermediaries) at the time of purchase. IBM, Otis Elevator and General Motors extended their franchises to include their aftermarkets for service. Federal Express restructured its internal operations to permit 100 percent positive tracking of en route packages."

26. Organizations must emphasize strategic planning for IRM in order to gain a competitive advantage as they move into an era of increased automation and global competition. Information systems can help streamline business functions, improve managerial decision making, create new products and businesses and enhance relationships with suppliers and customers.

DEVELOPING THE IRM STRATEGIC PLAN

27. The ultimate goal of an effective IRM strategic plan is the design, delivery and maintenance of a seamless, integrated information resource environment that responds successfully to the need for cross-functional flows of information while providing the flexibility and adaptability to respond to incessant business and technological change. The requirement is for a set of data transport capabilities and data management interfaces that are usable by each business function, but unique to and owned exclusively by none of them.[10] Without a plan there are no objectives, no measures and, ultimately, no results.

---

[9] Norton, David P. *Whatever Happened to the Systems Approach.* Nolan, Norton & Co., Stage by Stage. (1989), 1-12.

[10] McKay, David T., and Douglas W. Brockway. *Building I/T Infrastructure for the 1990s.* (Nolan, Norton & Co., Stage by Stage, 9, 3).

28. There are three key steps involved in planning for the introduction of IRM practices into an organization:

- 1) Determine strategic information resource requirements.
- 2) Baseline the existing environment.
- 3) Design the IRM.

Exhibit 1

The Planning Process

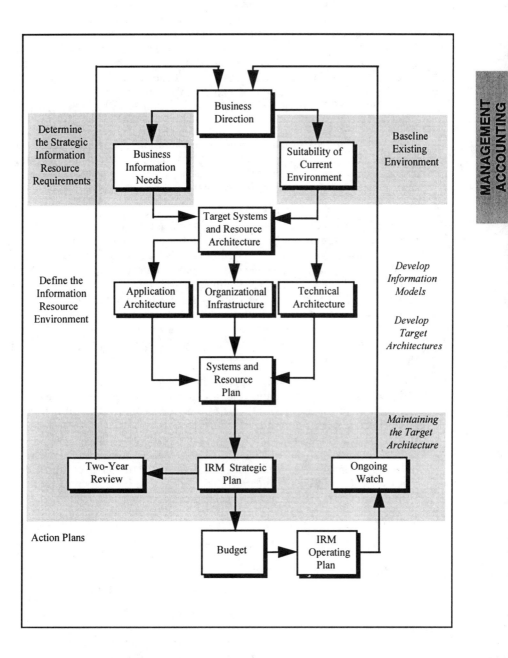

29.	As shown in Exhibit 1, the planning process starts with a definition of the business direction, this is the foundation for all subsequent steps. The strategic business planning process ensures that an organization understands its critical success factors, what it must do well to succeed and how it will measure success. Conversely, the strategic planning process provides an opportunity to identify areas of vulnerability, areas that may need to be monitored more closely and potentially subjected to stringent controls. All of this helps an organization to plot its course for the future. Critical success factors and the measurement criteria will vary from one organization to another, and will also change over time for a particular organization, depending upon the business environment and on the organization's direction. Typical examples of what an organization must do well to succeed in the next decade are customer service, new product development and cost control.

30.	The business strategy drives the process of determining what information the business requires to support its objectives and how well the existing environment (systems, processes, information, organizational structure, etc.) supports, or has the potential to support, the achievement of the business objectives.

31.	Technological issues are addressed in the third step, where a blueprint of the organization's future computing infrastructure is designed. The blueprint takes the form of a set of "target architectures," i.e., systems and resource architecture, application architecture and the technical architecture, each of which describes a particular component of the infrastructure to be constructed. This is a plan, conceptually similar to an architect's blueprint, describing what hardware, software and databases are necessary to satisfy the strategic information requirements previously identified. The target architectures also drive the design of the organizational infrastructure and the systems and resource plan.

32.	This set of target architectures supports the development of the IRM strategic plan, which, in turn, ensures the appropriate enabling technology and information infrastructure. It articulates how the organization will make the most effective use of information, computers, database technology, decision support tools and telecommunications in combination with other resources to achieve its mission. The IRM Plan reflects the organization's business focus, mirroring its emphasis on customer service, becoming the least-cost provider, expansion, decentralization goals and objectives and clearly states how the IRM organization will support the business mission.

33.	The following principles guide the development of an effective IRM strategy:

- It must be linked to the business strategy.

- Cross-functional business processes are central to the planning dimension.

- The technology infrastructure must represent a "model of the business."

34.	Once the IRM environment has been designed, the action plan is developed and, as shown, because it is recursive, it will be followed by a review cycle. Since the economy, markets and the information technology landscape shift every 12 to 18 months, it is important to repeat this exercise at least every two years. The entire IRM planning and implementation process is iterative; the cycles are dependent on business requirements, environment changes and information technology advances. If the IRM environment is to mirror the business, the review cycles must not be neglected and adjustments must be made to the environment as needed.

Determine Strategic Information Resource Requirements

35. It is important to identify specific initiatives that will help to achieve the business vision. Based on long-term return to the business, this provides the justification for moving forward with IRM implications. Effective IRM requires that information systems be designed to support the critical success factors and core business processes identified in the organization's strategic business plan.

36. For example, a core business process might be "product marketing" and a critical success factor in an organization's strategic plan might be expanding its customer base. Studying this factor carefully in the context of the organization could reveal that sales promotion and strategies need to be revised. Critical data to support this revision might include information on prospective customers.

37. The challenge will be to encourage business management to become involved in the information resource planning process and to increase the information technology group's knowledge of the business planning process. Understanding the technology and basic information building blocks is integral to designing something that will facilitate the business.

38. It is suggested that a planning group, consisting of the information systems executive and senior managers from key functional areas, should set up a series of planning workshops to examine the critical success factors. It is important to allow for refining the process to ensure that the analysis is complete and to determine areas where attention should be focused. This entire process is much simplified in the organizations that have a Chief Information Officer (CIO), who is a member of the senior management group and, as such, is involved in the business planning cycle from the beginning.

39. In the past, the focus of information systems planning may have been limited to determining how to apply technology to automate a task. Using the IRM approach more relevant questions might be: "How do I apply technology to competitive advantage? How do I get the right information to the decision makers? Where are the best opportunities to add value through information resources?"

40. The output of this stage of the planning process is a specific list of the processes and data critical to the organization's strategic direction and objectives. They are the strategic requirements to be satisfied in subsequent stages of the information planning and development process.

Baseline Existing Environment

41. The base point for developing the new IRM plan is a combination of existing plans, budgets, processes and systems. The purpose of baselining is to develop a complete and adequate assessment of the current environment. Information gathered at this time will provide the framework for assessing the risk/benefit of proposed changes, for structuring a transition plan and for changing the management approach. It will also act as an important feedback mechanism for users to provide input on needed improvements or opportunities for improvement.

42. Ongoing and planned projects should be reviewed and a summary of the project description, its status, planned completion, and estimate of cost prepared. Some projects may be put on a "hold" status if they depend upon technology or direction that could change radically because of the IRM plan.

43. The review of budgets should focus upon existing costs to determine what relates to sustaining current operations, maintaining existing systems, developing new systems and managing the department. It is also useful at this time to review long-term leases and licensing agreements to determine cancellation costs or upgrade penalties.

44. The systems review should focus on obtaining information about:

    - *System demographics* — its age, the language used to develop it, number of programs, file access or database management system used, hardware environment, etc.

    - *Maintenance status* — date of last major enhancement, planned maintenance, technical quality, currency and quality of existing system documentation.

    - *System functionality* — user problems, unmet needs, availability and usability of data and outputs, data security and integrity, future and present business relevance of the system.

45. Core business processes and activities will be defined and described according to:

    - *Desired outcome* — what are the measurable outputs or outcomes?

    - *Beginning point* — where does the activity "begin"; how is it triggered?

    - *Technology interfaces* — within the activity where, why and how does it need to interface with existing technology?

    - *Inter- and intra-organizational interfaces* — where, why and how does the activity interface with other business units?

    - *External interfaces* — where, why and how does the activity interface with external agencies, suppliers and customers?

    - *Ownership and accountability* — who "owns" the activity; who is accountable for achievement of the overall outcome?

    - *End point* — where and how does the activity end; what measures are applied to its completion, timeframes, volumes, targets?

Exhibit 2

Questions Addressed During Baselining

- Are our assets being preserved?
- How do we control information systems without crippling innovation?
- Is the information systems department appropriately organized?
- Are the organization and its human resources "ready for change?"
- Where should we invest?
- Do our information systems link to our business strategy?
- Are we getting a return on investment?
- Are we taking advantage of strategic technologies?
- Do we have the right mix of skills?
- Are we committed to a single vendor?
- Do we have the right architecture of applications, data, networks and computers?
- Can our customers use our systems?

46.   The baselining activity will, of necessity, be iterative in nature and, answering the questions listed in Exhibit 2 early in the planning process, will assist the planners to develop a much better understanding of:

- staffing levels and skills inventory and anticipated changes;
- facilities and resources and anticipated changes;
- in-force policies and procedures;
- information technology — current and planned environment;
- information flow;
- linkages with other infrastructure responsibilities and external agencies, including their information systems; and
- inputs, deliverables, customers and key performance indicators.

Define the Information Resource Environment

47.   There are many methodologies and approaches available to assist in planning, defining, designing and constructing an IRM environment. What is important is for the organization to select a consistent approach to be used in

all IRM initiatives across the organization. The approach employed in this Statement adds activity modeling to the well-established information engineering approach to business modeling, data modeling, process modeling and enterprise modeling. In this way, we ensure that enterprise-wide requirements are considered, information resources are directly linked to business strategy and goals, and the necessary balance between information, technology, process and organization is maintained.

48. Modeling is the act of developing an accurate description of a system, i.e., a set of interacting components and the relationships amongst them, a description that includes a definition of all of the important components of the system and how they interact. The reason for building a model is to make it possible to answer questions about a system without having to deal with the system itself. A series of models — business models, activity models, data models, process models and enterprise models — needs to be developed in order to fully appreciate what information resources exist, what are needed and where there are gaps.

Develop Information Models

49. The modeling process is somewhat labor intensive, requiring significant input from the business units. The models build on one another, each providing a view of information that is somewhat different from, but complementary to, its predecessor model. It must be understood that each model represents a "snapshot in time," a view of the situation as it is seen at the time the model is being developed. Although it appears that an organization's processes change much more frequently than the data it uses or the information it needs, the models should be revisited on a regular basis, for example, on an annual basis when the IRM plan is reviewed. It is suggested that development of the following models be undertaken:

- Business modeling is a technique for defining the information generated and received by departments in a company. This is the first step toward understanding the nature of the information flow within an organization. Business models serve as a bridge between identifying the strategic requirements and defining the technological infrastructure. They describe how the organization will operate once the strategic plans for IRM have been implemented.

- Activity modeling is a structured technique for defining who or what performs an activity, what tells them how to do it, what triggers the activity, and what the activity produces. Activity modeling can be used to ensure that information/data is directed to those who need it for their work, minimizing the risk of information overload and redundancy. It also uncovers potential overlaps across the organization. This phase of IRM will require the development of a model of current and future business activities. A series of activities combine to make a business process and an organization is comprised of a network of business processes.

- Data modeling is a systematic way of identifying the data categories or types that comprise the information flows defined in the business and activity models. Data modeling builds a picture of the interrelationships

886

among a company's data. This phase of IRM will require the development of a conceptual data model, representing the high-level view of the business's databases in the form of an entity-relationship model.

- Process modeling is used to document the way in which data is manipulated within an organization, i.e., it defines those functions of the system that will evolve into computer programs. This phase of IRM will require the development of the following elements:

  - conceptual transaction model, representing a high-level view of the create, retrieve, update and delete operations required to support the business;

  - distribution model, representing a high-level view of how databases and transactions are, or will be, distributed and where they will reside geographically.

- Enterprise modeling maps business activity to logical and physical descriptions of data, applications and locations, i.e., it is a method for integrating previously defined data, activity and process models into a consolidated whole, which will assist in sharing information across the company. It may take a very long time to complete an enterprise-wide model, but it is important to make every effort to develop the broadest view possible of the organization's information requirements.

50. While the modeling process can be completed manually, the use of computer-based tools is recommended. In this way, information that is gathered can be stored in an electronic repository for later use. Since we are in a period of continuous change, a static approach to IRM design is inadequate. Business environments continue to be dynamic, and determining which is the most appropriate mix of technologies, human resources, applications, databases, etc. is complex. Powerful simulation and prototyping tools are available to assist systems architects and designers to develop a living model of the business that can be maintained over time as a point of reference for defining the business and information architectures.

51. The Appendix to this Statement provides more detail about the modeling process and some of the more common modeling techniques.

Develop Target Architectures

52. The objective of this task is to prepare a suite of system architectures, based upon the requirements defined through the information models developed in the previous stage of the planning process. Target architectures are developed to provide a shared vision of the information resource environment needed to meet the business needs of the organization. The process of designing the architecture organizes the decision steps from business need to technical solution. The term "architectures" is used because the products of the process are analogous to building blueprints, i.e., they specify what the final product will look like once the plans have been implemented. In other words, target architectures describe the organization's future technological infrastructure.

53. The specific system architectures to be defined include:

- application architecture
- system software
- telecommunications
- hardware

54. The business value of the target architecture is considerable. Its purpose is to provide guidance and direction for building and integrating applications, data, technology and network communications. Just as sales forecasts provide a target for production and, in turn, for raw materials procurement and labor planning, the target architectures provide a target for systems development and, in turn, for the acquisition of hardware, software and databases to support systems development. It provides the foundation needed to ensure that the different technological components are compatible and can be integrated with each other.

55. Exhibit 3 provides a list of some of the architectural considerations that are tremendously important if an appropriate IRM environment is to be developed.[11]

---

[11] ibid

Exhibit 3

Architecture Considerations

- Hardware, including peripherals — predefined standards, environmental issues.
- Distributed versus centralized — existing standards, organizational preference.
- Network configuration — existing network(s), capacity, requirements.
- Communications protocols — existing standards, protocols being used today.
- System software — existing standards, options available on anticipated hardware and communications platforms.
- Database software — existing standards, what is in use today.
- Application development tools, CASE for example — tools in use today, tools available for potential platforms, database engine, operating system, communications platform.
- Development environment — standards in place for users/developers, other platform tools being considered, architectural priorities.
- Application software, make or buy, package selection, etc. — existing standards, industry-standard products, consistency with potential architecture, available support.
- Human interface — requirements, user expectations.

---

56. System architecture is usually determined by how the individual system designer chooses to use the various data processing technologies to meet user information requirements. The underlying data processing technologies can be divided into five major categories:

- applications
- data
- system software
- hardware
- network

57. There are a number of questions to be answered early in the process of architecture definition in order to ensure that the design proceeds in an appropriate context:[12]

---

[12] Smith, Patrick. *Client/Server Computing.* (Sams Publishing, 1992), 165-166.

MANAGEMENT ACCOUNTING

- How much can the organization afford?

- What is the level of skill, computer-literacy and ability of the potential system users?

- What are the real response time requirements?

- Is it essential that the system be available 24 hours per day, 7 days per week or will something less suffice?

- What is the security requirement? What is the potential impact of unauthorized access?

- How frequently might the application(s) change?

- What is the existing investment?

- What systems must the application(s) interface with?

58. It is possible that the target architectures will point toward replacement of old platforms. This can be complex, time-consuming, costly, disruptive and generally fraught with risk. The advantages of planning such a migration based on an architectural approach are many, but perhaps the most important is that it provides the blueprint necessary to plan for an orderly transition, weighing risks vs benefits at every stage.

59. **Applications and Data Architectures** — The objective of the data architecture is to package data into databases. The objective of the applications architecture is to package processes and the data associated with them into applications systems. These architectures are designed using a worksheet in matrix form. An example of such a matrix, based on previously developed business and data models, is shown in Exhibit 4.

60. There should only be one process responsible for creating any particular data attribute. This reduces redundancy and increases data integrity. The matrix therefore provides information about the correct sequence for constructing applications. An application that needs to retrieve a particular piece of data should be developed *after* the application that is responsible for creating that piece of data.

61. In addition, this matching of data and processes in a matrix provides information about the data and processing requirements of various levels and functional areas within an organization. It highlights which requirements are common to several areas or levels and which are different. This makes it easier to package applications so they best reflect the structure of the organization.

Exhibit 4

Example of a Matrix Relating Data and Applications

DATA Processes	Customer	Customer Order	Delivery	Product	Supplier	Supplier Order
1.1 Maintain Customer Account	A, D	R	R			
1.2 Receive Orders	R, U	A, D	R	R		R
1.3 Plan/Monitor Sales	R	R	R	R	R	R
1.4 Plan Sales Calls	R, U	R	R	R		
2.1 Manage A/R	R	R, U	R			
2.2 Manage A/P				R	R	R, U
2.3 Perform Financial Analyses	R	R	R	R	R	R
3.1 Maintain Product Information				A, D	R	R
3.2 Receive Products				R, U	R	R, U
3.3 Ship Products	R	R, U	A, D	R, U	R	
4.1 Maintain Supplier Accounts				R	A, D	R
4.2 Analyze Suppliers				R	R	R
4.3 Place Orders				R	R	A, D

A = adds (creates) the data
R = retrieves/accesses the data
U = updates the data
D = deletes the data

Each column in the matrix corresponds to an entity in a data model (or to a grouping of entities), and each row corresponds to a process in a process model. The entries in the cell indicate whether or not each process relates to the data and, if so, how. A process might:

- add data — for example, the process Maintain Customer Account is responsible for adding a customer to the database

- access data — for example, Plan/Monitor Sales might retrieve information about customers, products and suppliers

- update data — for example, Ship Products might update data about customer orders

- delete data — for example, Receive Orders might delete customer orders once they have been filled

62. **Technology Architecture** — The technology architecture, comprised of systems software, hardware and networks, is developed *after* the data and applications architectures. This represents a high-level specification of the processors, storage devices, network hardware and software, and local and remote operating systems required to support and implement the other architectures.

63. In order to develop a technology architecture, planners need to know the service requirements of each application and database. Service requirements for applications include response time, turnaround time, hours of availability, volume of traffic, accessibility and backups. Service requirements for databases are the degree of security and data integrity required. Exhibit 5 shows the service requirements for some of the data used in previous examples.

Exhibit 5

Example of the Specification of Service Requirements

DATA Processes		Customer	Customer Order	Delivery	Product	Supplier	Supplier Order
1.1	Maintain Customer Account	3 secs	30 secs	8-8	Medium	Central	24 hrs
1.2	Receive Orders	3 secs	30 secs	8-8	High	Remote	24 hrs
1.3	Plan/Monitor Sales	5 secs	1 hr	8-8	Low	Remote	7 days
1.4	Plan Sales Calls	5 secs	1 hr	8-8	Low	Remote	7 days
2.1	Manage A/R	5 secs	1 hr	8-5	High	Central	24 hrs
2.2	Manage A/P	5 secs	1 hr	8-5	High	Central	24 hrs
2.3	Perform Financial Analyses	5 secs	24 hrs	8-5	Low	Remote	24 hrs
3.1	Maintain Product Information	5 secs	1 hr	8-5	Medium	Central	3 days
3.2	Receive Products	5 secs	1 hr	8-5	High	Central	24 hrs
3.3	Ship Products	5 secs	1 hr	8-5	High	Central	24 hrs
4.1	Maintain Supplier Accounts	5 secs	1 hr	8-5	Low	Central	3 days
4.2	Analyze Suppliers	5 secs	24 hrs	8-5	Low	Central	7 days
4.3	Place Orders	5 secs	1 hr	8-5	Medium	Central	24 hrs

Database Service Requirements

	Data Integrity	Security (Loss of Data)	Access Security
Customer Data	High	High	High
Product Data	High	Medium	Low
Supplier Data	High	Medium	Medium

64. For any given set of data and applications architecture there are likely to be a number of alternative technology architectures that will satisfy service requirements. Prior to embarking on the actual development of the architectures, it is helpful if a series of "architectural principles" is developed to ensure that the overall objectives of the IRM program are consistently satisfied. Exhibit 6 is one example of a Statement of General Architectural Principles.

Exhibit 6

General Architectural Principles[13]

Stakeholders. The architecture will be designed to serve private citizens, corporate citizens, private business partners, public employees, county and municipal governments, federal agencies and other public service organizations.

A.   Citizen focus. All architectural decisions should support the delivery of citizen-oriented systems that are responsive to citizen demands, adaptable to changing business/program requirements, promote high quality service, and are easy to use.

B.   Consistency. Common business and technical requirements should be treated in a consistent way.

C.   Sharing. Architecture components will be sharable.

D.   Openness. Architecture components and associated specifications will use industry standards with preference for vendor-neutral implementations.

E.   Modularity. The architecture will be based on modular components with standardized interfaces.

F.   Buy versus make. Purchasable and integratable components are preferred over custom built or extensively modified products.

G.   Cost of compliance. Compliance with architectural standards may incur higher initial cost.

H.   Measurement. Measuring the use and performance of the architectural components will be performed continuously as normal practice.

I.   Operations. The preferred method of conducting business transactions (both internal and external) is through electronic means, e.g., Electronic Data Interchange (EDI), Electronic Funds Transfer (EFT), Electronic Mail (E-Mail), etc.

J.   Location. Geographic location must not be a constraint to accessing services or be used as the basis for charging for services.

K.   Flexibility for growth/change. The technical architecture needs to be designed for accommodating continuous change and must take into consideration possible future capabilities, as well as meeting maximum current requirements.

---

[13] General Architectural Principles was published by the state of North Carolina in early 1994.

65. Consideration must also be given to trends in information systems technology, adherence to or establishment of corporate standards, e.g., system network architecture (SNA), open systems interface (OSI), etc., and to what elements of the current systems can be modified for inclusion in the architecture. Since it may take an organization several years to reach the desired IRM environment, the potential for including emerging technologies should also be considered in the technology architecture design. Information systems planners need to evaluate emerging technologies and their potential impact on the organization on a continuing basis. This consists of developing an outline of each kind of technology, assessing where it might be used within the organization and estimating a timeframe within which it could be used. The Information Systems Steering Committee should receive an evaluation of any emerging technologies that are likely to have significant potential impact on the business.

66. Other issues to be considered during architecture design are:

- *Current technology assets* — hardware, software and applications portfolios.

- *Distribution of databases and transactions* — in the distributed computing approach, databases and transactions are often located at the point where business activities are performed; this can have significant implications for the technology architecture.

- *Best technology* — in preference to one common standard, select the best type of technology for the work to be done.

- *Interchangeability* — technology components selected on the basis of easy substitution without service disruption.

- *Workstation orientation* — desktop devices that are intelligent multi-functional workstations.

- *Networked environment* — all workstations networked, either locally or through wide area networks.

67. The *system software* architecture is determined by a number of technical products that are used to facilitate the operation of, and user interaction with, application programs. Major components of system software are:

- operating system(s)

- telecommunications monitor

- network software

- file access method

- database management system

- fourth-generation language

- programming languages

68. System software architecture and *hardware architecture* must be evaluated together, since the choice of system software may be influenced by the

hardware choice and vice versa. The hardware architecture in most computer configurations consists of:

- central processing unit
- disk drives
- tape drives
- terminals/workstations
- printers
- controllers

69. The *network architecture* involves the definition of both local area networks and remote telecommunications lines and controllers to support distributed terminals and printers and to link remote central processing units.

70. As the proclivity for client/server computing increases, so does the potential for multiple hardware and software components from multiple vendors as well as many related interfaces and interconnections. The potential for complexity is enormous; there are many issues to be resolved: communications, data management, security, maintenance, backup and recovery. In the IRM environment, the system architecture defines all technology components throughout the organization. This is particularly valuable in a distributed computing or client/server environment because it helps to:

- identify duplication and redundancy in existing technologies
- pinpoint dependence on specific vendors or technologies
- identify pockets of under-utilized or improperly applied technology
- highlight inconsistencies and incompatibilities amongst technologies

Maintaining the Target Architecture

71. Target architectures describe what the information resources in the organization will look like in the future (usually within a period of two to five years), not what they look like presently. As information needs and the information landscape change, target architectures must be revisited and updated just as sales forecasts are modified to reflect changing business conditions. An organization therefore needs a policy for maintaining its target architectures. Responsibility for this lies with the Information Systems Planning function.

72. The target architectures specify what the technological infrastructure will look like, but not how it is to be constructed. The final stage of the planning process, therefore, is creating the strategic implementation plan, which specifies how these architectures are to be constructed. It maps the organization's transition from its current portfolio through the implementation of particular systems development projects.

PREPARE THE IRM IMPLEMENTATION PLAN

73. The first stage in developing the IRM implementation plan is to define each project and assign priorities. Essentially, organizing priorities is based on these key factors: management need, benefit/cost, and risk. The development of project priorities and the definition of project interdependencies should result in the production of a project schedule that describes the sequence in which projects will be completed.

Project Selection Mechanism

74. The project selection mechanism should have three characteristics:

- It should rank projects according to how well they match the strategic business plan of the organization.

- It should be a formal mechanism, to ensure that planning is systematic and rigorous.

- It should take unquantifiable costs and benefits into account.

75. Traditional cost-benefit analyses using economic calculations such as return on investment, internal rate of return and net present value exhibit the first two characteristics, but not the third. Such analyses compare the expected investment required for a project with the benefits expected to result if it is implemented. Since they consider only financial benefits, any other kinds of benefits expected to result from the project must be either converted to financial terms (often arbitrarily) or considered independently from the formal analysis.

76. Neither of these solutions is satisfactory when it comes to information systems, since unquantifiable benefits are often significant. A better solution is to use a new formal project selection process that explicitly takes unquantifiable costs and benefits into account, such as the one outlined below.[14] This description highlights the general principles involved; specific features (such as specific scoring criteria) may be modified for different organizations.

Scoring Criteria

77. The formal project selection process described here uses nine criteria to prioritize projects for selection. It extends the concept of a "benefit" to include a wide range of factors that affect a system's business value. Likewise, it extends the concept of "cost" to include an evaluation of risk.

78. The criteria are divided into two groups: business criteria and technological criteria. All are used to rate every project.

[14] The project selection process described here is based on concepts presented in Parker, M.M., and R.J. Benson. *Information Economics: Linking Business Performance to Information Technology.* (Englewood Cliffs, NJ: Prentice Hall, 1988).

79. **Business Criteria** — The business criteria are:

- *Economic impact* — the traditional economic criteria used to rank projects, such as internal rate of return and net present value, as described above.

- *Strategic alignment* — the extent to which the project will achieve the strategic goals of the organization.

- *Competitive advantage* — the extent to which the project will give the organization an advantage over its competition.

- *Improved management information* — the extent to which the project will improve management information for the core activities of the business.

- *Competitive risk* — the extent to which postponement of the project will result in a net loss in the organization's competitive position.

- *Organizational risk* — the extent to which the organization will be disrupted by the project or will need to adapt if it is implemented.

80. **Technological Criteria** — The technological criteria are:

- *Strategic architecture* — the extent to which the project is an integral part of the target architecture and is necessary for the implementation of subsequent projects.

- *Definitional uncertainty* — the extent to which the requirements and specifications of the project are defined, have been approved, and are unlikely to change.

- *Infrastructure risk* — the extent to which the existing information systems environment must be modified to accommodate the project in terms of existing hardware, software, staff, skills and delivery of services. It may, for example, be necessary to implement a formal education and training program to ensure that the organization always has the technical expertise needed to plan and introduce carefully constructed technology infrastructures, particularly when complex technologies are involved.

The Scoring Process

81. Selecting projects is a joint process undertaken by users and information systems staff. Proposal ranking emphasizes high business impact (relationship of system to business objectives), tangible benefits (expected financial return to the level of investment required), intangible benefits (benefits derived as a result of implementing the system), low implementation risk (likelihood the system will fail to achieve the intended objectives), and quality of existing systems (ability of existing system to perform function efficiently and effectively).

82. A variety of people should participate in the scoring process, depending on their responsibilities and expertise. Project sponsors from the user community are responsible for the business implications, i.e., business value and business risk, of the projects they sponsor and understand these implications the most, so they score the business criteria. Information systems specialists are most responsible for and knowledgeable about the technological implications, i.e.,

technical value and technical risk, of the projects, so they score the technological criteria.

83.   The Information Systems Steering Committee is also a participant in the scoring process since it is responsible for the strategic direction of IRM. Periodically, the Committee assigns a weighted value to each of the project selection criteria. The value of the assigned weight depends on the *overall* contribution or element of risk each individual criterion is expected to introduce to the organization. For example, in Exhibit 7, avoidance of net loss in competitive position (competitive risk) and achieving the strategic goals of the organization (strategic alignment) are both considered to be major contributors to the organization's success and are therefore given a high weighted value. Conversely, disruption to the organization (organizational risk) and the fact that the requirements and specifications of the project have not yet been completed (definitional uncertainty) are considered to pose a threat. Because of the risk factor they are given a negative weighted value. These assigned weights are the same for all projects in any one time period, if they are updated the revisions are applied consistently to all outstanding projects.

84.   Exhibit 7 shows an example of a scored project.

Exhibit 7

Example of a Scored Project

	Weight	Score	Total Score
Business Criteria			
Economic impact	5	5	25
Strategic alignment	10	3	30
Competitive advantage	3	2	6
Management information	7	4	28
Competitive risk	8	3	24
Organizational risk	–2	1	-2
Technological Criteria			
Strategic architecture	5	5	25
Definitional uncertainty	–1	2	–2
Infrastructure risk	–2	1	–2
Total Project Score			**132**

Notes:

1. Weights are set by the Information Systems Steering Committee and are the same for all the projects to be ranked in a given time period.

2. Scores on the business criteria are determined by project sponsors for each project individually. A score can have a value from 0 to 5.

3. Scores on the technological criteria are determined by information systems specialists for each project individually. A score can have a value of 0 to 5.

4. The total score for each criteria is the weight of the criteria multiplied by the score assigned to that criteria.

5. The total project score is the sum of the total scores for each criteria.

85. Unfortunately, the appropriate assignment of weights is complex and the scoring procedure for the nine selection criteria is subjective. Although the process is structured and will be completed by professionals, it is still subject to manipulation and affected by personal preferences and biases, albeit unintentional.

86. Many efforts have been made to eliminate the level of subjective influence, including the use of "economic" appraisal of projects as opposed to "financial" appraisal, which precludes direct attribution of large benefits and costs that cannot be quantified. Assigning weights and scores requires managerial judgment and subjective assessment; but when conducted according to a structured and consistent formula it is possible to strive for maximum objectivity.

87. Regardless of the mechanism used, the following topics need to be discussed within the context of assessing each project's level of benefit and risk:

- *Are we addressing the appropriate business needs?* — Alignment with business objectives and market opportunities; balance between short- and long-term perspectives; investment across multiple business opportunities; sensitivity to organizational development issues; reaching beyond traditional views and business habits.

- *Are we containing the overall risk of our projects?* — Assessing risks of both action and inaction; looking at risks of projects both individually and collectively; technology, project and organization risks; focusing on ways to reduce risk; analyzing contingencies; managing adverse consequences.

- *Are the projects providing the optimum economic return?* — Capital appropriation; NPV, IRR, payback, SVA, ROI; using appropriate discounting factors; determining what is measurable; management confidence in analysis; consistency in cost and benefit estimation; considering all costs not only systems costs.

- *Are we deploying our scarce resources in the most effective manner?* — Up-front opportunities for systems integration; re-assessing existing resource commitments; focusing on allocation of critical resources where most appropriate; costing scarce resources at a true opportunity cost.

Selection Process

88. In its most objective state, the selection process requires each sponsor of a project to submit a project description to the Committee, with the project scored against each of the business criteria. Each project submitted is then scored on the basis of the technological criteria and projects are ranked according to the total project scores. Based on these rankings, projects are selected for implementation.

89. In the real world, however, there are other factors that contribute to and influence the decision-making process. For example, if there are budget constraints, the cost of a project can have a significant effect on its ranking or if a competitor is known to have taken steps that could have a negative impact on an organization's well-being this can cause a shift in direction. The objective is to select the best mix of projects, taking all relevant factors into consideration, recognizing that on occasion it will be necessary to invoke "emergency" measures in order to ensure the best "fit" with the organization's strategy and culture.

90. Project selection will take place on a regular basis, such as annually or quarterly. The timing of the process should correspond to the time periods used by the organization in making other budgeting decisions. More frequent selections have the advantage of being more responsive to changing business needs.

91. In addition to the ranked projects, the budget must accommodate changes for hardware, software, telecommunications and human resources, based on the project schedule and resource requirements identified in the project descriptions used as the basis for prioritization. If the personnel requirements exceed current staffing, then the recruitment and training of additional staff or the use of consultants should be anticipated. The budget must recognize the need to continue maintenance and minor enhancement of ongoing existing systems. It must also make accommodation for unforeseen "emergency" projects.

IMPLEMENTING THE STRATEGIC PLAN

92. Approval for the IRM plan must be obtained from the Information Systems Steering Committee (as representatives of the senior and middle management group). A walk through meeting should be held and each of the plan's major components reviewed. Following approval, the plan is "frozen" and final project schedules and budgets are prepared.

93. It is inevitable that new needs will continue to emerge and that priorities will need to be re-assigned. The plan must be flexible enough to accommodate these unforeseen circumstances. The Information Systems Steering Committee is responsible for adjusting project priorities, and possibly resources.

94. Projects are implemented according to the organization's systems development practices. The Information Systems Steering Committee and, in particular, the information systems planning representative, serves as a liaison with the different development groups to ensure that systems development conforms to the target architectures.

95. It is extremely important to consider the organizational impact of change when preparing the implementation plan. Did the baselining process indicate that the organization was "ready for change?" Are the sponsoring managers willing and able to champion the change process? Managing the human and organizational factors is extremely important to the overall success of the IRM initiative. To ensure a smooth roll out of the program, with minimal disruption resulting from lack of employee commitment and "buy-in," a formal, structured change management program must form part of the implementation strategy.

MEASURING SUCCESS — POST-IMPLEMENTATION REVIEW

Strategic Review

96. Since the economy, markets and information technology landscape are prone to radical shifts, the IRM plan should be reviewed at a strategic level at least once every two years, or more often if the corporate strategy is on a shorter review schedule. This review should assess whether the IRM strategy continues to support the business direction of the organization. If the organization has entered new businesses or new markets, then the IRM plan needs to be reviewed immediately; it should not wait until the scheduled biennial review.

97. Also at a strategic level, one of the key benefits of an IRM environment is that, as it matures, the organization will be able to capitalize on the increased level of knowledge, improved technology and collections of corporate data, enhanced interoperability of the systems, etc., in previously unthought of ways. It is important to organize a method of capturing this learning so that it can be used on a continuing basis to improve the overall IRM environment.

98. The framework for capturing this intellectual asset could be as simple as scheduled "information exchange" meetings with an attending scribe to document the lessons learned, or it could be something much more sophisticated, for example, installed on groupware such as Lotus Notes. In this latter case the "discussion" can be ongoing; it is time and geography independent and the information is captured electronically for future use.

Tactical Review

99. At a more tactical level, the impact of the IRM strategy on the organization should be assessed at regular (3-6 month) intervals. The following are indications of a successful and effective IRM implementation:

- The Information Systems Steering Committee continues to be active and involved.

- Management throughout the organization is enthusiastic about the new applications developed.

- The new applications are supporting strategic and operational business plans.

- Customers are being well served by the organization's information resources.

- Information systems can now be modified easily to accommodate changing decision-making and reporting requirements.

- The organization's hardware, databases, systems software and applications systems are compatible with each other and can be integrated as needed.

- Functional areas across the organization can access shared data and processing capabilities.

- The internal auditors have made positive assessments of the controls, safeguards and standards that relate to information resources.

100. Ultimately, the success of the IRM function is judged on the basis of its ability to move the organization effectively in the desired direction at an acceptable cost.

IRM POLICIES, STANDARDS AND PROCEDURES

101. Policies represent the basic ground rules of IRM. High-level, formal, written policies, standards and procedures must be established and disseminated throughout the company, adopted formally and enforced like any other business policy.[15]

102. The IRM operating principles/policies might include the following points:

- There must be full and active participation by user departments to ensure that systems meet the organization's mission-related information needs.

- Useful, timely, accurate, consistent and accessible data and information will be provided.

- Compatible and integrated information and data systems will be provided through the use of Data Base Management System (DBMS) technology.

- A capacity management program will be developed and implemented to manage equipment capacity and plan for upgrades.

- An ongoing assessment of ways new technology can be used to realize cost savings or other benefits.

- A combination of traditional and new concepts will be used to manage information resources, e.g., an integrated planning, budgeting and project tracking process; ongoing systems security reviews and follow-up audits; application systems inventory, etc.

103. The adoption of common industry standards is vitally important to the success of IRM because it is this that facilitates the ready exchange of information and supports the interoperability of systems. In order to effectively control and facilitate interoperability and data sharing among platforms, both generic and platform-specific standards need to be identified to support distributed processing/databases in a networked environment. Some of the standards that will be needed are identified in the following list:

- Security will become an increasingly important issue as an organization implements enterprise-wide networks to support distributed access to physically distributed data. Policies must be developed to address confidentiality, integrity and availability of data, hardware and software.

- A standard, structured systems development methodology is important; it would provide:
  - a standard approach to all aspects of development for systems staff
  - a consistent process for users to participate in systems development/ enhancements

---

[15] Custer, Jeffrey A. Six Ingredients of a Successful IRM Environment. *Data Base Newsletter* (March/April 1995).

- overall improved productivity
- a more stable end product
- a reduction in specification errors
- improvements in the ability to integrate systems

- To support the ability for porting applications and data on a variety of vendor platforms, generic and platform-specific standards for each hardware platform will be required. A minimum level of standards will be required for the purpose of rating packaged software.

- Documentation is a critical requirement for the operation and maintenance of applications. Standards for both generic and specific documentation for all software/hardware platforms will need to be established.

IRM ROLES AND RESPONSIBILITIES

104. The 1990s have produced a dramatic change in the information systems organizational structure and in associated accountabilities. Because the convergence of business strategy and information systems strategy is still evolving, many roles are in transition. Individuals with a thorough grounding in the business of the organization are increasingly required to understand how best to deploy technology. Similarly, individuals with extensive technical knowledge are increasingly being asked to interpret and apply business strategies. However, it is important that the roles and responsibilities associated with IRM be understood and that there be a common agreement on the allocation of accountabilities. The architects, developers, user department managers, etc., must work as a team with other stakeholders to manage the opportunity from its inception through to the realization of the business benefits.

Chief Information Officer

105. The evolution of tightly linked corporate and information systems strategies has been driven by the need to support the Chief Executive Officer (CEO) in his or her effort to maintain a watch on the company and its progress. The position of CIO has been established to provide this link between the senior management group and the information systems group. The CIO is the senior manager in charge of information systems, a peer of the CFO (Chief Financial Officer) and the COO (Chief Operating Officer). The difference between the CIO and the traditional MIS director is the scope of the CIO's influence.[16]

106. The CIO is a business person first and a technical expert second. He or she is a full member of the management team and is a peer of other chief executives who report directly to the Board of Directors or to the CEO. The CIO's mandate is to develop and promote IRM, linking information systems to the strategic plan of the business.

---

[16] Kerr, James M. *Strategies for Managing Information Resources.* In The IRM Imperative. (Toronto, ON: John Wiley & Sons, Inc., 1991), 1`7.

107. The CIO position is relatively new and has met with some resistance; however, as the opportunities for exploiting technology increase and the linkage between business strategy and information systems becomes more important, it is expected that a similar role will be needed in every major organization. In smaller organizations, the Information Systems Director will need to fulfill the strategic role as well as having the responsibility for day-to-day management of the Information Systems Department.

Information Systems Steering Committee

108. Executive level leadership is important — executive level involvement in IRM is achieved through the Information Systems Steering Committee.[17] The Committee's role is essential for first developing the strategic plans and, second, prioritizing the projects for the tactical plans. The Committee's main role is to keep the IRM strategy consistent with the organization's overall business strategy. The Committee is composed of the senior executive in each functional area.

109. The Committee resolves business issues and is responsible for mediating the information resource requirements of various areas of the organization. The Committee is also responsible for the review, approval and adoption of IRM policy and standards and for the review, approval and commitment of funding for IRM.

110. In small and medium-sized companies, the resources may not be available to support an Information Systems Steering Committee and in this instance the Committee's responsibilities could be undertaken by a sub-committee of the Management or Executive Committee. Regardless of the organization's size, it is absolutely essential that a representative group of senior managers be formed to direct the IRM program.

111. A multidisciplinary, multifunctional team is essential. Problems that cross traditional functional lines cannot be resolved unless each function and discipline is involved in developing the solution.

User Department Management

112. Involvement on the part of user department management (and staff) is important. They are key to identifying opportunities for the application of technology and ultimately for sponsoring IRM initiatives. The objective is to bring user departments into full partnership in managing information resources, providing strategic direction to the IRM architects. Information resources require significant capital investment, are built for the long term and have a relatively long life. They need to be managed in a fashion that allows the using communities to influence their construction and operation so that they add value to the community as a whole, which is much more effective than individual systems acquired by individual communities of interest, i.e., departments.

---

[17] This concept is discussed further in Porter, G.L. The Rise of the CIO. Financial Executive (August 1985), 41-44.

113. Managers are responsible for effective operations and strategic planning in their areas. This is equally as pertinent to information resources as it is to any other resource.[18] Managers should identify opportunities for streamlining and automating operations in their areas, sponsoring projects which they deem appropriate. They should participate in the formulation of systems requirements, manage each system's implementation, and ensure that the organization's portfolio of information systems and projects is consistent with its strategic plans.

114. In terms of day-to-day operations, managers are responsible for participating in planning for computer use in their areas, for hiring and training people who will use computers, for encouraging the development of end-user capabilities and for the cost-effectiveness of computer use.

115. Eventually, the user departments will "own" the results of the IRM planning process. This implies the evaluation and coordination of many changes, including redesigned business processes, changes in roles and responsibilities, new systems, etc. Their involvement, commitment and "buy in" are essential elements of success.

Management Accountants

116. The management accountant's role in the strategic planning process depends on whether the management accountant is an executive who is a member of the Information Systems Steering Committee, a project sponsor from the management community or an information systems specialist. A management accountant in any of these three roles can provide valuable insights about information and decision making throughout the organization and thus, through IRM, help improve decision making and realize the organization's strategic business plan.

117. In strategic planning for IRM, the management accountant should ensure that databases, information systems and related computerized decision support systems are designed to help:

- quantify and interpret the effects of economic events related to the organization;
- evaluate data for trends and relationships that help assess the implication of events;
- assure the integrity and accuracy of information concerning an organization's activities and resources;
- monitor and measure performance and induce corrective action where necessary;
- implement a reporting system that provides people throughout the organization with timely information relevant to their responsibilities; and
- prepare financial statements and reports.

---

[18] This point is discussed further in Rockart, J.F. The Line Takes the Leadership — IS Management in a Wired Society. *Sloan Management Review* (Summer 1988), 57-64.

Internal Auditors

118.　Internal auditors are responsible for the following:

- assessing information system controls, starting at the analysis and design stages of a project and continuing throughout the life of each system;

- determining whether information resources are adequately safeguarded; and

- monitoring information system activity to ensure that it takes place according to specified standards and procedures.

Information Systems Specialists

119.　Information systems specialists are responsible for the following:

- working with the management team to identify opportunities to gain strategic business advantage through the use of automated systems;

- understanding the business impact of current and emerging technologies, and facilitating their introduction into the organization where appropriate;

- planning for systems development, which includes developing standards, managing data, creating a blueprint for the information systems infrastructure (hardware, software, databases and communications) that the organization intends to put in place and developing a specific plan for achieving this infrastructure;

- developing and maintaining the information systems infrastructure so that it supports current requirements and facilitates the support of new requirements;

- developing individual information systems, which includes analyzing, designing, programming and testing new applications;

- ensuring that various systems development projects are consistent with each other and avoiding unnecessary duplication in data and processing;

- working with the end users when planning for systems development to ensure that the system is utilized effectively; and

- understanding the business objectives and functional responsibilities of the organizations serviced by the application systems, e.g. finance, marketing, etc.

Appendix

Business Models

Business models serve as a bridge between identifying the strategic requirements (stage 1) and defining the technological infrastructure (stage 3). They describe how the organization will operate once the strategic plans for IRM have been implemented.

There are three basic objectives in constructing business models:

- to add relevant detail to the critical processes and data already identified;

- to specify how critical processes and data are related to each other, since up until this stage they have been examined individually; and

- to describe existing operations, so that newly identified requirements can be integrated with current business functions and requirements.

In the example in paragraph 36, sales and promotion strategies and information about prospective customers were identified as strategic requirements. Before the technological implications of these requirements can be specified, they must be examined in further detail through the construction of business models. Business models describe how these processes are carried out currently and how they might be made more effective in the future. The model specifies who would develop the strategies, and what activities and decisions are involved in developing them. Similarly, the models would specify what information is currently gathered, what information should be gathered, and how this information would be used to expand knowledge about prospective customers. The rigorous process of constructing business models can also identify non-value-added activities that are currently performed.

Characteristics of Business Models

Business models have characteristics that make them especially effective descriptive tools:

- They are independent of specific hardware and software technologies, so they do not need to be changed if the organization adopts new technologies.

- They are independent of current organizational structure, and therefore highlight areas where the structure might be effectively modified.

- They separate business processes from the automated systems used to process data, which facilitates the development of systems servicing various areas of the organization.

- They are constructed in a hierarchical top-down manner, which limits the amount of detail that has to be gathered and absorbed at any one time.

- They provide a common language for discussing business data and process, which facilitates communication among participants in the planning and development processes.

- They provide the documentation in diagram form that can be understood by people without technical expertise. Thus, they enhance communication between managers and information systems specialists.

Business models are based on information collected throughout the organization. Sources of data may include:

- planning documents

- interviews with management and staff

- examination of existing forms, files and records

- examination of operating procedure manuals

- small group discussions with key employees

There are a variety of specific techniques for producing business models, although they all share the characteristics outlined above. Many organizations and consulting companies have set up their own standards for business model construction and there are also automated computer packages, called Computer-Aided Software Engineering (CASE) tools, that analyze the integrity and consistency of the business models and produce the required documentation.

An organization constructs two types of business models: *process* models and *data* models.

Safeguarding the Business Model Data

Because the development of business models involves a large quantity of data collected by different individuals over a period of time, it is necessary to manage and safeguard the information collected. The primary tool for doing this is a *data dictionary*. Information systems specialists are responsible for maintaining the data dictionary and for developing policies as standards for its control.

A data dictionary is a central repository of information about each element in the business model (processes, data flows, external and internal sources of data, entities, relationships and attributes).

For example, the data flow Purchase Order could be defined as:[19]

Purchase Order = Purchase Order Number + Vendor Name + Vendor Address + POI Date + Ship to Address + {Item Number + Item + Description + Quantity + Price + Amount} + Total + Authorization

where {} indicates that these components are repeated multiple times. There would be data dictionary entries for each component of this definition. For example, Quantity might be defined as an integer greater than zero.

---

[19] This example has been taken from Armitage. H.M. *Linking Management Accounting Systems With Computer Technology.* (Hamilton, ON: The Society of Management Accountants of Canada, 1985).

The data dictionary ensures that:

- each element is named and defined uniquely and consistently;

- elements are used consistently throughout the collection of business models constructed; and

- it is possible to determine the effects of a change in one element on the rest of the system.

A data dictionary can be maintained either manually, using file cards or loose-leaf pages in a binder, or automatically, using a commercial data dictionary system. The CASE tools for business model construction come with their own data dictionary facilities.

Process Models

Process models describe activities performed by the organization. If we think of an organization as a system of interdependent parts, the objective in developing a process model (or data flow diagram) is to specify how the system operates.

A process model consists of four components:

1. processes or activities (shown as circles)

2. data flows, which represent the flow of information into, out of or between processes (shown as arrows)

3. sources of information outside the system being examined (shown as rectangles)

4. sources of information within the system being examined (shown between parallel lines)

The following diagram is an example of a process model. It is a simplified diagram of the relationships between four major activities of a distributing firm, which are labeled as follows: Manage Sales, Manage Financial Resources, Manage Products and Manage Suppliers.

Note that three important sources of information external to the organization are shown: industry sources, customers and suppliers. Three important internal sources of information are the Customer File, the Supplier File and the Product File.

Note also that each activity consists of subactivities. For example, the activity Manage Products in this diagram includes the subactivities Maintain Product Information, Receive Products and Ship Products. Each subactivity will have its own process model; a model of the subactivity Maintain Product Information, for example, might include the following subactivities: Create New Product, Update Inventory Levels and Cost Product.

Defining the subactivities in a process model is called *decomposition.* It limits the amount of detail that has to be gathered and absorbed at any one time, because detail about a subactivity is specified in a separate process model for that activity.

Example of a Data Flow Diagram
(Process Model)

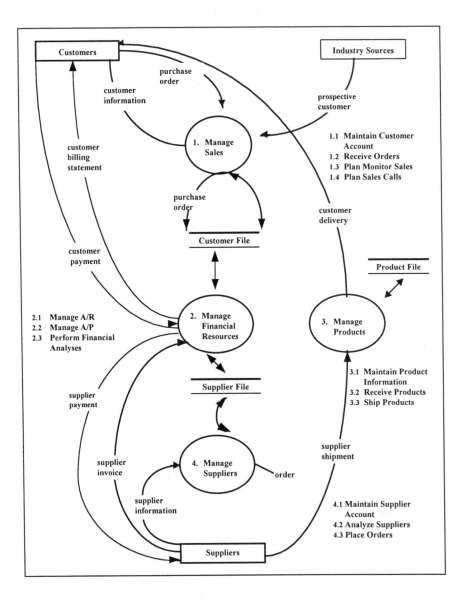

Data Models

Data models are used to describe the pieces of information that must be gathered by an organization and how these pieces interrelate. A data model (or entity-relationship diagram) consists of three components:

- entities, which are the concepts of primary interest to the organization (shown as boxes)

- relationships, which link the various entities (shown as box lines)

- attributes, which are characteristics of entities (written inside the box of the entity they describe)

**Example of an Entity-Relationship Diagram
(Data Model)**

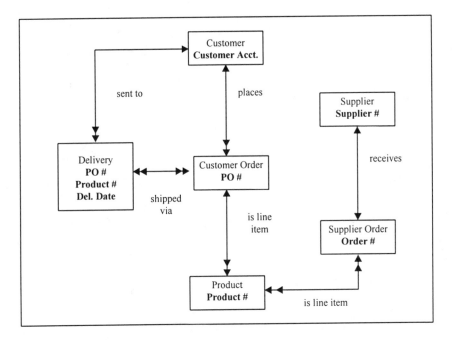

A simplified example of a data model is shown in the data model diagram. It describes a portion of the information relevant to the distributor represented in the process model diagram. Note that for each entity, one attribute (or sometimes more) has been shown in bold type; this is its primary key, the characteristic that uniquely identifies it. For example, customers are uniquely identified by a Customer Account; for deliveries, the primary key includes a PO Number, Product Number and Delivery Date.

The relationships among entities describe the business rules of the organization, which are represented by arrows on the lines. Note that some arrows are double and others are single; for example, the relationship "places" between a customer and a customer order shows a single arrowhead on the top and a double one on the bottom. This is to show that each order is associated with only one customer, while a customer can be associated with more than one order.

Glossary

Attribute	An element of a data model. Attributes are used to specify characteristics of entities.
CASE tools	Computer-Aided Software Engineering tools. Software packages that aid in the design and development of computer systems. They allow documentation (such as data model diagrams, process model diagrams and data dictionaries) to be created and stored by computer.
Data dictionary	A central repository of information about elements in data and process models. It contains the definition of each element.
Data flow	An element of a process model. A data flow represents information entering into or exiting from a process.
Data model	A diagram that describes the organization's data and how different pieces of data are interrelated. A variety of techniques are available to produce data models. The specific kind of data model in this guideline is an Entity-Relationship Model.
Decomposition	Dividing a particular process in a process model into subprocesses so that further detail about the subprocesses can be defined.
Entity	An element of a data model. An entity is a category of object that is of interest to the organization and about which data will be maintained, such as a customer and an employee.
Information centre	An organizational unit that helps end-users develop computer applications.
Network architecture	Involves the definition of both local area networks and remote telecommunications lines and controllers to support distributed terminals and printers and to link remote central processing units.
Primary key	An attribute of an entity in a data model that serves to identify the entity uniquely, such as an employee number.
Process	An element of a process model. A process represents an activity in the organization.
Process model	A diagram that describes the organization's activities and how different activities are interrelated. A variety of techniques are available to produce process models. The specific kind of process model shown in this guideline is a Data Flow Diagram.

Relationship	An element of a data model. A relationship is an association between or among entities.
System software architecture	It is determined by a number of technical products that are used to facilitate the operation of, and user interaction with, application programs.
Target architecture	A blueprint of the organization's technologies, showing what they will look like once implementation has been completed. There is a target architecture for data, applications systems and hardware, and communications technology.
Technology architecture	It is the specifications for systems software, hardware and networks. It is developed after the data and application architectures.

SUMMARY OF STUDIES

The Committee has issued nine studies, as summarized below. Note that Study 2 has been superseded by Practice Statement 3.

Study 1
Control of Computer Applications
Issued October 1985

This study is no longer applicable given the advancement of information technology.

Study 3
Revised — An Introduction to Strategic Financial Management
Issued January 1995

Enterprises of all kinds (whether private or public sector, whether for profit or not for profit) are finding that the environment in which they operate is subject to an increasing rapid rate of change. As a consequence, there has been a shift of emphasis, towards the strategic level of management (concerned with the making and monitoring of decisions as to what to do) as distinct from the tactical level (concerned with the making and monitoring of decisions as to how to do what is done).

The more one gets involved with strategy, however, the more limitations of the traditional accounting model become apparent. Being designed for reporting on what has happened, it is backward looking, inward looking and static. People who are proactively involved in making things happen, on the other hand, must necessary be forward looking, outward looking and dynamic. As a consequence, we have now reached the stage where the accounting model is not only inappropriate, but seriously misleading, as a basis for strategic decision making and monitoring: any management team in the private sector, for example, which sets out to maximize this year's profit will almost certainly damage the long-term health of the organization.

This paper makes the point that there is more to accountancy than accounting. Specifically, as well as accounting, which is concerned with the objectively verifiable truth about a certain past, there is financial management, which is concerned with subjective judgments about an uncertain future. Creating a structure which enables strategic choices to be evaluated, and their implementation monitored, is a crucial task in today's conditions and one for which the skills of the management accountant are appropriate.

This paper puts the need to offer the prospect of an adequate return at the pivot of economic endeavor. Only those enterprises capable of doing so will be able to attract the funds necessary to survive and grow; those incapable must inevitably shrink—perhaps to extinction. Strategic Financial Management (SFM) translates this imposed discipline into self discipline within an organization: what the treasurer sees as the rate of return necessary to warrant the employment of funds, the financial controller sees the criterion for their deployment. These two aspects of financial management are harmonized through the promulgation of a financial objective: to maximize net present value. In a distributable profit seeking organization, this is expressed in terms of the net value of projected cash flows.

Cash flow, in this context, is a simple concept, i.e., the excess of income from customers over payments to suppliers and employees, or the excess of distributions (interest, tax and dividends) over financing. As such, it does not depend on weeks or months of applying and accounting conventions like depreciation and provisions. Likewise, the cost of capital is a reflection of society's relative preferences for cash flows arising in different time frames, augmented to allow for perceived uncertainty, and the extent of the enterprise's risk aversion. It does not depend on backward looking analyses of the fluctuations in small lot share prices.

The principles of SFM are outlined in this paper, together with brief examples showing its application to individual dimensions of strategy, to their blending into coherent business strategies, and their combination into optimum corporate strategies. Most importantly, the idea of strategic monitoring is introduced, i.e., the establishment of a benchmark (derived from a previous evaluation, updated for the passage of time and the flow of cash) against which to assess a current evaluation. One cannot wait until a strategy has been played out before measuring the outcome and taking any action; strategic monitoring needs to be continuous and forward looking. The numbers produced by the SFM model are significantly different from accounting ones, but this paper shows how they can be reconciled to highlight the perceived 'intangible assets' of an organization—which, in a rapidly changing environment, are likely to be the key sources of competitive advantage and barriers to entry.

The paper aims to stimulate debate amongst those concerned to provide financial input to the strategic level of management.

Study 4
Reporting Treasury Performance —
A Framework for the Treasury Practitioner
Issued September 1995

Treasury activities have become increasingly significant with the development and deregulation of financial markets and complex derivative instruments. These developments necessitate setting clear objectives for corporate treasuries, senior management understanding the underlying risks and control environment, and regular reporting of performance relative to those objectives to the highest level of corporate management. This study addresses the key areas in establishing a system of reporting on the activities of a centralized treasury which manages a group's foreign exchange exposures, its liquidity, equity and debt fund raising and its relationship with key financial institutions such as banks and rating agencies.

Dramatic changes are occurring in the workplace. Largely in response to pressures arising from increasing domestic and global competition, organizations are scrutinizing all aspects of their functioning, from their product market strategies to their operations, in order to increase value creation for customers, owners and other stakeholders. Major changes are taking place to remove activities and processes which do not contribute to value creation, and to align value creating processes with strategies.

Substantial delayering of organizational hierarchies has occurred, along with greater empowerment of employees are the operational level. Empowered employees, working in "teams" perform many of the key value-adding activities of an organization, supported by technologies which help align their activities with organizational strategy and goals.

Self-directed or semi-autonomous work teams have been seen to be of increasing relevance in competitive and changing environments. Team-based work design has the potential to create greater flexibility and responsiveness to customers or clients; it can enable team members to perform broader operational responsibilities, and some of what would previously have been regarded as management or technical support tasks. Work teams are seen to generate greater productivity as well as improved workforce motivation.

The work team approach is gaining momentum in both manufacturing and service organizations: greater autonomy, control and broader responsibilities are being given to work teams. However, substantially increased support and training are required to ensure that the teams have the necessary skills and information to enact these new responsibilities — to be self-directed, productive and effective.

Team members also need to be imbued with a greater awareness of the resources they command and consume, and of how the consumption of these resources is linked to the creation of value (for customers, owners and other stakeholders) through the work they perform. How does this awareness become manifest — in the way they operative collectively as a team, in what is regarded as important, what is focused on, or who team members interact with? How does or can "resource awareness" become either implicit or explicit in the activities and interactions of teams?

Is there an important role that can be performed by the management accounting function in organizations in adding value to both teams and team-based organizations? This question is the subject of this study. It is explored by examining the structures, processes, responsibilities and goals of self-directed work teams (SDWT) using current views from the literature on SDWT and examples from an organization in the process of implementing and developing a SDWT structure for its manufacturing operations.

In examining the organizational roles of management accounting where SDWT are operative, the study also sheds light on the skills and tools needed by Management Accountants to support such initiatives. It also raises the question of how management accounting can add value to *organizational* processes in this situation, as well as to teams and team processes.

Study 6
Environmental Management in Organizations —
The Role of the Management Accountant
Issued March 1998

This study discusses the role of management accountants in corporate environmental management and the relevance of their expertise in furthering the corporate sustainable development agenda. In doing so, it draws upon the work of the member bodies of the International Federation of Accountants (IFAC), as well as the growing body of theoretical, case study, and empirical literature of leading accounting researchers around the world. As it is impossible to address all of the major issues, arguments, and methodologies involved in environmental management accounting within the scope of this paper, its aim is to provide non-environmental accountants with the general concepts they will need to begin to understand the scope and nature of the field.

This study is divided into two distinct parts. Part I provides a brief overview of some of the key challenges and objectives of corporate environmental management within the framework of sustainable development. It discusses the responses from business, industry, non-profit organizations and the IFAC member bodies to the recommendations of Agenda 21 as adopted by the Rio Summit in 1992. It does not focus on one particular environmental management system per se, but talks to the general aim of corporate environmental management and accounting practices in industry. Part II discusses the accountant's role in corporate environmental management. It first describes how sustainable development extends the objectives of the firm and discusses the resulting implications for management. It then defines the domain of *environmental accounting* and discusses the major challenges and objectives management accountants face in accounting for the environment. The Concluding Remarks section synthesizes the study and makes some final observations on the role of the accountancy profession in furthering the global sustainable development agenda.

Study 7
The Measurement and Management of
Intellectual Capital: An Introduction
Issued October 1998

It is recognized that the intellectual capital of a firm plays a significant role in creating competitive advantage, and thus managers and other stakeholders in organizations are asking, with increasing frequency, that its value be measured and reported for planning, control, reporting, and evaluation purposes. However, at this point, there is still a great deal of room for experimentation in quantifying and reporting on the intellectual capital of the firm. Given the potential for both complexity and diversity, developing intellectual capital measures and reporting practices that are comparable between firms remains one of the key challenges for the accounting profession. The international accounting bodies represented by the International Federation of Accountants have begun to examine the role of the accounting profession in managing and reporting the intellectual capital of the firm.

In publishing this study, the Financial and Management Accounting Committee (FMAC) of IFAC supports the growing effort to understand the complexities of intellectual capital management, accounting and reporting, yet recognizes that there is a long way to go for generally accepted and endorsed practices to evolve. The three general measures of the intellectual capital of the firm that have been described within this study (i.e., market-to-book ratios, Tobin's "q", and CIV) may be the first to be considered by the accounting community.

Although the emerging frameworks of intellectual capital management have provided a new holistic perspective on the firm, its resources, and ways of managing them, this study introduces the view that established management accounting practices and techniques can be readily applied to this area. A wide variety of precedents and principles are currently available to assist in the management of the human, organizational and customer capital of the firm that draw upon a broad range of disciplines and management perspectives. Identifying and applying this wealth of information in a cohesive and appropriate way may be a major contribution that the accounting profession can make to managing for the success of organizations.

Study 8
Codifying Power and Control:
Ethical Codes in Action
Issued May 1999

Corporations draw power from the overarching systems of ethics and moral principles which are proclaimed or used in the societies or communities in which they operate. Within these societies or communities, such ethical systems or moral principles are seen as just, fair, normal or even uncontestable; they represent 'correct' or commendable ways of thinking and acting. Accordingly, when they are drawn into use within corporations, they are unlikely to be rejected; they will be more likely to be accepted voluntarily and willingly by the constituents of corporations – by employees, customers, suppliers, agencies of government, and the community at large.

Corporations draw the power of ethical systems and moral principles into use in a number of ways - as implicit or explicit guiding values, as decision premises, or as preferred forms of conduct or behavior. Often these norms or notions are formalized in codes which are given various labels; in this study they are referred to generically as Corporate Codes of Ethics. Different types of Codes of Ethics frame ethical or moral power differently, and focus on different organizational variables.

The power deployed in corporations through the use of Codes of Ethics is designed to establish patterns of thought and patterns of action that are appropriate to the corporation's circumstances. Such patterning should produce corporate responses that are appropriate to the imperatives and requirements of the fast-changing, competitive contexts in which they operate. For example, dynamic, innovative responses might be called for in some contexts; in other contexts, reinforcement of existing actions or marginal adaptations may be sufficient responses.

This study argues, and seeks to illustrate if not demonstrate, that different types of context and their underlying conditions will produce different uses of Codes of Ethics and the power they embody.

Controls are associated with the use of power in Codes of Ethics, to ensure that appropriate responses to contextual conditions faced by a corporation occur. It is one thing to (seek to) induce a response through the use of power; it is another thing to secure the desired outcome – that is, to secure control. Just as different sets of contextual conditions occasion different uses of the power in Codes of Ethics, different types of control will be associated with these different uses of power. More than likely, Codes of Ethics will be used also to focus such controls.

This study seeks to demonstrate that Corporate Codes of Ethics are not ornamental expressions of good intent. Instead, they are practical instruments of management, designed to capture the power of social or community morality and put it to good corporate use. Used selectively, Codes of Ethics assist corporations in fashioning effective responses to the different types of contextual condition they might face.

As practical instruments of management Corporate Codes of Ethics are of central interest to accountants concerned with managing. How are they used? Why are they used? When are they used differently? And when is their use effective? This study seeks to provide answers to such questions, for the benefit of managers and accountants alike.

Study 9
Enhancing Shareholder Wealth by
Better Managing Business Risk
Issue June 1999

Developed in conjunction with PricewaterhouseCoopers' Global Risk Management Solutions group, the study was written in response to an increasing demand for information on risk management issues. It is intended to extend awareness of some of the leading edge issues, provide practical guidance on best practice and convey current thought leadership in regard to risk management.

Until recently, risk has been viewed by business as a negative concept. However, CEOs have recognized that managing risk is an integral part of generating sustainable shareholder value. This positive interpretation of risk reflects the new understanding of the connection between well-managed risk and improved performance. That is, where management mobilize the linkage between risk management, achievement of corporate goals and reduced volatility of outcomes, the organization's economic performance can be enhanced significantly.

The risks faced by organizations are part of a risk continuum. They can be evaluated in terms of hazard, uncertainty and opportunity and by the degree of influence they have on conformance, operating performance and strategic objectives. Effective risk management practices can identify and evaluate risks across all levels of the continuum and can deliver realistic assessments of the likelihood and impact of risks on the organization's value.

Risk response ensures that resource allocation responds to the continuum of risks faced by the organization. For its success, the response is reliant upon gaining commitment from executive management and the Board of Directors, establishing the business process including assigning responsibilities for change, resoucing, communication, training and reinforcing a risk culture throughout the organization via human resources mechanisms.

New international expectations and in some cases, standards, are emerging and additional tools and techniques are becoming available for better measurement of risks and value.

Study 10
Targeting Costing for Effective Cost Management
Issued June 1999

This study analyses the target costing (or product cost planning system) used at Toyota Motor Corporation Australia (TMCA). At TMCA, target costing forms an integral part of the design and introduction of new products, and ongoing cost management processes. By focusing on the participants in the target costing process (including personnel from accounting, engineering, purchasing and sales) the study details the techniques and processes used to manage costs in the product design stages and during production – throughout the life-cycle of a product.

The study provides a series of contributions to our understanding of target costing systems.

First, the study illustrates how target costing may be adapted to a Western 'culture'. Many of the existing published accounts of target costing are situated in Japanese companies.

Second, it explains how target costing may still operate effectively when most of the product design is provided by an overseas parent company. While this might be expected to constrain opportunities for product cost planning, at TMCA the cost management activities are intense despite these constraints.

Third, the TMCA case illustrates in detail how value engineering (VE) - an important tool used in target costing - works in practice, and the degree of creativity and innovation that underlies its operation.

Fourth, the description of the product cost planning processes at TMCA demonstrates how pre-production VE techniques that focus on the design of a new product can integrate with the ongoing cost management activities of currently produced products.

Fifth, this study provides a detailed example of the cross-functional nature of an effective target costing process.

Finally, the TMCA case provides an illustration of how the finance function can provide an effective coordination and integrative role to focus organizational efforts towards effective cost management.

OTHER PUBLICATIONS

Annual Theme Booklets

As part of its mission to encourage the development of management accounting and to encourage research into matters of importance to management accountants, the FMAC established in 1993 the production of an annual booklet gathering multi-nation comments on a common topic.

Each year, a theme is chosen with a future orientation and articles dealing with this important topic, but from different viewpoints, are requested from authors around the globe. As well as being for publication, these articles provide an important input to FMAC in establishing its future work plan. FMAC sees the scope of the professional accountant in business as having a broad orientation, which encompasses information and knowledge management.

Previous publications in the series have been:

- 1994 A View of Tomorrow - Management Accountancy in the Year 2004

- 1995 A View of Tomorrow - The Senior Financial Officer in the Year 2005

- 1996 Performance Management in Small Businesses

- 1997 Preparing Organizations to Manage the Future

- 1998 Into the 21st Century with Information Management

- 1999 The Role of Management Accounting in Creating Value

Article Award for Distinguished Contribution to Management Accounting

The FMAC Article Award for Distinguished Contribution to Management Accounting is designed to give an author or authors particular recognition for an article published in a member body publication that is judged to have made, or be likely to make, a distinct and valuable contribution to the advancement of management accounting. In addition, the program rewards nine other meritorious articles published in member body publications. The FMAC Article Award for Distinguished Contribution to Management Accounting was designed to pursue the goals of the FMAC which include:

      i) encouraging the development of management accounting and increasing the recognition of professional contribution, and

     ii) encouraging research into matters important to management accountants and disseminating the results of such research on an international basis.

The winning article and other meritorious articles are assembled in a booklet on an annual basis and distributed to all IFAC member bodies who are encouraged to reprint the articles. All reprinted articles identify where the publication originally appeared.

The FMAC has published five annual booklets from 1994 to 1998.

Financial Management Fundamentals
Issued June 1998

This booklet is intended to help financial management small and medium enterprises. The small and medium enterprise (SME) is built on challenges - challenges to find the necessary resources, to attract and to retain talent, and challenges to find a defendable niche in the marketplace. In as much as the survival rate of the SME through its formative years is as low as 1 in 4 (a U.S. statistic), it is important that good ideas and good approaches that are applied in one nation be disseminated to others without delay.

The FMAC published in March 1996 a booklet containing the views of a number of authors from countries around the world on the subject of "Performance Management in Small Businesses." The subject was selected because of the significance of the SME to economic growth and new job creation in all nations.

At the same time, work was progressing at the Fédération des Experts Comptables Européens (FEE) on the development of a guide on financial management fundamentals for small businesses. FEE recently completed that guide and distributed it in Europe. In producing it, considerable reliance has been placed on *Making a Success of your Business: The Toolkit*, produced by the Chartered Institute of Management Accountants (CIMA).

One of the objectives of the FMAC is to disseminate on an international basis, documents that do an excellent job in assisting managers in the field of financial and management accounting. The content of the FEE guide is considered by the FMAC to be worthy of a broader distribution, for use by managers of small businesses in all parts of the world. It is an easy-to-read, useful and practical guide to improving financial management and control.

INFORMATION TECHNOLOGY

CONTENTS OF THIS SECTION

	Page
Guidelines:	
1. Managing Security of Information	928
2. Managing Information Technology Planning for Business Impact	945

For additional information on the Information Technology Committee, recent developments, and/or to obtain outstanding exposure drafts, visit the Committee's page at http://www.ifac.org/Committees/ITC.

1

January 1998

MANAGING SECURITY OF INFORMATION

CONTENTS

Paragraphs

Preface

Executive Summary .... 1—5

Key definitions 6

Why is Information Security Important? .... 7—11

What is Information Security? .... 12—13

What are the Principles of Information Security? .... 14—22

What is the Best Approach to Implement Information Security? .... 23—38

**Appendix A: Information Security Policy Statement
     Example**

Appendix B: Acknowledgments

In a digital world, the effective management of information, information systems and communications is of critical importance to the success and survival of an organization. This criticality arises from:

- the increasing dependence on information and the systems and communications that deliver the information;

- the scale and cost of the current and future investments in information; and

- the potential for technologies to dramatically change organizations and business practices, create new opportunities, and reduce costs.

Many organizations recognize the potential benefits that technology can yield. Successful organizations, however, understand and manage the risks associated with implementing new technologies. Executive management needs to have an appreciation for and a basic understanding of the risks and constraints of information technology in order to provide effective direction and adequate controls.

This guideline is intended to assist management to implement policy and procedures within an overall internal control framework. Additional technical guidance may be necessary as management seeks to implement these guidelines.

This guideline is based upon best practices recommended in selected primary publications of the Department of Trade and Industry (United Kingdom), the Department of Commerce (USA), the Government of New South Wales (Australia) and the Organization for Economic Cooperation and Development.

EXECUTIVE SUMMARY

WHY?

1. In a global information society, where information travels through cyberspace on a routine basis, the significance of information is widely accepted. In addition, information and the information systems and communications that deliver the information are truly pervasive throughout organizations—from the user's platform to local and wide area networks to servers to mainframe computers. Accordingly, executive management has a responsibility to ensure that the organization provides all users with a secure information systems environment. Sound security is fundamental to achieving this assurance. Furthermore, there is a need for organizations to protect themselves against the risks inherent with the use of information systems while simultaneously recognizing the benefits that can accrue from having secure information systems. Thus, as dependence on information systems increases, security is universally recognized as a pervasive, critically needed, quality.

WHAT?

2. The concept of security applies to all information. Security relates to the protection of valuable assets against loss, disclosure, or damage. In this context, valuable assets are the data or information recorded, processed, stored, shared, transmitted, or retrieved from an electronic medium. The data or information must be protected against harm from threats that will lead to its loss, inaccessibility, alteration or wrongful disclosure. The protection is through a layered series of technological and non-technological safeguards such as physical security measures, background checks, user identifiers, passwords, smart cards, biometrics, firewalls, etc. Security applies to all information. The security concept is summarized in the security objective.

Security Objective: The objective of information security is "the *protection of the interests of those relying on information, and the information systems and communications that deliver the information, from harm resulting from failures of availability, confidentiality, and integrity."* [*]

The security objective is supported by the eight core principles.

CORE PRINCIPLES

Accountability: Responsibility and accountability must be explicit.

Awareness: Awareness of risks and security initiatives must be disseminated.

Multidisciplinary: Security must be addressed taking into consideration both technological and non-technological issues.

Cost Effectiveness: Security must be cost-effective.

Integration: Security must be coordinated and integrated.

Reassessment: Security must be reassessed periodically.

Timeliness: Security procedures must provide for monitoring and timely response.

Societal Factors: Ethics must be promoted by respecting the rights and interests of others.

HOW?

3. To meet the security objective and develop and maintain adequate controls in compliance with generally accepted core principles, an ongoing and integrated approach is necessary.

---

[*] Adapted from "Guidelines for the Security of Information Systems" by the Organization for Economic Cooperation & Development, 1992.

APPROACH

Policy Development: The security objective and core principles provide a framework for the first critical step for any organization—developing a security policy.

Roles and Responsibilities: For security to be effective, it is imperative that individual roles, responsibilities, and authority are clearly communicated and understood by all.

Design: Once a policy has been approved by the governing body of the organization and related roles and responsibilities assigned, it is necessary to develop a security and control framework that consists of standards, measures, practices, and procedures.

Implementation: Once the design of the security standards, measures, practices, and procedures has been approved, the solution should be implemented on a timely basis, and then maintained.

Monitoring: Monitoring measures need to be established to detect and ensure correction of security breaches, such that all actual and suspected breaches are promptly identified, investigated, and acted upon, and to ensure ongoing compliance with policy, standards, and minimum acceptable security practices.

Awareness, Training, and Education: Awareness of the need to protect information, training in the skills needed to operate information systems securely, and education in security measures and practices are of critical importance for the success of an organization's security program.

WHEN?

4. With the ever changing technological environment, what is considered state-of-the-art today will be obsolete tomorrow, and security must keep pace with these changes. Security must be considered as an integral part of the systems development life cycle process and explicitly considered during each phase of the process. Security must be dealt with in a proactive manner in order for it to be effective. Timeliness is critical in ensuring information security.

WHO?

5. Executive management, information systems security professionals, data owners, process owners, technology providers, users, and information systems auditors all have roles and responsibilities in ensuring the effectiveness of information security. Due diligence must be exercised by all individuals involved in the management, use, design, development, maintenance, operation, or monitoring of information systems.

INFORMATION TECHNOLOGY

KEY DEFINITIONS

6. **Availability** means the characteristic of data, information and information systems being accessible and useable on a timely basis in the required manner.

   Communications is the transmission and reception of signals and includes both voice and data communications.

   Confidentiality means the characteristic of data and information being disclosed only to authorized persons, entities, and processes at authorized times and in an authorized manner.

   Cyberspace means the global information and communications network where time, distance, and space are not a limitation.

   Data means a representation of facts, concepts, or instructions, in a formalized manner suitable for communication, interpretation, or processing by human beings or by automatic means.

   Information is the meaning assigned to data by means of conventions applied to that data.

   Information Systems means the computers, communications facilities, computer and communications networks, and data and information that may be recorded, processed, stored, shared, transmitted, or retrieved by them, including programs, specifications, and procedures for their operation, use, and maintenance.

   Information Systems Auditor is and auditor—either internal or external—who possesses the knowledge, skill, and abilities to review and evaluate the development, maintenance, and operation of components of information systems.

   Integrity means the characteristic of data and information being accurate and complete and the preservation of accuracy and completeness by protecting the data and information from unauthorized, unanticipated, or unintentional modification.

WHY IS INFORMATION SECURITY IMPORTANT?

7. In a global information society, where information travels through cyberspace on a routine basis, the significance of information is widely accepted. In addition, information and the information systems and communications that deliver the information are truly pervasive throughout organizations—from the user's platform to local and wide area networks to servers to mainframe computers. Organizations depend on timely, accurate, complete, valid, consistent, relevant, and reliable information. Accordingly, executive management has a responsibility to ensure that the organization provides all users with a secure information systems environment.

8. There are many direct and indirect benefits from the use of information systems. There are also many direct and indirect risks relating to these

information systems. These risks have led to a gap between the need to protect systems and the degree of protection applied. This gap is caused by:

- Widespread use of technology;

- Interconnectivity of systems;

- Elimination of distance, time, and space as constraints;

- Unevenness of technological change;

- Devolution of management and control;

- Attractiveness of conducting unconventional electronic attacks over more conventional physical attacks against organizations; and

- External factors such as legislative, legal, and regulatory requirements or technological developments.

9. Security failures may result in both financial losses and/or intangible losses such as unauthorized disclosure of competitive or sensitive information.

10. Threats to information systems may arise from intentional or unintentional acts and may come from internal or external sources. The threats may emanate from, among others, technical conditions (program bugs, disk crashes), natural disasters (fires, floods), environmental conditions (electrical surges), human factors (lack of training, errors, and omissions), unauthorized access (hacking), or viruses. In addition to these, other threats, such as business dependencies (reliance on third party communications carriers, outsourced operations, etc.) that can potentially result in a loss of management control and oversight are increasing in significance.

11. Adequate measures for information security help to ensure the smooth functioning of information systems and protect the organization from loss or embarrassment caused by security failures.

WHAT IS INFORMATION SECURITY?

12. Security relates to the protection of valuable assets against loss, disclosure, or damage. Securing valuable assets from threats, sabotage, or natural disaster with physical safeguards such as locks, perimeter fences, and insurance is commonly understood and implemented by most organizations. However, security must be expanded to include logical and other technical safeguards such as user identifiers, passwords, firewalls, etc. which are not understood nearly as well by organizations as physical safeguards. In organizations where a security breach has been experienced, the effectiveness of security policies and procedures has had to be reassessed.

13. This concept of security applies to all information. In this context, the valuable assets are the data or information recorded, processed, stored, shared, transmitted, or retrieved from an electronic medium. The data or information is protected against harm from threats that will lead to its loss, inaccessibility, alteration, or wrongful disclosure. The protection is achieved through a layered series of technological and non-technological safeguards

such as physical security measures, user identifiers, passwords, smart cards, biometrics, firewalls, etc.

Security Objective: The objective of information security is "the *protection of the interests of those relying on information, and the information systems and communications that deliver the information, from harm resulting from failures of availability, confidentiality, and integrity.*"

For any organization, the security objective is met when:

- information systems are available and usable when required (availability);

- data and information are disclosed only to those who have a right to know it (confidentiality); and

- data and information are protected against unauthorized modification (integrity). The relative priority and significance of availability, confidentiality, and integrity vary according to the data within the information system and the business context in which it is used.

WHAT ARE THE PRINCIPLES OF INFORMATION SECURITY?

14.   The security objective is supported by eight core principles—accountability, awareness, multidisciplinary, cost effectiveness, integration, reassessment, timeliness, and societal factors. Each core principle is briefly discussed below.

ACCOUNTABILITY—*Responsibility and accountability must be explicit.*

15.   Security of information requires an express and timely apportionment of responsibility and accountability among data owners, process owners, technology providers, and users. This accountability should be formalized and communicated.

Issues to consider include:

- specification of ownership of data and information;

- identification of users and others who access the system in a unique manner;

- recording of activities through the provision of management audit trails;

- assignment of responsibility for maintenance of data and information; and

- institution of investigative and remedial procedures when a breach or attempted breach of the security objective occurs.

AWARENESS—*Awareness of risks and security initiatives must be disseminated.*

16.   In order to foster confidence in information, data owners, process owners, technology providers, users, and other parties, with a legitimate interest to learn or be informed, must be able to gain knowledge of the existence and general extent of the risks facing the organization and its systems and the

organization's security initiatives and requirements. Security measures are only effective if all involved are aware of their proper functioning and of the risks they address.

Issues to consider include:

- level of detail disclosed must not compromise security;

- appropriate knowledge is available to all parties, not just users, who have a legitimate right to be informed;

- awareness is part of the induction program for new recruits to an organization so as to build security awareness as part of the corporate culture; and

- recognition that maintaining awareness is an on-going process.

MULTIDISCIPLINARY—*Security must be addressed taking into consideration both technological and non-technological issues.*

17. Security is more than just technology. It also covers administrative, organizational, operational, and legal issues. Accordingly, technical standards should be developed with and, be reinforced by, codes of practice; audit; legislative, legal, and regulatory requirements; and awareness, education, and training.

Issues to consider include:

- business value or sensitivity of the information asset;

- impact of the organizational and technological changes on the administration of security;

- technologies that are available to meet the security objectives;

- requirements of legislation and industry norms; and

- requirements to carefully manage advanced security techniques.

COST EFFECTIVENESS—*Security must be cost-effective.*

18. Different levels and types of security may be required to address the risks to information. Security levels and associated costs must be compatible with the value of the information.

Issues to consider include:

- value to and dependence of the organization on particular information assets;

- value of the data or information itself, based on a pre-defined level of confidentiality or sensitivity;

- threats to the information, including the severity and probability of such threats;

935

- safeguards that will minimize or eliminate the threats, including the costs of implementing the safeguards;

- costs and benefits of incremental increases to the level of security;

- safeguards that will provide an optimum balance between the harm arising from a security breach and the costs associated with the safeguards; and

- where available and appropriate, the benefit of adopting established minimum security safeguards as a cost-effective alternative to balancing costs and risks.

INTEGRATION—*Security must be coordinated and integrated.*

19. Measures, practices, and procedures for the security of information should be coordinated and integrated with each other and with other measures, practices, and procedures of the organization, and third parties on whom the organization's business processes depend, so as to create a coherent system of security. This requires that all levels of the information cycle—gathering, recording, processing, storing, sharing, transmitting, retrieving, and deleting—are covered.

Issues to be considered include:

- security policy and management included as an integral part of the overall management of the organization;

- concurrent development of security systems with information systems or, at least, harmonization of all security processes to provide a consistent security framework;

- review of inter-related systems to ensure that the level of security is compatible; and

- risks relating to third parties on whom the organization's business processes depend.

REASSESSMENT—*Security must be reassessed periodically.*

20. The security of information systems should be reassessed periodically, as information systems and the requirements for their security vary over time.

Issues to consider include:

- increase in dependence on the information systems requiring an upgrade to the business continuity plans and arrangements;

- changes to the information systems and their infrastructure;

- new threats to the information systems requiring better safeguards;

- emerging security technologies providing more cost effective safeguards than were possible earlier; and

- different business focus, or organizational structure, or legislation necessitating a change in the existing level of security.

TIMELINESS—*Security procedures must provide for monitoring and timely response.*

21. Organizations must establish procedures to monitor and respond to real or attempted breaches in security in a timely manner in proportion with the risk. The increasingly interconnected real-time and transborder nature of information and the potential for damage to occur rapidly require that organizations react swiftly.

   Issues to consider include:

   • instantaneous and irrevocable character of business transactions;

   • volume of information generated from the increasingly interconnected and complex information systems;

   • automated tools to support real-time and after-the-fact monitoring; and

   • expediency of escalating breaches to the appropriate decision making level.

SOCIETAL FACTORS—*Ethics must be promoted by respecting the rights and interests of others.*

22. Information and the security of information should be provided and used in such a manner that the rights and interests of others are respected and that the level of security must be consistent with the use and flow of information that is the hallmark of a democratic society.

   Issues to consider include:

   • ethical use and/or disclosure of data or information obtained from others;

   • fair presentation of the data or information to users; and

   • secure destruction of data or information that is sensitive but no longer required.

WHAT IS THE BEST APPROACH TO IMPLEMENT INFORMATION SECURITY?

23. To meet the security objective, and develop and maintain adequate controls in compliance with generally accepted core principles, an ongoing and integrated approach is necessary. Executive management and especially chief executive officer support is essential for the successful development, design, implementation, and monitoring of security controls.

24. Policy Development: The security objective and core principles provide a framework for the first critical step for any organization—developing a security policy (see example information security policy statement in appendix A). The security policy should support and complement existing organizational policies. The thrust of the policy statement must be to recognize the underlying value of, and dependence on, the information within an organization. The information security policy should describe:

INFORMATION TECHNOLOGY

- The importance of information security to the organization;

- A statement from the chief executive officer in support of the goals and principles of effective information security;

- Specific statements indicating minimum standards and compliance requirements for specific areas:

    - Assets classification;
    - Data security;
    - Personnel security;
    - Physical, logical, and environmental security;
    - Communications security;
    - Legal, regulatory, and contractual requirements;
    - System development and maintenance life cycle requirements;
    - Business continuity planning;
    - Security awareness, training, and education;
    - Security breach detection and reporting requirements; and
    - Violation enforcement provisions.

- Definitions of responsibilities and accountabilities for information security, with appropriate separation of duties;

- Particular information system or issue specific areas; and

- Reporting responsibilities and procedures.

25. **Roles and Responsibilitie**: For security to be effective, it is imperative that individual roles, responsibilities, and authority are clearly communicated and understood by all. Since every organization will have its own unique needs, it is not possible to provide a generic approach. Organizations must assign security related functions in the appropriate manner to nominated employees. Responsibilities to consider include:

- Executive Management—assigned overall responsibility for the security of information;

- Information Systems Security Professionals—responsible for the design, implementation, management, and review of the organization's security policy, standards, measures, practices, and procedures;

- Data Owners—responsible for determining sensitivity or classification levels of the data as well as maintaining accuracy and integrity of the data resident on the information system;

- Process Owners—responsible for ensuring that appropriate security, consistent with the organization's security policy, is embedded in their information systems;

- Technology providers—responsible for assisting with the implementation of information security;

- Users—responsible for following the procedures set out in the organization's security policy; and

- Information Systems Auditors—responsible for providing independent assurance to management on the appropriateness of the security objectives, and on whether the security policy, standards, measures, practices, and procedures are appropriate and comply with the organization's security objectives.

26. **Design**: Once a policy has been approved by the governing body of the organization and related roles and responsibilities assigned, it is necessary to develop a security and control framework. This consists of standards, measures, practices, and procedures within which individual systems are then introduced and maintained.

27. When designing new or improved standards, measures, practices and procedures for the security of information systems it is important to consider individual business requirements and the risks related to the particular system in order to identify the specific security requirements. Assessments of the risks must include both business and technical risks and the analysis of control objectives, standards, and techniques needed to provide an integrated control framework.

28. The process concludes with the design of an integrated security system that is compatible with the needs of the organization, given technical and cost constraints.

29. **Implementation**: Once the design of the security standards, measures, practices and procedures has been approved, the solution should be implemented on a timely basis, and then maintained. The security standards, measures, practices, and procedures will cover a number of subject areas including:

- managerial controls, such as span of control, separation of duties, background checks, and personnel awareness, training, and education to ensure that personnel act appropriately to prevent, detect, or correct problems.

- identification and authentication controls to establish accountability and to prevent unauthorized persons from gaining access to the systems through, for example, passwords or smart tokens;

- logical access controls to establish who or what has access to a specific type of information resources and the type of access permitted, such as read, write, update, or delete;

- accountability controls through management audit trails that maintain a record of all user and system activity;

- controls, such as cryptography, over information transmitted and stored to ensure confidentiality, authenticity, integrity, and non-repudiation;

- systems development life cycle process controls to ensure that security is considered as an integral part of the process and explicitly considered during each phase of the process;

- physical and environmental controls (encompassing physical access, fire detection and prevention, air-conditioning and power supply continuity, structural soundness, and the physical security of data transmission lines) to ensure that adequate measures are taken against threats emanating from the physical environment;

- computer support and operations controls to ensure that these routine but critical activities (user support, software support, change management, configuration management, media controls, backups, documentation, and maintenance) enhance the overall level of security; and

- business continuity planning controls to ensure that an organization can prevent interruptions, and recover and resume processing in the event of a partial or total interruption to information systems availability.

30. **Monitoring**: Information systems are subject to a wide range of disruptive incidents of varying degrees of intensity. The business processes that rely on these systems and the environment in which both these systems and processes operate, are also continually subject to change and new risks.

31. Preventive measures may not always be feasible or cost-effective to minimize loss, disclosure, damage, or disruption. Hence, monitoring measures need to be established to detect and ensure correction of security breaches, such that all actual and suspected breaches are promptly identified, investigated, and acted upon. This will also ensure ongoing compliance with policy, standards, and minimum acceptable security practices.

32. The immediate benefit of instituting monitoring measures and procedures over systems, processes, and their environment, is to promptly identify, contain damage, and expedite recovery. The most important consequential benefit is that it increases the ability to prevent future damage and inconvenience, while increasing the predictability of actions involving failures or breaches of security. An associated benefit is the deterrence value of effective monitoring processes. Actions that may result from monitoring practices are:

- disciplinary or corrective actions;

- minimization and recovery of losses;

- refinement of security levels;

- changes to policy or standards;

- changes to design and implementation of security;

- initiation of reassessment programs, including root cause and pattern analysis;

- initiation of intelligent monitoring systems with interactive feedback; and

- initiation of network or system penetration studies.

33. Follow up of security is as important as its implementation, especially in the light of new technological developments, whether those adopted by the system owner or those available for use by others. Issues that need to be addressed in achieving effective monitoring include:

- the appointment of a responsible manager with adequate tools and resources;

- the performance of independent and objective assessments of security controls such as provided by security audits;

- the establishment of clear and expedient investigative procedures;

- the massive amount of management audit trail information from a large variety of system components that may need to be examined;

- the timeliness of escalation processes when electronic transactions are practically instantaneous; and

- the dynamic and ever changing business and information systems environment.

34. **Awareness, Training, and Education**: People are often the weakest link in securing information. Awareness of the need to protect information, training in the skills needed to operate them securely, and education in security measures and practices are of critical importance for the success of an organization's security program.

35. The overriding benefits of awareness, training, and education, are in improving employee behavior and attitudes towards information security and in increasing the ability to hold employees accountable for their actions.

36. Raising the collective awareness level of the organization regarding security matters can be achieved through a variety of training methods—videos, newsletters, posters, briefings, etc. To be effective, the campaign must be creative and frequently changed.

37. Training and communication are usually focused on security-related job skills and stimulate practices such as protecting the physical area and equipment (caring for media such as diskettes), protecting passwords, and reporting security violations. Advanced training may be needed for managers and specialized training necessary for system administrators and information systems auditors.

38. Education is more in-depth and typically targeted for information systems security professionals to gain expertise. It is normally achieved through external programs and should be regarded as part of career development.

INFORMATION SECURITY POLICY STATEMENT EXAMPLE

- The purpose of the Information Security Policy is to protect the organization's information assets from all types of threats, whether internal or external, deliberate, or accidental. Information systems security is critical to the organization's survival.

- The Chief Executive Officer supports and has approved the Information Security Policy.

- It is the Policy of the organization to ensure that:
  - Assets will be classified as to the level of protection required;
  - Information will be protected against unauthorized access;
  - Confidentiality of information will be assured;
  - Integrity of information will be maintained;
  - Personnel security requirements will be met;
  - Physical, logical, and environmental security (including communications security) will be maintained;
  - Legal, regulatory, and contractual requirements will be met;
  - Systems development and maintenance will be performed using a life cycle methodology;
  - Business continuity plans will be produced, maintained, and tested.
  - Information security awareness training will be provided to all staff;
  - All breaches of information systems security, actual or suspected, will be reported to, and promptly investigated by Information Systems Security;
  - Violations of Information Security Policy will result in penalties or sanctions.

- Standards, practices, and procedures will be produced, and measures implemented to support the Information Security Policy. These may include, but are not limited to, virus protection, passwords, and encryption.

- Business requirements for the availability of information and information systems will be met.

- The roles and responsibilities regarding information security are defined for:
  - Executive management;
  - Information systems security professionals;
  - Data owners;
  - Process owners;
  - Technology providers;
  - Users;
  - Information systems auditors.

- The Information Systems Security function has direct responsibility for maintaining the Information Security Policy and providing guidance and advice on its implementation.

- All managers are directly responsible for implementing the Information Security Policy within their areas of responsibility, and for adherence by their staff.

- It is the responsibility of each employee to adhere to the Information Security Policy.

Signed: _____

Title: _____ Date: _____

Appendix B

ACKNOWLEDGMENTS

Primary Sources

"The Business Manager's Guide To Information Security," Department Of Trade And Industry, UK, 1996.

"An Introduction To Computer Security: The NIST Handbook," Department Of Commerce, USA 1995.

"Security Of Information Systems," Government Of New South Wales, Australia, 1994.

"Guidelines for the Security Of Information Systems," The Organization for Economic Cooperation And Development, 1992.

Other Sources

"British Standards Institute: Code of practice for information security management BS 7799," British Standards Institute, London, 1995.

Cadbury Commission, The Institute of Chartered Accountants of England and Wales, 1992.

"COBIT: Control Objectives for Information *and* Related Technology," Information Systems Audit and Control Foundation, 1996.

"Criteria On Control," The Canadian Institute of Chartered Accountants, 1996.

"Internal Control-Integrated Framework," the report of the Committee of Sponsoring Organizations of the Treadway Commission (COSO), the American Institute of Certified Public Accountants, the Financial Executives Institute, the Institute of Management Accountants, the Institute of Internal Auditors, and the American Accounting Association, 1994.

"Standards Australia and Standards New Zealand: Information security management AS/NZS 4444," Standards Australia/Standards New Zealand, Homebush NSW, 1996.

"Systems Auditability and Control Report," Institute of Internal Auditors Research Foundation, 1991.

2

January 1999

MANAGING INFORMATION TECHNOLOGY PLANNING FOR BUSINESS IMPACT

CONTENTS

	Paragraphs
Preface	
Executive Summary	1-5
Key definitions	6
Why is Information Technology Planning Important?	7-10
What is Information Technology Planning?	11-14
What are the Key Principles in Developing an Information Technology Plan?	15-25
What is the Best Approach for Information Technology Planning?	26-44

Appendix:

Key Control Objectives and Assessment Issues for Information Technology Planning

Preface

In a digital world, the management and use of information, information systems and communications is of critical importance to the success of an organization. The criticality arises from:

- *the increasing dependence on information and the systems and communications that deliver the information;*

- *the scale and cost of the current and future investments in information; and*

- *the potential of technologies to dramatically change organizations and business practices, create new opportunities and reduce costs.*

Many organizations recognize the potential benefits that technology can yield. Successful organizations, however, understand and manage the risks associated with implementing new technologies. Executive management needs to have an appreciation of the benefits, risks and constraints of information technology in order to provide effective direction and adequate control.

In this guideline series, the International Federation of Accountants, through its Information Technology Committee, seeks to promote executive understanding of key issues affecting the management of information and communications. This series of guidelines is written for management.

*This guideline is the second of the series and covers **managing information technology planning**. In addition to emphasizing the nature and need for information technology planning and its impact on business strategy, these guidelines provide an understanding of the main principles on which plans should be formulated, and a generic approach for implementing effective planning.*

Executives in various capacities – for example, accountants, financial controllers, auditors, or business managers – are frequently called upon to manage, participate in, assess, or comment on the information technology planning process. It is, therefore, essential for executives to have a sound knowledge of the principles and practices of managing information technology planning.

EXECUTIVE SUMMARY

WHY?

1. For most organizations, the rapid developments in information technology provide management with an opportunity to develop and implement new or improved products and services. To take advantage of this opportunity, management must first recognize the potential represented by information technologies, and, next, identify and implement information systems which assist in better meeting the organisation's business objectives. Information technology planning, as described in these guidelines, is an effective approach to assist management in this process since it provides:

   - a structured basis for evaluating the impact of technologies in the broader context of business objectives and comparative assessment with similar organizations;

   - a framework for scheduling necessary information system projects in an integrated manner while recognizing available resources and constraints; and

   - assurance that investments in the information system projects are justified in terms of realizable benefits and represent the most appropriate option to the organization.

WHAT?

2. An information technology plan supports the business goals and strategies within the business plan. The objective of the information technology plan is to provide a road-map of the information technology required to support the business direction of an organization, outlining the resources that are required and the benefits that will be realized on implementation of the plan. While each information technology plan is unique to the needs and circumstances of an organization, it is generally formulated using the following ten principles:

CORE PRINCIPLES

- *ALIGNMENT*—The plan should support and complement the business direction of an organization.

- *RELEVANT SCOPE*—The scope of the plan should be established to facilitate formulation of effective strategies.

- *RELEVANT TIMEFRAME*—A planning horizon should be formulated that provides long-term direction and short-to-medium term deliverables in a manner consistent with the business strategy.

- *BENEFITS REALIZATION*—Costs of implementation should be justified through tangible and intangible benefits that can be realized.

INFORMATION TECHNOLOGY

- *ACHIEVABILITY*—The planning process should recognize the capability and capacity of the organization to deliver solutions within the stated planing timeframe.

- *MEASURABLE PERFORMANCE*—The plan should provide a basis for measuring and monitoring performance.

- *REASSESSMENT*—The plan should be reassessed periodically.

- *AWARENESS*—The plan should be disseminated widely.

- *ACCOUNTABILITY*—Responsibility for implementing the plan should be explicit.

- *COMMITMENT*—Management commitment in implementing the plan should be exhibited.

HOW?

3. Although information technology plans are unique, the planning process and the underlying activities are similar. Usually, the plan will be developed in four phases:

APPROACH—Phase I: Orientation

This start-up phase is required to establish the scope of the plan and the methodology and techniques to be applied. In this phase the resources that are required for developing the plan are mobilized.

APPROACH—Phase II: Assessment

The focus of this phase is to establish the broad information technology requirements of the organization and compare these with the current information technology usage. Also, this phase provides an opportunity to identify other potential uses of technologies which may assist in meeting business objectives. Major steps in this phase are: confirm business direction and drivers; review technology trends; outline future requirements; inventory existing information systems; and develop an assessment of what is needed. In the concluding step of this phase there should be a well-developed assessment of the current and future business needs, the benefits available from implementing technologies, the gap between what is desired and what is required by the organization, and a list of the key issues to be considered in the formulation of the information technology strategies.

APPROACH—Phase III: Strategic Plan

This phase commences with developing the vision and desired future positioning of information technology within the organization. This is followed by an analysis of the options that are available with respect to information, applications, technology infrastructure, communications, business process re-engineering, and organizational resources. The option analysis culminates in the selection of appropriate, justified and compatible strategies which, collectively, form the strategic plan.

APPROACH—Phase IV: Tactical Plan

In this phase, the selected strategies are divided into a series of projects which are scheduled for implementation depending upon relative priorities and resource availability. The planning process is concluded by recommending a monitoring and control mechanism that will ensure that the plan is implemented in a timely, efficient and effective manner.

WHEN?

4. The information technology plan necessarily complements the business plan of an organization. A new information technology plan is necessary when there is a fundamental change in the business strategies; or when most of the projects comprising the existing plan have been implemented; or when the business and technology assumptions of the existing plan have changed to the extent that the plan is no longer viable. Even if a new plan is not necessary, the existing plan must be reassessed on a periodic basis.

WHO?

5. The information technology plan is usually prepared under the direction of a steering committee that is headed by the Chief Executive Officer, Chief Information Officer, or another senior business executive. The steering committee may comprise senior business executives, key business unit managers, the information technology manager and the information systems audit manager. The steering committee is supported by a specifically formed project team—which may include external consultants with expertise in developing information technology plans.

KEY DEFINITIONS

6. **Applications** means the computer programs, specifications, and procedures for their operation, use and maintenance that are required to input, store, process, share, transmit, or retrieve data and information relating to one or more groups of business processes.

   Communications is the transmission and reception of messages and includes both voice and data communications.

   Data means a representation of facts, concepts, or instructions in a formalized manner suitable for communication, interpretation or processing by human beings or by automatic means.

   Information is the meaning assigned to data by means of conventions applied to that data.

   Information Systems means the technology infrastructure and applications together with the data and information that may be recorded, stored, processed, shared, retrieved, or transmitted by them.

Information Technology refers to information systems and the organizational resources required to plan, acquire, implement, deliver and monitor them.

Technology Infrastructure refers to the hardware and software components and their interconnections required to support the applications.

WHY IS INFORMATION TECHNOLOGY PLANNING IMPORTANT?

7. Effective management of information technology is a business imperative and increasingly a source of competitive advantage. The rapid pace of technological changes together with the declining unit costs, are providing organizations with increasing potential for:

   - enhancing the value of existing products or services;

   - providing new products and services; and

   - introducing alternative delivery mechanisms.

   To benefit from information technology requires: foresight to prepare for the changes; planning to provide an economical and effective approach; as well as, effort and commitment in making it happen.

8. Information technology planning provides a structured means of addressing the impact of technologies, including emerging technologies, on an organization. Through the planning process, relevant technologies are identified and evaluated in the context of broader business goals and targets. Based on a comparative assessment of relevant technologies, the direction for the organization can be established.

9. The implementation of information technologies may be a complex, time consuming and expensive process for organizations. Information technology planning provides a framework to approach and schedule, wherever possible, necessary information technology projects in an integrated manner. Through this process, performance milestones can be agreed upon, scope of specific projects established, resources mobilized and constraints or limitations identified. Without effective planning, the implementation of information technologies may be misguided, haphazard, delayed and more expensive than justified.

10. Good governance requires that all investments be justified—including any information technology investments. Information technology planning provides a process for not only evaluating alternative approaches, but also for justifying the selected approach in terms of benefits, both tangible and intangible, that will be realized by an organization. This is an important dimension when many of the underlying projects may be difficult to support on an individual basis.

WHAT IS INFORMATION TECHNOLOGY PLANNING?

11. Business planning is an accepted responsibility of management. Plans provide a direction and framework for action. Plans enunciate business goals

and the actions that need to be initiated to achieve those goals including related benefits, resources and timeframes.

12. Increasingly, information technologies not only supports but, also, may drive or enable business strategies. In this context information technologies are an integral part of the business planning process itself. If such potential is evident after the completion of the business plan, then the business plan must be revisited and, if appropriate, revised.

13. An information technology plan is supportive of the business plan. It is based on the business goals and strategies. It provides a framework for information technology investments so that the desired outcome, in terms of benefits, can be obtained with the most effective and efficient use of available resources.

14. The objective of information technology planning is to "provide a **road-map** of the information technology required to support and enhance the business direction of an organization, outlining the **resources** that are required and **benefits** that will be realized on implementation of the plan."

In this context:

- *road-map* defines the desired position for the organization's use of information technology at a future point in time (*strategies*) and the manner in which the position will be attained over the intervening period (*tactics*);

- *resources* encompass existing information technology, and on-going expenditures on information systems, related facilities and personnel, as well as any additional investments proposed within the plan; and

- *benefits* to be realized may include incremental revenue or reduced costs of operations or improved service quality that will arise from the implementation of the plan.

WHAT ARE THE KEY PRINCIPLES IN DEVELOPING AN INFORMATION TECHNOLOGY PLAN?

15. Each organization should develop information technology plans which reflect its business strategy and match its information technology needs for a given future period. Notwithstanding the uniqueness of a business perspective, an information technology plan must be based on the following ten principles. Each of these is briefly discussed below.

ALIGNMENT—The plan should support and complement the business direction of an organization.

16. An information technology plan must be integrated to the needs and direction of the organization. To achieve this alignment, the key drivers of the information technology plan are the desired short- and long-term business targets as contained in the current business plan. Throughout the planning process, the focus must remain on the information and services/processes to be provided and the technology infrastructure required to provide effective and efficient services which meet business and organizational requirements.

A successful information technology plan must be prioritized and executed within the framework of these business strategies.

Issues to consider include:

- business direction and any changes that are anticipated—for example, new product launches, emerging delivery channels, or alternate business scenarios;
- legal and regulatory framework and changes thereto—the impact of likely changes must be factored into the planning process;
- competitive environment and the corresponding challenges and opportunities such as an alliance with third-parties through inter-organizational systems;
- key business strategies and the related information technology support requirements;
- risks and costs of adopting more flexible information technology plans that are adaptable to evolving business strategies; and
- service-level requirements of the business in terms of, for example, security (availability, integrity, and confidentiality), information system response times—particularly during peak periods—and data storage and archiving requirements.

RELEVANT SCOPE—The scope of the plan should be established to facilitate formulation of effective strategies.

17. The scope of the information technology plan has a major impact on the effort required to prepare it, as well as the plans acceptance and ultimate success. An inadequate scope would inhibit the formulation of effective strategies and an excessively wide scope will mitigate against implementation of the plan.

Issues to consider include:

- extent to which the plan should address the business needs of geographically dispersed units or autonomous business units;
- linkages with other business or functional strategies—for example, a business process re-engineering program may require extensive dovetailing with human resource and workplace redesign strategies; and
- requirements to incorporate linkages to third parties (customers, suppliers, partners, etc.) and the manner in which joint plans should be established.

RELEVANT TIMEFRAME—A planning horizon should be formulated that provides long-term direction and short-to-medium term deliverables in a manner consistent with the business strategy.

18. Information technology initiatives can take a long period, even years, to implement. The duration of the plan depends upon the complexity of the

projects required to support business strategies and the certainty of the business direction itself. The more complex the projects, and the more certainty in direction, the further the planning horizon can be. Typically, plans have a three-to-five year strategic horizon and a two-to-three year tactical horizon. This timeframe may vary according to the type of the industry or an organizations circumstances.

Issues to consider include:

- recognition of the planning horizon of the business plan and business cycle;

- anticipated life cycle of the technology infrastructure—for example, an existing industry standard may become obsolete in the foreseeable future;

- impact of business objectives on the timeframe for an information technology initiative—for example, a product launch date will require that the corresponding information systems are operational prior to that date; and

- requirement to adopt a building block approach, where a consecutive series of projects is required to achieve the end result, may necessitate a longer planning timeframe.

BENEFITS REALIZATION—Costs of implementation should be justified through tangible and intangible benefits that can be realized.

19. The implementation of information technologies can lead to considerable cost savings or other strategic benefits, for example, increased market share through better service delivery. These benefits, both tangible and intangible, must be realized to ensure that an organization receives value-for-money from its information technology investments. Occasionally, the plan or specific strategies within it may be justified as being necessary for the survival of the business—for example, the cost of implementing an information system required to support a product or service or meet a new legal or regulatory requirement.

Issues to consider include:

- manner in which the benefits enumerated in the plan will be realized. For instance, if the expenditure in a particular area is justified on efficiency grounds, then the plan must specify the amount, nature, and timing of cost savings that arise with the implementation of the strategy;

- extent to which the proposed expenditures within the plan are necessary to support the business. This needs to be differentiated from other incremental expenditures. For example, essential but obsolete information systems and equipment may need to be systematically replaced as part of the cost of staying in business;

- degree of uncertainty, if any, that applies to the benefits. For example, if the primary benefit from the strategy is to provide information for improved decision-making, then this intangible benefit may be both difficult to assess and realize; and

- return on capital provided by the investment and the impact of not pursuing or delaying the implementation of specific strategies.

ACHIEVABILITY—The planning process should recognize the capability and capacity of the organization to deliver solutions within the stated planning timeframe.

20. Information technology related initiatives can require major investments in terms of capital and people. It is essential that the strategies and tactics in the information technology plan not only offer a high payback but are also within the means of an organization. At times, this limitation may necessitate adoption of a less than ideal solution, or a delayed or phased implementation of the ideal solution.

    Issues to consider include:

    - availability of additional resources (capital, technology infrastructure, people) required to implement the plan—for example, if the plan is based on a significant increase in capital expenditure on information technology, then the source of such capital must be considered before the plan is fully developed; and

    - compatibility of proposed information technology-related initiatives with the organizational culture—for example, if a given initiative requires a high level of user experience in information technology, then this requirement must be compared to the user skill level within the organization.

MEASURABLE PERFORMANCE—The plan should provide a basis for measuring and monitoring performance.

21. A successful plan must provide a yardstick for measuring progress and serve as a benchmark for modifying objectives to improve and provide input for corrective action—either to improve performance or revise the plan. Typically, an information technology plan will provide performance milestones against which performance can be measured.

    Issues to consider include:

    - setting realistic and specific performance milestones that facilitate periodic review of performance against the plan;

    - formalizing a process for the periodic review of progress against established milestones;

    - assessing benefits realized against benefits anticipated on completion of the projects;

    - providing for progress reporting against plans on an on-going basis, including early warning of any problem areas; and

- linking information technology plan deliverables to business targets and budgets so that the impact of any delay is apparent and leads to a corresponding revision of the business plan.

REASSESSMENT—The plan should be reassessed periodically.

22. Plans are based on business and information technology assumptions. If these assumptions change, the existing initiatives and projects may be inappropriate or more effective alternatives may have emerged. An effective plan must be flexible and provide for periodic reassessment of the validity and effectiveness of both strategies and tactics.

Issues to consider include:

- establish a check list of business and information technology assumptions on which the plan is formulated;

- incorporate a mechanism to periodically confirm validity of planning assumptions (against the above check list) and critical success factors—for example, if a selected information technology becomes obsolete, then the plan should be immediately evaluated and appropriate revisions made; and

- volatility of the business environment and its impact on project priorities— for example, if a new business line is to be launched, then the information technology plan may need to be changed to reflect this business imperative.

AWARENESS—The plan should be disseminated widely.

23. Once the information technology plan has been approved, it should be disseminated to all concerned parties to ensure there is broad understanding of the direction and strategy. This may be assisted through the use of an easy to read summary of the plan.

Issues to consider include:

- elements of the plan which contain sensitive information—for example, competitive strategy should not be disclosed beyond those who need to know; and

- providing relevant information to third-parties with an interest in the information technology strategies—without compromising the competitive needs or other sensitivities of the organization.

ACCOUNTABILITY—Responsibility for implementing the plan should be explicit.

24. All plans require translation into action. Therefore, it is imperative to establish roles and responsibilities with respect to the execution and monitoring of the plans.

INFORMATION TECHNOLOGY

Issues to consider include:

- identifying sponsors for each planned project—usually a senior executive for the business area most effected by the project; and

- specifying the technical and business team leaders together with other appropriately skilled team members for each project and establishing clear areas of responsibility of key team members with agreed dates for delivery.

COMMITMENT—Management commitment in implementing the plan should be exhibited.

24. The implementation of the projects contained in the plan usually requires significant resources. These resources are only likely to be available on a timely basis if there is strong support for the plan and its objectives from executive management. Further, implementation of the plan may be hindered by unforeseen impediments. Management intervention may be necessary to circumvent these difficulties.

Issues to consider include:

- active executive management participation in the formulation of key strategies is imperative—for example, management participation is needed through interviews and workshops, in order to both contribute to the planning process and develop a progressive buy-in to the plan; and

- progressive executive management approvals and endorsements are needed at the end of each phase of the planning process.

WHAT IS THE BEST APPROACH FOR INFORMATION TECHNOLOGY PLANNING?

25. While organizations develop information technology plans that are matched to their needs, the planning process and the activities undertaken are similar. The sequence and importance of the planning activity may vary, but the conceptual information technology planning process is generic. This process entails that organizations will develop information technology plans in four phases – an orientation phase, an assessment phase, a strategy phase and a tactical phase.

PHASE I: ORIENTATION

27. The first phase is required to establish or confirm the scope of the information technology for the planning process, the methodology and techniques to be applied, mobilization of the planning team, and the reporting lines for the planning process. The planning process may have been initiated in response to a major change in the business strategies, or the implementation of most of the projects in the tactical plan, or where the business or information technology assumptions of the existing plan have

changed significantly. Major steps in this phase and the key activities are described below.

28. **Establish scope:** The scope of the information technology plan normally follows the business plan of the organization and represents an essential starting point to the planning process. Key activities include:

- determining if the plan incorporates all business units or that separate plans will be developed for selected business units;

- assessing the impact, if any, of organizational structure and policies on the scope—for example, for autonomous business units the practicality of formulating centralized strategies;

- evaluating the extent of third-party involvement in the planning process— for example, to support inter-organizational systems; and

- establishing an overall timeframe for the strategic and tactical plans.

At the end of this step, the scope and timeframe for the information technology plan will have been established.

29. **Establish methodology/techniques and mobilize resources**: Information technology planning can be a time-consuming process depending on the size of the organization, and the scale of its current or desired information technology usage. Once the scope has been established, the methodology and techniques need to be established and the background information and resources necessary for the planning effort need to be mobilized, including a clear delineation of reporting lines. Key activities include:

- gathering necessary background information on the organization, its information technology profile and capabilities and any impending changes that may impact the planning process;

- selecting a proven methodology to support the planning activities. This may be provided by external consultants, internally developed, or acquired from a third party;

- determining techniques that will be used for collecting and analyzing information, including questionnaires, interviews, workshops, etc.;

- developing a specific timetable for the completion of the plan, particularly the key phases;

- establishing an information technology project team. Typically, this will be a multidisciplinary team, comprised of persons with both information technology and business skills. Frequently, the team is supplemented by external consultants with expertise in information technology planning; and

- formalizing the reporting mechanism for the project team. Generally, the team reports to a steering committee which is headed by the Chief Executive Officer, Chief Information Officer, or another senior business executive and comprises key business unit managers, the information technology manager, and an information systems audit manager.

At the end of this step, a methodology, approach and timetable will have been established, background information gathered and an information technology planning team will be in place for the planning activities remaining.

PHASE II: ASSESSMENT

30. In the second phase of the information technology planning process the focus is on establishing a base line. During this phase, data is collected and analyzed to describe the existing usage and management of information technology and the extent to which they are unable, or may be unable, to support business objectives. Also, this phase provides an opportunity to identify other potential uses of information technologies which may assist in meeting business objectives. Major steps in this phase and key activities are briefly described below.

31. **Confirm business direction and drivers:** This step is necessary to ensure that the key driver for the information technology plan is the business direction of the organization. Typically, this information will be extracted from the business plan of the organization. Key activities include:

    - identifying core business goals, strategies and priorities, critical success factors, business and information technology assumptions, external relationships, trading partners or information technology providers, conceptual business models, launch of new or improved lines of products, current or changing regulatory requirements, major business opportunities and threats;

    - developing a competitive profile of the business, through a business planning methodology, with respect to strengths, weaknesses, opportunities, and threats.

    - developing a competitive profile of the business in the use of information technology, preferably by reference to available benchmarks, such as expenditure on information technology as a percentage of total expenditure or total assets, service delivery times or customer satisfaction levels; and

    - analyzing the current and future organizational structures of the business and determining the impact of these structures and their distribution on the information and information system needs and related assumptions.

    At the end of this step, a perspective will have been developed of the direction of the business and its impact on information technology usage, given competitive pressures.

32. **Review technology trends:** In this step, a view is formulated of the technologies from, for instance, discussions with vendors and other third parties. Key activities include:

    - establishing the cost, complexity, applicability and practicality of each major technology; and

- assessing, at a high level, the benefits, costs and risks from leading the technology direction for the industry compared to established practice within the industry.

At the end of this step a view will have been developed on the impact of information technologies and the potential they represent.

33. **Outline future requirements:** Based on the business direction and the technology trends, the high-level existing and future requirements of the organization should be established. Key activities include:

- identifying the information and related data needs of an organization through high-level data modeling and business process analysis;

- determining the broad applications areas that are required to support the information needs; and

- determining current and future service-level requirements, such as security, response times, and problem resolution procedures.

At the end of this step there should be a clear understanding of the business requirements that will need to be met over the planning horizon.

34. **Inventory existing information systems:** In this step, information technology usage is described. Key activities include:

- documenting existing information flows to support operations and decision making;

- describing current applications—nature, scope, source, language and hardware requirements, functionality, interfaces, dependencies, age, operating cost, complexity and known limitations;

- documenting linkages and interfaces between internal information systems and to external information systems;

- listing technology infrastructure—processors, peripheral and storage devices, communications and network equipment, terminals and personal computers—and associated operating system software, protocols and communications software. The nature, use, age, cost, residual life and limitation of each group should also be identified; and

- identifying organizational resources, including skills, experiences, methodologies and tools.

At the end of this step there should be a factual description of information technology usage within the organization.

35. **Develop an assessment:** In this step, the information gathered in the preceding steps is analyzed so that a baseline is established. Key activities include:

- comparing what information technology is required by the business against what exists so that an understanding of the major gaps is formulated;

- evaluating each major area of the existing information systems to identify areas where there are significant deficiencies or, apparent, user dissatisfaction with function, availability and service delivery;

- identifying business areas or practices where significant new or improved information systems are required; and

- preparing a list of major issues that need to be addressed in the formulation of the strategies—for example, capital constraints; infrastructure development; change management; exploitation of new technologies; business and information technology assumptions; improved service levels; risks and other obstacles to successful completion.

In the concluding step of this phase there should be a well developed assessment of the current and future business needs, the benefits available from implementing technologies, the gap between what is desired and what is required by the organization, and a list of the key issues to be considered in the formulation of the information technology strategies. (To assist in this assessment effort, the appendix includes key control objectives and assessment issues that should be considered.)

PHASE III: STRATEGIC PLAN

36.   In the third phase of the information technology planning process appropriate strategies are formulated. These strategies are founded on the assessment of the business needs and priorities, information technology direction and other related issues considered in the assessment phase. Major steps in the phase and the corresponding activities are described below.

37.   **Develop a vision:** Before any strategies are formulated it is useful to establish the desired position in terms of information technology at the end of the planning horizon—namely, where do we want to be? Usually, this is accomplished by developing a vision for the future which encompasses the desired information technology-related position in alignment with the business strategies. Key activities include:

- determining the information technology critical success factors and related business and information technology assumptions;

- identifying areas of emphasis in developing the strategies—for example, to out perform the competition in the use of technology may be an important objective, or to meet agreed service-levels may be more critical; and

- developing a realistic vision and supporting goals for the plan which recognize both the critical success factors and areas of emphasis.

At the end of this step a vision, in terms of information technology matching organizational objectives, will have been established.

38.   **Conduct option analysis:** This step is critical to the formulation of an effective plan. Alternatives must be analyzed for meeting the information needs of the organization. The alternatives must cover information, applications, technology infrastructure, communications and organizational resources that are required. Also, the alternatives must recognize mutual

dependencies. For example, if the decision is to acquire package solutions, then the information and technology infrastructure needs are, to a large extent, driven by the package selected. Alternatively, if the decision is to adopt a particular technology infrastructure standard, then the information, application, and the business process needs are driven by the most appropriate solution available for the standard selected. Key activities include:

- developing alternate models for assessing and delivering the data and information requirements of the organization—what, why, when, and where information is required;

- identifying alternative application approaches for meeting the information needs of the organization for each business segment—for example, custom develop, retain existing information system, acquire a package, or a hybrid solution;

- assessing alternate approaches and associated risks for meeting the technology infrastructure needs which are compatible with the chosen application and satisfy the service level requirements of the organization, including technology infrastructure standards;

- evaluating alternate approaches for meeting the communication needs— for example, a centralized communications network management model against a distributed network model; and

- identifying organizational processes and policies needed to support the acquisition, development, implementation, operation and maintenance of the information systems and the various ways that these needs may be met—for example, defining new policies, re-engineering business processes, recruitment of additional personnel; and outsourcing of implementation and/or delivery of new functionality.

At the end of this step, there should be a clear understanding of the alternatives that are available to the organization and the relative merits, including risks, costs and benefits, represented by each alternative.

39. **Develop a strategic plan:** Once all the alternative options are identified, the most effective strategic options should be selected, providing they are within the resource capacity and capability of the organization and all the selected options are compatible with each other to the extent necessary. Key activities include:

- justifying selection of the strategy—degree of fit to the business needs, compatibility with other strategies selected, flexibility to adapt to changing circumstances, adherence to industry standards, speed of implementation, organizational capability and learning curve required, and relative costs and benefits;

- developing an integrated planning framework to bring together the individual strategies culminating in a cohesive overall strategy covering information, applications, technology infrastructure, and organization perspectives in a manner that meets business objectives; and

- developing a broad implementation plan as a prelude to more detailed planning in the next phase.

At the conclusion of this phase, there should be a well-developed strategic plan. There should also be an overall justification for pursuing the plan and a broad implementation timetable.

PHASE IV: TACTICAL PLAN

40. In the last phase of the planning process, the tactical (or implementation) plan is developed. In the tactical plan, the focus is on the projects that need to be undertaken to implement each of the strategies. Major steps in this phase and corresponding activities are described below.

41. **Identify and specify projects:** In this step, each strategy is broken into specific projects—to facilitate control, implementation and matching to the resource capability of the organization. Also, the projects may need to be integrated to business related projects such as business re-engineering. These projects include any transitional projects that are required as a bridge between the new and existing information systems. Key activities include:

- specifying the nature, functionality, and scope of each project;

- establishing interdependencies between projects;

- identifying the costs and benefits of individual projects; and

- estimating the implementation timeframe for each project.

At the end of this step, all the projects required to support the implementation of the strategic plan will have been specified.

42. **Prioritize projects:** The strategic plan provides only broad guidance on the priorities of the projects. Now that the projects are specified, their priorities must be confirmed. Criteria to consider include:

- strategic impact of the project in supporting the business strategy;

- dependencies on other projects—for example, a communication network may be the foundation project for a new service delivery offering and would need to be scheduled and completed prior to the new service delivery offering;

- business imperatives—for example, the launch date of a new product or changes to regulatory requirements or meeting competitive or customer needs;

- benefits that can be realized—projects with high benefits or quick results should be fast-tracked; and

- resource requirements—for example, funding may constrain the concurrent implementation of major projects.

At the end of this step all the projects in the tactical plan will have been prioritized.

43. **Develop the tactical plan:** In this step, each project is scheduled for implementation based on its priority, the resources required, the resources available and the implementation timeframe. The implementation plan should:

- schedule all projects, specifying who does what and when;

- identify the critical path and performance milestones for key deliverables;

- provide the underlying assumptions and constraints; and

- develop financial, resource allocation, and benefit realization plans to support the implementation of the projects.

At the end of this activity, the organization will have formulated a plan for translating the strategy into actions.

44. **Recommend monitoring and control process:** In this concluding step, the monitoring and control mechanisms need to be established to ensure that the plan is implemented in a timely, efficient, and effective manner. Typically, the overall responsibility for the continuing approval and oversight of the plan rests with an executive level committee—the Information Technology Steering Committee. Key activities include:

- developing a monitoring and control mechanism that will ensure that the plan implementation as well as business and information technology assumptions are periodically reviewed and, where appropriate, corrective action is taken;

- assigning accountabilities for the implementation of specific projects within the plan—for example, a project sponsor and project manager; and

- assigning responsibilities for delivering estimated benefits from those parts of the information technology plan that have been implemented—for example, the senior business executives responsible for areas where the new or enhanced system is being used.

This step marks the conclusion of the information technology planning process.

Key Control Objectives and Assessment Issues
for Information Technology Planning

(For use by the Information Technology control professional
as an assessment guide)

Key Control Objectives

Define a Strategic Information Technology Plan
1. Information Technology as Part of the Organization's Long- and Short-Range Plan **
2. Information Technology Long-Range Plan
3. Information Technology Long-Range Planning -- Approach and Structure
4. Information Technology Long-Range Plan Changes
5. Short-Range Planning for the Information Services Function
6. Assessment of Existing Systems

1. Information Technology as Part of the Organization's Long- and Short-Range Plan

    Senior management is responsible for developing and implementing long- and short-range plans that fulfill the organization's mission and goals. In this respect, senior management should ensure that information technology issues as well as opportunities are adequately assessed and reflected in the organization's long- and short-range plans.

2. Information Technology Long-Range Plan

    Management of the information services function is responsible for regularly developing information technology long-range plans supporting the achievement of the organization's overall missions and goals. Accordingly, management should implement a long-range planning process, adopt a structured approach and set up a standard plan structure.

3. Information Technology Long-Range Planning -- Approach and Structure

    Management of the information services function should establish and apply a structured approach regarding the long-range planning process. This should result in a high-quality plan which covers the basic questions of what, who, how, when and why. Aspects which need to be taken into account and adequately addressed during the planning process are the organizational model and changes to it, geographical distribution, technological evolution, costs, legal and regulatory requirements, requirements of third-parties or the market, planning horizon, business process re-engineering, staffing, in- or out-sourcing, etc. Benefits of the choices made should be clearly identified. The plan itself should also refer to other plans such as the organization quality plan and the information risk management plan.

4. Information Technology Long-Range Plan Changes

Management of the information services function should ensure a process is in place to timely and accurately modify the information technology long-range plan to accommodate changes to the organization's long-range plan and changes in information technology conditions.

5. Short-Range Planning for the Information Services Function

Management of the information services function should ensure that the information technology long-range plan is regularly translated into information technology short-range plans. Such short-range plans should ensure that appropriate information services function resources are allocated on a basis consistent with the information technology long-range plan. The short-range plans should be reassessed periodically and amended as necessary in response to changing business and information technology conditions. The timely performance of feasibility studies should ensure that the execution of the short-range plans is adequately initiated.

6. Assessment of Existing Systems

Prior to developing or changing the strategic information technology plan, management of the information services function should assess the existing information systems in terms of degree of business automation, functionality, stability, complexity, costs, strengths and weaknesses, in order to determine the degree to which the existing systems support the organization's business requirements.

Key Assessment Issues

Consider whether:

- Information services function or business enterprise policies and procedures address a structured planning approach

- A methodology is in place to formulate and modify the plans and at a minimum, they cover:

  - organization mission and goals

  - information technology initiatives to support the organization mission and goals

  - opportunities for information technology initiatives

  - feasibility studies of information technology initiatives

  - risk assessments of information technology initiatives

  - optimal investment of current and future information technology investments

965

- re-engineering of information technology initiatives to reflect changes in the organization's mission and goals
- evaluation of the alternative strategies for data applications, technology and organization

- Organizational changes, technology evolution, regulatory requirements, business process re-engineering, staffing, in- and out-sourcing, etc. are taken into account and adequately addressed in the planning process

- Long- and short-range information technology plans exist, are current, adequately address overall enterprise, its mission and key business functions

- Information technology projects are supported by the appropriate documentation as identified in the information technology planning methodology

- Checkpoints exist to ensure that information technology objectives and long- and short-range plans continue to meet organizational objectives and long- and short-range plans

- Review and sign-off occurs by process owners and senior management of information technology plans

- The information technology plan assesses the existing information systems in terms of degree of business automation, functionality, stability, complexity, costs, strengths and weaknesses

Test whether:

- Minutes from information services function planning/steering committee meetings reflect the planning process

- Planning methodology deliverables exist and are as prescribed

- Relevant information technology initiatives are included in the information services function long- and short- range plans (i.e., hardware changes, capacity planning, information architecture, new system development or procurement, disaster recovery planning, installation of new processing platforms, etc.)

- Information technology initiatives support the long- and short-range plans and consider requirements for research, training, staffing, facilities, hardware and software

- Technical implications of information technology initiatives have been identified

- Consideration has been given to optimizing current and future information technology investments

- Information technology long- and short-range plans are consistent with the organization's long- and short-range plans and organization requirements

- Plans have been changed to reflect changing conditions

- Information technology long-range plans are periodically translated into short-range plans

- Tasks exist to implement the plans

Substantiate the risk of control objectives not being met by:

- Benchmarking of strategic information technology plans against similar organizations or appropriate international standards/recognized industry best practices

- A detailed review of the IT plans to ensure that IT initiatives reflect the organization's mission and goals

- A detailed review of the IT plans to determine if known areas of weakness within the organization are being identified for improvement as part of the IT solutions contained in the plans

* abstracted from "Control Objectives for Information and related Technology (COBIT) 2nd Edition" published by the Information Systems Audit and Control Foundation (ISACF), 1996, 1998

** the term "long-range" is comparable to "strategic" and the term "short-range" is comparable to "tactical"

MEMBERSHIP

CONTENTS OF THIS SECTION

	Page
Summary of Documents:	
Items to Consider for Inclusion in Charters and/or By-laws of Professional Accountancy Bodies	970
Guidance on the Formation and Organization of a Professional Accountancy Body	970

For additional information on the Membership Committee, recent developments, and/or to obtain outstanding exposure drafts, visit the Committee's page at http://www.ifac.org/Committees/Membership.

**Items to Consider for Inclusion in Charters and/or By-laws
of Professional Accountancy Bodies
Issued July 1997**

This document was prepared by the Membership Committee of IFAC in order to assist any professional accountancy organization which is in the process of drafting or amending its basic governance documents. Although there are differences in the legal environments of various countries, there are certain items and issues that should be addressed, regardless of the legal system. This document is an easy to follow check list of those items to consider, including alternatives, for the development of an organization's constitution and By-laws.

**Guidance on the Formation and Organization of a
Professional Accountancy Body
Issued April 1998**

This paper provides assistance in the formation, development and administration of a professional accountancy body. It charts basic considerations in forming a professional accountancy body from the legal and organizational structure, relations with government, membership requirements and recruitment to governance. It summarizes the basic issues that should be considered by a professional accountancy body as it goes through a number of stages towards its maturity. Although it is useful to consider these typical stages in preparing long-term plans, and although this paper includes guidance that may be useful even to long-established organizations, it focuses primarily on organizations in their formative and start-up phases.

PUBLIC SECTOR

CONTENTS OF THIS SECTION

	Page
Introduction to the Public Sector Committee of the International Federation of Accountants	972

Guidelines:

1.	Financial Reporting by Government Business Enterprises	976
2.	Applicability of International Standards on Auditing to Audits of Financial Statements of Government Business Enterprises	979

Summary of Other Documents:

Study 1	Financial Reporting by National Governments	983
Study 2	Elements of the Financial Statements of National Governments	984
Study 3	Auditing for Compliance with Authorities—A Public Sector Perspective	984
Study 4	Using the Work of Other Auditors—A Public Sector Perspective	984
Study 5	Definition and Recognition of Assets	985
Study 6	Accounting for and Reporting Liabilities	985
Study 7	Performance Reporting by Government Business Enterprises	986
Study 8	The Government Financial Reporting Entity	987
Study 9	Definition and Recognition of Revenues	987
Study 10	Definition and Recognition of Expenses/Expenditures	988

Selected Bibliography of Public Sector Accounting and Auditing Material	988

PUBLIC SECTOR

Introduction to the Public Sector Committee of the International Federation of Accountants

CONTENTS

	Paragraphs
Objectives and Terms of Reference	1-4
Appointment of Members	5
Nature, Scope and Authority of Pronouncements	6-7
Working Procedures	8-10
Language	11

For additional information on the Public Sector Committee, recent developments, and/or to obtain outstanding exposure drafts, visit the Committee's page at http://www.ifac.org/Committees/Public Sector.

INTRODUCTION TO THE PUBLIC SECTOR COMMITTEE
OF THE INTERNATIONAL FEDERATION OF ACCOUNTANTS

Objectives and Terms of Reference

1. The mission of the International Federation of Accountants (IFAC) as set out in paragraph 2 of its Constitution is "the worldwide development and enhancement of an accountancy profession with harmonized standards, able to provide services of consistently high quality in the public interest."

2. The Public Sector Committee (PSC) is a standing committee of the Council of IFAC formed to address, on a coordinated worldwide basis, the needs of those involved in public sector financial reporting, accounting and auditing. In this regard, the term "public sector" refers to national governments, regional (e.g., state, provincial, territorial) governments, local (e.g., city, town) governments and related governmental entities (e.g., agencies, boards, commissions and enterprises).

3. At present, governments and other public sector entities follow widely diverse accounting and auditing practices and, in many countries, there are no authoritative standards for the public sector. For those countries where standards do exist, the body of standards may be either at an early stage of development or limited in application to specific types of entities in the public sector.

4. The terms of reference of PSC require it to develop programs aimed at improving public sector financial management and accountability including:

   - developing accounting and auditing standards and promoting their acceptance;
   - developing and coordinating programs to promote education and research; and
   - encouraging and facilitating the exchange of information among member bodies and other interested parties.

Appointment of Members

5. The members of PSC are nominated by the member bodies in the countries selected by the Council of IFAC to serve on the committee. Countries are appointed for an initial term of two and a half years which may be renewed for further two and a half year terms. In addition, the Council may also appoint one or more international organizations to serve on the committee; such appointment would also be for a period of two and a half years which may be renewed for further two and a half year terms. The members of the committee will be primarily engaged in the public sector. For voting purposes, each country and organization represented on the committee has one vote.

PUBLIC SECTOR

Nature, Scope and Authority of Pronouncements

6. PSC has been given the authority, on behalf of the Council, to issue standards, guidelines, studies and occasional papers on financial reporting, accounting and auditing in the public sector.

Standards

International Public Sector Standards contain individual requirements on financial reporting, accounting and auditing in the public sector with related guidance in the form of explanatory and other material. National standards differ in form and content. PSC takes cognizance of such documents, and their differences and, in the light of these issues, International Standards which are recommended for international adoption. In order to assist IFAC member bodies in the implementation of International Public Sector Standards, PSC will, with the support of the Council, seek to promote their acceptance by national standard-setting authorities.

Guidelines

International Public Sector Guidelines recommend practices to be followed in the public sector on financial reporting, accounting and auditing. In order to assist IFAC member bodies in the implementation of International Public Sector Guidelines, PSC will, with the support of the Council, seek to promote their acceptance by national standard-setting authorities.

Studies

International Public Sector Studies are intended to provide advice on financial reporting, accounting and auditing issues in the public sector. They are based on study of the best practices and most effective methods for dealing with the issues being addressed.

Occasional Papers

Occasional Papers are intended to provide information that contributes to some segments of the body of public sector financial reporting, accounting and auditing knowledge. They are aimed at providing new information or fresh insights into public sector issues and generally result from research activities such as: literature searches, questionnaire surveys, interviews, experiments, case studies and analysis.

7. PSC pronouncements are aimed at developing and harmonizing public sector financial reporting, accounting and auditing practices. To achieve this aim, PSC considers and makes use of pronouncements issued by:

- the International Accounting Standards Committee (IASC) and the International Auditing Practices Committee (IAPC) to the extent they are applicable to the public sector;

- national regulatory authorities;

- professional accounting bodies; and

- other organizations interested in financial reporting, accounting and auditing in the public sector.

International Public Sector Standards are not intended to, and do not, override authoritative national standards for the public sector issued by governments, regulatory or professional accounting bodies. PSC will ensure that its pronouncements are consistent with those of IASC and IAPC to the extent those pronouncements are applicable and appropriate to the public sector.

Working Procedures

8. While PSC is ultimately responsible for selecting the subject matters to be addressed by its standards, guidelines, studies and occasional papers, suggestions and proposals from interested individuals and organizations are encouraged. The responsibility for carrying out the necessary research and for preparing exposure drafts of proposed standards and guidelines or drafts of studies may be delegated by the committee to subcommittees or individuals. Such subcommittees are always chaired by a member of the committee but may include persons who are not members of a member body of IFAC.

9. The committee issues exposure drafts of all proposed standards and guidelines for comment by IFAC member bodies and others who may be interested in the pronouncements. This provides an opportunity for those affected by PSC pronouncements to present their views on them before the pronouncements are finalized and approved by the committee. The committee considers all comments received on exposure drafts and makes such modifications as it considers appropriate. Exposure drafts of proposed standards and guidelines must be approved for issue by vote of at least two-thirds of the total voting rights of PSC present at a meeting. A quorum of nine committee members is requested for a vote to be held.

10. The draft of a standard or guideline duly revised after the exposure period, or a study is submitted to the PSC for approval. If approved by at least three-quarters of the total voting rights of PSC present at a meeting, the pronouncement is published and released. A quorum of nine committee members is required for a vote to be held.

Language

11. The approved text of a pronouncement is that published by PSC in the English language. Member bodies of IFAC are authorized to prepare, after obtaining IFAC approval, translations of such pronouncements at their own cost, to be issued in the language of their own countries as appropriate. These translations should indicate the name of the body that prepared the translation and that it is a translation of the approved text.

1

July 1989

Financial Reporting by Government Business Enterprises

CONTENTS

	Paragraphs
Introduction	1-3
Government Business Enterprises	4-7
Requirements for Financial Statements	8-10

Introduction

1. The Introduction to the Public Sector Committee states that Public Sector Committee (PSC) pronouncements are aimed at developing and harmonizing public sector financial reporting and accounting practices. Where appropriate, the PSC will consider and make use of pronouncements issued by the International Accounting Standards Committee (IASC) to the extent they are applicable to the public sector. International Accounting Standards (IASs), as well as International Public Sector Guidelines, are not intended to, and do, not override authoritative national standards issued by governments, regulatory or professional accounting bodies.

2. The purpose of this Guideline is to specify the accounting standards that should be used in the preparation and presentation of the published financial statements of government business enterprises.

3. The term 'government' refers to national governments, regional (e.g., state, provincial, territorial) governments and local (e.g., city, town) governments.

Government Business Enterprises

4. The Guideline is designed to include such government business enterprises as national railways, energy utilities, and communication services. It does not exclude less commercial activities. The characteristics which government business enterprises usually possess are set out in paragraphs 5, 6 and 7.

5. Government business enterprises are businesses which operate within the public sector ordinarily to meet a political or social interest objective. They are normally required to operate commercially, that is to make profits or to recoup, through user charges, a substantial proportion of their operating costs.

6. In many countries, the public sector includes business enterprises that are owned or controlled by government. The principal activity of these government business enterprises is similar to that of private sector business enterprises, that is to sell goods or services to individuals and nongovernment organizations as well as other public sector entities. All government business enterprises have the financial and operating authority to carry on business, usually including the power to contract in their own name, and some are able to raise finance from nongovernment sources.

7. Government business enterprises usually take the same legal form as private sector business enterprises. In some countries, however, government business enterprises may be subject to specific legislation; as a result, they may have a legal form different from business enterprises in the private sector.

Requirements for Financial Statements

8. Government business enterprises issue financial statements to legislators and government departments, outside investors, employees, lenders, the public and other users. When such financial statements are issued, they should be presented in accordance with accounting principles, accounting standards and other requirements that are generally accepted for other business enterprises.

9. Financial statements provide information on financial performance and financial position. The IASC has developed standards for business enterprises relevant to reporting financial performance and position. Since these concepts apply to government business enterprises, the enterprises should present financial statements that conform, in all material respects, with IASs and comply with the appropriate national accounting standards and requirements applicable to other business enterprises.

10. Observance of the above requirements represents a minimum level of reporting necessary to provide adequate information to users. Circumstances in which it may be appropriate to report additional information would include:

- When there are additional requirements for published financial statements mandated by governments, government business enterprises should also report in accordance with such requirements.

- When government business enterprises operate to a financial target which is set on a basis other than the historical cost model, government business enterprises should also prepare financial statements on this other basis so as to provide information on financial performance in relation to targets.

- In the case of government business enterprises operating in a non-competitive or monopolistic environment, financial results alone may be an inadequate measure of performance; thus, it may be appropriate to provide information on productivity/efficiency as additional performance measures.

- When government business enterprises have nonfinancial or social objectives which conflict with their commercial objectives, it may be appropriate for them to report on the extent to which they have achieved these other objectives and the impact on financial performance.

2

July 1990

Applicability of International Standards on Auditing to Audits of Financial Statements of Government Business Enterprises

CONTENTS

	Paragraphs
Introduction	1-2
Government Business Enterprises	3
Requirements for Audits of Financial Statements	4-10

Introduction

1. The Introduction to the Public Sector Committee states that Public Sector Committee (PSC) pronouncements are aimed at developing and harmonizing public sector[1] financial reporting, accounting, and auditing practices. The PSC will consider and make use of pronouncements issued by the International Auditing Practices Committee (IAPC) to the extent they are applicable to the public sector. International Standards on Auditing (ISAs) issued by the IAPC and International Public Sector Guidelines (IPSGs) are not intended to, and do not, override authoritative national standards issued by governments, regulatory or professional accounting bodies.

2. The purpose of this Guideline is to describe the applicability of ISAs to audits of financial statements[2] of government business enterprises.

Government Business Enterprises

3. This Guideline is applicable to such government business enterprises as national railroads, energy utilities, and communication services. Government business enterprises are normally required to operate commercially, that is, to make profits or to recoup, through user charges, a substantial proportion of their operating costs. In many countries, the public sector includes business enterprises that are owned or controlled by government. The principal activity of these government business enterprises is similar to that of private sector business enterprises, that is, to sell goods or services to individuals and nongovernment organizations as well as other public sector entities. Additional characteristics which government business enterprises usually possess are set out in IPSG 1 "Financial Reporting by Government Business Enterprises" (paragraphs 5 to 7).

Requirements for Audits of Financial Statements

4. Government business enterprises prepare financial statements for the use of legislators and government departments, outside investors, employees, lenders, the public and other users. Auditors are often required to express an opinion on such financial statements. IAPC has developed ISAs for auditors to use whenever an independent audit of financial statements is carried out.

5. The audit objectives for auditing and reporting on financial statements of government business enterprises are similar to those for private sector entities. As such, the same standards should apply regardless of the nature of the enterprise. Users of financial statements are entitled to a uniform quality of assurance and would not be well served by the application of differing

---

[1] As described in the Introduction to the PSC, "the term 'public sector' refers to national governments, regional (e.g., state, provincial, territorial) governments, local (e.g., city, town) governments and related governmental entities (e.g., agencies, boards, commissions and enterprises)."

[2] The term "financial statements," as defined in the Preface to Statements of International Accounting Standards, covers balance sheets, income statements or profit and loss accounts, statements of changes in financial position, notes and other statements and explanatory material which are identified as being part of the financial statements.

standards. Therefore, audits of financial statements of government business enterprises should conform, in all material respects, with ISAs.

6. ISAs describe:

- The basic principles which govern the auditor's professional responsibilities.

- The qualifications or essential characteristics of auditors (e.g., adequate training, independence, and due care in performing audits of financial statements).

- The standards and practices for performing audits of financial statements (e.g., adequate planning and supervision, the assessments of inherent and control risks and their impact on substantive procedures, and the process by which the auditor determines the procedures to be performed when carrying out the audit).

- The form and content of audit reports.

7. Financial statements of government business enterprises may include information that is different from, or in addition to, that contained in the financial statements of business enterprises in the private sector (e.g., comparison of expenditures in the period with limits established by legislation). In such circumstances, appropriate modifications may be required to the nature, timing and extent of audit procedures, and the auditor's report.

8. Some government business enterprises employ resources to achieve a variety of nonfinancial or social objectives in addition to their commercial objectives. While their audited financial statements provide an accounting of their financial position, results of operations and changes in financial position, these financial statements, by themselves, may not adequately report on the results of their non-commercial activities. Auditors may be required to audit and report on information relating to:

(a) compliance with legislation and regulatory requirements (including applicable local public sector pronouncements);

(b) the adequacy of the enterprise's internal control structure; and

(c) economy, efficiency, and effectiveness of programs, projects and activities.

This information may either be included in, or may be in addition to, the enterprise's financial statements. The audit of such information may require auditors to perform work that is in addition to that required solely for the purpose of auditing and reporting on the financial statements.

9. Some government business enterprises may include in their annual reports information on performance in terms of achieving objectives as measured by specified financial or other indicators. Auditors may also be required to audit and report on this additional performance information.

10. This Guideline is not specifically designed to apply to the audit of the information set out in paragraphs 7 to 9; however, this Guideline and ISAs may be useful.

11. A Public Sector Perspective (PSP) on the applicability of ISAs to the audit of financial statements of public sector entities other than government business enterprises is included at the end of each ISA. Where no PSP is added the ISA is applicable in all material respects to the public sector.

The application of ISAs in the public sector was previously dealt with in International Public Sector Guideline 3.

SUMMARY OF OTHER DOCUMENTS

The Committee has issued ten other documents, as summarized below.

Study 1
Financial Reporting by National Governments
Issued March 1991

The scope of the Study is to consider:

- financial reporting by national governments and their major governmental units;

- financial reports that provide information on government plans, performance and compliance with relevant authorities;

- information needs of the principal users of government financial reports, with primary emphasis on the needs of external users; and

- the forms of reporting best suited to meeting those information needs.

This Study is of particular interest to senior financial officers in government, politicians, legislative auditors and others who use government financial reports because it addresses the fundamental underpinnings of governmental financial reporting.

Comparative summaries of users, user needs and objectives were prepared. They illustrate that there is concurrence on who users are, what their needs are and, accordingly, the objectives of financial reporting.

The Study develops a logical progression from users and user needs to the objectives of government financial reporting. It provides further context for the discussion of objectives by exploring the governmental environment and the limits of financial reporting.

The Study then discusses financial reporting. Rather than recommending a single, preferred financial reporting model, the Study describes the spectrum of possible bases of accounting and different reporting models (types of reports). It then illustrates their strengths and weaknesses in meeting the objectives of financial reporting. The Study demonstrates that in moving from single displays of cash receipts and disbursements to summary financial reports that account for total economic resources, more of the objectives of financial reporting are met. Since those objectives are derived from user needs, more complete and better information will better meet those needs.

The Study recognizes that financial reporting by national governments is influenced by government financial reporting policies and practices which are embedded in the provisions of legislation and legal prescription.

Study 2
Elements of the Financial Statements of National Governments
Issued July 1993

This Study considers the elements (types or classes of financial information) to be reported in financial statements prepared under the different bases of accounting that may be employed by national governments and their major units and the way in which those elements may be defined. It also considers the implications of reporting particular elements, or subsets thereof, for the messages communicated by financial statements and the achievement of the objectives identified in Study 1.

The Study aims to assist in developing the full potential of the accounting models currently employed in individual jurisdictions to communicate financial information to users. That is useful for accountability and decision making purposes.

This Study focuses on reporting the elements in the financial statements prepared for national governments. However, it is acknowledged that aspects of the delivery of goods and services and the achievement of government objectives will in some cases, be best achieved through the display of financial or non-financial information in notes, schedules or statements other than the statement of financial position or statement of financial performance in the financial report.

Study 3
Auditing for Compliance with Authorities—A Public Sector Perspective
Issued October 1994

This Study addresses aspects of the audit for compliance in the public sector which, in many countries, is subject to very different mandates and objectives than in the private sector. In a democratic system of government, accountability to the public and particularly, to its designated representatives, is an overriding aspect of the management of a public sector entity. Public sector entities are usually established by legislation and their operations governed by various authorities derived from legislation. Management of public sector entities is accountable for operating in accordance with the provisions of the relevant laws, regulations and other authorities governing them. Since legislation and other authorities are the primary means by which legislators control the raising and spending of money by the public sector, auditing for compliance with relevant authorities is usually an important and integral part of the audit mandate, or terms of engagement, for most audits of public sector entities. Because of the variety of authorities, their provisions may be conflicting with one another and may be subject to differing interpretations. Also, subordinate authorities may not adhere to the directions or limits prescribed by the enabling legislation. As a result, an assessment of compliance with authority in the public sector requires considerable professional judgment and is of particular importance.

Study 4
Using the Work of Other Auditors—A Public Sector Perspective
Issued October 1994

This Study addresses using the work of other auditors, including both other external and internal auditors, in financial attest and compliance audits. It considers the matters an auditor has to take into consideration when using the work of another auditor and provides a public sector perspective to International Standard on Auditing (ISA) 600 "Using the Work of Another Auditor" and ISA 610 "Considering the Work of Internal Auditing."

The Study considers the principles stated in the ISAs noted above and describes their applicability to the public sector. It also discusses some of the particular issues arising in the public sector when a principal auditor considers using the work of another auditor. The areas discussed deserving special attention are the autonomy of different tiers of government, the differing mandates of Higher Audit Institutions (HAI), and the particular problems surrounding using the work of other auditors in an international context.

Study 5
Definition and Recognition of Assets
Issued August 1995

This Study identifies and describes the variety of views which exist about whether, when and how specific assets should be measured and reported in the public sector. It considers and explores:

- the definition and recognition of assets;

- the effect of different bases of accounting on the definition and recognition of assets; and

- the issues associated with certain types of assets.

The Study acknowledges that the demand for government services has increased. This growth in demand has meant increasing competition for government services, stimulated by education standards, communication and community interest in government actions. Consequently, governments are under pressure to manage their assets efficiently and effectively. Accountability for efficiency and effectiveness of public sector asset management can be shown through better financial reporting. Better reporting provides a basis of understanding by the public, elected decision makers and by management. This, in turn, supports better decision making and asset allocation.

Study 6
Accounting for and Reporting Liabilities
Issued August 1995

This Study provides a public sector perspective on the definition and recognition of liabilities. It identifies, considers and explores views held on:

- the definition and classification of liabilities;

- the effect of different bases of accounting on accounting for and reporting liabilities; and

- the issues associated with certain types of liabilities.

The Study describes the variety of views which exist about whether, when and how certain liabilities should be measured and reported. Historically, governments have focused on their outstanding debt as a primary measure of the government's liabilities or indebtedness, particularly in formulating or assessing economic policy. However, governments assume a variety of commitments and obligations that give rise to other liabilities that are often unreported by governments. Yet information about all of a government's liabilities and exposure to potential liabilities is vital if governments are to manage their cash flow and make informed decisions about the financing of future services and resource allocation. While governments have liabilities similar to business enterprises, they also have other potential liabilities, such as recurring commitments under established social programs, guarantees and promises made by politicians. The study distinguishes liabilities, commitments and contingencies.

Study 7
Performance Reporting by Government Business Enterprises
Issued January 1996

This Study identifies principal users of performance information, considers the needs of those users, and outlines forms of reporting that could be available to meet those needs. The Study is thereby concerned primarily with the provision of information about an enterprise's performance (covering both financial and non-financial aspects of performance) supplementary to the information provided in financial statements, in the context of general purpose financial statements.

The need for this Study arises from the fact that financial standards on their own are not always sufficient to give an indication of the overall performance of a particular organization. Public sector bodies can differ from private sector enterprises in both their objectives and finance. Although government business enterprises are normally required to operate commercially and usually take the same legal form as private sector business enterprises, the combination of the fact that they often enjoy a monopoly position and the political context in which they operate means that the user of financial reports can rely less on measures of performance such as return on capital employed. As a result, groups with an interest in the performance such as return on capital employed. As a result, groups with an interest in the performance of government business enterprises — governments, legislators, taxpayers and consumers — may have difficulty in making informed judgments about the efficiency and effectiveness of government business enterprises.

Government business enterprises may not be delivering services in circumstances that are even close to being a competitive market. So the test of relative market efficiency and effectiveness cannot always be applied. The issue therefore is how to formulate performance measures that will enable judgments about efficiency and effectiveness to be made. This Study considers how such measures might be defined and how a government business enterprise's performance in relation to these measures might best be reported to those with an interest in its performance.

Study 8
The Government Financial Reporting Entity
Issued July 1996

This Study considers the implications of different approaches to the definition of the government financial reporting entity and different techniques for the construction of government financial reports to the achievement of objectives of financial reports.

This Study is a companion to Study 1, *Financial Reporting by National Governments,* issued in March 1991, and Study 2, *Elements of the Financial Statement of National Governments,* issued in July 1993. Study 8 builds on the discussions and definitions from Studies 1 and 2. Consistent with Studies 1 and 2, the primary focus of this Study is on financial reporting of national governments. However, the matters it addresses may be equally applicable for other levels of governments (state, provincial and local governments).

It is hoped that this Study will lead to improvements in financial reporting by governments and greater comparability of financial reports both within and between jurisdictions.

Study 9
Definition and Recognition of Revenues
Issued December 1996

This Study examines concepts, principles and issues related to the definitions and recognition of revenues in the general purpose financial statements of national governments and other non-business public sector entities. Specifically, this Study identifies and discusses the definition and classification of revenues, issues with certain types of revenue and the effect of different bases of accounting on the definition and recognition of revenues.

Information on revenues is important in assisting users to assess the financial condition and performance of governments. Comparing revenues with expenses helps users to assess interperiod equity (that is, whether current revenues are sufficient to cover the costs of programs and services provided in the current period).

This Study extends Study 1, *Financial Reporting by National Governments,* issued in March 1991, and Study 2, *Elements of the Financial Statement of National Governments,* issued in July 1993. It is also a companion to Study 5, *Definition and Recognition of Assets,* Study 6, *Accounting for and Reporting Liabilities,* and Study 10, *Definition and Recognition of Expenses/Espenditures.*

The primary focus of this Study is on the financial statements prepared for national governments and for the entities and units they establish for the delivery of goods and services and the achievement of government objectives. However, the matters it addresses may be equally applicable for other levels of governments (state, provincial and local governments).

Study 10
Definition and Recognition of Expenses/Expenditures
Issued December 1996

This Study examines the concepts, principles and issues related to the treatment of expenses/expenditures in general purpose financial statements of governments and other non-business public sector entities.

Governments are under growing pressures not only to manage their funds effectively, but also to show their management has been effective. To achieve this, governments need complete information about their expenses/expenditures in order to assess their revenue requirements, the sustainability of their programs and their flexibility.

This Study extends Study 1, *Financial Reporting by National Governments,* issued in March 1991, and Study 2, *Elements of the Financial Statement of National Governments,* issued in July 1993. It is also a companion to Study 5, *Definition and Recognition of Assets,* Study 6, *Accounting for and Reporting Liabilities,* and Study 9, *Definition and Recognition of Revenues..*

The primary focus of this Study is on the financial statements prepared for national governments and for the entities and units they establish for the delivery of goods and services and the achievement of government objectives. However, the matters it addresses may be equally applicable for other levels of governments (state, provincial and local governments).

Selected Bibliography of Public Sector Accounting and Auditing Material
Issued January 1993

To help developing and coordinating programs to promote education and research and for encouraging and facilitating the exchange of information among member bodies and other interested parties, the PSC issued a Selected Bibliography of Public Sector Accounting and Auditing Material. The Bibliography has been designed to include all authoritative and non-authoritative public sector accounting and auditing material issued by standard-setting bodies and Supreme Audit Institutions.

The listings of publications included in the Bibliography have been provided by the organizations themselves and are currently updated as of June 30, 1992.